Index to Vital Data

in

Local Newspapers

of

Sonoma County

California

Volume 3
1881-1885

Sonoma County Genealogical Society, Inc.

HERITAGE BOOKS
2015

HERITAGE BOOKS
AN IMPRINT OF HERITAGE BOOKS, INC.

Books, CDs, and more—Worldwide

For our listing of thousands of titles see our website
at
www.HeritageBooks.com

Published 2015 by
HERITAGE BOOKS, INC.
Publishing Division
5810 Ruatan Street
Berwyn Heights, Md. 20740

International Standard Book Numbers
Paperbound: 978-0-7884-1941-6
Clothbound: 978-0-7884-6086-9

Contents

Surname Index to Vital Data in Newspapers

Sonoma County, California

1881-1885: Volume III

This indexing project was undertaken to help fill the gaps in some of the early records in Sonoma County. Volume I, which covers the period from 1854 through 1875, was published early in 2001.[1] Volume II, which covers the period from 1876-1880, was published in the summer of 2001.[2]

The present volume contains an index of surnames found in those papers published in Sonoma County between 1881 and 1885. Other volumes are planned for the future. Some of the entries include residents from the surrounding counties of Marin, Napa, Solano, Lake, and Mendocino. Abstracts of some of the articles found in local newspapers appear on-line at <www.newspaperabstracts.com>.

Newspapers indexed

CR	Cloverdale Reveille	1881 - 1885
DD	Daily Democrat	July 1883 - 1885
DR	Daily Republican	1881 - 1885
HE	Healdsburg Enterprise	1881 - 1883
PCo	Petaluma Courier	1881 - 1885
PWA	Petaluma Weekly Argus	1881 - 1885
RRF	Russian River Flag	1881 - 1885
SD	Sonoma Democrat	1881 - 1885
SI	Sonoma Index Tribune	15 August - December 1885
SRR	Santa Rosa Republican	1881 - 1885
SWI	Sonoma Weekly Index	24 November 1882 - 5 April 1884

Other newspapers published during this time period
Other newspapers were published during this period, but no copies could be located. They include the Daily Morning Imprint, Echo, Echo de Santa Rosa (Italian), Outlook, Pacific Sentinel, Santa Rosa Journal (German), L'etoile des pouvies et de souffrants (not indexed, but issues for 1881-1883 are available at the Sonoma County Library Annex).

---

[1]Sonoma County Genealogy Society, *Surname Index to Vital Data in Newspapers, Sonoma County, California, 1854-1875: Volume I* (Bowie, Md.: Heritage Books, 2001).

[2]Sonoma County Genealogy Society, *Surname Index to Vital Data in Newspapers, Sonoma County, California, 1876-1880: Volume II* (Bowie, Md.: Heritage Books, 2001).

Microfilm copies of the newspapers may be found at these libraries

Cloverdale Public Library   CR
401 North Cloverdale Blvd.
Cloverdale, CA 95425
707-894-5271

Healdsburg Museum   HE, RRF
221 Matheson
Healdsburg, CA   95448
707-431-3325

Healdsburg Public Library   HE, RRF
Piper and Center Streets
Healdsburg, CA   95448
707-433-3772

Petaluma Public Library   PC, PWA
100 Fairgrounds Drive
Petaluma, CA 94952
707-763-9801

Sonoma County Library Annex   DD, DR , SD, SRR
3rd and E Streets
Santa Rosa, CA 95404
707-545-0831   ext. 562

Sonoma State Library   SD
1801 E. Cotati Ave.
Rohnert Park, CA   94928
707-664-2161

Sonoma Valley Regional Library   SI, SWI
755 West Napa Street
Sonoma, CA 95476
707-996-5217

Aids to interpreting the data

This third volume contains more than 13,000 entries. There are many typographical errors in these early papers and although every effort has been made to ensure the accuracy of the names, the reader will note variations in spelling of both surnames and given names. If the name you are researching does not appear where you expect it, consider variant spellings. Just as may be found in other early vital records—birth, death, marriage, and the like—newspapers also include errors of fact or transcription. Some microfilms of the early papers are difficult to read and while our abstractors did their best, some inaccuracies may have occurred. The serious researcher is always encouraged to go to the original source if at all possible, and to check other local sources if they exist. In particular, consider variations in spelling or spacing of surnames and given names, as well as possible initials, which may occur in the various sources. We have not attempted to make a decision about which format is correct or commonly used; that is up to the individual researcher.

Be aware that a particular type of record, i.e., a marriage record, may contain the names of persons other than the bride and groom, such as the minister or parents. A death record may also include the names of family members. Occasionally, a birth or a marriage announcement is given years after the event. These births and marriages did not take place in Sonoma County, but elsewhere in the country.

In order to conserve space we have used some standard abbreviations:

Code	Type of Record
b.	Birth record. The entry will almost always be under the name of the father, as the child's name is seldom given in the newspaper. Birth records were first recorded in Sonoma County in 1871.
d.	Death record. Some of the names listed may be family members as well as the deceased. Deaths were first recorded in Sonoma County in 1871.
m.	Marriage record. Marriages were first recorded in 1847.
p.	Probate record. In many cases this is the only indication of a person's death in Sonoma County.
o.	Other record. This may be a divorce, or any other type of article giving some genealogical information about the individual.
s.	The article appears in a supplement to the newspaper of that date.

Comments

In some cases the last column in the chart contains comments. This may include the name of a cemetery if known, a location mentioned in the item, special circumstances, where additional information can be found, and the like. A list of Sonoma County cemeteries follows, as does a map of the county, and a list of Sonoma County place names. *Place names which do not include a state abbreviation should be assumed to be California and are often Sonoma County.*

Historical information on towns and villages in Sonoma County is reprinted here from *The Sonoma Searcher.*[3]

SONOMA COUNTY TOWNS
AND VILLAGES: VINTAGE 1890

America is ten miles north of Santa Rosa; including the immediate vicinity; it has a population of 250. It is more widely known as Mark West Springs. It has a hotel and post office and is a resort for tourists and invalids. A stage line affords communication with Santa Rosa.

Bloomfield is a thriving community at the head of Big Valley, twelve miles north of Petaluma. The population is about 350. The village has a full complement of stores, churches and societies; a good hotel is maintained. It has communication by stage with Petaluma. It is growing and offers inducements to settlers.

Bodega is eighteen miles north of Petaluma, and located on Bodega Bay in the midst of a fine dairy country from which, with the fishing business, it derives its support. It boasts of a hotel, post office and express office.

Clairville is located twenty-three miles northwest from Santa Rosa on the line of the S. F. & N. P. R. R. It is in the midst of a farming and vine growing district. There are several wineries in the immediate neighborhood. It has a population of 150. Skaggs' Springs are six miles distant from this point with which communication is maintained by stage.

Cloverdale is fourth in point of wealth and population amongst the towns of Sonoma County. It is the present terminus of the San Francisco and North Pacific Railroad, and is distant thirty-three miles northwest of Santa Rosa and eighty-four miles from San Francisco. It is in the midst of a large and productive region, and is the center of trade for the wool interest and extensive hop fields of this part of the country. The climate here is more bracing than in the southern portion of Sonoma, and is especially adapted to the growth of the hardier varieties of fruits. The population is about 1,400 and is steadily growing. The leading denominations have places of worship with good congregations. All the leading secret and fraternal orders and societies have flourishing organizations. Hotel accommodations are good. The town is amply supplied with water furnished by the Cloverdale Water Company. Real estate is low, and the opportunities offered to the settler are unexcelled by those of other places. Stages leave here for Ukiah, Mendocino City, Eureka and other points on the North Coast, and for all points in Lake County and northern Napa. A railroad will, in a few months, connect it with Ukiah, Mendocino County. The Cloverdale *Reveille* ably advocates the interest of the community. It is published weekly.

Cozzens. A small burg located a few miles distant from Healdsburg. It has a population of 150 and is surrounded by a prosperous farming and wine growing community. A saw mill is located here and a general merchandise store supplies the needed requirements of the village.

Duncan's Mills is located thirty miles north from Petaluma. It has communication with San Francisco by the North Pacific Coast Railroad. It is supported by important lumber, dairy and stock raising interests. The Duncan's Mill's Land and Lumber Company saw mills are located here. The population is about 250. The surrounding country is noted for its romantic and picturesque scenery, and abundance of game and fish. It is a favorite resort for the tourist, the sportsman and for camping parties during the summer months. Stages leave here for all points in Mendocino and Humboldt counties.

Fisherman's Bay is located on the coast above Fort Ross. A population of 200 is supported by the

---

[3]"Sonoma County Towns and Villages: Vintage 1890," *The Sonoma Searcher*, volume 23 (June 1996): 52; reprinted from *Illustrated History of Sonoma County* (Chicago: Lewis Publishing, 1889), pp. 168-170.

farming interest and employment at the saw and shingle mills which are located here.

Fisk's Mills is a small village of about 150 population, in Salt Point Township, distant about twelve miles north of Fort Ross. Communication is had with Duncan's Mills by stage.

Forestville is distant twelve miles northwest of Santa Rosa, on the S. F. & N. P. R. R. Large quantities of tan-bark are shipped from this point. A rustic chair factory is located here. The business community consists of a hotel, blacksmith shops and two general merchandise stores. The surrounding country is devoted to farming.

Fort Ross is a small settlement forty-two miles north of Petaluma. It contains many reminders of the early days when a Russian colony was located here. It is one of the oldest settlements on the northern coast of California. The population is about 130, who are principally engaged in stock raising and farming. It is connected with Duncan's Mills by stage.

Freestone is on the line of the North Pacific Coast Railroad. The population is about 175, supported by the dairying and farming carried on in the vicinity.

Fulton. An ambitious and growing village on the line of the S. F. & N. P. R. R., four miles from Santa Rosa, is surrounded by a rich agricultural district. Considerable fruit is raised here. The population is 200, dependent upon the fruit and farming interests of the vicinity. From this place a branch of the S. F. & N. P. R. R. extends to Guerneville.

Geyser Springs is located sixteen miles from Cloverdale, from which place they are reached by stage. It is a noted health and pleasure resort. The numerous mineral springs in the vicinity are the chief attraction.

Guerneville. The progressive and prosperous town of Guerneville is situated in the midst of a large lumber producing district, and is surrounded by forests of redwood; a branch of the S. F. & N. P. R. R. has its terminus at this point. The town derived its name from one of its pioneer residents who is engaged in the large milling interests of the town. There are four extensive lumber mills located in the town, employing a large number of men. The present population is variously estimated at from 750 to 900. As the forests are being cleared off the land is put under cultivation, producing fine crops of vegetables and cereals, and a large yield of fruit. The Korbel mills located about three miles up the Russian River, are the most extensive lumber mills in the county. Considerable attention has of late been paid to the vine, and many acres have been set out. In addition to the lumber mills, there is also a box factory and shingle mill in active operation. The prospects of this town are very bright. Its rapid growth and prosperity are assured.

Kellogg. A summer resort, sixteen miles from Santa Rosa, with which it is connected by stage.

Lakeside is a thriving and growing village, twenty-two miles southeast of Santa Rosa. There are large farming, dairy and stock raising interests in the vicinity; the population is about 150.

Litton Springs. A noted health and pleasure resort, four miles from Healdsburg, on the S. F. & N. P. R. R. The water of the mineral springs located here is bottled and finds a market all over the State. The Litton Springs College is located at this point. The country in the neighborhood is rich and productive, and inviting to settlement.

Mark West is on the line of the S. F. & N. P. R. R. six miles north of Santa Rosa. The leading interests of the vicinity are farming, fruit and vine growing. The population is about 100. The surrounding country is rich and fertile and excellently adapted to the growth of vines and fruit.

Occidental. This growing and prosperous town is located on the line of the North Pacific Coast Railroad, about thirty miles north of Petaluma. Farming, fruit growing and lumber manufacturing are the principal industries in which the inhabitants are engaged. The population is 225.

Penn's Grove is a small settlement five miles north of Petaluma on the line of the S. F. & N. P. R. R. It is in the midst of a large vine growing and wine producing district. The population is 125.

Timber Cove is forty-five miles north of Petaluma, and has a population of 160. The occupation of the residents is mainly farming, stock raising, and dairying. It is known by the Post Office Department as Seaview.

Skaggs' Springs. Has long been noted as a health and pleasure resort, twenty-nine miles distant from Santa Rosa. A stage connects it with Clairville, six miles distant. The population is about 115, who are principally engaged in wool raising.

Smith's Ranch, or more generally known as Bodega Roads, is twenty-five miles north of Petaluma, and is on the line of the North Pacific Coast Railroad. The people of the surrounding country are principally engaged in dairying and farming, from which their support is chiefly derived. The population is about 250.

Stony Point. Is located seven miles north of Petaluma in the midst of a large fruit, dairy and farming region. The population is about 200, including those residing in the immediate vicinity.

Valley Ford is one of the prosperous communities of Sonoma. It is on the line of the North Pacific Coast R. R., eighteen miles north of Petaluma. It boasts of a flouring mill. The population is about 250. It is supported by the large dairying, farming, and stock raising interest by which it is surrounded.

Windsor is another of the large and thrifty villages of Sonoma County. It is ten miles northwest of Santa Rosa, in the midst of a large farming and fruit growing section. There are many vineyards in the neighborhood and several nurseries. It has a population of 400. The village boasts of a brick manufactory, several fruit-drying establishments, and other industries of minor importance.

Other Sonoma County Towns and Townships

Alexander Valley	Knights Valley	Salt Point
Altruria	Lakeville	Salt Point Township
Analy Township	Lewis	San Antonio
Annapolis	Liberty	San Luis/Louis
Asti	Llano	Santa Rosa
Bennett Valley	Los Guilicos	Santa Rosa Township
Bodega Corners	Lytton	Schellville
Bodega Township	Markham	Sea View
Cloverdale Township	Matanzas	Sebastopol
Donahue	Mendocino Township	Soda Rock
Dry Creek	Ocean Township	Sonoma
El Verano	Petaluma	Sonoma Township
Elmore	Petaluma Township	Stewarts Point
Forestville Station	Pocket Canyon	Table Mountain
Geysers	Redwood Township	Two Rock
Geyserville	Rincon	Vallejo Township
Glen Ellen	Rincon Valley	Washington
Green Valley	Rio Nido	Washington Township
Healdsburg	Roblar	West Windsor
Kenwood	Russian River Township	

Sonoma County, California
Townships
Map — Circa 1896-1897

Sonoma County Cemeteries

Alexander (Cyrus) Family Cemetery
Alpine Valley Graves
Annapolis Church Cemetery
Asti Family Cemetery
Beeson Cemetery
Bennett Valley Cemetery
Bloomfield Cemetery
Bodega Bay Cemetery
Bodega Town Calvary Cemetery
Canfield Cemetery
Catron Family Cemetery
Chanate
Cloverdale Cemetery
Druids Cemetery
Duncans Mill Cemetery
Evergreen Cemetery
Faudre Family Records
Faught
Forestville Odd Fellows Cemetery
Fulton Cemetery
General Vallejo Ranch Cemetery
Geyserville Hill Cemetery
Gilliam Cemetery
Green Valley M.E. Church Cemetery
Guerneville Cemetery
Hall Cemetery
Healdsburg Oak Mound Cemetery
Holliday Ranch Graves
Joy Ranch Graves
Liberty Cemetery
London Ranch Graves
Long Family Ranch Cemetery
Macedonia M.E. Church South Cemetery
Manzanita or Hagen Ranch Cemetery
Mark West Cemetery
McPeak Cemetery

Nobels Ranch Cemetery
Nun Canyon Grave
O'Farrell (Jasper) Ranch Grave
Patten (Charles) Ranch Cemetery
Petaluma Cypress Hill Cemetery
Petaluma Calvary Cemetery
Petaluma Jewish Cemetery
Petaluma Cypress Hill Cemetery - Elmore Plot
Peterson Ranch Graves, Bennett Valley
Pioneer Cemetery
Pleasant Hill Cemetery
Preston Cemetery
Russian Cemetery (Fort Ross)
San Jacinto Battle Veteran
Santa Rosa Rural Cemetery
Santa Rosa Catholic Cemetery
Santa Rosa Odd Fellows Cemetery
Santa Rosa Odd Fellows Lawn Cemetery
Santa Rosa Odd Fellows Mausoleum
Sebastopol Cemetery
Sharp Cemetery
Shiloh Cemetery
Skaggs Family Cemetery
Sonoma Mountain Cemetery
Sonoma Valley Cemetery
Sonoma Catholic Cemetery
Spring Hill Cemetery
Steele Family Cemetery
Thompson Family Cemetery
Two Rock Church Cemetery
Upper Dry Creek Cemetery
Warneke Ranch Cemetery

Acknowledgments

This project was prepared using a four-step process. First, microfilm of the early newspapers was read and the information was abstracted onto prepared forms. Next, the information on the forms was entered into table format by data entry persons using their own hardware and software at home. Then the data was sent online to a person who acted as the central data collector. Finally, camera-ready copy was prepared and proofread against the abstracted information.

Persons contributing to this effort included the following:

Project Coordinator
Audrey Herman

Abstractors
Esther Mott
Ray Owen
Audrey Phillips
June Smith
Jeanne Taylor
Lenora Williams

Data Entry
Maggi Andrews
Anna Conley
Didi DeGolia
Denise Mills
Melba Newman
Lois Nimmo
Lorraine Parmer
Audrey Phillips
Debra Sapp
Mary Smith
Helen Strickley

Proof Readers
Doris Dickenson
Audrey Herman

Camera-Ready Copy
Carmen Finley

A

(1) Surname	(2) Given Name	(3)	(4)	(5) Date	(6) Pg	(7) Col	(8) Comments
Abbey	Alfred	m.	RRF	24 May 1883	2	3	
Abbey	Alfred	m.	SD	26 May 1883	2	7	
Aborn	Mrs.	m.	SD	10 Oct. 1885	1	5	
Abraham	L.	b.	PCo	14 May 1884	3	4	
Abraham	Louis	m.	CR	19 May 1883	3	2	
Abraham	Louis	b.	RRF	8 May 1884	5	6	
Abraham	P.	b.	PCo	30 Apr. 1884	2	6	
Abraham	P.	b.	PWA	3 May 1884	3	6	
Abraham	P.	b.	SD	10 May 1884	2	4	
Abrams	Frederick G.	d.	CR	19 Mar. 1881	4	3	
Abrams	Frederick G.	d.	PCo	16 Mar. 1881	3	4	son of Peter
Abrams	Frederick G.	d.	SD	19 Mar. 1881	3	8	
Abrams	Henrietta	d.	DR	18 Nov. 1881	3	2	
Abrams	Nettie L.	m.	DR	15 Nov. 1882	2	3	
Abrams	Nettie L.	m.	PCo	8 Nov. 1882	3	6	
Abrams	Nettie L.	m.	SD	4 Nov. 1882	3	6	
Abramsky	B.	b.	PCo	19 Dec. 1883	3	4	
Abshere	Margaret	d.	CR	2 Aug. 1884	3	1	
Abshier	Maggie B.	d.	DR	28 July 1884	3	3	
Abshier	Maggie B.	d.	PCo	30 July 1884	3	6	
Abshier	Maggie B.	d.	PWA	2 Aug. 1884	3	4	
Ackerman	Ethel M.	d.	DR	3 Oct. 1881	2	3	
Ackerman	Ethel M.	d.	PCo	28 Sept. 1881	3	5	
Ackerman	Ethel M.	d.	SD	8 Oct. 1881	3	8	
Adams	(female)	b.	DR	17 Mar. 1884	3	3	
Adams	A. H.	d.	PCo	1 Apr. 1885	3	6	
Adams	A. H.	d.	SD	4 Apr. 1885	2	5	
Adams	Andrew J.	d.	DR	22 Oct. 1881	2	4	
Adams	Andrew J.	d.	PCo	26 Oct. 1881	3	4	
Adams	Andrew J.	d.	SD	22 Oct. 1881	3	6	
Adams	Belle	m.	PC	4 July 1883	3	5	
Adams	Belle	m.	SD	30 June 1883	3	5	
Adams	Ellen	m.	PCo	28 June 1882	3	5	
Adams	Ellen	m.	SD	24 June 1882	3	5	
Adams	Emma	m.	CR	5 Mar. 1881	4	2	
Adams	Emma	m.	DR	1 Mar. 1881	3	2	
Adams	Emma	m.	PCo	9 Mar. 1881	3	4	
Adams	Emma	m.	SD	5 Mar. 1881	3	8	

(1) Surname	(2) Given Name	(3)	(4)	(5) Date	(6) Pg	(7) Col	(8) Comments
Adams	Eva Lulu	d.	PWA	25 Apr. 1885	3	4&6	
Adams	F. M.	d.	DR	8 Sept. 1882	3	1	
Adams	Frank E.	m.	DR	13 July 1885	3	4	
Adams	Frank E.	m.	PCo	15 July 1885	3	6	
Adams	Frank	b.	DR	29 July 1885	3	4	
Adams	Frank	b.	PCo	22 July 1885	3	6	
Adams	Frank	b.	SD	18 July 1885	5	5	
Adams	H.	m.	PCo	16 July 1884	3	6	
Adams	Henry	d.	DR	18 July 1882	3	2	
Adams	Henry	d.	PCo	28 June 1882	3	5	
Adams	Henry	d.	SD	8 July 1882	2	5	
Adams	J. H.	m.	DR	5 July 1884	3	4	
Adams	J. S.	m.	SD	22 Aug. 1885	6	2	
Adams	James F.	d.	DR	2 Feb. 1882	2	3	
Adams	James F.	d.	PCo	15 Feb. 1882	3	4	
Adams	James F.	d.	SD	4 Feb. 1882	3	6	
Adams	Jerusha	m.	SD	25 Mar. 1882	3	6	
Adams	John	b.	DR	22 Aug. 1881	2	3	
Adams	John	b.	SD	3 Sept. 1881	3	8	
Adams	John	b.	SD	20 Aug. 1881	3	8	
Adams	Joshua	b.	SD	22 Aug. 1885	6	2	
Adams	L.	b.	SWI	29 Mar. 1884	3	5	
Adams	Lora Z.	m.	DR	25 Nov. 1881	2	3	
Adams	Lora Z.	m.	PCo	23 Nov. 1881	3	5	
Adams	Lucy K.	m.	PCo	24 June 1885	3	6	
Adams	Lucy K.	m.	SD	27 June 1885	5	4	
Adams	Lynchburg	b.	PCo	19 Mar. 1884	3	6	
Adams	Lynchburg	b.	PWA	22 Mar. 1884	3	6	
Adams	Lynchburg	b.	SD	22 Mar. 1884	2	4	
Adams	May	d.	DR	9 July 1884	3	3	
Adams	Sophrona	m.	SD	16 Apr. 1881	3	8	
Adams	T. J.	b.	PCo	27 July 1881	3	5	
Adams	W. E.	b.	RRF	10 Feb. 1881	2	5	
Adams	W. E.	b.	SD	19 Feb. 1881	3	8	
Adamson	I. N.	b.	RRF	28 July 1881	2	5	
Adamson	Isaac Newton	m.	DR	9 Nov. 1885	2	2	
Adamson	Isaac Newton	m.	SD	14 Nov. 1885	3	5	
Adamson	Milton	d.	PWA	28 Mar. 1885	3	4&5	
Adamson	Milton	d.	SD	4 Apr. 1885	2	5	also p. 5 col. 5
Adamson	Rena	m.	DR	4 Sept. 1885	3	4	
Adamson	Rena	m.	PCo	2 Sept. 1885	3	6	
Adel	Frank	d.	DR	16 Oct. 1885	3	4	

(1) Surname	(2) Given Name	(3)	(4)	(5) Date	(6) Pg	(7) Col	(8) Comments
Adel	Frank	d.	PCo	21 Oct. 1885	3	4	
Adel	Frank	d.	SD	24 Oct. 1885	5	4	
Aglala	M., Miss	m.	SD	19 July 1884	2	5	
Agnew	Lizzie F.	m.	PCo	10 Jan. 1883	3	6	
Agnew	Lizzie F.	m.	PWA	5 Jan. 1883	2	5	
Ahbrigi	Peter	b.	PCo	3 May 1882	3	5	
Ahbrigi	Peter	b.	SD	6 May 1882	3	6	
Aiken	Alice E.	d.	PCo	21 June 1882	3	5	
Aiken	Edith	m.	DR	24 May 1884	3	2	
Aiken	Edward	d.	DR	6 Dec. 1884	3	2	
Aiken	Ellen	m.	DD	10 Nov. 1883	3	3	
Aiken	H. S.	b.	PWA	23 Aug. 1884	3	4	
Aiken	H. S.	b.	SD	6 Sept. 1884	2	5	
Aiken	Henry	b.	PCo	20 Aug. 1884	3	4	
Aiken	Henry S.	m.	PC	30 May 1883	3	4	
Aiken	Henry S.	m.	SD	26 May 1883	2	7	
Aiken	Martha	d.	PCo	4 Mar. 1885	3	6	
Aiken	Martha	d.	PWA	28 Feb. 1885	3	5	
Aiken	Martha	d.	SD	14 Mar. 1885	5	5	
Aiken	Minnie E.	m.	SD	28 Jan. 1882	3	6	
Aiken	William E.	d.	PCo	10 Dec. 1884	3	1&5	
Aiken	William E.	d.	PWA	6 Dec. 1884	3	4	
Aiken	William E.	d.	SD	27 Dec. 1884	2	4	
Aiken	William	d.	SD	24 June 1882	3	5	
Aikin	Edith	m.	PCo	28 May 1884	2	4	
Aikin	Edith	m.	SD	31` May 1884	1	5	also p. 2 col. 3
Ainsby	Eleanor A.	m.	PCo	21 June 1882	3	5	
Ainsby	Eleanor A.	m.	SD	17 June 1882	2	4	
Ainsworth	A. S.	d.	DR	4 Nov. 1881	2	3	
Aitken	W.	b.	RRF	23 June 1881	2	4	
Aitken	W.	b.	SD	2 July 1881	3	8	
Akers	S.	o.	SIT	22 Aug. 1885	2	2	
Albee	Aurel	p.	DD	11 July 1883	3	2	
Albee	Aurel	d.	PCo	17 Jan. 1883	3	5	
Albee	Fred I.	m.	PCo	21 June 1882	3	5	
Albee	Fred I.	m.	SD	17 June 1882	2	4	
Albertson	Frank	m.	RRF	22 June 1882	3	6	
Albertson	Joseph	d.	RRF	28 July 1881	3	6	
Albertson	Martha A.	d.	DR	25 July 1881	2	3	
Albertson	Martha	d.	RRF	28 July 1881	3	6	
Alderson	H. E.	o.	RRF	3 Aug. 1882	3	6	
Alexander	Gertrude	d.	RRF	20 Dec. 1883	2	2	family cemetery

(1) Surname	(2) Given Name	(3)	(4)	(5) Date	(6) Pg	(7) Col	(8) Comments
Alexander	William H.	d.	PC	13 June 1883	3	6	
Allen	Alta	m.	DR	27 July 1882	2	3	
Allen	Ann W.	d.	DR	30 Dec. 1884	2	2	
Allen	Ann W.	d.	SD	3 Jan. 1885	2	4	
Allen	D. C.	b.	DR	31 Dec. 1881	2	3	
Allen	D. C.	b.	PCo	11 Jan. 1882	3	6	
Allen	D. C.	b.	SD	7 Jan. 1882	3	8	
Allen	D. C.	b.	SD	21 Jan. 1882	3	6	
Allen	Edward A.	b.	DR	16 Nov. 1885	3	4	
Allen	Edward A.	b.	PCo	11 Nov. 1885	3	4	
Allen	Frank	b.	SD	19 Mar. 1881	3	8	
Allen	George R.	m.	PCo	19 Nov. 1884	3	5	
Allen	George W.	d.	DD	4 Dec. 1883	3	3	
Allen	Henry	d.	DR	25 Aug. 1885	3	4	
Allen	Henry	d.	SD	29 Aug. 1885	2	4	
Allen	Jane	m.	PCo	22 Apr. 1885	3	6	
Allen	Jane	m.	SD	25 Apr. 1885	2	5	
Allen	John	b.	PCo	7 Dec. 1881	3	5	
Allen	John	b.	SD	17 Dec. 1881	3	7	
Allen	Julia	d.	SD	7 May 1881	3	8	
Allen	Julia	d.	SD	23 Apr. 1881	3	8	
Allen	Mary	d.	DR	17 May 1884	3	2	
Allen	Mary	d.	RRF	15 May 1884	5	6	
Allen	Mattie M.	m.	DD	2 Aug. 1883	3	2	
Allen	Mattie M.	m.	PC	1 Aug. 1883	3	6	
Allen	Mattie M.	m.	SD	4 Aug. 1883	2	5	
Allen	Mattie	m.	PWA	28 July 1883	3	7	
Allen	O. S.	d.	CR	1 Dec. 1883	3	1	
Allen	Oliver	d.	PCo	31 May 1882	3	5	
Allen	Oliver	d.	PCo	31 May 1882	3	1	Cypress Hill Cemetery
Allen	Orrick Sterling	d.	DD	27 Nov. 1883	3	1&2	
Allen	Orrick Sterling	d.	HE	29 Nov. 1883	2	4	
Allen	Orrick Sterling	d.	RRF	29 Nov. 1883	2	3	
Allen	Orrick Sterling	d.	SD	1 Dec. 1883	3	2&4	Rural Cemetery
Allen	Otis	o.	DR	4 Aug. 1882	3	1	
Allen	Otis	b.	SD	14 Mar. 1885	5	5	
Allen	S. I.	m.	DR	28 Dec. 1881	2	2	
Allen	S. I.	m.	PCo	4 Jan. 1882	3	7	
Allen	S. I.	m.	SD	31 Dec. 1881	3	6	
Allison	Hester L.	m.	SD	9 Apr. 1881	3	8	
Allison	Louisa	m.	DR	21 Nov. 1882	3	2	

(1) Surname	(2) Given Name	(3)	(4)	(5) Date	(6) Pg	(7) Col	(8) Comments
Allison	Louisa	m.	PCo	29 Nov. 1882	3	6	
Allison	Samuel F.	m.	DR	23 Mar. 1884	3	3	
Allison	Samuel	m.	PCo	26 Mar. 1884	3	6	
Alloway	Mary	m.	DR	2 Oct. 1885	3	4	
Alloway	Mary	m.	PCo	30 Sept. 1885	3	6	
Alvard	Harriet W.	d.	SD	27 Jan. 1883	3	6	
Alward	Harriet W.	d.	PCo	24 Jan. 1883	3	5	
Ambler	John	m.	PCo	12 Aug. 1885	3	6	
Amen	Mrs.	m.	CR	11 Oct. 1884	3	3	
Ames	Annie L.	m.	PWA	2 June 1883	3	8	
Ames	Annie L.	m.	SD	2 June 1883	2	7	
Amon	Rebecca J.	m.	SD	7 Jan. 1882	3	8	
Amos	Francis	d.	SD	19 Sept. 1885	2	4	
Amos	Orvilla	m.	SD	2 July 1881	3	8	
Amos	Ovilla	m.	DR	1 July 1881	2	2	
Amos	R. C.	d.	CR	16 Apr. 1881	5	3	
Amos	R. C.	d.	CR	16 Apr. 1881	5	2	
Amos	Robert C.	d.	DR	12 Apr. 1881	2	3	
Amos	Robert C.	d.	SD	16 Apr. 1881	3	8	
Amos	Villa	m.	RRF	30 June 1881	3	1	
Anderson	Allen J.	m.	SD	5 May 1883	3	1	
Anderson	Andrew	b.	SD	11 July 1885	5	6	
Anderson	C.	b.	DR	1 Feb. 1882	2	3	
Anderson	C.	b.	SD	4 Feb. 1882	3	6	
Anderson	Freida F.	d.	SD	29 Aug. 1885	2	4	
Anderson	Frieda F.	d.	DR	20 Aug. 1885	3	4	
Anderson	George	d.	CR	15 Oct. 1881	1	2	
Anderson	George	d.	DD	13 Aug. 1883	3	3	
Anderson	George	d.	SD	18 Aug. 1883	2	6	
Anderson	Irene E.	m.	DD	4 Oct. 1883	3	2	
Anderson	J. T.	b.	PCo	22 Apr. 1885	3	6	
Anderson	James	d.	DR	19 May 1884	3	2	
Anderson	James	b.	PCo	8 Mar. 1882	3	5	
Anderson	James	b.	RRF	2 Mar. 1882	2	4	
Anderson	James	b.	SD	11 Mar. 1882	3	6	
Anderson	James	d.	SD	24 May 1884	1	5	Rural Cemetery
Anderson	James	d.	SD	24 May 1884	2	3	
Anderson	John A.	b.	RRF	12 Oct. 1882	2	3	
Anderson	John A.	b.	SD	30 Sept. 1882	3	6	
Anderson	Josie A.	b.	DR	2 Oct. 1882	2	3	
Anderson	T. J.	b.	SD	25 Apr. 1885	2	5	
Andrae	Jennie	m.	DR	8 Mar. 1882	2	3	

(1) Surname	(2) Given Name	(3)	(4)	(5) Date	(6) Pg	(7) Col	(8) Comments
Andreson	J. F.	b.	DR	16 Sept. 1881	3	2	
Andrews	George	m.	RRF	25 Aug. 1881	2	4	
Andrews	C. N.	m.	SD	5 Jan. 1884	1	4	
Andrews	Cyrus N.	m.	PCo	2 Jan. 1884	3	6	
Andrews	Cyrus N.	m.	PWA	29 Dec. 1883	3	6	
Andrews	George	m.	SD	3 Sept. 1881	3	8	
Andrews	Howard	m.	PCo	6 May 1885	3	6	
Andrews	Howard	m.	SD	9 May 1885	2	5	
Angellotti	Emma T.	m.	DR	2 Oct. 1885	3	4	
Angle	Rench	b,	DD	6 Oct. 1883	3	3	
Angle	Rench	b.	SD	13 Oct. 1883	3	4	
Angwin	William	b.	RRF	13 July 1882	2	3	
Anker	Annie	m.	CR	21 Apr. 1883	3	1	
Anker	Annie	m.	PC	25 Apr. 1883	3	5	
Anker	Annie	d.	PCo	4 Oct. 1882	3	6	
Anker	Neil	b.	CR	13 Aug. 1885	3	2	
Anker	Yocum	d.	CR	29 Mar. 1883	3	2	Riverside Cem.
Anker	Yokum	d.	PCo	2 Apr. 1884	3	6	
Annette	James	m.	DD	19 Nov. 1883	3	3	
Annette	James	m.	SD	24 Nov. 1883	3	4	
Anthony	Josiah	d.	SD	23 Apr. 1881	3	8	
Anthony	Nellie M.	m.	PCo	5 July 1882	3	5	
Apperson	John A.	m.	SD	8 Jan. 1881	3	8	
Apple	J. H.	b.	SD	5 Mar. 1881	3	8	
Appleton	H.	b.	PCo	15 Mar. 1882	3	4	
Appleton	H.	b.	SD	25 Mar. 1882	3	6	
Aradou	J. (son of)	d.	DD	26 July 1883	3	2	
Aradou	J. (son of)	d.	PC	25 July 1883	3	6	
Aradou	J. (son of)	d.	RRF	19 July 1883	2	4	
Aradou	J. (son of)	d.	SD	28 July 1883	2	5	
Arbuckle	Adila	d.	DR	24 Dec. 1884	2	2	
Archer	Henry	b.	DR	12 Nov. 1885	3	4	twins
Archer	Henry	b.	PCo	18 Nov. 1885	3	4	
Archer	Henry	b.	SD	21 Nov. 1885	3	5	
Archer	William H.	m.	DR	18 Dec. 1884	2	2	
Armstrong	Emma	d.	PCo	9 Nov. 1881	3	5	
Armstrong	Wiliam	d.	SD	12 Nov. 1881	3	7	
Armstrong	William Scott	d.	DD	8 Sept. 1883	3	3	
Armstrong	William	d.	DR	7 Nov. 1881	2	3	
Arneke	Minnie	m.	DR	22 Dec. 1882	3	3	
Arneke	Minnie	m.	PCo	27 Dec. 1882	3	6	
Arneke	Minnie	m.	SD	30 Dec. 1882	3	6	

(1) Surname	(2) Given Name	(3)	(4)	(5) Date	(6) Pg	(7) Col	(8) Comments
Arnold	Brad, Mrs.	d.	SD	7 July 1883	2	5	
Arnold	Edward	d.	SD	21 Mar. 1885	2	5	
Arnold	Emma	m.	PCo	14 Jan. 1885	3	6	
Arnold	Emma	m.	SD	10 Jan. 1885	2	6	
Arnold	Florence L.	m.	SD	24 Jan. 1885	5	5	
Arnold	George	d.	DR	30 Jan. 1882	2	3	
Arnold	George	d.	SD	4 Feb. 1882	3	6	
Arnold	Harley	d.	DR	4 Apr. 1882	2	2	
Arnold	Marshall	m.	DD	29 Dec. 1883	3	3	
Arntruster	Herbert	b.	SD	19 Jan. 1884	3	6	
Arntruster	Hubert	b.	PCo	9 Jan. 1884	3	6	
Arntruster	Hubert	b.	PWA	5 Jan. 1884	3	7	
Arsnip	Sarah	m.	DR	10 Aug. 1885	3	4	
Arsnip	Sarah	m.	SD	22 Aug. 1885	6	2	
Arthur	Charles R.	m.	SD	22 Jan. 1881	3	8	
Arthur	Emma R.	d.	SD	19 Feb. 1881	3	8	
Aserson	Annie Erika	m.	SD	21 Jan. 1882	3	6	
Ashley	Frank	m.	RRF	20 Oct. 1881	2	4	
Ashley	Frankie	m.	DR	7 Oct. 1881	2	3	
Ashley	Frankie	m.	PCo	12 Oct. 1881	3	5	
Ashley	Frankie	m.	SD	15 Oct. 1881	3	8	
Ashley	Mary A.	m.	DR	3 Dec. 1881	2	3	
Ashley	Mary A.	m.	PCo	7 Dec. 1881	3	5	
Ashley	Mary A.	m.	SD	17 Dec. 1881	3	7	
Ashley	W. T.	m.	PCo	5 Apr. 1882	3	5	
Ashley	William T.	m.	DR	23 Mar. 1882	2	3	
Ashley	William T.	m.	SD	8 Apr. 1882	3	6	
Ashton	C., Miss	m.	PWA	23 Aug. 1884	3	4	
Atherson	Carrie	m.	DD	5 Nov. 1883	3	2	
Atherson	Carrie	m.	SD	10 Nov. 1883	3	5	
Atherton	A. W.	m.	PCo	16 Jan. 1884	3	6	
Atherton	A. W.	m.	RRF	10 Jan. 1884	2	4	
Atherton	A. W.	m.	SD	19 Jan. 1884	3	6	
Atkins	W. G.	o.	DR	21 Oct. 1882	3	2	
Atkins	W. G.	o.	SD	30 Apr. 1881	3	4	
Atkins	W. G.	d.	SD	20 Jan. 1883	3	4	
Atkinson	(male)	b.	DR	23 Apr. 1884	3	2	
Atkinson	T. A.	b.	PCo	30 Apr. 1884	2	6	
Atkinson	T. A.	b.	RRF	1 May 1884	5	6	
Atkinson	T. A.	b.	SD	26 Apr. 1883	3	5	
Atterbury	Bessie	m.	DR	29 May 1884	3	2	
Atterbury	Bessie	m.	PCo	11 June 1884	3	5	

(1) Surname	(2) Given Name	(3)	(4)	(5) Date	(6) Pg	(7) Col	(8) Comments
Atterbury	Bessie	m.	SD	31` May 1884	2	3	
Atterbury	Eva	m.	SD	7 Jan. 1882	3	4&8	
Atterbury	Evelyn	m.	PCo	11 Jan. 1882	3	6	
Atwater	Elizabeth S.	d.	PCo	13 Sept. 1882	3	7	
Atwater	F. H.	b.	PC	8 Aug. 1883	3	6	
Atwater	F. H.	b.	PWA	11 Aug. 1883	3	8	
Atwater	F. H.	b.	SD	11 Aug. 1883	2	7	
Atwater	Frank H.	m.	PCo	26 July 1882	3	6	
Atwater	Frank H.	m.	SD	29 July 1882	3	7	
Atwater	Henry M.	d.	PC	25 Apr. 1883	3	5	
Aubrey	Robert	d.	DR	1 Nov. 1881	2	3	filed aft. Nov. 29
Austin	Charles	m.	SD	11 July 1885	1	7	
Austin	Harry	o.	DR	20 June 1881	2	2	
Austin	Herbert	b.	DR	13 Aug. 1881	2	3	
Austin	Herbert	b.	SD	20 Aug. 1881	3	8	
Austin	Howard	d.	SD	19 Apr. 1884	3	4	
Austin	Howard James	d.	DR	14 Apr. 1884	3	3	
Austin	Howard James	d.	PCo	16 Apr. 1884	3	5	
Austin	Howard James	d.	PCo	23 Apr. 1884	2	6	
Austin	Howard James	d.	RRF	17 Apr. 1884	2	4	
Austin	James	o.	DR	26 Oct. 1882	2	1	
Austin	James, Mrs.	d.	DR	14 June 1884	3	3	
Austin	Maud Alice	d.	DR	20 Jan. 1882	3	2	
Averell	A.	b.	PCo	1 July 1885	3	6	
Avery	C. N.	b.	DR	18 Aug. 1884	3	3	
Avery	C. N.	b.	PCo	20 Aug. 1884	3	4	
Avery	M., Mr. & Mrs.	d.	CR	12 July 1884	3	1	
Avery	M., Mrs.	d.	DR	17 July 1884	3	3	
Avery	M., Mrs.	d.	PCo	23 July 1884	3	6	
Ayer	George	b.	PCo	31 May 1882	3	5	
Ayer	George	b.	SD	27 May 1882	3	5	
Ayers	Andrew	m.	DD	10 Sept. 1883	3	3	
Ayers	Andrew	m.	PWA	8 Sept. 1883	3	8	
Ayers	Andrew	m.	SD	15 Sept. 1883	2	4	
Ayers	Anna M.	m.	PCo	10 Dec. 1884	3	5	
Ayers	Anna M.	m.	PWA	6 Dec. 1884	3	4	
Ayers	B. F.	m.	SD	29 Jan. 1881	3	8	
Ayers	George	b.	DR	23 May 1882	2	3	
Ayers	Henry	m.	RRF	28 July 1881	2	3	
Ayers	Henry	m.	SD	13 Aug. 1881	3	8	
Ayers	Ida Matilda	d.	PCo	26 Oct. 1881	3	4	
Ayers	John	b.	PCo	21 Mar. 1883	3	5	

(1) Surname	(2) Given Name	(3)	(4)	(5) Date	(6) Pg	(7) Col	(8) Comments
Ayers	John	b.	PWA	24 Mar. 1883	3	7	
Ayres	Ben	d.	RRF	20 Oct. 1881	2	4	
Ayres	Henry	m.	DR	8 Aug. 1881	3	2	
Ayres	Henry	m.	RRF	4 Aug. 1881	2	5	
Ayres	Ida Matilda	d.	DR	19 Oct. 1881	3	2	
Ayres	Ida Matilda	d.	RRF	20 Oct. 1881	2	4	
Ayres	Ida Matilda	d.	SD	29 Oct. 1881	3	6	

B

(1) Surname	(2) Given Name	(3)	(4)	(5) Date	(6) Pg	(7) Col	(8) Comments
Babb	Hugh	d.	SD	9 July 1881	3	8	
Babcock	L. W.	m.	SD	10 Jan. 1885	2	6	
Babcock	Robert	b.	DD	15 Dec. 1883	3	1	
Babstock	John	d.	SD	29 Aug. 1885	2	4	
Baciagalupi	L.	p.	DR	9 July 1884	3	3	
Bacon	Frank	b.	DD	4 Dec. 1883	3	3	
Bacon	Frank	b.	SD	8 Dec. 1883	3	1	
Bacon	S. W.	b.	PCo	6 Sept. 1882	3	7	
Badger	Benjamin D.	b.	DD	27 Sept. 1883	3	3	
Badger	Benjamin D.	b.	SD	29 Sept. 1883	2	6	
Badger	Douglas	m.	DR	27 Dec. 1882	3	3	
Badger	Douglas	m.	PCo	3 Jan. 1883	3	4	
Badger	George W.	d.	PCo	30 Jan. 1884	3	6	
Badger	George W.	d.	PWA	26 Jan. 1884	3	6	
Badger	Mary E.	m.	DR	1 Aug. 1884	3	3	
Badger	Mary E.	m.	PCo	6 Aug. 1884	2	4	
Badger	Mary E.	m.	PWA	9 Aug. 1884	2	4	
Badger	Mary E.	m.	SD	9 Aug. 1884	3	4	
Badger	Robert A.	m.	DR	10 Dec. 1884	3	2	
Badger	Robert A.	m.	PCo	17 Dec. 1884	2	4	
Badger	Robert A.	m.	SD	13 Dec. 1884	2	5	
Badger	William N.	d.	SD	18 Aug. 1883	3	2	Rural Cemetery
Baechtel	Mart	b.	SD	15 Jun. 1881	3	8	
Baettge	Charles	b.	DR	31 Oct. 1881	2	3	
Baettge	Charles	b.	PC	4 July 1883	3	5	
Baettge	Charles	b.	PWA	7 July 1883	3	6	
Baettge	Charles	b.	SD	5 Nov. 1881	3	6	
Bagge	F.	b.	CR	11 June 1881	5	5	
Bagge	F. C. S.	b.	DD	27 Dec. 1883	3	3	
Bagge	F. C. S.	b.	PCo	2 Jan. 1884	3	6	
Bagge	F. C. S.	b.	RRF	2 June 1881	2	3	
Bagge	F. C. S.	b.	RRF	27 Dec. 1883	2	2	
Bagge	F. C. S.	b.	SD	11 June 1881	3	8	
Bagge	F. C. S.	b.	SD	5 Jan. 1884	1	8	
Bagley	Daniel	b.	PCo	9 Nov. 1881	3	5	
Bagliotti	Paul	b.	SD	7 July 1883	2	5	
Bahn	Selma	m.	SD	25 Mar. 1882	3	6	
Bahnsen	John	d.	CR	9 May 1885	3	1	

(1) Surname	(2) Given Name	(3)	(4)	(5) Date	(6) Pg	(7) Col	(8) Comments
Bahrs	Herman	d.	DR	25 Nov. 1881	2	3	
Bahrs	Herman	d.	PCo	23 Nov. 1881	3	5	
Bahrs	Herman	d.	SD	3 Dec. 1881	3	8	
Bailey	B. H.	b.	SD	8 Nov. 1884	2	5	
Bailey	B. H.	b.	SD	15 Nov. 1884	2	5	
Bailey	Burton H.	m.	CR	1 Jan. 1881	5	5	
Bailey	Mira E.	m.	DR	6 July 1885	3	3	
Bailey	Mira E.	m.	PCo	15 July 1885	3	6	
Bailey	Nina E.	m.	SD	11 July 1885	5	6	
Bailey	T. E. C.	m.	PWA	4 Apr. 1885	3	6	
Bailhache	J. N.	b.	HE	2 Feb. 1882	2	3	
Bailhache	John N.	b.	DR	4 Feb. 1882	2	3	
Bailhache	John N.	d.	DR	30 Nov. 1882	3	2	
Bailhache	John N.	b.	RRF	2 Feb. 1882	3	7	
Bailhache	John N.	b.	SD	4 Feb. 1882	3	6	
Bailhache	Robert	d.	DR	5 May 1884	3	2	
Bailhache	Robert	d.	PCo	7 May 1884	3	5	
Bailhache	Robert	d.	RRF	8 May 1884	5	6	
Bailhache	Robert	d.	SD	10 May 1884	1	5	
Bailhache	Robert	d.	SD	17 May 1884	3	5	
Bailhache	Ruth	m.	RRF	24 May 1883	2	3	
Bailhache	Ruth	m.	SD	26 May 1883	2	7	
Bailiff	Frank	d.	DR	30 Nov. 1882	2	3	Santa Rosa Cem.
Bailiff	Georgie	m.	SD	19 Sept. 1885	2	4	
Bailiff	Geranie	m.	DR	16 Sept. 1882	3	4	
Bailiff	John	d.	RRF	28 Dec. 1882	2	2	
Bain	James	b.	SD	21 Jan. 1882	3	6	
Bain	Robert (dau. of)	d.	DR	13 Dec. 1882	3	2	
Baker	A. M.	b.	CR	29 Aug. 1885	3	1	
Baker	A. M.	b.	PC	2 May 1883	3	5	
Baker	A. M.	b.	RRF	4 Aug. 1881	2	5	
Baker	A. M.	b.	RRF	26 Apr. 1883	2	3	
Baker	A. M.	b.	SD	5 May 1883	3	6	
Baker	J. C.	b.	PC	4 Apr. 1883	3	5	
Baker	J. C.	b.	RRF	29 Mar. 1883	2	4	
Baker	P. S.	m.	DR	21 May 1884	3	2	
Baker	Peter S.	m.	PCo	21 May 1884	3	4	
Baker	Peter S.	m.	PWA	24 May 1884	3	5	
Baker	Peter S.	m.	SD	24 May 1884	2	3	
Baker	T.	b.	SD	1 July 1882	2	3	
Baker	Theodore	b.	SD	28 Feb. 1885	5	6	
Baker	William	d.	DD	31 Oct. 1883	3	3	

(1) Surname	(2) Given Name	(3)	(4)	(5) Date	(6) Pg	(7) Col	(8) Comments
Baker	William	d.	SD	3 Nov. 1883	3	3	
Baldwin	C. A.	m.	DR	2 Oct. 1885	3	4	
Baldwin	C. A.	m.	PCo	30 Sept. 1885	3	6	
Baldwin	G. T.	b.	PC	11 July 1883	3	5	
Baldwin	Josephine L.	m.	PCo	2 Jan. 1884	3	6	
Baldwin	Josephine L.	m.	PWA	5 Jan. 1884	3	7	
Baldwin	Josephine L.	m.	SD	5 Jan. 1884	1	4	
Baldwin	O.T.	b.	PWA	14 July 1883	3	6	
Bale	E.	b.	PC	4 Apr. 1883	3	5	
Bale	E.	b.	SD	7 Apr. 1883	2	6	
Ball	John W.	d.	RRF	4 Aug. 1881	2	5	
Ballou	D. W.	d.	SD	14 Mar. 1885	5	5	
Balny	A. J.	m.	PCo	22 Mar. 1882	3	5	
Balny	A. J.	m.	SD	1 Apr. 1882	3	6	
Balzari	C. P.	b.	PCo	23 Jan. 1884	3	5	
Bamford	Mary L.	m.	DR	30 Dec. 1882	2	1	
Bancroft	Neva	d.	SD	13 June 1885	3	5	
Bane	D. C. (son of)	d.	SD	29 July 1882	3	7	
Bane	D. C.	b.	DR	24 Apr. 1882	2	2	
Bane	D. C.	b.	PCo	3 May 1882	3	5	
Bane	D. C.	b.	SD	6 May 1882	3	6	
Bane	D. C. (son of)	d.	DR	24 July 1882	2	2	
Bane	D. C. (son of)	d.	PCo	2 Aug. 1882	3	6	
Banfield	Isaac N.	m.	DR	12 May 1882	3	2	
Banfield	Isaac N.	m.	HE	11 May 1882	2	3	
Banfield	Isaac N.	m.	PCo	17 May 1882	3	5	
Banfield	Isaac N.	m.	RRF	11 May 1882	2	3	
Banfield	Isaac N.	m.	SD	20 May 1882	2	4	
Banks	Willie	d.	SD	5 Feb. 1881	3	8	
Bannon	Christopher	d.	SD	30 July 1881	3	8	
Barber	W. E.	m.	PCo	28 Dec. 1881	3	6	
Barber	W. E.	m.	SD	24 Dec. 1881	2	3	
Barbetta	N. J.	m.	PCo	27 May 1885	3	6	
Barboni	Lodovina	m.	SD	23 Dec. 1882	2	5	
Barham	Hattie S.	m.	DR	10 Jan. 1884	3	3	
Barham	Hattie S.	m.	PCo	16 Jan. 1884	3	6	
Barker	Bettie	m.	CR	18 Apr. 1885	5	2	
Barker	J. H.	b.	CR	27 Sept. 1884	3	1	
Barker	J. H.	b.	PCo	1 Oct. 1884	3	5	
Barlow	Eva R.	m.	DR	22 Dec. 1881	2	2	
Barlow	Eva R.	m.	PCo	21 Dec. 1881	3	5	
Barlow	Eva R.	m.	SD	24 Dec. 1881	2	3	

(1) Surname	(2) Given Name	(3)	(4)	(5) Date	(6) Pg	(7) Col	(8) Comments
Barlow	Fannie D.	m.	PWA	19 Mar. 1884	3	6	
Barlow	Fannie	m.	DR	25 Apr. 1884	3	2	
Barlow	Fannie	m.	PCo	23 Apr. 1884	2	6	
Barlow	Fannie	m.	RRF	1 May 1884	5	6	
Barlow	Fannie	m.	SD	26 Apr. 1883	3	5	
Barlow	Hulda	d.	SD	1 Dec. 1883	3	2	
Barlow	Huldah	d.	DD	4 Dec. 1883	3	3	
Barlow	Huldah L.	d.	PWA	1 Dec. 1883	3	6	
Barlow	Hulduh	d.	SD	8 Dec. 1883	3	1	
Barlow	S. Q.	b.	DR	5 Apr. 1882	3	2	
Barlow	S. Q.	b.	PCo	29 Mar. 1882	3	5	
Barlow	S. Q.	b.	PCo	5 Mar. 1884	3	6	
Barlow	S. Q.	b.	PWA	1 Mar. 1884	3	6	
Barlow	S. Q.	b.	SD	1 Apr. 1882	3	6	
Barnes	Aaron	m.	DR	20 July 1885	3	4	
Barnes	Aaron	m.	PCo	29 July 1885	3	4	
Barnes	Aaron	m.	SD	25 July 1885	3	5	
Barnes	Aaron, Jr.	m.	DR	8 Dec. 1882	3	2	
Barnes	Aaron, Jr.	m.	PCo	13 Dec. 1882	3	4	
Barnes	Bettie	m.	SD	1 Oct. 1881	3	8	
Barnes	Carrie	d.	DD	14 Nov. 1883	3	3	
Barnes	Carrie	d.	SD	17 Nov. 1883	3	4&5	Pleasant Hill Cem.
Barnes	Grover Cleveland	b.	SD	4 July 1885	5	4	
Barnes	Ida M.	m.	CR	27 Oct. 1883	3	1	
Barnes	Ida M.	m.	RRF	25 Oct. 1883	2	4	
Barnes	J.	d.	DR	24 Sept. 1882	3	2	
Barnes	J. J.	b.	PWA	24 Feb. 1883	3	7	
Barnes	J. K.	b.	DR	29 July 1885	3	4	
Barnes	J. K.	b.	PCo	22 July 1885	3	6	
Barnes	James	b.	DD	26 July 1883	3	2	
Barnes	James	b.	PC	25 July 1883	3	6	
Barnes	James	b.	PWA	28 July 1883	3	7	
Barnes	James	b.	SD	28 July 1883	2	5	
Barnes	John	m.	SD	8 Jan. 1881	3	8	
Barnes	Laura E.	d.	PCo	21 June 1882	3	5	
Barnes	Laura E.	d.	SD	24 June 1882	3	5	
Barnes	Lydia	d.	SD	27 June 1885	5	4	
Barnes	Mattie	m.	DR	19 Nov. 1885	3	4	
Barnes	Mattie	m.	PCo	23 Nov. 1885	3	4	
Barnes	Mattie	m.	SD	21 Nov. 1885	3	5	
Barnes	Nellie Cox	m.	DD	28 Aug. 1883	3	3	
Barnes	Retta	m.	RRF	29 Sept. 1881	2	6	

(1) Surname	(2) Given Name	(3)	(4)	(5) Date	(6) Pg	(7) Col	(8) Comments
Barnes	Rettie	m.	DR	24 Sept. 1881	2	3	
Barnes	Rudolph	b.	PC	4 Apr. 1883	3	5	
Barnes	Rudolph	b.	PWA	7 Apr. 1883	2	3	
Barnes	S. George	d.	PCo	15 Nov. 1882	3	5	
Barnes	W. P.	b.	PCo	1 July 1885	3	6	
Barnes	William H.	b.	DR	24 Nov. 1882	2	3	
Barnes	William H.	b.	RRF	23 Nov. 1882	2	4	
Barnes	Zilla	m.	CR	18 Nov. 1882	3	3	
Barnes	Zilla	m.	PCo	29 Nov. 1882	3	6	
Barnes	Zilpha	d.	PCo	27 Sept. 1882	3	6	
Barnett	G. W.	b.	SD	26 Nov. 1881	3	8	
Barnett	J. D.	b.	DR	12 July 1884	3	3	
Barnett	J. D.	b.	PCo	16 July 1884	3	6	
Barnett	J. D.	b.	PCo	23 July 1884	3	6	
Barney	Carey E.	m.	PCo	17 Sept. 1884	3	6	
Barney	Carey E.	m.	SD	20 Sept. 1884	2	5	
Barnhill	M. K.	d.	RRF	26 Jan. 1882	2	2	
Barnhill	M. K.	d.	SD	11 Feb. 1882	3	6	
Barnhill	Robert	d.	RRF	26 Jan. 1882	2	2	
Barr	E. H.	m.	RRF	19 July 1883	2	4	
Barr	Nettie M.	m.	SD	1 June 1881	3	7	
Barret	David E.	m.	SD	5 Mar. 1881	3	8	
Barrett	David E.	m.	PCo	9 Mar. 1881	3	4	
Barrett	Mr. & Mrs.	b.	DR	17 Sept. 1881	2	3	
Barrett	Mr. & Mrs.	b.	PCo	14 Sept. 1881	2	4	
Barrett	Mr. & Mrs.	b.	SD	24 Sept. 1881	3	8	
Barron	T. J.	b.	SD	24 Jan. 1885	5	5	
Barron	William	o.	RRF	17 Jan. 1884	3	3	
Barrow	Peter	d.	CR	10 Dec. 1881	1	3	
Barrow	Peter	d.	CR	17 Dec. 1881	1	3	
Barthlome	M.	b.	SD	28 Feb. 1885	5	6	
Bartholme	M.	b.	PCo	25 Feb. 1885	3	6	
Bartholme	M.	b.	PWA	28 Feb. 1885	3	5	
Bartlett	Alexander	m.	DR	27 Mar. 1884	3	3	
Bartlett	Alexander	m.	PCo	2 Apr. 1884	3	6	
Bartlett	Eldredge	b.	SD	8 Dec. 1883	3	1	
Bartlett	Eldridge	b.	DD	4 Dec. 1883	3	3	
Bartlett	Eldridge	b.	PCo	21 Dec. 1881	3	5	
Bartlett	Eldridge	b.	PCo	26 Jan. 1881	3	4	
Bartlett	Eldridge	d.	PCo	30 Dec. 1885	3	2	
Bartlett	Eldridge	b.	PWA	1 Dec. 1883	3	6	
Bartlett	Eldridge	b.	SD	5 Feb. 1881	3	8	

(1) Surname	(2) Given Name	(3)	(4)	(5) Date	(6) Pg	(7) Col	(8) Comments
Bartlett	Eldridge	b.	SD	31 Dec. 1881	3	6	
Bartolani	P.	b.	PCo	1 Apr. 1885	3	6	
Bartolani	P.	b.	SD	4 Apr. 1885	2	5	
Barton	Annie A.	m.	DR	18 Aug. 1885	3	4	
Barton	Annie A.	m.	SD	22 Aug. 1885	5	5	
Barton	Charles H.	d.	PCo	18 Feb. 1885	3	6	
Barton	Charles H.	d.	SD	21 Feb. 1885	2	5	
Bartram	Robert W.	m.	SD	10 Dec. 1881	3	2	
Baruh	Herman	d.	DD	18 Aug. 1883	3	3	
Baruh	Herman	d.	PC	15 Aug. 1883	3	6	
Baruh	Herman	d.	PWA	18 Aug. 1883	3	7	
Baruh	Herman	d.	PWA	25 Aug. 1883	3	8	
Baruh	Herman	d.	SD	18 Aug. 1883	3	3	
Baruh	Herman	d.	SD	25 Aug. 1883	2	5	
Baruh	Moses	m.	PCo	26 July 1882	3	6	
Basford	Ida	m.	RRF	28 June 1883	2	3	
Bass	Augustus	d.	DR	16 Dec. 1882	2	3	
Bass	Augustus	d.	PCo	20 Dec. 1882	3	5	
Bass	Augustus	d.	SD	16 Dec. 1882	3	6	
Bass	Seymore	d.	RRF	14 Dec. 1882	2	3	
Bassett	Mattie	d.	PCo	9 Dec. 1885	3	6	
Bassoni	Louie	b.	SD	12 Mar. 1881	3	8	
Batcher	Mariam Isabell	d.	PCo	4 Feb. 1885	3	6	
Bateman	Mary L.	m.	DR	3 May 1881	2	2	
Bateman	Mary Luce	m.	SD	16 Apr. 1881	3	8	
Bateman	Mary	m.	CR	7 May 1881	5	5	
Bates	Hattie	d.	CR	24 Feb. 1883	3	1	
Bates	John D.	d.	DR	7 June 1882	3	2	
Bates	John D.	d.	PCo	31 May 1882	3	5	
Bates	John D.	d.	SD	10 June 1882	2	3	
Bates	Theodore	b.	DR	29 Aug. 1882	3	2	
Bates	Theodore	b.	SD	2 Sept. 1882	3	6	
Bauer	Florentine	m.	PCo	23 Apr. 1884	2	6	
Bauer	Florentine	m.	PWA	26 Apr. 1884	3	6	
Bauer	Florentine	m.	RRF	1 May 1884	5	6	
Bauer	Florentine	m.	SD	26 Apr. 1883	3	5	
Bauer	J. W.	b.	PWA	9 June 1883	3	7	
Bauer	John	b.	PCo	16 Mar. 1881	3	4	
Bauer	William	b.	PC	6 June 1883	3	4	
Bauer	William	m.	PCo	6 Sept. 1882	3	7	
Bauer	William	b.	SD	16 June 1883	2	6	
Baur	Elsie	d.	DR	4 Apr. 1881	2	3	

(1) Surname	(2) Given Name	(3)	(4)	(5) Date	(6) Pg	(7) Col	(8) Comments
Baur	Elsie	d.	SD	16 Apr. 1881	3	8	
Baur	Florentine	m.	DR	25 Apr. 1884	3	2	
Baur	John	b.	CR	19 Mar. 1881	4	3	
Baur	John	b.	DR	21 Nov. 1881	2	3	
Baur	John	b.	SD	19 Mar. 1881	3	8	
Baur	Lester	d.	PCo	6 July 1881	3	5	
Baur	Lester	d.	SD	16 July 1881	3	8	
Baux	Victoria C.	d.	PCo	7 Dec. 1881	3	5	
Baxman	Louis	o.	SD	9 Sept. 1882	3	2	
Baxter	E. Louisa	m.	DR	16 Sept. 1881	3	2	
Baxter	E. Louisa	m.	PCo	14 Sept. 1881	2	4	
Baxter	Louise	m.	SD	17 Sept. 1881	3	8	
Bayler	W. (Mrs. Joseph)	d.	PCo	18 Jan. 1882	3	5	
Bayler	Wilhelmina	d.	SD	14 Jan. 1882	3	8	
Beach	William	b.	PCo	11 Oct. 1882	3	6	
Beach	William	m.	SD	1 Oct. 1881	3	8	
Beals	C.	o.	SIT	22 Aug. 1885	2	2	
Beam	J., Mrs.	d.	CR	8 Apr. 1882	1	3	
Beam	Jere	d.	PCo	8 July 1885	3	6	
Beam	Jeremiah	d.	DR	8 July 1885	3	3	2 articles from Masonic Lodge
Beam	Jeremiah	d.	SD	4 July 1885	5	3&4	also p. 5 col. 1
Bean	A. A.	o.	SD	30 Apr. 1881	3	3	
Bean	Mary	d.	PCo	16 Aug. 1882	3	6	
Bean	Mary	d.	SD	19 Aug. 1882	3	5	
Bear	Catharine	d.	RRF	29 Mar. 1883	2	4	
Bear	Catherine	d.	PC	4 Apr. 1883	3	5	
Bear	Catherine	d.	PC	28 Mar. 1883	3	5	
Beardin	George A.	m.	PC	4 July 1883	3	5	
Beardin	George A.	m.	SD	30 June 1883	3	5	
Beardin	Martha E.	m.	PCo	13 Sept. 1882	3	7	
Beardin	Martha E.	m.	SD	9 Sept. 1882	3	6	
Beardon	George	b.	DR	21 Nov. 1884	3	2	
Beardon	George	b.	PCo	19 Nov. 1884	3	5	
Beardon	George	b.	SD	15 Nov. 1884	2	5	
Beasley	J.	b.	CR	28 May 1881	5	1	
Beasley	J.	b.	CR	28 Nov. 1885	3	2	
Beasley	J.	b.	DR	16 May 1882	3	2	
Beasley	J.	b.	PCo	17 May 1882	3	5	
Beasley	J.	b.	SD	20 May 1882	2	4	
Beattge	Charles	b.	PCo	9 Nov. 1881	3	5	
Beaver	Bird	d.	PC	9 May 1883	3	5	

(1) Surname	(2) Given Name	(3)	(4)	(5) Date	(6) Pg	(7) Col	(8) Comments
Beaver	Thomas	b.	DD	23 Nov. 1883	3	2	
Beaver	Thomas	b.	SD	1 Dec. 1883	3	4	
Beavers	Frankie	d.	PCo	8 July 1885	3	6	
Beavers	Frankie	d.	SD	4 July 1885	5	4	
Beck	Anna	d.	RRF	1 Mar. 1883	2	4	Oak Mound Cemetery
Beck	Annie	d.	PCo	7 Mar. 1883	3	5	
Beck	Kate	m.	SD	10 May 1884	1	4	
Beckley	Ira M.	m.	PCo	10 Jan. 1883	3	6	
Beckley	Ira M.	b.	PCo	9 Jan. 1884	3	6	
Beckley	Ira M.	b.	PWA	5 Jan. 1884	3	7	
Beckley	Ira M.	m.	SD	13 Jan. 1883	3	5	
Beckley	Ira M.	b.	SD	19 Jan. 1884	3	6	
Beckley	M.	m.	PWA	12 Jan. 1883	3	6	
Beckner	Laura A.	m.	DR	15 July 1884	3	3	
Beckner	W. S.	m.	DR	4 Oct. 1881	2	3	
Beckner	William	m.	SD	8 Oct. 1881	3	8	
Bedwell	Selina McMinn	d.	SD	12 May 1883	2	6	also p. 3 col. 2
Bedwell	Selina	d.	PC	16 May 1883	3	5	
Bee	Millard	b.	PCo	21 Mar. 1883	3	5	
Bee	Millard	b.	SD	7 Apr. 1883	2	6	
Beebe	F. M.	m.	PCo	9 Nov. 1881	3	5	
Beebe	Henry C.	m.	DR	31 Mar. 1884	3	3	
Beeck	Hans C.	m.	SD	10 Jan. 1885	2	6	
Beeler	Frank	d.	DR	14 July 1884	3	3	
Beeler	Frank	d.	PCo	16 July 1884	3	6	
Beeson	Annie	m.	PCo	9 Dec. 1885	3	6	
Beeson	Caroline	d.	DR	9 May 1881	2	2	
Beeson	Caroline	d.	RRF	5 May 1881	2	4	
Beeson	Emma	m.	PC	18 Apr. 1883	3	5	
Beeson	Emma	m.	RRF	12 Apr. 1883	2	5	
Beeson	Emma	m.	RRF	19 Apr. 1883	2	3	
Beeson	Henry, Mrs.	d.	SD	13 Dec. 1884	2	5	
Beeson	Ida	m.	PCo	12 Mar. 1884	3	6	
Beeson	Ida	m.	RRF	6 Mar. 1884	2	3	
Beeson	Isaac R.	b.	DR	24 Feb. 1882	2	3	
Beeson	Mrs.	d.	CR	6 Dec. 1884	3	2	
Beeson	O. W.	m.	RRF	23 Aug. 1883	2	4	
Beeson	Rhoda M.	m.	SD	30 July 1881	3	8	
Beeson	Willis	b.	DR	24 Feb. 1882	2	3	
Beggs	John	d.	CR	16 Apr. 1881	5	3	
Beggs	John	d.	DR	18 Apr. 1881	3	2	
Beggs	John	d.	PCo	13 Apr. 1881	3	6	

(1) Surname	(2) Given Name	(3)	(4)	(5) Date	(6) Pg	(7) Col	(8) Comments
Beggs	John	d.	SD	16 Apr. 1881	3	8	
Beggs	W. I.	m.	DR	16 May 1884	3	2	
Beggs	W. I.	m.	PCo	14 May 1884	3	4	
Beggs	W. I.	m.	PWA	10 May 1884	3	5	
Beggs	W. I.	m.	SD	17 May 1884	3	5	
Beggs	William J.	b.	DR	29 July 1885	3	4	
Beggs	William J.	b.	PCo	22 July 1885	3	6	
Behmer	Annie E.	m.	DR	5 Apr. 1881	2	3	
Behmer	John	m.	DR	16 Oct. 1885	3	4	
Behmer	John	m.	PCo	28 Oct. 1885	3	4	
Behmer	John	m.	SD	24 Oct. 1885	5	4	
Behmer	Lizzie	m.	SD	9 Apr. 1881	3	8	
Behrens	Walter N.	m.	PCo	24 Aug. 1881	3	5	
Behrens	Walter N.	m.	SD	3 Sept. 1881	3	8	
Belden	C. C.	b.	PCo	8 Mar. 1882	3	5	
Belden	C. C.	b.	SD	4 Mar. 1882	3	6	
Belden	Charles	b.	DR	15 Feb. 1882	2	3	
Belisle	Mr. & Mrs.	b.	DR	18 Dec. 1884	2	2	
Belisle	Mr. & Mrs.	b.	PCo	24 Dec. 1884	3	4	
Belisle	Mr. & Mrs.	b.	PWA	20 Dec. 1884	3	4	
Belisle	Mr. & Mrs.	b.	SD	27 Dec. 1884	2	4	
Bell	Catharine	d.	SD	6 Aug. 1881	3	8	
Bell	Catherine	d.	PCo	20 July 1881	3	5	
Bell	Catherine	d.	SD	30 July 1881	3	8	
Bell	Francisca Theresa	d.	DR	26 May 1884	3	2	
Bell	Francisca Theresa	d.	PCo	28 May 1884	2	4	
Bell	Horace	b.	PWA	12 July 1884	3	6	
Bell	Ida M.	m.	PCo	4 Mar. 1885	3	6	
Bell	Ida M.	m.	SD	14 Mar. 1885	5	5	
Bell	Josie M.	m.	DR	28 Sept. 1881	3	2	
Bell	Josie M.	m.	RRF	22 Sept. 1881	2	5	
Bell	Lucinda	m.	DR	9 Nov. 1885	2	2	
Bell	Lucinda	m.	SD	14 Nov. 1885	3	5	
Bell	Mary	d.	SD	7 May 1881	3	8	
Bell	Robert Benjamin	m.	SD	19 Mar. 1881	3	8	
Bell	W.	b.	DR	22 Dec. 1882	3	3	
Bell	W.	b.	PCo	27 Dec. 1882	3	6	
Bell	Warner	m.	RRF	7 July 1881	2	4	
Bell	Warren	m.	DR	11 July 1881	2	3	
Bellingham	Maggie	m.	SD	10 Jan. 1885	2	6	
Belloni	George	m.	PCo	18 Oct. 1882	3	6	
Belvail	John H.	m.	DD	25 Sept. 1883	3	3	

(1) Surname	(2) Given Name	(3)	(4)	(5) Date	(6) Pg	(7) Col	(8) Comments
Belvail	John H.	m.	SD	29 Sept. 1883	2	6	
Bendietti	Francisco	m.	DR	20 Oct. 1885	3	4	
Benjamin	Kate	d.	RRF	17 Aug. 1882	2	3	
Benjamin	Kate	d.	SD	19 Aug. 1882	3	5	
Benjamin	Ursula	d.	PC	16 May 1883	3	5	
Benjamin	Ursula	d.	RRF	10 May 1883	2	3	
Benjamin	Ursula	d.	SD	19 May 1883	3	5	
Bennett	D.	d.	PCo	16 Jan. 1884	3	6	
Bennett	D.	d.	SD	19 Jan. 1884	3	6	
Bennett	Daniel	p.	DR	9 July 1884	3	3	
Bennett	Daniel	d.	RRF	10 Jan. 1884	2	4	
Bennett	Eunice	m.	DR	5 Apr. 1882	3	2	
Bennett	Eunice	m.	PCo	29 Mar. 1882	3	5	
Bennett	Eunice	m.	SD	25 Mar. 1882	3	6	
Bennett	James Jasper	m.	DR	2 Dec. 1881	2	3	
Bennett	Silas F.	d.	DR	27 Jan. 1882	3	1	
Bennett	Silas F.	d.	DR	28 Jan. 1882	2	3	
Bennett	Silas F.	d.	PCo	25 Jan. 1882	3	6	
Bennett	William J.	d.	DR	1 Apr. 1884	3	3	
Bennett	William J.	d.	PCo	9 Apr. 1884	3	6	
Bennett	William	d.	DR	9 Apr. 1884	3	3	
Bennetti	B.	o.	PCo	16 Dec. 1885	3	2	
Benson	Andrew	d.	SD	19 July 1884	2	5	
Benson	Charles	m.	PCo	21 Mar. 1883	3	5	
Bentley	A.	b.	PCo	1 Oct. 1884	3	5	
Bently	A.	b.	PCo	9 Nov. 1881	3	5	
Bently	A.	b.	SD	19 Nov. 1881	4	8	
Benton	Celia	m.	DD	20 Oct. 1883	3	3	
Benton	Hubbard	d.	PCo	5 July 1882	3	5	
Benton	L. M., Mrs.	m.	DR	8 Mar. 1882	2	3	
Benton	Lewis	m.	PC	6 June 1883	3	4	
Bercini	Peter	d.	DR	16 Nov. 1885	3	4	
Bergman	Minnie	m.	PCo	16 Dec. 1885	3	6	
Bernert	Fred	b.	PCo	11 Oct. 1882	3	6	
Bernert	Fred	b.	SD	7 Oct. 1882	3	6	
Bernstein	J. A.	m.	CR	15 Jan. 1881	5	5	
Bernstein	J. A.	m.	DR	12 Jan. 1881	3	2	
Bernstein	J. A.	m.	SD	15 Jun. 1881	3	8	
Berri	V.	b.	PCo	21 Mar. 1883	3	5	
Berry	S. B.	b.	DR	28 Nov. 1881	2	3	
Berry	S. B.	b.	PCo	7 Dec. 1881	3	5	
Berry	S. B.	b.	SD	3 Dec. 1881	3	8	

(1) Surname	(2) Given Name	(3)	(4)	(5) Date	(6) Pg	(7) Col	(8) Comments
Berryhill	G. H.	b.	DD	11 Aug. 1883	3	1	
Berton	Albert	m.	PC	4 July 1883	3	5	
Bertron	Albert	m.	RRF	28 June 1883	2	3	
Berwick	John C.	b.	SWI	29 Mar. 1884	3	5	
Berwick	John Charles	b.	PCo	19 Mar. 1884	3	6	
Berwick	John Charles	b.	PWA	22 Mar. 1884	3	6	
Berwick	John Charles	b.	SD	22 Mar. 1884	2	4	
Bethane	John	b.	DR	21 Dec. 1881	2	2	
Bethane	John	b.	PCo	4 Jan. 1882	3	7	
Bethane	John	b.	SD	24 Dec. 1881	2	3	
Bethune	Juanita	d.	DR	25 May 1882	2	3	
Bethune	Juanita	d.	PCo	31 May 1882	3	5	
Bethune	Juanita	d.	SD	27 May 1882	3	5	
Bever	Annie	m.	DD	4 Dec. 1883	3	3	
Bever	R. W.	m.	DD	22 Sept. 1883	3	2	
Bever	T. J.	m.	PCo	10 Jan. 1883	3	6	
Bever	Thomas J.	m.	RRF	4 Jan. 1883	2	2	
Bever	Thomas	b.	RRF	22 Nov. 1883	2	3	
Biaggi	B. B.	m.	PCo	17 June 1885	3	6	
Biaggi	B.	m.	SD	13 June 1885	3	5	
Bice	John W.	d.	PC	20 June 1883	3	6	
Bice	Samuel	b.	DR	17 Sept. 1881	2	3	
Bice	Samuel	b.	SD	24 Sept. 1881	3	8	
Bicknell	C. N.	m.	PCo	17 Dec. 1884	2	4	
Bicknell	Clifford N.	m.	DR	11Dec. 1884	3	2	
Bicknell	Clifford N.	m.	SD	13 Dec. 1884	2	5	
Biddings	Henry A.	m.	PCo	4 Mar. 1885	3	6	
Biddings	Henry A.	m.	SD	14 Mar. 1885	5	5	
Biddle	B. R.	d.	PCo	27 Sept. 1882	3	6	
Biddle	B. R.	d.	SD	30 Sept. 1882	3	6	
Biddle	Benjamin R.	d.	RRF	21 Sept. 1882	2	4	
Bidwell	Franklin	o.	SD	5 Aug. 1882	3	1	
Bidwell	James	b.	DR	24 Feb. 1882	2	3	
Bidwell	John	b.	DR	24 Feb. 1882	2	3	
Bidwell	May	d.	RRF	10 May 1883	2	3	Oak Mound Cemetery
Bieuchini	Louisa	m.	DR	21 July 1885	3	4	
Bieuchini	Louisa	m.	PCo	15 July 1885	3	6	
Bigelow	C. P.	d.	RRF	11 May 1882	2	3	
Bigelow	Josie Austin	d.	DR	13 May 1882	2	3	
Bigelow	Josie Austin	d.	RRF	11 May 1882	2	3	
Bigerstaff	Hattie C.	m.	DD	29 Dec. 1883	3	3	
Bigsby	W. S.	m.	SD	20 Aug. 1881	3	8	

(1) Surname	(2) Given Name	(3)	(4)	(5) Date	(6) Pg	(7) Col	(8) Comments
Bigsby	Wilson	m.	DR	6 Aug. 1881	2	3	
Bill	C.	b.	DR	14 Nov. 1882	2	3	
Bill	C.	b.	PCo	22 Nov. 1882	3	5	
Bill	C.	b.	RRF	16 Nov. 1882	2	4	
Bills	A. C.	b.	CR	4 Apr. 1885	3	1	
Bills	A. C.	b.	SD	18 Apr. 1885	2	4	
Bilow	John D.	m.	DD	6 Oct. 1883	3	3	
Bilow	John D.	m.	SD	13 Oct. 1883	3	4	
Bingham	A. W.	d.	CR	15 Jan. 1881	5	3	
Bingham	A. W.	d.	CR	15 Jan. 1881	5	4	
Bingham	A. W.	d.	PCo	12 Jan. 1881	3	2	
Bingham	A. W.	d.	PCo	12 Jan. 1881	2	1	
Bingham	A. W.	d.	SD	15 Jan. 1881	3	8	
Birch	A. J.	d.	SD	18 Feb. 1882	3	3	
Birchfield	Sarah	m.	PCo	20 July 1881	3	5	
Birchfield	Sarah	m.	SD	23 July 1881	3	8	
Bird	Jesse	m.	PCo	14 Mar. 1883	3	5	
Bird	Jesse	m.	SD	10 Mar. 1883	2	6	
Birkle	Marie	m.	DR	13 June 1884	3	3	
Birkle	Marie	m.	PCo	11 June 1884	3	5	
Birkle	Marie	m.	PWA	14 June 1884	3	6	
Birkle	Marie	m.	SD	28 June 1884	3	4	
Birotra	John	m.	PCo	26 Oct. 1881	3	4	
Bishop	Charles E.	m.	DR	23 Jan. 1882	2	3	
Bishop	Charles E.	m.	SD	28 Jan. 1882	3	6	
Bishop	Elijah	m.	DR	8 Mar. 1882	2	3	
Bishop	Tennessee	o.	SD	28 Oct. 1882	1	5	
Bither	Annie	m.	PCo	9 Mar. 1881	3	4	
Bither	Annie	m.	SD	5 Mar. 1881	3	8	
Bither	Annie M.	m.	SD	25 Oct. 1884	2	5	
Bither	Mr. & Mrs.	b.	PCo	8 Oct. 1884	3	6	
Bither	Mr. & Mrs.	b.	PWA	11 Oct. 1884	3	4	
Bizzini	Julius	m.	DR	16 Sept. 1882	3	4	
Bizzini	Julius	m.	SD	19 Sept. 1885	2	4	
Black	Bud	b.	PCo	24 Jan. 1883	3	5	
Black	Bud	b.	RRF	18 Jan. 1883	2	3	
Black	Bud	b.	SD	27 Jan. 1883	3	6	
Black	George	b.	CR	8 Jan. 1881	5	5	
Black	George	b.	CR	6 Dec. 1884	3	1	
Black	George	b.	PCo	10 Dec. 1884	3	5	
Black	George	b.	RRF	13 Jan. 1881	2	5	
Black	George	b.	SD	15 June 1881	3	8	

(1) Surname	(2) Given Name	(3)	(4)	(5) Date	(6) Pg	(7) Col	(8) Comments
Black	Lorens	d.	DR	5 Nov. 1884	2	2	
Black	Maggie	d.	DD	13 Aug. 1883	3	3	
Black	Maggie	d.	SD	18 Aug. 1883	2	6	
Black	Mary E.	d.	PCo	29 Nov. 1882	3	6	
Black	Mollie J.	m.	DR	30 May 1881	2	3	
Black	Mollie J.	m.	RRF	26 May 1881	2	5	
Black	Mollie J.	m.	SD	4 June 1881	3	8	
Black	Mollie	m.	CR	28 May 1881	5	5	
Black	S.	m.	SD	23 Sept. 1882	3	6	
Black	William, Mrs.	d.	CR	25 Nov. 1882	3	1	Cloverdale Cemetery
Black	William	m.	RRF	17 May 1883	2	3	
Blackburn	Lillie M.	m.	DR	11 Feb. 1882	2	3	
Blackburn	Lillie M.	m.	SD	18 Feb. 1882	3	6	
Blackie	James	m.	SD	5 Mar. 1881	3	8	
Blackington	Cora A.	m.	CR	22 Jan. 1881	5	5	
Blackington	Cora	m.	SD	29 Jan. 1881	3	8	
Blackinton	Cora A.	m.	DR	25 Jan. 1881	3	2	
Blackinton	Cora A.	m.	RRF	20 Jan. 1881	2	5	
Blackwell	A. J.	p.	DR	29 Nov. 1884	3	2	
Blackwell	A. J.	d.	PC	30 May 1883	3	2	
Blackwell	A. J.	d.	PWA	2 June 1883	3	8	
Blackwell	A. J.	d.	SD	2 June 1883	3	4	
Blackwell	A. J.	d.	SD	2 June 1883	1	5	Stony Point
Blain	Alpharetta	m.	DD	6 Oct. 1883	3	3	
Blain	Alpharetta	m.	SD	13 Oct. 1883	3	4	
Blair	Mary	m.	SD	24 Dec. 1881	2	3	
Blair	W. J.	b.	DD	1 Sept. 1883	3	2	
Blaizier	Joseph	d.	SD	14 Mar. 1885	1	5	also p. 5 col. 2
Blake	George E.	b.	SD	16 June 1883	2	6	
Blake	John	m.	PCo	16 Feb. 1881	3	4	
Blake	John	m.	SD	19 Feb. 1881	3	8	
Blakely	Thomas H.	m.	PCo	13 Sept. 1882	3	7	
Blakely	Thomas H.	m.	SD	9 Sept. 1882	3	6	
Blanchard	D. N.	m.	DR	16 Nov. 1885	3	4	
Blanche	Carl	d.	PCo	5 Nov. 1884	3	5	
Blanche	Carl	b.	SD	8 Nov. 1884	2	5	
Blank	August	d.	PC	22 Aug. 1883	3	5	
Blank	John	b.	PWA	8 Sept. 1883	3	8	
Blazer	Charles	m.	PCo	21 Mar. 1883	3	5	
Blazer	Charles	b.	PCo	30 Jan. 1884	3	6	
Blazer	J. S.	d.	RRF	28 Sept. 1882	3	6	
Blazer	Joseph	d.	PCo	11 Mar. 1885	3	4	

(1) Surname	(2) Given Name	(3)	(4)	(5) Date	(6) Pg	(7) Col	(8) Comments
Bledsoe	John H.	m.	DD	25 Sept. 1883	3	3	
Bledsoe	John H.	m.	RRF	27 Sept. 1883	2	2	
Bledsoe	John H.	m.	SD	29 Sept. 1883	2	6	
Bledsoe	Robert R.	m.	SD	22 Aug. 1885	6	2	
Bledsoe	Robert	m.	DR	15 Aug. 1885	3	4	
Bliss	William D.	m.	PCo	14 Sept. 1881	2	4	
Bliss	William D.	m.	PCo	14 Sept. 1881	2	4	
Bliss	William D.	m.	PCo	14 Sept. 1881	2	4	
Bliss	William D.	m.	SD	17 Sept. 1881	3	8	
Bliss	William W.	m.	DR	16 Sept. 1881	3	2	
Block	George	b.	DR	26 Aug. 1885	3	4	
Block	George	m.	PCo	21 Mar. 1883	3	5	
Block	Rosa	m.	SD	11 July 1885	1	7	
Bloom	Rebecca	m.	CR	19 May 1883	3	2	
Bloomer	A. C.	m.	PCo	2 Jan. 1884	3	6	
Bloomington	Henrietta	d.	DR	22 July 1882	3	2	
Bloomington	Henrietta	d.	PCo	2 Aug. 1882	3	6	
Bloomington	Henrietta	d.	SD	5 Aug. 1882	3	5	
Bloomington	I., Mrs.	d.	SD	22 July 1882	3	1	San Francisco
Blow	James	m.	SD	27 June 1885	5	4	
Blued	Leon	b.	PCo	25 Feb. 1885	3	6	
Blued	Leon	b.	PWA	28 Feb. 1885	3	5	
Blued	Leon	b.	SD	14 Mar. 1885	5	5	
Blumenthal	Moses	b.	PCo	7 Jan. 1885	3	6	
Blundell	Vance D.	b.	HE	20 Apr. 1882	2	2	
Blundell	Vance D.	b.	RRF	8 June 1882	2	3	
Blundell	Vance D.	b.	SD	3 June 1882	2	4	
Blythe	Benjamin F.	d.	DD	23 July 1883	3	2	
Board	(female)	b.	DR	4 Apr. 1884	3	3	
Board	Evart	d.	SD	27 Jan. 1883	3	6	
Board	Evart (son of)	d.	RRF	18 Jan. 1883	2	3	
Board	H. D. (son of)	d.	PCo	24 Jan. 1883	3	5	
Board	Willia A.	m.	RRF	4 Oct. 1883	2	3	
Board	William	b.	PCo	9 Apr. 1884	3	6	
Board	William	b.	RRF	3 Apr. 1884	2	4	
Board	Willie	m.	HE	4 Oct. 1883	2	3	
Boardman	Walter	b.	SD	14 Mar. 1885	5	5	
Bock	George L.	d.	DD	12 Oct. 1883	3	3	
Bock	George L.	d.	PWA	6 Oct. 1883	3	8	
Bock	George L.	d.	SD	20 Oct. 1883	3	4	
Bock	Kate	m.	PCo	7 May 1884	3	5	
Bock	Kate	m.	PWA	3 May 1884	3	6	

(1) Surname	(2) Given Name	(3)	(4)	(5) Date	(6) Pg	(7) Col	(8) Comments
Bock	Katie	m.	DR	8 May 1884	3	2	
Bockius	W. L.	b.	PCo	17 June 1885	3	6	
Body	Mark	b.	CR	28 May 1881	5	5	
Body	Mark	b.	DR	21 May 1881	2	3	
Boenel	William	d.	SD	15 Oct. 1881	3	1	Lower Lake
Bogers	Theo J.	m.	SD	10 Sept. 1881	3	8	
Boggs	Panthia	m.	SD	7 May 1881	3	8	
Bolla	G.	d.	PCo	3 Aug. 1881	3	5	
Bolles	W. A.	m.	HE	29 Dec. 1881	2	3	
Bolles	W.	m.	PCo	11 Jan. 1882	3	6	
Bolton	Bridget	d.	DD	23 Nov. 1883	3	2	
Bolton	Bridget	d.	PWA	24 Nov. 1883	3	6	
Bolton	Bridget	d.	SD	1 Dec. 1883	3	4	
Bolton	Josie	m.	DD	29 Sept. 1883	3	2	
Bonbier	Charles	m.	PCo	9 Dec. 1885	3	6	
Bondietti	Francisco	m.	PCo	28 Oct. 1885	3	4	
Bondietti	Francisco	m.	SD	24 Oct. 1885	5	4	
Bone	Frank	d.	PCo	3 June 1885	3	6	
Bone	Frank	m.	SD	23 May 1885	2	5	
Bone	James C.	d.	PCo	12 Oct. 1881	3	5	
Bone	James O.	d.	DR	12 Oct. 1881	2	3	
Bone	James O.	d.	SD	15 Oct. 1881	3	8	
Bonee	Rosa F.	m.	SD	17 Nov. 1883	3	5	
Bonee	Rose F.	m.	DD	10 Nov. 1883	3	3	
Bones	Frank	o.	CR	23 Apr. 1881	1	3	
Bones	J.	b.	PWA	28 Mar. 1885	3	5	
Bones	James C.	d.	SD	8 Oct. 1881	3	8	
Bones	James G.	d.	DR	5 Oct. 1881	2	3	
Bones	Mr. & Mrs.	b.	DR	26 Mar. 1884	3	3	
Bonham	B. B.	d.	RRF	14 Feb. 1884	2	2	Masonic Cemetery, Los Angeles
Bonham	B. B.	d.	RRF	21 Feb. 1884	2	1	
Bonham	D. B.	d.	PWA	9 Feb. 1884	3	2	
Bonham	Dr.	d.	CR	16 Feb. 1884	3	1	
Bonham	Mattie	m.	DR	27 Dec. 1881	2	2	
Bonham	Mattie	m.	PCo	4 Jan. 1882	3	7	
Bonham	Mattie	m.	SD	31 Dec. 1881	3	6	
Bonneau	Clarence V.	d.	PCo	14 Mar. 1883	3	5	
Bonner	Jean C.	m.	SD	25 Oct. 1884	2	5	
Bonner	John	d.	DR	27 June 1882	2	3	Rural Cemetery
Bonner	John	d.	SD	1 July 1882	2	3	
Bonnesell	Charles	b.	PCo	21 Jan. 1885	2	5	

(1) Surname	(2) Given Name	(3)	(4)	(5) Date	(6) Pg	(7) Col	(8) Comments
Bonnesell	Charles	b.	PWA	24 Jan. 1885	3	5	
Boone	(family)	o.	DR	26 Oct. 1882	1	4	history of family back to 1699
Boothby	(female)	d.	DR	25 Apr. 1884	3	2	
Boothby	(female)	b.	DR	25 Apr. 1884	3	2	
Boothby	B. F.	b.	PCo	23 Apr. 1884	2	6	
Boothby	B. F.	b.	PWA	19 Apr. 1884	3	5	
Boothby	B. F.	b.	RRF	1 May 1884	5	6	
Boothby	B. F. (dau. of)	d.	PCo	23 Apr. 1884	2	6	
Boothby	B. F. (dau. of)	d.	RRF	1 May 1884	5	6	
Boothby	B. F. (dau. of)	d.	SD	26 Apr. 1884	3	5	
Boothy	B. F. (dau. of)	d.	PWA	19 Apr. 1884	3	6	
Borouck	Fannie	m.	PWA	20 Oct. 1883	3	2	
Bosasco	John	b.	DR	29 July 1885	3	4	
Boss	George W.	m.	DR	6 Dec. 1884	3	2	
Bostwick	William	b.	SD	26 Aug. 1882	3	5	
Bosworth	Etta	m.	DR	28 Aug. 1882	3	2	
Bosworth	Etta	m.	RRF	31 Aug. 1882	2	4	
Bosworth	Etta	m.	SD	2 Sept. 1882	3	6	
Bosworth	Fannie L.	m.	DR	24 Nov. 1885	3	4	
Bosworth	Fannie L.	m.	PCo	18 Nov. 1885	3	4	
Boudin	Pierre	b.	HE	8 June 1882	2	3	
Bound	Joseph	m.	SD	18 Apr. 1885	2	4	
Bourns	M. J., Miss	m.	DR	9 Nov. 1885	2	2	
Bowden	Isaac	d.	PCo	19 Dec. 1883	3	4	
Bowden	Isaac	d.	PWA	15 Dec. 1883	3	6	
Bowen	W. N.	m.	SD	12 Mar. 1881	3	8	
Bower	Daniel	m.	DD	25 July 1883	3	2	
Bower	Daniel	m.	PC	1 Aug. 1883	3	6	
Bower	Daniel	m.	SD	28 July 1883	2	5	
Bower	M. J.	b.	SD	10 Jan. 1885	2	6	
Bowles	Bourbon	m.	PCo	28 June 1882	3	5	
Bowles	Bourbon	m.	SD	1 July 1882	2	3	
Bowles	Jesse	b.	PCo	4 Oct. 1882	3	6	"to Jesse Bowles, a stem-winder"
Bowles	Lizzie	m.	DR	1 Dec. 1885	3	4	
Bowles	Lizzie	m.	PCo	23 Nov. 1885	3	4	
Bowles	P. E.	m.	SD	8 Dec. 1883	3	1	
Bowles	Philip E.	m.	PWA	24 Nov. 1883	3	2	
Bowles	Scott	m.	DR	1 Dec. 1885	3	4	
Bowles	Scott	m.	PCo	23 Nov. 1885	3	4	
Bowles	W. A.	m.	DR	23 Dec. 1881	2	2	

(1) Surname	(2) Given Name	(3)	(4)	(5) Date	(6) Pg	(7) Col	(8) Comments
Bowles	W. A.	m.	PCo	28 Dec. 1881	3	6	
Bowles	W. A.	m.	RRF	22 Dec. 1881	2	3	
Bowles	W. A.	m.	RRF	5 Jan. 1882	3	1	
Bowles	W. A.	m.	SD	31 Dec. 1881	3	6	
Bowman	Abbie	m.	PCo	20 Sept. 1882	3	6	
Bowman	Abbie	m.	RRF	7 Sept. 1882	2	4	
Bowman	J. H.	d.	RRF	2 Nov. 1882	2	4	
Bowman	John H.	p.	DD	11 July 1883	3	2	
Bowman	John H.	d.	DR	7 Nov. 1882	2	2	
Bowman	John H.	d.	PCo	1 Nov. 1882	3	5	
Bowman	John	o.	CR	10 Mar. 1883	3	1	
Bowman	Leonard	d.	DR	30 Dec. 1884	2	2	
Box	Samuel P.	m.	DR	8 Dec. 1884	3	2	
Boxall	Miss	m.	SD	18 Apr. 1885	2	5	
Boy	William	b.	SD	20 Aug. 1881	3	8	
Boyce	Rush O.	d.	DR	30 Aug. 1884	3	3	art. col. 1 "sad news"
Boyce	Rush O.	d.	PCo	3 Sept. 1884	2	5	
Boyce	Rush O.	d.	PWA	6 Sept. 1884	3	4	
Boyce	Rush	d.	SD	6 Sept. 1884	1	7	also p. 2 col. 5 Rural Cemetery
Boyce	Spaulding	d.	SD	6 June 1885	2	4	
Boyd	Emma Jean	d.	DR	29 Nov. 1882	3	2	
Boyd	Emma Jean	d.	PCo	22 Nov. 1882	3	5	
Boyd	Emma Jean	d.	RRF	16 Nov. 1882	2	4	
Boyd	George	m.	DR	12 July 1882	3	2	
Boyd	George	m.	PCo	28 June 1882	3	5	
Boyd	George	m.	SD	1 July 1882	2	3	
Boyes	J. F.	b.	SD	23 Apr. 1881	3	8	
Boyes	J. B., Mrs	m.	SD	3 June 1882	2	4	
Boyes	J. P.	d.	PCo	23 Dec. 1885	2	4	
Boyes	John B.	d.	SD	12 Dec. 1885	3	1	
Boyes	Laura Belle	m.	SD	8 Jan. 1881	3	8	
Boylan	Terrence	p.	DD	19 July 1883	3	2	
Boynton	A. A.	o.	DR	3 Aug. 1882	3	2	
Bracket	Joshua H.	m.	PCo	1 Mar. 1882	2	4	
Brackett	J. A., Mrs.	d.	PC	28 Mar. 1883	3	5	
Brackett	J. S., Mrs.	d.	PWA	24 Mar. 1883	3	7	
Brackett	Joshua H.	m.	DR	8 Mar. 1882	2	3	
Brackett	Joshua S.	m.	SD	25 Feb. 1882	3	6	
Braden	William	d.	PWA	22 Mar. 1884	3	6	
Bradford	Cynthia	d.	PCo	7 Mar. 1883	3	5	
Bradford	Cynthia	d.	RRF	1 Mar. 1883	2	4	Oak Mound Cemetery

(1) Surname	(2) Given Name	(3)	(4)	(5) Date	(6) Pg	(7) Col	(8) Comments
Bradford	D .W.	d.	RRF	1 Mar. 1883	2	4	Oak Mound Cemetery
Bradford	D. W.	d.	PCo	7 Mar. 1883	3	5	
Bradford	D. W.	d.	RRF	12 May 1881	2	4	
Bradford	Mary A.	d.	DR	14 May 1881	2	3	
Bradford	Mary A.	d.	RRF	12 May 1881	2	4	Oak Mound, Healdsburg
Bradford	Mary A.	d.	SD	14 May 1881	3	8	
Bradford	Robert	b.	DR	2 Nov. 1885	3	4	
Bradley	Henry L.	m.	SD	1 Aug. 1885	2	3	also p. 5 col. 6
Brady	Anna Marie	m.	DR	26 June 1884	3	3	
Brady	Erwin	b.	PCo	19 Oct. 1881	3	5	
Brady	Erwin	b.	SD	29 Oct. 1881	3	6	
Brady	Lottie	d.	PCo	28 June 1882	3	5	
Brady	Lottie	d.	SD	1 July 1882	2	3	
Brady	P.	d.	SD	20 Dec. 1884	2	2	
Brain	William	m.	CR	17 Feb. 1883	3	1	
Brainard	H. P.	b.	PWA	23 Aug. 1884	3	4	
Brainerd	H. P.	b.	PCo	20 Aug. 1884	3	4	
Brainerd	H. P.	b.	SD	6 Sept. 1884	2	5	
Brammer	Frederick	b.	PCo	14 Oct. 1885	3	6	
Brammer	Frederick	b.	SD	17 Oct. 1885	4	5	
Bramord	H.	b.	DR	21 Aug. 1884	3	4	
Brandt	Anna M. C.	m.	PCo	1 Mar. 1882	2	4	
Brandt	Anna M. C.	m.	SD	11 Mar. 1882	3	6	
Brannan	James	b.	SD	3 Dec. 1881	3	8	
Brannon	James	b.	DR	18 Nov. 1881	3	2	
Brannon	James	b.	PCo	30 Nov. 1881	3	5	
Bransford	Z. W.	b.	PCo	7 Feb. 1883	3	6	
Bransford	Z. W.	b.	SD	10 Feb. 1883	2	7	
Brant	Anna M. C.	m.	DR	8 Mar. 1882	2	3	
Brasford	Ida	m.	PC	4 July 1883	3	5	
Brawley	Evaline May	m.	SD	23 June 1883	3	5	
Brawley	Eveline May	m.	PC	27 June 1883	3	6	
Bray	E. J.	m.	PWA	11 Oct. 1884	3	4	
Bray	Elisha J.	m.	PCo	8 Oct. 1884	3	6	
Bray	Elisha J.	m.	SD	4 Oct. 1884	3	5	
Bray	Leonard Zaddock	d.	DR	13 May 1882	2	3	
Bray	Leonard Zadock	d.	PCo	24 May 1882	3	5	
Bray	Leonard Zaddock	d.	SD	20 May 1882	2	4	
Breekwaldt	Joahim	m.	PCo	12 Oct. 1881	3	5	
Breekwoldt	Joahim	m.	DR	14 Oct. 1881	2	3	
Breekwoldt	Joahim	m.	SD	22 Oct. 1881	3	6	
Breitenstein	Theodore	b.	PCo	23 Dec. 1885	3	4	

(1) Surname	(2) Given Name	(3)	(4)	(5) Date	(6) Pg	(7) Col	(8) Comments
Breitenstein	Theodore	b.	SD	19 Dec. 1885	3	4	
Bremmer	Fredrick	b.	DD	8 Dec. 1883	3	3	
Brendel	F. W.	b.	SD	19 Feb. 1881	3	8	
Bresee	Elizabeth W.	d.	DR	24 June 1881	2	3	
Bresee	Elizabeth W.	d.	SD	25 June 1881	3	8	
Bresson	Joseph	b.	SD	12 Mar. 1881	3	8	
Bresson	Pauline	d.	SD	9 Apr. 1881	3	8	
Brewer	(male)	b.	DR	5 Feb. 1884	3	3	
Brewer	A. G.	b.	PCo	13 Feb. 1884	3	6	
Brewer	A. G.	b.	SD	9 Feb. 1884	7	2	
Brians	Olive May	m.	PCo	30 July 1884	3	6	
Brichetto	Antonio	d.	SIT	29 Aug. 1885	3	2&5	
Brien	John	b.	SD	19 Feb. 1881	3	8	
Brier	K. W.	d.	PWA	19 Jan. 1883	2	2	
Briggs	Hiram	m.	PCo	26 Dec. 1883	3	5	
Briggs	Nellie	d.	PC	8 Aug. 1883	3	6	
Briggs	Nellie	d.	PWA	11 Aug. 1883	3	8	
Briggs	Nellie	d.	SD	11 Aug. 1883	2	7	
Briggs	Robert W.	m.	SD	19 Feb. 1881	3	8	
Bright	C.	d.	DR	17 May 1881	2	2	
Bright	C., Mrs.	d.	SD	21 May 1881	3	8	
Brightenstine	Theodore	m.	SD	13 June 1885	3	5	
Britt	Eugene W.	m.	DD	29 Dec. 1883	3	3	
Brittain	Harvey	m.	PCo	8 Mar. 1882	3	5	
Brittain	Harvey	m.	SD	4 Mar. 1882	3	6	
Brittain	Martin Adams	d.	DR	8 July 1884	3	1	
Brittan	Martin A.	d.	SD	28 June 1884	3	4	
Britton	Duke	m.	PCo	12 Mar. 1884	3	6	
Britton	Duke`	m.	DR	4 Mar. 1884	3	3	
Britton	Harvey	m.	DR	3 Mar. 1882	2	3	
Britton	Harvey	m.	DR	8 Mar. 1882	2	3	
Britton	Martin Adams	d.	DR	19 June 1884	3	3	
Britton	Norman A.	m.	DR	1 May 1884	3	2	
Britton	Norman A.	m.	PCo	7 May 1884	3	5	
Britton	Norman A.	m.	PWA	10 May 1884	3	2&5	
Britton	Norman A.	m.	RRF	8 May 1884	5	6	
Broaddus	O. J.	m.	SD	26 Feb. 1881	3	8	
Broadwell	Susan	m.	DD	15 Dec. 1883	3	1	
Brogan	May	m.	CR	1 Jan. 1881	5	5	
Brogan	May	m.	CR	1 Jan. 1881	5	5	
Brogan	May	m.	SD	8 Jan. 1881	3	8	
Brolley	Daniel	d.	SD	5 Feb. 1881	3	8	

(1) Surname	(2) Given Name	(3)	(4)	(5) Date	(6) Pg	(7) Col	(8) Comments
Broocke	Minnie L.	m.	PWA	1 Dec. 1883	3	6	
Brookfield	Marie	m.	CR	9 June 1883	3	1	
Brookfield	Marie	m.	PC	13 June 1883	3	6	
Brooks	E. K.	p.	DR	6 Aug. 1884	3	2	
Brooks	Henry C.	m.	DR	20 June 1884	3	3	
Brooks	Henry C.	m.	SD	5 July 1884	2	3	
Brooks	Jay	b.	PCo	18 Feb. 1885	3	6	
Brooks	Jay	b.	SD	21 Feb. 1885	2	5	
Brooks	John S.	b.	PCo	11 June 1884	3	5	
Brooks	John S.	b.	SD	14 June 1884	2	4	
Brooks	Mary	m.	DD	25 Sept. 1883	3	3	
Brooks	Mary	m.	SD	29 Sept. 1883	2	6	
Brooks	Minnie C.	m.	PCo	26 Nov. 1884	3	5	
Brooks	Minnie C.	m.	SD	23 Nov. 1884	2	6	also p. 3 col. 2
Brooks	Minnie	m.	DR	25 Nov. 1884	3	2	
Brooks	Mr. & Mrs.	b.	SD	18 Apr. 1885	2	4	
Brooks	Silas	b.	SD	14 May 1881	3	8	
Brooks	T. J.	b.	DR	12 Oct. 1881	2	3	
Brooks	T. J.	b.	SD	15 Oct. 1881	3	8	
Brooks	Thomas J.	d.	DR	13 Oct. 1882	3	1	
Brooks	Thomas J.	d.	PCo	18 Oct. 1882	3	6	
Brooks	Thomas J.	d.	RRF	12 Oct. 1882	2	3	
Brooks	Thomas	b.	RRF	13 Oct. 1881	2	4	
Brooks	Thomas	b.	SD	22 Oct. 1881	3	6	
Brooks	W. E.	m.	SD	10 Sept. 1881	3	8	
Brookshire	E. S.	d.	CR	25 Feb. 1882	1	3	
Brookshire	E. S.	d.	RRF	16 Feb. 1882	3	7	
Brookshire	E. S.	d.	SD	18 Feb. 1882	3	2	
Brown	Albert	m.	RRF	19 Apr. 1883	2	3	
Brown	Birdie E. N.	m.	PCo	1 Nov. 1882	3	5	
Brown	Birdie Estella Nevada	m.	DR	30 Oct. 1882	3	1	
Brown	Birdie Estrella Nevada	m.	SD	28 Oct. 1882	3	5	
Brown	C. H.	d.	RRF	16 June 1881	2	5	Oak Mound, Healdsburg
Brown	Callie E.	m.	DD	8 Sept. 1883	3	3	
Brown	Carrie	m.	SD	18 July 1885	5	5	also p. 5 col. 5
Brown	Carrie R.	m.	DR	11 July 1885	3	4	
Brown	Carrie R.	m.	PCo	15 July 1885	3	6	
Brown	Charles	b.	DR	26 July 1882	2	2	
Brown	D.	b.	DD	4 Dec. 1883	3	3	
Brown	D.	b.	SD	8 Dec. 1883	3	1	
Brown	Dan	b.	DD	23 Nov. 1883	3	2	
Brown	Dan	b.	DR	6 Sept. 1881	2	3	

(1) Surname	(2) Given Name	(3)	(4)	(5) Date	(6) Pg	(7) Col	(8) Comments
Brown	Dan	b.	RRF	22 Nov. 1883	2	3	
Brown	Dan	b.	SD	10 Sept. 1881	3	8	
Brown	Dan	b.	SD	1 Dec. 1883	3	4	
Brown	Daniel	b.	PCo	9 Dec. 1885	3	6	
Brown	Daniel	b.	SD	19 Dec. 1885	3	4	
Brown	Eliza	d.	PCo	6 Apr. 1881	3	5	
Brown	G. C.	m.	DR	8 Apr. 1884	3	2	
Brown	G. C.	m.	PCo	16 Apr. 1884	3	5	
Brown	G. C.	m.	SD	12 Apr. 1884	2	5	
Brown	G. P.	b.	DD	16 July 1883	3	2	
Brown	Hattie B.	m.	PC	23 May 1883	3	5	
Brown	Hattie B.	m.	RRF	17 May 1883	2	3	
Brown	Hugh	o.	SD	24 Mar. 1883	3	3	
Brown	Jessie	m.	PCo	11 June 1884	3	5	
Brown	Jessie	m.	PWA	14 June 1884	3	6	
Brown	Joseph G.	m.	DR	1 Apr. 1881	2	3	
Brown	Joseph G.	m.	RRF	31 Mar. 1881	2	3	
Brown	Joseph G.	b.	RRF	18 Jan. 1883	2	3	
Brown	Lulu	m.	PCo	31 May 1882	3	5	
Brown	Lulu	m.	SD	10 June 1882	2	3	
Brown	Maggie	m.	DR	8 Aug. 1881	3	2	
Brown	Maggie	m.	RRF	4 Aug. 1881	2	5	
Brown	Maggie	m.	RRF	28 July 1881	2	3	
Brown	Maggie	m.	SD	13 Aug. 1881	3	8	
Brown	Mary E.	m.	SD	19 Feb. 1881	3	8	
Brown	Mary	d.	PC	25 Apr. 1883	3	5	
Brown	Mary	d.	PWA	28 Apr. 1883	3	8	
Brown	Mary	m.	PWA	4 Apr. 1885	3	6	
Brown	Mary	m.	SD	18 Apr. 1885	2	4	
Brown	Mattie	m.	DR	20 Oct. 1885	3	4	
Brown	Sarah A.	m.	SD	23 Nov. 1884	2	6	
Brown	T. H.	b.	DR	27 Oct. 1885	3	4	under died heading
Brown	Thomas	d.	SD	8 Nov. 1884	2	5	
Brown	W. A.	d.	PWA	10 Jan. 1885	3	4	
Brown	W. C.	d.	PCo	14 Jan. 1885	3	6	
Brownsberger	Bessie	d.	DD	12 Oct. 1883	3	3	
Brownsberger	Bessie	d.	HE	11 Oct. 1883	2	2	
Brownsberger	Bessie	d.	RRF	11 Oct. 1883	2	5	Oak Mound Cemetery
Brownsberger	Bessie	d.	SD	20 Oct. 1883	3	4	
Brownsberger	S.	b.	PCo	14 Mar. 1883	3	5	
Brownsberger	S.	b.	RRF	15 Mar. 1883	2	4	
Brownsberger	S.	b.	SD	17 Mar. 1883	3	3	

(1) Surname	(2) Given Name	(3)	(4)	(5) Date	(6) Pg	(7) Col	(8) Comments
Bruce	Bell A.	m.	SD	5 Nov. 1881	3	6	
Bruce	Mary W.	d.	HE	18 May 1882	2	3	
Bruce	Mary W.	d.	RRF	16 Mar. 1882	2	4	
Bruegge	H. F.	b.	DR	6 Dec. 1884	3	2	
Bruggeman	(female)	b.	DR	17 Mar. 1884	3	3	
Bruggeman	C. F.	b.	PCo	19 Mar. 1884	3	6	
Brumfield	Charles A.	m.	DR	3 Nov. 1885	3	4	
Brumfield	Priscilla	m.	SD	16 July 1881	3	8	
Brummer	Adolph	m.	DR	4 Dec. 1881	2	3	
Brummer	Adolph	m.	PCo	30 Nov. 1881	3	5	
Brummer	Adolph	m.	SD	3 Dec. 1881	3	8	
Brummer	William	b.	CR	22 Jan. 1881	5	5	
Brummer	William	b.	PCo	19 Jan. 1881	3	4	
Brummer	William	b.	SD	29 Jan. 1881	3	8	
Bruning	Annie M. C.	d.	DR	6 June 1882	3	2	
Brunner	Louise C.	m.	DD	28 July 1883	2	2	
Brush	E. B.	b.	PCo	9 Feb. 1881	3	4	
Brush	G. M.	b.	PCo	14 June 1882	3	5	
Brush	G. M.	b.	SD	17 June 1882	2	4	
Brush	William P.	m.	DR	26 Jan. 1882	2	3	
Brush	William P.	m.	SD	4 Feb. 1882	3	6	
Bryan	F. J.	m.	PCo	31 Aug. 1881	3	5	
Bryan	Mary A.	m.	SD	30 July 1881	3	8	
Bryan	Mary	m.	DR	8 Aug. 1882	3	2	
Bryan	Mary	m.	PCo	9 Aug. 1882	3	6	
Bryan	Mary	m.	SD	12 Aug. 1882	3	5	
Bryan	T. W.	b.	PCo	21 June 1882	3	5	
Bryan	T. W.	b.	PCo	2 Apr. 1884	3	6	
Bryan	T. W.	b.	PWA	29 Mar. 1884	3	6	
Bryan	T. W.	b.	SD	17 June 1882	2	4	
Bryan	Thomas J.	d.	PCo	26 Apr. 1882	3	4	
Bryan	Thomas J.	d.	SD	29 Apr. 1882	3	6	
Bryan	Thomas	m.	SD	3 Sept. 1881	3	8	
Bryan	Thomas	m.	SD	10 Sept. 1881	3	8	
Bryan	Thomas W.	m.	DR	30 Aug. 1881	3	2	
Bryant	A.	b.	DR	10 Jan. 1882	2	3	
Bryant	A. (inf. son)	d.	DR	29 July 1884	3	3	
Bryant	Anna A.	m.	PWA	22 Dec. 1883	3	6	
Bryant	Annie A.	m.	PCo	26 Dec. 1883	3	5	
Bryant	C. G.	b.	PCo	17 Jan. 1883	3	5	
Bryant	C. G.	b.	PWA	19 Jan. 1883	3	7	
Bryant	Helen	m.	DR	1 May 1882	3	2	

(1) Surname	(2) Given Name	(3)	(4)	(5) Date	(6) Pg	(7) Col	(8) Comments
Bryant	Helen R.	m.	PCo	26 Apr. 1882	3	4	
Bryant	Helen R.	m.	SD	29 Apr. 1882	3	6	
Bryant	John J.	m.	CR	1 Dec. 1883	3	1	
Bryant	John J.	m.	DD	4 Dec. 1883	3	3	
Bryant	John J.	m.	HE	29 Nov. 1883	3	3	also p. 2 col. 4
Bryant	John J.	m.	RRF	29 Nov. 1883	2	3	
Bryant	John J.	m.	SD	8 Dec. 1883	3	1	
Bryant	T. H.	o.	DR	26 Oct. 1882	2	2	
Buchan	James A.	m.	PCo	28 Dec. 1881	3	6	
Buchan	James E.	m.	DR	17 Dec. 1881	2	2	
Buchan	James E.	m.	SD	24 Dec. 1881	2	3	
Buchanan	J. C.	b.	SD	12 Nov. 1881	3	7	
Buchanan	Lida Ann	d.	SD	9 Aug. 1884	3	4	
Buckius	Willard L.	m.	DD	24 Sept. 1883	3	2	
Buckius	Willard L.	m.	PWA	22 Sept. 1883	3	6	
Buckius	Willard L.	m.	SD	29 Sept. 1883	2	6	
Buckle	(female)	b.	DR	25 Apr. 1884	3	2	
Buckle	John	b.	PCo	23 Apr. 1884	2	6	
Buckle	John	m.	RRF	30 Nov. 1882	2	3	
Buckle	John	b.	RRF	17 Apr. 1884	2	4	
Buckle	John	b.	SD	26 Apr. 1883	3	5	
Buckley	Bruce	b.	SD	12 Mar. 1881	3	8	
Budans	H.	b.	DR	1 Nov. 1881	2	3	filed after Nov. 29
Budans	H.	b.	PCo	9 Nov. 1881	3	5	
Budans	H.	b.	SD	19 Nov. 1881	4	8	
Buell	Cora	m.	SD	26 Feb. 1881	3	8	
Buell	Guy A.	m.	DR	26 May 1884	3	2	
Buell	Guy A.	m.	PCo	28 May 1884	2	4	
Buffett	C. C.	m.	CR	28 Feb. 1885	3	1	
Buffett	C. C.	m.	PCo	4 Mar. 1885	3	6	
Buffett	Charles C.	m.	SD	14 Mar. 1885	5	5	
Bumbaugh	Elizabeth	d.	DR	19 Nov. 1885	3	4	
Bumer	William	m.	DR	17 Dec. 1881	2	2	
Bumer	William	m.	HE	15 Dec. 1881	2	4	
Bumer	William	m.	PCo	21 Dec. 1881	3	5	
Bumer	William	m.	SD	24 Dec. 1881	2	3	
Bundy	Elizabeth	d.	SD	16 Apr. 1881	3	8	
Bunker	E. A.	m.	DR	18 June 1884	3	3	
Bunker	E. A.	m.	PCo	15 June 1884	3	4	
Burchard	Daniel T.	m.	CR	12 Mar. 1881	5	5	
Burchard	Daniel T.	m.	DR	9 Mar. 1881	3	2	
Burchard	Daniel W.	m.	SD	12 Mar. 1881	3	8	

(1) Surname	(2) Given Name	(3)	(4)	(5) Date	(6) Pg	(7) Col	(8) Comments
Burckhalter	Abraham	d.	DR	18 July 1882	3	1&2	
Burckhalter	J.	d.	CR	3 Nov. 1883	3	1	
Burckhalter	Jeremiah	d.	DD	29 Oct. 1883	3	3	
Burckhalter	Jeremiah	d.	SD	3 Nov. 1883	3	3	
Burdick	S. W.	d.	RRF	15 May 1884	5	6	
Burdick	Stephen W.	d.	DR	12 May 1884	3	2	
Burdick	Stephen W.	d.	PCo	7 May 1884	3	1	Cypress Hill
Burdick	Stephen W.	d.	PCo	7 May 1884	3	5	
Burdick	Stephen W.	d.	PWA	10 May 1884	3	5	
Burdick	Stephen W.	d.	SD	17 May 1884	3	5	
Burgard	G. F.	m.	PWA	23 Aug. 1884	3	4	
Burge	George (son of)	d.	SD	16 Apr. 1881	3	8	
Burger	C. H.	b.	PCo	1 Apr. 1885	3	6	
Burger	C. H.	b.	SD	4 Apr. 1885	2	5	
Burger	C. H. (son of)	d.	PCo	12 Apr. 1882	3	5	
Burger	C. H. (son of)	d.	SD	8 Apr. 1882	3	6	
Burger	G. N.	m.	SD	31 Dec. 1881	3	6	
Burger	John R.	m.	SD	30 July 1881	3	8	
Burger	Mary A.	m.	SD	8 Jan. 1881	3	8	
Burger	Mary E.	m.	RRF	9 Mar. 1882	2	4	
Burger	Miss	m.	CR	4 Mar. 1882	1	4	
Burgess	Frank	b.	DD	4 Dec. 1883	3	3	
Burgess	Jennie	m.	CR	17 Feb. 1883	3	1	
Burgess	Samuel	m.	DD	20 Oct. 1883	3	3	
Burgett	William	b.	CR	28 May 1881	5	5	
Burgett	William	b.	DD	21 Aug. 1883	3	3	
Burgett	William	b.	PC	22 Aug. 1883	3	5	
Burgett	William	b.	RRF	26 May 1881	2	5	
Burgett	William	b.	RRF	16 Aug. 1883	2	4	
Burgett	William	b.	SD	4 June 1881	3	8	
Burgett	William	b.	SD	25 Aug. 1883	2	5	
Burghard	G. F.	m.	DR	18 Aug. 1884	3	3	
Burgren	Erick	d.	SD	5 Jan. 1884	1	8	
Burgren	Erick J.	d.	DD	27 Dec. 1883	3	3	
Burgtorf	Minnie	d.	DR	10 June 1881	2	2	
Burgtorf	Minnie	d.	SD	25 June 1881	3	8	
Burk	George	d.	PCo	11 Mar. 1885	2	2	
Burk	Jessie	m.	SD	25 July 1885	3	5	
Burke or Berg	George	d.	SD	14 Mar. 1885	1	5	
Burke	(children of)	d.	SD	24 Mar. 1883	2	5	
Burke	(twin children)	d.	PC	28 Mar. 1883	3	5	
Burke	(win children)	d.	PWA	31 Mar. 1883	2	4	

(1) Surname	(2) Given Name	(3)	(4)	(5) Date	(6) Pg	(7) Col	(8) Comments
Burke	Alice	d.	SD	18 Mar. 1882	3	5	
Burke	Clarence	d.	SD	30 Apr. 1881	3	8	
Burke	Jessie	m.	DR	20 July 1885	3	4	
Burke	Jessie	m.	PCo	29 July 1885	3	4	
Burke	John	b.	PCo	12 July 1882	3	5	
Burke	John	b.	SD	15 July 1882	2	4	
Burke	Katie	d.	PCo	18 Oct. 1882	3	6	
Burke	Mr. & Mrs.	b.	PCo	21 Mar. 1883	3	5	
Burke	Mr. & Mrs.	b.	SD	24 Mar. 1883	2	5	
Burke	Thomas (dau. of)	d.	PCo	15 Mar. 1882	3	4	
Burke	Thomas (dau. of)	d.	SD	25 Mar. 1882	3	6	
Burke	Thomas	d.	RRF	9 Mar. 1882	2	4	
Burling	George W.	b.	DR	15 Nov. 1884	3	2	
Burling	George W.	m.	PCo	26 Dec. 1883	3	5	
Burling	George W.	b.	PCo	12 Nov. 1884	3	5	
Burling	George W.	m.	PWA	29 Dec. 1883	3	6	
Burling	George W.	b.	PWA	15 Nov. 1884	3	4	
Burling	George W.	m.	SD	29 Dec. 1883	3	6	
Burner	William	m.	RRF	22 Dec. 1881	2	3	
Burnett	A. G.	b.	CR	25 June 1881	4	3	
Burnett	A. G.	b.	DD	27 Dec. 1883	3	3	
Burnett	A. G.	b.	DR	17 June 1881	2	3	
Burnett	A. G.	o.	DR	26 Oct. 1882	2	1	
Burnett	A. G.	b.	PCo	2 Jan. 1884	3	6	
Burnett	A. G.	b.	RRF	9 June 1881	2	5	
Burnett	A. G.	b.	RRF	27 Dec. 1883	2	2	
Burnett	A. G.	b.	SD	18 June 1881	3	8	
Burnett	A. G.	b.	SD	5 Jan. 1884	1	8	
Burnett	J. A.	b.	DR	25 Apr. 1881	3	2	
Burnett	Sarah E.	d.	PCo	1 Nov. 1882	3	5	
Burnett	Sarah Elouise	d.	DR	26 Oct. 1882	3	1	
Burnett	Sarah Elouise	d.	SD	28 Oct. 1882	3	5	
Burney	John	d.	DR	29 Apr. 1884	3	2	
Burney	John	d.	PCo	30 Apr. 1884	2	6	
Burney	John	d.	RRF	1 May 1884	5	6	
Burney	John	d.	SD	3 May 1884	3	3	
Burnham	J. C.	m.	DR	19 June 1884	3	3	
Burnham	J. C.	m.	PCo	18 June 1884	3	4	
Burnham	J. C.	m.	PWA	14 June 1884	3	6	
Burnham	J. C.	m.	SD	28 June 1884	3	4	
Burnham	Joseph	b.	DR	1 Dec. 1885	3	4	
Burnham	Joseph	b.	PCo	23 Nov. 1885	3	4	

(1) Surname	(2) Given Name	(3)	(4)	(5) Date	(6) Pg	(7) Col	(8) Comments
Burns	Anna	m.	PWA	11 Oct. 1884	3	4	
Burns	C. S.	b.	PCo	21 Mar. 1883	3	5	
Burns	C. S.	b.	PWA	24 Mar. 1883	3	7	
Burns	Charles S.	m.	PCo	3 May 1882	3	5	
Burns	Eugene F.	m.	SD	22 Sept. 1883	1	6	
Burns	John	b.	PCo	26 Mar. 1884	3	6	
Burns	John	b.	PWA	29 Mar. 1884	3	6	
Burns	John	m.	SD	29 Jan. 1881	3	8	
Burns	John	b.	SD	29 Mar. 1884	2	5	
Burns	Robert	m.	DR	29 Nov. 1882	3	2	
Burris	(male)	b.	DR	18 Jan. 1884	3	3	
Burris	Bettie	m.	HE	4 Oct. 1883	2	3	
Burris	D.	b.	DR	23 Jan. 1882	2	3	
Burris	D.	b.	PCo	25 Jan. 1882	3	6	
Burris	D.	b.	SD	28 Jan. 1882	3	6	
Burris	Jennie L.	m.	SD	12 May 1883	2	6	
Burris	L. W.	b.	PCo	23 Jan. 1884	3	5	
Burris	L. W.	b.	SD	26 Jan. 1884	3	5	
Burris	Luther W.	m.	SD	30 Sept. 1882	3	1	
Burris	Mary	m.	SD	30 Sept. 1882	3	1	
Burris	William M.	o.	DR	3 Nov. 1882	3	1	
Burrus	Jennie L.	m.	PC	9 May 1883	3	5	
Burrus	Jennie L.	m.	RRF	10 May 1883	2	3	
Burtchael	Effie C.	d.	PCo	16 Nov. 1881	3	5	
Burtchael	P. T.	b.	PCo	9 Nov. 1881	3	5	
Burtcher	W. P.	m.	DR	26 Dec. 1884	2	2	
Burton	Noah	d.	DR	17 Jan. 1882	2	3	
Burton	Noah	d.	PCo	18 Jan. 1882	3	5	
Burzhard	S. F.	m.	SD	23 Aug. 1884	2	4	
Busch	J. G.	b.	DD	23 July 1883	3	2	
Busch	J. G.	b.	SD	28 July 1883	2	5	
Bush	Eli	m.	SD	24 May 1884	2	3	
Bush	Giles	b.	PCo	25 Feb. 1885	3	6	
Bush	Giles	m.	RRF	24 Apr. 1884	1	4	
Bush	Giles	b.	SD	21 Feb. 1885	2	5	
Bush	Giles H.	m.	DR	25 Apr. 1884	3	2	
Bush	Giles H.	m.	PCo	23 Apr. 1884	2	6	
Bush	Giles H.	m.	SD	26 Apr. 1883	3	5	
Bush	Margaret	m.	SD	2 May 1885	2	5	
Bush	William (son of)	d.	PCo	28 Feb. 1883	3	5	
Bush	William (son of0	d.	RRF	22 Feb. 1883	2	3	
Bush	William P.	m.	HE	26 Jan. 1882	2	3	

(1) Surname	(2) Given Name	(3)	(4)	(5) Date	(6) Pg	(7) Col	(8) Comments
Bush	William P.	m.	RRF	26 Jan. 1882	2	2	
Bush	William	b.	PCo	28 Feb. 1883	3	5	
Bush	William	b.	RRF	22 Feb. 1883	2	3	
Bushnell	William	d.	DR	30 Apr. 1881	2	3	
Butcher	Nettie V. Seawell	d.	SD	17 Jan. 1885	5	3	Rural Cemetery
Butcher	William P.	m.	PCo	7 Jan. 1885	3	6	
Butcher	William P.	m.	SD	3 Jan. 1885	2	4	also p. 2 col. 7
Butler	A. B.	m.	PCo	22 Feb. 1882	3	5	
Butler	A. B.	m.	SD	11 Feb. 1882	3	6	
Butler	A. C.	m.	DR	9 Feb. 1882	2	3	
Butler	Alida	m.	DR	3 Dec. 1881	2	3	
Butler	Alida	m.	PCo	7 Dec. 1881	3	5	
Butler	Alida	m.	SD	17 Dec. 1881	3	7	
Butler	Bessie	m.	DR	12 Aug. 1884	3	3	
Butler	Bessie	m.	PWA	16 Aug. 1884	3	4	
Butler	Bessie	m.	SD	13 Aug. 1884	2	4	
Butler	E. A.	b.	DR	19 Sept. 1885	3	4	
Butler	E. F.	d.	SD	14 Jan. 1882	3	5	
Butler	John W.	d.	DR	25 Nov. 1881	2	3	
Butler	John W.	d.	PCo	7 Dec. 1881	3	5	
Butler	John W.	d.	SD	17 Dec. 1881	3	7	
Butler	Sarah A.	m.	DD	31 July 1883	3	2	
Butler	Sarah A.	m.	PC	8 Aug. 1883	3	6	
Butler	Sarah A.	m.	SD	4 Aug. 1883	2	5	
Butler	Thomas B.	m.	DR	17 Nov. 1884	3	2	
Butler	Thomas B.	b.	PCo	9 Apr. 1884	3	6	
Butler	Thomas B.	b.	SD	5 Apr. 1884	3	4	
Butterfield	Carrie	m.	DD	25 Sept. 1883	3	3	
Butterfield	Carrie	m.	SD	29 Sept. 1883	2	6	
Button	Catharine H. V.	d.	PCo	7 May 1884	3	5	
Button	Catherine H.	d.	RRF	15 May 1884	5	6	
Button	Catherine H. V.	d.	DR	10 May 1884	3	2	
Button	Catherine V.	d.	PWA	10 May 1884	3	5	
Button	Katie	m.	PWA	12 Jan. 1884	3	7	
Button	Norman A.	m.	SD	3 May 1884	3	1	
Butts	Cecil	d.	DR	16 Oct. 1885	3	4	
Butts	Cecil	d.	SD	24 Oct. 1885	5	4	
Butts	Josephine	m.	SD	27 Sept. 1884	2	5	
Butts	T. J.	b.	DR	1 Nov. 1881	2	3	filed after Nov. 29
Butts	T. J.	b.	PCo	9 Nov. 1881	3	5	
Butts	T. J.	b.	SD	19 Nov. 1881	4	8	
Buzzell	Lucinda	m.	SD	17 June 1882	3	1	

(1) Surname	(2) Given Name	(3)	(4)	(5) Date	(6) Pg	(7) Col	(8) Comments
Buzzill	L.	b.	SD	16 Apr. 1881	3	8	
Bynum	Thomas	m.	SD	16 June 1883	2	6	
Byon	Timothy	b.	SD	23 Apr. 1881	3	8	

C

(1) Surname	(2) Given Name	(3)	(4)	(5) Date	(6) Pg	(7) Col	(8) Comments
Cadose	Mr.	b.	DR	31 July 1885	3	4	
Cadosèr	Mr. & Mrs.	b.	PCo	5 Aug. 1885	3	6	
Cadwell	Carrie	m.	SD	29 July 1882	3	7	
Cadwell	Carrie L.	m.	PCo	26 July 1882	3	6	
Cahalin	Mamie E.	d.	PCo	19 July 1882	3	6	
Cahalin	Mamie E.	d.	RRF	13 July 1882	2	4	
Cahoon	Louise B.	m.	DR	22 Nov. 1884	3	2	
Cahoon	Louise B.	m.	PCo	26 Nov. 1884	3	5	
Cahoon	Louise B.	m.	SD	23 Nov. 1884	2	6	also p. 3 col 4.
Cairns	John, Mrs.	d.	DR	30 Dec. 1884	2	2	
Calaghan	Mary	m.	DR	29 Aug. 1882	3	2	
Calaghan	Mary	m.	SD	2 Sept. 1882	3	6	
Calder	Isaac	d.	SD	2 Dec. 1882	3	2	
Caldwell	S. C.	m.	DR	5 Aug. 1881	2	2	
Caldwell	S. T.	b.	PCo	20 Sept. 1882	3	6	
Caldwell	S. T.	b.	PCo	12 Mar. 1884	3	6	
Caldwell	S. T.	b.	RRF	14 Sept. 1882	2	4	
Caldwell	S. T.	b.	RRF	6 Mar. 1884	2	3	
Caldwell	S. T.	m.	SD	6 Aug. 1881	3	8	
Caldwell	S. T.	b.	SD	23 Sept. 1882	3	6	
Caldwell	Samuel T.	m.	RRF	11 Aug. 1881	2	5	
Caldwell	Samuel T.	m.	SD	20 Aug. 1881	3	8	
Caldwell	William	b.	CR	20 Sept. 1884	3	1	
Caldwell	William	b.	PCo	1 Nov. 1882	3	5	
Caldwell	William	b.	PCo	24 Sept. 1884	3	5	
Call	Olive	m.	DR	22 May 1884	3	2	
Call	Ollie	m.	SD	24 May 1884	2	3	
Callalan	Mary A.	m.	SD	27 Sept. 1884	2	5	
Callaway	C. M.	b.	PCo	14 Feb. 1883	3	6	
Callaway	C. M.	b.	SD	10 Feb. 1883	2	7	
Calloway	C. M.	b.	RRF	8 Feb. 1883	2	4	
Calzascia	Frances	m.	DR	21 May 1884	3	2	
Calzaseia	Frances	m.	PWA	24 May 1884	3	5	
Calzaseia	Frances	m.	SD	24 May 1884	2	3	
Cameron	Edwin H.	m.	SD	10 Jan. 1885	2	6	
Cameron	G.	d.	RRF	20 July 1882	2	4	
Cameron	G. (son of)	d.	CR	13 July 1882	5	2	
Cameron	G. (son of)	d.	PCo	19 July 1882	3	6	

(1) Surname	(2) Given Name	(3)	(4)	(5) Date	(6) Pg	(7) Col	(8) Comments
Cameron	G. (son of)	d.	SD	22 July 1882	3	5	
Cameron	Gordon	b.	CR	13 May 1882	5	1	
Cameron	Gordon	b.	DR	16 May 1882	3	2	
Cameron	Gordon	b.	PCo	17 May 1882	3	5	
Cameron	Gordon	b.	SD	20 May 1882	2	4	
Cameron	J. W.	m.	RRF	27 Sept. 1883	2	2	
Camm	John	m.	PWA	12 Jan. 1884	3	7	
Camm	John L.	b.	PCo	14 Jan. 1885	3	6	
Camm	John L.	b.	PWA	17 Jan. 1885	2	4	
Campbell	B. F.	o.	SWI	24 Nov. 1882	3	2	
Campbell	Bessie	d.	RRF	24 Mar. 1881	2	4	
Campbell	Claud	d.	DR	25 Jan. 1882	2	3	
Campbell	Edgar	m.	RRF	8 Feb. 1883	2	4	also p. 3 col. 3
Campbell	George	d.	RRF	26 Jan. 1882	2	2	
Campbell	George (son of)	d.	SD	4 Feb. 1882	3	6	
Campbell	George S.	b.	DR	15 Nov. 1881	2	3	
Campbell	George S.	b.	PCo	16 Nov. 1881	3	5	
Campbell	George S.	b.	SD	19 Nov. 1881	4	8	
Campbell	I. R. F.	m.	PCo	14 Feb. 1883	3	6	
Campbell	Matilda C.	d.	DR	4 Oct. 1881	2	3	
Campbell	Matilda C.	d.	SD	8 Oct. 1881	3	8	
Campbell	Nellie	d.	DR	13 June 1884	3	3	
Campbell	Nellie	d.	PCo	18 June 1884	3	4	
Campbell	R. B.	d.	DR	2 Nov. 1885	3	4	
Campbell	R. B.	d.	PCo	28 Oct. 1885	3	4	
Campbell	R. B.	d.	SD	24 Oct. 1885	5	4	
Campbell	R. E.	m.	CR	10 Feb. 1883	3	1	
Campbell	R. E.	b.	PCo	6 Aug. 1884	2	4	
Campbell	R. E.	m.	SD	10 Feb. 1883	2	7	
Campbell	R. E.	b.	SD	9 Aug. 1884	3	4	
Campbell	Thomas	b.	PCo	14 June 1882	3	5	twins
Campbell	Thomas	m.	PCo	15 Oct. 1884	3	6	
Campbell	Thomas	b.	RRF	8 June 1882	2	3	
Campbell	Thomas	b.	SD	17 June 1882	2	4	
Camphausen	Ina Becenil	m.	DR	21 July 1882	3	2	
Canaiga	George	b.	SD	9 July 1881	3	8	
Canaway	Agnes	m.	SD	9 Apr. 1881	3	8	
Cane	Ella	m.	SD	10 June 1882	3	2	
Canepa	Darwin C.	o.	DR	26 Oct. 1882	2	2	
Canepa	G.	b.	PCo	16 Nov. 1881	3	5	
Canepa	G.	b.	SD	26 Nov. 1881	3	8	
Cannon	James	m.	SD	1 Oct. 1881	3	8	

(1) Surname	(2) Given Name	(3)	(4)	(5) Date	(6) Pg	(7) Col	(8) Comments
Cannon	James P.	m.	DR	24 Sept. 1881	2	3	
Cannon	James P.	m.	PCo	21 Sept. 1881	3	5	
Cannon	Jerome	b.	PCo	17 June 1885	3	6	
Cannon	Jerome	b.	SD	27 June 1885	5	4	
Canright	Josie	m.	SWI	7 Apr. 1883	3	5	
Cantel	Eugene J. B.	m.	PCo	15 Apr. 1885	3	6	
Cantel	J. B.	m.	PWA	18 Apr. 1885	3	6	
Cantel	Josephine Louise	m.	PCo	5 July 1882	3	5	
Cantel	Mary	m.	PCo	22 Mar. 1882	3	5	
Cantel	Mary	m.	SD	1 Apr. 1882	3	6	
Canwright	Josie	m.	PWA	7 Apr. 1883	2	3	
Capell	Charles	m.	DR	26 Aug. 1885	3	4	
Capell	Minnie O.	m.	DR	3 Nov. 1885	3	4	
Capell	Walter B.	m.	SD	1 June 1881	3	7	
Carah	J. H.	m.	DR	16 July 1884	3	3	
Carah	John H.	m.	PCo	23 July 1884	3	6	
Carah	John H.	m.	SD	19 July 1884	2	5	also p. 3 col. 3
Carberry	Katie	m.	PCo	22 Oct. 1884	3	6	
Carberry	Katie	m.	PWA	25 Oct. 1884	3	4	
Carberry	Katie	m.	SD	8 Nov. 1884	2	5	
Carey	Nora	m.	DR	8 Dec. 1884	3	2	
Cargile	J. L.	d.	PCo	15 Mar. 1882	3	4	
Cargile	J. L., Mrs.	d.	SD	11 Mar. 1882	3	6	
Carle	Emma	d.	CR	1 Sept. 1883	3	1&3	San Francisco
Carle	Emma	d.	DD	8 Sept. 1883	3	3	
Carleton	John W.	d.	PCo	30 Apr. 1884	2	6	
Carleton	John W.	d.	RRF	1 May 1884	5	6	
Carleton	John W.	d.	SD	3 May 1884	3	3	
Carlson	Elizabeth	m.	SD	4 Feb. 1882	3	6	
Carlton	J. M.	m.	DR	6 Aug. 1881	2	3	
Carlton	J. M.	d.	DR	28 Apr. 1884	3	2	
Carlton	J. M.	m.	SD	20 Aug. 1881	3	8	
Carlton	J. W.	b.	DR	9 June 1881	2	2	
Carlton	J. W.	b.	SD	11 June 1881	3	8	
Carlton	James	d.	DR	5 Apr. 1881	2	3	
Carlton	James	d.	SD	9 Apr. 1881	3	8	
Carlton	James	d.	SD	16 Apr. 1881	3	8	
Carlton	Mary M.	m.	SD	2 July 1881	3	8	
Carmenito	Antonio	b.	PCo	12 July 1882	3	5	
Carmenito	Antonio	b.	SD	15 July 1882	2	4	
Carmody	James	m.	DR	10 Apr. 1882	2	2	
Carmody	James	m.	PCo	5 Apr. 1882	3	5	

(1) Surname	(2) Given Name	(3)	(4)	(5) Date	(6) Pg	(7) Col	(8) Comments
Carmody	John	d.	CR	30 Apr. 1881	5	5	
Carmody	John	d.	DR	29 Apr. 1881	3	2	
Carmody	John	d.	PCo	27 Apr. 1881	3	5	
Carmody	John	d.	SD	7 May 1881	3	8	
Carmody	P. C.	b.	PCo	25 Oct. 1882	3	5	
Carmody	Patrick C.	m.	PCo	30 Nov. 1881	3	5	
Carmody	Patrick C.	m.	SD	31 Dec. 1881	3	6	
Carmody	Thomas	b.	PCo	13 May 1885	3	6	
Carnaige	Mr.	b.	RRF	30 June 1881	3	2	
Carner	Retta J.	m.	DR	11 Jan. 1881	3	2	
Carner	Retta J.	m.	SD	15 Jun. 1881	3	8	
Carnwell	Henry	d.	DR	18 July 1884	3	3	
Carothers	J. H.	b.	DD	4 Dec. 1883	3	3	
Carothers	J. H.	b.	SD	8 Dec. 1883	3	1	
Carothers	John W.	m.	PCo	14 Oct. 1885	3	6	
Caroway	Edna	m.	DR	2 Dec. 1881	2	3	
Carpenter	Frankie E.	m.	d.	28 July 1883	2	5	
Carpenter	Frankie E.	m.	DD	26 July 1883	3	2	
Carpenter	Frankie E.	m.	PC	25 July 1883	3	6	
Carpenter	Frankie E.	m.	PWA	28 July 1883	3	7	
Carpenter	May	m.	DR	23 Jan. 1882	2	3	
Carr	F. B.	d.	SD	15 Nov. 1884	2	5	
Carr	Frank P.	d.	DR	14 Nov. 1884	3	2	
Carr	Frank P.	d.	PCo	19 Nov. 1884	3	5	
Carr	James E.	m.	PCo	21 Jan. 1885	2	5	
Carr	James E.	m.	PWA	24 Jan. 1885	3	5	
Carr	Mark, Jr.	m.	DD	5 Nov. 1883	3	2	
Carr	Mark, Jr.	m.	PWA	3 Nov. 1883	3	8	
Carr	Mark, Jr.	m.	SD	10 Nov. 1883	3	5	
Carr	Mark	b.	PWA	23 Aug. 1884	3	4	
Carr	Thomas	b.	DR	15 Nov. 1882	2	3	
Carr	Thomas	b.	PCo	15 Nov. 1882	3	5	
Carr	Ursula A.	m.	PWA	22 Nov. 1884	3	4	
Carr	Vesula A.	m.	DR	21 Nov. 1884	3	2	
Carr	Vesula	m.	PCo	19 Nov. 1884	3	5	
Carrie	Annie	m.	PCo	10 Dec. 1884	3	5	
Carrie	J. A.	o.	CR	1 Sept. 1883	3	3	
Carriger	Nicholas	d.	PCo	8 July 1885	3	6	
Carriger	Nicholas	o.	PCo	15 July 1885	2	2	text of will
Carriger	Nicholas	d.	SD	4 July 1885	5	3&4	also p. 5 col. 1; Sonoma
Carriger	Nicholas	p.	SD	15 Aug. 1885	3	6	
Carriger	Nicholas	p.	SD	18 July 1885	1	4	text of will

(1) Surname	(2) Given Name	(3)	(4)	(5) Date	(6) Pg	(7) Col	(8) Comments
Carriger	S. J., Mrs.	m.	DR	5 Nov. 1881	2	3	
Carriger	S. J., Mrs.	m.	PCo	9 Nov. 1881	3	5	
Carriger	S. J., Mrs.	m.	SD	12 Nov. 1881	3	7	
Carrillo	Albert	m.	DR	11 Feb. 1884	3	3	
Carrillo	Joseph	m.	PCo	24 June 1885	3	6	
Carrillo	Joseph	m.	SD	27 June 1885	5	4	
Carroll	James	b.	PC	20 June 1883	3	6	
Carroll	James	b.	PWA	23 June 1883	3	7	
Carroll	James (son of)	d.	CR	13 June 1885	1	3	
Carroll	James (son of)	d.	PCo	10 June 1885	3	6	
Carroll	John	d.	PCo	30 Sept. 1885	3	6	
Carroll	John	d.	SD	17 Oct. 1885	4	5	
Carroll	Johnny	d.	DR	30 Sept. 1885	3	4	
Carroll	Johnny	d.	SD	3 Oct. 1885	5	4	
Carroll	Johnny	d.	SRR	1 Oct. 1885	3	3	
Carroll	Katherine	d.	PCo	1 Nov. 1882	3	5	
Carroll	Katherine	d.	RRF	26 Oct. 1882	2	3	
Carroll	Mary	d.	DR	23 May 1882	2	3	
Carroll	Mary	d.	PCo	17 May 1882	3	5	
Carroll	Mary	d.	SD	20 May 1882	2	4	
Carroll	Mary	d.	SD	17 Oct. 1885	4	5	
Carroll	Nellie	d.	PCo	14 Oct. 1885	3	6	
Carsin	John	b.	PCo	27 Dec. 1882	3	6	
Carsin	John	b.	SD	23 Dec. 1882	2	5	
Carson	Dorothy	d.	DR	8 Mar. 1882	2	3	
Carson	Dorothy	d.	PCo	15 Mar. 1882	3	4	
Carson	Dorothy	d.	SD	11 Mar. 1882	3	6	
Carson	Dorothy	d.	SD	25 Mar. 1882	3	6	
Carson	J. A.	b.	DD	28 Aug. 1883	3	3	
Carson	J. A.	b.	PWA	25 Aug. 1883	3	8	
Carson	J. A.	b.	SD	1 Sept. 1883	2	7	
Carson	Moses	o.	SD	14 Nov. 1885	3	3	
Carson	Moses	o.	SD	17 Oct. 1885	5	1	
Carter	C. F.	b.	DR	24 Oct. 1882	3	2	
Carter	C. F.	b.	PCo	18 Oct. 1882	3	6	
Carter	Hariet F.	d.	DR	27 May 1884	3	2	
Carter	M. M.	b.	SD	25 June 1881	3	8	
Carter	Mary I.	m.	SD	12 Mar. 1881	3	8	
Carter	S. L.	d.	DD	29 Dec. 1883	3	3	
Carter	S. L., Mrs.	d.	SD	5 Jan. 1884	1	4&8	
Carter	Susan	d.	PCo	2 Jan. 1884	3	6	
Carty	Charles	d.	PWA	28 Mar. 1885	3	5	

(1) Surname	(2) Given Name	(3)	(4)	(5) Date	(6) Pg	(7) Col	(8) Comments
Carty	Charles, Jr.	d.	SD	4 Apr. 1885	2	5	
Carver	H. E., Mrs.	d.	CR	17 Mar. 1883	3		
Carver	H. E., Mrs.	d.	PCo	21 Mar. 1883	3	5	
Carver	H. E., Mrs.	d.	RRF	15 Mar. 1883	2	4	Beeson Burying Ground
Carver	H. E., Mrs.	d.	SD	17 Mar. 1883	3	5	
Cary	Franklin L.	d.	SD	2 May 1885	2	5	
Case	Carrie B.	m.	PCo	21 June 1882	3	5	
Case	Hattie	d.	CR	2 Apr. 1881	5	3	
Case	Hattie	d.	DR	30 Mar. 1881	3	2	
Case	Hattie	d.	PCo	23 Mar. 1881	3	4	
Case	Hattie	d.	SD	2 Apr. 1881	3	8	
Case	Susie	m.	PC	27 June 1883	3	6	
Case	Susie	m.	RRF	21 June 1883	2	3	
Case	Susie	m.	SD	23 June 1883	3	5	
Caseres	G. A.	b.	DR	14 Nov. 1881	2	3	
Caseres	George	b.	DR	22 Sept. 1885	3	4	
Caseres	Mr. & Mrs.	b.	PCo	23 Sept. 1885	3	6	
Caseres	Mr. & Mrs.	b.	SD	19 Nov. 1881	4	8	
Caseres	Mr. & Mrs.	b.	SD	26 Sept. 1885	5	4	
Casey	Edward O.	m.	CR	22 Oct. 1881	5	3	
Casey	Edward O.	m.	DR	25 Oct. 1881	3	2	
Casey	Edward O.	m.	PCo	2 Nov. 1881	3	5	
Casey	Edward O.	m.	SD	29 Oct. 1881	3	6	
Casey	John	b.	PCo	26 Mar. 1884	3	6	
Casey	John	b.	PWA	29 Mar. 1884	3	6	
Casey	John	b.	SD	29 Mar. 1884	2	5	
Casey	John	b.	SWI	29 Mar. 1884	3	5	
Casey	Mary	m.	DR	22 July 1884	3	3	
Casey	Mary	m.	PCo	30 July 1884	3	6	
Casey	Mary	m.	PWA	26 July 1884	2	3	
Casey	Mary	m.	SD	26 July 1884	1	4	
Casey	Mathew	d.	PCo	30 July 1884	3	6	
Casey	Mathew	d.	PWA	2 Aug. 1884	3	4	
Casey	Matthew	d.	DR	1 Aug. 1884	3	3	
Casley	Patrick	d.	DR	30 July 1881	2	3	
Cassel	F. L.	b.	PC	25 Apr. 1883	3	5	
Cassel	F. L.	b.	SD	28 Apr. 1883	3	6	
Cassiday	Bardey	d.	RRF	16 Mar. 1882	2	4	
Cassiday	Bardey, Mrs.	d.	SD	25 Mar. 1882	3	6	
Cassidy	Barney, Mrs.	d.	PCo	22 Mar. 1882	3	5	
Cassidy	Nellie	m.	DR	20 Nov. 1885	3	4	
Cassidy	Nellie	m.	PCo	23 Nov. 1885	3	4	

(1) Surname	(2) Given Name	(3)	(4)	(5) Date	(6) Pg	(7) Col	(8) Comments
Castagnaso	Andrew	d.	SD	7 Nov. 1885	3	4	
Castagnaso	Andrew (son of)	d.	SIT	31 Oct. 1885	2	3	
Castanisco	Henry	b.	PCo	13 Aug. 1884	3	4	
Castanisco	Henry	b.	PWA	16 Aug. 1884	3	4	
Castanisco	Henry	b.	SD	13 Aug. 1884	2	4	
Castelli	Louis	d.	SD	25 July 1885	3	3	
Castle	Frank I.	m.	DR	8 Aug. 1882	3	2	
Castle	Frank L.	m.	RRF	3 Aug. 1882	2	4	
Castle	Frank L.	b.	RRF	19 Apr. 1883	2	3	
Castlio	Madora	m.	DD	29 Dec. 1883	3	3	
Casto	Mamie	m.	DD	11 Oct. 1883	3	3	
Cauckwell	John	b.	CR	30 Apr. 1881	5	5	
Cauckwell	John	b.	DR	26 Apr. 1881	2	2	
Cauckwell	John	b.	SD	7 May 1881	3	8	
Caughey	A.	b.	SD	29 Aug. 1885	2	4	
Caughey	Robert	b.	SD	19 Feb. 1881	3	8	
Cauldin	W. W.	b.	DR	15 Nov. 1884	3	2	
Cavanagh	T. J.	m.	DR	21 Jan. 1884	3	2	
Cavanagh	T. J.	m.	PWA	19 Jan. 1884	3	7	
Cavanagh	Thomas	m.	PCo	23 Jan. 1884	3	5	
Cavanagh	Thomas	m.	SD	26 Jan. 1884	3	5	
Cerini	John	m.	DR	21 May 1884	3	2	
Cerini	John	m.	SD	24 May 1884	2	3	
Cerini	John	d.	SD	18 Apr. 1885	2	5	
Chadbourne	S. W.	m.	DR	28 Sept. 1881	3	2	
Chadbourne	S. W.	m.	RRF	22 Sept. 1881	2	5	
Chadwick	Bell	m.	PC	25 July 1883	3	6	
Chadwick	Belle	m.	DD	23 July 1883	3	2	
Chadwick	Belle	m.	SD	28 July 1883	2	5	
Chaffee	E. S.	m.	SD	27 June 1885	5	4	
Chaffee	F. S.	m.	PCo	24 June 1885	3	6	
Chalfant	Mattie	m.	DR	30 May 1884	3	2	
Chalfant	Mattie	m.	PCo	4 June 1884	3	5	
Chambaud	John	d.	DR	9 Dec. 1884	3	2	
Chambaud	John	d.	SD	13 Dec. 1884	2	5	
Chamberlain	Annie C.	m.	DR	8 Mar. 1882	2	3	
Chamberlain	Annie C.	m.	PCo	1 Mar. 1882	2	4	
Chamberlain	Annie C.	m.	SD	25 Feb. 1882	3	6	
Chamberlain	Kittie	m.	SD	27 June 1885	5	4	
Chamberland	Kittie	m.	PCo	24 June 1885	3	6	
Chambers	Charles R.	d.	PCo	29 Mar. 1882	3	5	
Chambers	Edward	m.	CR	18 Feb. 1882	5	1	

(1) Surname	(2) Given Name	(3)	(4)	(5) Date	(6) Pg	(7) Col	(8) Comments
Chambers	Edward	m.	RRF	2 Mar. 1882	4	1	
Chambers	J. K.	b.	SD	21 Apr. 1883	2	6	
Champlin	Charles P.	b.	PCo	2 Dec. 1885	3	4	
Champlin	Charles P.	b.	SIT	28 Nov. 1885	2	3	
Champlin	Charles V.	m.	PCo	10 Jan. 1883	3	6	
Champlin	Charles V.	m.	PWA	5 Jan. 1883	2	5	
Chandler	Jane	d.	SD	21 Feb. 1885	2	5	
Chandler	Joseph	m.	CR	18 Nov. 1882	3	3	
Chandler	Joseph	d.	CR	4 Apr. 1885	3	2	
Chandler	Joseph	m.	PCo	29 Nov. 1882	3	6	
Chandler	Joseph	d.	PCo	1 Apr. 1885	3	6	
Chandler	Joseph	d.	SD	4 Apr. 1885	1	6	also p. 2 col. 5
Chandler	Josiah	d.	PCo	26 July 1882	3	2	
Chandler	Josiah	d.	SD	29 July 1882	3	1&7	
Chandler	W. R.	m.	CR	11 Apr. 1885	3	2	
Chandler	W. R.	m.	SD	18 Apr. 1885	2	5	
Chapman	Henrietta	m.	SD	10 Dec. 1881	3	2	
Chapman	Lizzie Frances	d.	DR	5 May 1882	2	2	Santa Rosa Cem.
Chapman	Lizzie Frances	d.	SD	6 May 1882	3	6	
Chapman	Lizzie Frances	d.	SD	13 May 1882	3	1	
Chapman	Lizzie Francis	d.	PCo	17 May 1882	3	5	
Chapman	Lizzie N.	d.	DR	12 Sept. 1882	2	2	
Chapman	Thomas A.	m.	DR	26 Sept. 1881	3	2	
Chapman	Thomas A.	m.	DR	28 Sept. 1881	3	2	
Chapman	Thomas A.	m.	RRF	22 Sept. 1881	2	5	
Chapman	Thomas M.	d.	DR	24 Feb. 1882	2	3	
Chapman	Thomas M.	d.	PCo	22 Feb. 1882	3	5	
Chapman	Thomas M.	o.	SD	1 Apr. 1882	3	2	text of will
Chapman	Thomas M.	d.	SD	25 Feb. 1882	3	6	
Charles	G. A.	d.	CR	15 Jan. 1881	5	5	
Charles	G. A.	d.	DR	5 Jan. 1881	3	2	
Charles	G. A.	d.	DR	11 Jan. 1881	3	2	
Charles	G. A.	d.	SD	8 Jan. 1881	3	8	
Chase	Emily	d.	DR	8 Sept. 1882	3	4	
Cheibold	Mr. & Mrs.	b.	CR	30 Apr. 1881	5	5	
Cheibold	Mr. & Mrs.	b.	DR	26 Apr. 1881	2	2	
Cheney	T.	o.	SIT	22 Aug. 1885	2	2	
Chenowith	Charles	m.	DR	25 Apr. 1884	3	2	
Chenowith	Charles	m.	PCo	7 May 1884	3	5	
Chenowith	Charles	m.	RRF	1 May 1884	5	6	
Chester	Charles	m.	SD	29 Jan. 1881	3	8	
Chester	Theodore	b.	DD	4 Dec. 1883	3	3	

(1) Surname	(2) Given Name	(3)	(4)	(5) Date	(6) Pg	(7) Col	(8) Comments
Chick	A.	m.	PCo	30 July 1884	3	6	
Chick	D. A.	m.	DR	25 July 1884	3	3	
Chiebold	Mr. & Mrs.	b.	CR	30 Apr. 1881	5	5	
Chiebold	Mr. & Mrs.	b.	SD	7 May 1881	3	8	
Childers	Emma	m.	CR	9 June 1883	3	1	
Childers	Emma	m.	PC	13 June 1883	3	6	
Childers	Gussie	m.	DD	24 Dec. 1883	3	2	
Childers	Gussie	m.	PCo	26 Dec. 1883	3	5	
Childers	Gussie	m.	SD	29 Dec. 1883	3	6	
Chinn	L. F.	d.	DR	7 Dec. 1882	2	3	
Chinn	L. F.	d.	PCo	13 Dec. 1882	3	4	
Chinn	L. F., Mrs.	d.	SD	16 Dec. 1882	3	6	
Chisholm	A. J.	m.	RRF	15 Sept. 1881	2	5	
Chitwood	James M.	m.	DR	31 Oct. 1881	2	3	
Chitwood	James M.	m.	PCo	2 Nov. 1881	3	5	
Chitwood	James M.	m.	SD	5 Nov. 1881	3	6	
Chitwood	John H.	m.	DD	25 Sept. 1883	3	3	
Chitwood	John H.	m.	SD	29 Sept. 1883	2	6	
Chitwood	Monroe	m.	RRF	27 Oct. 1881	2	5	
Chopard	Louis M.	d.	PWA	1 Dec. 1883	3	3&6	
Christian	Mary A.	m.	PCo	2 Aug. 1882	3	6	
Christian	Mary A.	m.	RRF	27 July 1882	2	4	
Christianson	Peter	b.	SD	26 Nov. 1881	3	8	
Christie	A.	b.	PC	25 Apr. 1883	3	5	
Christie	A.	b.	PWA	28 Apr. 1883	3	8	
Christie	D.	o.	SIT	22 Aug. 1885	2	2	
Christie	J. B.	d.	PCo	17 Sept. 1884	3	4&6	
Christie	J. B.	d.	PWA	13 Sept. 1884	3	1&6	
Christie	John B.	d.	PCo	10 Sept. 1884	3	2&1	Cypress Hill
Christie	W. E. B.	d.	DR	10 Jun. 1881	2	2	
Christlich	Albert	d.	PCo	2 July 1884	3	4	
Christlich	Albert	d.	PWA	5 July 1884	3	6	
Christlich	Albert	d.	SD	12 July 1884	6	8	
Christlich	Fred	d.	HE	30 Mar. 1882	3	5	
Christlich	Frederick	d.	PCo	29 Mar. 1882	3	2&5	
Christlich	Frederick	d.	SD	1 Apr. 1882	3	6	
Christlich	Fredrick	d.	CR	8 Apr. 1882	1	3	
Church	Douglas	d.	SWI	5 Apr. 1884	3	4	
Church	John L.	m.	SD	6 June 1885	2	4	
Church	Walter	m.	DR	20 Mar. 1882	2	3	
Church	Walter	m.	PCo	15 Mar. 1882	3	4	
Church	Walter	b.	PCo	17 Sept. 1884	3	6	

(1) Surname	(2) Given Name	(3)	(4)	(5) Date	(6) Pg	(7) Col	(8) Comments
Church	Walter	b.	PWA	20 Sept. 1884	3	4	
Church	Walter	m.	SD	25 Mar. 1882	3	6	
Church	Walter	b.	SD	27 Sept. 1884	2	5	
Churchill	H. H.	b.	PCo	22 Oct. 1884	3	6	
Churchman	William	b.	SD	13 Aug. 1881	3	8	
Clarey	Annie J.	m.	SD	22 Sept. 1883	1	6	
Clark	A. W.	b.	DR	2 Nov. 1885	3	4	
Clark	Allie S.	m.	PCo	14 May 1884	3	4	
Clark	Allie S.	m.	RRF	8 May 1884	5	6	also p. 8 col. 1
Clark	Allie S.	m.	SD	17 May 1884	3	5	
Clark	Annie	d.	RRF	2 Mar. 1882	2	4	
Clark	Charles	p.	DR	6 Aug. 1884	3	2	
Clark	D. C.	b.	DR	5 Nov. 1881	2	3	
Clark	D. C.	b.	PCo	9 Nov. 1881	3	5	
Clark	D. C.	b.	RRF	3 Nov. 1881	2	3	
Clark	D. M.	o.	DR	28 Jan. 1882	2	2	
Clark	Emma	m.	DR	12 Nov. 1881	2	2	
Clark	Emma	m.	RRF	17 Nov. 1881	3	3	
Clark	Emma N.	m.	PCo	18 Oct. 1882	3	6	
Clark	Emma N.	m.	SD	14 Oct. 1882	3	6	
Clark	George C.	b.	PCo	6 Aug. 1884	2	4	
Clark	George C.	b.	SD	9 Aug. 1884	3	4	
Clark	H. F.	d.	SD	26 Feb. 1881	3	8	
Clark	Howard	d.	DR	9 Dec. 1884	3	2	
Clark	Howard	p.	DR	26 Dec. 1884	2	2	
Clark	Howard	d.	PWA	13 Dec. 1884	3	4	
Clark	Howard	d.	SD	13 Dec. 1884	2	5	
Clark	J. H. H.	m.	DR	17 May 1881	2	2	
Clark	J. H.	d.	DR	8 Mar. 1882	2	3	
Clark	J. H.	m.	RRF	26 May 1881	2	5	
Clark	J. H. H.	m.	SD	21 May 1881	3	8	
Clark	J. M.	b.	DR	4 Mar. 1882	2	3	
Clark	J. B. (son of)	d.	DR	31 Oct. 1881	2	3	
Clark	J. B. (son of)	d.	SD	5 Nov. 1881	3	6	
Clark	James H.	b.	RRF	2 Mar. 1882	2	4	
Clark	James H.	b.	SD	11 Mar. 1882	3	6	
Clark	James	b.	DR	10 July 1885	3	4	
Clark	James	d.	PCo	7 Oct. 1885	2	1	
Clark	James	b.	PCo	8 July 1885	3	6	
Clark	James	d.	SIT	10 Oct. 1885	3	3	
Clark	James M.	d.	SD	10 Oct. 1885	1	3	
Clark	James H., Mrs.	d.	DR	24 Feb. 1882	2	3	

(1) Surname	(2) Given Name	(3)	(4)	(5) Date	(6) Pg	(7) Col	(8) Comments
Clark	James H. H., Mrs.	d.	PCo	1 Mar. 1882	2	4	
Clark	James H. H., Mrs.	d.	SD	25 Feb. 1882	3	6	
Clark	John L.	m.	SD	5 Feb. 1881	3	8	
Clark	Leona	m.	PCo	28 June 1882	3	5	
Clark	Leona	m.	RRF	6 July 1882	2	4	
Clark	Leona	m.	SD	8 July 1882	2	5	
Clark	Lillie	d.	DR	8 Feb. 1884	3	3	
Clark	Lillie	d.	PCo	13 Feb. 1884	3	6	
Clark	Lillie	d.	SD	16 Feb. 1884	2	5	
Clark	Margaret	m.	SD	11 Feb. 1882	3	6	
Clark	Mathew	m.	DR	12 Jan. 1882	3	2	
Clark	Mathew	m.	PCo	18 Jan. 1882	3	5	
Clark	Mathew	m.	SD	14 Jan. 1882	3	8	
Clark	Richard C.	m.	DD	20 July 1883	3	2	
Clark	Richard C.	m.	PC	18 July 1883	3	5	
Clark	Richard O.	m.	SD	28 July 1883	2	5	
Clark	S. P.	d.	SD	3 Nov. 1883	1	6	
Clark	Samuel B.	m.	PC	4 July 1883	3	5	
Clark	Samuel B.	m.	PWA	30 June 1883	3	7	
Clark	Samuel B.	m.	SD	30 June 1883	3	5	
Clark	Susie	m.	SD	27 June 1885	5	4	
Clark	Tillie	m.	PCo	16 Dec. 1885	3	6	
Clark	William	d.	DR	20 Sept. 1881	2	3	
Clarke	John S.	b.	SD	5 Feb. 1881	3	8	
Clarke	Richard C.	m.	PWA	21 July 1883	3	7	
Claussen	May	m.	PCo	24 Sept. 1884	3	5	
Claussen	May	m.	PWA	20 Sept. 1884	3	4	
Clay	Fred	d.	CR	8 Aug. 1885	3	4	
Clay	Henry	d.	PCo	3 May 1882	3	5	
Clay	Henry	d.	SD	29 Apr. 1882	3	6	
Claypool	J.	b.	CR	28 May 1881	5	5	
Claypool	J.	b.	DR	24 May 1881	2	2	
Claypool	J.	b.	SD	28 May 1881	3	8	
Claypool	Jere	b.	RRF	2 June 1881	2	3	
Claypool	Robert Lee	d.	DD	31 Dec. 1883	3	3	
Claypool	Robert Lee	d.	PCo	2 Jan. 1884	3	6	
Claypool	Robert Lee	d.	SD	5 Jan. 1884	1	8	
Clayton	Amy R.	m.	DR	12 Oct. 1881	2	3	
Clayton	Amy R.	m.	PCo	12 Oct. 1881	3	5	
Clayton	Amy R.	m.	SD	15 Oct. 1881	3	1&8	
Clayton	Frank	b.	DR	16 July 1881	2	2	
Clayton	Frank	b.	SD	23 July 1881	3	8	

(1) Surname	(2) Given Name	(3)	(4)	(5) Date	(6) Pg	(7) Col	(8) Comments
Clemenson	C. J.	d.	DR	5 Sept. 1885	3	4	
Cleverly	Henry C.	m.	SD	31 Dec. 1881	3	6	
Clewe	F.	b.	SD	13 Aug. 1881	3	8	
Clifford	M. H.	m.	DR	1 Dec. 1885	3	4	
Clisbee	Maggie G.	d.	DR	24 July 1884	3	3	
Clover	Martha J.	m.	SD	21 Feb. 1885	2	5	
Clover	Martha	m.	PCo	25 Feb. 1885	3	6	
Clover	Martha	m.	PWA	28 Feb. 1885	3	5	
Cluver	Anna C.	m.	PCo	10 Dec. 1884	3	5	
Cluver	Anna C.	m.	PWA	13 Dec. 1884	3	4	
Cluver	Annie	m.	SD	13 Dec. 1884	2	5	
Clyman	James	d.	SD	7 Jan. 1882	3	2	
Cnopius	John, Jr.	m.	DR	5 June 1884	3	3	
Cnopius	John, Jr.	m.	SD	14 June 1884	2	4	
Cnopius	Maria E.	m.	CR	2 Apr. 1881	5	3	
Cnopius	Maria E.	m.	DR	30 Mar. 1881	3	2	
Cnopius	Maria E.	m.	SD	2 Apr. 1881	3	8	
Cnopius	Maria	m.	CR	2 Apr. 1881	5	3	
Coates	Harry	b.	PWA	24 Mar. 1883	3	7	
Coats	Elenora	m.	PC	4 July 1883	3	5	
Coats	Elenora	m.	SD	7 July 1883	2	5	
Coats	Harry	b.	PCo	21 Mar. 1883	3	5	
Coats	Harry	b.	SD	24 Mar. 1883	2	5	
Coats	William H.	m.	DR	6 May 1882	2	3	
Cobb	D. L.	m.	DR	19 Nov. 1885	3	4	
Cobb	L. D.	d.	SD	10 Feb. 1883	3	3	
Cobb	L. D.	d.	SD	24 Feb. 1883	3	2	
Cochran	A. E.	m.	DD	8 Sept. 1883	3	3	
Cochran	A. E.	m.	RRF	13 Sept. 1883	2	4	
Cochran	A. E.	m.	SD	15 Sept. 1883	2	4	
Cochran	Lillian	m.	DD	4 Dec. 1883	3	3	
Cochran	Lillian	m.	PWA	1 Dec. 1883	3	6	
Cochran	Lillian	m.	SD	8 Dec. 1883	3	1	
Cocke	Frances	d.	SD	23 Sept. 1882	3	2	
Cocke	W. E.	p.	DD	24 July 1883	3	2	
Cocke	W. E.	p.	DR	6 Dec. 1884	2	1	
Cocke	William Ewing	d.	SD	21 Apr. 1883	3	2	Rural Cemetery
Cockrill	(female)	b.	DR	6 June 1884	3	3	
Cockrill	B. T.	b.	PC	6 June 1883	3	4	
Cockrill	B. T.	b.	PWA	9 June 1883	3	7	
Cockrill	C. T.	b.	SD	16 June 1883	2	6	
Cockrill	Ida J.	m.	DR	13 Sept. 1881	2	3	

(1) Surname	(2) Given Name	(3)	(4)	(5) Date	(6) Pg	(7) Col	(8) Comments
Cockrill	Ida J.	m.	DR	24 Sept. 1881	2	3	
Cockrill	Ida J.	m.	PCo	21 Sept. 1881	3	5	
Cockrill	Ida J.	m.	SD	1 Oct. 1881	3	8	
Cockrill	Ida J.	m.	SD	17 Sept. 1881	3	8	
Cockrill	Prof. & Mrs.	b.	PCo	14 Dec. 1881	3	4	
Cockrill	Prof.	b.	SD	10 Dec. 1881	3	7	
Cockrill	W. C.	b.	PCo	11 June 1884	3	5	
Cockrill	Zachariah	d.	DR	29 Nov. 1884	3	2	
Cockrill	Zachariah	d.	PCo	3 Dec. 1884	3	5	
Codding	G. R.	p.	DR	6 Aug. 1884	3	2	
Codding	G. R.	d.	DR	7 July 1884	3	3	
Codding	G. R.	d.	PCo	2 July 1884	3	2&4	
Codding	G. R.	d.	PWA	5 July 1884	3	1&6	
Codoni	Ida Lucia	d.	PCo	28 Dec. 1881	3	6	
Codoni	Luela	d.	SD	31 Dec. 1881	3	6	
Codoni	Quinto	b.	SD	5 Mar. 1881	3	8	
Coe	Frank A.	o.	CR	21 Nov. 1885	1	4	
Coen	James	b.	PCo	14 Dec. 1881	3	4	
Coen	James	b.	SD	10 Dec. 1881	3	7	
Coffer	Lucy A.	m.	SD	14 Mar. 1885	5	5	
Coffman	N. B.	m.	DR	13 Nov. 1885	3	2	article on marriage
Coffman	N. B.	m.	DR	16 Nov. 1885	3	4	article on marriage
Coggeshall	F. R.	m.	DR	11 Jan. 1881	3	2	
Coggeshall	F. R.	m.	SD	15 Jun. 1881	3	8	
Coggshall	Fred	m.	PCo	5 Jan. 1881	3	4	
Cohen	Nettie	m.	RRF	21 Dec. 1882	3	4	
Cohn	Samuel	b.	PCo	29 Mar. 1882	3	5	
Cohn	Samuel	b.	RRF	23 Mar. 1882	2	5	
Cohn	Samuel	b.	SD	1 Apr. 1882	3	6	
Colburn	Ida C.	m.	DD	8 Dec. 1883	3	3	
Colburn	Orlin F.	m.	DD	8 Dec. 1883	3	3	
Colburn	Orlin F.	m.	PWA	8 Dec. 1883	3	6	
Colburn	Orville P.	m.	DD	8 Dec. 1883	3	3	
Colburn	Orville P.	m.	PWA	8 Dec. 1883	3	6	
Colby	Anna Jewell	d.	DR	8 Mar. 1882	2	3	
Colby	Anna Jewell	d.	PCo	1 Mar. 1882	2	4	
Colby	Anna Jewell	d.	SD	11 Mar. 1882	3	6	
Colby	Edwin	m.	PCo	22 Apr. 1885	3	6	
Colby	Edwin	m.	SD	25 Apr. 1885	2	5	
Colby	George J.	d.	DD	26 July 1883	3	2	
Colby	George J.	d.	PC	25 July 1883	3	6	
Colby	George J.	d.	PWA	28 July 1883	3	7	

(1) Surname	(2) Given Name	(3)	(4)	(5) Date	(6) Pg	(7) Col	(8) Comments
Colby	George J.	d.	SD	28 July 1883	2	5	
Coldwell	Alexander	m.	PCo	21 Feb. 1883	3	5	
Coldwell	Alexander	m.	PWA	24 Feb. 1883	3	7	
Cole	A. C.	b.	DR	5 Dec. 1885	3	4	
Cole	A. L.	b.	PCo	15 Apr. 1885	3	6	
Cole	Charles L.	m.	SD	17 Nov. 1883	3	5	
Cole	Dora	m.	SD	15 Aug. 1885	1	7	
Cole	Dora	m.	SD	22 Aug. 1885	6	2	
Cole	Eva	d.	DR	16 July 1884	3	3	
Cole	Eva	d.	PCo	23 July 1884	3	6	
Cole	F. N.	b.	SD	22 Oct. 1881	3	6	
Cole	H. L.	b.	PCo	12 Mar. 1884	3	6	
Cole	H. L.	b.	PWA	8 Mar. 1884	3	6	
Cole	H. L.	b.	SD	8 Mar. 1884	6	5	
Cole	Henry I.	m.	PC	16 May 1883	3	5	
Cole	Mary	m.	RRF	20 Jan. 1881	2	5	
Cole	Richard	b.	SD	12 Feb. 1881	3	8	
Coleman	Gary	m.	SD	9 May 1885	2	5	
Coleman	James	b.	SD	23 Nov. 1882	3	6	
Coleman	James	b.	SD	21 Feb. 1885	2	5	
Coleman	Thomas	d.	SD	15 Sept. 1883	3	1	
Coles	Mary	m.	CR	22 Jan. 1881	5	5	
Colgan	Ed P.	b.	SD	1 Aug. 1885	5	6	
Colgan	Edward	b.	DR	27 July 1885	3	4	
Colhurn	Eugene	m.	PCo	29 Nov. 1882	3	6	
Collier	D.	b.	SD	16 June 1883	2	6	
Collier	F.	m.	PC	25 July 1883	3	6	
Collier	Frank	b.	PCo	15 Oct. 1884	3	6	
Collier	Frank	b.	SD	11 Oct. 1884	2	5	
Collier	S. F.	m.	DD	23 July 1883	3	2	
Collier	S. F.	m.	SD	28 July 1883	2	5	
Collier	Susan	d.	PCo	29 Mar. 1882	3	5	
Collier	Susan	d.	SD	1 Apr. 1882	3	6	
Collins	J. J., Mrs.	d.	DR	21 July 1885	3	4	
Collins	Matthew	d.	PCo	21 Mar. 1883	3	5	
Collins	Matthew	d.	PWA	24 Mar. 1883	3	7	
Collins	Matthew	d.	SD	24 Mar. 1883	2	5	
Collins	Zilla	d.	DR	12 Aug. 1881	3	2	
Collins	Zilla	d.	PCo	10 Aug. 1881	3	5	
Colter	J. H.	b.	DD	27 Dec. 1883	3	3	
Colter	J. H.	b.	SD	5 Jan. 1884	1	8	
Colvin	Anthony J.	d.	SD	19 May 1883	3	5	

(1) Surname	(2) Given Name	(3)	(4)	(5) Date	(6) Pg	(7) Col	(8) Comments
Colvin	Arthur J.	d.	PC	9 May 1883	3	5	
Colvin	Arthur J.	m.	PWA	12 May 1883	3	8	
Colvin	Libbie	m.	SD	1 June 1881	3	7	
Combs	A. R.	b.	CR	29 Jan. 1881	5	5	
Combs	A. R.	b.	DR	20 Oct. 1885	3	4	
Combs	A. R.	b.	PCo	28 Oct. 1885	3	4	
Combs	A. R.	b.	RRF	27 Jan. 1881	2	4	
Combs	A. R.	b.	SD	5 Feb. 1881	3	8	
Combs	B. S.	d.	PCo	25 Feb. 1885	3	6	
Combs	Frank B.	d.	SD	28 Feb. 1885	5	6	
Compton	E. G.	b.	DD	13 Oct. 1883	3	3	
Compton	Green	b.	SD	25 June 1881	3	8	
Compton	Rebecca	m.	DD	22 Sept. 1883	3	2	
Comstock	Philena	p.	DR	26 Dec. 1884	2	2	
Condron	James	b.	RRF	10 Feb. 1881	2	5	
Conger	(infant son of)	d.	DR	24 Sept. 1885	3	4	
Conger	C. C.	b.	SD	23 May 1885	2	5	
Conger	C. C. (son of)	d.	SRR	1 Oct. 1885	3	3	
Conger	Cornelia C.	m.	DD	25 Sept. 1883	3	3	
Conger	Cornelia C.	m.	RRF	27 Sept. 1883	2	2	
Conger	Cornelia C.	m.	SD	29 Sept. 1883	2	6	
Conger	John	b.	RRF	19 May 1881	2	4	
Conger	Senator	b.	DR	17 June 1882	3	2	
Conger	Senator	b.	PCo	21 June 1882	3	5	
Conger	Senator	b.	RRF	15 June 1882	2	4	
Conger	Senator	b.	SD	17 June 1882	2	4	
Congleton	A. A.	d.	PCo	24 Sept. 1884	3	5	
Congleton	George	b.	PCo	14 Dec. 1881	3	4	
Congleton	George	b.	RRF	8 Dec. 1881	2	4	
Congleton	George	b.	SD	10 Dec. 1881	3	7	
Conklin	J.	d.	DR	10 May 1884	3	2	
Conklin	J.	d.	PCo	14 May 1884	3	4	
Conklin	J.	d.	PWA	17 May 1884	3	6	
Conley	Mr.	b.	SD	14 Mar. 1885	5	5	
Conley	Mr. & Mrs.	b.	PCo	25 Feb. 1885	3	6	
Connell	David	m.	DR	10 July 1884	3	3	
Connell	David	m.	SD	5 July 1884	2	3	
Conner	J.	b.	DR	9 Feb. 1882	2	3	
Conner	J.	b.	HE	9 Feb. 1882	2	3	
Conner	J.	b.	RRF	16 Feb. 1882	2	4	
Conner	Jerusha	d.	PC	18 July 1883	3	5	
Conner	Jerusha	d.	RRF	12 July 1883	2	4	

(1) Surname	(2) Given Name	(3)	(4)	(5) Date	(6) Pg	(7) Col	(8) Comments
Conner	M., Miss	m.	DR	5 Aug. 1884	3	4	
Conniff	Ellen	d.	DR	11 Jan. 1881	3	2	
Conniff	John	d.	CR	15 Jan. 1881	5	5	.
Connolly	B. J.	b.	PWA	22 Sept. 1883	3	6	
Connolly	Barnard J.	b.	PWA	21 Feb. 1885	3	5	
Connolly	Barnard J.	b.	SD	28 Feb. 1885	5	6	
Connolly	Bernard	b.	PCo	25 Oct. 1882	3	5	
Connolly	Bernard J.	m.	DR	13 Sept. 1881	2	3	
Connolly	Bernard J.	m.	PCo	7 Sept. 1881	2	4	
Connolly	Bernard J.	b.	PCo	18 Feb. 1885	3	6	
Connolly	J.	m.	SD	17 Sept. 1881	3	8	
Connor	J.	b.	PCo	15 Feb. 1882	3	4	
Connor	J.	b.	SD	11 Feb. 1882	3	6	
Connor	M., Miss	m.	PCo	13 Aug. 1884	3	4	
Connor	M., Mrs.	m.	PWA	9 Aug. 1884	2	4	
Conway	D.	o.	CR	15 Apr. 1882	5	2	
Conway	M.	b.	PC	27 June 1883	3	6	
Conway	M.	b.	PWA	30 June 1883	3	7	
Conway	M.	b.	SD	30 June 1883	3	5	
Cook	Adam	d.	DR	26 Nov. 1884	3	2	
Cook	Adam	d.	PCo	26 Nov. 1884	3	5	
Cook	Adam	d.	PWA	29 Nov. 1884	3	4	
Cook	Adam	d.	SD	23 Nov. 1884	2	6	
Cook	Catherine	d.	DR	23 Oct. 1885	3	4	
Cook	Catherine	d.	PCo	21 Oct. 1885	3	4	
Cook	David	d.	PCo	9 Apr. 1884	3	6	
Cook	David	d.	PWA	12 Apr. 1884	3	6	
Cook	David	d.	SWI	5 Apr. 1884	3	3&4	
Cook	Edward	m.	DD	4 Dec. 1883	3	3	
Cook	Edward	m.	SD	8 Dec. 1883	3	1	
Cook	Frank W.	m.	DR	23 Feb. 1882	2	3	
Cook	G. A.	d.	PWA	25 Apr. 1885	3	6	
Cook	G. A.	d.	SD	25 Apr. 1885	2	5	
Cook	G. L.	b.	DD	12 Nov. 1883	3	3	
Cook	George	m.	CR	28 May 1881	5	5	
Cook	George	m.	DR	21 May 1881	2	3	
Cook	George	m.	RRF	19 May 1881	2	4	
Cook	George	m.	SD	4 June 1881	3	8	
Cook	George M.	m.	SD	28 May 1881	3	8	
Cook	H. E.	b.	CR	29 Jan. 1881	5	5	
Cook	H. E.	b.	DR	26 Jan. 1881	3	2	
Cook	H. E.	b.	SD	5 Feb. 1881	3	8	

(1) Surname	(2) Given Name	(3)	(4)	(5) Date	(6) Pg	(7) Col	(8) Comments
Cook	Israel	d.	SD	18 Aug. 1883	3	4	
Cook	J.	b.	DR	17 Aug. 1882	3	2	
Cook	J.	b.	SD	2 Sept. 1882	3	6	
Cook	John G.	m.	DR	24 Oct. 1884	3	3	
Cook	John G.	m.	PWA	25 Oct. 1884	3	4	
Cook	John G.	m.	SD	8 Nov. 1884	2	5	
Cook	John	m.	PCo	22 Oct. 1884	3	6	
Cook	John	b.	RRF	10 Aug. 1882	2	4	
Cook	John S.	d.	DR	30 Dec. 1881	2	3	
Cook	John S.	d.	HE	29 Dec. 1881	2	3	
Cook	John S.	d.	SD	31 Dec. 1881	3	6	
Cook	John Silas	d.	RRF	29 Dec. 1881	2	3	
Cook	Maggie	d.	DD	15 Sept. 1883	3	3	
Cook	Marcus Raphael	d.	DD	21 Aug. 1883	3	3	
Cook	Marcus Raphael	d.	RRF	16 Aug. 1883	2	4	
Cook	Marcus Raphael	d.	SD	25 Aug. 1883	2	5	
Cook	Margaret	d.	DD	14 Sept. 1883	3	2	
Cook	Martha	d.	DR	24 June 1884	3	3	
Cook	Martha	d.	PCo	25 June 1884	3	4	
Cook	Mary J.	m.	DR	24 Oct. 1884	3	3	
Cook	Mary J.	m.	PCo	22 Oct. 1884	3	6	
Cook	Mary J.	m.	PWA	25 Oct. 1884	3	4	
Cook	Mary J.	m.	SD	8 Nov. 1884	2	5	
Cook	Philip	d.	CR	2 Dec. 1882	3	2	
Cook	Philip	d.	PCo	6 Dec. 1882	3	6	
Cook	Philip	d.	SD	16 Dec. 1882	3	6	
Cook	W. W.	m.	CR	10 Nov. 1883	3	1	
Cook	William W.	m.	DD	10 Nov. 1883	3	3	
Cook	William W.	m.	RRF	8 Nov. 1883	2	3	
Cook	William W.	m.	SD	17 Nov. 1883	3	5	
Cooke	Carrie	m.	CR	2 June 1883	3	3	
Cooley	John	b.	DR	31 Jan. 1882	2	3	
Cooley	John	b.	RRF	2 Feb. 1882	3	7	
Cooley	John	b.	SD	4 Feb. 1882	3	6	
Cooley	M. V. (dau. of)	d.	DD	16 July 1883	3	2	
Cooley	M. V. (dau. of)	d.	PC	18 July 1883	3	5	
Cooley	M. V.	m.	CR	3 Sept. 1881	5	2	
Cooley	M. V.	b.	DD	16 July 1883	3	2	
Cooley	M. V.	b.	PC	18 July 1883	3	5	
Cooley	Van	b.	DR	10 July 1884	3	3	
Coon	N. L.	m.	PWA	1 Dec. 1883	3	6	
Coon	N. L.	m.	SD	8 Dec. 1883	3	1	

(1) Surname	(2) Given Name	(3)	(4)	(5) Date	(6) Pg	(7) Col	(8) Comments
Coon	Robert (son of)	d.	CR	12 Feb. 1881	5	5	
Coon	Robert (son of)	d.	DR	7 Feb. 1881	3	2	
Coon	Robert (son of)	d.	SD	12 Feb. 1881	3	8	
Coon	Robert	b.	CR	12 Feb. 1881	5	5	
Coon	Robert	b.	DR	7 Feb. 1881	3	2	
Coon	Robert	d.	RRF	10 Feb. 1881	2	5	
Coon	Robert	b.	RRF	10 Feb. 1881	2	5	
Coon	Robert	b.	SD	12 Feb. 1881	3	8	
Cooney	Ellen	m.	DD	8 Sept. 1883	3	3	
Cooney	Ellen	m.	SD	15 Sept. 1883	2	4	
Cooney	James	b.	PWA	17 Nov. 1883	3	8	
Cooney	James	b.	SD	17 Nov. 1883	3	5	
Cooper	Emma	m.	PCo	27 May 1885	3	6	
Cooper	H. H.	o.	SD	24 Dec. 1881	3	4	
Cooper	J. O.	o.	DR	1 Sept. 1882	3	2	
Cooper	James	b.	PCo	26 Mar. 1884	3	6	
Cooper	James	b.	PWA	22 Mar. 1884	3	6	
Cooper	Jimmy	b.	SD	22 Mar. 1884	2	4	
Cooper	W. H.	m.	DR	19 Nov. 1881	2	3	
Cooper	W. H.	b.	PCo	21 Feb. 1883	3	5	
Cooper	W. H.	b.	PWA	24 Feb. 1883	3	7	
Cooper	William M.	d.	DR	1 Apr. 1884	3	3	
Cooper	William M.	d.	PCo	9 Apr. 1884	3	6	
Cooper	William M.	d.	SD	5 Apr. 1884	3	4	
Copeland	Archibald	d.	CR	18 Apr. 1885	5	1	Cloverdale Cem.
Copeland	Archibald	d.	PCo	22 Apr. 1885	3	6	
Copeland	Archibald	d.	SD	25 Apr. 1885	2	5	
Coppel	Annie	m.	RRF	26 May 1881	2	5	
Copple	Annie	m.	DR	17 May 1881	2	2	
Copple	Annie	m.	SD	21 May 1881	3	8	
Copple	Maggie	m.	RRF	1 Dec. 1881	2	3	
Copple	Maggie	m.	SD	3 Dec. 1881	3	2	
Copsey	Charles C.	d.	SD	2 Apr. 1881	3	8	
Copsey	H. B.	m.	SD	17 Oct. 1885	4	5	
Corbaley	John A.	b.	DR	17 Feb. 1882	2	3	
Corbaley	John A.	b.	RRF	16 Feb. 1882	2	4	
Corbaley	John A.	d.	RRF	28 Dec. 1882	2	2	
Corbaley	John A.	b.	SD	18 Feb. 1882	3	6	
Corbaley	Platt M.	b.	DR	2 Dec. 1882	3	2	
Corbaley	Platt M.	m.	HE	29 Dec. 1881	2	3	
Corbaley	Platt M.	b.	RRF	30 Nov. 1882	2	3	
Corbaley	Platte M.	m.	DR	23 Dec. 1881	2	2	

(1) Surname	(2) Given Name	(3)	(4)	(5) Date	(6) Pg	(7) Col	(8) Comments
Corbaley	Platte M.	m.	PCo	28 Dec. 1881	3	6	
Corbaley	Platte M.	m.	RRF	22 Dec. 1881	2	3	
Corbaley	Platte M.	m.	SD	31 Dec. 1881	3	6	
Corbaley	Richard	o.	SD	26 Dec. 1885	3	2	
Corbaley	W. G.	b.	HE	4 Oct. 1883	2	3	
Corbaley	William G.	b.	RRF	4 Oct. 1883	2	3	
Cord	Mahala	m.	SD	10 Sept. 1881	3	8	
Corey	Matilda	d.	DR	7 Apr. 1881	2	3	
Corey	Matilda	d.	SD	16 Apr. 1881	3	8	
Corey	Nora E.	m.	PCo	3 Dec. 1884	3	5	
Corey	Nora E.	m.	PWA	29 Nov. 1884	3	4	
Corey	Nora E.	m.	SD	13 Dec. 1884	2	5	
Corini	John	m.	PWA	24 May 1884	3	5	
Corless	Albert	m.	PCo	4 Mar. 1885	3	6	
Corless	Albert	m.	PWA	28 Feb. 1885	3	5	
Corliss	Margaret	d.	PCo	27 Feb. 1884	3	6	
Corliss	Margaret	d.	PWA	1 Mar. 1884	3	6	
Cornelius	George	b.	PCo	14 Dec. 1881	3	4	
Cornelius	George	b.	SD	17 Dec. 1881	3	7	
Cornelius	George H. H.	b.	DD	12 Oct. 1883	3	3	
Cornelius	George H.	b.	PWA	13 Oct. 1883	3	8	
Cornelius	George H. H.	b.	SD	20 Oct. 1883	3	4	
Cornelius	George H. H.	b.	SWI	6 Oct. 1883	3	4	
Cornett	George	b.	DR	5 Nov. 1881	2	3	
Cornett	George	b.	PCo	9 Nov. 1881	3	5	
Cornett	George	b.	RRF	10 Nov. 1881	2	4	
Cornett	George	b.	SD	12 Nov. 1881	3	7	
Cornue	B. F.	b.	DD	17 Oct. 1883	3	3	
Cornue	B. F.	b.	SD	20 Oct. 1883	3	4	
Cornwell	C. C.	d.	PCo	15 Oct. 1884	3	6	
Cornwell	C. C.	d.	PWA	18 Oct. 1884	3	4	
Cornwell	Henry	d.	PCo	16 July 1884	3	6	
Cornwell	Henry	d.	PWA	19 July 1884	3	3&4	
Cortez	John	d.	SD	14 June 1884	2	4	
Costello	Louis	d.	CR	25 July 1885	3	3	
Costello	Mr.	d.	CR	7 Nov. 1885	3	3	
Costello	William	d.	PCo	11 Nov. 1885	3	2	
Cottle	D. W.	b.	DR	18 July 1884	3	3	
Cottle	D. W.	b.	PCo	16 July 1884	3	6	
Cottrill	Fidelia	m.	SD	8 Dec. 1883	3	1	
Cottrill	Fidella	m.	DD	4 Dec. 1883	3	3	
Coul	John B.	p.	DR	29 Nov. 1884	3	2	

(1) Surname	(2) Given Name	(3)	(4)	(5) Date	(6) Pg	(7) Col	(8) Comments
Coul	Peter	b.	RRF	4 Aug. 1881	2	5	
Coul	Peter	m.	RRF	6 Jan. 1881	2	5	
Coulter	J. H.	b.	PCo	2 Jan. 1884	3	6	
Coulter	J. H.	b.	RRF	27 Dec. 1883	2	2	
Coulter	Olivia J.	m.	PCo	28 Dec. 1881	3	6	
Coulter	Olivia J.	m.	SD	24 Dec. 1881	2	3	
Couniff	Ellen	d.	PCo	5 Jan. 1881	3	4	
Couniff	Ellen	d.	SD	8 Jan. 1881	3	8	
Coventry	Adele	m.	RRF	6 Jan. 1881	2	5	
Coventry	Adele	m.	SD	8 Jan. 1881	3	8	
Coventry	Adelia	m.	CR	15 Jan. 1881	5	5	
Coventry	Adelia	m.	DR	11 Jan. 1881	3	2	
Covey	Mary M.	m.	DD	21 Sept. 1883	3	3	
Covey	Mary M.	m.	SD	29 Sept. 1883	2	6	
Covey	Mary	m.	RRF	27 Sept. 1883	2	2	
Cowan	Safa T.	m.	DR	18 Oct. 1881	3	1&2	
Cowan	Safa T.	m.	SD	22 Oct. 1881	3	6	
Cowan	Safatate	m.	PCo	26 Oct. 1881	3	4	
Cowden	James	d.	DR	21 Aug. 1882	3	2	
Cowen	Sam (son of)	d.	PWA	28 Mar. 1885	3	5	
Cowie	Mr.	d.	SD	17 Oct. 1885	5	1	murdered 1846
Cowie	T.	d.	SD	3 Oct. 1885	5	3	murdered 1846
Cowles	J. A.	b.	SD	19 Mar. 1881	3	8	
Cowles	J. Q.	b.	PCo	7 Mar. 1883	3	5	
Cowles	J. Q.	b.	PWA	10 Mar. 1883	3	6	
Cowles	Maggie	m.	PCo	19 Jan. 1881	3	4	
Cowles	Maggie	m.	SD	29 Jan. 1881	3	8	
Cox	A. B.	d.	DR	18 Jan. 1884	3	3	
Cox	A. B.	d.	PCo	23 Jan. 1884	3	5	
Cox	A. B.	d.	SD	19 Jan. 1884	3	6	
Cox	Arabell Florence	d.	CR	1 Aug. 1885	3	3	
Cox	George	b.	PCo	21 June 1882	3	5	
Cox	George	b.	RRF	29 June 1882	2	5	
Cox	George	b.	SD	24 June 1882	3	5	
Cox	George W.	m.	CR	25 Aug. 1883	3	2	
Cox	James	m.	DR	29 Nov. 1884	3	2	
Cox	James M.	m.	PCo	3 Dec. 1884	3	5	
Cox	Jim	d.	SD	1 Nov. 1884	1	5	
Cox	Mary Ann	d.	DD	15 Sept. 1883	3	3	
Cox	Mary Ann	m.	DD	27 Sept. 1883	3	3	
Cox	Mattie A.	m.	RRF	27 July 1882	2	4	
Cox	Mattie	m.	CR	22 July 1882	5	3	

(1) Surname	(2) Given Name	(3)	(4)	(5) Date	(6) Pg	(7) Col	(8) Comments
Cox	Mattie	m.	DR	25 July 1882	2	3	
Cox	Mattie	m.	PCo	2 Aug. 1882	3	6	
Cox	Mattie	m.	SD	5 Aug. 1882	3	5	
Cox	Nate	b.	PCo	8 July 1885	3	6	
Cox	Nate	b.	PCo	24 June 1885	3	6	
Cox	Nate	b.	SD	27 June 1885	5	4	
Coy	Will B.	m.	PCo	18 Feb. 1885	3	6	
Coy	Will B.	m.	PWA	21 Feb. 1885	3	5	
Coy	Will B.	m.	SD	21 Feb. 1885	2	5	
Cozad	John	b.	DR	16 Dec. 1885	3	4	
Cozad	John	b.	PCo	23 Dec. 1885	3	4	
Cozad	Samuel O.	d.	SD	21 Feb. 1885	2	5	
Cozens	D.	m.	RRF	7 Sept. 1882	2	4	
Cozzens	D.	b.	PC	6 June 1883	3	4	
Cozzens	D.	m.	PCo	20 Sept. 1882	3	6	
Cozzens	D.	b.	RRF	31 May 1883	2	4	
Crabb	Mella A.	m.	DR	22 Aug. 1881	2	3	
Craig	Archibald	d.	PCo	18 Jan. 1882	3	5	
Craig	Archie	d.	DR	17 Jan. 1882	2	3	
Craig	Archie	d.	SD	21 Jan. 1882	3	6	
Craig	D. N.	b.	PCo	31 Jan. 1883	3	5	
Craig	D. N.	b.	PWA	28 Mar. 1885	3	5	
Craig	O. W.	o.	SIT	22 Aug. 1885	2	2	
Craig	Peter	d.	RRF	4 Aug. 1881	2	2	
Cramer	(female)	b.	DR	16 May 1884	3	2	
Cramer	A. M.	m.	CR	29 Jan. 1881	5	5	
Cramer	A. M.	m.	RRF	27 Jan. 1881	2	4	
Cramer	A. M.	m.	SD	5 Feb. 1881	3	8	
Cramer	John F.	m.	PCo	18 Nov. 1885	3	4	
Cramer	Lorinda	m.	DD	18 Aug. 1883	3	3	
Cramer	Lorinda	m.	PC	15 Aug. 1883	3	6	
Cramer	Lorinda	m.	PWA	11 Aug. 1883	3	8	
Cramer	Lorinda	m.	SD	25 Aug. 1883	2	5	
Cramer	M. A.	b.	PCo	14 May 1884	3	4	
Cramer	M. A.	b.	PWA	17 May 1884	3	6	
Cramer	M. A.	b.	SD	17 May 1884	3	5	
Cramer	Maria	d.	DD	3 Nov. 1883	3	3	
Cramer	Maria	d.	PWA	3 Nov. 1883	3	3&8	
Cramer	Sadie	d.	DR	22 Sept. 1885	3	4	
Crandall	Frank	m.	CR	26 Mar. 1881	5	5	
Crandall	Frank	m.	CR	26 Mar. 1881	5	5	
Crandall	Frank L.	m.	SD	2 Apr. 1881	3	8	

(1) Surname	(2) Given Name	(3)	(4)	(5) Date	(6) Pg	(7) Col	(8) Comments
Crandall	Frank P.	m.	DR	26 Mar. 1881	3	2	
Crandall	Frank P.	m.	RRF	24 Mar. 1881	2	4	
Crandall	Frank T.	m.	SD	26 Mar. 1881	3	8	
Crane	Adeline P.	d.	PCo	2 Jan. 1884	3	6	
Crane	Adeline P.	d.	PWA	5 Jan. 1884	3	1&7	Cypress Hill
Crane	Adeline P.	d.	SD	5 Jan. 1884	1	4	
Crane	C. B.	b.	DR	5 May 1882	2	2	
Crane	C. B.	b.	RRF	4 May 1882	2	4	
Crane	E. T.	b.	PCo	23 July 1884	3	6	
Crane	E. T.	b.	SD	19 July 1884	2	5	
Crane	Ella	m.	PCo	14 Mar. 1883	3	5	
Crane	Ella	m.	SD	10 Mar. 1883	3	3	
Crane	Ellis T.	b.	DR	10 July 1884	3	3	
Crane	George L.	d.	CR	23 Aug. 1884	3	1	
Crane	George L.	d.	DR	16 Aug. 1884	3	2	
Crane	George L.	d.	PCo	20 Aug. 1884	3	4	
Crane	Olive	m.	DR	30 July 1884	3	3	
Crane	Olive	m.	PCo	6 Aug. 1884	2	4	
Crane	Olive	m.	SD	2 Aug. 1884	3	1	
Crane	T. L.	m.	DR	26 Dec. 1882	3	1	
Crane	Tarleton L.	m.	PCo	3 Jan. 1883	3	4	
Crane	Tarleton L.	m.	SD	30 Dec. 1882	3	6	
Crane	W.	b.	RRF	20 Jan. 1881	2	5	
Crantz	F.	m.	CR	21 Apr. 1883	3	1	
Crantz	F.	m.	PC	25 Apr. 1883	3	5	
Cranz	F.	d.	CR	27 Dec. 1884	3	2&3	Cloverdale Cem.
Cranz	F.	d.	PCo	7 Jan. 1885	3	6	
Cranz	F.	d.	SD	10 Jan. 1885	2	6	
Crapser	Isabella S.	m.	DR	28 Jan. 1882	2	3	
Crapser	Isabella S.	m.	PCo	25 Jan. 1882	3	6	
Crawford	Adam	o.	SD	9 Feb. 1884	1	3	
Crawford	Alex G.	m.	SD	25 July 1885	3	5	
Crawford	Alice Amelia	d.	PC	8 Aug. 1883	3	6	
Crawford	Alice Amelia	d.	RRF	2 Aug. 1883	2	4	Oak Mound Cemetery
Crawford	Alice F.	m.	DR	1 Feb. 1884	3	3	
Crawford	Alice F.	m.	PCo	6 Feb. 1884	3	6	
Crawford	Alice F.	m.	PWA	9 Feb. 1884	3	6	
Crawford	Alice F.	m.	SD	9 Feb. 1884	1	3	
Crawford	Alice M.	d.	PC	18 July 1883	3	5	
Crawford	Alice M.	d.	RRF	12 July 1883	2	4	Oak Mound Cemetery
Crawford	Edith	d.	RRF	26 July 1883	2	4	
Crawford	J. A.	d.	CR	19 Dec. 1885	3	4	

(1) Surname	(2) Given Name	(3)	(4)	(5) Date	(6) Pg	(7) Col	(8) Comments
Crawford	J. A.	b.	PCo	16 Jan. 1884	3	6	
Crawford	J. A.	b.	SD	19 Jan. 1884	3	6	
Crawford	James A.	m.	SD	21 Apr. 1883	2	6	
Crawford	Lena	d.	DD	23 July 1883	3	2	
Crawford	Lena	d.	SD	28 July 1883	2	5	
Crawford	Mary	m.	CR	25 Aug. 1883	3	2	
Crawford	Mr.	m.	CR	14 Apr. 1883	3	1&2	
Crawford	Susan A.	m.	CR	27 Dec. 1884	3	1	
Crawford	Thomas	d.	CR	27 Aug. 1881	5	2	
Creagh	B., Mrs.	d.	PCo	21 May 1884	3	4	
Creagh	B., Mrs.	d.	SD	24 May 1884	2	3	
Creigh	John	d.	DR	19 May 1884	3	2	
Crescenzo	Louis	m.	RRF	15 Nov. 1883	2	3	
Crigler	A. P.	b.	PCo	7 June 1882	3	5	
Crigler	A. P.	b.	PCo	18 June 1884	3	4	
Crigler	A. P.	b.	SD	10 June 1882	2	3	
Crigler	A. P.	b.	SD	28 June 1884	3	4	
Crigler	T.	b.	DR	27 Jan. 1882	2	3	
Crigler	T.	b.	SD	28 Jan. 1882	3	6	
Crigler	Thomas	b.	PCo	25 Feb. 1885	3	6	
Crigler	Thomas	b.	SD	28 Feb. 1885	5	6	
Crigler	William E. (son of)	d.	DR	8 July 1881	3	1	
Crill	Ecce	m.	DR	8 Aug. 1881	3	2	
Crill	Eden	m.	RRF	4 Aug. 1881	2	5	
Crilly	Nicholas	d.	PCo	1 June 1881	3	4	
Crilly	Nicholas	m.	SD	4 June 1881	3	8	
Crippen	Mary E.	m.	DR	5 June 1884	3	3	
Cripper	Mary E.	m.	PCo	11 June 1884	3	5	
Crisp	Sarah J	m.	SD	21 Mar. 1885	2	4&5	
Crittenden	Parker L.	b.	SD	1 Oct. 1881	3	8	
Crocket	I. P.	b.	SD	8 Jan. 1881	3	8	
Crockett	Margaret	m.	SD	5 Mar. 1881	3	8	
Crockett	Nettie	m.	PCo	22 Mar. 1882	3	5	
Cromer	John F.	m.	DR	24 Nov. 1885	3	4	
Crommett	Sarah A.	m.	PCo	18 Oct. 1882	3	6	
Crommett	Sarah A.	m.	SD	14 Oct. 1882	3	6	
Cromwell	F. H.	b.	DR	24 Nov. 1885	3	4	
Cromwell	F. H.	b.	PCo	18 Nov. 1885	3	4	
Cromwell	Frank	m.	PCo	2 Jan. 1884	3	6	
Cromwell	Frank	m.	PWA	5 Jan. 1884	3	7	
Cropper	Harvey	d.	CR	8 Jan. 1881	5	5	
Cropper	Harvey N.	d.	DR	5 Jan. 1881	3	2	

(1) Surname	(2) Given Name	(3)	(4)	(5) Date	(6) Pg	(7) Col	(8) Comments
Cropper	Harvey N.	d.	SD	8 Jan. 1881	3	8	
Cross	(female)	b.	DR	9 June 1884	3	3	
Cross	(female)	b.	DR	13 June 1884	3	3	
Cross	Emma	m.	PCo	28 Dec. 1881	3	6	
Cross	Emma	m.	SD	24 Dec. 1881	2	3	
Cross	John C.	b.	PCo	11 June 1884	3	5	
Cross	John C.	b.	PWA	7 June 1884	3	6	
Cross	John C.	b.	SD	28 June 1884	3	4	
Cross	Mary Eliza	d.	PCo	7 Dec. 1881	3	5	
Cross	William E.	d.	PCo	22 Mar. 1882	3	5	
Cross	William E.	d.	SD	18 Mar. 1882	3	5	
Crosson	Mary	m.	PCo	15 Oct. 1884	3	6	
Crowe	Annie L.	m.	PWA	27 Oct. 1883	3	8	
Crowell	Albert	b.	DR	17 Dec. 1881	2	2	
Crowell	Albert	b.	PCo	21 Dec. 1881	3	5	
Crowell	Albert	b.	PCo	28 Dec. 1881	3	6	
Crowell	Albert	b.	RRF	15 Dec. 1881	2	4	
Crowell	Albert	b.	SD	24 Dec. 1881	2	3	
Crowell	Albert	b.	SD	7 Jan. 1882	3	8	
Crross	Emma	m.	DR	19 Dec. 1881	2	2	
Crutcher	J. W.	b.	SD	5 Mar. 1881	3	8	
Crystal	Vina	m.	DR	10 Dec. 1884	3	2	
Crystal	Vina	m.	PCo	17 Dec. 1884	2	4	
Crystal	Vina	m.	SD	13 Dec. 1884	2	5	
Cullum	Alice	m.	SD	24 May 1884	2	3	
Cullum	Carrie Watson	m.	DD	31 Aug. 1883	3	3	
Cullum	Carrie Watson	m.	RRF	30 Aug. 1883	2	4	
Cummings	Ellis	b.	DD	25 Oct. 1883	3	2	
Cummings	Ellis	b.	SD	27 Oct. 1883	3	4	
Cummings	Frank	m.	PCo	2 Aug. 1882	3	6	
Cummings	Frank	m.	PCo	16 Aug. 1882	3	6	
Cummings	Frank	b.	PCo	15 Oct. 1884	3	6	
Cummings	Frank	m.	RRF	27 July 1882	2	4	
Cummings	Frank	m.	SD	5 Aug. 1882	3	5	
Cummings	George	b.	SD	1 Apr. 1882	3	6	
Cummings	George W.	b.	RRF	23 Mar. 1882	2	5	
Cummings	Isabel	m.	DR	16 Nov. 1882	2	3	
Cummings	Isabel	m.	PCo	22 Nov. 1882	3	5	

(1) Surname	(2) Given Name	(3)	(4)	(5) Date	(6) Pg	(7) Col	(8) Comments
Cummings	Isabel	m.	RRF	16 Nov. 1882	2	4	
Cummings	Mamie	m.	HE	11 Oct. 1883	2	2	
Cummings	Mamie	m.	RRF	4 Oct. 1883	2	3	
Cummins	D. B.	b.	PC	15 Aug. 1883	3	6	
Cummins	D. B.	b.	RRF	6 Jan. 1881	2	5	
Cummins	D. B.	b.	RRF	9 Aug. 1883	2	4	
Cummins	D. B.	b.	SD	1 June 1881	3	7	
Cummins	Ellis	b.	PCo	11 Oct. 1882	3	6	
Cummins	Ellis	b.	SD	7 Oct. 1882	3	6	
Cummins	G. W.	m.	SD	19 Feb. 1881	3	8	
Cunningham	Arthur	d.	DR	28 July 1885	3	4	
Cunningham	Arthur C.	m.	DD	10 Oct. 1883	3	3	
Cunningham	Arthur S.	m.	SD	13 Oct. 1883	3	4	
Cunningham	J. J.	d.	PWA	18 Oct. 1884	3	1	Healdsburg Cemetery
Cunningham	Minnie J.	m.	DR	24 Sept. 1885	3	4	
Cunningham	Minnie J.	m.	SRR	1 Oct. 1885	3	3	
Cunningham	W. J.	b.	DR	21 July 1884	2	2	
Cunningham	W. J.	b.	PCo	23 July 1884	3	6	
Cunningham	W. J.	b.	PWA	26 July 1884	2	3	
Curran	Frank	m.	DR	24 Oct. 1882	3	2	
Curran	Frank	m.	PCo	18 Oct. 1882	3	6	
Curran	Frank	b.	PWA	8 Dec. 1883	3	6	
Curran	Frank	b.	SD	8 Dec. 1883	3	1	
Currier	Mr. & Mrs.	b.	DR	10 July 1885	3	4	
Currier	W. H.	b.	PCo	8 July 1885	3	6	
Currier	William H.	m.	PCo	14 May 1884	3	4	
Currier	William H.	m.	RRF	8 May 1884	5	6	also p. 8 col. 1
Currier	William H.	m.	SD	17 May 1884	3	5	
Curry	Belle	m.	DR	9 Nov. 1882	3	1 & 2	
Curry	Belle	m.	PCo	15 Nov. 1882	3	5	
Curry	Belle	m.	SD	11 Nov. 1882	3	7	
Curry	J. H.	d.	CR	2 July 1881	5	5	
Curry	J. H.	d.	DR	25 June 1881	2	3	
Curtis	Francis	o.	SIT	5 Sept. 1885	2	3	
Curtis	James	d.	PCo	28 June 1882	3	5	
Curtis	James	d.	SD	8 July 1882	2	5	
Curtis	Joseph	m.	CR	9 June 1883	3	1	
Curtis	Joseph	m.	PC	13 June 1883	3	6	

(1) Surname	(2) Given Name	(3)	(4)	(5) Date	(6) Pg	(7) Col	(8) Comments
Curtis	Kate L. D.	m.	RRF	31 Mar. 1881	2	3	
Curtis	Katie L. D.	m.	SD	2 Apr. 1881	3	8	
Curtis	Maria L.	o.	SIT	5 Sept. 1885	2	3	
Curtis	Mary J.	m.	SD	18 Apr. 1885	2	5	
Curtis	Mollie	m.	CR	11 Apr. 1885	3	2	
Cyco	Lorenze	d.	CR	3 Sept. 1881	5	1	Cloverdale Cemetery

D

(1) Surname	(2) Given Name	(3)	(4)	(5) Date	(6) Pg	(7) Col	(8) Comments
Dabner	A.	b.	PCo	12 Mar. 1884	3	6	
Dabner	A.	b.	PWA	8 Mar. 1884	3	6	
Dabner	A.	b.	SD	15 Mar. 1884	2	5	
Dabner	Frank	b.	DR	23 Oct. 1885	3	4	
Dabner	Frank	b.	PCo	21 Oct. 1885	3	4	
Dabner	Frank	m.	SD	25 Oct. 1884	2	5	
Dabner	John	d.	DR	24 Feb. 1882	2	3	
Dabner	John	d.	PCo	22 Feb. 1882	3	5	
Dabner	John	d.	SD	4 Mar. 1882	3	6	
Dabner	Rosa	d.	PCo	22 Feb. 1882	3	5	
Dabner	Rose	d.	SD	4 Mar. 1882	3	6	
Dailey	Useal	m.	SD	13 Aug. 1881	3	8	
Daily	J. B.	m.	CR	15 Jan. 1881	5	5	
Daily	J. B.	m.	CR	15 Jan. 1881	5	5	
Daily	James B.	m.	DR	11 Jan. 1881	3	2	
Daivdson	Adam	b.	PCo	9 Mar. 1881	3	4	
Dalton	Benton	m.	PC	4 July 1883	3	5	
Dalton	F. H. B.	m.	SD	7 July 1883	1	5	
Dalton	Thomas Benton	m.	PWA	30 June 1883	3	2&7	
Dalton	W. H.	d.	RRF	9 June 1881	2	4	
Dalton	W. W.	d.	CR	4 June 1881	5	4	
Dalton	William H.	d.	DR	4 June 1881	2	2	
Dalton	William H.	d.	PCo	1 June 1881	3	4	
Dalton	William H.	m.	SD	4 June 1881	3	8	
Daly	Thomas	m.	CR	22 Mar. 1884	3	1	
Daly	Thomas	m.	SD	29 Mar. 1884	2	5	
Dampier	Emily F. A.	m.	PCo	6 Aug. 1884	2	4	
Dana	A. W.	b.	DD	26 Dec. 1883	3	3	
Dana	A. W.	b.	DR	24 Jan. 1882	3	2	
Dana	A. W.	b.	PCo	2 Jan. 1884	3	6	
Dana	A. W.	b.	SD	28 Jan. 1882	3	6	
Dana	A. W.	b.	SD	29 Dec. 1883	3	6	
Daniel	James P.	b.	DR	16 Nov. 1885	3	4	
Daniel	James P.	b.	PCo	11 Nov. 1885	3	4	
Daniels	M. J., Mrs.	m.	DR	26 Aug. 1884	3	4	
Daniels	M. J., Mrs.	m.	PCo	3 Sept. 1884	2	5	
Daniels	Stephen	d.	DR	5 Nov. 1884	2	2	
Dankert	J. A.	d.	DR	23 Oct. 1885	3	4	

(1) Surname	(2) Given Name	(3)	(4)	(5) Date	(6) Pg	(7) Col	(8) Comments
Dankert	J. A.	d.	PCo	21 Oct. 1885	3	4	
Darden	Rosa	m.	PCo	9 Jan. 1884	3	6	
Darden	Rosa	m.	SD	5 Jan. 1884	1	4	
Darden	W. H.	m.	DR	25 Apr. 1884	3	2	
Darden	W. H.	m.	PCo	23 Apr. 1884	2	6	
Darden	W. H.	m.	PWA	19 Mar. 1884	3	6	
Darden	W. H.	m.	RRF	1 May 1884	5	6	
Darden	W. H.	m.	SD	26 Apr. 1883	3	5	
Darmody	Patrick	d.	PCo	7 Feb. 1883	3	6	also col. 3
Darting	Martin	d.	CR	26 Nov. 1881	1	3	
Dasheills	Benjamin	b.	DD	6 Oct. 1883	3	3	
Dasheills	Benjamin	b.	SD	13 Oct. 1883	3	4	
Daugherty	Sarah	d.	DD	1 Sept. 1883	3	2	
Davidson	(male)	b.	DR	25 Apr. 1884	3	2	
Davidson	A. T.	b.	PCo	23 Apr. 1884	2	6	
Davidson	A. T.	b.	RRF	1 May 1884	5	6	
Davidson	Alex T.	b.	SD	19 Apr. 1884	3	4	
Davidson	Etta	m.	SD	16 June 1883	2	6	
Davidson	Jacob E.	d.	DR	25 Nov. 1884	3	2	
Davidson	Jacob E.	d.	PCo	3 Dec. 1884	3	5	
Davidson	Jacob E.	d.	SD	23 Nov. 1884	2	6	also p. 3 col .1
Davidson	Jane	m.	SD	10 Jan. 1885	2	6	
Davidson	Maggie	m.	CR	7 Nov. 1885	3	5	
Davidson	Maggie	m.	DR	9 Nov. 1885	2	2	
Davidson	Mary B.	d.	PC	6 June 1883	3	4	
Davidson	Mary B.	d.	SD	2 June 1883	2	7	
Davies	Nettie M.	d.	DR	8 Dec. 1881	3	2	
Davies	Nettie	d.	CR	10 Dec. 1881	1	3	
Davies	Nettie	d.	CR	17 Dec. 1881	1	3	
Davies	Nettie	d.	SD	17 Dec. 1881	3	7	
Davies	S. W.	d.	PCo	10 Sept. 1884	3	6	
Davies	S. W.	d.	SD	13 Sept. 1884	1	5	also p. 3 col. 4
Davis	A.	d.	DR	27 Aug. 1884	3	2	article "killed"
Davis	A.	d.	SD	30 Aug. 1884	3	1	San Francisco
Davis	Amanda	d.	PCo	14 Mar. 1883	3	5	
Davis	Amanda	d.	RRF	8 Mar. 1883	2	3	
Davis	C. A.	m.	CR	29 Apr. 1882	1	2	
Davis	C. A.	m.	PCo	26 Apr. 1882	3	4	
Davis	C. A.	m.	SD	22 Apr. 1882	3	3	
Davis	Charles H.	m.	DR	22 Apr. 1882	3	1	
Davis	D. O., Jr.	b.	DR	30 Apr. 1881	2	2	
Davis	D. O., Jr.	b.	RRF	13 July 1882	2	3	

(1) Surname	(2) Given Name	(3)	(4)	(5) Date	(6) Pg	(7) Col	(8) Comments
Davis	D. O., Jr.	d.	RRF	13 July 1882	2	4	
Davis	D. O., Jr.	b.	RRF	31 May 1883	2	4	
Davis	D. O., Jr.	b.	SD	22 July 1882	3	5	
Davis	D. O.	b.	PC	6 June 1883	3	4	
Davis	D. O.	b.	PCo	19 July 1882	3	6	
Davis	D. O.	b.	PCo	29 July 1885	3	4	
Davis	D. O.	b.	SD	16 June 1883	2	6	
Davis	Dan, Jr.	b.	CR	30 Apr. 1881	5	5	
Davis	Dan, Jr.	b.	CR	30 Apr. 1881	5	5	
Davis	Daniel O.	b.	RRF	28 Apr. 1881	2	3	
Davis	E. W.	b.	DR	9 May 1881	2	2	
Davis	E. W.	o.	DR	26 Oct. 1882	2	2	
Davis	E. W.	b.	PCo	24 June 1885	3	6	
Davis	E. W.	b.	RRF	19 May 1881	2	4	
Davis	E. W.	b.	SD	14 May 1881	3	8	
Davis	E. W.	b.	SD	27 June 1885	5	4	
Davis	Eliza S.	m.	DR	28 Dec. 1881	2	2	
Davis	Eliza S.	m.	PCo	4 Jan. 1882	3	7	
Davis	Eliza S.	m.	SD	31 Dec. 1881	3	6	
Davis	Elizabeth E.	d.	DR	26 May 1884	3	2	
Davis	Elizabeth E.	d.	PCo	28 May 1884	2	4	
Davis	Elizabeth	d.	SD	31` May 1884	1	5	also p. 2 col. 3
Davis	Elmira	m.	PCo	10 May 1882	3	5	
Davis	Elmira	m.	SD	13 May 1882	2	4	
Davis	G. V.	b.	CR	26 Mar. 1881	5	5	
Davis	G. V.	b.	SD	2 Apr. 1881	3	8	
Davis	George A.	b.	DR	21 July 1885	3	4	
Davis	George A.	b.	PCo	22 July 1885	3	6	
Davis	George	m.	PCo	1 Oct. 1884	3	5	
Davis	George	b.	SD	18 July 1885	5	5	
Davis	Harriet	m.	DD	15 Sept. 1883	3	3	
Davis	J. B.	b.	DR	6 Sept. 1881	2	3	
Davis	Jennie E.	m.	PCo	2 Jan. 1884	3	6	
Davis	Jennie E.	m.	PWA	29 Dec. 1883	3	6	
Davis	Jennie E.	m.	SD	5 Jan. 1884	1	4	
Davis	John B.	b.	PC	20 June 1883	3	6	
Davis	John B.	b.	SD	16 June 1883	2	6	
Davis	L. T.	o.	DR	31 July 1882	3	1	
Davis	M. J.	m.	PC	27 June 1883	3	6	
Davis	M. J.	m.	RRF	21 June 1883	2	3	
Davis	Mana J.	m.	SD	23 June 1883	3	5	
Davis	Mary	d.	DD	12 Dec. 1883	3	2	

(1) Surname	(2) Given Name	(3)	(4)	(5) Date	(6) Pg	(7) Col	(8) Comments
Davis	Mary	d.	PCo	19 Dec. 1883	3	4	
Davis	Mary	d.	SD	15 Dec. 1883	3	2	Fresno
Davis	Mattie	d.	DR	20 Aug. 1881	2	3	
Davis	Mollie E.	m.	PCo	27 Dec. 1882	3	6	
Davis	Mollie E.	m.	SD	30 Dec. 1882	3	6	
Davis	Nettie M.	d.	PCo	21 Dec. 1881	3	5	
Davis	S. C.	d.	DR	1 July 1884	3	3	
Davis	Walter S.	o.	DR	26 Oct. 1882	2	2	
Davis	Will	b.	PCo	10 Dec. 1884	3	5	
Davis	William	b.	PCo	10 May 1882	3	5	
Davis	William	b.	SD	13 May 1882	2	4	
Davisson	D. D.	o.	DR	3 July 1882	3	1	
Dawson	Emma	m.	DD	8 Dec. 1883	3	3	
Dawson	Emma	m.	PWA	8 Dec. 1883	3	6	
Day	A., Miss	m.	PCo	12 Nov. 1884	3	5	
Day	Alice	m.	DR	6 Nov. 1884	2	2	
Day	Alice	m.	SD	8 Nov. 1884	2	5	
Day	L. T.	m.	DD	24 Dec. 1883	3	2	
Dayton	Nettie	d.	CR	2 Apr. 1881	5	3	
Dayton	Nettie	d.	DR	30 Mar. 1881	3	2	
Dayton	Nettie	d.	SD	2 Apr. 1881	3	8	
De Coe	T. C.	b.	PCo	30 Apr. 1884	2	6	
De Free	George	d.	PCo	16 Nov. 1881	3	5	
De Fries	William John	d.	SD	21 Feb. 1885	2	5	
De Hay	A.	b.	PC	4 July 1883	3	5	
De May	Mary	d.	DD	13 Oct. 1883	3	3	
De Nise	Conover	d.	PCo	7 Mar. 1883	3	5	
De Spain	Lulu	m.	PCo	2 Apr. 1884	3	6	
Dean	Eugene F.	m.	SD	16 Apr. 1881	3	8	
Dearborn	Jonathan B.	d.	SD	12 Mar. 1881	3	8	
DeBolt	Lottie	m.	PCo	20 July 1881	3	5	
DeBolt	Lottie	m.	SD	9 July 1881	3	8	
Deckey	H. W.	m.	SD	25 Mar. 1882	3	6	
Decoe	(female)	b.	DR	22 Apr. 1884	3	2	
Decoe	T. C.	m.	DR	24 Sept. 1881	2	3	
Decoe	T. C.	b.	DR	12 July 1882	3	2	
Decoe	T. C.	b.	PCo	19 July 1882	3	6	
Decoe	T. C.	m.	SD	1 Oct. 1881	3	8	
Decoe	T. C.	b.	SD	22 July 1882	3	5	
Decoe	T. C.	b.	SD	26 Apr. 1883	3	5	
DeCoe	T. C.	m.	RRF	29 Sept. 1881	2	6	
DeCostas		d.	DR	22 Oct. 1882	3	2	

(1) Surname	(2) Given Name	(3)	(4)	(5) Date	(6) Pg	(7) Col	(8) Comments
DeCostaz	Henri	m.	SD	28 Oct. 1882	3	3	
Deegand	Michael	m.	DR	31 Dec. 1881	2	3	
Deegand	Michael	m.	SD	7 Jan. 1882	3	8	
Dees	Berdena	m.	PCo	8 July 1885	3	6	
Dees	Berdena	m.	PCo	15 July 1885	3	6	
Defrates	Vincent	d.	PC	4 Apr. 1883	3	5	
Defrates	Vincent	d.	SD	7 Apr. 1883	2	6	
DeFree	George	d.	DR	2 Nov. 1881	2	3	
DeFree	George	d.	SD	12 Nov. 1881	3	7	
DeFries	Dr.	b.	DR	10 July 1884	3	3	
DeFries	W.	b.	PCo	9 July 1884	3	5	
DeFries	W.	b.	PWA	5 July 1884	3	6	
DeFries	William John	d.	PCo	18 Feb. 1885	3	6	
DeFries	William John	d.	PWA	14 Feb. 1885	3	5	
Degand	Michael	m.	PCo	4 Jan. 1882	3	7	
Dehay	Mr. & Mrs.	b.	CR	23 June 1883	3	1	
DeHay	A.,	b.	SD	7 July 1883	2	5	
DeHay	Mary	d.	SD	20 Oct. 1883	3	4	
Deily	James B.	m.	RRF	6 Jan. 1881	2	5	
Deily	James B.	m.	SD	8 Jan. 1881	3	8	
Delanehanty	Minnie	d.	DR	1 Aug. 1885	3	4	
Delanehanty	Minnie	d.	PCo	12 Aug. 1885	2	4	
Delanehanty	Minnie	d.	PCo	29 July 1885	3	4	
Delaney	James	d.	PCo	15 Oct. 1884	3	6	
Delaney	James	d.	PWA	18 Oct. 1884	3	1&4	
DeLong	Francis	d.	PWA	14 Feb. 1885	3	3&5	Novato
Delzelle	D. S.	b.	DR	22 Oct. 1881	2	4	
Delzelle	Maggie	m.	DR	27 Mar. 1884	3	3	
Delzelle	Maggie	m.	PCo	2 Apr. 1884	3	6	
Delzelle	William R.	m.	PCo	2 Nov. 1881	3	5	
DeMartini	Ansonia	d.	DR	1 July 1881	2	2	
DeMartini	Ansonia	d.	PCo	29 June 1881	3	5	
DeMartini	Ansonia	d.	SD	9 July 1881	3	8	
Demetz	Carl	d.	DR	5 Oct. 1881	2	3	
Demetz	H.	b.	SD	22 Jan. 1881	3	8	
Demetz	Henry (son of)	d.	SD	8 Oct. 1881	3	8	
Deming	Clara	m.	DR	10 Nov. 1884	2	2	
Deming	Colonel	d.	SD	16 Sept. 1822	3	3	
Deming	Horace	d.	DR	12 Sept. 1882	3	2&1	
Deming	Horace	d.	PCo	20 Sept. 1882	3	6	
Demmon	Oscar Leonidas	d.	SD	26 Mar. 1881	3	8	
Dempsey	James	b.	PC	2 May 1883	3	5	

(1) Surname	(2) Given Name	(3)	(4)	(5) Date	(6) Pg	(7) Col	(8) Comments
Dempsey	James	b.	PC	25 Apr. 1883	3	5	
Dempsey	James	b.	RRF	26 Apr. 1883	2	3	
Dempsey	James	b.	SD	5 May 1883	3	6	
Dempsey	James	b.	SD	28 Apr. 1883	3	6	
Dempsey	Mr. & Mrs.	b.	SD	21 Mar. 1885	2	5	
Dempsey	P.	m.	PCo	17 Jan. 1883	3	5	
Dempsey	P.	m.	RRF	11 Jan. 1883	2	2	
Denicke	Hugo	m.	PCo	10 Dec. 1884	3	5	
Denicke	Hugo L.	m.	DR	3 Dec. 1884	3	2	
DeNise	Conover	d.	CR	3 Mar. 1883	3	1	Cloverdale Cem.
Denker	Henry (infant dau.)	d.	DR	8 Dec. 1884	3	2	
Denker	Henry (dau. of)	d.	PCo	3 Dec. 1884	3	5	
Denker	Henry (son of)	d.	PWA	6 Dec. 1884	3	4	
Denker	Henry (dau. of)	d.	SD	13 Dec. 1884	2	5	
Denker	Rebecca	d.	PCo	1 July 1885	3	6	
Denman	Frank	o.	DR	26 Oct. 1882	2	2	
Denman	Frank H.	m.	PCo	11 Feb. 1885	3	6	
Denner	William W.	d.	DR	1 Oct. 1885	3	4	
Dennes	Rosa	m.	CR	17 Mar. 1883	3		
Dennes	Rosa	m.	PCo	21 Mar. 1883	3	5	
Dennes	Rosa	m.	RRF	15 Mar. 1883	3	4	
Dennis	Rosa	m.	SD	17 Mar. 1883	3	5	
Dennis	Samuel	b.	DR	9 Apr. 1882	3	2	
Dennis	Samuel	b.	PCo	5 Apr. 1882	3	5	
Dennis	Samuel	b.	PCo	29 Mar. 1882	3	5	
Dennis	Samuel	b.	RRF	6 Apr. 1882	2	4	
Dennis	Samuel	b.	SD	1 Apr. 1882	3	6	
Denny	Emma A.	m.	SD	28 July 1883	2	5	
Denny	Emma	m.	PC	1 Aug. 1883	3	6	
Denny	Emma	m.	PWA	4 Aug. 1883	3	7	
Densmore	Clara Edna	d.	DR	10 Apr. 1882	2	2	
Densmore	Clara Edna	d.	PCo	5 Apr. 1882	3	5	
Densmore	J. E.	b.	DR	29 July 1885	3	4	
Densmore	J. E.	b.	PCo	22 July 1885	3	6	
Derby	Laura	d.	CR	15 Jan. 1881	5	5	
Derby	Laura	d.	DR	11 Jan. 1881	3	2	
Derby	Lora	d.	PCo	5 Jan. 1881	3	4	
Derby	Lora	d.	SD	8 Jan. 1881	3	8	
Derrick	G .W.	b.	DD	20 Oct. 1883	3	3	
Derrick	G. W.	b.	SD	27 Oct. 1883	3	4	
Derrick	George W.	b.	DR	1 July 1882	2	2	
Derrick	George W.	b.	PCo	12 July 1882	3	5	

(1) Surname	(2) Given Name	(3)	(4)	(5) Date	(6) Pg	(7) Col	(8) Comments
Derrick	George W.	b.	SD	8 July 1882	2	5	
Derrick	Joseph	b.	RRF	10 Aug. 1882	2	4	
DeRussy	Melinda T.	d.	SD	19 May 1883	3	5	
Despain	Lulu E.	m.	DR	31 Mar. 1884	3	3	
DeTurk	I.	o.	DR	26 Oct. 1882	2	2	
Devilbiss	H. W.	b.	DD	28 Aug. 1883	3	3	
Devilbiss	Henry	b.	SD	2 Apr. 1881	3	8	
Devoto	Louis	b.	PCo	7 Mar. 1883	3	5	
Dewey	Edward	m.	DR	21 Apr. 1884	3	2	
Dewey	Edward	m.	SD	19 Apr. 1884	3	4	
Diamon	I. H.	b.	SD	16 Apr. 1881	3	8	
Dias	I. L.	m.	PCo	14 Feb. 1883	3	6	
Dias	I. L.	b.	SD	31 May 1884	2	3	
Dias	Isaac L.	d.	PCo	3 Dec. 1884	3	5	also col. 1 & 2
Dias	Isaac L.	d.	PWA	6 Dec. 1884	3	4	
Dias	Isaac L.	d.	PWA	13 Dec. 1884	2	4	
Dias	Isaac L.	d.	SD	13 Dec. 1884	2	5	
Dias	J. L.	m.	SD	10 Feb. 1883	2	7	
Dias	L. L.	b.	PCo	28 May 1884	2	4	
Dias	L. L.	m.	PWA	10 Feb. 1883	3	7	
Dibble	Helen	m.	DR	27 Oct. 1884	3	3	
Dibble	Helen	m.	PCo	29 Oct. 1884	3	5	
Dibble	Helen	m.	SD	8 Nov. 1884	2	5	
Dibble	Jerome	d.	DR	18 Nov. 1882	3	1	
Dibble	N. P.	b.	DR	19 Dec. 1884	3	2	
Dibble	N. P.	b.	PCo	17 Dec. 1884	2	4	
Dibble	N. P.	b.	PWA	20 Dec. 1884	3	4	
Dibble	W. I.	b.	PCo	12 Aug. 1885	3	6	
Dibble	W. I.	b.	SD	22 Aug. 1885	6	2	
Dibble	W. J.	b.	DR	7 Aug. 1885	3	4	
Dibble	William I.	m.	DR	12 Aug. 1884	3	3	
Dibble	William L.	m.	PWA	16 Aug. 1884	3	4	
Dibble	William L.	m.	SD	13 Aug. 1884	2	4	
Dickinson	Fred Renard	d.	PCo	15 June 1881	3	5	
Dickinson	Fred Renard	d.	SD	25 June 1881	3	8	
Dickinson	Freddie	d.	SD	18 June 1881	3	8	
Dickinson	G. D.	b.	PC	20 June 1883	3	6	
Dickinson	G. D.	b.	PWA	23 June 1883	3	7	
Dickson	(male)	b.	DR	16 May 1884	3	2	
Dickson	C. J.	b.	PCo	16 Nov. 1881	3	5	
Dickson	Emma C.	d.	DD	11 Oct. 1883	3	3	
Dickson	Emma C.	d.	SD	13 Oct. 1883	3	4	also p. 3 col. 2

(1) Surname	(2) Given Name	(3)	(4)	(5) Date	(6) Pg	(7) Col	(8) Comments
Dickson	Emma Church	d.	SD	20 Oct. 1883	1	4	Rural Cemetery
Dickson	J. M.	m.	DR	4 Nov. 1885	3	4	
Dickson	J. M.	m.	SD	7 Nov. 1885	3	1	
Dickson	James	d.	SD	20 Jan. 1883	3	3	
Dickson	Sallie	m.	PCo	20 Sept. 1882	3	6	
Dickson	Sallie	m.	SD	23 Sept. 1882	3	6	
Dickson	W. H.	m.	DR	25 Aug. 1881	2	3	
Dickson	W. H.	m.	SD	27 Aug. 1881	3	8	
Dickson	W. M.	b.	PCo	16 Aug. 1882	3	6	
Dickson	W. M.	b.	SD	19 Aug. 1882	3	5	
Dickson	W.	b.	PCo	14 May 1884	3	4	
Dickson	W.	b.	SD	17 May 1884	3	5	
Dickson	William	m.	DR	25 Nov. 1881	2	3	
Dickson	William	m.	PCo	23 Nov. 1881	3	5	
Dickson	William	b.	PWA	17 May 1884	3	6	
Dickson	William	m.	SD	26 Nov. 1881	3	8	
Dille	C. F.	b.	SD	19 July 1884	2	5	
Diller	C. W.	b.	DR	16 Nov. 1881	2	3	
Diller	C. W.	b.	PCo	23 Nov. 1881	3	5	
Diller	C. W.	b.	SD	19 Nov. 1881	4	8	
Dillingham	W. K.	m.	CR	4 Mar. 1882	1	4	
Dillingham	W. K.	b.	CR	4 Aug. 1883	3	1	
Dillingham	W. K.	b.	DD	28 July 1883	3	2	
Dillingham	W. K.	b.	PC	8 Aug. 1883	3	6	
Dillingham	W. K.	m.	RRF	9 Mar. 1882	2	4	
Dillingham	W. K.	b.	SD	4 Aug. 1883	2	5	
Dillon	Charles	m.	DR	16 Sept. 1882	3	4	
Dillon	Charles	m.	SD	19 Sept. 1885	2	4	
Dillon	Sarah M.	m.	SD	13 June 1885	3	5	
Dimmick	F. M.	o.	SD	22 Sept. 1883	1	5	
Dimmie	George M.	d.	RRF	7 Apr. 1881	2	5	
Dimmie	Joseph	d.	RRF	7 Apr. 1881	2	5	Oak Mound, Healdsburg
Dinning	Arzelia	m.	DD	27 Oct. 1883	3	3	
Dinwiddie	J. I.	o.	DR	26 Oct. 1882	2	1	
Dinwiddie	J. L.	o	PWA	17 Nov. 1883	3	2	
Dinwiddie	R. R.	d.	PC	13 June 1883	3	6	
Dinwiddie	R. R.	d.	RRF	7 June 1883	2	3	
Dinwiddie	R. R.	d.	SD	16 June 1883	2	6	
Dittmer	William	b.	SD	19 Mar. 1881	3	8	
Divenger	Frederick	d.	SD	4 Oct. 1884	3	5	
Dixon	Eugene F.	m.	CR	28 June 1884	3	1	
Dixon	Eugene F.	m.	DR	1 July 1884	3	3	

(1) Surname	(2) Given Name	(3)	(4)	(5) Date	(6) Pg	(7) Col	(8) Comments
Dixon	Eugene F.	m.	PCo	9 July 1884	3	5	
Dixon	Samuel L.	d.	DD	13 Aug. 1883	3	3	
Dixon	Samuel L.	d.	SD	18 Aug. 1883	2	6	
Dixon	Thomas H.	d.	SD	21 Feb. 1885	2	5	
Dock	Ah	o.	DR	13 Nov. 1882	3	1	
Dodge	Susan G.	d.	RRF	31 Aug. 1882	2	4	
Dodson	Charles	b.	DR	9 Apr. 1882	3	2	
Dodson	Charles	b.	PCo	29 Mar. 1882	3	5	
Dodson	Charles	b.	RRF	6 Apr. 1882	2	4	
Dodson	Charles	b.	SD	1 Apr. 1882	3	6	
Doescher	Charles	b.	SD	8 Jan. 1881	3	8	
Dohn	George	b.	CR	1 Jan. 1881	5	5	
Dolan	Anna	m.	PCo	12 Aug. 1885	3	6	
Dolan	Annie	p.	DD	11 July 1883	3	2	
Dolan	Honora	d.	DR	8 June 1882	3	2&1	
Dolan	Honora	d.	PCo	14 June 1882	3	5	
Dolan	Honora	d.	RRF	15 June 1882	2	4	
Dolan	Honora	d.	SD	10 June 1882	2	3	
Dolan	Mary E.	d.	SD	28 Apr. 1883	3	4	
Dolan	Michael	b.	SD	4 June 1881	3	8	
Dolan	Mr.	m.	SD	12 Mar. 1881	3	8	
Domine	Fred	d.	PC	18 July 1883	3	5	
Domine	Frederic	d.	DD	16 July 1883	3	2	
Dominici	D.	b.	PWA	18 Apr. 1885	3	6	
Dominici	D.	b.	SD	7 Apr. 1883	2	6	
Dominici	Domenico	b.	SD	6 Aug. 1881	3	8	
Dominici	Dommico	b.	DR	2 Aug. 1881	2	2	
Donahue	John	d.	PC	4 July 1883	3	5	
Donahue	John	d.	SD	7 July 1883	2	5	
Donahue	John	b.	SD	2 May 1885	2	5	
Donahue	Peter	d.	SD	5 Dec. 1885	1	3	
Donavan	Francis	m.	DR	30 Sept. 1881	2	3	
Donley	Ambrose	d.	DR	22 Dec. 1881	2	2	
Donley	Ambrose	d.	DR	31 Dec. 1881	2	3	
Donley	Ambrose	d.	PCo	21 Dec. 1881	3	5	
Donley	John	d.	SD	31 Dec. 1881	3	6	
Donnelly	Annie E.	m.	DR	5 June 1884	3	3	
Donnelly	Annie Elizabeth	m.	SD	14 June 1884	2	4	
Donnelly	John	d.	PC	4 Apr. 1883	3	5	
Donnelly	Mr.	d.	SD	31 Mar. 1883	3	1	Petaluma
Donnelly	W. A.	b.	SD	12 Mar. 1881	3	8	
Donovan	Mary	m.	DR	13 Feb. 1882	2	3	

(1) Surname	(2) Given Name	(3)	(4)	(5) Date	(6) Pg	(7) Col	(8) Comments
Donovan	Mary	m.	SD	11 Feb. 1882	3	3&6	
Dooley	Hambleton	m.	DR	30 Jan. 1882	2	3	
Dooley	Hambleton	m.	PCo	25 Jan. 1882	3	6	
Dooley	Maggie	m.	PWA	15 Dec. 1883	3	6	
Doran	A.	b.	SD	22 Aug. 1885	6	2	
Dorman	William	b.	PCo	9 Nov. 1881	3	5	
Dornin	Thomas J.	d.	SD	18 Oct. 1884	1	5	
Doss	Emma	m.	PCo	24 Jan. 1883	3	5	also col. 3
Doss	Emma R.	m.	PWA	19 Jan. 1883	3	7	
Doss	Emma R.	m.	SD	27 Jan. 1883	3	6	
Doss	John R.	b.	PCo	27 Dec. 1882	3	6	
Doss	John R.	b.	SD	30 Dec. 1882	3	6	
Dota	L.	b.	DD	31 Aug. 1883	3	3	
Dougherty	A. J.	d.	PWA	26 Jan. 1884	3	6	
Dougherty	A. J., Mrs.	d.	PCo	23 Jan. 1884	3	5	
Dougherty	Anna	m.	DR	4 Dec. 1881	2	3	
Dougherty	Anna	m.	PCo	30 Nov. 1881	3	5	
Dougherty	Annie	m.	SD	3 Dec. 1881	3	4&8	
Dougherty	B. G., Mrs.	d.	DR	14 Jan. 1884	3	3	
Dougherty	Julia Ann	d.	SD	19 Jan. 1884	3	2&6	Odd Fellows
Dougherty	Maria T.	m.	SD	29 Sept. 1883	2	6	
Dougherty	Marie T.	m.	DD	25 Sept. 1883	3	3	
Doughty	Charles Edward	m.	DR	21 Sept. 1885	3	4	
Dovey	Margaret	m.	DR	9 May 1881	2	2	
Dovey	Margaret	m.	SD	14 May 1881	3	8	
Dow	C. H.	b.	DR	25 July 1882	2	3	
Dow	C. H.	b.	RRF	20 July 1882	2	4	
Dow	George	b.	PCo	20 Sept. 1882	3	6	
Dow	George	b.	PCo	22 Apr. 1885	3	6	
Dow	George	b.	PWA	25 Apr. 1885	3	6	
Dow	George	b.	RRF	14 Sept. 1882	2	4	
Dow	George	d.	RRF	14 Sept. 1882	2	4	
Dow	George	b.	SD	23 Sept. 1882	3	6	
Dow	George (dau. of)	d.	PCo	20 Sept. 1882	3	6	
Dow	J. G.	d.	PCo	8 July 1885	3	6	
Dowdall	J.	o.	SIT	22 Aug. 1885	2	2	
Dowease	J.	b.	CR	25 July 1885	3	2	
Downer	H. A.	b.	PCo	21 Mar. 1883	3	5	
Downer	H. A.	b.	PWA	24 Mar. 1883	3	7	
Downey	A. J.	b.	DR	21 July 1885	3	4	
Downey	A. J.	b.	PCo	15 July 1885	3	6	
Downing	C. V. B.	b.	RRF	10 Aug. 1882	2	4	

(1) Surname	(2) Given Name	(3)	(4)	(5) Date	(6) Pg	(7) Col	(8) Comments
Downing	C. V. B.	b.	SD	12 Aug. 1882	3	5	
Downing	Clarence V. B.	d.	DR	7 Dec. 1882	2	3	
Downing	Clarence V. B.	d.	RRF	7 Dec. 1882	2	4	Oak Mound
Downing	Delia	m.	PCo	6 Dec. 1882	3	6	
Downing	J. M.	m.	SD	5 Mar. 1881	3	8	
Downing	Joseph H.	b.	RRF	4 Jan. 1883	2	2	
Downing	Wesley C.	d.	DR	11 Sept. 1882	3	1	Ohio
Downing	Wesley	d.	SD	16 Sept. 1822	3	3	
Doyle	Daniel	m.	DD	8 Sept. 1883	3	3	
Doyle	Daniel	m.	SD	15 Sept. 1883	2	4	
Doyle	Louise	m.	PCo	19 July 1882	3	6	
Doyle	Louise	m.	SD	15 July 1882	2	4	
Dozier	Elizabeth E.	d.	PCo	1 Oct. 1884	3	5	
Dozier	Elizabeth Edwards	d.	SD	27 Sept. 1884	2	5	also p. 3 col .2 Rural Cem.
Drahms	A.	b.	DR	31 May 1881	2	2	
Drake	George	m.	RRF	31 Mar. 1881	2	3	
Drake	George	m.	SD	2 Apr. 1881	3	8	
Drees	August H.	d.	DR	21 July 1882	3	2	
Drees	August H.	d.	PCo	19 July 1882	3	6	
Drees	August H.	d.	SD	22 July 1882	3	5	
Dresser	Charles	b.	PCo	13 Sept. 1882	3	7	
Dresser	Charles	b.	RRF	7 Sept. 1882	2	4	
Driscoll	Cornelius	d.	SD	1 Sept. 1883	1	6	
Driscoll	James Joseph	m.	PCo	17 Jan. 1883	3	5	
Driscoll	James Joseph	m.	PWA	12 Jan. 1883	3	2&6	
Driscoll	L.	d.	PC	18 Apr. 1883	3	5	
Driscoll	L. R.	d.	CR	14 Apr. 1883	3	1&2	
Driscoll	Lemuel R.	d.	SD	21 Apr. 1883	2	6	
Drube	Louis	b.	PCo	14 Oct. 1885	3	6	
Drube	Louis	b.	SD	10 Oct. 1885	5	5	
Drummond	(female)	b.	DR	6 Feb. 1884	3	2	
Drummond	(female)	b.	DR	18 Mar. 1884	3	3	
Drummond	J. H.	b.	PCo	13 Feb. 1884	3	6	
Drummond	J. H.	b.	PWA	9 Feb. 1884	3	6	
Drummond	J. H.	b.	SD	16 Feb. 1884	2	5	
Dubois	J. C.	m.	SD	13 June 1885	3	5	
Duboise	William S.	m.	DD	4 Oct. 1883	3	2	
Duck	Ah	d.	DR	9 Dec. 1882	3	2	
Ducker	A.	b.	PC	27 June 1883	3	6	
Ducker	A.	b.	PWA	30 June 1883	3	7	
Ducker	A.	b.	SD	30 June 1883	3	5	
Ducker	Catherine	d.	SD	22 Aug. 1885	6	2	

(1) Surname	(2) Given Name	(3)	(4)	(5) Date	(6) Pg	(7) Col	(8) Comments
Ducker	William, Sr.	d.	SD	27 June 1885	1	4	
Ducker	William	d.	PCo	17 June 1885	3	6	
Dudley	W. S.	m.	PCo	21 Feb. 1883	3	5	also 28 Feb. p. 3 col.2
Dudley	W. S.	m.	RRF	15 Feb. 1883	2	3	
Dudley	W. S.	m.	SD	17 Feb. 1883	3	1	
Duerson	J. H.	b.	DR	19 Dec. 1884	3	2	
Duerson	J. H.	b.	SD	27 Dec. 1884	2	4	
Duerson	J.	b.	PWA	27 Dec. 1884	2	5	
Duerson	John A.	b.	CR	19 Mar. 1881	4	3	also 26 Mar. 1881 p. 5 col. 4
Duerson	John H.	b.	CR	19 Mar. 1881	4	3	
Duerson	John H.	b.	DR	15 Mar. 1881	2	3	
Duerson	John	b.	PCo	31 Dec. 1884	3	4	
Duerson	John	b.	SD	19 Mar. 1881	3	8	
Duescher	Charles	b.	PCo	5 Jan. 1881	3	4	
Duffey	Edward	d.	SD	25 Apr. 1885	2	5	
Dunbar	Alexander	d.	DR	24 June 1884	3	3	
Dunbar	Alexander	d.	PCo	25 June 1884	3	4	
Dunbar	Alexander	d.	SD	28 June 1884	3	4	
Dunbar	Edith M.	d.	DD	4 Aug. 1883	3	2	
Dunbar	Edith M.	d.	SD	11 Aug. 1883	2	7	
Dunbar	Eva	m.	DR	9 Nov. 1885	2	2	
Dunbar	Eva	m.	PCo	4 Nov. 1885	2	5	
Dunbar	Eva	m.	SD	7 Nov. 1885	3	4	
Dunbar	J. (dau. of)	d.	PC	8 Aug. 1883	3	6	
Dunbar	John	b.	PCo	21 Mar. 1883	3	5	
Dunbar	John	m.	PCo	1 Oct. 1884	3	5	
Dunbar	John	m.	SD	4 Oct. 1884	3	5	
Dunbar	Mary H.	d.	DD	21 Sept. 1883	3	3	
Dunbar	Mary H.	d.	DD	22 Sept. 1883	3	2	
Dunbar	Mary H.	d.	SD	29 Sept. 1883	1	4	also p. 2 col. 6
Dunbar	Nicholas	d.	SD	14 Mar. 1885	5	5	
Duncan	(female)	b.	DR	7 Feb. 1884	3	3	
Duncan	(female)	b.	DR	8 Mar. 1884	3	2	
Duncan	Charles A.	m.	DR	24 Sept. 1885	3	4	
Duncan	Charles A.	m.	SRR	1 Oct. 1885	3	3	
Duncan	Charles H.	m.	CR	17 Mar. 1883	3		
Duncan	Charles H.	m.	PCo	21 Mar. 1883	3	5	
Duncan	E. B.	b.	SD	12 Feb. 1881	3	8	
Duncan	Eva	d.	SD	12 Mar. 1881	3	8	
Duncan	F. L.	m.	PCo	12 Nov. 1884	3	5	
Duncan	F. L.	m.	SD	8 Nov. 1884	2	5	
Duncan	George B.	b.	DR	28 Dec. 1885	3	4	

(1) Surname	(2) Given Name	(3)	(4)	(5) Date	(6) Pg	(7) Col	(8) Comments
Duncan	George B.	b.	PCo	12 Mar. 1884	3	6	
Duncan	George B.	b.	PCo	30 Dec. 1885	3	4	
Duncan	George	m.	CR	9 June 1883	3	1	
Duncan	George	m.	PC	13 June 1883	3	6	
Duncan	Lallie H.	d.	RRF	5 Oct. 1882	2	3	
Duncan	Lallie H.	d.	SD	7 Oct. 1882	1	3	also p. 3 col. 6
Duncan	Lyod.	m.	CR	18 Apr. 1885	5	2	
Duncan	S. M.	b.	DR	20 June 1881	2	2	
Duncan	S. M.	b.	PCo	13 Feb. 1884	3	6	
Duncan	S. M.	b.	SD	25 June 1881	3	8	
Duncan	S. M.	b.	SD	9 Feb. 1884	7	2	
Duncan	S.	b.	CR	25 June 1881	4	3	
Duncan	Sallie H.	d.	PCo	11 Oct. 1882	3	6	
Duncan	Samuel	b.	PCo	16 Sept. 1885	3	6	
Duncan	Samuel	m.	RRF	1 Dec. 1881	2	3	
Duncan	Samuel	m.	SD	3 Dec. 1881	3	2	
Duncan	Sue	m.	SD	2 June 1883	2	7	
Duncan	T. L.	m.	DR	5 Nov. 1884	2	2	
Duncan	Thomas	d.	CR	1 Dec. 1883	3	1	Hopland
Duncan	Thomas	d.	CR	10 Nov. 1883	3	1	
Duncan	Thomas	d.	DD	12 Nov. 1883	3	3	
Duncan	Thomas	d.	SD	17 Nov. 1883	3	5	
Dunckley	L. E., Mrs.	m.	PCo	5 Aug. 1885	3	6	
Dunckley	L. E., Mrs.	m.	SD	22 Aug. 1885	6	2	
Dunkley	Joseph	d.	PCo	24 Dec. 1884	3	4	
Dunkley	Mattie	m.	DR	5 July 1884	3	4	
Dunkley	Mattie	m.	PCo	16 July 1884	3	6	
Dunlap	J. L.	b.	SD	21 Apr. 1883	2	6	
Dunn	D. J.	m.	PCo	12 Nov. 1884	3	5	
Dunn	Daisy	m.	DR	16 Dec. 1881	2	2	
Dunn	Daisy	m.	PCo	28 Dec. 1881	3	6	
Dunn	Daisy	m.	SD	24 Dec. 1881	2	3	
Dunn	James Marshall	d.	DD	26 Oct. 1883	3	3	
Dunn	James Marshall	d.	PWA	27 Oct. 1883	3	8	
Dunn	John	d.	PCo	2 July 1884	3	4	
Dunn	Marshall	d.	SD	3 Nov. 1883	3	3	
Dunn	William	m.	DR	29 Dec. 1881	2	3	
Dunn	William	m.	PCo	11 Jan. 1882	3	6	
Dunn	William	m.	SD	7 Jan. 1882	3	8	
Dunsing	Georgia	m.	DD	21 Aug. 1883	3	3	
Dunsing	Georgia	m.	SD	25 Aug. 1883	2	5	
Dunwoody	E., Mrs.	m.	SD	25 Oct. 1884	2	5	

(1) Surname	(2) Given Name	(3)	(4)	(5) Date	(6) Pg	(7) Col	(8) Comments
Dunwoody	Emeline	d.	PCo	15 Oct. 1884	3	6	
Dunwoody	Seth M.	m.	DD	1 Aug. 1883	3	2	
Dunwoody	Seth M.	m.	SD	4 Aug. 1883	2	5	
Dunwoody	Seth	m.	PC	8 Aug. 1883	3	6	
Dupont	Albert	m.	DD	25 Sept. 1883	3	3	
Dupont	Albert	m.	PWA	29 Sept. 1883	3	8	
Dupont	Albert	m.	SD	29 Sept. 1883	2	6	
Durie	Robert H.	m.	DD	26 July 1883	3	2	
Durie	Robert H.	m.	PC	25 July 1883	3	6	
Durie	Robert H.	m.	PWA	28 July 1883	3	7	
Durie	Robert H.	m.	SD	28 July 1883	2	5	
Dutel	John	b.	SIT	19 Dec. 1885	2	3	
Dutton	Emma	m.	PCo	10 Dec. 1884	3	5	
Dutton	Emma J.	m.	DR	3 Dec. 1884	3	2	
Dutton	G. W.	d.	PCo	20 May 1885	3	6	also 27 May p. 3 col. 4
Dutton	George W.	d.	SD	30 May 1885	5	4	
Dutton	W. N.	b.	SD	9 Aug. 1884	3	4	
Dwenger	Fritz	d.	PCo	1 Oct. 1884	3	5	
Dwinelle	Charles H.	m.	SD	13 June 1885	3	5	
Dwinelle	John W.	d.	CR	5 Mar. 1881	1	4	
Dwinelle	John W.	d.	DR	21 Feb. 1881	3	2	
Dyer	Delia Ann	p.	DD	19 July 1883	3	2	
Dyer	K.	b.	SD	25 June 1881	3	8	
Dyer	R. D.	d.	DR	26 Jan. 1882	2	3	

E

(1) Surname	(2) Given Name	(3)	(4)	(5) Date	(6) Pg	(7) Col	(8) Comments
Eagleson	Annie May	m.	SD	21 Mar. 1885	1	4	also p. 2 col. 5
Eakle	Henry T.	b.	SD	12 Feb. 1881	3	8	
Eardley	Bedson R.	m.	PWA	1 Nov. 1884	3	4	
Earl	E. T.	m.	DR	14 Feb. 1884	3	2	
Earl	Edwin T.	m.	PCo	20 Feb. 1884	3	6	
Earl	Edwin T.	m.	PWA	23 Feb. 1884	3	2&6	
Earl	Edwin T.	m.	SD	16 Feb. 1884	2	5	also p. 3 col. 4, 5, 6
Eastlich	A.	m.	DR	25 July 1882	2	3	
Eastlich	A.	m.	PCo	2 Aug. 1882	3	6	
Eastlich	A.	m.	SD	5 Aug. 1882	3	5	
Eastlick	A.	m.	CR	22 July 1882	5	3	
Eastlick	A.	b.	PC	13 June 1883	3	6	
Eastlick	A. D.	m.	RRF	27 July 1882	2	4	
Eastlick	Al	b.	CR	27 June 1885	3	1	
Eastlick	Al	b.	PCo	1 July 1885	3	6	
Eastman	Frank	d.	RRF	13 July 1882	1	6	
Eastman	H. L.	m.	SWI	22 Sept. 1883	2	3	
Eaton	Bettie	m.	PCo	17 Jan. 1883	3	5	
Eaton	Bettie	m.	PCo	24 Jan. 1883	3	5	
Eaton	Bettie	m.	RRF	18 Jan. 1883	2	3	
Eaton	Bettie	m.	SD	13 Jan. 1883	3	5	
Eaton	Elizabeth M.	d.	DD	23 July 1883	3	2	
Eaton	Elizabeth M.	d.	PC	25 July 1883	3	6	
Eaton	Elizabeth M.	d.	SD	28 July 1883	2	5	
Ebbert	Henrietta	d.	DR	8 Mar. 1882	2	3	
Ebbert	Henrietta	d.	PCo	22 Mar. 1882	3	5	
Ebbert	Henrietta	d.	SD	18 Mar. 1882	3	5	
Eberle	(female)	b.	DR	28 June 1884	3	2	
Eccleston	Julia	m.	DD	23 July 1883	3	2	
Eckert	(male)	b.	DR	7 Apr. 1884	3	3	
Eckert	Peter	b.	DR	11 Feb. 1882	2	3	
Eckert	Peter	b.	PCo	22 Feb. 1882	3	5	
Eckert	Peter	b.	PCo	9 Apr. 1884	3	6	
Eckert	Peter	b.	SD	11 Feb. 1882	3	6	
Eckert	Peter	b.	SD	12 Apr. 1884	2	5	
Eddy	George	m.	DR	14 Dec. 1881	2	2	
Eddy	George	m.	PCo	7 Dec. 1881	3	5	
Eddy	George	m.	SD	17 Dec. 1881	3	7	

(1) Surname	(2) Given Name	(3)	(4)	(5) Date	(6) Pg	(7) Col	(8) Comments
Edelman	Emily	d.	PCo	24 Aug. 1881	3	5	
Edelmann	Emily	d.	SD	3 Sept. 1881	3	8	
Edmeads	Effie	d.	DR	7 July 1884	3	3	
Edmeads	Effie	d.	PCo	2 July 1884	3	4	
Edmeads	Effie	d.	PWA	5 July 1884	3	6	
Edmeads	Effie	d.	SD	12 July 1884	6	8	
Edmondson	Edward	d.	DR	7 Jan. 1884	3	3	
Edmondson	Edward	d.	DR	18 Jan. 1884	3	2	Rural cemetery
Edmondson	Edward	d.	PCo	9 Jan. 1884	3	6	
Edrington	Barrett	d.	PCo	9 Nov. 1881	3	5	
Edward	Lottie	m.	PCo	11 Feb. 1885	3	6	
Edwards	Ben	b.	PCo	26 Oct. 1881	3	4	
Edwards	Ben	b.	SD	5 Nov. 1881	3	6	
Edwards	C. S.	b.	SD	12 Mar. 1881	3	8	
Edwards	Helen R.	m.	DR	16 Nov. 1885	3	4	
Edwards	John	b.	CR	22 July 1882	5	3	
Edwards	John	b.	DR	25 July 1882	2	3	
Edwards	John	b.	PCo	2 Aug. 1882	3	6	
Edwards	John	b.	RRF	27 July 1882	2	4	
Edwards	Joseph	b.	PCo	4 Mar. 1885	3	6	
Edwards	Joseph	b.	PWA	7 Mar. 1885	3	5	
Edwards	Laura V.	m.	DR	18 May 1882	2	2	also p. 3 col. 1
Edwards	Laura V.	m.	PCo	31 May 1882	3	5	
Edwards	Laura V.	m.	SD	10 June 1882	2	3	
Edwards	M. W.	b.	SD	10 Dec. 1881	3	7	
Edwards	Matilda	d.	SWI	5 Apr. 1884	3	4	
Egbert	Mrs.	m.	SD	8 Jan. 1881	3	8	
Ehlers	Henry	m.	CR	15 Jan. 1881	5	5	
Ehlers	Henry	m.	DR	11 Jan. 1881	3	2	
Ehlers	Henry	b.	PCo	25 Jan. 1882	3	6	
Ehlers	Henry	m.	SD	15 Jan. 1881	3	8	
Eichler	Lillie	d.	DR	14 Sept. 1882	3	2	
Eichler	Lillie	d.	PCo	13 Sept. 1882	3	7	
Eichler	Lillie	d.	RRF	7 Sept. 1882	2	4	
Einhorn	J. H.	m.	DR	5 Nov. 1885	3	4	
Einhorn	J. H.	m.	SD	7 Nov. 1885	2	2	also p. 3 col. 4
Elder	Emma	m.	PCo	5 Jan. 1881	3	4	
Elder	Emma	m.	SD	15 Jan. 1881	3	8	
Elder	Emma S.	m.	DR	11 Jan. 1881	3	2	
Eldred	J. J.	d.	DR	15 Oct. 1885	3	4	
Eldredge	J. B.	m.	PC	9 May 1883	3	5	

(1) Surname	(2) Given Name	(3)	(4)	(5) Date	(6) Pg	(7) Col	(8) Comments
Eldredge	Joseph B.	m.	SD	12 May 1883	2	6	
Eldridge	J.	b.	PCo	2 Jan. 1884	3	6	
Eldridge	J.	b.	RRF	27 Dec. 1883	2	2	
Eldridge	Joseph	b.	DD	27 Dec. 1883	3	3	
Eldridge	Joseph	b.	SD	5 Jan. 1884	1	8	
Eldridge	Mary	m.	DD	23 Nov. 1883	3	2	
Eldridge	Mary	m.	PWA	24 Nov. 1883	3	6	
Eldridge	Mary	m.	SD	1 Dec. 1883	3	4	
Elfick	Frank (son of)	d.	SD	29 Oct. 1881	3	1	
Elkins	Frank E.	m.	PWA	17 Nov. 1883	3	2&8	
Elkins	Frank E.	m.	SD	17 Nov. 1883	3	5	
Elliot	E.	d.	PCo	26 Apr. 1882	3	1	
Elliot	Ellis	d.	PCo	26 Apr. 1882	3	4	
Elliot	Ellis	d.	SD	29 Apr. 1882	3	6	
Elliott	Ellis	d.	DR	1 May 1882	3	2	
Elliott	James Monroe	m.	DR	30 Sept. 1881	2	3	
Elliott	William B.	o.	CR	21 Nov. 1885	1	4	
Ellis	George	d.	SD	18 Apr. 1885	2	5	
Ellis	John E.	m.	DR	23 Jan. 1882	2	3	
Ellis	Leander	b.	PCo	3 Sept. 1884	2	5	
Ellis	Leander`	b.	SD	6 Sept. 1884	2	5	
Ellis	W. C.	b.	CR	22 Jan. 1881	5	5	
Ellis	W. C.	b.	SD	29 Jan. 1881	3	8	
Ellis	William	b.	DR	11 July 1885	3	4	
Ellis	William	b.	RRF	20 Jan. 1881	2	5	
Ellis	William	b.	SD	18 July 1885	5	5	
Elmore	Orvis	m.	PCo	3 Sept. 1884	2	5	
Elmore	Orvis	m.	PWA	30 Aug. 1884	3	5	
Elmore	Orvis	m.	SD	6 Sept. 1884	2	5	
Elmore	Ovis	b.	DR	21 July 1885	3	4	
Elmore	Ovis	b.	PCo	15 July 1885	3	6	
Elphick	Frank	d.	PCo	26 Oct. 1881	3	4	
Elphick	Frank (son of)	d.	SD	5 Nov. 1881	3	6	
Elphick	George	m.	DD	4 Dec. 1883	3	3	
Elphick	J. T.	b.	PCo	21 Mar. 1883	3	5	
Elphick	J. T.	b.	PWA	31 Mar. 1883	2	4	
Elphick	J. T.	b.	SD	7 Apr. 1883	2	6	
Elphick	Lottie	d.	PC	18 Apr. 1883	2	2	also p. 3 col. 5
Elphick	Lottie	d.	PWA	21 Apr. 1883	3	8	
Ely	A. N., Mrs.	d.	DR	1 July 1882	2	2	
Ely	A. N., Mrs.	d.	RRF	29 June 1882	2	5	Oak Mound, Healdsburg
Ely	A. N., Mrs.	d.	SD	1 July 1882	2	3	

(1) Surname	(2) Given Name	(3)	(4)	(5) Date	(6) Pg	(7) Col	(8) Comments
Ely	A. N.	d.	PCo	28 June 1882	3	5	
Ely	Edmund F.	d.	SD	1 Sept. 1883	2	7	
Ely	Edmund F.	d.	SD	8 Sept. 1883	1	5	Rural Cemetery
Ely	Elisha	d.	RRF	29 June 1882	2	5	
Ely	Sarah E.	m.	SD	1 Aug. 1885	2	3	also p. 5 col. 6
Emerson	Bessie	m.	PCo	2 Aug. 1882	3	6	
Emerson	Bessie	m.	RRF	15 June 1882	3	4	
Emerson	Bessie	m.	RRF	27 July 1882	2	4	
Emerson	Bessie	m.	SD	5 Aug. 1882	3	5	
Emerson	John Albert	m.	SD	21 Jan. 1882	3	6	
Emerson	Sarah A.	d.	DR	12 May 1884	3	2	
Emerson	Sarah A.	d.	PCo	7 May 1884	3	5	
Emerson	Sarah A.	d.	PWA	10 May 1884	3	5	
Emerson	Sarah A.	d.	RRF	15 May 1884	5	6	
Emerson	Sarah A.	d.	SD	17 May 1884	3	5	
Emery	Eva J.	m.	PCo	11 Oct. 1882	3	6	
Emmett	Temple	b.	SD	14 May 1881	3	8	
Emparan	Mr. & Mrs.	b.	SWI	9 June 1883	2	4	
Emparan	Ricardo	b.	PWA	16 June 1883	3	7	
Emparan	Ricardo	b.	SD	7 Nov. 1885	3	4	
Emparan	Ricardo	b.	SIT	31 Oct. 1885	2	3	
Emparan	Richardo	b.	DR	11 Nov. 1885	2	2	
England	Charles	b.	PCo	18 June 1884	3	4	
England	Charles	b.	SD	28 June 1884	3	4	
England	Marian L.	m.	PCo	10 Jan. 1883	3	6	
England	Maron L.	m.	SD	6 Jan. 1883	2	5	
England	Willard A.	m.	SD	12 Feb. 1881	3	8	
England	William A.	m.	DR	21 Feb. 1881	3	1	
Englehardt	John	b.	DR	9 Nov. 1885	2	2	
Englehardt	John	b.	PCo	4 Nov. 1885	2	5	
Englehart	S. A.	b.	PCo	7 May 1884	3	5	
Englehart	S. A.	b.	SD	22 Oct. 1881	3	6	
Englehart	Sam A.	b.	DR	3 Oct. 1881	2	3	
Englehart	Sam A.	b.	RRF	1 May 1884	5	6	
Englehart	Sam A.	b.	SD	10 May 1884	2	4	
Englehart	Samuel A.	b.	RRF	29 Sept. 1881	2	6	
Engler	George	b.	PCo	20 Feb. 1884	3	6	
Engler	George	b.	PWA	23 Feb. 1884	3	6	
Engler	George	b.	SD	1 Mar. 1884	6	6	
Engler	George	b.	SIT	26 Sept. 1885	2	2	
English	John	d.	DR	22 Oct. 1881	2	4	
English	John	d.	PCo	26 Oct. 1881	3	4	

(1) Surname	(2) Given Name	(3)	(4)	(5) Date	(6) Pg	(7) Col	(8) Comments
English	John	d.	SD	22 Oct. 1881	3	6	
English	John M.	m.	SD	19 Mar. 1881	3	1	
English	Nancy T.	m.	SD	10 Jan. 1885	2	6	
Ennis	C. L.	m.	CR	15 Jan. 1881	5	5	
Ennis	C. L.	b.	CR	21 Feb. 1885	3	1	
Ennis	C. L.	m.	DR	11 Jan. 1881	3	2	
Ennis	C. L.	b.	PCo	18 Feb. 1885	3	6	
Ennis	C. L.	b.	SD	21 Feb. 1885	2	5	
Ennis	Charles L.	m.	SD	8 Jan. 1881	3	8	
Enos	John	b.	PCo	10 Sept. 1884	3	6	
Enos	John	b.	PWA	6 Sept. 1884	3	4	
Enos	John	b.	SD	20 Sept. 1884	2	5	
Enos	John (son of)	d.	PWA	20 Sept. 1884	3	4	
Equi	Joseph	b.	SD	14 Mar. 1885	5	5	
Erringer	E. E., Mrs.	d.	DR	25 July 1881	2	3	
Erringer	E. E., Mrs.	d.	RRF	21 July 1881	2	4	
Erringer	E. E., Mrs.	d.	SD	6 Aug. 1881	3	8	
Erwin	May	m.	DR	19 Dec. 1884	3	2	
Erwin	May	m.	PCo	17 Dec. 1884	2	4	
Erwin	May	m.	PWA	20 Dec. 1884	3	4	
Erwin	May	m.	SD	13 Dec. 1884	2	5	
Erwin	N.	b.	PCo	6 Apr. 1881	3	5	
Erwin	N.	b.	SD	16 Apr. 1881	3	8	
Erwin	Nicholas	b.	PC	1 Aug. 1883	3	6	
Erwin	Nicholas	b.	PWA	4 Aug. 1883	3	7	
Erwin	Nicholas	b.	SD	4 Aug. 1883	2	5	
Estes	George	b.	SIT	21 Nov. 1885	2	3	
Estes	George W.	b.	SWI	26 May 1883	3	4	
Estes	Lucinda	m.	DR	28 Nov. 1881	2	3	
Eustace	Ernest W.	m.	SD	10 Jan. 1885	2	6	
Eustace	Maggie	m.	PCo	31 Dec. 1884	3	4	
Eustace	Maggie	m.	PWA	27 Dec. 1884	2	5	
Evans	Abraham	d.	PCo	17 Sept. 1884	3	6	
Evans	Abraham	d.	SD	27 Sept. 1884	2	5	
Evans	Abram	d.	PWA	20 Sept. 1884	3	2&4	
Evans	Charles J.	p.	DD	19 July 1883	3	2	
Evans	E. W. M.	m.	PC	18 July 1883	3	5	
Evans	E. W. M.	b.	PCo	10 Dec. 1884	3	5	
Evans	E. W. M.	m.	PWA	14 July 1883	3	6	
Evans	E. W. M.	b.	PWA	13 Dec. 1884	3	4	
Evans	E. W. M.	b.	SD	27 Dec. 1884	2	4	
Evans	Edward W. M.	m.	DD	13 July 1883	3	3	

(1) Surname	(2) Given Name	(3)	(4)	(5) Date	(6) Pg	(7) Col	(8) Comments
Evans	Rose	m.	SD	6 June 1885	2	4	
Evart	John B.	d.	PC	9 May 1883	3	5	
Evart	John B.	d.	SD	19 May 1883	3	5	
Evart	John R.	m.	PWA	12 May 1883	3	8	
Eveleth	Cornelia C.	d.	PCo	25 Feb. 1885	3	6	
Eveleth	Cornelia	d.	SD	21 Feb. 1885	2	5	
Eveleth	J. A.	b.	PCo	6 Aug. 1884	2	4	
Evelith	J. A.	b.	DR	4 Aug. 1884	3	3	
Everts	Clifford	b.	SD	7 Apr. 1883	2	6	
Ewell	P. D. F.	d.	SIT	21 Jan. 1888	3	2	
Ewell	P. J.	m.	SD	11 Aug. 1883	2	7	
Ewing	E. P.	o.	CR	21 Nov. 1885	1	4	

F

(1) Surname	(2) Given Name	(3)	(4)	(5) Date	(6) Pg	(7) Col	(8) Comments
Fairbanks	Frank	m.	DD	6 Oct. 1883	3	3	
Fairbanks	Frank	m.	PCo	5 Aug. 1885	3	6	
Fairbanks	Frank	m.	SD	13 Oct. 1883	3	4	
Fairbanks	Hattie J.	d.	PCo	12 Nov. 1884	3	5	
Fairbanks	Hattie J.	d.	PWA	15 Nov. 1884	3	4	
Fairbanks	Percy M.	m.	DR	19 Dec. 1884	3	2	
Fairbanks	Percy M.	m.	PCo	17 Dec. 1884	2	4	
Fairbanks	Percy M.	m.	PWA	20 Dec. 1884	3	4	
Fairbanks	Percy M.	m.	SD	13 Dec. 1884	2	5	
Fairbrother	George H.	m.	PCo	16 Jan. 1884	3	6	also 23 Jan. p. 3 col. 3
Fairbrother	George H.	m.	PWA	19 Jan. 1884	3	7	
Fairbrother	George H.	m.	SD	19 Jan. 1884	3	6	
Fairman	(female)	b.	DR	25 Mar. 1884	3	3	
Fairman	Reathe	d.	PCo	26 Mar. 1884	3	6	
Fairman	Reathe	d.	SD	29 Mar. 1884	2	5	
Fairman	William (dau. of)	d.	RRF	27 Mar. 1884	2	3	Fulton
Fairman	William (dau. of)	d.	SD	5 Apr. 1884	3	4	
Faith	Mary	m.	PC	16 May 1883	3	5	
Faith	Mary	m.	PWA	19 May 1883	3	8	
Falker	F. D.	d.	RRF	13 Oct. 1881	3	6	
Fanning	Carrie	m.	SD	11 Aug. 1883	2	7	
Fanning	May	m.	PWA	18 Aug. 1883	3	2	
Fannon	Peter	d.	SD	5 Mar. 1881	3	8	
Farley	Lizzie	d.	DR	9 Nov. 1885	2	2	
Farley	Lizzie	d.	PCo	4 Nov. 1885	2	5	
Farley	Lizzie	d.	SD	7 Nov. 1885	3	4	
Farley	R. K.	m.	DR	22 Dec. 1884	2	2	
Farley	R. K.	m.	PCo	24 Dec. 1884	3	4	
Farley	R. K.	m.	PWA	20 Dec. 1884	3	4	
Farley	W. F.	b.	PC	2 May 1883	3	5	
Farley	W. F.	b.	SD	12 May 1883	2	6	
Farmer	(female)	b.	DR	5 Feb. 1884	3	3	
Farmer	B. F.	m.	PCo	7 Mar. 1883	3	5	
Farmer	Benjamin F.	m.	SD	10 Mar. 1883	3	1	
Farmer	C. L.	m.	CR	2 June 1883	3	3	
Farmer	Charles R.	m.	SD	15 Aug. 1885	1	7	
Farmer	Charles R.	m.	SD	22 Aug. 1885	6	2	
Farmer	E. T. (dau. of)	d.	PCo	3 Sept. 1884	2	5	

(1) Surname	(2) Given Name	(3)	(4)	(5) Date	(6) Pg	(7) Col	(8) Comments
Farmer	E. T.	d.	CR	24 Oct. 1885	3	3	
Farmer	E. T.	b.	PCo	13 Feb. 1884	3	6	
Farmer	E. T.	d.	PCo	28 Oct. 1885	3	4	
Farmer	E. T.	d.	SD	24 Oct. 1885	3	3	also p. 5 col. 3&4
Farmer	Enna Mary	d.	DR	10 July 1885	3	4	
Farmer	Euna Mary	d.	SD	11 July 1885	5	6	
Farmer	G. W.	m.	HE	23 Feb. 1882	2	4	
Farmer	George	m.	DR	24 Feb. 1882	2	3	
Farmer	George	m.	PCo	1 Mar. 1882	2	4	
Farmer	George	m.	SD	25 Feb. 1882	3	6	
Farmer	George L.	m.	RRF	8 May 1884	5	6	
Farmer	John H.	d.	SD	15 Jan. 1881	3	8	
Farmer	John Parton	d.	DR	6 July 1882	3	2	
Farmer	John Paxton	d.	PCo	28 June 1882	3	5	
Farmer	John Paxton	d.	SD	8 July 1882	2	5	
Farmer	Martha	d.	PCo	10 Sept. 1884	3	6	
Farmer	Martha	d.	SD	13 Sept. 1884	3	4	
Farmer	Mr.	m.	CR	18 Feb. 1882	5	2	
Farmer	Mr.	m.	RRF	16 Feb. 1882	3	6	
Farmer	Rebecca	d.	DR	23 Aug. 1884	3	4	
Farmer	Rebecca	d.	SD	6 Sept. 1884	2	5	
Farmer	Samuel	b.	SD	11 Mar. 1882	3	6	
Farmer	William	d.	SD	26 May 1883	3	2	
Farmschlag	Peter	d.	DD	10 Sept. 1883	3	3	
Farmschlag	Peter	d.	SD	15 Sept. 1883	2	4	
Farnell	William	m.	CR	11 Aug. 1883	3	1	
Farnell	William	m.	DD	11 Aug. 1883	3	1	
Farnell	William	m.	PC	8 Aug. 1883	3	6	
Farnell	William	m.	SD	18 Aug. 1883	2	6	
Farnsworth	Clara	m.	DD	10 Sept. 1883	3	3	
Farnsworth	Clara	m.	PWA	8 Set. 1883	3	8	
Farnsworth	Clara	m.	SD	15 Sept. 1883	2	4	
Farnsworth	Lizzie B.	m.	PCo	23 Nov. 1881	3	5	
Farnsworth	Lizzie B.	m.	SD	26 Nov. 1881	3	8	
Farnsworth	Lizzie E.	m.	DR	25 Nov. 1881	2	3	
Farnsworth	Mamie	m.	PCo	10 June 1885	3	6	
Farnsworth	May	m.	SD	13 June 1885	3	5	
Farquar	C. S.	b.	CR	30 Apr. 1881	5	5	
Farquar	C. S.	b.	DR	30 Apr. 1881	2	2	
Farquar	C. S.	b.	PCo	27 Apr. 1881	3	5	
Farquar	C. S.	b.	SD	7 May 1881	3	8	
Farrel	James	b.	SD	13 Aug. 1881	3	8	

(1) Surname	(2) Given Name	(3)	(4)	(5) Date	(6) Pg	(7) Col	(8) Comments
Farrell	Michael	m.	SD	27 Sept. 1884	2	5	
Farrington	George	d.	SD	5 May 1883	1	7	Valley Ford
Faught	Ella	m.	DD	27 Aug. 1883	3	3	
Faught	Ella	m.	SD	1 Sept. 1883	2	7	
Faught	L. C.	b.	DR	26 July 1884	3	3	
Faught	L. C.	b.	PCo	30 July 1884	3	6	
Faulds	P. K.	m.	DD	16 July 1883	3	2	
Faulkner	James	p.	DD	24 July 1883	3	2	
Faulkner	James	m.	DR	1 Mar. 1882	2	3	
Faulkner	James	d.	DR	2 Oct. 1882	3	2	
Faulkner	James	m.	PCo	8 Mar. 1882	3	5	
Faulkner	James	d.	RRF	5 Oct. 1882	3	1	
Faulkner	James	d.	SD	7 Oct. 1882	1	4	Masonic Cem., Sebastopol
Faulkner	James	m.	SD	25 Feb. 1882	3	6	
Fauste	Mary	m.	SD	25 Oct. 1884	2	5	
Favalai	Roseina	m.	PCo	1 Apr. 1885	3	6	
Favalai	Roseina	m.	PWA	4 Apr. 1885	3	6	
Favalai	Roseina	m.	SD	4 Apr. 1885	2	5	
Faylor	Mary J.	d.	PWA	12 July 1884	3	6	
Faylor	Mary	d.	DR	7 July 1884	3	3	
Faylor	Mary	d.	PCo	16 July 1884	3	6	
Fedderson	M.	b.	PCo	3 May 1882	3	5	
Fedderson	M.	b.	SD	6 May 1882	3	6	
Feehan	Mary	d.	DR	25 Aug. 1885	3	4	
Feehan	Mary	d.	SD	29 Aug. 1885	2	4	
Feehan	William	d.	DR	29 Nov. 1881	2	3	
Feehan	William	d.	PCo	7 Dec. 1881	3	5	
Feehan	William	d.	SD	26 Nov. 1881	3	8	
Felker	Henry	d.	DR	7 Oct. 1881	2	3	
Felker	Henry	d.	SD	15 Oct. 1881	3	8	
Fell	Erastus	d.	DR	8 May 1882	2	3	
Felt	Theodore D.	d.	PCo	20 Feb. 1884	3	6	
Felt	Theodore D.	d.	RRF	21 Feb. 1884	2	3	
Felt	Theodore	d.	DR	7 Feb. 1884	3	3	
Felton	Levi	m.	DD	22 Sept. 1883	3	2	
Fengar	Annie	m.	DR	24 Oct. 1882	3	2	
Fenger	Annie	m.	PCo	18 Oct. 1882	3	6	
Fenn	Frederick	d.	RRF	6 July 1882	3	1	
Ferguson	Charles F.	m.	PC	4 Apr. 1883	3	5	
Ferguson	David	m.	HE	11 Oct. 1883	2	2	
Ferguson	David	m.	RRF	11 Oct. 1883	2	5	
Ferguson	David	m.	RRF	25 Oct. 1883	2	4	

(1) Surname	(2) Given Name	(3)	(4)	(5) Date	(6) Pg	(7) Col	(8) Comments
Ferguson	W. W., Jr.	m.	RRF	27 Dec. 1883	2	2	
Ferguson	W. W.	o.	RRF	16 Nov. 1882	2	4	
Ferguson	W. W.	o.	SWI	24 Nov. 1882	2	3	
Ferguson	William W., Jr.	m.	PCo	16 Jan. 1884	3	6	
Ferguson	William W., Jr.	m.	SD	19 Jan. 1884	3	6	
Ferguson	William	o.	RRF	23 Nov. 1882	3	2	
Fernald	Allen Johnson	m.	PWA	1 Dec. 1883	3	6	
Fernald	Johnson	m.	DD	4 Dec. 1883	3	3	
Fernald	Johnson	b.	PCo	10 Dec. 1884	3	5	
Fernald	Johnson	b.	PWA	13 Dec. 1884	3	4	
Fernald	Johnson	m.	SD	8 Dec. 1883	3	1	
Fernn	Frederick	d.	CR	8 July 1882	5	3	San Francisco
Ferral	John	m.	PCo	4 Feb. 1885	3	6	
Ferry	John	b.	CR	6 May 1882	5	1	
Ferry	John	b.	DR	13 May 1882	2	3	
Ferry	John	b.	PCo	10 May 1882	3	5	
Ferry	John	b.	SD	13 May 1882	2	4	
Fessenden	G. I.	d.	PCo	5 Mar. 1884	3	6	
Fessenden	G. L.	d.	RRF	28 Feb. 1884	2	3	also 6 Mar, p. 2 col. 2
Fewell	Ella Jane	m.	DR	26 Sept. 1881	3	2	
Fewell	Ella Jane	m.	RRF	22 Sept. 1881	2	5	
Fewell	Ella Jane	m.	SD	8 Oct. 1881	3	8	
Field	Jennie	d.	PCo	4 June 1884	3	5	
Field	Jennie Racilla	d.	SD	14 June 1884	2	4	
Field	W. E.	b.	RRF	27 Dec. 1883	2	2	
Field	Walter	b.	PCo	19 Dec. 1883	3	4	
Fields	Olive	m.	CR	18 Feb. 1882	5	1	
Fields	Olive	m.	RRF	2 Mar. 1882	4	1	
Fields	Walter E.	m.	PCo	20 Sept. 1882	3	6	
Fields	Walter E.	m.	RRF	14 Sept. 1882	2	4	
Fields	Walter E.	m.	SD	23 Sept. 1882	3	6	
Filben	Thomas	m.	SD	10 June 1882	3	2	
Filben	Thomas	b.	SD	6 Sept. 1884	2	5	
Filippini	G.	d.	PWA	5 Jan. 1883	3	3	
Fillipini	James	d.	SD	2 Dec. 1882	3	1	
Fillippini	James	d.	DR	1 Dec. 1882	3	1	
Fillippini	James	d.	PCo	29 Nov. 1882	3	2	Cypress Hill Cemetery
Fillmore	Wing H.	m.	PCo	6 Aug. 1884	2	4	
Filton	Edward	d.	PCo	30 Dec. 1885	3	2	
Finch	Cyrilla J.	d.	DR	8 Aug. 1881	3	2	
Fine	Emsley	b.	PCo	16 Apr. 1884	3	5	
Fine	Emsley	b.	PWA	19 Apr. 1884	3	6	

(1) Surname	(2) Given Name	(3)	(4)	(5) Date	(6) Pg	(7) Col	(8) Comments
Fine	Mary	m.	CR	29 Apr. 1882	1	2	
Fine	Mary	m.	DR	22 Apr. 1882	3	1	
Fine	Mary	m.	PCo	26 Apr. 1882	3	4	
Fine	Mary	m.	SD	22 Apr. 1882	3	3	
Fine	Mr. & Mrs.	b.	SD	9 Apr. 1881	3	2	birth occurred in 1845
Finegan	Anna	m.	DR	21 Apr. 1884	3	2	
Finlay	Josie	m.	RRF	13 Jan. 1881	2	5	
Finlay	Josie	m.	SD	22 Jan. 1881	3	8	
Finley	W. A.	b.	DR	13 Mar. 1882	2	2	
Finley	W. A.	b.	PCo	22 Mar. 1882	3	5	
Finley	W. A.	b.	SD	18 Mar. 1882	3	5	
Finnegan	Anna	m.	SD	19 Apr. 1884	3	4	
Finnegan	James Clinton	d.	DR	13 Feb. 1884	3	3	
Finnegan	James Clinton	d.	PCo	20 Feb. 1884	3	6	
Finnegan	James Clinton	d.	SD	16 Feb. 1884	2	5	
Finnegan	James	d.	DR	15 Feb. 1884	3	2	
Finnerty	Thomas	m.	SD	13 Aug. 1881	3	8	
Finney	P.	d.	SD	26 Nov. 1881	3	2	
Finney	T. B.	b.	PC	1 Aug. 1883	3	6	
Finney	T. B. C.	b.	DD	28 July 1883	3	2	
Finney	T. B. C.	b.	SD	4 Aug. 1883	2	5	
Firebaugh	H. C.	b.	RRF	3 Feb. 1881	3	4	
Fiscus	George W.	m.	SD	3 Jan. 1885	2	7	
Fish	John R.	m.	SD	6 Sept. 1884	2	5	
Fisher	A. L.	o.	PWA	16 Feb. 1884	3	2	
Fisher	Helen A.	d.	DR	20 Aug. 1885	3	4	
Fisher	Helen A.	d.	SD	29 Aug. 1885	2	4	
Fisher	Sam, Jr.	m.	DR	21 May 1884	3	2	
Fisher	Sam, Jr.	m.	PWA	24 May 1884	3	5	
Fisher	Sam, Jr.	m.	SD	24 May 1884	1	6	also p. 2 col. 3
Fisk	George S.	m.	PCo	16 Dec. 1885	3	6	
Fitch	Bessie	d.	DR	26 Mar. 1881	3	2	
Fitch	Bessie	d.	RRF	31 Mar. 1881	2	4	
Fitch	Earnest	d.	DD	20 Oct. 1883	3	3	
Fitch	Ernest	d.	SD	27 Oct. 1883	3	4	
Fitch	John B.	m.	HE	23 Feb. 1882	2	4	
Fitch	John B.	m.	PCo	15 Feb. 1882	3	4	
Fitch	John B.	d.	RRF	31 Mar. 1881	2	4	
Fitch	John B.	m.	RRF	16 Feb. 1882	2	4	
Fitch	John B.	m.	SD	18 Feb. 1882	3	6	
Fitch	John E.	m.	DR	11 Feb. 1882	2	3	
Fitch	John B., Mrs.	d.	RRF	24 Mar. 1881	2	4	Mendocino City

(1) Surname	(2) Given Name	(3)	(4)	(5) Date	(6) Pg	(7) Col	(8) Comments
Fitch	Joseph	b.	DR	5 Nov. 1881	2	3	
Fitch	Joseph	b.	DR	24 Sept. 1885	3	4	
Fitch	Joseph	d.	DR	24 Sept. 1885	3	4	
Fitch	Joseph	b.	PCo	9 Nov. 1881	3	5	
Fitch	Joseph	b.	PCo	16 Nov. 1881	3	5	
Fitch	Joseph	b.	PCo	10 Jan. 1883	3	6	
Fitch	Joseph	b.	PCo	22 Apr. 1885	3	6	
Fitch	Joseph	b.	RRF	10 Nov. 1881	2	4	
Fitch	Joseph	b.	RRF	4 Jan. 1883	2	2	
Fitch	Joseph	b.	SD	12 Nov. 1881	3	7	
Fitch	Joseph	b.	SD	6 Jan. 1883	2	5	
Fitch	Joseph	b.	SRR	1 Oct. 1885	3	3	
Fitch	Joseph (son of)	d.	RRF	18 Oct. 1883	2	4	
Fitch	Joseph (son of)	d.	SRR	1 Oct. 1885	3	3	
Fitch	Juce	d.	CR	26 Mar. 1881	5	5	
Fitch	Nettie	d.	DR	12 Aug. 1882	3	2	
Fitch	Nettie	d.	RRF	17 Aug. 1882	2	3	
Fitts	Mary M.	d.	DR	6 Sept. 1881	2	3	
Fitzgerald	A. L., Mrs.	d.	DR	11 Dec. 1882	3	1	San Jose
Fitzgerald	A. L., Mrs.	d.	SD	16 Dec. 1882	3	6	
Fitzgerald	Willie	d.	PCo	31 Jan. 1883	3	5	
Fitzgerald	Willie	d.	SD	27 Jan. 1883	3	6	
Fitzroy	Mary E.	m.	SD	12 Mar. 1881	3	8	
Flag	F.	b.	DR	31 Jan. 1882	2	3	
Flage	Mary A.	m.	RRF	23 Aug. 1883	2	4	
Flaherty	Patrick	d.	SD	4 Apr. 1885	2	5	
Flanagan	John P.	b.	SD	22 Jan. 1881	3	8	
Flannery	Margaret	d.	PCo	26 Oct. 1881	3	4	
Flannery	Margaret	d.	SD	22 Oct. 1881	3	6	
Fletcher	William R.	m.	DR	9 May 1881	2	2	
Fletcher	William R.	m.	SD	14 May 1881	3	8	
Flint	Isaac A.	o.	SD	11 Apr. 1885	1	3	
Flint	Sarah E.	o.	SD	11 Apr. 1885	1	3	
Flippen	John Wilson	d.	SD	8 Nov. 1884	2	5	
Flippin	Wilson	d.	DR	2 Nov. 1884	2	2	
Flood	Michael	m.	DD	10 Oct. 1883	3	3	
Flood	Michael	m.	SD	13 Oct. 1883	1	3	also p. 3 col. 4
Florizone	Henry	m.	PWA	22 Nov. 1884	3	4	
Florizoone	Henry	m.	DR	21 Nov. 1884	3	2	
Florizoone	Henry	m.	PCo	19 Nov. 1884	3	5	
Flournoy	W. H.	b.	PCo	15 Mar. 1882	3	4	
Flournoy	W. H.	b.	SD	11 Mar. 1882	3	6	

(1) Surname	(2) Given Name	(3)	(4)	(5) Date	(6) Pg	(7) Col	(8) Comments
Fluger	William	d.	PCo	16 Dec. 1885	3	6	
Flynn	Maria A.	m.	PCo	21 Jan. 1885	2	5	
Flynn	Maria A.	m.	PWA	24 Jan. 1885	3	5	
Focha	Manuel	b.	PCo	21 Dec. 1881	3	5	
Focha	Manuel	b.	SD	31 Dec. 1881	3	6	
Fochetti	Julius	b.	PCo	13 Aug. 1884	3	4	
Fochetti	Julius	b.	PWA	16 Aug. 1884	3	4	
Fochetti	Julius	b.	SD	13 Aug. 1884	2	4	
Fogerty	Michael	d.	PC	1 Aug. 1883	3	6	
Fogerty	Michael (son of)	d.	RRF	26 July 1883	2	4	
Fogg	David	d.	DR	25 Aug. 1881	2	3	
Fogg	David	d.	SD	27 Aug. 1881	3	8	
Foley	Dennis	b.	PCo	26 Oct. 1881	3	4	
Foley	Dennis	b.	SD	5 Nov. 1881	3	6	
Foley	Dennis	b.	SD	22 Oct. 1881	3	6	
Folks	Charles	d.	SD	6 June 1885	2	4	
Folks	John, Mrs.	d.	DR	30 Mar. 1881	2	2	
Folks	Louise	d.	SD	9 Apr. 1881	3	8	
Folks	Nellie	m.	SD	24 Jan. 1885	5	5	
Folks	Victoria L.	d.	RRF	31 Mar. 1881	3	4	
Folsom	Stephen M.	m.	DR	22 Nov. 1884	3	2	
Folsom	Stephen M.	m.	PCo	26 Nov. 1884	3	5	
Folsom	Stephen M.	m.	SD	23 Nov. 1884	2	6	also p. 3 col. 4.
Footman	Henry E.	m.	SD	1 June 1881	3	7	
Foppiano	John	b.	RRF	4 Jan. 1883	2	2	
Foppiano	Louisa	d.	HE	4 Oct. 1883	2	4	
Foppiano	Louisa	d.	PC	18 Apr. 1883	3	5	
Foppiano	Louisa	d.	RRF	12 Apr. 1883	2	5	
Ford	George	m.	DR	4 Mar. 1884	3	3	
Ford	George	b.	DR	5 Sept. 1885	3	4	
Ford	George	m.	PCo	12 Mar. 1884	3	6	
Ford	George	b.	PCo	16 Sept. 1885	3	6	
Ford	Mary	d.	PCo	22 Oct. 1884	3	6	
Ford	Mary	d.	PWA	25 Oct. 1884	3	4	
Ford	Mary	d.	SD	25 Oct. 1884	2	5	
Ford	Mr. & Mrs.	b.	CR	13 Oct. 1883	3	1	
Foreman	Kate	m.	PCo	15 July 1885	3	6	
Foreman	Kate	m.	SD	11 July 1885	5	6	
Forman	Mr.	b.	CR	18 Nov. 1882	3	3	
Forman	Mr.	b.	RRF	30 Nov. 1882	2	3	
Forman	Mr. & Mrs.	b.	DR	20 Nov. 1882	3	2	
Forman	Mr. & Mrs.	b.	PCo	22 Nov. 1882	3	5	

(1) Surname	(2) Given Name	(3)	(4)	(5) Date	(6) Pg	(7) Col	(8) Comments
Formschlag	Peter	d.	PWA	8 Sept. 1883	3	8	
Forpiano	John	b.	PCo	3 Jan. 1883	3	4	
Forpiano	John	b.	SD	30 Dec. 1882	3	6	
Forrest	Lucy L.	d.	DR	21 July 1884	2	2	
Forrest	Lucy L.	d.	PCo	23 July 1884	3	6	
Forsman	Kate	m.	DR	6 July 1885	3	3	
Forster	Annie	d.	CR	26 Mar. 1881	5	5	
Forster	Annie	d.	DR	26 Mar. 1881	3	2	
Forster	Annie	d.	RRF	24 Mar. 1881	2	4	Oak Mound, Healdsburg
Forster	Annie	d.	SD	2 Apr. 1881	3	8	
Forsyth	T.	b.	DR	20 Mar. 1882	2	3	
Forsyth	T.	b.	PCo	29 Mar. 1882	3	5	
Forsyth	T.	b.	SD	25 Mar. 1882	3	6	
Forsythe	William H.	o.	DR	28 Aug. 1882	3	1	
Forsythe	William H.	d.	PCo	8 Oct. 1884	3	6	
Forsythe	William H.	d.	SD	4 Oct. 1884	3	5	
Forsythe	William	o.	SD	2 Sept. 1882	3	2	
Foss	Charley	m.	HE	12 Jan. 1882	3	2	
Foss	Clark	d.	SD	29 Aug. 1885	5	3	
Foss	Clark	d.	SIT	29 Aug. 1885	3	3	
Foss	Harriet L.	m.	SD	21 Jan. 1882	3	6	
Foss	Sarah	d.	SD	23 Nov. 1884	2	6	
Foster	Ada R.	d.	DR	24 Oct. 1884	3	3	
Foster	Ada R.	d.	PCo	22 Oct. 1884	3	6	
Foster	Ada R.	d.	PWA	25 Oct. 1884	3	4	
Foster	Blanche	m.	DD	23 Nov. 1883	3	2	
Foster	Blanche	m.	RRF	22 Nov. 1883	2	3	
Foster	Blanche	m.	SD	1 Dec. 1883	3	4	
Foster	Charles	d.	CR	25 Feb. 1882	1	2	
Foster	Charles	d.	RRF	23 Feb. 1882	2	3	
Foster	Charles H.	m.	SD	23 Nov. 1884	2	6	
Foster	Ida R.	d.	SD	8 Nov. 1884	2	5	
Foster	Joseph	d.	SD	9 June 1883	3	2	
Foster	W. B.	d.	SD	21 Mar. 1885	1	7	also p. 5 col. 2
Foster	Winston E.	d.	DR	4 Mar. 1882	2	3	
Foster	Winston E.	d.	PCo	8 Mar. 1882	3	5	
Foster	Winston E.	d.	RRF	2 Mar. 1882	2	4	
Foster	Winston E.	d.	SD	11 Mar. 1882	3	6	
Fouchek	Maria	d.	PC	18 Apr. 1883	3	5	
Fouchey	Maria	d.	PWA	21 Apr. 1883	3	8	
Fowler	Annie	m.	DR	18 June 1884	3	3	
Fowler	Annie	m.	PCo	15 June 1884	3	4	

(1) Surname	(2) Given Name	(3)	(4)	(5) Date	(6) Pg	(7) Col	(8) Comments
Fowler	H. R.	d.	PC	18 July 1883	3	5	
Fowler	H. R.	d.	PWA	14 July 1883	3	6	
Fowler	John, Mrs.	o.	SD	4 Feb. 1882	2	4	
Fowler	Laura E.	m.	SD	4 Feb. 1882	3	6	
Fowler	Mr.	d.	SD	3 Oct. 1885	5	3	murdered 1846
Fowler	Mr.	d.	SD	17 Oct. 1885	5	1	murdered 1846
Fowler	W.	m.	DR	7 Nov. 1881	2	3	
Fox	(female)	b.	DR	7 June 1884	3	3	
Fox	C. M.	b.	PC	9 May 1883	3	5	
Fox	C. M.	b.	PCo	11 June 1884	3	5	
Fox	Charles Marshall	d.	PCo	4 Oct. 1882	3	6	
Fox	Henry	b.	CR	28 May 1881	5	5	
Fox	Henry	b.	RRF	26 May 1881	2	5	
Fox	Henry	b.	SD	4 June 1881	3	8	
Fox	Sadie L.	m.	PCo	13 Sept. 1882	3	7	
Fox	Sadie L.	m.	SD	9 Sept. 1882	3	6	
Fox	Thomas H.	d.	DR	22 Dec. 1884	2	2	
Foy	Hugh	b.	SD	25 Feb. 1882	3	6	
Foy	Mr. & Mr.	b.	PCo	22 Feb. 1882	3	5	
Foy	Mr. & Mrs.	b.	DR	13 Feb. 1882	2	3	
Foy	Mr. & Mrs.	b.	SD	11 Feb. 1882	3	6	
Foye	Mr. & Mrs.	b.	DD	27 Dec. 1883	3	3	
Fragolia	G. B. (dau. of)	d.	PC	20 June 1883	3	6	
Fragolia	G. B. (dau. of)	d.	RRF	14 June 1883	2	3	
Frain	Mr. & Mrs.	b.	CR	11 Oct. 1884	3	1	
Frain	Mr. & Mrs.	b.	PCo	15 Oct. 1884	3	6	
Frain	Mr. & Mrs.	b.	SD	25 Oct. 1884	2	5	
Fraiser	M.	b.	DR	11 Sept. 1885	3	4	
Frame	R. A.	m.	DR	28 Dec. 1881	2	2	
Frame	R. A.	m.	PCo	4 Jan. 1882	3	7	
Frame	R. A.	m.	SD	31 Dec. 1881	3	6	
France	Andrew	b.	DD	8 Sept. 1883	3	3	
France	Andrew	b.	RRF	6 Sept. 1883	2	4	
France	Andrew	b.	SD	15 Sept. 1883	2	4	
France	Jennie E.	d.	DR	29 July 1885	3	4	
France	Jennie E.	d.	PCo	29 July 1885	3	4	
Francisco	Imperial	d.	DR	7 Mar. 1882	3	1	
Frank	B. F.	m.	DR	15 June 1881	2	3	
Frank	B. F.	m.	PCo	22 June 1881	3	5	
Frank	B. F.	m.	SD	18 June 1881	3	8	
Frank	Samuel	m.	DR	31 Oct. 1881	2	3	
Frank	Samuel	m.	PCo	2 Nov. 1881	3	5	

(1) Surname	(2) Given Name	(3)	(4)	(5) Date	(6) Pg	(7) Col	(8) Comments
Frank	Samuel	m.	SD	29 Oct. 1881	3	6	
Franke	Emil	m.	SD	17 Dec. 1881	3	7	
Franklin	B. F.	b.	PCo	12 July 1882	3	5	
Franklin	B. F.	b.	SD	15 July 1882	2	4	
Franz	Minnie	m.	PC	4 July 1883	3	5	
Franz	Minnie	m.	PWA	30 June 1883	3	7	
Franz	Minnie	m.	SD	30 June 1883	3	5	
Fraser	Bruce	m.	PWA	8 Sept. 1883	3	8	
Fraser	Julia M.	d.	SD	24 June 1882	3	2&5	
Frasier	Jessie J.	d.	PCo	1 June 1881	3	4	
Frasier	Jessie J.	d.	SD	11 June 1881	3	8	
Frasier	M.	b.	PCo	9 Sept. 1885	3	6	
Frasier	Mary E.	m.	SD	25 June 1881	3	8	
Frasier	Mary J.	m.	DR	10 June 1881	2	2	
Frazier	E. H.	m.	CR	26 Feb. 1881	5	3	
Frazier	E. H.	m.	CR	26 Feb. 1884	5	2	
Frazier	E. H.	m.	DR	1 Mar. 1881	3	2	
Frazier	E. H.	m.	SD	5 Mar. 1881	3	8	
Frazier	Edna	d.	DD	7 Sept. 1883	3	3	
Free	R. H.	b.	DR	6 May 1882	2	3	
Freeborn	John G.	d.	PCo	22 Mar. 1882	3	5	
Freeborn	John Green	d.	RRF	9 Mar. 1882	2	4	
Freeborn	John Green	d.	SD	18 Mar. 1882	3	5	
Freeborn	John	d.	RRF	2 Mar. 1882	3	3	
Freeman	Edward A.	m.	SD	19 Mar. 1881	3	8	
Freeman	Henry	d.	DR	3 July 1884	2	2	
Freeman	Henry	d.	PCo	16 July 1884	3	6	
Freeman	James D.	d.	CR	2 May 1885	5	2	
Freeman	Laura L.	m.	DD	4 Oct. 1883	3	2	
Freeman	Laura L.	m.	PWA	6 Oct. 1883	3	8	
Freeman	Lucretia	m.	DR	12 Mar. 1884	3	2	
Freeman	Lucretia	m.	PCo	19 Mar. 1884	3	6	
Freeman	Lucretia	m.	SD	22 Mar. 1884	2	4	
Freeman	Marilla	m.	PCo	6 May 1885	3	6	
Freeman	Marilla	m.	SD	9 May 1885	2	5	
Freeman	Nadien J.	m.	PCo	7 Sept. 1881	2	4	
Freeman	Nadien	m.	DR	13 Sept. 1881	2	3	
Freeman	Nadien	m.	SD	24 Sept. 1881	3	8	
Frehe	Louis	b.	DR	8 Nov. 1884	2	2	
Frehe	Louis	b.	PCo	12 Nov. 1884	3	5	
French	Charles F.	m.	PCo	11 Oct. 1882	3	6	
French	Minnie	d.	CR	10 Sept. 1881	5	2	

(1) Surname	(2) Given Name	(3)	(4)	(5) Date	(6) Pg	(7) Col	(8) Comments
Freshhower	C. C.	b.	PCo	23 Nov. 1881	3	5	
Freshour	C. C.	b.	RRF	17 Nov. 1881	2	3	
Freshour	C. C.	b.	SD	26 Nov. 1881	3	8	
Freshower	C. C.	b.	SD	3 Dec. 1881	3	8	
Fressenden	G. L.	d.	SD	8 Mar. 1884	6	5	
Friedlander	Fannie	m.	PCo	6 July 1881	3	5	
Friedlander	Fannie	m.	SD	16 July 1881	3	8	
Friend	Mary	m.	PCo	16 Aug. 1882	3	6	
Friend	Mary	m.	SD	5 Aug. 1882	3	5	
Frisbie	Levi	b.	SD	22 Oct. 1881	3	6	
Frisch	Nellie	m.	SD	3 Dec. 1881	3	8	
Fritch	J. Homer	b.	PCo	21 Mar. 1883	3	5	
Fritsch	Nellie	m.	DR	25 Nov. 1881	2	3	
Fritsch	Nellie	m.	PCo	23 Nov. 1881	3	5	
Frohlking	William F.	m.	DD	24 Sept. 1883	3	2	
Frohlking	William F.	m.	PWA	22 Sept. 1883	3	6	
Frohlking	William F.	m.	SD	29 Sept. 1883	2	6	
Frost	B. F.	d.	RRF	23 Mar. 1882	3	3	
Frost	C. W.	b.	DR	22 July 1882	3	2	
Frost	Charles	b.	PCo	2 Aug. 1882	3	6	
Frost	Charles	b.	SD	22 July 1882	3	5	
Frost	Corda	m.	DR	9 Dec. 1881	2	3	
Frost	Corda	m.	HE	8 Dec. 1881	2	3	
Frost	Cordie	m.	PCo	14 Dec. 1881	3	4	
Frost	Cordie	m.	RRF	1 Dec. 1881	2	3	
Frost	Cordie	m.	SD	10 Dec. 1881	3	7	
Frost	Frank	b.	RRF	29 Nov. 1883	2	3	
Frost	G. W.	b.	CR	19 Sept. 1885	3	1	
Frost	G. W.	b.	DR	21 Sept. 1885	3	4	
Frost	Martin	d.	SD	12 Jan. 1884	1	7	
Frost	Martin V.	m.	DR	9 Apr. 1882	3	2	
Frost	Martin V.	m.	PCo	12 Apr. 1882	3	5	
Frost	Martin V.	m.	RRF	6 Apr. 1882	2	4	
Frost	V.	m.	SD	15 Apr. 1882	3	6	
Fruits	Delia	m.	PCo	21 May 1884	3	4	
Fruits	Delia	m.	PWA	24 May 1884	3	5	
Fruits	Delia	m.	SD	24 May 1884	2	3	
Fruits	Delia I.	m.	DR	21 May 1884	3	2	

(1) Surname	(2) Given Name	(3)	(4)	(5) Date	(6) Pg	(7) Col	(8) Comments
Frye	Bonnie	m.	DR	26 May 1884	3	2	
Frye	Bonnie	m.	PCo	28 May 1884	2	4	
Fulkerson	Abner	d.	RRF	23 Mar. 1882	3	4	
Fulkerson	Anna Leigh	d.	DR	16 Sept. 1882	3	4	
Fulkerson	Anna Leigh	d.	SD	19 Sept. 1885	2	4	
Fulkerson	J. William	d.	SD	15 Aug. 1885	3	6	
Fulkerson	John	b.	PCo	19 Mar. 1884	3	6	
Fulkerson	John	d.	RRF	23 Mar. 1882	3	4	
Fulkerson	John	b.	SD	15 Mar. 1884	2	5	
Fulkerson	Laura E	m.	PCo	3 Jan. 1883	3	4	
Fulkerson	Laura	m.	DR	27 Dec. 1882	3	3	
Fulkerson	Richard	d.	RRF	23 Mar. 1882	3	3	
Fulkerson	Robert Edward Lee	b.	SD	13 June 1885	3	5	
Fulkerson	Robert	m.	DR	15 July 1884	3	3	
Fulkerson	S. T.	b.	DR	3 Aug. 1881	2	3	
Fulkerson	S. T.	b.	SD	6 Aug. 1881	3	8	
Fulkerson	Sally	d.	DR	18 Mar. 1882	2	3	
Fulkerson	Sally	d.	PCo	29 Mar. 1882	3	5	
Fulkerson	Sarah	d.	RRF	23 Mar. 1882	3	3	
Fulkerson	Sarah	d.	SD	1 Apr. 1882	3	6	
Fulkerson	William	d.	DD	21 July 1883	3	2	
Fulkerson	William	d.	PC	1 Aug. 1883	3	6	
Fulkerson	William	d.	SD	28 July 1883	2	5	
Fullager	William	d.	DR	7 Dec. 1885	3	4	
Fuller	Ellen	m.	PCo	22 July 1885	3	6	
Fuller	Ellen	m.	SD	18 July 1885	5	5	
Fuller	H. S.	d.	DR	19 June 1884	3	3	
Fuller	H. S.	d.	PCo	18 June 1884	3	4	
Fuller	H. S.	d.	SD	28 June 1884	3	4	
Fuller	Hattie	m.	DR	24 Oct. 1882	3	2	
Fuller	Hattie	m.	PCo	18 Oct. 1882	3	6	
Fuller	Rachael M.	d.	SD	10 June 1882	2	3	
Fuller	Rachel M.	d.	PCo	7 June 1882	3	5	
Fuller	W. F. H.	m.	SD	2 Apr. 1881	3	8	
Fuller	William F. A.	m.	RRF	26 May 1881	2	5	
Fuller	William F. A.	m.	SD	21 May 1881	3	8	
Fulton	David	d.	DR	5 Feb. 1884	3	3	
Fulton	David	p.	DR	13 Nov. 1884	3	2	

(1) Surname	(2) Given Name	(3)	(4)	(5) Date	(6) Pg	(7) Col	(8) Comments
Fulton	David	d.	PCo	13 Feb. 1884	3	6	
Fulton	David	d.	SD	9 Feb. 1884	1	6	also p. 7 col. 2
Fulton	Retta	m.	PCo	2 Jan. 1884	3	6	
Fulweidar	Harvey	d.	CR	8 Jan. 1881	5	5	

G

(1) Surname	(2) Given Name	(3)	(4)	(5) Date	(6) Pg	(7) Col	(8) Comments
Gable	Ella	m.	DR	7 Nov. 1881	2	3	
Gable	Ella	m.	PCo	2 Nov. 1881	3	5	
Gable	Ella	m.	SD	29 Oct. 1881	3	6	
Gaby	Emma A.	m.	PCo	23 July 1884	3	6	
Gaby	Emma A.	m.	SD	19 July 1884	2	5	also p. 3 col. 3
Gaby	Emma	m.	DR	16 July 1884	3	3	
Gaffney	B.	m.	SD	19 July 1884	2	5	
Gafney	Mr.	d.	SD	23 Apr. 1881	3	1	
Gaines	Eugene	d.	DR	19 June 1884	3	3	
Gaines	Eugene	d.	PCo	18 June 1884	3	4	
Gaines	Eugenie	d.	SD	28 June 1884	3	4	
Gale	Alice	m.	PC	2 May 1883	3	5	
Gale	Alice	m.	PWA	28 Apr. 1883	3	8	
Gale	Alice	m.	SD	12 May 1883	2	6	
Gale	Arthur	d.	DR	7 June 1882	3	2	
Gale	Arthur	d.	PCo	7 June 1882	3	5	
Gale	Arthur	d.	SD	10 June 1882	2	3	
Gale	L. L.	b.	DR	14 May 1881	2	3	
Gale	L. L.	b.	PCo	24 Jan. 1883	3	5	
Gale	L. L.	b.	SD	27 Jan. 1883	3	6	
Gale	Lester L.	b.	RRF	12 May 1881	2	4	
Gale	Lester	b.	RRF	18 Jan. 1883	2	3	
Gale	Mary D.	m.	DR	13 Sept. 1881	2	3	
Gale	Mary D.	m.	PCo	7 Sept. 1881	2	4	
Gale	Mary D.	m.	SD	17 Sept. 1881	3	8	
Gale	Mr. & Mrs.	b.	SD	14 May 1881	3	8	
Gallagher	A. R.	m.	DD	22 Sept. 1883	3	2	
Gallagher	Louisa	m.	DR	13 Sept. 1881	2	3	
Gallagher	Louisa	m.	PCo	7 Sept. 1881	2	4	
Gallagher	Louisa	m.	SD	17 Sept. 1881	3	8	
Gallagher	Patrick	b.	PCo	23 Jan. 1884	3	5	
Gallagher	Thomas	b.	SD	16 Apr. 1881	3	8	
Gallagher	Thomas	b.	SD	23 Apr. 1881	3	8	
Gamble	(female)	b.	DR	28 Mar. 1884	3	3	
Gamble	John	b.	CR	29 Mar. 1883	3	1	
Gamble	John	b.	PCo	2 Apr. 1884	3	6	
Gamble	John	b.	RRF	27 Mar. 1884	2	3	
Gamble	John	b.	SD	5 Apr. 1884	3	4	

(1) Surname	(2) Given Name	(3)	(4)	(5) Date	(6) Pg	(7) Col	(8) Comments
Gamboni	S.	b.	DD	12 Nov. 1883	3	3	
Gammon	G. P. (son of)	d.	PCo	10 Jan. 1883	3	6	
Gammon	G. P. (son of)	d.	PCo	31 Jan. 1883	3	5	
Gammon	G. P. (son of)	d.	RRF	4 Jan. 1883	2	2	
Gammon	G. P. (son of)	d.	RRF	25 Jan. 1883	2	4	
Gammon	G. P. (son of)	d.	SD	6 Jan. 1883	2	5	
Gammon	G. P. (son of)	d.	SD	27 Jan. 1883	3	6	
Gammon	G. P.	b.	PCo	10 Jan. 1883	3	6	
Gammon	G. P.	b.	RRF	4 Jan. 1883	2	2	
Gammon	G. P.	b.	SD	6 Jan. 1883	2	5	
Garcia	Jose	d.	CR	25 July 1885	3	2	
Garcia	Jose	d.	SD	25 July 1885	1	6	
Gardner	Charles	m.	SD	3 Oct. 1885	5	4	also 10 Oct., p. 1 col. 3
Gardner	Ida	m.	SD	25 Oct. 1884	2	5	
Gardner	Jacob	b.	DR	10 July 1885	3	4	
Gardner	Lizzie	m.	DD	1 Aug. 1883	3	2	
Gardner	Lizzie	m.	PC	8 Aug. 1883	3	6	
Gardner	Lizzie	m.	SD	4 Aug. 1883	2	5	
Gardner	Willie	d.	SD	14 Mar. 1885	5	5	
Garfield	Charles E.	b.	SD	3 Sept. 1881	3	8	
Garratt	William	m.	DR	6 July 1885	3	3	
Garratt	William	m.	PCo	15 July 1885	3	6	
Garrett	Eliza J.	d.	DR	22 Dec. 1884	2	2	
Garrett	Eliza J.	d.	PCo	24 Dec. 1884	3	4	
Garrett	Eliza J.	d.	PWA	20 Dec. 1884	3	4	
Gartman	Annie	m.	SD	11 Aug. 1883	2	7	
Gartmann	Annie	m.	PC	22 Aug. 1883	3	5	
Gartmann	Annie	m.	PWA	18 Aug. 1883	3	7	
Gartmann	Annie	m.	SWI	11 Aug. 1883	3	3	
Garwood	W.	m.	DR	7 Nov. 1881	2	3	
Garwood	W.	m.	PCo	2 Nov. 1881	3	5	
Garwood	Wondus	m.	SD	29 Oct. 1881	3	6	
Gassman	Sarto	m.	DR	2 May 1881	2	2	
Gaston	John W.	m.	DR	13 Sept. 1881	2	3	
Gaston	John W.	m.	PCo	7 Sept. 1881	2	4	
Gaston	John W.	m.	SD	24 Sept. 1881	3	8	
Gaston	Nadian	d.	DR	4 Apr. 1884	3	3	
Gaston	Nadie Freeman	d.	PWA	29 Mar. 1884	3	6	
Gaston	Nadien	d.	PCo	2 Apr. 1884	3	6	
Gasts	Mamie	m.	SD	13 Oct. 1883	3	4	
Gates	Celestia C.	m.	CR	8 Jan. 1881	5	5	

(1) Surname	(2) Given Name	(3)	(4)	(5) Date	(6) Pg	(7) Col	(8) Comments
Gates	Celestia C.	m.	DR	11 Jan. 1881	3	2	
Gates	Celestia C.	m.	SD	15 Jan. 1881	3	8	
Gates	Celestia	m.	CR	8 Jan. 1881	5	4&5	
Gates	E. H.	b.	PCo	23 Jan. 1884	3	5	
Gates	E. H.	b.	RRF	17 Jan. 1884	2	4	
Gates	E. H.	b.	SD	26 Jan. 1884	3	5	
Gates	W. F.	m.	DR	20 Jan. 1882	3	2	
Gates	W. F.	m.	HE	19 Jan. 1882	2	3	
Gates	W. F.	d.	PCo	24 Sept. 1884	3	5	
Gates	W. F.	m.	RRF	19 Jan. 1882	2	3	
Gates	W. F.	d.	SD	27 Sept. 1884	2	5	
Gauldin	Samuel Grover Cleavland	b.	PCo	19 Nov. 1884	3	5	
Gauldin	W. W.	b.	SD	23 Nov. 1884	2	6	
Gautier	L.	d.	DR	11 Dec. 1882	3	2	
Gautier	Leonidas	d.	PCo	27 Dec. 1882	3	6	
Gautier	Leonidas	d.	SD	16 Dec. 1882	3	6	
Gaver	Henry	d.	SD	21 May 1881	3	8	
Gaver	Tilman B.	d.	DR	24 Oct. 1884	3	3	
Gaver	Tilman B.	d.	PWA	25 Oct. 1884	3	4	
Gaver	Tilman B.	d.	SD	8 Nov. 1884	2	5	
Gaver	Tilman E.	d.	PCo	22 Oct. 1884	3	6	
Gavin	J.	b.	DD	21 Sept. 1883	3	3	
Gavin	J.	b.	RRF	20 Sept. 1883	2	4	
Gavin	J.	b.	SD	29 Sept. 1883	2	6	
Gearhart	L. C.	m.	DR	13 Sept. 1881	2	3	
Gearhart	L. C.	m.	RRF	8 Sept. 1881	2	4	
Geary	Edward Bartholomew	d.	DR	18 June 1881	2	3	
Geary	T. J.	b.	DR	25 Aug. 1884	3	4	
Geary	T. J.	b.	PCo	3 Sept. 1884	2	5	
Geary	Thomas J.	m.	PCo	21 Mar. 1883	3	5	
Geary	Thomas J.	m.	RRF	29 Mar. 1883	2	4	
Geary	Thomas J.	m.	SD	24 Mar. 1883	2	5	also p. 3 col. 2
Geer	Cyrus	b.	DR	25 Nov. 1881	2	3	
Geer	Cyrus	b.	HE	24 Nov. 1881	2	3	
Geer	Cyrus	b.	PCo	30 Nov. 1881	3	5	
Geer	Cyrus	b.	RRF	24 Nov. 1881	2	4	
Geer	Cyrus	b.	SD	3 Dec. 1881	3	8	
Gemmer	J. E.	m.	DR	5 Apr. 1881	2	3	
Gemmer	John	m.	SD	9 Apr. 1881	3	8	
Gemmill	J. D.	b.	SD	8 Nov. 1884	2	5	
Gemmill	J. D. (son of)	d.	SD	8 Nov. 1884	2	5	
Gemmill	J. D. (infant son)	d.	DR	24 Oct. 1884	3	3	

(1) Surname	(2) Given Name	(3)	(4)	(5) Date	(6) Pg	(7) Col	(8) Comments
George	Ella A.	m.	PWA	31 Mar. 1883	2	4	
Gepsen	Peter	m.	PCo	8 July 1885	3	6	
Gepsen	Peter	m.	SD	4 July 1885	5	4	
Gerald	Mr. & Mrs.	b.	PC	1 Aug. 1883	3	6	
Gerald	Mr. & Mrs.	b.	RRF	26 July 1883	2	4	
Gerckens	H. L.	m.	PWA	2 June 1883	3	8	
Gerckens	Henry	b.	PCo	27 Feb. 1884	3	6	
Gerckens	Henry	b.	PWA	1 Mar. 1884	3	6	
Gerckens	J. H. L.	m.	PC	30 May 1883	3	4	
German	William W.	m.	DR	17 Nov. 1882	2	3	
German	William W.	m.	PCo	22 Nov. 1882	3	5	
Geurkink	Lizzie C.	d.	DR	17 Sept. 1885	3	4	
Geurkirk	Lizzie C.	d.	PCo	16 Sept. 1885	3	6	
Giacomi	(infant dau.)	d.	DR	19 June 1884	3	3	
Giacomini	J. B.	b.	PCo	3 Aug. 1881	3	5	
Giacomini	J. B.	b.	SD	13 Aug. 1881	3	8	
Gibb	Florena H.	m.	DR	7 Nov. 1881	2	3	
Gibb	Florence H.	m.	PCo	2 Nov. 1881	3	5	
Gibb	Florence H.	m.	SD	12 Nov. 1881	3	7	
Gibbens	C.	m.	PCo	29 Nov. 1882	3	6	
Gibbens	John C.	m.	CR	18 Nov. 1882	3	3	
Gibbons	Patrick	d.	PWA	10 Jan. 1885	3	1	
Gibbs	E. C.	m.	DR	24 Oct. 1884	3	3	
Gibbs	E. C.	m.	PCo	22 Oct. 1884	3	6	
Gibbs	E. C.	m.	SD	8 Nov. 1884	2	5	
Gibbs	J. M.	m.	PWA	25 Oct. 1884	3	4	
Gibbs	Jennie	m.	CR	19 Jan. 1884	3	2	
Giberson	A. M.	m.	PCo	16 Mar. 1881	3	4	
Giberson	A. M., Miss	m.	CR	19 Mar. 1881	4	3	
Giberson	A. M., Miss	m.	DR	21 Nov. 1881	2	3	
Giberson	A. M., Miss	m.	SD	19 Mar. 1881	3	8	
Giberson	Annie M.	m.	CR	19 Mar. 1881	4	3	
Gibney	P. J.	d.	DR	7 July 1881	2	3	
Gibney	P. J.	d.	SD	9 July 1881	3	8	
Gibson	(female)	b.	DR	28 June 1884	3	2	
Gibson	A. J.	b.	DD	6 Oct. 1883	3	3	
Gibson	Catherine F.	d.	SD	6 June 1885	2	4	
Gibson	Henry	m.	DD	31 July 1883	3	2	
Gibson	Henry	m.	PC	8 Aug. 1883	3	6	
Gibson	Henry	m.	SD	4 Aug. 1883	2	5	
Gibson	J. W., Mrs.	d.	CR	30 May 1885	4	1	
Gibson	John	m.	DR	5 Aug. 1884	3	4	

(1) Surname	(2) Given Name	(3)	(4)	(5) Date	(6) Pg	(7) Col	(8) Comments
Gibson	John	m.	PCo	13 Aug. 1884	3	4	
Gibson	John	m.	PWA	9 Aug. 1884	2	4	
Gibson	Katherine	d.	PCo	27 May 1885	3	6	
Gibson	Loraine	d.	DR	15 Nov. 1881	2	3	
Gibson	Loraine	d.	SD	26 Nov. 1881	3	8	
Gibson	Loranie	d.	PCo	23 Nov. 1881	3	5	
Gibson	Lydia	d.	PCo	26 Oct. 1881	3	4	
Gibson	Nancy J.	m.	PCo	19 Nov. 1884	3	5	
Gibson	Robert W.	b.	DD	13 Oct. 1883	3	3	
Gila	Dominik	d.	SD	8 Jan. 1881	3	8	
Gilbert	E.	b.	SD	30 July 1881	3	8	
Gilbert	J. A., Mrs.	d.	PCo	20 May 1885	3	2&6	
Gilbert	Piatt B.	b.	SD	1 Sept. 1883	2	7	
Gilbert	Platt B.	b.	DD	28 Aug. 1883	3	3	
Gilbert	Platt B.	m.	PCo	18 Oct. 1882	3	6	
Gilbert	Platt B.	b.	PWA	25 Aug. 1883	3	8	
Gilbert	Platt P.	m.	DR	24 Oct. 1882	3	2	
Gilbride	Mary Ellen	d.	PCo	15 Oct. 1884	3	6	
Gilbride	R.	b.	RRF	20 Oct. 1881	2	4	
Gilbride	R.	b.	SD	29 Oct. 1881	3	6	
Gilbridge	R.	b.	PCo	26 Oct. 1881	3	4	
Giles	Bud	m.	DD	4 Dec. 1883	3	3	
Giles	Bud	m.	SD	8 Dec. 1883	3	1	
Giles	L. R.	d.	PC	2 May 1883	3	5	
Giles	Lewis R.	o.	RRF	19 Apr. 1883	3	4	
Giles	Lewis R.	d.	RRF	26 Apr. 1883	3	4	Oak Mound Cem.
Giles	Lewis R.	d.	SD	5 May 1883	3	6	
Gilham	Washington	d.	PCo	29 Mar. 1882	3	5	
Gilham	Washington	d.	SD	1 Apr. 1882	3	6	
Gill	Nettie	m.	PCo	3 Jan. 1883	3	4	
Gill	Nettie	m.	PWA	5 Jan. 1883	2	5	
Gill	Nettie	m.	SD	6 Jan. 1883	2	5	
Gillam	Michael	d.	PCo	2 Aug. 1882	3	2	
Gillett	R. M., Mrs	d.	PC	20 June 1883	3	6	
Gillett	R. M., Mrs.	d.	SD	23 June 1883	3	5	
Gillette	Ralph J.	m.	CR	7 May 1881	5	5	
Gillette	Ralph J.	m.	DR	30 Apr. 1881	2	2	
Gillette	Ralph J.	m.	SD	16 Apr. 1881	3	8	
Gilliam	Mitchell	d.	DR	27 July 1882	3	1	
Gilliam	Mitchell	d.	SD	5 Aug. 1882	3	1	his home property
Gilliam	Mitchell	d.	SD	29 July 1882	3	1	
Gillian	Mitchell	d.	RRF	10 Aug. 1882	3	1	

(1) Surname	(2) Given Name	(3)	(4)	(5) Date	(6) Pg	(7) Col	(8) Comments
Gillispee	Eleanor	m.	CR	5 Feb. 1881	4	1	description of 1831 wedding
Gillmore	Effie A.	m.	DR	8 Mar. 1882	2	3	
Gillmore	Penn	m.	DR	8 Mar. 1882	2	3	
Gimbel	Katherine	m.	CR	28 May 1881	5	5	
Gimbel	Katherine	m.	DR	20 May 1881	2	3	
Gimbel	Katherine	m.	PCo	18 May 1881	3	5	
Gimbel	Katherine	m.	SD	28 May 1881	3	8	
Ginger	D.	d.	CR	30 May 1885	4	2	
Gist	John	b.	PCo	26 Dec. 1883	3	5	
Gist	John	b.	PWA	29 Dec. 1883	3	6	
Gist	John	b.	SD	29 Dec. 1883	3	6	
Git	Ah	o.	DR	13 Nov. 1882	3	1	
Given	T.	b.	CR	2 Apr. 1881	5	3	
Given	T.	b.	SD	16 Apr. 1881	3	8	
Givin	George	d.	PC	30 May 1883	3	2	
Gladden	J. W.	m.	DR	9 Dec. 1881	2	3	
Gladden	J. W.	m.	HE	8 Dec. 1881	3	2	
Gladden	Jerrie W.	m.	RRF	8 Dec. 1881	2	4	
Gladden	Mary Ella	m.	RRF	27 Sept. 1883	2	2	
Gladden	Sadie E.	d.	CR	19 Feb. 1881	4	2	
Gladden	Sadie	d.	DR	19 Feb. 1881	3	2	
Gladden	Sadie	d.	RRF	17 Feb. 1881	2	4	
Gladden	W. N.	d.	CR	19 Feb. 1881	4	2	
Gladden	W. N.	d.	RRF	17 Feb. 1881	2	4	
Glass	E., Mrs.	d.	DR	1 Aug. 1885	3	4	
Glass	Emilie	d.	PCo	5 Aug. 1885	3	6	
Gleason	C. S.	b.	CR	7 May 1881	5	5	
Gleason	C. S.	b.	DR	29 Apr. 1881	3	2	
Gleason	C. S.	b.	SD	14 May 1881	3	8	
Gleason	P. H.	b.	DR	22 Apr. 1882	3	2	
Gleason	P. H.	b.	PCo	19 Apr. 1882	3	5	
Gleason	P. H.	b.	SD	15 Apr. 1882	3	6	
Gleason	W. Irving	m.	DR	24 June 1884	3	3	
Gleason	W. Irving	m.	PWA	21 June 1884	3	5	
Gleeson	Annie	m.	SD	29 Jan. 1881	3	8	
Glenn	J. D.	m.	DR	9 Nov. 1885	2	2	
Glenn	J. D.	m.	PCo	4 Nov. 1885	2	5	
Glenn	J. D.	m.	SD	7 Nov. 1885	3	4	
Glenn	J. H.	o.	DR	16 Aug. 1882	3	1	
Glenn	J. H.	m.	SD	10 Oct. 1885	1	5	
Glenn	John	d.	DD	12 Nov. 1883	3	3	

(1) Surname	(2) Given Name	(3)	(4)	(5) Date	(6) Pg	(7) Col	(8) Comments
Glenn	John	d.	SD	17 Nov. 1883	3	5	
Glenn	Minnie	d.	SD	21 Mar. 1885	1	5	also p. 2 col. 5
Glidden	William	m.	SD	24 Jan. 1885	5	5	
Gline	E. M.	d.	SD	7 May 1881	3	1	
Glines	E. M.	d.	DR	6 May 1881	3	2	
Glines	Julia	m.	CR	24 Sept. 1881	1	3	
Glover	Delia A.	m.	PWA	1 Dec. 1883	3	6	
Glover	Delia A.	m.	SD	8 Dec. 1883	3	1	
Gluyas	Reesa	d.	PCo	26 Apr. 1882	3	4	
Gluyas	Ressa	d.	DR	17 Apr. 1882	3	2	
Glynn	Nellie M.	m.	PWA	16 Aug. 1884	3	4	
Glynn	Nellie M.	m.	SD	13 Aug. 1884	2	4	
Glynn	Nellie	m.	DR	15 Aug. 1884	3	2	
Glynn	Nellie	m.	PCo	20 Aug. 1884	3	4	
Gness	F. M.	m.	PWA	25 Aug. 1883	3	8	
Gobbi	P.	b.	PCo	14 May 1884	3	4	
Gobbi	P.	b.	RRF	8 May 1884	5	6	
Gobbi	P.	b.	SD	17 May 1884	3	5	
Gober	Emma	d.	RRF	23 Aug. 1883	2	4	
Gober	Frank	m.	CR	19 Mar. 1881	4	3	
Gober	Frank	m.	DR	14 Mar. 1881	2	3	
Gober	Frank	m.	RRF	17 Feb. 1881	2	5	
Gober	Kittie	m.	RRF	28 Dec. 1882	2	2	
Goddard	Dan	b.	DR	20 Jan. 1882	3	2	
Goddard	Dan	b.	HE	19 Jan. 1882	2	3	
Goddard	Dan	b.	SD	28 Jan. 1882	3	6	
Goddard	Daniel	b.	RRF	26 Jan. 1882	2	2	
Goddard	Frank	m.	DD	29 Dec. 1883	3	3	
Goddard	Frank	m.	PCo	2 Jan. 1884	3	6	
Goddard	Frank	m.	RRF	27 Dec. 1883	2	2	
Goddard	Frank	m.	SD	5 Jan. 1884	1	8	
Godfrey	Addie	m.	PCo	1 Oct. 1884	3	5	
Goess	George A.	b.	PCo	9 Apr. 1884	3	6	
Goess	George A.	b.	PWA	12 Apr. 1884	3	6	
Goess	George A.	b.	SWI	5 Apr. 1884	3	4	
Goess	John	m.	SD	5 Dec. 1885	1	8	
Goetzelman	Andrew	m.	PCo	21 June 1882	3	5	
Goetzelman	Andrew	m.	SD	24 June 1882	3	5	
Goforth	Lavina C.	d.	PCo	27 Feb. 1884	3	6	
Goforth	Lavina C.	d.	SD	1 Mar. 1884	6	6	
Gohes	Kittie	m.	DR	21 Dec. 1882	2	2	
Gohes	Kittie	m.	PCo	27 Dec. 1882	3	6	

(1) Surname	(2) Given Name	(3)	(4)	(5) Date	(6) Pg	(7) Col	(8) Comments
Gohes	Kittie	m.	SD	30 Dec. 1882	3	6	
Golden	George	b.	PCo	22 Mar. 1882	3	5	
Golden	George	m.	SD	14 May 1881	3	8	
Goldfish	B.	b.	DR	1 Sept. 1882	3	2	
Goldfish	B.	b.	SD	2 Sept. 1882	3	6	
Goldsmith	Samuel	m.	SD	26 Sept. 1885	5	4	
Goldstein	D.	d.	RRF	5 May 1881	3	6	
Good	Harry Carlton	m.	PCo	15 Apr. 1885	3	6	
Good	John, Mrs.	d.	DR	26 Apr. 1881	3	1	
Goode	Rosa	m.	SD	16 June 1883	2	6	
Goodfellow	Thomas C.	m.	SD	10 May 1884	2	4	
Goodfellow	Thomas	m.	DR	8 May 1884	3	2	
Goodman	Thomas F.	m.	SD	20 Jan. 1883	2	5	
Goodman	Thomas	d.	CR	1 Aug. 1885	3	3	
Goodman	Thomas	d.	DR	21 July 1885	3	4	
Goodman	Thomas	m.	PCo	24 Jan. 1883	3	5	
Goodman	Thomas	d.	PCo	29 July 1885	3	4	
Goodman	Thomas	d.	SD	25 July 1885	3	5	
Goodman	Thomas	d.	SD	25 July 1885	1	4	Lakeport
Goodrich	Elizabeth	m.	DR	6 Sept. 1881	2	3	
Goodspeed	Charles A.	d.	DR	2 July 1881	3	2	
Goodspeed	Charley A.	m.	RRF	30 June 1881	2	4	
Goodspeed	Georgia	m.	PCo	6 Feb. 1884	3	6	
Goodspeed	Georgia	m.	RRF	31 Jan. 1884	2	3	
Goodwin	E. W.	m.	SD	28 Jan. 1882	3	6	
Goodwin	E. W.	b.	SD	9 Aug. 1884	3	4	
Goodwin	F. W.	b.	SD	13 Aug. 1884	2	4	
Goodwin	Minnie	d.	SD	23 Aug. 1884	2	4	
Goodwin	Mr. & Mrs.	b.	SD	14 May 1881	3	8	
Gordon	J. B.	d.	CR	28 May 1881	5	5	
Gordon	J. B.	d.	CR	28 May 1881	4	2	also p. 5 col. 5
Gordon	J. B.	d.	RRF	26 May 1881	2	5	Santa Rosa
Gordon	J. B.	d.	SD	28 May 1881	3	4&8	
Gordon	Jackson	o.	DR	22 Apr. 1882	3	1	
Gordon	James Burns	d.	DR	24 May 1881	2	2	also p. 3 col. 2
Gordon	James	d.	RRF	31 Mar. 1881	2	3	
Gordon	James	d.	SD	2 Apr. 1881	3	8	
Gordon	Joseph William	d.	SD	29 Oct. 1881	3	6	
Gordon	Laura de Force	o.	SD	5 Dec. 1885	3	3	
Gordon	Levi B.	m.	DR	10 Apr. 1882	2	2	
Gordon	Levi B.	m.	PCo	5 Apr. 1882	3	5	
Gordon	Mary J.	m.	RRF	26 May 1881	2	5	

(1) Surname	(2) Given Name	(3)	(4)	(5) Date	(6) Pg	(7) Col	(8) Comments
Gordon	Melissa	m.	SD	3 Sept. 1881	3	8	
Gordon	Mellissa	m.	RRF	25 Aug. 1881	2	4	
Gordon	W. H.	b.	CR	26 Mar. 1881	5	5	
Gordon	W. H.	b.	SD	2 Apr. 1881	3	8	
Gore	Fred A.	m.	DR	17 July 1885	3	4	
Gore	Fred A.	m.	PCo	22 July 1885	3	6	
Gore	Fred A.	m.	SD	25 July 1885	3	5	
Gorensky	J.	b.	PWA	21 Feb. 1885	3	5	
Gorman	Adelaide	m.	PC	11 July 1883	3	5	
Gorman	Frank	m.	DD	22 Sept. 1883	3	2	
Gorman	Frank	m.	SD	29 Sept. 1883	2	6	
Goss	John	m.	DR	28 Nov. 1885	3	4	
Goss	John	m.	PCo	9 Dec. 1885	3	6	
Gossage	Addie	m.	DR	24 Sep. 1881	2	3	
Gossage	Addie	m.	PCo	21 Sept. 1881	3	5	
Gossage	Addie	m.	SD	1 Oct. 1881	3	8	
Gossage	Joseph	b.	PCo	10 Jan. 1883	3	6	
Gossage	Joseph	b.	PWA	12 Jan. 1883	3	6	
Gossage	Joseph	b.	SD	13 Jan. 1883	3	5	
Gossage	William	d.	PWA	16 Aug. 1884	3	4	
Gott	William H.	d.	DR	29 Jan. 1884	3	3	
Gott	William H.	d.	PCo	30 Jan. 1884	3	6	
Gott	William (son of)	d.	PCo	3 Jan. 1883	3	4	
Gott	William (son of)	d.	SD	6 Jan. 1883	2	5	
Gott	William	b.	PCo	3 Jan. 1883	3	4	
Gott	William	b	SD	6 Jan. 1883	2	5	
Gould	George F.	m.	DR	10 June 1884	3	3	
Gould	George W.	m.	SD	16 Apr. 1881	3	8	
Gould	Thomas J.	d.	PC	16 May 1883	3	5	
Gould	Thomas J.	d.	RRF	17 May 1883	2	3	
Gould	Thomas J.	d.	SD	19 May 1883	3	5	
Goulett	Nelson	d.	SD	28 Mar. 1885	5	1	
Gounsky	J.	b.	DR	17 Sept. 1881	2	3	
Gounsky	J.	b.	PCo	18 Feb. 1885	3	6	
Gounsky	J.	b.	PWA	8 Sept. 1883	3	8	
Gounsky	J.	b.	SD	17 Sept. 1881	3	8	
Gounsky	J.	b.	SD	28 Feb. 1885	5	6	
Gounsky	J. (dau. of)	d.	DD	18 Oct. 1883	3	3	
Gounsky	J. (dau. of)	d.	PWA	13 Oct. 1883	3	8	
Gounsky	J. (dau. of)	d.	SD	20 Oct. 1883	3	4	
Grabow	Mrs.	m.	PCo	21 June 1882	3	5	
Grabow	Mrs.	m.	SD	24 June 1882	3	5	

(1) Surname	(2) Given Name	(3)	(4)	(5) Date	(6) Pg	(7) Col	(8) Comments
Grace	Mary A.	d.	SD	1 June 1881	3	7	
Grace	Perry O.	d.	DR	24 Nov. 1884	3	2	
Grace	Perry	d.	PCo	3 Dec. 1884	3	5	
Grace	Perry	d.	SD	23 Nov. 1884	2	6	
Grady	W. D.	m.	SD	18 Apr. 1885	2	5	
Graham	E.	b.	DR	13 Sept. 1881	2	3	
Graham	E.	b.	SD	17 Sept. 1881	3	8	
Graham	Edwin	b.	DR	17 Sept. 1881	2	3	
Graham	Edwin	b.	PCo	14 Sept. 1881	2	4	
Graham	Edwin	b.	SD	24 Sept. 1881	3	8	
Graham	Ida	m.	PCo	15 Apr. 1885	3	6	
Graham	Ida	m.	PWA	18 Apr. 1885	3	6	
Graham	J. P.	b.	PCo	10 Sept. 1884	3	6	
Graham	J. W.	m.	SD	2 July 1881	3	8	
Graham	James	m.	DR	1 July 1881	2	2	
Graham	James W.	m.	RRF	30 June 1881	2	4	
Graham	Jane P.	d.	DD	31 Oct. 1883	3	3	
Graham	Jane P.	d.	SD	3 Nov. 1883	3	3	
Graham	Joseph	b.	PCo	15 Apr. 1885	3	6	
Graham	Joseph M.	m.	SD	17 Nov. 1883	3	5	
Graham	L. F.	m.	DR	11 Feb. 1882	2	3	
Graham	L. F.	m.	RRF	16 Feb. 1882	2	4	
Graham	L. F., Miss	m.	SD	18 Feb. 1882	3	6	
Graham	Libbie	m.	HE	23 Feb. 1882	2	4	
Graham	Libbie	m.	PCo	15 Feb. 1882	3	4	
Graham	Maggie J.	m.	DD	4 Dec. 1883	3	3	
Graham	Mary	m.	SD	13 Aug. 1881	3	8	
Graham	W. F.	m.	DD	29 Sept. 1883	3	2	
Grandi	John	b.	DD	20 July 1883	3	2	
Grandi	John	b.	PC	18 July 1883	3	5	
Grandi	Sylvia	d.	DD	2 Aug. 1883	3	2	
Grandi	Sylvia	d.	SD	4 Aug. 1883	2	5	
Grandrot	Othella	m.	SD	12 Mar. 1881	3	8	
Granger	Grace A.	d.	PCo	21 Oct. 1885	3	4	
Granger	Grace B.	d.	DR	23 Oct. 1885	3	4	
Granger	Mr. & Mrs.	b.	DR	26 Aug. 1885	3	4	
Granger	Mr. & Mrs.	b.	PCo	19 Aug. 1885	3	6	
Grant	John D.	o.	CR	2 Dec. 1882	3	3	
Gravatt	William	m.	SD	11 July 1885	5	6	
Gray	Carrie	m.	RRF	13 Jan. 1881	2	5	
Gray	Charles T.	m.	SD	5 Mar. 1881	3	8	
Gray	D.	b.	SD	1 Oct. 1881	3	8	

(1) Surname	(2) Given Name	(3)	(4)	(5) Date	(6) Pg	(7) Col	(8) Comments
Gray	Georgiana R.	m.	PCo	20 May 1885	3	6	
Gray	Isaac	d.	RRF	28 Sept. 1882	2	3	
Gray	J. W.	b.	DR	27 Dec. 1884	2	3	
Gray	J. W.	b.	PCo	14 Jan. 1885	3	6	
Gray	Jacob	d.	RRF	28 Sept. 1882	2	3	
Gray	Lester D.	m.	DR	22 May 1884	3	2	
Gray	Lester D.	m.	SD	24 May 1884	2	3	
Gray	Lester	b.	PCo	1 Apr. 1885	3	6	
Gray	Lester	b.	SD	4 Apr. 1885	2	5	
Greason	C. S.	b.	CR	7 May 1881	5	5	
Greaver	Andrew J.	m.	PCo	18 Oct. 1882	3	6	
Greaver	Andrew J.	m.	RRF	12 Oct. 1882	2	3	
Greaver	Andrew J.	m.	SD	14 Oct. 1882	3	6	
Greek	John H.	m.	PCo	21 June 1882	3	5	
Greek	John H.	m.	SD	17 June 1882	2	4	
Greek	John H.	m.	SD	24 June 1882	3	5	
Greeley	F. H.	b.	CR	3 Dec. 1881	5	2	
Greely	F. H.	d.	CR	3 Dec. 1881	5	2	
Greely	F. H.	b.	DR	4 Dec. 1881	2	3	
Green	Charles	d.	PCo	17 Dec. 1884	2	4	
Green	Charles	d.	PWA	20 Dec. 1884	3	4	
Green	Charles	d.	SD	13 Dec. 1884	2	5	
Green	Henry H.	m.	DD	25 Sept. 1883	3	3	
Green	Henry H.	m.	SD	29 Sept. 1883	2	6	
Green	L. B.	m.	DD	21 Sept. 1883	3	3	
Green	L. B.	m.	SD	29 Sept. 1883	2	6	
Green	L. R.	m.	RRF	27 Sept. 1883	2	2	
Green	Mary Ann	d.	DR	8 May 1882	2	3	
Green	W. C.	m.	PWA	16 Aug. 1884	3	4	
Green	W. C.	m.	SD	13 Aug. 1884	2	4	
Green	W. C., Jr.	b.	DR	21 July 1885	3	4	
Green	W. C., Jr.	b.	PCo	29 July 1885	3	4	
Green	Warren	b.	CR	22 Nov. 1884	3	1	
Green	William C.	m.	DR	15 Aug. 1884	3	2	
Green	William C.	m.	PCo	20 Aug. 1884	3	4	
Greene	Rosa H.	m.	DR	10 Jan. 1884	3	3	
Greene	Warren	b.	PCo	26 Nov. 1884	3	5	
Greening	Belle	m.	PCo	6 Sept. 1882	3	7	
Greening	Laura A.	m.	SD	22 Aug. 1885	6	2	
Greenwell	Mr. & Mrs.	b.	CR	28 July 1883	3	1	
Greenwell	Mr. & Mrs.	b.	PC	1 Aug. 1883	3	6	
Greenwell	Mr. & Mrs.	b.	SD	4 Aug. 1883	2	5	

(1) Surname	(2) Given Name	(3)	(4)	(5) Date	(6) Pg	(7) Col	(8) Comments
Greenwood	Hannah	d.	DR	21 Dec. 1882	2	2	
Greenwood	Hannah	d.	PCo	27 Dec. 1882	3	6	
Greenwood	Hannah	d.	SD	30 Dec. 1882	3	6	
Greenwood	Louisa	d.	SD	29 Oct. 1881	3	6	
Greevey	Thomas	b.	DD	8 Dec. 1883	3	3	
Greevey	Thomas	b.	RRF	6 Dec. 1883	2	3	
Gregg	G. T.	o.	DR	1 July 1882	3	1	
Gregg	George	b.	SD	4 June 1881	3	8	
Gregory	L.	b.	DR	24 Nov. 1882	2	3	triplets
Gregory	L.	b.	RRF	23 Nov. 1882	3	4	
Gregory	L. (son of)	d.	DR	24 Nov. 1882	2	3	
Gregory	L. (son of)	d.	PCo	29 Nov. 1882	3	6	
Gregory	L. (dau. of)	d.	PCo	14 Feb. 1883	3	6	
Gregory	L. (dau. of)	d.	SD	10 Feb. 1883	2	7	
Gregory	Myrtle	d.	RRF	15 Feb. 1883	2	3	
Gregson	Henry	m.	PCo	10 Jan. 1883	3	6	
Gregson	Henry	m.	PWA	12 Jan. 1883	3	6	
Gregson	James	o.	SD	9 Apr. 1881	3	2	
Grider	D. S.	b.	PCo	27 Dec. 1882	3	6	
Grider	T. S.	b.	CR	26 Mar. 1881	5	5	
Grider	T. S.	b.	DR	23 Mar. 1881	3	2	
Grider	T. S.	b.	SD	12 Mar. 1881	3	8	
Grider	T. S.	b.	SD	16 Dec. 1882	3	6	
Griest	Agnes	d.	SD	5 Aug. 1882	3	5	
Griest	Alice Florence	m.	RRF	5 Jan. 1882	3	1	
Griest	Allie	m.	DR	23 Dec. 1881	2	2	
Griest	Allie	m.	PCo	28 Dec. 1881	3	6	
Griest	Allie	m.	RRF	22 Dec. 1881	2	3	
Griest	Allie	m.	SD	31 Dec. 1881	3	6	
Griest	Allie F.	m.	HE	29 Dec. 1881	2	3	
Griest	Leah Agnes	d.	PCo	2 Aug. 1882	3	6	
Griest	Leah Agnes	d.	RRF	27 July 1882	2	4	Healdsburg
Griest	Leah	d.	DR	1 Aug. 1882	2	2	Oak Mound Cem.
Griest	Lewis	d.	RRF	2 Mar. 1882	3	6	
Griest	Peter	d.	DR	18 Feb. 1884	3	3	
Griest	Peter	d.	PCo	20 Feb. 1884	3	6	
Griest	Peter	m.	RRF	22 Dec. 1881	2	3	
Griest	Peter	d.	RRF	2 Mar. 1882	3	6	
Griest	Peter	m.	RRF	15 Nov. 1883	2	3	
Griest	Peter	d.	RRF	6 Mar. 1884	3	4	
Griest	Peter	d.	RRF	21 Feb. 1884	2	3	also col. 2
Griest	Peter	d.	SD	1 Mar. 1884	6	6	

(1) Surname	(2) Given Name	(3)	(4)	(5) Date	(6) Pg	(7) Col	(8) Comments
Griffen	Belle May	d.	PCo	8 Nov. 1882	3	6	
Griffen	Belle May	d.	RRF	2 Nov. 1882	2	4	
Griffen	G. W.	b.	SD	3 June 1882	2	4	
Griffen	George W.	d.	RRF	2 Nov. 1882	2	4	
Griffin	Bell	d.	SD	4 Nov. 1882	3	6	
Griffin	Belle May	d.	DR	1 Nov. 1882	3	2	
Griffin	G. W.	b.	DR	23 May 1882	2	3	
Griffin	G. W.	b.	PCo	31 May 1882	3	5	
Griffin	G. W.	b.	RRF	25 May 1882	2	3	
Griffin	Ida S.	b.	DR	1 Dec. 1884	3	2	
Griffin	Kate	m.	SD	30 Apr. 1881	3	8	
Griffin	Mr. & Mrs.	b.	PCo	3 Dec. 1884	3	5	
Griffin	Mr. & Mrs.	b.	PWA	6 Dec. 1884	3	4	
Griffin	P. L. (infant dau.)	d.	DR	8 Dec. 1884	3	2	
Griffith	A.	b.	PCo	9 Nov. 1881	3	5	
Griffith	A.	b.	SD	19 Nov. 1881	4	8	
Griffith	E. J.	b.	DD	12 Dec. 1883	3	2	
Griffith	E. J.	b.	DR	15 Mar. 1882	2	2	
Griffith	Hattie M.	m.	SD	16 Apr. 1881	3	8	
Griffith	Jessie E.	m.	SD	16 Apr. 1881	3	8	
Griffiths	Charles	d.	RRF	16 Mar. 1882	2	4	
Griffiths	W. L.	d.	RRF	16 Mar. 1882	2	4	
Griggs	Hattie C.	m.	DR	22 Dec. 1881	2	2	
Griggs	Hattie	m.	SD	24 Dec. 1881	2	3	
Griggs	W. B.	b.	DR	1 Oct. 1885	3	4	
Grigsby	P. D.	b.	SD	21 May 1881	3	8	
Grimley	William	d.	SD	30 July 1881	3	8	
Grimsby	Eva	m.	DR	16 Nov. 1881	2	3	
Grimsby	Eva	m.	PCo	23 Nov. 1881	3	5	
Grimsby	Eva	m.	PCo	30 Nov. 1881	3	5	
Grimsby	Eva	m.	SD	3 Dec. 1881	3	8	
Grist	Alice H.	m.	PCo	11 Jan. 1882	3	6	
Groff	W. R.	b.	PCo	13 Aug. 1884	3	4	
Groff	W. R.	b.	PWA	16 Aug. 1884	3	4	
Groff	William R.	m.	PCo	8 Mar. 1882	3	5	
Grosh	A.	b.	DR	21 July 1885	3	4	
Grosh	A.	b.	PCo	15 July 1885	3	6	
Grosh	A.	b.	SD	18 July 1885	5	5	
Groshong	George	d.	DR	4 Aug. 1884	3	3	
Groshong	George	d.	PWA	9 Aug. 1884	2	4	
Groshong	Georgie	d.	CR	2 Aug. 1884	3	2	
Groshong	Hiram	b.	CR	3 Mar. 1883	3	1	

(1) Surname	(2) Given Name	(3)	(4)	(5) Date	(6) Pg	(7) Col	(8) Comments
Groshong	Jennie Esther	d.	CR	26 Sept. 1885	3	3	
Groskopf	Albert	m.	PC	22 Aug. 1883	3	5	
Groskopf	Albert	m.	PWA	18 Aug. 1883	3	7	
Groskopf	Albert	m.	SD	11 Aug. 1883	2	7	
Groskopf	Albert	m.	SWI	11 Aug. 1883	3	3	
Grove	Arvil T.	m.	SD	14 Mar. 1885	5	5	
Grove	C. C.	b.	PC	1 Aug. 1883	3	6	
Grove	C. C.	b.	RRF	26 July 1883	2	4	
Grove	Catharine	d.	CR	28 May 1881	5	5	
Grove	Catharine	d.	DR	24 May 1881	2	2	
Grove	Catherine	d.	SD	28 May 1881	3	8	
Grove	Christopher	b.	DR	13 Aug. 1881	2	3	
Grove	Christopher	b.	RRF	11 Aug. 1881	2	5	
Grove	Christopher	b.	SD	20 Aug. 1881	3	8	
Grove	David	m.	PCo	10 May 1882	3	5	
Grove	David	d.	RRF	24 Nov. 1881	3	5	
Grove	David	m.	SD	13 May 1882	2	4	
Grove	Edward	m.	SD	11 Aug. 1883	2	7	
Grove	G. W.	m.	RRF	17 Nov. 1881	3	3	
Grove	George	m.	DR	12 Nov. 1881	2	2	
Grove	John	d.	RRF	30 Mar. 1882	2	5	
Grove	Lewis	d.	RRF	1 Dec. 1881	2	3	Oak Mound Cem.
Grove	Lewis	d.	RRF	24 Nov. 1881	3	5	
Grove	Lewis S.	d.	DR	3 Dec. 1881	3	2	
Grove	Lewis S.	d.	DR	23 Nov. 1881	3	1	
Grove	Lewis S.	d.	DR	25 Nov. 1881	2	3	
Grove	Lewis S.	d.	PCo	7 Dec. 1881	3	5	
Grove	Louis	d.	CR	3 Dec. 1881	1	3	
Grove	Louis	d.	HE	24 Nov. 1881	2	3	
Grove	Louis S.	d.	SD	26 Nov. 1881	3	2	
Grove	Mary C.	d.	DR	5 Apr. 1882	3	2	
Grove	Mary C.	d.	PCo	5 Apr. 1882	3	5	
Grove	Mary C.	d.	RRF	30 Mar. 1882	2	5	
Grove	Mary C.	d.	SD	1 Apr. 1882	3	6	
Grover	C. D.	b.	CR	30 Apr. 1881	5	5	
Grover	C. D.	b.	DR	3 May 1881	2	2	
Grover	C. D.	b.	PCo	27 Apr. 1881	3	5	
Grover	C. D.	b.	SD	7 May 1881	3	8	
Grover	Isaac W.	m.	SD	8 Jan. 1881	3	8	
Groves	David, Mrs.	d.	RRF	26 May 1881	3	2	Shiloh
Groves	Phoebe	m.	DR	6 Dec. 1884	3	2	
Groves	Phoebe	m.	PCo	3 Dec. 1884	3	5	

(1) Surname	(2) Given Name	(3)	(4)	(5) Date	(6) Pg	(7) Col	(8) Comments
Groves	Phoebe	m.	PWA	6 Dec. 1884	3	4	
Grundy	Ida E.	m.	DR	17 Nov. 1881	2	3	
Grundy	Ida E.	m.	RRF	17 Nov. 1881	2	3	
Gudmundson	K.	d.	SD	10 Sept. 1881	3	8	
Gudmundson	Knud	d.	DR	21 Sept. 1881	2	3	
Guess	M. F.	m.	DD	23 Aug. 1883	3	2	
Guess	M. F.	m.	PC	22 Aug. 1883	3	5	
Guess	M. F.	m.	SD	25 Aug. 1883	2	5	
Guinan	Nora	m.	SD	8 Oct. 1881	3	8	
Guist	Nola	d.	PCo	18 Oct. 1882	3	6	
Guiteau	Mr.	d.	DR	3 July 1882	3	1	jail yard
Gum	I.	b.	SD	21 Mar. 1885	2	5	
Gummer	James	m.	PCo	11 June 1884	3	5	
Gummer	James	m.	PWA	14 June 1884	3	6	
Gumpertz	Jacob	m.	SD	29 Jan. 1881	3	8	
Gunning	Ann	p.	SD	9 May 1885	1	4	will contested
Gunning	Anna	d.	PWA	28 Mar. 1885	3	3&5	
Gunning	Annie	d.	PCo	1 Apr. 1885	3	1&6	
Gunning	William C.	d.	PCo	11 Feb. 1885	3	1&6	Cypress Hill
Gunning	William Crawford	d.	PWA	14 Feb. 1885	3	1&5	Cypress Hill
Guntley	Caroline	m.	DD	4 Aug. 1883	3	2	
Gwinn	Edward	m.	SD	6 June 1885	2	4	
Gwinn	Fannie E.	m.	SD	11 Feb. 1882	3	6	
Gwinn	George	p.	DD	11 July 1883	3	2	
Gwinn	George W.	p.	DD	24 July 1883	3	2	
Gwinn	George W.	d.	PWA	2 June 1883	3	8	

H

(1) Surname	(2) Given Name	(3)	(4)	(5) Date	(6) Pg	(7) Col	(8) Comments
Haas	Charles (dau. of)	d.	SD	19 Mar. 1881	3	8	
Haehl	J. J.	p.	DR	16 July 1884	3	2	
Haeckl	L.	b.	SD	12 Mar. 1881	3	8	
Haeckl	Willie	d.	SD	9 Apr. 1881	3	8	
Haegan	J. J.	d.	PC	30 May 1883	3	2	
Haehl	Catherine	d.	DR	16 Dec. 1882	2	3	
Haehl	Ella M.	d.	DR	20 Nov. 1882	3	2	
Haehl	Ella M.	d.	PCo	22 Nov. 1882	3	5	
Haehl	Henry	b.	CR	12 Mar. 1881	5	5	
Haehl	Henry	b.	CR	24 Nov. 1883	3	1	
Haehl	Henry	b.	DD	4 Dec. 1883	3	3	
Haehl	Henry	b.	SD	19 Mar. 1881	3	8	
Haehl	Henry	b.	SD	8 Dec. 1883	3	1	
Haehl	J. J.	d.	CR	23 Feb. 1884	3	3	Cloverdale Cem.
Hagan	J. J.	d.	PWA	2 June 1883	3	8	
Hagan	John M.	d.	DD	3 Dec. 1883	3	2	
Hagan	John M.	d.	SD	15 Dec. 1883	1	3&5	
Hagan	Mr.	d.	SD	2 June 1883	1	5	
Hagen	Mr.	d.	PWA	26 May 1883	3	1	
Hahman	F. G.	d.	DD	2 Oct. 1883	3	3	
Hahman	F. G.	d.	SD	6 Oct. 1883	1	7	Rural Cem, also col. 6 & p. 3 col. 4, 3
Hahman	Feodor Gustave	d.	CR	6 Oct. 1883	3	1&3	
Hahman	Feodore G.	d.	PWA	6 Oct. 1883	3	2&8	
Haigh	J. B., Mrs.	d.	DR	18 July 1884	3	3	
Haigh	J. B., Mrs.	d.	PCo	30 July 1884	3	6	
Haigh	Robert	b.	PC	2 May 1883	3	5	
Haigh	Robert	b.	SD	5 May 1883	3	6	
Hale	Evert W.	m.	PWA	5 Jan. 1883	3	2	
Hale	George E.	d.	PCo	12 Mar. 1884	3	6	
Hale	George E.	d.	RRF	6 Mar. 1884	2	3	
Hale	J. H.	m.	DR	28 Aug. 1882	3	2	
Hale	J. H.	m.	RRF	31 Aug. 1882	2	4	
Hale	J. H.	m.	SD	2 Sept. 1882	3	6	
Hale	Susie	m.	DR	1 Mar. 1882	2	3	
Hale	Susie	m.	PCo	8 Mar. 1882	3	5	
Hale	Susie	m.	SD	25 Feb. 1882	3	6	
Hall	A. W.	m.	RRF	27 Mar. 1884	2	3	

(1) Surname	(2) Given Name	(3)	(4)	(5) Date	(6) Pg	(7) Col	(8) Comments
Hall	A. W.	m.	SD	5 Apr. 1884	3	4	
Hall	Albert	b.	PCo	21 Feb. 1883	3	5	
Hall	Albert	b.	PCo	3 Sept. 1884	2	5	
Hall	Albert	b.	PWA	24 Feb. 1883	3	7	
Hall	Albert	b.	PWA	30 Aug. 1884	3	5	
Hall	Albert	b.	SD	13 Sept. 1884	3	4	
Hall	Albert S.	b.	PCo	16 Nov. 1881	3	5	
Hall	C. T.	b.	DR	29 July 1885	3	4	
Hall	C. T.	b.	PCo	22 July 1885	3	6	
Hall	Clarence C.	m.	RRF	8 Nov. 1883	2	3	
Hall	E. G.	b.	RRF	7 Apr. 1881	2	4	
Hall	E. G.	b.	SD	16 Apr. 1881	3	8	
Hall	E., Mrs.	m.	PC	11 July 1883	3	5	
Hall	E., Mrs.	m.	DD	3 July 1883	3	3	
Hall	E., Mrs.	m.	SD	7 July 1883	2	5	
Hall	Ed	m.	DR	4 June 1881	3	2	
Hall	Ed F.	m.	DR	3 June 1881	2	3	also p. 3 col. 1
Hall	Edward	m.	RRF	16 Feb. 1882	3	5	
Hall	Emma	m.	CR	30 May 1885	4	1	
Hall	Emma	m.	PCo	27 May 1885	3	6	
Hall	Evelyn	d.	DR	5 June 1882	3	2	
Hall	Evelyn	d.	SD	10 June 1882	2	3	also p. 3 col. 3
Hall	Fanny	d.	DR	25 July 1882	2	3	
Hall	Fanny	d.	RRF	20 July 1882	2	4	
Hall	G. H.	b.	PCo	4 Oct. 1882	3	6	
Hall	G. P.	b.	DD	26 July 1883	3	2	
Hall	G. P.	b.	PC	25 July 1883	3	6	
Hall	G. P.	b.	PWA	28 July 1883	3	7	
Hall	G. P.	b.	SD	28 July 1883	2	5	
Hall	George	b.	SD	30 Sept. 1882	3	6	
Hall	Gilbert P.	m.	PCo	31 May 1882	3	5	
Hall	Gilbert P.	m.	SD	10 June 1882	2	3	
Hall	Henry	d.	RRF	20 July 1882	2	4	
Hall	Henry, Mrs.	d.	SD	22 July 1882	3	5	
Hall	J. E.	m.	CR	11 June 1881	5	5	
Hall	J. E.	b.	DD	20 Dec. 1883	2	2	
Hall	J. E.	b.	DR	13 Apr. 1882	3	2	
Hall	J. E.	b.	PCo	19 Apr. 1882	3	5	
Hall	J. E.	b.	PCo	26 Apr. 1882	3	4	
Hall	J. E.	b.	PCo	26 Dec. 1883	3	5	
Hall	J. E.	m.	RRF	16 June 1881	2	5	
Hall	J. E.	m.	SD	4 June 1881	3	8	

(1) Surname	(2) Given Name	(3)	(4)	(5) Date	(6) Pg	(7) Col	(8) Comments
Hall	J. E.	b.	SD	15 Apr. 1882	3	6	
Hall	J. E.	o.	SD	21 June 1883	1	3	
Hall	J. E.	b.	SD	22 Dec. 1883	3	5	
Hall	Julia	d.	CR	13 July 1882	5	2	
Hall	Julia	d.	DR	21 July 1882	3	2	
Hall	Julia	d.	PCo	19 July 1882	3	6	
Hall	Julia	d.	RRF	20 July 1882	2	4	
Hall	L. B.	d.	PCo	14 Mar. 1883	3	5	
Hall	Laura J.	m.	PCo	3 Dec. 1884	3	5	
Hall	Laura	m.	DR	6 Dec. 1884	3	2	
Hall	Lizzie B.	m.	DD	17 Oct. 1883	3	3	
Hall	Lizzie B.	m.	SD	20 Oct. 1883	3	4	
Hall	Luke	b.	RRF	29 June 1882	2	5	
Hall	Luke	b.	SD	1 July 1882	2	3	
Hall	Luke (dau. of)	d.	PC	13 June 1883	3	6	
Hall	Luke (dau. of)	d.	RRF	7 June 1883	2	3	
Hall	Luke (dau. of)	d.	SD	16 June 1883	2	6	
Hall	P. L.	b.	SD	5 Mar. 1881	3	8	
Hall	S. W.	d.	DR	23 June 1884	3	3	
Hall	Sallie E.	m.	PCo	2 Jan. 1884	3	6	
Hall	Sallie	m.	PWA	5 Jan. 1884	3	7	
Hall	Samantha	d.	CR	22 Jan. 1881	5	5	
Hall	Samantha	d.	SD	29 Jan. 1881	3	8	
Hall	Samantha	d.	PCo	19 Jan. 1881	3	4	
Hall	Samuel A.	d.	DR	9 Nov. 1885	2	2	
Hall	Samuel	d.	CR	1 Jan. 1881	5	4	also 8 Jan. 1881, p. 5 col. 5
Hall	Samuel	d.	CR	8 Jan. 1881	5	5	
Hall	Samuel	d.	DR	1 Jan. 1881	3	2	
Hall	Samuel	d.	SD	15 Jun. 1881	3	8	
Hall	W. P.	b.	DR	18 Feb. 1882	2	3	
Hall	W. P.	b.	PCo	15 Feb. 1882	3	4	
Hall	W. R.	m.	SD	7 Jan. 1882	3	4 & 8	
Hall	Walter R.	m.	PCo	11 Jan. 1882	3	6	
Hall	Wiley	b.	CR	10 Sept. 1881	5	3	
Hall	Wiley	b.	DR	13 Sept. 1881	2	3	
Halsell	J. T.	m.	SD	19 Feb. 1881	3	8	
Haltinner	Babette	m.	DR	27 May 1882	2	3	
Haltinner	Babette	m.	PCo	31 May 1882	3	5	
Haltinner	Babette	m.	SD	27 May 1882	3	5	
Ham	Charles M.	b.	SD	26 Feb. 1881	3	8	
Hambree	L.	b.	CR	12 Feb. 1881	5	5	

(1) Surname	(2) Given Name	(3)	(4)	(5) Date	(6) Pg	(7) Col	(8) Comments
Hambree	L.	b.	DR	10 Feb. 1881	3	2	
Hamill	Charles B.	m.	DR	17 June 1882	3	2	
Hamill	Charles B.	m.	PCo	21 June 1882	3	5	
Hamill	Charles B.	m.	RRF	15 June 1882	2	4	
Hamill	Charles B.	m.	SD	17 June 1882	2	4	
Hamilton	C. C.	b.	DD	15 Sept. 1883	3	3	
Hamilton	Charlotte E.	d.	DR	28 June 1884	3	2	
Hamilton	G. W.	o.	SD	24 Dec. 1881	3	3	
Hamilton	George W.	b.	PCo	13 Sept. 1882	3	7	
Hamilton	James H.	m.	SD	19 Mar. 1881	3	8	
Hamilton	Sallie	d.	DR	16 Nov. 1882	2	3	
Hamilton	Sallie	d.	PCo	22 Nov. 1882	3	5	
Hamilton	Sallie	d.	RRF	16 Nov. 1882	2	4	
Hamm	Gussie	m.	PCo	10 Sept. 1884	3	6	
Hamm	Gussie	m.	PWA	13 Sept. 1884	3	6	
Hamm	Gussie	m.	SD	20 Sept. 1884	2	5	
Hammel	Charles	b.	PC	2 May 1883	3	5	
Hammel	Charles	b.	SD	5 May 1883	3	6	
Hammell	Henry	b.	PCo	16 Mar. 1881	3	4	
Hammell	Henry	b.	SD	19 Mar. 1881	3	8	
Hammell	Mr. & Mrs.	b.	CR	19 Mar. 1881	4	3	
Hammett	Martha	m.	DD	25 July 1883	3	2	
Hammett	Martha	m.	PC	1 Aug. 1883	3	6	
Hammett	Martha	m.	SD	28 July 1883	2	5	
Hammock	Miss	m.	CR	2 Dec. 1882	3	2	
Hammond	Frank	b.	CR	2 Apr. 1881	5	3	
Hammond	Frank	b.	PCo	30 Mar. 1881	3	4	
Hammond	Frank	b.	PCo	21 Mar. 1883	3	5	
Hammond	Frank	b.	PWA	31 Mar. 1883	2	4	
Hammond	Frank	b.	SD	9 Apr. 1881	3	8	
Hammond	Frank	b.	SD	7 Apr. 1883	2	6	
Hammonds	S. T.	d.	SD	14 May 1881	3	8	
Hancock	(male)	b.	DR	12 Mar. 1884	3	2	
Haney	Frank	b.	PC	13 June 1883	3	6	
Haney	Frank	m.	PCo	21 June 1882	3	5	
Haney	Frank	b.	PWA	16 June 1883	3	7	
Haney	Frank	m.	SD	24 June 1882	3	5	
Haney	Frank (son of)	d.	DD	12 Oct. 1883	3	3	
Haney	Frank (son of)	d.	PWA	13 Oct. 1883	3	8	
Haney	Frank (son of)	d.	SD	20 Oct. 1883	3	4	
Haney	John W.	m.	PCo	10 Sept. 1884	3	6	
Haney	John W.	m.	SD	20 Sept. 1884	2	5	

(1) Surname	(2) Given Name	(3)	(4)	(5) Date	(6) Pg	(7) Col	(8) Comments
Hanna	W. E.	b.	PC	16 May 1883	3	5	
Hanna	W. E.	b.	PWA	19 May 1883	3	8	
Hannah	Nettie	m.	PCo	21 Feb. 1883	3	5	
Hannah	Nettie	m.	PWA	24 Feb. 1883	3	7	
Hannon	James P.	m.	DR	13 Sept. 1881	2	3	
Hannon	James P.	m.	SD	17 Sept. 1881	3	8	
Hansen	Edward	m.	PWA	4 Apr. 1885	3	6	
Hansen	Edward	m.	SD	18 Apr. 1885	2	4	
Hansen	Pelar	m.	SD	31 Dec. 1881	3	6	
Hanson	E. P.	b.	DD	12 Oct. 1883	3	3	
Hanson	Cora	m.	SD	9 May 1885	2	5	
Hanson	E. P.	b.	PWA	13 Oct. 1883	3	8	
Hanson	E. P.	b.	SD	20 Oct. 1883	3	4	
Hanson	Louis	b.	DD	15 Sept. 1883	3	3	
Hanson	Michael	b.	PCo	21 Feb. 1883	3	5	
Haraszthy	A. F.	d.	SIT	4 Feb. 1888	2	4	also p. 3 col. 2
Haraszthy	Otella	m.	DD	10 Oct. 1883	3	3	
Haraszthy	Otella	m.	SD	13 Oct. 1883	1	3	also p. 3 col. 4
Harbison	Luther J.	m.	SD	9 Apr. 1881	3	8	
Hardesty	Polly S.	d.	DD	2 Aug. 1883	3	2	
Hardesty	Polly S.	d.	SD	4 Aug. 1883	2	5	
Hardin	(male)	b.	DR	22 May 1884	3	2	
Hardin	George	b.	DR	2 Oct. 1885	3	4	
Hardin	George M.	m.	PCo	14 Jan. 1885	3	6	
Hardin	George M.	b.	PCo	30 Sept. 1885	3	6	
Hardin	George M.	m.	PWA	17 Jan. 1885	2	4	
Hardin	J. M.	b.	DD	23 Nov. 1883	3	2	
Hardin	J. M.	b.	PWA	24 Nov. 1883	3	6	
Hardin	J. M.	b.	SD	1 Dec. 1883	3	4	
Hardin	John M.	m.	PCo	4 Oct. 1882	3	6	
Hardin	L. B.	b.	DR	9 Nov. 1885	2	2	
Hardin	Labon	b.	PC	25 Apr. 1883	3	5	
Hardin	Labon	b.	PWA	28 Apr. 1883	3	8	
Hardin	Lester B.	m.	PCo	11 Oct. 1882	3	6	
Hardin	Lester B.	m.	SD	7 Oct. 1882	1	3	also p. 3 col. 6
Hardin	Lester	b.	PCo	21 May 1884	3	4	
Hardin	Lester	b.	PWA	24 May 1884	3	5	
Hardin	Lester	b.	SD	24 May 1884	2	3	
Hardin	Mary F.	d.	PCo	4 Jan. 1882	3	7	
Hardin	Mary F.	d.	SD	14 Jan. 1882	3	8	
Hardin	Robert	m.	DR	1 Aug. 1882	3	2	
Hardin	Robert	m.	PCo	2 Aug. 1882	3	6	

(1) Surname	(2) Given Name	(3)	(4)	(5) Date	(6) Pg	(7) Col	(8) Comments
Hardin	Robert	m.	SD	29 July 1882	3	7	
Hardin	T. S.	m.	DD	27 Oct. 1883	3	3	
Harford	Rev. and Mrs.	b.	PWA	3 Mar. 1883	3	6	
Harford	Rev.	b.	PCo	28 Feb. 1883	3	5	
Harford	Rev.	b.	SD	3 Mar. 1883	2	6	
Harford	Robert I.	d.	PWA	9 June 1883	3	1&7	also 16 June, p. 2 col. 3
Harford	Robert L.	d.	PC	6 June 1883	3	4	
Harford	Robert L.	d.	SD	16 June 1883	2	6	
Hargrave	Emma	m.	DR	13 Sept. 1881	2	3	
Hargrave	Emma	m.	RRF	8 Sept. 1881	2	4	
Harley	W. N.	b.	SD	5 Feb. 1881	3	8	
Harlow	C. A.	m.	PCo	16 Nov. 1881	3	5	
Harlow	Charles A.	m.	DR	8 Nov. 1881	2	3	
Harlow	Charles A.	m.	RRF	10 Nov. 1881	2	4	
Harlow	Cleora Ann	d.	DR	20 Aug. 1881	2	3	
Harlow	Cleora Ann	d.	PCo	17 Aug. 1881	3	5	
Harlow	Cleora Ann	d.	SD	27 Aug. 1881	3	8	
Harlow	James	d.	DR	4 Feb. 1882	2	3	
Harlow	James	d.	PCo	15 Feb. 1882	3	4	
Harlow	James	d.	SD	4 Feb. 1882	3	6	
Harmon	Jennie	m.	DD	24 Sept. 1883	3	2	
Harmon	William	m.	DR	9 Feb. 1882	2	3	
Harmon	William	d.	DR	3 Dec. 1884	3	2	
Harmon	William	m.	HE	9 Feb. 1882	2	3	
Harnett	Ella	d.	SD	5 Mar. 1881	3	8	
Harrington	(female)	b.	DR	21 June 1884	3	3	
Harrington	(male)	b.	DR	17 Mar. 1884	3	3	
Harrington	Cas.	b.	PCo	15 June 1884	3	4	
Harrington	Charles	b.	SD	5 July 1884	2	3	
Harrington	Katie	d.	DR	25 Nov. 1884	3	2	inf. daughter of Charles J.
Harrington	Katie	d.	PCo	3 Dec. 1884	3	5	
Harrington	P. J.	d.	SD	5 Mar. 1881	3	8	
Harris	E. D.	m.	PCo	18 Oct. 1882	3	6	
Harris	E. D.	m.	SD	14 Oct. 1882	3	6	
Harris	E. D.	b.	SD	6 June 1885	2	4	
Harris	Emily Isabella	d.	DR	1 Oct. 1885	3	4	
Harris	Emily Isabella	d.	SD	3 Oct. 1885	5	4	also 10 Oct., p. 1 col. 5
Harris	Granville S.	m.	PCo	7 Oct. 1885	3	6	
Harris	Granville S.	m.	SD	10 Oct. 1885	5	5	
Harris	Granville S.	m.	SIT	3 Oct. 1885	2	3	
Harris	Jacob	o.	DR	9 Mar. 1882	3	1	

(1) Surname	(2) Given Name	(3)	(4)	(5) Date	(6) Pg	(7) Col	(8) Comments
Harris	John L.	b.	SD	4 Apr. 1885	2	5	
Harris	John W.	m.	DD	10 Oct. 1883	3	3	
Harris	John W.	m.	SD	13 Oct. 1883	3	4	
Harris	Mattie	m.	DD	24 Dec. 1883	3	2	
Harris	Phoebe B.	o.	DR	9 Mar. 1882	3	1	
Harris	R. A.	b.	PCo	30 Sept. 1885	3	6	
Harris	R. A.	b.	SD	3 Oct. 1885	5	4	
Harris	Richard A.	m.	DR	17 Nov. 1884	3	2	
Harris	Richard A.	m.	PCo	26 Nov. 1884	3	5	
Harris	Richard A.	m.	SD	23 Nov. 1884	2	6	
Harris	Thomas M.	b.	DD	1 Sept. 1883	3	2	
Harris	Thomas M.	b.	SD	8 Sept. 1883	2	7	
Harris	Thomas M.	b.	SD	10 Oct. 1885	5	5	
Harris	Thomas	b.	SD	18 June 1881	3	8	
Harris	W. F.	b.	CR	16 June 1883	3	1	
Harris	W. F.	b.	DR	9 Nov. 1885	2	2	
Harris	W. F.	b.	PC	20 June 1883	3	6	
Harris	W. F.	b.	RRF	14 June 1883	2	3	
Harris	W. F.	b.	SD	23 June 1883	3	5	
Harrison	Jacob	m.	DD	15 Sept. 1883	3	3	
Harrison	Judith	d.	SD	28 Oct. 1882	3	5	
Harrison	Robert H.	m.	DD	10 Oct. 1883	3	3	
Harrison	Robert H.	m.	SD	13 Oct. 1883	3	4	
Harrison	Thomas	b.	SD	6 Sept. 1884	2	5	
Hart	Carl	d.	RRF	19 July 1883	3	4	
Hart	George	d.	CR	28 May 1881	4	1	
Hart	George	d.	DR	30 May 1881	2	3	
Hart	George	d.	RRF	26 May 1881	3	4	
Hart	George	m.	SD	4 June 1881	3	8	
Hart	Mary L.	m.	PCo	7 Jan. 1885	3	6	
Hart	Mary L.	m.	SD	3 Jan. 1885	2	7	
Hartnett	Morris M.	d.	PCo	1 Nov. 1882	3	1	
Hartnett	Morris M.	d.	SD	4 Nov. 1882	3	1	
Hartnett	Morris	d.	DR	30 Oct. 1882	3	1	also 1 Nov., p. 2 col. 1
Hartnett	Mr.	d.	CR	12 Aug. 1882	3	2	
Hartsock	Adolphus	d.	PCo	8 July 1885	3	6	
Hartsock	Adolphus	d.	SD	27 June 1885	5	4	
Hartsock	Mr. & Mrs.	b.	SD	21 Mar. 1885	2	5	
Harvey	A. A.	m.	DR	22 Aug. 1881	2	3	
Harvey	Amelia A.	m.	SD	13 Aug. 1881	3	8	
Harvey	Lulu	m.	PCo	2 Nov. 1881	3	5	
Haselton	C. O.	m.	PCo	30 Dec. 1885	3	4	

(1) Surname	(2) Given Name	(3)	(4)	(5) Date	(6) Pg	(7) Col	(8) Comments
Haskell	A. A., Mrs.	d.	PCo	16 Jan. 1884	3	6	
Haskell	A. A., Mrs.	d.	PWA	19 Jan. 1884	3	3&7	
Haskell	A. A., Mrs.	d.	SD	19 Jan. 1884	3	6	
Haskell	W. B.	m.	PC	1 Aug. 1883	3	6	
Haskell	W. B.	m.	PWA	4 Aug. 1883	3	7	
Haskell	William B.	m.	SD	28 July 1883	2	5	
Haskins	Arthur M.	d.	DR	2 Nov. 1885	3	4	
Haskins	Arthur M.	d.	PCo	28 Oct. 1885	3	4	
Haskins	Flora B.	d.	PCo	27 Sept. 1882	3	6	
Haskins	Lizzie	d.	PCo	2 Dec. 1885	3	4	
Haskins	Ruth A.	d.	PWA	22 Sept. 1883	3	2&6	
Haskins	T. J.	b.	CR	1 Jan. 1881	5	5	
Haskins	T. J.	b.	DR	5 Jan. 1881	3	2	
Haskins	T. J.	b.	SD	8 Jan. 1881	3	8	
Haskins	W. W.	b.	DR	4 Sept. 1885	3	4	
Haskins	W. W.	b.	PCo	2 Sept. 1885	3	6	
Haskins	William W.	m.	PCo	31 Dec. 1884	3	4	
Haskins	William W.	m.	PWA	3 Jan. 1885	3	4	
Haskins	William W.	m.	SD	10 Jan. 1885	2	6	
Hasper	Mary	d.	PWA	28 Mar. 1885	3	5	
Hasper	Mary	d.	SD	4 Apr. 1885	2	5	
Hassett	Aaron	b.	DR	7 Dec. 1882	2	3	
Hassett	Aaron	b.	PCo	13 Dec. 1882	3	4	
Hassett	Aaron	b.	RRF	7 Dec. 1882	2	3	
Hassett	Aaron	b.	SD	16 Dec. 1882	3	6	
Hassett	Lulu C.	m.	CR	13 May 1882	5	1	
Hassett	Lulu C.	m.	RRF	11 May 1882	3	4	
Hassett	Lulu	m.	DR	12 May 1882	3	2	
Hassett	Lulu	m.	HE	11 May 1882	2	3	
Hassett	Lulu	m.	PCo	17 May 1882	3	5	
Hassett	Lulu	m.	SD	20 May 1882	2	4	
Hastings	Emma	m.	PCo	25 Feb. 1885	3	6	
Hastings	S. C.	m.	CR	3 Oct. 1885	3	2	
Hastings	S. C.	m.	CR	11 Apr. 1885	3	2	
Hatch	Ed	b.	SD	9 Aug. 1884	3	4	
Hatch	Frederick	m.	DD	20 Oct. 1883	3	3	
Hatton	C. B.	m.	DR	21 Dec. 1882	2	2	
Hatton	C. B.	m.	PCo	27 Dec. 1882	3	6	
Hatton	C. B.	m.	SD	30 Dec. 1882	3	6	
Hatton	Charles	m.	RRF	28 Dec. 1882	2	2	
Hatton	Charles	b.	RRF	25 Oct. 1883	2	4	
Hatton	Mary	d.	DR	22 Apr. 1882	3	2	

(1) Surname	(2) Given Name	(3)	(4)	(5) Date	(6) Pg	(7) Col	(8) Comments
Hatton	Mary	d.	PCo	19 Apr. 1882	3	5	
Haubert	Jacob	d.	PCo	7 June 1882	3	5	
Haubrich	Sarah Andrew	d.	PCo	19 Aug. 1885	3	6	
Haubrich	W. F.	d.	PC	27 June 1883	3	6	
Haubrich	Sarah Andrew	d.	DR	26 Aug. 1885	3	4	nee Hill
Hauert	H. F.	b.	PWA	13 Oct. 1883	3	8	
Haupt	J.	b.	CR	25 Mar. 1882	5	1	
Haupt	J.	b.	CR	27 June 1885	3	1	
Haupt	J.	b.	DD	8 Sept. 1883	3	3	
Haupt	J.	b.	DR	28 Mar. 1882	2	3	
Haupt	J.	b.	SD	15 Sept. 1883	2	4	
Haupt	J. (son of)	d.	DD	8 Sept. 1883	3	3	
Haupt	J. (son of)	d.	SD	15 Sept. 1883	2	4	
Haupt	Julius	b.	PCo	1 July 1885	3	6	
Hauto	P.	b.	SIT	7 Jan. 1888	2	5	
Haven	George	b.	SD	7 Oct. 1882	3	6	
Hawkins	Alice M.	d.	DR	10 May 1881	2	2	
Hawkins	Alice M.	d.	SD	14 May 1881	3	8	
Hawkins	Elijah	d.	CR	12 Feb. 1881	5	5	
Hawkins	Elijah	d.	DR	7 Feb. 1881	3	2	
Hawkins	Elijah	d.	SD	5 Feb. 1881	3	8	
Hawkins	Maria	d.	PC	9 May 1883	3	5	
Hawkins	Maria	d.	SD	12 May 1883	2	6	
Hawles	A. H.	m.	SD	27 Aug. 1881	3	8	
Hayden	Alice A.	m.	CR	8 Jan. 1881	5	5	
Hayden	Alice A.	m.	DR	1 Jan. 1881	3	2	
Hayden	Lewis H.	d.	DR	10 Dec. 1881	2	3	
Hayden	Lewis H.	d.	PCo	21 Dec. 1881	3	5	
Hayes	Alice	m.	DR	3 July 1884	2	2	
Hayes	Alice	m.	PCo	16 July 1884	3	6	
Hayes	Alice	m.	SD	5 July 1884	2	3	
Hayes	Anna	m.	SD	9 May 1885	2	5	
Hayes	Ellen	m.	PCo	24 May 1882	3	5	
Hayes	Ellen	m.	SD	20 May 1882	2	4	
Hayes	G. H.	o.	CR	2 Apr. 1881	4	1	
Hayes	Jennie	m.	PCo	20 Sept. 1882	3	6	
Hayes	Jennie	m.	RRF	14 Sept. 1882	2	4	
Hayes	Jennie	m.	SD	23 Sept. 1882	3	6	
Hayes	Mary	m.	DR	15 Feb. 1881	3	1	
Hayes	Mary	m.	SD	19 Feb. 1881	3	8	
Hayes	W. C.	m.	SD	26 Mar. 1881	3	8	
Hayne	W. H.	b.	PWA	2 May 1885	3	6	

(1) Surname	(2) Given Name	(3)	(4)	(5) Date	(6) Pg	(7) Col	(8) Comments
Hays	H. G.	m.	RRF	16 Nov. 1882	2	4	
Hays	Hattie C.	m.	RRF	21 Sept. 1882	2	4	
Hays	Hattie	m.	SD	30 Sept. 1882	3	6	
Hayward	Anabel Stuart	d.	PC	20 June 1883	3	6	
Hayward	Anabel Stuart	d.	SD	16 June 1883	2	6	
Hayward	Darwin L.	b.	PC	20 June 1883	3	6	
Hayward	Darwin L.	b.	SD	16 June 1883	2	6	
Hazell	Will H.	m.	DD	24 Sept. 1883	3	2	
Head	Robert	d.	SD	27 Jan. 1883	3	5&6	
Head	Robertson	d.	PCo	31 Jan. 1883	3	5	
Headley	E.	m.	DR	28 Sept. 1885	3	4	
Headley	E., Miss	m.	SRR	1 Oct. 1885	3	3	
Headley	Louisa E.	m.	SD	3 Oct. 1885	5	4	
Headrick	Rena Roberts	d.	DR	7 Feb. 1884	3	3	
Heald	Georgiana	m.	PCo	11 Mar. 1885	3	6	
Heald	Oliver	d.	PC	16 May 1883	3	5	
Healey	W. E.	b.	SD	12 Apr. 1884	2	5	
Healy	Edward	b.	PCo	13 Sept. 1882	3	7	
Healy	Edwin B.	m.	SD	1 Oct. 1881	3	8	
Healy	Edwin H.	m.	DR	24 Sept. 1881	2	3	
Healy	Edwin R.	m.	PCo	21 Sept. 1881	3	5	
Healy	Mary	m.	DD	29 Dec. 1883	3	3	
Healy	W. E.	b.	PCo	9 Apr. 1884	3	6	
Heaney	John W.	m.	PWA	6 Sept. 1884	3	4	
Heath	B. M., Mrs.	d.	PCo	7 Oct. 1885	3	6	
Heath	B. M., Mrs.	d.	SD	10 Oct. 1885	5	5	
Heath	William A.	b.	SD	18 June 1881	3	8	
Heath	William	b.	CR	11 June 1881	5	5	
Heath	William	b.	SD	25 June 1881	3	8	
Hebbing	Frank	d.	RRF	15 Nov. 1883	2	3	
Hebron	Ann	d.	CR	19 Feb. 1881	4	2	
Hebron	Ann	d.	SD	19 Feb. 1881	3	8	
Hedden	R. H. K.	b.	SD	8 Jan. 1881	3	8	
Hedges	Charles B.	d.	DD	28 Aug. 1883	3	3	
Hedges	Charles B.	d.	PWA	25 Aug. 1883	3	8	
Hedges	Charles E.	d.	SD	1 Sept. 1883	2	7	
Hedges	E. D.	b.	PCo	16 Apr. 1884	3	5	
Hedges	E. D.	b.	PWA	12 Apr. 1884	3	6	
Hedges	Ed	b.	PCo	3 Jan. 1883	3	4	
Hedges	Ed	b.	PWA	5 Jan. 1883	2	5	
Hedges	Ed	b.	SD	6 Jan. 1883	2	5	
Hedges	Edward	m.	DR	25 Nov. 1881	2	3	

(1) Surname	(2) Given Name	(3)	(4)	(5) Date	(6) Pg	(7) Col	(8) Comments
Hedges	Edward	m.	PCo	23 Nov. 1881	3	5	
Hedges	Edward	m.	SD	3 Dec. 1881	3	8	
Hedges	S. H.	b.	DD	26 Dec. 1883	3	3	
Hedges	S. H.	b.	SD	29 Dec. 1883	3	6	
Hedges	Stephen H.	m.	PC	9 May 1883	3	5	
Hedges	Stephen H.	m.	PWA	12 May 1883	3	8	
Hedges	Steven H.	m.	SD	12 May 1883	2	6	
Hedges	W. H.	b.	DD	12 Nov. 1883	3	3	
Hedrick	J., Mrs.	d.	CR	25 June 1881	4	3	
Hedrick	J., Mrs.	d.	SD	2 July 1881	3	8	
Hedrick	James	d.	RRF	16 June 1881	2	5	
Hedrick	James	d.	RRF	30 Mar. 1882	2	5	
Hedrick	James	d.	SD	1 Apr. 1882	3	6	
Hedrick	James, Mrs.	d.	DR	18 June 1881	2	3	
Hedrick	James, Mrs.	d.	SD	18 June 1881	3	8	
Hedrick	Jane	d.	DR	28 June 1881	2	2	
Heffelfinger	Emma	d.	DR	20 Dec. 1881	2	2	
Heffelfinger	Emma	d.	SD	7 Jan. 1882	3	8	
Heffelfinger	Laura J.	d.	DR	5 Nov. 1885	3	4	
Heffelfinger	Laura J.	d.	SD	7 Nov. 1885	3	4	
Heffelfinger	W. J.	b.	DR	14 Dec. 1881	2	2	
Heffelfinger	W. J.	b.	PCo	28 Dec. 1881	3	6	
Heffelfinger	W. J.	b.	SD	24 Dec. 1881	2	3	
Heffelfinger	W. J. (dau. of)	d.	PCo	28 Dec. 1881	3	6	
Hegler	G. H.	m.	CR	5 Mar. 1881	4	2	
Hegler	G. H.	m.	DR	1 Mar. 1881	3	2	
Hegler	G. H.	b.	DR	4 Aug. 1885	3	4	
Hegler	G. H.	m.	PCo	9 Mar. 1881	3	4	
Hegler	G. H.	m.	SD	5 Mar. 1881	3	8	
Hegner	Edward	b.	PCo	10 Sept. 1884	3	6	
Hegner	Edward	b.	PWA	13 Sept. 1884	3	6	
Hegner	Edward	b.	SD	20 Sept. 1884	2	5	
Heisel	Paul	o.	DR	21 Oct. 1882	3	2	
Helbush	Mr. & Mrs.	b.	DR	17 Sept. 1885	3	4	
Helbush	Mr. & Mrs.	b.	PCo	23 Sept. 1885	3	6	
Held	Georginia	m.	PWA	7 Mar. 1885	3	5	
Held	Henrietta G.	m.	SD	14 Mar. 1885	5	5	
Helm	Elizabeth P.	d.	DR	17 Jan. 1882	2	3	
Hembreys	Samuel	d.	DR	9 Nov. 1885	2	2	
Hendley	H. E., Mrs.	d.	SD	3 May 1884	3	3	Rural Cemetery
Hendley	H. E., Mrs.	d.	SD	26 Apr. 1884	3	5	
Hendley	John	p.	DD	11 July 1883	3	2	

(1) Surname	(2) Given Name	(3)	(4)	(5) Date	(6) Pg	(7) Col	(8) Comments
Hendley	John, Mrs.	d.	DR	21 Apr. 1884	3	2	
Hendley	John, Mrs.	d.	PCo	30 Apr. 1884	2	6	
Hendley	Nannie V.	m.	DR	16 Dec. 1885	3	4	
Hendley	Nannie V.	m.	PCo	23 Dec. 1885	3	3&4	
Hendley	Nannie V.	m.	SD	19 Dec. 1885	3	1&4	
Hendrick	Ed	b.	SD	28 Jan. 1882	3	6	
Hendrick	J., Mrs.	d.	CR	25 June 1881	4	3	
Hendrick	W. W.	m.	CR	19 Jan. 1884	3	1	
Hendrick	William W.	m.	SD	26 Jan. 1884	3	5	
Hendricks	J.	b.	RRF	24 Mar. 1881	2	4	
Hendricks	Mary Ann	m.	DD	29 Dec. 1883	3	3	
Hendricks	Mary C.	m.	PCo	22 Nov. 1882	3	5	
Hendricks	Mary	m.	CR	18 Nov. 1882	3	3	
Hendricks	Mary	m.	DR	16 Nov. 1882	2	3	
Hendricks	Mary	m.	RRF	23 Nov. 1882	2	4	
Hendricks	W. W.	m.	PCo	23 Jan. 1884	3	5	
Hendricks	W. W.	m.	RRF	17 Jan. 1884	2	4	
Hendricks	Wallace	b.	SD	15 Nov. 1884	2	5	
Hendrickson	D.	b.	SD	25 June 1881	3	8	
Henle	Albert	d.	SD	14 May 1881	3	8	
Henley	B.	b.	CR	30 Apr. 1881	5	5	
Henley	B.	b.	DR	25 Apr. 1881	3	2	
Henley	B.	b.	SD	23 Apr. 1881	3	8	
Henley	D.	o.	DR	12 Aug. 1881	3	1	erroneous report of d.
Henley	G. W.	d.	DR	6 Aug. 1881	3	1	
Henley	George W.	d.	CR	13 Aug. 1881	1	4	
Henley	George W.	d.	SD	6 Aug. 1881	3	2&8	
Henley	Susan J.	d.	SD	23 Nov. 1882	3	2	
Henley	W. N., Mrs.	d.	SD	3 Sept. 1881	3	8	
Hennessy	Daniel	b.	DR	10 Apr. 1882	2	2	
Hennessy	Daniel	b.	PCo	12 Apr. 1882	3	5	
Hennessy	Daniel	b.	SD	15 Apr. 1882	3	6	
Henning	Frank	d.	CR	17 Nov. 1883	3	1	
Henning	Frank	d.	DD	17 Nov. 1883	3	3	
Henning	Frank	d.	RRF	22 Nov. 1883	3	4	
Henrickson	John C.	m.	PCo	28 June 1882	3	5	
Henrickson	John C.	m.	SD	1 July 1882	2	3	
Henry	Ali	d.	DD	28 Aug. 1883	3	3	
Henry	Ali	d.	PWA	25 Aug. 1883	3	3&8	
Henry	Ali	d.	SD	1 Sept. 1883	2	7	
Henry	Anna Maria	d.	DR	31 Mar. 1884	3	3	
Henry	Anna Maria	d.	PCo	9 Apr. 1884	3	6	

(1) Surname	(2) Given Name	(3)	(4)	(5) Date	(6) Pg	(7) Col	(8) Comments
Henry	Anna Maria	d.	RRF	17 Apr. 1884	2	4	
Henry	Anna Maria	d.	SD	5 Apr. 1884	3	4	
Henry	C.	b.	SD	12 Mar. 1881	3	8	
Henry	John	d.	CR	24 Dec. 1881	1	2	
Henry	Lennie	m.	PCo	15 Oct. 1884	3	6	
Henzel	George S.	m.	DR	28 Jan. 1882	2	3	
Henzel	George S.	m.	PCo	25 Jan. 1882	3	6	
Herald	M. & Mrs.	b.	SD	27 June 1885	5	4	
Herald	Mr. & Mrs.	b.	PCo	24 June 1885	3	6	
Herbert	John	m.	SD	3 Dec. 1881	3	8	
Herin	Owen	b.	PWA	6 Oct. 1883	3	8	
Herman	J. F.	b.	DR	23 May 1881	2	2	
Herman	J. F.	b.	SD	28 May 1881	3	8	
Hervey	Kate	m.	DR	1 Nov. 1881	2	3	filed after Nov. 29
Hervey	Kate	m.	PCo	9 Nov. 1881	3	5	
Heslep	Josephine	d.	DR	31 May 1881	2	2	
Heslep	Josephine	d.	PCo	1 June 1881	3	4	
Heslep	Josephine	m.	SD	4 June 1881	3	8	
Hesse	Christian	d.	DR	26 July 1884	3	3	
Hesse	Frederick	b.	PCo	7 Dec. 1881	3	5	
Hesse	Frederick	b.	SD	26 Nov. 1881	3	8	
Hesse	Mr.	d.	CR	19 July 1884	3	1	
Hesse	Mr.	d.	PCo	23 July 1884	3	6	
Hester	Catherine	d.	CR	12 Feb. 1881	5	5	
Hester	Catherine	d.	DR	7 Feb. 1881	3	2	
Hester	Catherine	d.	PCo	2 Feb. 1881	3	4	
Hester	Catherine	d.	SD	12 Feb. 1881	3	8	
Hewitt	Belle	m.	SD	5 Mar. 1881	3	8	
Hewitt	C. E.	d.	SD	15 Apr. 1882	3	6	
Hewitt	C. E., Mrs.	d.	DR	9 Apr. 1882	3	2	
Hewitt	C. E., Mrs.	d.	PCo	12 Apr. 1882	3	5	
Hewitt	C. E., Mrs.	d.	RRF	6 Apr. 1882	2	4	
Hewitt	George B. M.	d.	PCo	21 Jan. 1885	2	5	
Hewitt	George B. M.	d.	SD	24 Jan. 1885	5	5	
Hewitt	Josie	d.	DD	26 Sept. 1883	3	2	
Hewitt	Josie	d.	SD	29 Sept. 1883	2	6	
Hewlett	Frederick Whitney	d.	PCo	23 Feb. 1881	3	4	son of Frederick
Hewlett	Frederick Whitney	d.	SD	26 Feb. 1881	3	8	
Heyerman	John Frederick	d.	SIT	4 Feb. 1888	3	3	
Heyermann	Sophie	d.	SD	28 Feb. 1885	5	6	
Heyward	Frank	m.	DR	25 Nov. 1884	3	2	
Heyward	Frank	m.	PCo	26 Nov. 1884	3	5	

(1) Surname	(2) Given Name	(3)	(4)	(5) Date	(6) Pg	(7) Col	(8) Comments
Heyward	Frank	m.	SD	23 Nov. 1884	2	6	also p. 3 col. 2
Hickey	Maurice	b.	CR	2 July 1881	5	5	
Hickey	Maurice	b.	DR	24 June 1881	2	3	
Hickey	Maurice	b.	DR	16 Nov. 1885	3	4	
Hickey	Maurice	b.	PCo	22 June 1881	3	5	
Hickey	Maurice	b.	PCo	11 Nov. 1885	3	4	
Hickey	Maurice	b.	SD	2 July 1881	3	8	
Hickman	Nettie	m.	SD	10 Jan. 1885	2	6	
Hicks	E	m.	DR	18 Apr. 1884	3	2	
Hicks	E.	m.	PWA	26 Apr. 1884	3	6	
Hicks	E.	m.	SD	19 Apr. 1884	3	4	
Hicks	E. S.	o.	SD	11 July 1885	5	5	
Hicks	Hattie	m.	SD	6 May 1882	3	6	
Hicks	Margaret	d.	PCo	22 Apr. 1885	3	6	
Hicks	Thomas	b.	SD	18 Apr. 1885	2	4	
Hickson	John	m.	PCo	22 Apr. 1885	3	6	
Hickson	John	m.	SD	25 Apr. 1885	2	5	
Higgins	B. F.	b.	PCo	19 July 1882	3	6	
Higgins	Charles B.	m.	PCo	11 Mar. 1885	3	6	
Higgins	Charles B.	d.	PWA	14 Mar. 1885	3	5	
Higgins	Charles R.	d.	SD	21 Mar. 1885	2	5	
Higgins	Leslie J.	b.	RRF	12 May 1881	2	4	
Higgins	Mary N.	m.	SD	2 Apr. 1881	3	8	
Hildreth	William H.	b.	SD	21 Apr. 1883	2	6	
Hill	A. E.	m.	SD	26 Jan. 1884	3	5	
Hill	A. E., Mrs.	m.	CR	19 Jan. 1884	3	1	
Hill	A. F., Mrs.	m.	PCo	23 Jan. 1884	3	5	
Hill	A. E., Mrs.	m.	RRF	17 Jan. 1884	2	4	
Hill	C. S.	m.	DD	22 Oct. 1883	3	3	
Hill	C. S.	b.	PCo	11 Feb. 1885	3	6	
Hill	C. S.	b.	PWA	14 Feb. 1885	3	5	
Hill	C. S.	m.	SD	27 Oct. 1883	3	4	
Hill	C. S.	b.	SD	21 Feb. 1885	2	5	
Hill	H. W.	m.	PCo	24 June 1885	3	6	
Hill	H. W.	m.	SD	27 June 1885	5	4	
Hill	Hannah K.	d.	SD	25 Oct. 1884	2	5	
Hill	J. W.	b.	CR	16 Apr. 1881	5	2	
Hill	J. W.	b.	CR	16 Apr. 1881	5	3	
Hill	James M.	m.	SD	3 June 1882	2	4	
Hill	John W.	b.	SD	16 Apr. 1881	3	8	
Hill	John W.	b.	SD	23 Apr. 1881	3	8	
Hill	Lindel	d.	SD	1 Mar. 1884	6	6	

(1) Surname	(2) Given Name	(3)	(4)	(5) Date	(6) Pg	(7) Col	(8) Comments
Hill	Lindel	d.	SD	23 Feb. 1884	3	4	
Hill	Lindel M.	d.	PCo	27 Feb. 1884	3	6	
Hill	Lindel	d.	DR	20 Feb. 1884	3	3	
Hill	Milton	d.	SD	18 Apr. 1885	2	5	
Hill	Rebecca	d.	SD	5 Mar. 1881	3	8	
Hill	Robert	b.	CR	22 Dec. 1883	3	1	
Hill	Robert	b.	PCo	2 Jan. 1884	3	6	
Hill	W. C.	m.	PCo	14 Jan. 1885	3	6	
Hill	W. C.	m.	SD	10 Jan. 1885	2	6	
Hill	William	o.	DR	26 Oct. 1882	2	1	
Hillis	J. A.	b.	PCo	14 Mar. 1883	3	5	
Hillis	J. A. (wife and child)	d.	RRF	22 Mar. 1883	3	3	
Hillis	John T.	d.	CR	26 Dec. 1885	3	5	
Himan	Jacob	m.	DD	15 Sept. 1883	3	3	
Himan	Jacob	m.	DD	27 Sept. 1883	3	3	
Himan	Jacob	m.	PWA	29 Sept. 1883	3	8	
Himan	Jacob	m.	SD	29 Sept. 1883	2	6	
Himebauch	Clara	d.	PCo	28 Dec. 1881	3	6	
Himebauch	Maria D.	d.	PC	6 June 1883	3	4	
Himebauch	Maria D.	d.	SD	16 June 1883	2	6	
Himebaugh	Eva	d.	CR	28 May 1881	5	5	
Himebaugh	Eva	d.	DR	20 May 1881	2	3	
Himebaugh	Eva	d.	SD	28 May 1881	3	8	
Himebaugh	William	d.	DR	14 Oct. 1881	2	3	
Himebaugh	William	d.	PCo	12 Oct. 1881	3	5	
Himebaugh	William	d.	SD	22 Oct. 1881	3	6	
Himebaugh	Eva	d.	PCo	18 May 1881	3	5	
Hinckley	E., Mrs.	m.	DR	3 Jan. 1884	3	2	
Hinckley	Elizabeth	m.	PCo	9 Jan. 1884	3	6	
Hinckley	Elizabeth	m.	RRF	3 Jan. 1884	2	4	
Hinckley	Elizabeth	m.	SD	5 Jan. 1884	1	1	
Hinds	Samuel D.	d.	SD	22 Aug. 1885	6	2	
Hindson	F. J.	b.	SD	6 Aug. 1881	3	8	
Hindson	F. J.	b.	SD	16 July 1881	3	8	
Hindson	Frank J.	b.	PCo	14 Mar. 1883	3	5	
Hindson	Frank J.	b.	SD	3 Mar. 1883	2	6	
Hines	Robert G.	d.	SD	30 June 1883	3	5	
Hinkel	Martha	m.	CR	10 Nov. 1883	3	1	
Hinkston	Harlow	d.	PCo	2 Mar. 1881	4	4	
Hinkston	Harlow	d.	RRF	17 Feb. 1881	2	4	
Hinkston	Harlow	d.	SD	5 Mar. 1881	3	8	
Hinkston	Nancy	d.	PCo	29 Oct. 1884	3	5	

(1) Surname	(2) Given Name	(3)	(4)	(5) Date	(6) Pg	(7) Col	(8) Comments
Hinrichs	Carl	m.	PCo	15 Oct. 1884	3	6	
Hinricks	Carl	m.	PWA	11 Oct. 1884	3	4	
Hinton	Otho	o.	DR	14 July 1881	3	1	
Hinton	Otho	d.	DR	25 Oct. 1882	3	1	Santa Rosa Cem.
Hirth	Fred	b.	DR	2 Oct. 1885	3	4	
Hirth	Fred	b.	PCo	7 Oct. 1885	3	6	
Hitchcock	Ida M.	m.	SD	29 Jan. 1881	3	8	
Hitchcock	Silas	d.	RRF	20 Oct. 1881	2	4	
Hixon	W.	b.	PCo	19 Mar. 1884	3	6	
Hixon	W.	b.	RRF	13 Mar. 1884	2	2	
Hoadley	E. A.	b.	PCo	31 May 1882	3	5	
Hoadley	E. A.	b.	SD	27 May 1882	3	5	
Hoadley	Gus	b.	RRF	25 May 1882	2	3	
Hoadley	Hattiem	m.	PC	22 Aug. 1883	3	5	
Hoadley	Ida	m.	PCo	7 Jan. 1885	3	6	
Hoadley	Ida	m.	SD	10 Jan. 1885	2	6	
Hoadley	J. F.	b.	RRF	4 Jan. 1883	2	2	
Hoadley	J. F., Jr.	b.	DR	2 Nov. 1885	3	4	
Hoadley	J. F., Jr.	b.	PCo	3 Jan. 1883	3	4	
Hoadley	J. F., Jr.	b.	PCo	16 Apr. 1884	3	5	
Hoadley	James F., Jr.	m.	CR	22 Oct. 1881	5	3	
Hoadley	James F., Jr.	m.	DR	25 Oct. 1881	3	2	
Hoadley	James F., Jr.	m.	PCo	2 Nov. 1881	3	5	
Hoadley	James F., Jr.	m.	SD	29 Oct. 1881	3	6	
Hoadley	Louisa E.	m.	PCo	7 Oct. 1885	3	6	
Hoag	Abigail	d.	DD	18 Oct. 1883	3	3	
Hoag	Abigail	d.	SD	20 Oct. 1883	3	4	
Hoar	Addie E.	m.	PCo	1 Nov. 1882	3	5	
Hoar	B. F.	b.	DR	30 Jan. 1882	2	3	
Hoar	B. F.	b.	PCo	25 Jan. 1882	3	6	
Hobbie	G.	b.	DR	20 July 1881	3	2	
Hobbie	G.	b.	SD	6 Aug. 1881	3	8	
Hobson	Mary L.	m.	RRF	31 Aug. 1882	2	4	
Hobson	Mary	m.	SD	2 Sept. 1882	3	6	
Hockheimer	Mariam	m.	PCo	26 July 1882	3	6	
Hockin	William	b.	DR	8 Mar. 1882	2	3	
Hockin	William	b.	PCo	1 Mar. 1882	2	4	
Hockin	William	b.	SD	25 Feb. 1882	3	6	
Hodgson	W. H.	m.	PCo	10 Jan. 1883	3	6	
Hodgson	W. H.	m.	SD	6 Jan. 1883	2	5	
Hoen	Berthold	d.	CR	13 Aug. 1885	3	2	
Hoen	Berthold	d.	DR	7 Aug. 1885	3	4	

(1) Surname	(2) Given Name	(3)	(4)	(5) Date	(6) Pg	(7) Col	(8) Comments
Hoen	Berthold	d.	PCo	12 Aug. 1885	3	6	
Hoen	Berthold	d.	SD	15 Aug. 1885	1	3	
Hoen	Berthold	d.	SD	22 Aug. 1885	6	2	
Hoen	Berthold	d.	SIT	15 Aug. 1885	3	1	
Hoesley	H. P. (dau. of)	d.	PCo	13 Aug. 1884	3	4	
Hoesley	H. P. (dau. of)	d.	PWA	9 Aug. 1884	2	4	
Hoesly	H. P. (inf. dau.)	d.	DR	5 Aug. 1884	3	4	
Hoesly	H. P. (dau. of)	d.	SD	9 Aug. 1884	3	4	
Hoffgard	Charles	d.	HE	29 Dec. 1881	3	1	
Hoffgard	Charles	d.	RRF	29 Dec. 1881	3	1	
Hoffgard	F.	p.	DR	13 Nov. 1884	3	2	
Hoffman	Carl A.	b.	PCo	4 Jan. 1882	3	7	
Hoffman	Carl A.	b.	SD	31 Dec. 1881	3	6	
Hoffman	Carl Adalbert	b.	DR	28 Dec. 1881	2	2	
Hoffman	Charles	d.	SD	31 Oct. 1885	1	5	
Hoffman	Charles	d.	SIT	31 Oct. 1885	3	5	
Hoffman	Eva Belle	m.	PCo	24 Jan. 1883	3	5	
Hoffman	Eva Belle	m.	SD	20 Jan. 1883	2	5	
Hoffman	George	m.	DD	29 Dec. 1883	3	3	
Hoffman	Lou	m.	SD	21 Apr. 1883	2	6	
Hoffman	W. A.	m.	DD	20 Oct. 1883	3	3	
Hoffstetter	Bernard	d.	PCo	21 Jan. 1885	2	5	
Hoffstetter	Bernard	d.	PWA	24 Jan. 1885	3	5	
Hoffstetter	Bernard	d.	SD	24 Jan. 1885	5	5	
Hofgard	C. F.	p.	DR	16 July 1884	3	2	
Hogan	Birdinia	m.	PWA	5 Jan. 1883	3	2	
Hogans	William B.	d.	DR	24 June 1881	2	2	
Hoit	Sarah M.	m.	DR	20 Jan. 1882	3	2	
Hoit	Sarah M.	m.	HE	19 Jan. 1882	2	3	
Hoit	Sarah M.	m.	RRF	19 Jan. 1882	2	3	
Holcomb	Edith B.	m.	SD	27 Jan. 1883	3	6	
Holcomb	Edith	m.	PCo	31 Jan. 1883	3	5	
Holcomb	Edith	m.	RRF	25 Jan. 1883	2	4	
Holcomb	Frankie	m.	CR	21 Apr. 1883	3	1	
Holcomb	Frankie	m.	RRF	19 Apr. 1883	3	4	
Holcomb	Frankie M.	m.	PC	25 Apr. 1883	3	5	
Holcomb	Frankie M.	m.	SD	21 Apr. 1883	2	6	
Holden	William	d.	DR	9 June 1884	3	3	
Holden	William	d.	PCo	11 June 1884	3	5	
Holden	William	d.	SD	14 June 1884	2	4	
Holenback	Henry G.	m.	SD	12 Mar. 1881	3	8	
Holland	Belle	m.	PCo	26 Dec. 1883	3	5	

(1) Surname	(2) Given Name	(3)	(4)	(5) Date	(6) Pg	(7) Col	(8) Comments
Holland	Belle	m.	PWA	29 Dec. 1883	3	6	
Holland	Belle	m.	SD	29 Dec. 1883	3	6	
Holland	Mary	m.	SD	10 Jan. 1885	2	6	
Holland	May	m.	PCo	31 Dec. 1884	3	4	
Holland	May	m.	PWA	3 Jan. 1885	3	4	
Holland	Rosa E.	m.	HE	11 May 1882	2	3	
Holland	Rosa E.	m.	PCo	17 May 1882	3	5	
Holland	Rosa E.	m.	RRF	11 May 1882	2	3	
Holland	Rosa E.	m.	SD	20 May 1882	2	4	
Holland	Rose E.	m.	DR	12 May 1882	3	2	
Holler	Henry (son of	d.	RRF	5 Apr. 1883	2	3	
Holler	Henry (son of)	d.	PC	28 Mar. 1883	3	5	
Holler	Henry (son of)	d.	SD	7 Apr. 1883	2	6	
Holliday	James E.	m.	RRF	29 June 1882	2	5	
Holliday	James E.	m.	SD	24 June 1882	3	5	
Holliday	W. F.	d.	DR	22 Sept. 1882	3	2	
Holliday	W. F.	d.	PCo	27 Sept. 1882	3	2	
Holliday	W. F.	d.	SD	23 Sept. 1882	3	1	
Holliday	W. F.	d.	SD	30 Sept. 1882	1	3	
Holling	F.	b.	DD	4 Aug. 1883	3	2	
Holly	R. S.	b.	CR	22 Jan. 1881	5	5	
Holly	S. B.	b.	PCo	12 Jan. 1881	3	2	
Holly	S. B.	b.	SD	22 Jan. 1881	3	8	
Holly	S. R.	b.	DR	17 Jan. 1881	3	2	
Holm	Jacob	b.	SD	30 Apr. 1881	3	8	
Holman	W. O.	o.	DR	8 Sept. 1882	3	1	
Holmes	Albert	d.	DR	5 Sept. 1882	3	2	
Holmes	Albert	p.	DR	9 July 1884	3	3	
Holmes	Albert	d.	PCo	13 Sept. 1882	3	7	
Holmes	Albert	d.	RRF	7 Sept. 1882	2	4	Petaluma
Holmes	Edward	m.	SD	17 Oct. 1885	2	7	
Holmes	Edward M.	m.	SD	24 Oct. 1885	1	3	
Holmes	Laura	m.	SD	19 Mar. 1881	3	8	
Holmes	Lucy T.	p.	DD	19 July 1883	3	2	
Holmes	Lucy T.	d.	DR	24 Feb. 1882	2	3	
Holmes	Lucy T.	d.	PCo	22 Feb. 1882	3	5	
Holmes	Lucy T.	d.	RRF	2 Mar. 1882	2	3	
Holmes	Lucy T.	d.	SD	4 Mar. 1882	3	6	
Holst	Caroline	d.	RRF	21 Sept. 1882	2	4	
Holst	Peter (son of)	d.	PCo	27 Sept. 1882	3	6	
Holst	Peter	b.	DR	28 Oct. 1884	2	3	
Holst	Peter	b.	PCo	29 Oct. 1884	3	5	

(1) Surname	(2) Given Name	(3)	(4)	(5) Date	(6) Pg	(7) Col	(8) Comments
Holst	Peter	d.	RRF	21 Sept. 1882	2	4	
Holst	Peter	b.	SD	19 Feb. 1881	3	8	
Holst	Peter	b.	SD	8 Nov. 1884	2	5	
Holton	Patrick	d.	PC	18 Apr. 1883	3	2&5	
Holtz	Peter	b.	DR	17 June 1882	3	2	
Holtz	Peter	b.	DR	2 Nov. 1885	3	4	
Holtz	Peter	b.	PCo	21 June 1882	3	5	
Holtz	Peter	b.	RRF	15 June 1882	2	4	
Holtz	Peter	b.	SD	17 June 1882	2	4	
Holverstot	Elizabeth	m.	SD	19 Mar. 1881	3	8	
Holverstot	John	m.	SD	19 Mar. 1881	3	8	
Holzer	E.	b.	DR	4 Sept. 1885	3	4	
Holzer	E.	b.	DR	29 Aug. 1885	3	4	
Holzer	E.	b.	PCo	2 Sept. 1885	3	6	
Hood	Alice	m.	DR	27 June 1884	3	3	
Hood	Alice	m.	PCo	15 June 1884	3	4	
Hood	Alice	m.	PWA	28 June 1884	3	5	
Hood	Carrie Smith	o.	SD	1 Dec. 1883	1	5	
Hood	Eva	m.	SD	8 Sept. 1883	3	4	
Hood	Lon	o.	SD	14 June 1884	1	6	
Hood	T. B.	o.	SD	1 Dec. 1883	1	5	
Hooper	George	m.	DR	29 July 1884	3	3	
Hooper	George	m.	PCo	30 July 1884	3	6	
Hooper	George	b.	PCo	6 May 1885	3	6	
Hooper	George	m.	PWA	2 Aug. 1884	3	4	
Hooper	George	m.	SD	9 Aug. 1884	3	4	
Hooper	George R.	m.	PCo	6 Dec. 1882	3	6	
Hooper	John F.	m.	PCo	21 June 1882	3	5	
Hooten	(female)	b.	DR	25 Apr. 1884	3	2	
Hooten	J. J.	b.	PCo	23 Apr. 1884	2	6	
Hooten	J. J.	b.	SD	26 Apr. 1883	3	5	
Hoover	Rosanna	d.	SD	26 Nov. 1881	3	8	
Hope	Ella	m.	SD	18 July 1885	5	5	
Hope	Ella R.	m.	DR	14 July 1885	3	4	
Hope	Ella R.	m.	PCo	15 July 1885	3	6	
Hopkins	M. D.	b.	PCo	11 Oct. 1882	3	6	
Hopper	Columbus	m.	SD	13 Aug. 1881	3	8	
Hopper	George R.	m.	CR	2 Dec. 1882	3	3	
Hopper	George R.	m.	DR	2 Dec. 1882	3	2	
Hopper	George R.	m.	SD	9 Dec. 1882	2	5	
Hopper	Henry T.	m.	SD	30 Sept. 1882	3	1	
Hopper	Jesse	m.	SD	1 June 1881	3	7	

(1) Surname	(2) Given Name	(3)	(4)	(5) Date	(6) Pg	(7) Col	(8) Comments
Hopper	Rose	m.	CR	21 Feb. 1885	3	1	
Hopper	Rose	m.	PCo	18 Feb. 1885	3	6	
Hopper	T. J.	b.	SD	23 Apr. 1881	3	8	
Horger	Rosina G.	m.	SD	10 Jan. 1885	2	6	
Hornberger	Charles	m.	PCo	19 July 1882	3	6	
Hornberger	Charles	m.	SD	15 July 1882	2	4	
Horst	Peter	b.	RRF	10 Feb. 1881	2	5	
Horstman	Sophia G. Denker	d.	SD	24 Oct. 1885	5	4	
Horstmen	Sophia C.	d.	PCo	14 Oct. 1885	3	6	
Hoskins	Annie	m.	CR	28 May 1881	5	5	
Hoskins	Annie	m.	SD	28 May 1881	3	8	
Hoskins	Annie E.	m.	DR	24 May 1881	2	2	
Hoskins	Annie E.	m.	PCo	25 May 1881	3	5	
Hoskins	Pauline	m.	DR	1 May 1882	3	2	
Hoskins	Pauline	m.	PCo	26 Apr. 1882	3	4	
Hoskins	Pauline	m.	SD	29 Apr. 1882	3	6	
Hotchkiss	Joseph	b.	DR	30 Sept. 1881	2	3	
Hotchkiss	Joseph	b.	SD	22 Oct. 1881	3	6	
Hotchkiss	W. J.	b.	PCo	14 Mar. 1883	3	5	
Hotchkiss	W. J.	b.	RRF	15 Mar. 1883	2	4	
Hotchkiss	W. J.	b.	SD	17 Mar. 1883	3	3	
Hottel	John F.	m.	SD	19 Mar. 1881	3	8	
Houda	B. A.	b.	PCo	22 Apr. 1885	3	6	
Houda	B. A.	b.	PWA	18 Apr. 1885	3	6	
Houda	B. A.	b.	SD	18 Apr. 1885	2	4	
Hovey	Theo	m.	PCo	27 May 1885	3	6	
Hovey	Theodore	m.	CR	30 May 1885	4	1	
Howard	A. C., Miss	m.	PCo	20 Aug. 1884	3	4	
Howard	A. C., Miss	m.	PWA	23 Aug. 1884	3	4	
Howard	C. L., Miss	m.	PCo	20 Aug. 1884	3	4	
Howard	C. L., Miss	m.	PWA	23 Aug. 1884	3	4	
Howard	C. L., Miss	m.	SD	6 Sept. 1884	2	5	
Howard	Caroline	d.	PCo	3 May 1882	3	5	
Howard	Caroline	d.	SD	29 Apr. 1882	3	6	
Howard	James	m.	DR	28 Sept. 1881	3	2	
Howard	James	m.	RRF	22 Sept. 1881	2	5	
Howard	James	m.	SD	8 Oct. 1881	3	8	
Howard	John	b.	CR	19 Jan. 1884	3	2	
Howard	John	b.	PCo	23 Jan. 1884	3	5	
Howard	Mack	m.	DR	8 Dec. 1884	3	2	
Howard	Mark	d.	PCo	5 Mar. 1884	3	6	
Howard	William	o.	SD	2 July 1881	3	1	

(1) Surname	(2) Given Name	(3)	(4)	(5) Date	(6) Pg	(7) Col	(8) Comments
Howard	William	o.	SD	27 Oct. 1883	3	2	
Howe	E., Mrs.	m.	CR	4 Mar. 1882	5	1&2	
Howe	E., Mrs.	m.	DR	28 Feb. 1882	2	3	
Howe	E., Mrs.	m.	PCo	8 Mar. 1882	3	5	
Howe	E., Mrs.	m.	SD	4 Mar. 1882	3	6	
Howe	Thomas	m.	PWA	11 Oct. 1884	3	4	
Howell	J. G.	b.	RRF	17 Feb. 1881	2	4	
Howell	J. G.	b.	SD	19 Feb. 1881	3	8	
Howell	John G.	d.	RRF	6 Apr. 1882	2	4	
Howell	Mary	m.	DD	29 Dec. 1883	3	3	
Howell	Miss	m.	DR	8 Dec. 1884	3	2	
Howell	O.	b.	SD	19 Feb. 1881	3	8	
Howell	Ruth	d.	RRF	6 Apr. 1882	2	4	
Howell	Thomas W.	b.	PCo	2 Dec. 1885	3	4	
Howell	Thomas W.	b.	SD	5 Dec. 1885	3	4	
Howland	Ada	m.	SD	29 Jan. 1881	3	8	
Hoyer	Cornelius	d.	PCo	14 Oct. 1885	3	2&6	
Hubbard	Ann A.	m.	PWA	17 Jan. 1885	2	4	
Hubbard	Anna A.	m.	PCo	14 Jan. 1885	3	6	
Hubbard	Daniel	b.	SD	25 June 1881	3	8	
Hubche	Henry	b.	SD	11 June 1881	3	8	
Huber	Charles C.	b.	SD	16 July 1881	3	8	
Hubert	William	d.	DR	18 July 1884	3	1&3	
Hubert	Willie	d.	PCo	23 July 1884	3	6	
Hubert	Willie	d.	SD	19 July 1884	2	5	
Hubsch	A. J.	b.	DD	12 Oct. 1883	3	3	
Hubsch	A. J.	b.	PWA	13 Oct. 1883	3	8	
Hubsch	A. J.	b.	SD	20 Oct. 1883	3	4	
Hubsch	A. J.	b.	SWI	6 Oct. 1883	3	4	
Hubsch	Joseph	m.	DR	13 Dec. 1882	2	3	
Hubsch	Joseph	m.	PCo	20 Dec. 1882	3	5	
Hudson	Elbert	b.	SD	19 Mar. 1881	3	8	
Hudson	F. J.	b.	SD	23 July 1881	3	8	
Hudson	George B.	d.	PWA	10 Nov. 1883	3	6	
Hudson	George P.	d.	SD	10 Nov. 1883	1	4	
Hudson	R. J.	m.	SD	7 May 1881	3	8	
Hudson	Samuel Kelsey	d.	PCo	3 Sept. 1884	2	5	
Hudson	Samuel Kelsey Nelson	d.	SD	6 Sept. 1884	2	5	
Hudson	Samuel Kelly Nilson	d.	DR	30 Aug. 1884	3	4	
Hudson	W. H.	m.	DR	16 July 1881	2	2	
Hudson	William H.	m.	PCo	20 July 1881	3	5	

(1) Surname	(2) Given Name	(3)	(4)	(5) Date	(6) Pg	(7) Col	(8) Comments
Hudson	William H.	m.	SD	16 July 1881	3	8	
Hudson	William H.	m.	SD	23 July 1881	3	8	
Hudspeth	William	b.	SD	18 Apr. 1885	2	4	
Huebner	O. C.	b.	CR	19 Mar. 1881	4	3	
Huebner	O. C.	b.	DR	23 Mar. 1881	3	2	
Huebner	O. C.	b.	RRF	17 Feb. 1881	2	5	
Huebner	O. C.	b.	SD	19 Mar. 1881	3	8	
Huff	Charles Edward	d.	DD	4 Aug. 1883	3	2	
Huff	Charles Edward	d.	SD	11 Aug. 1883	2	7	
Huffman	Aaron	b.	DD	31 Aug. 1883	3	3	
Huffman	Aaron	b.	RRF	30 Aug. 1883	2	4	
Huffman	G. W. (son of)	d.	CR	24 Jan. 1885	3	1	
Hughes	Balthazard	d.	SD	8 Oct. 1881	3	8	
Hughes	Avis Vivienne	d.	SD	21 Apr. 1883	2	6	
Hughes	C. W.	m.	DR	1 May 1882	3	2	
Hughes	James	d.	PC	4 July 1883	3	5	
Hughes	James	d.	SD	30 June 1883	3	5	
Hughes	R. C.	m.	SD	24 Jan. 1885	5	5	
Hughes	Balthazard	d.	DR	3 Oct. 1881	2	3	
Hughes	Balthazard	d.	PCo	28 Sept. 1881	3	5	
Hugues	Francis Josephine	d.	PCo	5 Apr. 1882	3	5	
Hugues	Josephine	d.	DR	10 Apr. 1882	2	2	
Hulbert	Henry	o.	DR	23 May 1882	3	1	
Hull	Andrew C.	m.	DR	10 Jun. 1881	2	2	
Hull	Andrew C.	m.	SD	25 June 1881	3	8	
Humbert	Charles E.	m.	PCo	7 Jan. 1885	3	6	
Humbert	Charles E.	m.	SD	10 Jan. 1885	2	6	
Hungar	Felix	b.	DR	26 Sept. 1881	3	2	
Hungar	Felix	b.	SD	1 Oct. 1881	3	8	
Hunt	Anna L.	m.	CR	22 Oct. 1881	5	3	
Hunt	Anna L.	m.	DR	25 Oct. 1881	3	2	
Hunt	Anna L.	m.	PCo	2 Nov. 1881	3	5	
Hunt	Anna L.	m.	SD	29 Oct. 1881	3	6	
Hunt	Cassandra M.	m.	PCo	1 July 1885	3	6	
Hunt	Charles	b.	DR	11 Sept. 1885	3	4	
Hunt	Charles	b.	PCo	9 Sept. 1885	3	6	
Hunt	F. W.	b.	DR	7 Oct. 1881	2	3	
Hunt	F. W.	b.	SD	15 Oct. 1881	3	8	
Hunt	Harry	d.	SD	19 Dec. 1885	1	6	
Hunt	J. B.	b.	SD	7 Jan. 1882	3	8	
Hunt	Julian H.	m.	SD	9 Apr. 1881	3	8	
Hunt	Lottie	m.	PCo	14 Mar. 1883	3	5	

(1) Surname	(2) Given Name	(3)	(4)	(5) Date	(6) Pg	(7) Col	(8) Comments
Hunt	Lottie	m.	PWA	17 Mar. 1883	3	7	
Hunt	Lottie	m.	SD	17 Mar. 1883	3	5	
Hunt	Manassa	b.	PCo	23 Mar. 1881	3	4	
Hunt	Manassa	b.	SD	2 Apr. 1881	3	8	
Hunt	Manassah	d.	PCo	6 Sept. 1882	3	1&7	
Hunt	Phoebe	p.	DD	24 July 1883	3	2	
Hunt	William L.	m.	PWA	19 Jan. 1883	3	7	
Hunter	Carrie	m.	DD	16 July 1883	3	2	
Hunter	Lutitia	m.	SD	18 July 1885	5	5	
Hunter	W. C.	m.	DR	29 Oct. 1885	3	4	
Hunter	William C.	m.	CR	31 Oct. 1885	3	4	
Hurley	(male)	b.	DR	21 June 1884	3	3	
Hurley	J. G.	b.	PCo	15 June 1884	3	4	
Huron	Lettie	m.	SD	1 Oct. 1881	3	8	
Hurry	Mary	m.	PCo	14 Mar. 1883	3	5	
Hurry	Mary	m.	SD	17 Mar. 1883	3	5	
Hursh	James	m.	SD	16 Apr. 1881	3	8	
Hurt	Boody	d.	SD	29 Dec. 1883	1	6	
Hurt	W. Irwin	m.	PCo	24 Jan. 1883	3	5	also col. 3
Hurt	W. Irwin	m.	SD	27 Jan. 1883	3	6	
Hussey	W. B.	m.	SD	16 July 1881	3	8	
Hussey	W. R.	m.	PCo	6 July 1881	3	5	
Hussy	Eugene	m.	PCo	18 Oct. 1882	3	6	
Hussy	Eugene	m.	SD	14 Oct. 1882	3	6	
Hutchings	Horatio	d.	DR	15 Nov. 1881	2	3	
Hutchings	Horatio	d.	PCo	16 Nov. 1881	3	5	
Hutchings	Horatio	d.	RRF	10 Nov. 1881	2	4	
Hutchinson	F. A.	b.	PCo	16 Apr. 1884	3	5	
Hutchinson	Francis A.	m.	PCo	2 Aug. 1882	3	6	
Hutchinson	Francis A.	m.	RRF	27 July 1882	2	4	
Hutchinson	Frank	b.	PCo	16 Sept. 1885	3	6	
Hutchinson	Johnson	d.	DR	16 Feb. 1884	3	3	
Hutchinson	Joseph	d.	DR	24 Nov. 1885	3	4	
Hutchinson	Joseph	d.	PCo	18 Nov. 1885	3	4	
Hutchinson	William	m.	CR	25 June 1881	4	3	
Hutchinson	William	m.	DR	18 June 1881	2	3	
Hutchinson	William	m.	SD	18 June 1881	3	8	
Hutchinson	William	m.	RRF	16 June 1881	2	5	
Hutt	James	b.	SD	26 Aug. 1882	3	5	
Hyde	Mary E.	m.	DR	18 July 1884	3	3	
Hyde	Mary E.	m.	PCo	16 July 1884	3	6	
Hyde	Mary E.	m.	PWA	19 July 1884	3	4	

(1) Surname	(2) Given Name	(3)	(4)	(5) Date	(6) Pg	(7) Col	(8) Comments
Hyde	Mary J.	m.	SD	24 June 1882	3	3&5	
Hyde	Mary	m.	DR	22 June 1882	3	1	
Hynes	James	d.	CR	18 Mar. 1882	5	3	Cypress Hill
Hynes	James	d.	DR	20 Mar. 1882	2	3	
Hynes	James	d.	PCo	15 Mar. 1882	3	2&3	Cypress Hill
Hynes	James	d.	PCo	15 Mar. 1882	3	4	
Hynes	James	d.	RRF	30 Mar. 1882	1	7	
Hynes	James	o.	SD	1 Apr. 1882	3	2	text of will
Hynes	James	d.	SD	25 Mar. 1882	3	6	

I & J

(1) Surname	(2) Given Name	(3)	(4)	(5) Date	(6) Pg	(7) Col	(8) Comments
Iles	Joseph	d.	DR	30 Oct. 1882	3	1	
Ilg	Ernest	b.	PCo	6 Dec. 1882	3	6	
Ilg	Ernest	b.	SD	9 Dec. 1882	2	5	
Ilg	Ernest	b.	SD	18 July 1885	5	5	
Indian	John	b.	RRF	22 June 1882	2	3	
Ingham	Andrew H.	m.	DR	21 July 1884	2	2	
Ingham	Andrew W.	m.	PCo	23 July 1884	3	6	
Ingle	J. A.	b.	SD	26 Mar. 1881	3	8	
Inglis	James	d.	DR	1 Nov. 1881	2	3	filed after Nov. 29
Inglis	James	d.	PCo	26 Oct. 1881	3	4	
Ingraham	John	m.	DR	13 Dec. 1884	1	4	
Ingram	Charles L.	m.	CR	13 June 1885	3	2	
Ingram	Charles L.	m.	PCo	24 June 1885	3	6	
Ingram	Charles L.	m.	SD	27 June 1885	5	4	
Ingram	D. H. (family)	d.	CR	15 Jan. 1881	5	4	
Ingram	Mary	m.	SD	31 Dec. 1881	3	6	
Ingston	Nancy	d.	PWA	25 Oct. 1884	3	4	
Inman	A. C.	d.	DR	1 Apr. 1884	3	3	
Inman	A. C.	d.	PCo	9 Apr. 1884	3	6	
Inman	Aaron	p.	DR	9 July 1884	3	3	
Inmon	Hiram K.	d.	PCo	13 Sept. 1882	3	7	
Irvin	Pauline A.	m.	DR	30 Jan. 1882	2	3	
Irvin	Pauline A.	m.	PCo	25 Jan. 1882	3	6	
Irving	J. O.	m.	SD	10 Mar. 1883	3	3	
Irving	Joseph O.	m.	PCo	14 Mar. 1883	3	5	
Irwin	(male)	b.	DR	8 Jan. 1884	3	3	
Irwin	James	b.	SIT	19 Dec. 1885	2	3	
Irwin	Mary L.	m.	DR	5 Dec. 1882	3	2	
Irwin	Mary L.	m.	PCo	6 Dec. 1882	3	6	
Irwin	Mary L.	m.	SD	9 Dec. 1882	2	5	
Isaacs	Jesse	d.	SD	1 Mar. 1884	3	3	
Isles	Alfred	b.	PCo	27 May 1885	3	6	
Isola	Alphonso	m.	DR	10 Aug. 1885	3	4	
Isola	Alphonso	m.	SD	22 Aug. 1885	6	2	
Jackson	A. L.	b.	SD	10 Sept. 1881	3	8	
Jackson	Allie	m.	PCo	28 Jan. 1885	3	6	
Jackson	Charles H.	m.	PWA	1 Dec. 1883	3	6	
Jackson	E. M.	b.	SD	24 Dec. 1881	2	3	

(1) Surname	(2) Given Name	(3)	(4)	(5) Date	(6) Pg	(7) Col	(8) Comments
Jackson	Emma	m.	RRF	22 June 1882	3	6	
Jackson	Lizzie	m.	DD	27 Oct. 1883	3	3	
Jackson	Lora B.	d.	SD	19 Feb. 1881	3	8	
Jackson	Lora H.	d.	SD	19 Feb. 1881	3	8	
Jacobs	Annie (son of)	d.	DD	8 Sept. 1883	3	3	
Jacobs	E.	b.	HE	8 June 1882	2	3	
Jacobs	E.	b.	PCo	14 June 1882	3	5	
Jacobs	E.	b.	PCo	6 Feb. 1884	3	6	
Jacobs	E.	b.	RRF	8 June 1882	2	3	
Jacobs	E.	b.	RRF	31 Jan. 1884	2	3	
Jacobs	E.	b.	SD	17 June 1882	2	4	
Jacobs	Ed	m.	PCo	30 Jan. 1884	3	6	
Jacobs	Edmond	m.	PCo	6 Feb. 1884	3	6	
Jacobs	G. H.	b.	SD	4 June 1881	3	8	
Jacobs	George W.	b.	DD	31 Aug. 1883	3	3	
Jacobs	George (son of)	d.	DD	8 Sept. 1883	3	3	
Jacobs	George (son of)	d.	RRF	6 Sept. 1883	2	4	
Jacobs	George (son of)	d.	SD	15 Sept. 1883	2	4	
Jacobs	George W.	b.	RRF	30 Aug. 1883	2	4	
Jacobs	Isaac	d.	DD	5 Nov. 1883	3	2	
Jacobs	Isaac	d.	SD	10 Nov. 1883	3	5	
Jacobs	James B.	m.	DR	6 July 1885	3	3	
Jacobs	James B.	m.	PCo	15 July 1885	3	6	
Jacobs	James B.	m.	SD	11 July 1885	5	6	
Jacobs	M.	b.	DR	4 July 1881	2	3	
Jacobs	M.	b.	SD	16 July 1881	3	8	
Jacobs	M.	b.	SD	14 Mar. 1885	5	5	
Jacobs	M. (son of)	d.	PCo	10 May 1882	3	5	
Jacobs	M. (son of)	d.	PCo	24 May 1882	3	5	
Jacobs	M. (son of)	d.	SD	20 May 1882	2	4	
Jacobs	Marks (son of)	d.	DR	1 May 1882	3	2	
Jacobs	Moses	d.	PCo	25 Feb. 1885	3	6	
Jacobs	Moses	o.	RRF	14 Feb. 1884	3	3	
Jacobs	Moses	d.	SD	21 Feb. 1885	2	5	
Jacobsen	C. A.	b.	DR	9 Nov. 1885	2	2	
Jacobsen	C. A.	m.	PCo	10 Dec. 1884	3	5	
Jacobsen	C. A.	b.	PCo	4 Nov. 1885	2	5	
Jacobsen	C. A.	m.	SD	13 Dec. 1884	2	5	
Jacobsen	Henry	d.	SD	14 Jan. 1882	3	8	
Jacobsen	Henry, Mrs.	d.	PCo	4 Jan. 1882	3	7	
Jacobsen	Jacob	d.	SD	27 June 1885	1	6	Mr. Haupt's place
Jacobson	C. A.	m.	PWA	13 Dec. 1884	3	4	

(1) Surname	(2) Given Name	(3)	(4)	(5) Date	(6) Pg	(7) Col	(8) Comments
Jacobson	H.	d.	PCo	16 Aug. 1882	3	2	drowned; Cypress Hill Cemetery
Jacobson	Henry	d.	PCo	16 Aug. 1882	3	6	
Jacobson	Henry	d.	SD	19 Aug. 1882	3	5	
Jahn	Emma	m.	SD	24 Oct. 1885	1	3	
James	Edward Albert	m.	SD	22 Jan. 1881	3	8	
James	Euphemia	d.	DD	20 Dec. 1883	2	2	
James	Euphemia	d.	PCo	19 Dec. 1883	3	4	
James	Euphemia	d.	PWA	22 Dec. 1883	3	6	
James	Euphemia	d.	SD	22 Dec. 1883	3	5	
James	R. L.	b.	SD	16 June 1883	2	6	
James	Rosa	m.	PCo	10 Sept. 1884	3	6	
James	Rosa	m.	PWA	6 Sept. 1884	3	4	
James	Rosa	m.	SD	20 Sept. 1884	2	5	
Jameson	William	b.	PCo	21 Jan. 1885	2	5	
Jameson	William	b.	PWA	24 Jan. 1885	3	5	
Jamison	Laura	m.	DR	19 Nov. 1881	2	3	
Jansen	John	m.	SD	19 Mar. 1881	3	8	
Jantillia	John	m.	DD	11 Aug. 1883	3	1	
January	Alice	d.	PCo	9 Dec. 1885	3	6	
Jaques	Belinda	m.	DR	2 May 1881	2	2	
Jarvis	A. E.	b.	DD	4 Aug. 1883	3	2	
Jarvis	Miles	b.	PWA	2 May 1885	3	6	
Jasent	Rosa	d.	PCo	3 May 1882	3	5	
Jefferson	Nellie	m.	DR	23 Dec. 1881	2	2	
Jefferson	Nellie	m.	HE	29 Dec. 1881	2	3	
Jefferson	Nellie	m.	RRF	22 Dec. 1881	2	3	
Jefferson	Nellie	m.	SD	31 Dec. 1881	3	6	
Jefferson	Nelly	m.	PCo	28 Dec. 1881	3	6	
Jeffress	James V.	m.	DR	27 Aug. 1881	2	3	
Jeffress	James V.	m.	RRF	25 Aug. 1881	2	4	
Jeffress	John K.	m.	DR	27 Aug. 1881	2	3	
Jeffress	John K.	m.	RRF	25 Aug. 1881	2	4	
Jeffreys	James V.	m.	SD	3 Sept. 1881	3	8	
Jeffries	James V.	m.	CR	27 Aug. 1881	5	4	
Jeffries	John R.	m.	CR	27 Aug. 1881	5	4	
Jenkins	Elizabeth	d.	PCo	7 Dec. 1881	3	5	
Jenkins	John	d.	SD	13 Aug. 1881	3	8	
Jensen	Lars	b.	SD	19 Mar. 1881	3	8	
Jensen	Matilda A.	m.	PCo	10 Dec. 1884	3	5	
Jensen	Matilda A.	m.	PWA	13 Dec. 1884	3	4	
Jensen	Matilda A.	m.	SD	13 Dec. 1884	2	5	
Jerald	Thomas	m.	CR	19 Feb. 1881	4	2	

(1) Surname	(2) Given Name	(3)	(4)	(5) Date	(6) Pg	(7) Col	(8) Comments
Jerald	Thomas	m.	SD	19 Feb. 1881	3	8	
Jespersen	Neils	b.	PCo	19 July 1882	3	6	
Jesse	J. E.	b.	PCo	6 Feb. 1884	3	6	
Jesse	J. E.	b.	PWA	9 Feb. 1884	3	6	
Jesse	J. E.	b.	SD	16 Feb. 1884	2	5	
Jessen	M. C.	d.	DR	3 Dec. 1881	2	3	
Jessen	M. C.	d.	PCo	30 Nov. 1881	3	5	
Jessen	M. C., Mrs.	d.	SD	10 Dec. 1881	3	7	
Jessup	Cassie	d.	PC	20 June 1883	3	6	
Jessup	Cassie	d.	RRF	14 June 1883	2	3	
Jessup	H. H.	b.	DR	26 July 1884	3	3	
Jessup	H. H.	b.	PCo	23 July 1884	3	6	
Jessup	H. H.	b.	RRF	31 Aug. 1882	2	4	
Jessup	H. H. (dau. of)	d.	SD	23 June 1883	3	5	
Jeter	W. P.	b.	CR	19 Jan. 1884	3	2	
Jeter	W. P.	b.	PCo	6 Feb. 1884	3	6	
Jeter	W. P.	b.	PCo	23 Jan. 1884	3	5	
Jeter	W. P.	b.	RRF	31 Jan. 1884	2	3	
Jewell	J. R.	o.	PWA	6 Oct. 1883	3	2&8	
Jewell	Samuel R.	m.	PCo	4 Mar. 1885	3	6	
Jewell	Samuel R.	m.	PWA	28 Feb. 1885	3	5	
Jewell	Samuel R.	m.	SD	14 Mar. 1885	5	5	
Jewett	Alice	m.	PCo	16 Feb. 1881	3	4	
Jewett	Alice	m.	SD	19 Feb. 1881	3	8	
Jewett	G. E.	b.	PCo	15 June 1881	3	5	
Jewett	G. E.	b.	SD	18 June 1881	3	8	
Jewett	G. E.	b.	SD	25 June 1881	3	8	
Jinkins	Mary A.	m.	DR	21 Sept. 1885	3	4	
Johannsen	Francisco	m.	DR	26 Aug. 1885	3	4	
Johnson	(male)	b.	DR	16 May 1884	3	2	
Johnson	Addie	m.	DR	14 Apr. 1882	3	2	
Johnson	Addie	m.	PCo	19 Apr. 1882	3	5	
Johnson	Addie	m.	SD	15 Apr. 1882	3	6	
Johnson	Bertha	d.	DR	18 Mar. 1882	2	3	
Johnson	Bertha	d.	PCo	29 Mar. 1882	3	5	
Johnson	Bertha	d.	SD	1 Apr. 1882	3	6	
Johnson	Carrie M. B.	m.	SD	31 Dec. 1881	3	6	
Johnson	Catharine	d.	SD	2 Dec. 1882	3	2	
Johnson	Catherine	d.	DR	29 Nov. 1882	3	1	
Johnson	Charles L.	m.	SD	14 Mar. 1885	5	5	
Johnson	Christie E.	d.	PCo	13 July 1881	3	5	
Johnson	Corry T.	d.	DR	30 June 1881	3	2	

(1) Surname	(2) Given Name	(3)	(4)	(5) Date	(6) Pg	(7) Col	(8) Comments
Johnson	Eliza	d.	CR	11 June 1881	5	5	
Johnson	Eliza	d.	DR	4 June 1881	2	2	
Johnson	Eliza	d.	RRF	2 June 1881	2	3	
Johnson	Eliza	d.	SD	11 June 1881	3	8	
Johnson	Elizabeth A.	d.	DR	23 May 1884	3	2	
Johnson	Elizabeth A.	d.	SD	31` May 1884	2	3	
Johnson	Elizabeth	m.	DR	26 Aug. 1885	3	4	
Johnson	Elizabeth J.	m.	SD	5 Feb. 1881	3	8	
Johnson	Emma	m.	DR	19 Nov. 1885	3	4	
Johnson	Hannah	d.	SD	25 Feb. 1882	3	3	
Johnson	Hattie	m.	DR	19 Dec. 1884	3	2	
Johnson	Hattie	m.	PCo	17 Dec. 1884	2	4	
Johnson	Henry	b.	PCo	23 Nov. 1885	3	4	
Johnson	J. B.	b.	SD	5 Mar. 1881	3	8	
Johnson	J. E.	b.	PCo	14 May 1884	3	4	
Johnson	J. E.	b.	PCo	14 Oct. 1885	3	6	
Johnson	J. E.	b.	PWA	10 May 1884	3	5	
Johnson	J. E.	b.	RRF	15 May 1884	5	6	
Johnson	J. E.	b.	SD	17 May 1884	3	5	
Johnson	James L.	m.	DD	29 Dec. 1883	3	3	
Johnson	John E.	b.	PCo	16 Feb. 1881	3	4	
Johnson	John E.	b.	SD	19 Feb. 1881	3	8	
Johnson	John	m	PC	2 May 1883	3	5	
Johnson	John	b.	PCo	16 Nov. 1881	3	5	
Johnson	John	m.	PWA	28 Apr. 1883	3	8	
Johnson	John	m.	SD	12 May 1883	2	6	
Johnson	John	d.	SIT	15 Aug. 1885	5	2	
Johnson	Katie	m.	SD	11 June 1881	3	8	
Johnson	Katy	m.	CR	11 June 1881	5	5	
Johnson	Katy	m.	DR	4 June 1881	2	2	
Johnson	Lavina	m.	SD	13 Oct. 1883	3	4	
Johnson	Lavinia	m.	DD	6 Oct. 1883	3	3	
Johnson	Lillian	m.	CR	25 Feb. 1882	1	2	
Johnson	Mamie	m.	DD	5 Nov. 1883	3	2	
Johnson	Mamie	m.	PWA	3 Nov. 1883	3	8	
Johnson	Mamie	m.	SD	10 Nov. 1883	3	5	
Johnson	Margaret	m.	SD	5 Mar. 1881	3	8	
Johnson	Mattie	m.	PWA	20 Dec. 1884	3	4	
Johnson	Miss	m.	RRF	26 May 1881	3	2	
Johnson	Mrs.	d.	RRF	23 Feb. 1882	2	3	
Johnson	Mrs. & son	d.	CR	25 Feb. 1882	1	2	
Johnson	Nancy L.	m.	DD	8 Dec. 1883	3	3	

(1) Surname	(2) Given Name	(3)	(4)	(5) Date	(6) Pg	(7) Col	(8) Comments
Johnson	Nancy L.	m.	PWA	8 Dec. 1883	3	6	
Johnson	Orrick	d.	DR	14 June 1881	3	2	
Johnson	Orrick	d.	RRF	9 June 1881	2	3	
Johnson	Orrick	d.	SD	11 June 1881	3	8	
Johnson	Peter	d.	CR	29 Jan. 1881	4	2	
Johnson	R. S. (dau. of)	d.	PWA	19 Jan. 1884	3	4	
Johnson	Rebecca T.	m.	DR	17 Aug. 1882	3	2	
Johnson	Rebecca T.	m.	SD	2 Sept. 1882	3	6	
Johnson	S., Mrs.	d.	CR	15 Jan. 1881	5	5	
Johnson	Sanborn, Mrs.	d.	DR	11 Jan. 1881	3	2	
Johnson	Sanborn	d.	SD	15 Jun. 1881	3	8	
Johnson	Silas S.	m.	SD	12 Jan. 1884	3	6	
Johnson	Thomas	o.	CR	5 Feb. 1881	4	1	50th anniversary
Johnson	Thomas	m.	CR	5 Feb. 1881	4	1	description of 1831 wedding
Johnson	W. T.	m.	DR	22 Aug. 1881	2	3	
Johnson	Wilhelmina	m.	SD	26 Dec. 1885	3	4	
Johnson	William A.	d.	DR	3 May 1881	2	2	
Johnston	C. B.	m.	PCo	6 Feb. 1884	3	6	
Johnston	C. B.	m.	RRF	31 Jan. 1884	2	3	
Johnston	Thomas M.	d.	SD	19 Mar. 1881	3	8	
Johnston	William H.	d	SD	5 Dec. 1885	1	4	
Jolly	Henry	d.	DR	28 Aug. 1882	3	2	
Jones	Caroline	m.	DR	18 Nov. 1882	3	2	
Jones	Carrie	m.	DR	13 July 1885	3	4	
Jones	Carrie	m.	PCo	22 Nov. 1882	3	5	
Jones	Carrie E.	m.	PCo	15 July 1885	3	6	
Jones	Charles	b.	CR	15 Jan. 1881	5	5	
Jones	Charles	b.	PCo	18 Oct. 1882	3	6	
Jones	Charles	b.	RRF	12 Oct. 1882	2	3	
Jones	Charles	b.	SD	22 Jan. 1881	3	8	
Jones	David	b.	SD	26 Feb. 1881	3	8	
Jones	David (son of)	d.	SD	5 Mar. 1881	3	8	
Jones	E. P.	m.	PCo	5 July 1882	3	5	
Jones	H. J.	d.	DD	12 Oct. 1883	3	3	
Jones	H. J., Mrs.	d.	CR	13 Oct. 1883	3	1	
Jones	H. J., Mrs.	d.	HE	11 Oct. 1883	2	2	
Jones	H. J., Mrs.	d.	SD	20 Oct. 1883	3	4	
Jones	Homer A.	m.	DD	2 Aug. 1883	3	2	
Jones	Homer A.	m.	PC	1 Aug. 1883	3	6	
Jones	Homer A.	m.	PWA	28 July 1883	3	7	
Jones	Homer A.	m.	SD	4 Aug. 1883	2	5	
Jones	Jennie	m.	DR	11 Dec. 1884	3	2	

(1) Surname	(2) Given Name	(3)	(4)	(5) Date	(6) Pg	(7) Col	(8) Comments
Jones	Jennie	m.	PCo	17 Dec. 1884	2	4	
Jones	Jennie	m.	SD	13 Dec. 1884	2	5	
Jones	John	b.	SD	5 May 1883	2	6	
Jones	L. D.	d.	DD	23 July 1883	3	2	
Jones	L. D.	b.	SD	4 Aug. 1883	2	5	
Jones	L. D., Mrs.	b.	DD	28 July 1883	3	2	
Jones	Laura	m.	DR	25 Aug. 1881	2	3	
Jones	Laura	m.	SD	27 Aug. 1881	3	8	
Jones	Mr. & Mrs.	b.	SD	21 Mar. 1885	2	5	
Jones	Nancy A.	d.	SD	18 July 1885	5	5	
Jones	Nancy	d.	DR	13 July 1885	3	4	
Jones	T. S.	b.	RRF	8 May 1884	5	6	
Jones	T. S.	b.	SD	17 May 1884	3	5	
Jones	Thad	b.	DR	1 Dec. 1884	3	2	
Jones	Thad	b.	DR	8 Dec. 1884	3	2	
Jones	Thad	b.	PCo	3 Dec. 1884	3	5	
Jones	Thad	m.	PCo	9 Jan. 1884	3	6	
Jones	Thad	m.	SD	5 Jan. 1884	1	4	
Jones	Thomas	d.	DR	31 May 1884	3	2	
Jones	Thomas	d.	PCo	4 June 1884	3	5	
Jones	Thomas	d.	PWA	7 June 1884	3	6	
Jones	William	b.	PCo	20 Dec. 1882	3	5	12th child
Jones	William	d.	SD	23 June 1883	2	1	
Joost	Henry Jacob	d.	PCo	24 June 1885	3	6	
Joost	Henry Jacob	d.	SD	27 June 1885	5	4	
Joost	Jacob	b.	SD	19 Jan. 1884	3	6	
Jordan	Charles	d.	SD	23 Apr. 1881	3	8	
Jordan	Dolly	m.	PCo	28 Feb. 1883	3	5	
Jordan	Dolly	m.	PWA	3 Mar. 1883	3	6	
Jordan	Dolly	m.	SD	3 Mar. 1883	2	6	
Jordan	James H.	m.	PCo	20 July 1881	3	5	
Jordan	James H.	m.	SD	9 July 1881	3	8	
Jordan	James	b.	PCo	26 Nov. 1884	3	5	
Jordan	James R.	d.	SD	13 June 1885	3	5	
Jordan	Leslie A.	b.	RRF	26 Oct. 1882	2	3	
Jordan	Nellie	m.	PCo	24 Aug. 1881	3	5	
Jordan	Nellie	m.	SD	3 Sept. 1881	3	8	
Jordan	Tense	d.	PCo	24 Jan. 1883	3	5	
Jordan	Tense	d.	SD	27 Jan. 1883	3	6	
Jordan	William F.	m.	PCo	6 Feb. 1884	3	6	
Jordan	William F.	m.	PWA	9 Feb. 1884	3	6	
Jordan	William F.	m.	SD	16 Feb. 1884	2	5	

(1) Surname	(2) Given Name	(3)	(4)	(5) Date	(6) Pg	(7) Col	(8) Comments
Jordon	Leslie A.	b.	PCo	1 Nov. 1882	3	5	
Joseph	James	b.	PCo	7 Dec. 1881	3	5	
Joyce	Charles	b.	PCo	15 Apr. 1885	3	6	
Joyce	Charles	b.	PWA	18 Apr. 1885	3	6	
Jud	Christian (son of)	d.	DR	3 June 1881	2	3	
Jud	Christian (son of)	m.	SD	4 June 1881	3	8	
Judd	C.	b.	DR	31 Jan. 1881	3	2	
Judd	C.	b.	RRF	10 Feb. 1881	2	5	
Judd	C.	b.	SD	5 Feb. 1881	3	8	
Juhl	Alma	d.	DR	29 Nov. 1882	3	2	
Juhl	Alma	d.	PCo	22 Nov. 1882	3	5	
Justi	Charles	d.	DR	7 July 1885	3	3	
Justi	Charles	d.	SD	11 July 1885	5	6	
Justie	H. H., Miss	m.	SD	1 July 1882	2	3	

K

(1) Surname	(2) Given Name	(3)	(4)	(5) Date	(6) Pg	(7) Col	(8) Comments
Kalbert	George	d.	RRF	23 Feb. 1882	2	3	
Kamp	Nicholas	b.	PCo	6 Aug. 1884	2	4	
Kamp	Nicholas	b.	PWA	9 Aug. 1884	2	4	
Kamp	Nicholas	b.	SD	9 Aug. 1884	3	4	
Kane	James	d.	SD	19 May 1883	3	5	
Kaplan	Mrs.	d.	RRF	23 Nov. 1882	3	5	
Kauffman	Catherine	p.	DR	16 July 1884	3	2	
Kauffman	Catherine	d.	DR	16 June 1884	3	3	
Kauffman	Catherine	d.	PCo	18 June 1884	3	4	
Kauffman	Frank A.	d.	DR	25 Oct. 1881	3	2	
Kauffmann	Kate	d.	SD	24 Jan. 1885	5	5	
Kaufman	Katherine	d.	SD	28 June 1884	3	4	
Kavanagh	H. H.	o.	DR	29 Mar. 1884	3	1	
Kean	J. B.	m.	PCo	8 Oct. 1884	3	6	
Kean	J. B.	m.	PWA	11 Oct. 1884	3	4	
Kean	J. B.	m.	SD	4 Oct. 1884	3	5	
Kean	Lizzie	m.	DD	19 Nov. 1883	3	3	
Kean	Lizzie	m.	SD	24 Nov. 1883	3	4	
Kearnes	Mary Ann	d.	DR	22 July 1881	3	2	
Keating	Wheeler	m.	PWA	28 Feb. 1885	3	5	
Keaton	Wheeler M.	m.	SD	21 Feb. 1885	2	5	
Keaton	Wheeler	m.	PCo	25 Feb. 1885	3	6	
Keays	Hannah	d.	DR	17 Nov. 1881	2	3	
Keays	Hannah	d.	PCo	16 Nov. 1881	3	5	
Keegan	D.	b.	DD	20 Dec. 1883	2	2	
Keegan	D.	b.	PCo	19 Dec. 1883	3	4	
Keegan	D.	b.	PWA	22 Dec. 1883	3	6	
Keegan	D.	b.	SD	22 Dec. 1883	3	5	
Keegan	Mr. & Mrs.	b.	SD	16 Apr. 1881	3	8	
Keegan	T.	b.	CR	16 Apr. 1881	5	3	
Keegan	T.	b.	PCo	13 Apr. 1881	3	6	
Keegan	T.	b.	PCo	19 Mar. 1884	3	6	
Keegan	T.	b.	SD	23 Apr. 1881	3	8	
Keegans	T.	b.	PWA	22 Mar. 1884	3	6	
Keegans	T.	b.	SD	22 Mar. 1884	2	4	
Keenan	A.	b.	PCo	11 May 1881	3	5	
Keenan	A.	b.	SD	21 May 1881	3	8	
Keenan	Alexander	b.	PCo	30 Jan. 1884	3	6	

(1) Surname	(2) Given Name	(3)	(4)	(5) Date	(6) Pg	(7) Col	(8) Comments
Keenan	Alexander	b.	PWA	2 Feb. 1884	3	6	
Keenan	Mary	m.	DR	27 Nov. 1885	3	4	
Keenan	Mary	m.	SD	5 Dec. 1885	1	7	
Keene	Emma Frank	m.	PCo	6 Dec. 1882	3	6	
Keene	F. C.	m.	DR	4 Jan. 1884	3	3	
Keene	F. C.	m.	PCo	23 Jan. 1884	3	5	
Kegan	Dennis	b.	PCo	15 Mar. 1882	3	4	
Kegan	Dennis	b.	SD	25 Mar. 1882	3	6	
Keifer	Cornelius	d.	PC	4 Apr. 1883	3	5	
Keifer	Cornelius	d.	PWA	7 Apr. 1883	2	3	
Keim	H. W.	m.	CR	12 Feb. 1881	5	5	
Keim	Henry W.	m.	DR	7 Feb. 1881	3	2	
Keim	Henry W.	m.	PCo	16 Feb. 1881	3	4	
Keim	Henry W.	m.	SD	12 Feb. 1881	3	8	
Keith	Capt.	b.	DR	29 July 1885	3	4	
Keith	Capt.	b.	PCo	29 July 1885	3	4	
Kellet	Ellie F.	m.	SD	19 Mar. 1881	3	8	
Kelley	Charlotte	d.	SD	18 Feb. 1882	3	6	
Kelley	Charlotte L.	d.	DR	17 Feb. 1882	2	3	
Kelley	Charlotte L.	d.	RRF	16 Feb. 1882	2	4	
Kelley	Ellinor	d.	RRF	25 Aug. 1881	2	4	
Kelley	Francis	d.	DR	28 Aug. 1882	3	2	
Kelley	James	b.	DR	29 July 1885	3	4	
Kelley	James	b.	PCo	22 July 1885	3	6	
Kelley	Luke	d.	DR	13 Mar. 1882	3	1	
Kelley	William H.	d.	RRF	25 Aug. 1881	2	4	
Kellogg	F. E.	m.	DR	8 Apr. 1884	3	2	
Kellogg	F. E., Mrs.	m.	PCo	16 Apr. 1884	3	5	
Kellogg	F. E., Mrs.	m.	SD	12 Apr. 1884	2	5	
Kellogg	William L.	m.	CR	21 Apr. 1883	3	1	
Kellogg	William L.	m.	PC	25 Apr. 1883	3	5	
Kellogg	William L.	m.	SD	21 Apr. 1883	2	6	
Kellogg	William	m.	RRF	19 Apr. 1883	3	4	
Kelly	Captain	o.	DR	8 Sept. 1882	3	1	
Kelly	Ellen	m.	PCo	26 Oct. 1881	3	4	
Kelly	Ellinor	d.	SD	3 Sept. 1881	3	8	
Kelly	J. A.	b.	SD	26 Mar. 1881	3	8	
Kelly	J. K., Miss	d.	DR	3 Oct. 1881	2	3	
Kelly	J. K., Miss	d.	SD	22 Oct. 1881	3	6	
Kelly	John J.	d.	PCo	26 Apr. 1882	3	4	
Kelly	John J.	d.	SD	22 Apr. 1882	3	2	
Kelly	John Joseph	d.	DR	19 Apr. 1882	3	2	Santa Rosa

(1) Surname	(2) Given Name	(3)	(4)	(5) Date	(6) Pg	(7) Col	(8) Comments
Kelly	John Joseph	d.	DR	20 Apr. 1882	3	1	
Kelso	Bell	m.	RRF	17 May 1883	2	3	
Kemp	John Charles	d.	SD	2 Aug. 1884	3	4	
Kempenski	John	d.	PWA	3 Nov. 1883	3	3	
Kempinski	John	d.	SD	3 Nov. 1883	1	6	
Kendall	Emma	m.	PCo	8 Mar. 1882	3	5	
Kenneally	(male)	b.	DR	13 June 1884	3	3	
Kenneally	James	b.	PCo	11 June 1884	3	5	
Kenneally	James	b.	SD	28 June 1884	3	4	
Kennedy	Alice C.	m.	SD	17 Feb. 1883	3	1	
Kennedy	Alice Carey	m.	PCo	21 Feb. 1883	3	5	also 28 Feb., p. 3 col. 2
Kennedy	Alice Carey	m.	RRF	15 Feb. 1883	2	3	
Kennedy	Almus	b.	SD	11 Mar. 1882	3	6	
Kennedy	Annie	m.	SD	28 Nov. 1885	3	5	
Kennedy	C. D.	m.	PCo	24 May 1882	3	5	
Kennedy	C. D.	m.	SD	20 May 1882	2	4	
Kennedy	D. S	b.	SD	11 Oct. 1884	2	5	
Kennedy	D. S.	b.	PCo	8 Oct. 1884	3	6	
Kennedy	David	m.	SD	6 May 1882	3	6	
Kennedy	Flora	m.	RRF	1 June 1882	1	6	
Kennedy	Flora	m.	SD	10 June 1882	2	3	
Kennedy	Georgie	d.	DR	17 Sept. 1881	2	3	
Kennedy	James	o.	SIT	22 Aug. 1885	2	2	
Kennedy	James	p.	DR	26 Dec. 1884	2	2	
Kennedy	James	d.	DR	2 Nov. 1885	3	4	
Kennedy	James	d.	PCo	14 Oct. 1885	3	6	
Kennedy	James	d.	PCo	28 Oct. 1885	3	4	
Kennedy	James	d.	SD	23 Aug. 1884	2	4	
Kennedy	James	d.	SD	24 Oct. 1885	5	4	
Kennedy	James	d.	SIT	10 Oct. 1885	2	3	also p. 3 col. 2
Kennedy	Mary	m.	DR	13 Dec. 1884	1	4	
Kennelly	James	d.	PCo	10 Dec. 1884	3	1&5	Catholic Cemetery
Kennelly	James	d.	PWA	13 Dec. 1884	3	2&4	
Kennelly	James	b.	PWA	14 June 1884	3	6	
Kennely	James	d.	DR	6 Dec. 1884	3	2	
Kenniston	Joseph	o.	SD	30 Sept. 1882	3	3	
Kenny	Kate M.	m.	DD	22 Sept. 1883	3	2	
Kenny	Kate M.	m.	SD	29 Sept. 1883	2	6	
Kenny	Thomas	m.	SD	30 July 1881	3	8	
Kent	Sarah A.	m.	RRF	16 Nov. 1882	2	4	
Kent	W. C.	b.	DR	21 Jan. 1882	3	2	
Kent	W. C.	b.	PCo	18 Jan. 1882	3	5	

(1) Surname	(2) Given Name	(3)	(4)	(5) Date	(6) Pg	(7) Col	(8) Comments
Kent	W. C.	b.	SD	28 Jan. 1882	3	6	
Kent	Wilhelmina	m.	SD	12 Jan. 1884	3	6	
Keran	J. N.	d.	RRF	3 Nov. 1881	3	4	
Keran	Jimmy	d.	DR	26 Oct. 1881	2	3	
Keran	Jimmy	d.	SD	29 Oct. 1881	3	6	
Kern	W.	m.	CR	19 Feb. 1881	4	2	
Kern	W.	m.	CR	19 Feb. 1881	4	2	
Kern	William	m.	DR	17 Feb. 1881	3	2	
Kern	William	m.	SD	19 Feb. 1881	3	8	
Kerr	R. A.	b.	PCo	10 Sept. 1884	3	6	
Ketsinger	G. W.	m.	SD	30 Dec. 1882	3	6	
Key	Hamilton	d.	PCo	15 Feb. 1882	3	4	
Key	William Hamilton	d.	DR	16 Feb. 1882	2	3	
Keyser	Myron N.	d.	SD	17 Mar. 1883	3	3	
Kiechler	Albert	d.	SIT	26 Sept. 1885	2	2	
Kilcorse	Mary	d.	DR	23 Sept. 1881	2	3	
Kilcorse	Mary	d.	PCo	21 Sept. 1881	3	5	
Kilcorse	Mary	d.	SD	1 Oct. 1881	3	8	
Kilcorse	Patrick	d.	DR	23 Sept. 1881	2	3	
Kilcorse	Patrick	d.	PCo	21 Sept. 1881	3	5	
Kilgore	A. C.	d.	PCo	14 Feb. 1883	3	6	
Kilgore	A. C.	d.	RRF	8 Feb. 1883	2	4	Big Plains Cemetery
Kilgore	A. C.	d.	SD	10 Feb. 1883	2	7	
Killam	A. F.	b.	PCo	31 Jan. 1883	3	5	
Killam	A. F.	b.	PWA	3 Feb. 1883	3	7	
Kimball	E. N.	b.	SD	2 Apr. 1881	3	8	
Kimes	D. M.	m.	SD	9 May 1885	2	5	also 16 May, p. 5 col. 4
King	E. W.	m.	DR	11 Jan. 1881	3	2	
King	Jesse	b.	RRF	26 Oct. 1882	2	3	
King	John	m.	PCo	19 Nov. 1884	3	5	
King	John	b.	PCo	23 Dec. 1885	3	4	
King	John	b.	SD	19 Dec. 1885	3	4	
King	Joseph L.	b.	DR	12 Oct. 1881	2	3	
King	Joseph L.	b.	PCo	12 Oct. 1881	3	5	
King	Joseph L.	b.	SD	15 Oct. 1881	3	8	
King	Joseph L.	b.	SD	22 Oct. 1881	3	6	
King	Louisa A.	d.	PCo	30 Dec. 1885	3	4	
King	M. W.	m.	CR	8 Jan. 1881	5	4&5	
King	M. W.	m.	SD	15 Jun. 1881	3	8	
King	Maria D.	d.	DR	25 July 1882	2	3	
King	Mariah D.	d.	PCo	26 July 1882	3	6	Cypress Hill Cemetery
King	Mariah	d.	SD	29 July 1882	3	7	

(1) Surname	(2) Given Name	(3)	(4)	(5) Date	(6) Pg	(7) Col	(8) Comments
King	Thomas M.	d.	CR	8 Dec. 1883	3	1	
King	Thomas	d.	PCo	12 Dec. 1883	2	4	
King	Thomas W.	d.	RRF	6 Dec. 1883	2	3	
King	William	m.	DR	25 Nov. 1881	2	3	
King	William	m.	PCo	23 Nov. 1881	3	5	
King	William	b.	RRF	3 Feb. 1881	2	4	
King	William	b.	SD	3 Feb. 1883	2	6	
Kingery	S. S.	d.	PC	20 June 1883	3	6	
Kingery	S. S.	d.	PWA	23 June 1883	3	7	
Kingsbury	Annie G.	d.	DR	26 Mar. 1884	3	3	
Kingwell	Mr. & Mrs.	b.	SD	4 Aug. 1883	2	5	
Kingwell	R.	b.	PC	1 Aug. 1883	3	6	
Kingwell	R.	b.	PWA	28 July 1883	3	7	
Kinloch	Charles S.	d.	SRR	1 Oct. 1885	3	3	
Kinloch	S.	d.	DR	26 Sept. 1885	3	4	
Kinney	Henry A.	d.	DR	31 May 1881	2	2	
Kinsey	George W.	b.	DD	22 Sept. 1883	3	2	
Kinslow	E.	b.	PCo	27 May 1885	3	6	
Kinslow	John F.	m.	DR	22 July 1884	3	3	
Kinslow	John F.	m.	PCo	30 July 1884	3	6	
Kinslow	John F.	m.	PWA	26 July 1884	2	3	
Kinslow	John F.	m..	SD	26 July 1884	1	4	
Kippetoe	David Archie	d.	DR	21 Sept. 1885	3	4	
Kirkman	W. C.	m.	DR	1 May 1882	3	2	
Kirkman	W. C.	m.	PCo	26 Apr. 1882	3	4	
Kirkman	W. C.	m.	SD	29 Apr. 1882	3	6	
Kirkpatrick	Cynthia	d.	DR	22 Aug. 1882	3	1	also 23 Aug., p. 2 col. 3
Kirkpatrick	Cynthia	d.	SD	26 Aug. 1882	3	2&5	
Kirloch	Charles S.	d.	DR	2 Oct. 1885	3	4	
Kise	Emma	d.	SD	7 Apr. 1883	2	6	
Kise	P. A. (dau. of)	d.	PC	16 May 1883	3	5	
Kise	P. A. (dau. of)	d.	RRF	17 May 1883	2	3	
Kise	P. A. (dau. of)	d.	SD	19 May 1883	3	5	
Kise	Philip	m.	DR	4 Mar. 1882	2	3	
Kise	Philip	b.	HE	12 Apr. 1883	2	4	
Kise	Philip	b.	PC	18 Apr. 1883	3	5	
Kise	Philip	m.	PCo	8 Mar. 1882	3	5	
Kise	Philip	m.	RRF	2 Mar. 1882	2	4	
Kise	Philip	b.	RRF	5 Apr. 1883	2	3	
Kise	Philip	m.	SD	25 Feb. 1882	3	6	
Kiser	E., Miss	m.	PWA	29 Sept. 1883	3	8	
Kiser	H. E.	m.	DD	25 Sept. 1883	3	3	

(1) Surname	(2) Given Name	(3)	(4)	(5) Date	(6) Pg	(7) Col	(8) Comments
Kiser	H. E., Miss	m.	SD	29 Sept. 1883	2	6	
Kiser	Joseph	b.	PWA	2 May 1885	3	6	
Kiser	Joseph	b.	SD	2 May 1885	2	5	
Kiser	Peter	b.	DR	29 July 1884	3	3	
Kiser	Peter	b.	PCo	30 July 1884	3	6	
Kiser	Peter	b.	PWA	2 Aug. 1884	3	4	
Kissack	Andrew	d.	SD	15 Sept. 1883	2	4	
Kissack	Margaret	d.	CR	8 Sept. 1883	3	1&2	
Kissack	Margaret	d.	DD	8 Sept. 1883	3	3	
Kissack	Margaret	d.	RRF	13 Sept. 1883	2	4	
Klahn	Anna	d.	SD	5 Mar. 1881	3	8	
Kleiser	J. A.	b.	CR	6 Aug 1881	5	2	
Kleiser	J. A.	b.	DR	6 Aug. 1881	2	3	
Kline	P. R.	b.	DD	15 Sept. 1883	3	3	
Kline	William Henry	d.	PCo	27 May 1885	3	6	
Klinger	Caroline	m.	PC	30 May 1883	3	4	
Klinger	Caroline W.	m.	PWA	2 June 1883	3	8	
Klinger	Marie	d.	PCo	21 Oct. 1885	3	4	
Klingler	Maria	d.	DR	23 Oct. 1885	3	4	
Klink	S. V. R.	d.	RRF	25 May 1882	2	3	
Klute	Carl	d.	CR	11 June 1881	5	5	
Klute	Carl Prior	d.	CR	11 June 1881	5	5	
Klute	Carl Prior	d.	DR	4 June 1881	2	2	
Klute	Henry	p	DR	26 Dec. 1884	2	2	
Klute	Henry	d.	PCo	1 Oct. 1884	3	5	
Klute	Henry	d.	SD	4 Oct. 1884	1	5	Rural Cemetery
Klute	Henry	d.	SD	27 Sept. 1884	2	5	also p. 3 col. 2
Knapp	Charles	b.	PCo	31 Jan. 1883	3	5	
Knapp	Charles	b.	PWA	3 Feb. 1883	3	7	
Knapp	Emma M.	m.	PC	25 July 1883	3	6	
Knapp	G. W.	b.	PWA	3 May 1884	3	6	
Knapp	Lena Maud	d.	DR	2 June 1882	3	2	
Knapp	Lena Maud	d.	PCo	31 May 1882	3	5	
Knapp	Lena Maud	d.	SD	10 June 1882	2	3	
Kneller	George	b.	DR	16 Nov. 1885	3	4	
Knight	Charles L.	m.	PC	4 July 1883	3	5	
Knight	Charles L.	m.	SD	7 July 1883	2	5	
Knowles	J. S.	d.	RRF	1 Dec. 1881	3	6	
Knowles	W. H.	b.	PCo	2 Apr. 1884	3	6	
Knowles	W. H.	b.	PWA	29 Mar. 1884	3	6	
Knowles	William H.	b.	PCo	18 Jan. 1882	3	5	
Knowlton	Louella	d.	PCo	8 Mar. 1882	3	5	

(1) Surname	(2) Given Name	(3)	(4)	(5) Date	(6) Pg	(7) Col	(8) Comments
Knox	C. W., Miss	d.	PCo	6 May 1885	3	6	
Knust	Lillie	m.	CR	11 Apr. 1885	3	2	
Knust	Miss	m.	CR	3 Oct. 1885	3	2	
Koch	A.	b.	DD	9 Oct. 1883	3	3	
Koch	A.	b.	SD	13 Oct. 1883	3	4	
Koch	Augustus	b.	PCo	23 Nov. 1881	3	5	
Koch	Augustus	b.	SD	19 Nov. 1881	4	8	
Koch	Franz	d.	RRF	28 July 1881	2	5	
Koch	William	d.	DR	20 Dec. 1884	3	2	
Kohle	Minnie	m.	SD	22 Aug. 1885	6	2	
Kohler	F. W.	b.	DR	11 Aug. 1882	3	2	
Kolbert	George	d.	CR	4 Mar. 1882	1	4	
Kolbert	George	d.	DR	18 Feb. 1882	3	1	
Kolliker	Fred	m.	PCo	22 Apr. 1885	3	6	
Kolliker	Fred	m.	SD	25 Apr. 1885	2	5	
Kopf	A. A.	b.	PCo	2 Nov. 1881	3	5	
Kopf	A. A.	b.	SD	5 Nov. 1881	3	6	
Kopf	A. A.	m.	SD	29 Jan. 1881	3	8	
Kopf	Bertha	d.	DR	13 Dec. 1882	3	1	
Korbel	A.	b.	CR	23 Apr. 1881	5	3	
Korbel	A.	b.	DR	14 Apr. 1881	2	3	
Korbel	A.	b.	SD	30 Apr. 1881	3	8	
Korbel	Miss	d.	PCo	1 Oct. 1884	3	5	
Kraft	E. H.	b.	DR	17 June 1881	2	3	
Kruse	James	d.	DR	22 Oct. 1885	3	4	
Kremer	Ann E.	d.	SD	21 Oct. 1882	3	6	
Kretsinger	G W.	m.	DR	22 Dec. 1882	3	3	
Kretsinger	G. W.	m.	PCo	27 Dec. 1882	3	6	
Kretsinger	G. W.	b.	PCo	19 Dec. 1883	3	4	
Kretsinger	G. W.	b.	RRF	13 Dec. 1883	2	2	
Kretzinger	G. W.	b.	DD	14 Dec. 1883	3	2	
Kridle	W. F.	d.	DR	31 Jan. 1881	3	2	
Kridle	W. F.	d.	SD	5 Feb. 1881	3	8	
Kroncke	Henry	b.	DR	2 Oct. 1882	2	3	
Kroncke	Henry	b.	DR	15 Sept. 1882	3	2	
Kroncke	Henry	b.	PCo	27 Sept. 1882	3	6	
Kronke	Henry	o.	DR	17 Aug. 1882	3	1	
Krueger	O. F.	b.	DD	8 Sept. 1883	3	3	
Krueger	O. F.	b.	SD	15 Sept. 1883	2	4	
Kruger	O. F.	b.	RRF	6 Sept. 1883	2	4	
Kruse	James	d.	PCo	28 Oct. 1885	3	4	
Kuffel	Emma May	m.	PCo	21 Mar. 1883	3	5	

(1) Surname	(2) Given Name	(3)	(4)	(5) Date	(6) Pg	(7) Col	(8) Comments
Kuffel	Emma May	m.	PWA	24 Mar. 1883	3	7	
Kuhl	Catharine	m.	SD	19 Sept. 1885	2	4	
Kuhl	Catherina	m.	DR	16 Sept. 1882	3	4	
Kurlander	J.	b.	PCo	25 Jan. 1882	3	6	
Kurlander	J.	b.	SD	21 Jan. 1882	3	6	
Kurlander	Mr. & Mrs.	b.	DR	19 Jan. 1882	2	3	
Kusiel	Sophia	d.	DD	15 Sept. 1883	3	3	
Kusiel	Sophie	d.	PWA	15 Sept. 1883	3	6	
Kuster	Charles H.	d.	CR	6 Aug. 1881	1	3	
Kuster	Charles Henry	m.	SD	6 Aug. 1881	3	8	
Kuster	Henry	b.	PCo	15 Oct. 1884	3	6	
Kuster	Henry	b.	PWA	18 Oct. 1884	3	4	
Kuster	Livia	m.	SD	17 Dec. 1881	3	7	
Kuykendall	J. O.	m.	RRF	8 May 1884	5	6	
Kuykendall	James	b.	PCo	4 Mar. 1885	3	6	
Kuykendall	James	b.	SD	14 Mar. 1885	5	5	
Kuykendall	James O	m.	SD	3 May 1884	3	3	
Kuykendall	James O.	m.	DR	30 Apr. 1884	3	2	
Kuykendall	Lulu	m.	SD	24 Feb. 1883	3	1	
Kyle	Lana	m.	PCo	28 Jan. 1885	3	6	
Kyle	Thomas A.	d.	DR	6 Dec. 1884	3	2	
Kyle	Thomas A.	d.	PCo	10 Dec. 1884	3	5	
Kyle	Thomas A.	d.	PWA	13 Dec. 1884	3	4	
Kyle	Thomas A.	d.	SD	27 Dec. 1884	2	4	
Kyle	Thomas	b.	PCo	10 June 1885	3	6	

L

(1) Surname	(2) Given Name	(3)	(4)	(5) Date	(6) Pg	(7) Col	(8) Comments
La Moore	Charley (father of)	d.	CR	31 Oct. 1885	3	2	
La Motte	A.	b.	PCo	7 Dec. 1881	3	5	
Labell	Julius	d.	PCo	22 Oct. 1884	3	6	
Labell	Julius	d.	SD	25 Oct. 1884	2	5	San Francisco
Lackey	Alexander	m.	PCo	20 July 1881	3	5	
Lackey	Alexander	m.	SD	23 July 1881	3	8	
Lacque	B. F.	m.	SD	3 Nov. 1883	3	3	
Laeque	B. F.	m.	DD	31 Oct. 1883	3	3	
Lafferty	H. H. (dau. of)	d.	PCo	21 Mar. 1883	3	5	
Lafferty	H. H. (dau. of)	d.	SD	17 Mar. 1883	3	5	
LaFranchi	Aneglina	m.	DR	2 Oct. 1882	2	3	
LaFranchi	Angelina	m.	PCo	27 Sept. 1882	3	6	
LaFranchi	Angelo	m.	DR	2 Oct. 1882	2	3	
LaFranchi	J. P. Angelo	m.	PCo	27 Sept. 1882	3	6	
Laird	T. F.	m.	SD	31 May 1884	1	5	also p. 2 col. 3
Laird	Thomas F.	m.	DR	24 May 1884	3	2	
Laird	Thomas F.	m.	PCo	28 May 1884	2	4	
Lamb	Horace G.	b.	PCo	27 May 1885	3	6	
Lamb	Mary A.	m.	CR	2 Dec. 1882	3	3	
Lamb	Mary A.	m.	DR	2 Dec. 1882	3	2	
Lamb	Mary A.	m.	PCo	6 Dec. 1882	3	6	
Lamb	Mary A.	m.	SD	9 Dec. 1882	2	5	
Lamb	William	m.	PWA	28 Apr. 1883	3	2	
Lamberrt	George	b.	DD	24 Dec. 1883	3	2	
Lambert	Miranda	d.	SD	15 Jan. 1881	3	8	
Lambert	Nevada	m.	DD	27 July 1883	3	2	
Lambert	Nevada	m.	PC	1 Aug. 1883	3	6	
Lambert	Nevada	m.	SD	4 Aug. 1883	2	5	
Lambert	William	o.	CR	27 Oct. 1883	3	3	
Lamont	Rolla	d.	PCo	15 Feb. 1882	3	4	
LaMont	Rolla	d.	DR	6 Feb. 1882	2	3	
LaMont	Rolla	d.	SD	11 Feb. 1882	3	6	
Landsborough	Thomas S.	d.	DR	15 Aug. 1882	2	2	
Landsborough	Thomas S.	d.	SD	2 Sept. 1882	3	6	
Lane	Frank T.	m.	DD	20 Oct. 1883	3	3	
Lane	Lucinda	d.	CR	10 Dec. 1881	5	2	Cloverdale Cemetery
Lane	Lucy Luella	d.	SD	12 Nov. 1881	3	7	
Langdon	C. W.	d.	CR	18 Feb. 1882	1	3	

(1) Surname	(2) Given Name	(3)	(4)	(5) Date	(6) Pg	(7) Col	(8) Comments
Langdon	C. W.	d.	DR	4 Feb. 1882	2	3	
Langdon	C. W.	d.	PCo	15 Feb. 1882	3	4	
Langdon	C. W.	d.	RRF	9 Feb. 1882	3	4	
Langdon	C. W.	d.	SD	4 Feb. 1882	2	4	also p. 3 col. 6
Langley	Michael	m.	DD	23 July 1883	3	2	
Langley	Michael	m.	SD	28 July 1883	2	5	
Lannan	P.	b.	CR	7 May 1881	5	5	
Lannan	P.	b.	DR	30 Apr. 1881	2	2	
Lannan	P.	b.	DR	2 Dec. 1882	3	2	
Lannan	P.	b.	PCo	6 Dec. 1882	3	6	
Lannan	P.	b.	RRF	5 May 1881	2	4	
Lannan	P.	b.	RRF	30 Nov. 1882	2	3	
Lannan	P.	b.	SD	7 May 1881	3	8	
Lardner	William B.	m.	RRF	20 Jan. 1881	2	5	
Lardner	William B.	m.	SD	29 Jan. 1881	3	8	
Laroux	Julius	b.	CR	16 June 1883	3	3	
Laroux	Julius	b.	PC	20 June 1883	3	6	
Larrison	Mr.	o.	CR	2 Dec. 1882	3	4	
Lassere	M., Miss	m.	CR	16 Apr. 1881	5	2	
Lassere	Maria	m.	CR	16 Apr. 1881	5	3	
Lassere	Marie	m.	DR	13 Apr. 1881	2	3	
Lasure	Marian	m.	SD	16 Apr. 1881	3	8	
Lathrop	Fannie R.	m.	DR	9 May 1881	2	2	
Lathrop	Fannie R.	m.	RRF	12 May 1881	2	4	
Lathrop	Miss	m.	RRF	16 Feb. 1882	3	5	
Latson	Walter R.	d.	PWA	24 Feb. 1883	3	7	
Laughlin	Adeline	m.	RRF	13 Sept. 1883	2	4	
Laughlin	C. W.	b.	PCo	9 Jan. 1884	3	6	
Laughlin	C. W.	b.	RRF	3 Jan. 1884	2	4	
Laughlin	Josephine	m.	DR	1 Aug. 1882	3	2	
Laughlin	Josephine	m.	PCo	2 Aug. 1882	3	6	
Laughlin	Josephine	m.	SD	29 July 1882	3	7	
Laughlin	L.	b.	SD	18 Apr. 1885	2	4	
Laughlin	Lee L.	b.	DD	31 Aug. 1883	3	3	
Laughlin	Lee	b.	RRF	30 Aug. 1883	2	4	
Laughlin	Malvina	m.	SD	16 Dec. 1882	3	6	
Laughlin	Mellvina	m.	RRF	7 Dec. 1882	2	3	
Laughlin	Melvina	m.	DR	7 Dec. 1882	2	3	
Laughlin	Melvina	m.	PCo	13 Dec. 1882	3	4	
Laughlin	S. (dau. of)	d.	RRF	17 Apr. 1884	2	4	
Laughlin	S. (dau. of)	d.	SD	26 Apr. 1884	3	5	
Laughlin	S.	b.	RRF	17 Apr. 1884	2	4	

(1) Surname	(2) Given Name	(3)	(4)	(5) Date	(6) Pg	(7) Col	(8) Comments
Laughlin	S.	b.	SD	26 Apr. 1883	3	5	
Laughlin	Samuel M.	m.	DR	1 Aug. 1882	3	2	
Laughlin	Samuel M.	m.	PCo	2 Aug. 1882	3	6	
Laughlin	Samuel M.	m.	SD	29 July 1882	3	7	
Laurence	Linnie Belle	m.	PWA	30 June 1883	3	2&7	
Lauritzen	J.	b.	DR	4 Sept. 1885	3	4	
Lauritzen	J.	b.	PCo	2 Sept. 1885	3	6	
Lauritzen	Jeppe C.	m.	PWA	20 Sept. 1884	3	4	
Lauritzen	Martin C.	b.	PCo	16 Sept. 1885	3	6	
Lauritzer	Else Leonora	m.	DR	2 Oct. 1885	3	4	
Lauritzer	Leonora	m.	DR	26 Sept. 1885	3	4	
Lauritzer	Leonora	m.	PCo	30 Sept. 1885	3	6	
Lauritzer	Leonora	m.	SRR	1 Oct. 1885	3	3	
Laurtzen	Jeppe C.	m.	PCo	24 Sept. 1884	3	5	
LaVine	Frank	m.	SD	11 Feb. 1882	3	6	
Law	Almira	m.	DR	13 Dec. 1882	2	3	
Law	Almira	m.	PCo	20 Dec. 1882	3	5	
Lawhead	Dollie	m.	DR	9 Feb. 1882	2	3	
Lawhead	Dollie	m.	HE	9 Feb. 1882	2	3	
Lawler	(female)	b.	DR	19 June 1884	3	3	
Lawler	John	b.	PCo	18 June 1884	3	4	
Lawler	John	b.	PWA	21 June 1884	3	5	
Lawrence	Charles, Mrs.	d.	DD	20 Oct. 1883	3	3	
Lawrence	Charles, Mrs.	d.	SD	27 Oct. 1883	3	4	
Lawrence	Josephine	d.	RRF	18 Oct. 1883	2	4	New York
Lawrence	Linnie Belle	m.	PC	4 July 1883	3	5	
Lawrence	Lulu	m.	PCo	29 Nov. 1882	3	6	
Lawrence	Minnie	m.	SD	7 July 1883	1	5	
Lawrence	Samuel B.	d.	SD	26 Mar. 1881	3	8	
Lawson	Nettie	m.	PCo	17 Sept. 1884	3	6	
Lawson	Nettie	m.	SD	20 Sep. 1884	2	5	
Laxman	P.	b.	CR	7 May 1881	5	5	
Laymance	Ella	m.	DR	8 Aug. 1882	3	2	
Laymance	Ella	m.	RRF	3 Aug. 1882	2	4	
Laymance	Francis	m.	PCo	28 June 1882	3	5	
Laymance	Francis	m.	RRF	6 July 1882	3	4	
Laymance	Francis	m.	SD	8 July 1882	2	5	
Laymance	Henry I.	m.	DR	30 Dec. 1882	2	1	
Laymance	Henry I.	m.	RRF	28 Dec. 1882	2	2	
Laymance	Henry T.	m.	SD	30 Dec. 1882	3	6	
Laymance	Mr. & Mrs.	b.	SD	18 Apr. 1885	2	4	
Lea	F.	d.	CR	30 July 1881	5	5	

(1) Surname	(2) Given Name	(3)	(4)	(5) Date	(6) Pg	(7) Col	(8) Comments
Leahey	Martyn E.	m.	DR	3 Nov. 1885	3	4	
Leard	Genevieve	d.	PC	28 Mar. 1883	3	5	
Leard	Genevieve	d.	RRF	22 Mar. 1883	2	4	
Leard	Genevieve	d.	SD	24 Mar. 1883	2	5	
Leard	J. B.	b.	PCo	20 Feb. 1884	3	6	
Leard	J. B.	b.	RRF	14 Feb. 1884	2	4	
Leard	J. B.	b.	SD	9 July 1881	3	8	
Leard	J. B.	b.	SD	1 Mar. 1884	6	6	
Leard	Phebe	d.	RRF	22 Feb. 1883	2	3	also 1 Mar. 1883; p. 2 col. 4; p. 3 col. 4
Leard	Phoebe	d.	CR	24 Feb. 1883	3	1	
Leard	Phoebe	d.	PCo	28 Feb. 1883	3	5	
Leary	James (dau. of)	d.	CR	27 June 1885	3	1	
Leary	Joseph	b.	SD	3 Dec. 1881	3	8	
Leballister	D. N.	b.	SD	15 Jun. 1881	3	8	
LeCornec	Marie	m.	SD	10 Feb. 1883	2	7	
Ledford	C. A.	b.	PCo	19 Dec. 1883	3	4	
Ledford	S. M.	b.	DD	6 Oct. 1883	3	3	
Ledford	S. M.	b.	SD	13 Oct. 1883	3	4	
Ledford	William R.	d.	CR	13 Oct. 1883	3	1	Cloverdale Cem.
Ledford	William R.	d.	DD	13 Oct. 1883	3	3	
Lee	Charles B.	d.	DR	10 Feb. 1882	2	3	
Lee	Charles B.	d.	SD	25 Feb. 1882	3	6	
Lee	Charles	b.	DR	3 Sept. 1885	3	4	
Lee	Charles	b.	PCo	29 Mar. 1882	3	5	
Lee	Charles	b.	PCo	16 Sept. 1885	3	6	
Lee	Charles	b.	SD	1 Apr. 1882	3	6	
Lee	Charles R.	d.	PCo	22 Feb. 1882	3	5	
Lee	Charlie	b.	DR	18 Mar. 1882	2	3	
Lee	Daniel	d.	DD	26 July 1883	3	2	
Lee	Daniel	p.	DR	9 July 1884	3	3	
Lee	Daniel	d.	PC	25 July 1883	3	6	
Lee	Daniel	d.	PWA	28 July 1883	3	7	
Lee	Daniel	d.	SD	28 July 1883	2	5	
Lee	Elias	m.	DR	21 Nov. 1882	3	2	
Lee	Elias	m.	PCo	29 Nov. 1882	3	6	
Lee	George S.	b.	SD	12 Mar. 1881	3	8	
Lee	Robert	b.	PCo	7 Feb. 1883	3	6	
Lee	Robert	b.	RRF	1 Feb. 1883	2	3	
Lee	Sarah	d.	DD	18 Aug. 1883	3	3	
Lee	W. H.	m.	DD	11 Oct. 1883	3	3	
Lee	W. H.	b.	DR	10 July 1884	3	3	

(1) Surname	(2) Given Name	(3)	(4)	(5) Date	(6) Pg	(7) Col	(8) Comments
Lee	W. H.	d.	HE	11 Oct. 1883	3	3	
Lee	W. H.	b.	PCo	23 July 1884	3	6	
Lee	W. H.	m.	SD	13 Oct. 1883	3	4	
Lee	W. H.	d.	SD	13 Oct. 1883	1	6	
Lee	William H.	o.	CR	20 Oct. 1883	3	1	
Leeds	E.	b.	PCo	1 Oct. 1884	3	5	
Leeper	A. G.	m.	PCo	19 July 1882	3	6	
Leffingwell	Joseph I.	d.	PCo	22 Oct. 1884	3	6	
Leffingwell	Joseph	d.	PWA	18 Oct. 1884	3	4	
Leffingwell	Joseph L.	d,	DR	24 Oct. 1884	3	3	
Leffingwell	Joseph L.	d.	SD	8 Nov. 1884	2	5	
Lefkowitz	P.	b.	DD	23 July 1883	3	2	
Lefkowitz	P.	b.	DD	28 July 1883	3	2	
Legg	Mary	d.	PCo	3 May 1882	3	5	
Legg	Mary	d.	SD	29 Apr. 1882	3	6	
Legg	Samuel	m.	DR	28 Mar. 1884	3	3	
Legg	Samuel	m.	PCo	2 Apr. 1884	3	6	
Legg	Samuel	m.	SD	5 Apr. 1884	3	4	
Leggett	Mr. & Mrs.	b.	DR	26 Aug. 1885	3	4	
Lehman	Angeline	d.	DR	17 Apr. 1882	3	1&2	
Lehman	Angeline	d.	PCo	26 Apr. 1882	3	4	
Lehman	Angeline	d.	SD	22 Apr. 1882	3	6	
Lehman	George	m.	DR	30 Dec. 1882	2	1	
Lehn	Charles	m.	CR	5 Mar. 1881	4	2	
Lehn	Charles	m.	DR	1 Mar. 1881	3	2	
Lehn	Charles	m.	PCo	9 Mar. 1881	3	4	
Lehn	Charles	m.	SD	5 Mar. 1881	3	8	
Leigh	A. G.	b.	PCo	11 Oct. 1882	3	6	
Leigh	A. G.	b.	RRF	5 Oct. 1882	2	3	
Leigh	Mr. & Mrs.	b.	DD	4 Dec. 1883	3	3	
Leigh	William	b.	DD	23 Nov. 1883	3	2	
Leigh	William	b.	RRF	28 Sept. 1882	2	3	
Leigh	William	b.	RRF	22 Nov. 1883	2	3	
Leigh	William	b.	SD	1 Dec. 1883	3	4	
Leisensen	Ida	m.	SD	10 June 1882	2	3	
Leiser	Leo	m.	SD	28 Mar. 1885	5	6	
Lemay	Daniel	d.	SD	21 Jan. 1882	3	6	
Lemay	Josiah	m.	PCo	28 June 1882	3	5	
Lemay	Josiah	m.	SD	24 June 1882	3	5	
Lemeau	August	b.	PCo	14 Feb. 1883	3	6	
Lemoine	E.	b.	CR	25 June 1881	4	3	
Lemoine	E.	b.	DR	24 Nov. 1882	2	3	

(1) Surname	(2) Given Name	(3)	(4)	(5) Date	(6) Pg	(7) Col	(8) Comments
Lemoine	E.	b.	RRF	9 June 1881	2	5	
Lemoine	E.	b.	RRF	23 Nov. 1882	2	4	
Lemoine	E.	b.	SD	2 July 1881	3	8	
Lemoine	E.	b.	SD	18 June 1881	3	8	
Lemon	Hetty J.	m.	DR	4 Dec. 1882	3	2	
Lemon	Hetty J.	m.	PCo	6 Dec. 1882	3	6	"Lemon-aid for one"
Lemon	Jennie H.	m.	SD	9 Dec. 1882	2	5	also p. 3 col. 6
Lemon	Thomas	p.	DR	6 Dec. 1884	2	1	
Lent	John F.	d.	DR	3 July 1884	2	2	
Lent	John R.	d.	PCo	16 July 1884	3	6	
Leppin	Dora H.	m.	DR	10 July 1885	3	4	
Leroux	Edgar	d.	PC	4 Apr. 1883	3	5	
Leroux	Edgar	d.	SD	7 Apr. 1883	2	6	
LeRoux	Jules	d.	SD	27 Oct. 1883	1	5	
Lescinskey	M.	b.	SD	26 Apr. 1883	3	5	
Lescinsky	M.	b.	RRF	17 Apr. 1884	2	4	
Leslie	Mr. & Mrs.	b.	PC	23 May 1883	3	5	
Leslie	Mr. & Mrs.	b.	RRF	17 May 1883	2	3	
Lester	John	d.	DR	22 Dec. 1884	2	2	
Lester	John	d.	PCo	17 Dec. 1884	2	4	
Lester	John	d.	PWA	20 Dec. 1884	3	4	
Lester	Peter	m.	PWA	24 Feb. 1883	3	7	
Levall	John	b.	PCo	14 Dec. 1881	3	4	
Levall	John	b.	SD	10 Dec. 1881	3	7	
Levey	E. D.	o.	CR	21 Nov. 1885	1	4	
Levie	Alice Jennie	d.	DR	16 Apr. 1884	3	2	
Levie	Alice Jennie	d.	PWA	19 Apr. 1884	3	6	
Lewis	Charles	b.	DR	9 Nov. 1885	2	2	
Lewis	Charles	b.	PCo	4 Nov. 1885	2	5	
Lewis	F. M.	d.	HE	26 Jan. 1882	3	4	
Lewis	F. M.	d.	PCo	25 Jan. 1882	3	2	Cypress Hill
Lewis	F. W.	b.	PCo	27 Dec. 1882	3	6	
Lewis	Frank W.	b.	PCo	10 Dec. 1884	3	5	
Lewis	Frank W.	b.	PWA	13 Dec. 1884	3	4	
Lewis	Frank W.	b.	SD	27 Dec. 1884	2	4	
Lewis	Harry	m.	CR	12 July 1884	3	1	
Lewis	Harry	m.	DR	17 July 1884	3	3	
Lewis	Harry	m.	PCo	23 July 1884	3	6	
Lewis	I. S.	b.	CR	19 Jan. 1884	3	1	
Lewis	John	d.	PCo	9 Dec. 1885	3	6	
Lewis	Lucy	m.	DR	12 July 1882	3	2	
Lewis	Lucy	m.	PCo	28 June 1882	3	5	

(1) Surname	(2) Given Name	(3)	(4)	(5) Date	(6) Pg	(7) Col	(8) Comments
Lewis	Lucy	m.	SD	1 July 1882	2	3	
Lewis	Mary	d.	PCo	2 Jan. 1884	3	6	
Lewis	Mary	d.	PWA	29 Dec. 1883	3	6	
Lewis	Mary	d.	SD	5 Jan. 1884	1	4	
Lewis	R. E.	b.	PCo	26 Dec. 1883	3	5	
Lewis	R. E.	b.	RRF	20 Dec. 1883	2	2	
Lewis	Rebecca	m.	DR	30 Dec. 1881	2	3	
Lewis	Rebecca	m.	HE	29 Dec. 1881	2	3	
Lewis	Rebecca	m.	PCo	11 Jan. 1882	3	6	
Lewis	Rebecca	m.	RRF	29 Dec. 1881	2	3	
Lewis	Rebecca	m.	SD	31 Dec. 1881	3	6	
Lewis	S. F.	b.	CR	2 Apr. 1881	5	3	
Lewis	S. F.	b.	DR	1 Apr. 1881	2	3	
Lewis	S. F.	b.	PCo	30 Mar. 1881	3	4	
Lewis	S. F.	b.	SD	9 Apr. 1881	3	8	
Lewis	S.	b.	SD	16 Apr. 1881	3	8	
Lewis	Sarah A.	m.	PCo	7 Jan. 1885	3	6	
Lewis	Sarah A.	m.	SD	3 Jan. 1885	2	7	
Lewis	W. A.	b.	DD	27 Sept. 1883	3	3	
Lewis	W. A.	b.	PWA	29 Sept. 1883	3	8	
Lewis	W. A.	b.	SD	29 Sept. 1883	2	6	
Lfferty	H. H. (dau. of)	d.	RRF	15 Mar. 1883	2	4	
Lichou	Henry	b.	PCo	3 Aug. 1881	3	5	
Lichou	Henry	b.	SD	13 Aug. 1881	3	8	
Lichou	Henry P.	b.	PWA	1 Sept. 1883	3	8	
Liddaker	William	b.	CR	12 Feb. 1881	5	5	
Liddaker	William	b.	DR	7 Feb. 1881	3	2	
Liddaker	William	b.	PCo	16 Feb. 1881	3	4	
Light	Ella	m.	DR	24 Oct. 1884	3	3	
Light	Ella	m.	PCo	22 Oct. 1884	3	6	
Light	Ella	m.	PWA	25 Oct. 1884	3	4	
Light	Ella	m.	SD	8 Nov. 1884	2	5	
Lightner	Dan	b.	PCo	5 Oct. 1881	3	5	
Lightner	John M.	d.	PCo	4 Oct. 1882	3	2&6	Cypress Hill Cemetery
Lightner	John S.	b.	DR	13 Dec. 1882	2	3	
Lightner	John S.	m.	DR	28 Jan. 1882	2	3	
Lightner	John S.	b.	PCo	6 Dec. 1882	3	6	
Lightner	John S.	m.	PCo	25 Jan. 1882	3	6	
Lightner	John S.	b.	PCo	1 Oct. 1884	3	5	
Lightner	John S.	b.	SD	16 Dec. 1882	3	6	
Likins	James W.	m.	DR	5 Aug. 1884	3	4	
Likins	James W.	m.	SD	9 Aug. 1884	3	4	

(1) Surname	(2) Given Name	(3)	(4)	(5) Date	(6) Pg	(7) Col	(8) Comments
Liljee	Charles P.	m.	SD	5 Mar. 1881	3	8	
Lillie	George	b.	SD	24 Sept. 1881	3	8	
Lillie	J. H.	m.	DR	26 June 1884	3	3	
Lillie	John H.	d.	SD	19 Dec. 1885	3	3	
Limebaugh	A.	b.	PCo	3 Jan. 1883	3	4	
Limebaugh	A.	b.	PCo	10 Sept. 1884	3	6	
Limebaugh	A.	b.	PWA	13 Sept. 1884	3	6	
Limebaugh	A.	b.	SD	13 Sept. 1884	3	4	
Limebaugh	Olive	d.	SD	13 Jan. 1883	3	5	
Lindig	Carl	o.	PCo	27 Aug. 1884	3	1	
Lindig	Carl	o.	SD	6 Sept. 1884	3	4	
Lindig	Carl	o.	SD	30 Aug. 1884	3	1	
Lindsay	J. J.	b.	SD	17 Mar. 1883	3	3	
Lindsay	J. J. (dau. of)	d.	RRF	15 Mar. 1883	2	4	
Lindsay	Robert	m.	SD	16 Apr. 1881	3	8	
Lindsey	R.	m.	CR	16 Apr. 1881	5	3	
Lindsey	R.	m.	CR	16 Apr. 1881	5	2	
Lindsey	Robert	m.	DR	13 Apr. 1881	2	3	
Line	Abel	d.	RRF	23 Feb. 1882	2	4	
Line	William A.	d.	RRF	23 Feb. 1882	2	4	Ferndale, CA
Linebaugh	A.	b.	PWA	5 Jan. 1883	2	5	
Linebaugh	A.	b.	SD	6 Jan. 1883	2	5	
Linebaugh	Columbus	m.	DR	1 Nov. 1881	2	3	filed after Nov. 29
Linebaugh	Columbus	m.	PCo	9 Nov. 1881	3	5	
Linebaugh	Henry	b.	DR	10 Nov. 1881	2	3	
Linebaugh	Maud	d.	PCo	5 Aug. 1885	3	6	
Linebaugh	Maud	d.	SD	22 Aug. 1885	6	2	
Linebaugh	Nellie	d.	DR	27 July 1881	3	2	
Linebaugh	Nellie	d.	SD	30 July 1881	3	1	
Linebaugh	Olive	d.	PCo	10 Jan. 1883	3	6	
Linebaugh	Olive	d.	PWA	12 Jan. 1883	3	6	
Linebaugh	Robert A.	b.	PCo	10 Dec. 1884	3	5	
Linebaugh	Robert A.	b.	PWA	13 Dec. 1884	3	4	
Linebaugh	Robert A.	b.	SD	27 Dec. 1884	2	4	
Linebaugh	Robert F.	m.	DR	16 Dec. 1881	2	2	
Linebaugh	Robert F.	m.	PCo	28 Dec. 1881	3	6	
Linebaugh	Robert F.	m.	SD	24 Dec. 1881	2	3	
Linney	T. B.	b.	PWA	4 Aug. 1883	3	7	
Linville	Lizzie	m.	PCo	31 May 1882	3	5	
Linville	Lizzie	m.	RRF	25 May 1882	2	3	
Linville	Lizzie	m.	SD	3 June 1882	2	4	
Liston	J. J.	m.	PCo	18 Mar. 1885	3	2	

(1) Surname	(2) Given Name	(3)	(4)	(5) Date	(6) Pg	(7) Col	(8) Comments
Liston	Jonathan J.	m.	PWA	28 Mar. 1885	3	5	
Little	Bridget	d.	PC	23 May 1883	3	5	
Little	Bridget	d.	PWA	26 May 1883	3	7	
Little	J. D.	b.	DR	2 Oct. 1882	2	3	
Little	J. D.	b.	PCo	27 Sept. 1882	3	6	
Little	Ray	d.	DR	21 Sept. 1881	2	3	
Little	Roy Wayne	d.	SD	10 Sept. 1881	3	8	
Littlefield	Mary A.	m.	DR	27 Oct. 1882	3	1	
Litzus	L.	b.	SD	12 Mar. 1881	3	8	
Livcy	C. R.	d.	HE	12 Jan. 1882	3	4	
Livcy	Charles Robert	d.	RRF	12 Jan. 1882	2	2	
Livcy	Mary	m.	PCo	21 June 1882	3	5	
Livcy	Mary	m.	SD	17 June 1882	2	4	
Livernash	J. H.	b.	CR	27 Oct. 1885	3	1	
Livernash	J. H.	b.	PC	4 July 1883	3	5	
Livernash	J. H.	b.	SD	7 July 1883	2	5	
Livernash	J. H.	b.	SD	24 Oct. 1885	5	4	
Livernash	J. H. (son of)	d.	CR	27 Oct. 1885	3	1	
Livey	C. R.	d.	PCo	18 Jan. 1882	3	5	
Livey	Mary	m.	DR	17 June 1882	3	2	
Livey	Mary	m.	RRF	15 June 1882	2	4	
Livingston	C. S.	b.	PCo	3 May 1882	3	5	
Livingston	C. S.	m.	SD	9 July 1881	3	8	
Livingston	C. S.	b.	SD	29 Apr. 1882	3	6	
Livy	C. R.	d.	SD	21 Jan. 1882	3	6	
Lloyd	James	b.	DD	21 Nov. 1883	3	3	
Lloyd	James	b.	SD	24 Nov. 1883	3	4	
Lloyd	Mary J.	m.	DR	7 Nov. 1881	2	3	
Lloyd	Mary J.	m.	PCo	2 Nov. 1881	3	5	
Lloyd	Mary J.	m.	SD	12 Nov. 1881	3	7	
Lobier	Louise	m.	SD	26 Sept. 1885	5	4	
Lockhart	Robert	m.	SD	3 Jan. 1885	2	7	
Lockie	John A.	b.	SD	5 Mar. 1881	3	8	
Lockwood	Linnie	m.	DR	4 Oct. 1881	2	3	
Lockwood	Lizzie	m.	SD	8 Oct. 1881	3	8	
Loeser	Amelia	m.	SD	29 Oct. 1881	3	6	
Loeser	Bertha A.	m.	DR	31 Oct. 1881	2	3	
Loeser	Bertha A.	m.	PCo	2 Nov. 1881	3	5	
Logan	Melvin	m.	SD	8 Jan. 1881	3	8	
Lombardi	S.	b.	PC	16 May 1883	3	5	
Lombardi	S.	b.	RRF	10 May 1883	2	3	
Lombardi	S.	b.	SD	19 May 1883	3	5	

(1) Surname	(2) Given Name	(3)	(4)	(5) Date	(6) Pg	(7) Col	(8) Comments
Lomont	Edwin H.	d.	DR	17 Apr. 1882	3	2	
Lomont	Edwin H.	d.	PCo	26 Apr. 1882	3	4	
Long	Alice	m.	DD	14 Sept. 1883	3	2	
Long	Alice	m.	RRF	13 Sept. 1883	2	4	
Long	Alice	m.	SD	22 Sept. 1883	2	4	
Long	Daniel L.	d.	PCo	19 July 1882	3	6	
Long	Daniel L.	d.	SD	22 July 1882	3	5	
Long	George Elmo	d.	DD	12 Oct. 1883	3	3	
Long	George Elmo	d.	HE	11 Oct. 1883	2	2	
Long	George Elmo	d.	RRF	11 Oct. 1883	2	5	
Long	George Elmo	d.	SD	20 Oct. 1883	3	4	
Long	George	b.	DR	21 Nov. 1884	3	2	
Long	George	b.	HE	2 Feb. 1882	2	3	
Long	George	b.	PCo	19 Nov. 1884	3	5	
Long	Harvey	d.	RRF	11 May 1882	3	1	
Long	John	b.	PCo	28 Feb. 1883	3	5	
Long	John	b.	PCo	8 July 1885	3	6	
Long	John	b.	RRF	22 Feb. 1883	2	3	
Long	W.	d.	CR	19 Dec. 1885	3	1	
Long	William	d.	PCo	23 Dec. 1885	3	4	
Long	William	d.	SD	19 Dec. 1885	3	4	
Longland	George	b.	DD	27 Oct. 1883	3	3	
Longmore	(infant son)	d.	DR	25 Feb. 1884	3	3	
Longmore	Edwin	d.	PCo	5 Mar. 1884	3	6	
Longmore	Edwin	d.	PWA	8 Mar. 1884	3	6	
Longmore	Edwin	d.	SD	1 Mar. 1884	6	6	
Longstreet	Elizabeth	d.	RRF	16 June 1881	2	5	
Loofborrow	Elias	d.	CR	11 June 1881	5	5	
Loofborrow	Elias	d.	DR	4 June 1881	2	2	
Loomis	Frank C.	m.	DR	10 Jan. 1884	3	3	
Loomis	Frank C.	b.	DR	18 Nov. 1884	3	2	
Loomis	Frank C.	b.	PCo	26 Nov. 1884	3	5	
Lopaz	Antone	b.	PC	20 June 1883	3	6	
Lopaz	Antone	b.	PWA	23 June 1883	3	7	
Loranger	John	b.	DR	30 Jan. 1882	2	3	
Loranger	John	b.	PCo	25 Jan. 1882	3	6	
Loring	Prescott	m.	DR	2 Oct. 1885	3	4	
Losee	Penryn	m.	RRF	9 Feb. 1882	3	4	
Losee	Perrine	d.	RRF	21 Sept. 1882	3	2	
Lottman	Clara M.	m.	PCo	8 Oct. 1884	3	6	
Lottman	Clara M.	m.	SD	11 Oct. 1884	2	5	
Lottman	W. B.	m.	SD	21 Mar. 1885	1	4	also p. 2 col. 5

(1) Surname	(2) Given Name	(3)	(4)	(5) Date	(6) Pg	(7) Col	(8) Comments
Loudon	R. B.	b.	SD	15 Oct. 1881	3	8	
Loughrey	F. X.	b.	SD	13 Aug. 1884	2	4	
Loughry	F. X.	b.	DR	12 Aug. 1884	3	3	
Lounibos	August	d.	SI	23 Oct. 1880	2	3	
Loux	Herman	b.	DR	16 Nov. 1882	2	3	
Loux	Herman	b.	PCo	15 Nov. 1882	3	5	
Lovejoy	A. P.	d.	CR	25 Apr. 1885	3	1	
Lovejoy	A. P.	d.	PCo	22 Apr. 1885	3	6	
Lovejoy	A. P.	d.	PWA	18 Apr. 1885	2	5	
Lovejoy	A. P.	d.	SD	2 May 1885	2	5	
Lovejoy	Allen P.	d.	SD	25 Apr. 1885	1	4	
Lovejoy	Frank E.	m.	DR	3 Dec. 1881	2	3	
Lovejoy	Frank E.	m.	PCo	7 Dec. 1881	3	5	
Lovejoy	Frank E.	m.	SD	3 Dec. 1881	3	8	
Lovejoy	Frank	b.	PCo	23 Jan. 1884	3	5	
Lovejoy	Frank	b.	PWA	26 Jan. 1884	3	6	
Lovejoy	Frank	b.	SD	26 Jan. 1884	3	5	
Lovejoy	Frank (son of)	d.	PCo	20 Aug. 1884	3	4	
Lovejoy	Frank (son of)	d.	PWA	23 Aug. 1884	3	4	
Lovejoy	Frank (son of)	d.	SD	6 Sept. 1884	2	5	
Lovejoy	Jane	m.	DR	26 Jan. 1882	2	3	
Lovejoy	Jane	m.	HE	26 Jan. 1882	2	3	
Lovejoy	Leonard	d.	DR	7 July 1884	3	3	
Lovejoy	Leonard	d.	PCo	2 July 1884	3	4	
Lovejoy	Leonard	d.	PWA	5 July 1884	3	6	
Lovejoy	Leonard	d.	SD	12 July 1884	6	8	
Lowell	R. D.	b.	PC	4 Apr. 1883	3	5	
Lowell	R. D.	b.	PWA	7 Apr. 1883	2	3	
Lowery	J. D.	d.	CR	10 Dec. 1881	1	2	
Lowery	T. J.	d.	RRF	1 Dec. 1881	3	1	
Lowery	T. J.	d.	SD	3 Dec. 1881	3	3	
Lowrey	Emma	d.	DD	4 Sept. 1883	2	2	
Lowrey	Emma	d.	SD	8 Sept. 1883	2	7	
Lowrey	William	m.	DR	13 July 1885	3	4	
Lowry	William	m.	CR	1 July 1885	3	2	
Lowry	Zerelda	m.	CR	19 Feb. 1881	4	2	
Lowry	Zerelda	m.	SD	19 Feb. 1881	3	8	
Lubeck	C.	o.	SIT	22 Aug. 1885	2	2	
Luce	Arthur S.	b.	RRF	6 July 1882	2	4	
Luce	Arthur S.	b.	SD	8 July 1882	2	5	
Luce	Charles F.	m.	DR	29 Oct. 1885	3	4	
Luce	Jirah	d.	CR	1 Jan. 1881	5	5	

(1) Surname	(2) Given Name	(3)	(4)	(5) Date	(6) Pg	(7) Col	(8) Comments
Luce	Jirah	d.	DR	1 Jan. 1881	3	2	
Luce	Jirah	d.	RRF	6 Jan. 1881	3	1	Healdsburg Cem.
Luce	Jirah	d.	SD	1 June 1881	3	7	
Luce	Lirah	d.	CR	1 Jan. 1881	5	5	
Luce	M. Y.	b.	PCo	30 Jan. 1884	3	6	
Luce	M. Y.	b.	RRF	22 June 1882	2	3	
Luce	Milton	b.	RRF	24 Jan. 1884	2	4	
Ludeman	Louise	d.	DR	17 Oct. 1881	2	3	
Ludeman	Louise	d.	PCo	26 Oct. 1881	3	4	
Ludeman	Louise	d.	SD	22 Oct. 1881	3	6	
Ludemann	John	b.	PCo	14 Oct. 1885	3	6	
Ludemann	John	b.	SD	10 Oct. 1885	5	5	
Ludemann	John	b.	SD	24 Oct. 1885	5	4	
Ludemann	John	b.	SIT	3 Oct. 1885	2	3	
Ludington	Charles C.	m.	CR	25 Feb. 1882	1	2	
Ludolph	Mary	d.	DR	8 Mar. 1884	3	2	
Ludolph	Mary	d.	PCo	12 Mar. 1884	3	6	
Ludolph	Mary	d.	PWA	15 Mar. 1884	3	6	
Ludolph	Mary	d.	SD	15 Mar. 1884	2	5	
Ludwig	Elmer	m.	CR	21 Feb. 1885	3	1	
Ludwig	J. Elmer	m.	PCo	18 Feb. 1885	3	6	
Ludwig	Mary	m.	CR	18 Aug. 1883	3	2	also 25 Aug., p. 3 col. 3
Ludwig	Roxa May	d.	DD	3 July 1883	3	3	
Ludwig	Roxa May	d.	SD	7 July 1883	2	5	also p. 3 col. 2
Ludwig	T. J.	b.	DR	14 May 1881	2	3	
Ludwig	T. J.	b.	SD	28 May 1881	3	8	
Ludwig	T. J. (dau. of)	d.	PC	11 July 1883	3	5	
Lufsky	Ida	d.	DR	24 Sept. 1885	3	4	
Lufsky	Ida	d.	SRR	1 Oct. 1885	3	3	
Luman	Mary	m.	PCo	10 Jan. 1883	3	6	
Luman	Mary	m.	SD	6 Jan. 1883	2	5	
Lunny	Patrick	b.	SD	15 Jun. 1881	3	8	
Lunsford	R. B.	o.	DR	3 Nov. 1882	3	1	
Lusk	Wallace F.	d.	PWA	16 Aug. 1884	3	2&4	
Lusk	Wallace T.	d.	PCo	13 Aug. 1884	3	4	
Lutitia	Miss	m.	DR	13 July 1885	3	4	
Lutrario	Maria	m.	PCo	13 May 1885	3	6	
Lutrario	Maria	m.	SD	23 May 1885	2	5	
Lutrell	Frank	b.	PWA	20 Sept. 1884	3	4	
Luttrell	Frank	b.	PCo	24 Sept. 1884	3	5	
Luttringer	Theresa	m.	DR	1 Feb. 1882	2	3	

(1) Surname	(2) Given Name	(3)	(4)	(5) Date	(6) Pg	(7) Col	(8) Comments
Luttringer	Theresa	m.	SD	4 Feb. 1882	3	6	
Lyman	James	b.	PC	15 Aug. 1883	3	6	
Lynch	Augusta	d.	DR	25 Aug. 1881	2	3	also p. 3 col. 1
Lynch	Augusta	d.	SD	17 Sept. 1881	3	8	
Lynch	Augusta	d.	SD	27 Aug. 1881	3	8	
Lynch	James M.	o.	DR	28 Aug. 1882	3	1	
Lynch	James M.	o.	SD	2 Sept. 1882	3	2	
Lynch	Mr. & Mrs.	b.	DD	15 Dec. 1883	3	1	
Lynch	Thomas	b.	SD	24 Dec. 1881	2	3	
Lynch	William	b.	DD	20 Oct. 1883	3	3	
Lynch	William	m.	PCo	22 Mar. 1882	3	5	
Lynn	Florence	m.	DR	2 Nov. 1881	2	3	
Lynn	Florence I.	m.	PCo	9 Nov. 1881	3	5	
Lynn	Florence I.	m.	SD	12 Nov. 1881	3	7	
Lyon	Nellia	m.	CR	15 Jan. 1881	5	5	
Lyon	Nellie	m.	DR	11 Jan. 1881	3	2	
Lyon	Nellie	m.	SD	8 Jan. 1881	3	8	
Lyons	A. J.	b.	PCo	14 Dec. 1881	3	4	
Lyons	A. J.	b.	SD	17 Dec. 1881	3	7	
Lyons	Ada	m.	DR	16 Nov. 1885	3	4	
Lyons	Ada	m.	SIT	14 Nov. 1885	2	3	
Lyons	H. C.	b.	SD	12 Mar. 1881	3	8	
Lyons	J.	b.	SD	2 Apr. 1881	3	8	
Lyons	M., Miss	m.	SD	26 Feb. 1881	3	8	
Lyons	Maggie	m.	CR	5 Mar. 1881	4	2	
Lyons	Maggie	m.	DR	25 Feb. 1881	3	2	
Lyth	George W.	m.	DR	15 Nov. 1882	2	3	
Lyth	George W.	m.	PCo	8 Nov. 1882	3	6	
Lyth	George W.	m.	SD	4 Nov. 1882	3	6	
Lyttaker	E. V.	m.	SD	13 June 1885	3	5	
Lyttaker	Valena	d.	DR	4 Feb. 1882	2	3	
Lyttaker	W. J.	b.	SD	12 Feb. 1881	3	8	
Lyttaker	Walena	d.	PCo	15 Feb. 1882	3	4	
Lyttaker	Walena	d.	SD	18 Feb. 1882	3	6	

M

(1) Surname	(2) Given Name	(3)	(4)	(5) Date	(6) Pg	(7) Col	(8) Comments
MacDonald	Alice F.	m.	DR	17 Sept. 1885	3	4	
MacDonald	Florence	d.	PCo	27 May 1885	3	6	
MacGregor	Freddie	d.	DR	31 May 1881	2	2	
Mackey	Virginia	m.	SD	12 Jan. 1884	3	6	
Mackie	Margaret F.	m.	DD	8 Sept. 1883	3	3	
Mackie	Margaret	m.	SD	15 Sept. 1883	2	4	
MacPherson	Richard	d.	CR	22 Oct. 1881	4	1	
MacWhinnie	J. Wallace	d.	PCo	6 May 1885	3	1	
MacWinnie	Helen A.	d.	PCo	8 July 1885	3	6	
Madden	Charles	p.	DR	26 Dec. 1884	2	2	
Madden	Edith	d.	SD	12 Mar. 1881	3	8	
Maddin	Charles	d.	PCo	16 Jan. 1884	3	6	
Maddin	Charles	d.	SD	19 Jan. 1884	3	6	
Maddock	Lute	m.	DR	19 Dec. 1884	3	2	
Maddock	Lute	m.	PCo	17 Dec. 1884	2	4	
Maddock	Lute	m.	PWA	20 Dec. 1884	3	4	
Maddux	A.	d.	SD	29 Dec. 1883	1	5	Rural Cem.; also p. 3 col. 6
Maddux	Florence	d.	DD	21 Dec. 1883	3	3	
Maddux	Florence	d.	PCo	2 Jan. 1884	3	6	
Madegan	Allie	m.	DD	7 Aug. 1883	3	2	
Madegan	Allie	m.	PC	8 Aug. 1883	3	6	
Madegan	Allie	m.	PWA	11 Aug. 1883	3	8	
Madegan	Allie	m.	SD	11 Aug. 1883	2	7	
Madegan	W. D.	m.	DD	7 Aug. 1883	3	2	
Madegan	W. D.	m.	PC	8 Aug. 1883	3	6	
Madegan	W. D.	m.	PWA	11 Aug. 1883	3	8	
Madegan	W. D.	m.	SD	11 Aug. 1883	2	7	
Madeira	Susan	d.	SD	25 Oct. 1884	2	5	
Magill	R. H., Mrs.	d.	DR	29 July 1884	3	3	
Magner	Othelia	m.	DR	17 Apr. 1884	3	2	
Magoon	W. H.	m.	PWA	3 May 1884	3	6	
Magoon	W. H.	m	SD	10 May 1884	1	4	
Magoon	William H.	m.	DR	8 May 1884	3	2	
Magoon	William H.	m.	PCo	7 May 1884	3	5	
Maguire	Louise G.	m.	SD	19 Mar. 1881	3	8	
Maher	N. C.	m.	DD	28 Aug. 1883	3	3	
Malcahy	William	b.	PCo	14 Dec. 1881	3	4	

(1) Surname	(2) Given Name	(3)	(4)	(5) Date	(6) Pg	(7) Col	(8) Comments
Malcom	Chester T.	m.	PC	11 July 1883	3	5	
Mallary	Eva E.	d.	CR	26 Mar. 1881	5	5	
Mallary	Eva E.	d.	DR	21 Nov. 1881	2	3	
Mallary	Eva E.	d.	SD	2 Apr. 1881	3	8	
Mallary	Eva E.	d.	SD	26 Mar. 1881	3	8	
Mallen	Edward	p.	DD	19 July 1883	3	2	
Malone	Ellen M.	m.	DR	28 Nov. 1885	3	4	
Malone	Ellen N.	m.	SD	5 Dec. 1885	1	8	
Malone	Nellie	m.	PCo	9 Dec. 1885	3	6	
Malony	Patrick	d.	DR	25 July 1881	2	3	
Manfredini	Angela	d.	PCo	20 Feb. 1884	3	6	
Manfredini	Angela	d.	PWA	23 Feb. 1884	3	6	
Manfredini	Angela	d.	SD	1 Mar. 1884	6	6	
Manion	Fannie	m.	DD	11 Dec. 1883	2	2	
Manion	Fannie	m.	PCo	19 Dec. 1883	3	4	
Manion	Jeff D.	d.	PCo	9 Sept. 1885	2	4	
Manion	Jefferson Davis	d.	SD	12 Sept. 1885	1	4	
Manion	Jefferson	d.	SIT	12 Sept. 1885	3	2	
Manney	James F.	b.	PCo	12 Mar. 1884	3	6	
Manney	James F.	b.	PWA	8 Mar. 1884	3	6	
Manney	James F.	b.	SD	15 Mar. 1884	2	5	
Manning	Albert	m.	SD	13 Aug. 1881	3	8	
Manning	Ella J.	m.	SD	6 June 1885	2	4	
Manning	J.	b.	SD	29 Apr. 1882	3	6	
Manning	James F.	m.	PCo	11 Jan. 1882	3	6	
Manning	James F.	m.	SD	21 Jan. 1882	3	6	
Mannon	J. M. (dau. of)	d.	DR	19 Nov. 1881	2	3	
Mansfield	Sophie	d.	RRF	16 Mar. 1882	2	4	
Marchant	George H.	b.	PCo	7 Dec. 1881	3	5	
Marcill	Napoleon	m.	DR	13 Feb. 1882	2	3	
Marcill	Napoleon	m.	SD	11 Feb. 1882	3	3&6	
Marcuchi	Abrami	b.	SD	23 Apr. 1881	3	8	
Marcy	J.	b.	PCo	3 Sept. 1884	2	5	
Marcy	J.	b.	PWA	6 Sept. 1884	3	4	
Marcy	J.	b.	SD	6 Sept. 1884	2	5	
Mardecai	Thomas	m.	PCo	21 Dec. 1881	3	5	
Mardon	C. W.	m.	PC	4 July 1883	3	5	
Mardon	C. W.	m.	SD	30 June 1883	3	5	
Mardon	Nellie	m.	CR	11 June 1881	5	5	
Mardon	Nellie	m.	DR	4 June 1881	2	2	
Mardon	Nellie	m.	RRF	2 June 1881	3	2	
Mardon	Nellie	m.	RRF	2 June 1881	2	3	

(1) Surname	(2) Given Name	(3)	(4)	(5) Date	(6) Pg	(7) Col	(8) Comments
Mardon	Nellie	m.	SD	11 June 1881	3	8	
Marea	Francis D.	d.	SD	21 May 1881	3	8	
Markham	A.	b.	SD	9 Feb. 1884	7	2	
Markham	Catherine	d.	PCo	8 Mar. 1882	3	5	
Markham	Catherine E.	d.	DR	24 Feb. 1882	2	3	
Markham	Catherine E.	d.	SD	4 Mar. 1882	3	6	
Markle	R. B.	b.	DD	4 Dec. 1883	3	3	
Marks	S.	b.	DR	27 Jan. 1882	2	3	
Marks	S.	b.	SD	28 Jan. 1882	3	6	
Marquardt	Fred	b.	SD	19 Feb. 1881	3	8	
Marriam	George M.	d.	SD	10 Oct. 1885	5	5	
Marron	James, Sr.	d.	DR	16 Nov. 1885	3	4	
Marrow	Maria A.	m.	CR	19 Feb. 1881	4	2	
Marrow	Maria A.	m.	DR	17 Feb. 1881	3	2	
Marrow	Maria A.	m.	SD	19 Feb. 1881	3	8	
Marsh	Ira M.	m.	DR	23 Aug. 1884	3	4	
Marsh	Ira M.	m.	PCo	3 Sept. 1884	2	5	
Marsh	Ira M.	m.	PWA	6 Sept. 1884	3	4	
Marsh	Ira M.	m.	SD	6 Sept. 1884	2	5	
Marshal	John	d.	DR	12 July 1882	3	1	
Marshal	Sarah A.	m.	DD	8 Sept. 1883	3	3	
Marshall	Annie	m.	CR	3 Sept. 1881	5	2	
Marshall	Hugh A.	m.	DR	1 June 1882	3	2	
Marshall	Hugh A.	m.	SD	10 June 1882	2	3	
Marshall	John	d.	CR	13 July 1882	5	2	
Marshall	John	d.	PCo	19 July 1882	3	6	
Marshall	John	d.	RRF	13 July 1882	3	1	
Marshall	John	d.	RRF	13 July 1882	2	4	
Marshall	John	d.	RRF	20 July 1882	3	1	Healdsburg
Marshall	John	d.	RRF	27 July 1882	3	5	
Marshall	John	p.	RRF	4 Jan. 1883	3	3	
Marshall	John	d.	SD	15 July 1882	3	3	
Marshall	John	d.	SD	22 July 1882	3	5	
Marshall	Lizzie	m.	PCo	28 May 1884	2	4	
Marshall	Sarah A.	m.	SD	15 Sept. 1883	2	4	
Marshall	Sarah	m.	RRF	13 Sept. 1883	2	4	
Marshall	William	m.	PWA	2 June 1883	3	8	
Marshall	William	m.	SD	2 June 1883	2	7	
Martens	Carrie	m.	PC	4 Apr. 1883	3	5	
Martens	Carrie	m.	PWA	7 Apr. 1883	2	3	
Marti	Joseph	d.	SD	2 July 1881	3	8	
Martin	A., Miss	m.	DR	29 Oct. 1885	3	4	

(1) Surname	(2) Given Name	(3)	(4)	(5) Date	(6) Pg	(7) Col	(8) Comments
Martin	Alexander	d.	PCo	7 Dec. 1881	3	5	
Martin	Alexander (son of)	d.	DR	16 Nov. 1885	3	4	
Martin	Alexander (son of)	d.	PCo	11 Nov. 1885	3	4	
Martin	E. E.	m.	PC	23 May 1883	3	5	
Martin	E. E.	m.	RRF	17 May 1883	2	3	
Martin	Edgaar	d.	RRF	10 Aug. 1882	2	4	Oak Mound Cem.
Martin	Edgar	d.	DR	12 Aug. 1882	3	2	
Martin	Edgar	d.	PCo	16 Aug. 1882	3	6	
Martin	Edgar	d.	SD	12 Aug. 1882	3	5	
Martin	Edna Bell	d.	DR	18 Nov. 1884	3	2	
Martin	Edna Bell	d.	PCo	26 Nov. 1884	3	5	
Martin	Edna Bell	d.	PWA	22 Nov. 1884	3	4	
Martin	Edward L.	m.	SD	10 Jan. 1885	2	6	
Martin	F., Mrs.	d.	PCo	3 Dec. 1884	3	5	
Martin	F., Mrs.	d.	SD	23 Nov. 1884	2	6	
Martin	H. P.	b.	DR	26 Nov. 1881	2	3	
Martin	H. P.	b.	PCo	30 Nov. 1881	3	5	
Martin	H. P.	b.	SD	3 Dec. 1881	3	8	
Martin	Ida M.	m.	DR	1 June 1882	3	2	
Martin	Ida M.	m.	SD	10 June 1882	2	3	
Martin	J. S.	d.	RRF	20 Apr. 1882	2	3	
Martin	J. S.	b.	RRF	26 Jan. 1882	2	2	
Martin	J. S.	b.	SD	4 Feb. 1882	3	6	
Martin	James	d.	PCo	27 May 1885	3	6	
Martin	John E.	b.	PCo	23 Dec. 1885	3	4	
Martin	John E.	b.	SD	19 Dec. 1885	3	4	
Martin	John	b.	DR	29 July 1882	3	2	
Martin	John	b.	PCo	26 July 1882	3	6	
Martin	John	b.	SD	29 July 1882	3	7	
Martin	John S.	d.	DR	22 Apr. 1882	3	2	
Martin	John S.	d.	HE	20 Apr. 1882	2	2	
Martin	John S.	d.	SD	29 Apr. 1882	3	6	
Martin	Joseph	b.	DD	8 Sept. 1883	3	3	
Martin	Joseph	b.	RRF	6 Sept. 1883	2	4	
Martin	Joseph	b.	SD	15 Sept. 1883	2	4	
Martin	Josiah	m.	DR	30 Dec. 1881	2	3	
Martin	Josiah	m.	HE	29 Dec. 1881	2	3	
Martin	Josiah	m.	PCo	11 Jan. 1882	3	6	
Martin	Josiah	m.	RRF	29 Dec. 1881	2	3	
Martin	Josiah	m.	SD	31 Dec. 1881	3	6	
Martin	Julius	b.	SD	9 Apr. 1881	3	2	birth in 1844
Martin	M.	m.	PCo	14 Dec. 1881	3	4	

(1) Surname	(2) Given Name	(3)	(4)	(5) Date	(6) Pg	(7) Col	(8) Comments
Martin	Marion	m.	DD	7 Dec. 1883	3	2	
Martin	Maud L.	d.	PCo	31 May 1882	3	5	
Martin	Maud L.	d.	RRF	25 May 1882	2	3	
Martin	Maud L.	d.	SD	3 June 1882	2	4	
Martin	Milton	m.	DR	9 Dec. 1881	2	3	
Martin	Milton	m.	HE	8 Dec. 1881	2	3	
Martin	Milton	m.	RRF	1 Dec. 1881	2	3	
Martin	Milton	m.	SD	10 Dec. 1881	3	7	
Martin	N.	b.	PC	1 Aug. 1883	3	6	
Martin	N.	b.	RRF	26 July 1883	2	4	
Martin	Pearl	d.	PCo	14 Feb. 1883	3	6	
Martin	Pearl	d.	RRF	8 Feb. 1883	2	4	also 15 Feb., p. 2 col. 3
Martin	Pearl	d.	SD	10 Feb. 1883	2	7	
Martin	R. J.	b.	DR	10 Jun. 1881	2	2	
Martin	R. J.	d.	RRF	25 May 1882	2	3	
Martin	R. J.	b.	SD	25 June 1881	3	8	
Martin	S. (dau. of)	d.	PWA	3 May 1884	3	6	
Martin	S.	b.	PCo	30 Apr. 1884	2	6	
Martin	S.	b.	PWA	3 May 1884	3	6	
Martin	S.	b.	SD	10 May 1884	2	4	
Martin	Sam (dau. of)	d.	PCo	30 Apr. 1884	2	6	
Martin	Thomas	d.	DD	18 Aug. 1883	3	3	
Martin	Thomas	d.	PC	15 Aug. 1883	3	6	
Martin	Thomas	d.	PWA	18 Aug. 1883	3	7	
Martin	Thomas	d.	SD	25 Aug. 1883	2	5	
Martini	A.	m.	SD	27 Oct. 1883	1	6	
Marzoff	Joseph	m.	PCo	30 Apr. 1884	2	6	
Marzoff	Joseph	m.	PWA	3 May 1884	3	6	
Marzolf	Joseph B.	m.	SD	10 May 1884	2	4	
Mason	Fred B.	m.	DR	10 Jan. 1884	3	3	
Mason	Fred B.	m.	PCo	16 Jan. 1884	3	6	
Mason	S. S.	b.	DR	20 May 1882	3	2	
Mason	S. S.	b.	HE	18 May 1882	2	3	
Mason	S. S.	b.	PCo	24 May 1882	3	5	
Mason	S. S.	b.	SD	20 May 1882	2	4	
Masrup	Andrew	m.	SD	4 Oct. 1884	3	5	
Maston	Emma J.	m.	SD	8 Jan. 1881	3	8	
Mastrop	Andrew	b.	DR	10 July 1885	3	4	
Mastrop	Andrew	b.	PCo	8 July 1885	3	6	
Mastrup	Andrew	m.	PCo	1 Oct. 1884	3	5	
Mastrup	Andrew	m.	PWA	27 Sept. 1884	2	4	

(1) Surname	(2) Given Name	(3)	(4)	(5) Date	(6) Pg	(7) Col	(8) Comments
Mastrup	Niels	b.	PCo	7 Feb. 1883	3	6	
Mastrup	Niels	b.	PWA	10 Feb. 1883	3	7	
Mastrup	Niels	b.	SD	10 Feb. 1883	2	7	
Mathers	John Thomas	d.	PWA	2 June 1883	3	8	
Mathers	W. F.	b.	PCo	11 Jan. 1882	3	6	
Mathers	W. F.	b.	SD	21 Jan. 1882	3	6	
Mathers	William F. (children of)	d.	PC	30 May 1883	3	2	
Matheson	David	b.	SD	26 Feb. 1881	3	8	
Mathews	Ann	d.	PCo	6 Dec. 1882	3	6	
Mathews	George J.	m.	DD	3 July 1883	3	3	
Mathews	George J.	m.	PC	11 July 1883	3	5	
Mathews	George J.	m.	SD	7 July 1883	2	5	
Mathews	Gerenia	m.	SD	5 Nov. 1881	3	6	
Mathews	J. R.	b.	SD	19 Feb. 1881	3	8	
Mathies	Henry	d.	DD	25 Sept. 1883	3	3	
Mathies	Henry	d.	SD	29 Sept. 1883	2	6	
Mathison	C.	b.	CR	19 Feb. 1881	4	2	
Mathison	C. T.	b.	DR	17 Feb. 1881	3	2	
Mathison	C. T.	b.	SD	19 Feb. 1881	3	8	
Mathison	Ellen C.	m.	PCo	11 Mar. 1885	3	6	
Mathison	Ellen C.	d.	PWA	14 Mar. 1885	3	5	
Mathorn	F. C.	m.	PCo	7 Jan. 1885	3	6	
Mathorn	F. C.	m.	SD	3 Jan. 1885	2	7	
Matson	A. T.	b.	PCo	23 Dec. 1885	3	4	
Matson	August	b.	PCo	26 Mar. 1884	3	6	
Matson	August	b.	PWA	29 Mar. 1884	3	6	
Matson	August	b.	SD	29 Mar. 1884	2	5	
Mattei	Vitore	d.	DD	15 Sept. 1883	3	3	
Mattei	Vitore	d.	PWA	15 Sept. 1883	3	6	
Mattei	Vitore	d.	SD	22 Sept. 1883	2	4	
Matteson	Erastus P.	m.	DD	5 Nov. 1883	3	2	
Matteson	Erastus P.	m.	SD	10 Nov. 1883	3	5	
Matthai	Edward G.	d.	DR	2 Nov. 1885	3	4	
Matthai	Edward G.	d.	PCo	28 Oct. 1885	3	4	
Matthai	Edward G.	d.	SD	31 Oct. 1885	3	3	
Matthews	Carmelita D.	m.	DR	1 July 1884	3	3	
Matthews	Carmelite	m.	CR	28 June 1884	3	1	
Matthews	Carmelite	m.	PCo	9 July 1884	3	5	
Matthews	George	d.	DR	4 Dec. 1882	3	1	
Matthews	Gerenia	m.	DR	31 Oct. 1881	2	3	
Matthews	Gerenia	m.	PCo	2 Nov. 1881	3	5	
Matthews	Jerenia E.	m.	RRF	27 Oct. 1881	2	5	

(1) Surname	(2) Given Name	(3)	(4)	(5) Date	(6) Pg	(7) Col	(8) Comments
Matthews	Laura	m.	SD	30 Sept. 1882	3	1	
Matthews	Susie	m.	PWA	2 Feb. 1884	3	2	
Matthies	Heinrich	d.	PWA	29 Sept. 1883	3	8	
Mattison	Mary	m.	PCo	8 July 1885	3	6	
Mattison	Mary	m.	SD	4 July 1885	5	4	
Mauk	E. A., Mrs.	d.	RRF	30 Nov. 1882	3	2	Oak Mound Cem.
Mauzy	Lucinda P.	d.	PCo	11 Feb. 1885	3	6	
Mauzy	Lucinda P.	d.	PWA	7 Feb. 1885	3	5	
Mauzy	S. H.	b.	SD	3 Sept. 1881	3	8	
Maxwell	John K.	d.	DR	31 Oct. 1881	2	3	
Maxwell	John K.	d.	PCo	2 Nov. 1881	3	5	
Maxwell	John K.	d.	RRF	27 Oct. 1881	2	5	
Maxwell	John K.	d.	SD	12 Nov. 1881	3	7	
Maxwell	Mr. & Mrs.	b.	PCo	24 Sept. 1884	3	5	
Maxwell	Samuel P.	d.	DR	29 July 1884	3	3	article col. 2
Maxwell	Samuel P.	d.	PCo	6 Aug. 1884	2	4	
Maxwell	Samuel P.	d.	SD	2 Aug. 1884	1	6	
Maybe	Mr.	m.	RRF	26 May 1881	3	2	
Maybee	Frank	m.	CR	11 June 1881	5	5	
Maybee	Frank	m.	DR	4 June 1881	2	2	
Maybee	Frank	m.	SD	11 June 1881	3	8	
Mayhood	John	b.	SD	11 June 1881	3	8	
Maynard	Eva	m.	PCo	5 Aug. 1885	3	6	
Maynard	J. H.	b.	CR	23 Apr. 1881	5	3	
Maynard	J. H.	b.	DR	20 Apr. 1881	3	2	
Maynard	J. H.	b.	SD	30 Apr. 1881	3	8	
Mays	B.	m.	PCo	10 Dec. 1884	3	5	
Mayse	John	b.	DR	8 Apr. 1881	2	3	
Mayse	John	b.	SD	16 Apr. 1881	3	8	
Mayse	John	b.	SD	30 Apr. 1881	3	8	
Mazzolini	Clementina	m.	DR	20 Oct. 1885	3	4	
Mazzolini	Clementina	m.	PCo	28 Oct. 1885	3	4	
Mazzolini	Clementina	m.	SD	24 Oct. 1885	5	4	
Mc Alister	John A.	m.	PC	16 May 1883	3	5	
Mc Kinna	P.	b.	PC	20 June 1883	3	6	
Mc Near	Jennie O.	d.	PC	30 May 1883	3	2	Cypress Hill
Mc Taggart	M. F.	b.	PC	1 Aug. 1883	3	6	
McAlester	John	b.	SD	4 July 1885	5	4	
McAllester	John	b.	PCo	1 July 1885	3	6	
McAllister	Anson E.	d.	SD	4 Mar. 1882	2	5	
McAllister	John A.	m.	PWA	19 May 1883	3	8	
McAllister	John	m.	SD	12 May 1883	2	6	

(1) Surname	(2) Given Name	(3)	(4)	(5) Date	(6) Pg	(7) Col	(8) Comments
McAnally	William W.	d.	DD	29 Oct. 1883	3	3	
McAnally	William W.	d.	SD	3 Nov. 1883	3	3	
McBride	Georgie	o.	CR	21 Nov. 1885	1	5	
McBride	H. B.	b.	DR	23 July 1881	3	2	
McBride	H. B.	b.	SD	14 June 1884	2	4	
McCabe	S.	b.	CR	22 July 1882	5	3	
McCabe	S.	b.	DR	25 July 1882	2	3	
McCabe	S.	b.	PCo	2 Aug. 1882	3	6	
McCabe	S.	b.	RRF	27 July 1882	2	4	
McCallum	Duncan	p.	DD	19 July 1883	3	2	
McCallum	William	m.	PCo	16 Aug. 1882	3	6	
McCallum	William	m.	SD	5 Aug. 1882	3	5	
McCann	John	d.	DR	15 July 1881	2	2	
McCann	John	d.	DR	20 July 1881	3	2	Santa Rosa Cem.
McCann	John	d.	SD	23 July 1881	3	8	
McCann	Joseph	d.	SD	4 Apr. 1885	2	5	
McCappin	James (son of)	d.	PWA	13 Dec. 1884	3	4	
McCarney	David	b.	DR	19 Dec. 1884	3	2	
McCartney	David	b.	PCo	17 Dec. 1884	2	4	
McCartney	David	b.	PWA	20 Dec. 1884	3	4	
McCartney	David	b.	SD	27 Dec. 1884	2	4	
McCartney	David, Jr.	m.	PWA	18 Aug. 1883	3	2	
McCelland	Ella	d.	SD	23 Dec. 1882	3	2	
McClary	W.	o.	SIT	22 Aug. 1885	2	2	
McCleave	Mary	m.	PCo	6 July 1881	3	5	
McClellan	Kate	d.	PCo	2 Sept. 1885	3	6	
McClellan	Kate	d.	SD	5 Sept. 1885	2	4	
McClellan	M. J.	d.	PC	2 May 1883	3	5	
McClellan	M. T.	p.	DR	26 Dec. 1884	2	2	
McClellan	M. T.	d.	SD	28 Apr. 1883	2	5	also p. 3 col. 6
McClelland	Anna	d.	DR	21 Dec. 1882	2	2	
McClelland	Anna	d.	PCo	27 Dec. 1882	3	6	
McClelland	Anna	d.	SD	30 Dec. 1882	3	6	
McClelland	Millie May	d.	DR	7 Aug. 1884	3	3	
McClelland	Millie	d.	PCo	13 Aug. 1884	3	4	
McClenny	W. S.	b.	RRF	22 Sept. 1881	2	6	
McClenny	W. S.	m.	SD	22 Jan. 1881	3	8	
McClenoy	W. S.	m.	RRF	13 Jan. 1881	2	5	
McCleve	Mary	m.	SD	16 July 1881	3	8	
McClintock	S. T. (dau. of)	d.	SD	2 Apr. 1881	3	8	
McClish	James	b.	CR	15 Jan. 1881	5	5	
McClish	James	b.	RRF	13 Jan. 1881	2	5	

(1) Surname	(2) Given Name	(3)	(4)	(5) Date	(6) Pg	(7) Col	(8) Comments
McClish	James	b.	SD	22 Jan. 1881	3	8	
McClure	W. F.	d.	PCo	4 May 1881	3	4	
McComas	Cora	m.	CR	12 Mar. 1881	5	5	
McComas	Cora	m.	DR	9 Mar. 1881	3	2	
McComas	Cora	m.	SD	12 Mar. 1881	3	8	
McConathy	James	d.	PCo	5 Mar. 1884	3	6	
McConathy	James	d.	SD	15 Mar. 1884	2	5	
McConathy	Mr.	d.	CR	1 Mar. 1884	3	1&2	Cloverdale Cem.
McConochie	(male)	b.	DR	9 Apr. 1884	3	3	
McConochie	Edward J.	d.	DR	5 Sept. 1885	3	4	
McConochie	Edward J.	d.	PCo	16 Sept. 1885	3	6	
McCool	T. A.	b.	PCo	18 Feb. 1885	3	6	
McCool	T. A.	b.	SD	21 Feb. 1885	2	5	
McCoppin	Walter K.	d.	DR	9 Dec. 1884	3	2	
McCormack	W. C.	b.	HE	20 Apr. 1882	2	2	
McCormack	W. C.	b.	PCo	26 Apr. 1882	3	4	
McCormack	W. C.	b.	SD	29 Apr. 1882	3	6	
McCormack	W.	b.	DR	22 Apr. 1882	3	2	
McCormack	William	b.	RRF	20 Apr. 1882	2	3	
McCormic	William	m.	CR	1 Jan. 1881	5	5	
McCormic	William	b.	PCo	9 Jan. 1884	3	6	
McCormic	William	m.	SD	8 Jan. 1881	3	8	
McCormick	William	b.	RRF	3 Jan. 1884	2	4	
McCornack	W. A.	b.	DD	4 Aug. 1883	3	2	
McCoy	Carrie B.	m.	DR	16 May 1884	3	2	
McCoy	Carrie B.	m.	PWA	10 May 1884	3	5	
McCoy	Carrie B.	d.	SD	17 May 1884	3	5	
McCoy	Carrrie H.	m.	PCo	14 May 1884	3	4	
McCoy	John	b.	SD	12 Mar. 1881	3	8	
McCoy	John	b.	SD	26 Feb. 1881	3	8	
McCoy	Sarah	d.	SD	15 Jun. 1881	3	8	
McCracken	Jasper	b.	CR	19 Feb. 1881	4	2	
McCracken	Jasper	b.	CR	19 Feb. 1881	4	2	
McCracken	Jasper	b.	DR	17 Feb. 1881	3	2	
McCracken	Jasper	b.	RRF	10 Feb. 1881	2	5	
McCracken	Jasper	b.	SD	19 Feb. 1881	3	8	
McCracken	Mr. & Mrs.	b.	SD	21 Mar. 1885	2	5	
McCraith	Nellie	m.	CR	22 Jan. 1881	5	5	
McCraith	Nellie	m.	DR	25 Jan. 1881	3	2	
McCraith	Nellie	m.	RRF	13 Jan. 1881	3	5	
McCraith	Nellie	m.	RRF	20 Jan. 1881	2	5	
McCraith	Nellie	m.	SD	29 Jan. 1881	3	8	

(1) Surname	(2) Given Name	(3)	(4)	(5) Date	(6) Pg	(7) Col	(8) Comments
McCray	Amanda	m.	CR	28 Feb. 1885	3	1	
McCray	Amanda	m.	PCo	4 Mar. 1885	3	6	
McCray	Amanda	m.	SD	14 Mar. 1885	5	5	
McCroden	James	d.	CR	10 Dec. 1881	1	2	
McCulloch	Edgar Robert	d.	CR	1 Jan. 1881	5	5	
McCulloch	Edgar Robert	d.	DR	1 Jan. 1881	3	2	
McCulloch	Edgar Robert	d.	SD	1 June 1881	3	7	
McCullough	Ebenezer A.	d.	DR	8 Nov. 1881	2	3	
McCullough	Ebenezer A.	d.	PCo	16 Nov. 1881	3	5	
McCullough	Ebenezer A.	d.	SD	12 Nov. 1881	3	7	
McCurdy	James, Mrs.	d.	DR	24 Feb. 1882	2	3	
McCurdy	James, Mrs.	d.	PCo	22 Feb. 1882	3	5	
McCurdy	Jane S.	d.	PCo	7 Dec. 1881	3	5	
McCutchan	Mattie F.	d.	DR	24 Oct. 1882	3	2	
McCutchan	Mattie F.	d.	PCo	25 Oct. 1882	3	5	
McCutchan	Mattie F.	d.	RRF	19 Oct. 1882	2	3	
McDaniel	L. J.	m.	DR	22 Dec. 1881	2	2	
McDaniel	L. J.	m.	SD	24 Dec. 1881	2	3	
McDannel	B. Frank	b.	SD	26 Feb. 1881	3	8	
McDevitt	Barnett	d.	CR	12 Feb. 1881	5	5	
McDevitt	Barnett	d.	DR	9 Feb. 1881	3	2	
McDevitt	Barnett	d.	SD	19 Feb. 1881	3	8	
McDevitt	S. Barnett	d.	PCo	16 Feb. 1881	3	4	
McDiarmid	Katie S.	m.	SD	12 Mar. 1881	3	8	
McDonald	Archie	d.	SD	18 Apr. 1885	2	5	
McDonald	George	b.	CR	12 Mar. 1881	5	5	
McDonald	George	b.	CR	27 Jan. 1883	3	1	
McDonald	George	b.	DR	23 Mar. 1881	3	2	
McDonald	George	b.	PCo	10 Jan. 1883	3	6	
McDonald	George	b.	PCo	2 Apr. 1884	3	6	
McDonald	George	b.	RRF	24 Mar. 1881	2	4	
McDonald	George	b.	SD	19 Mar. 1881	3	8	
McDonald	George H.	o.	CR	13 Oct. 1883	3	2	
McDonald	George H. (dau. of)	d.	CR	10 Feb. 1883	3	1	
McDonald	Hortense Nelson	m.	PCo	15 Apr. 1885	3	6	
McDonald	John	d.	DD	24 Nov. 1883	3	1&2	
McDonald	John	m.	RRF	26 May 1881	2	5	
McDonald	John	d.	SD	1 Dec. 1883	1	3	also p. 3 col. 4
McDonald	Mark L.	b.	SD	14 Mar. 1885	5	5	
McDonald	Martha Shephard	d.	SD	2 Aug. 1884	4	1	
McDonald	Ralph	d.	DR	17 Sept. 1885	3	4	
McDonald	Ralph	d.	PCo	16 Sept. 1885	3	6	

(1) Surname	(2) Given Name	(3)	(4)	(5) Date	(6) Pg	(7) Col	(8) Comments
McDonald	Ralph	d.	SD	19 Sept. 1885	2	4	
McDonald	Ronald	d.	PCo	10 Dec. 1884	3	2	
McDonald	William L.	m.	CR	8 Jan. 1881	5	5	
McDonald	William L.	m.	DR	1 Jan. 1881	3	2	
McDonnell	R. A.	d.	SD	20 Dec. 1884	1	5	
McDonnell	R. C.	d.	PWA	13 Dec. 1884	3	2	
McDonogh	Julia	d.	PWA	6 Oct. 1883	3	8	
McDonogh	Samuel	d.	PCo	27 July 1881	3	5	
McDonough	Samuel	d.	SD	6 Aug. 1881	3	8	
McDonough	Samuel	d.	SD	23 July 1881	3	8	
McDowall	Peter	d.	DR	23 Dec. 1885	3	4	
McDowell	James	m.	PCo	1 Nov. 1882	3	5	
McElroy	J. F.	b.	SD	28 Jan. 1882	3	6	
McElroy	Jane	d.	DR	7 June 1882	3	2	
McElroy	Jane	d.	PCo	31 May 1882	3	5	
McElroy	Jane	d.	SD	10 June 1882	2	3	
McElroy	John	d.	PCo	17 Jan. 1883	3	5	
McElroy	John	d.	PWA	19 Jan. 1883	3	7	
McEwen	Mary	m.	DR	15 May 1884	3	2	
McEwen	Mary	m.	SD	24 May 1884	1	6	
McFadden	Nellie	m.	DR	10 Apr. 1882	2	2	
McFadden	Nellie	m.	PCo	5 Apr. 1882	3	5	
McFarland	Lucy W.	m.	SD	20 May 1882	2	4	
McFarlane	George	m.	DR	30 July 1884	3	3	
McFarlane	George	m.	PCo	6 Aug. 1884	2	4	
McFarlane	George	m.	SD	2 Aug. 1884	3	1	
McFarling	Johnson H.	m.	SD	5 Nov. 1881	3	6	
McGah	Mary	m.	DR	29 Nov. 1882	3	2	
McGarry	John	m.	PCo	26 Oct. 1881	3	4	
McGarvey	Belle	m.	DD	24 Dec. 1883	3	2	
McGarvey	Mollie	m.	DD	20 Oct. 1883	3	3	
McGarvey	S. S.	b.	DD	28 Aug. 1883	3	3	
McGee	H. P.	m.	SD	10 May 1884	2	4	
McGee	Mr.	m.	DR	30 Sept. 1885	3	4	
McGee	Mr.	m.	SRR	1 Oct. 1885	3	3	
McGee	Olive	m.	SD	16 June 1883	2	6	
McGeorge	Robert	o.	DR	27 Feb. 1884	3	2	
McGill	A.	b.	DR	28 Mar. 1882	2	3	
McGill	A.	b.	PCo	29 Mar. 1882	3	5	
McGill	A.	b.	SD	1 Apr. 1882	3	6	
McGinn	Mary Grace	d.	SD	15 Sept. 1883	2	4	
McGinn	Mary	d.	DD	10 Sept. 1883	3	3	

(1) Surname	(2) Given Name	(3)	(4)	(5) Date	(6) Pg	(7) Col	(8) Comments
McGivney	Mary T.	m.	RRF	15 Sept. 1881	2	5	
McGlashan	C. F.	o.	RRF	14 Dec. 1882	3	4	
McGlenchy	Anthony	d.	DR	8 Nov. 1884	2	2	
McGlenchy	Anthony	d.	PCo	12 Nov. 1884	3	5	
McGlinn	Mary Grace	d.	PWA	8 Sept. 1883	3	8	
McGlinn	William J.	b.	PCo	28 May 1884	2	4	
McGlinn	William J.	b.	SD	31` May 1884	2	3	
McGlynn	Katie	d.	PCo	9 Nov. 1881	3	5	
McGlynn	William J.	m.	DR	24 Oct. 1882	3	2	
McGlynn	William J.	m.	PCo	18 Oct. 1882	3	6	
McGoubrick	John	m.	SD	11 Feb. 1882	3	6	
McGovern	D.	b.	DD	15 Sept. 1883	3	3	
McGovern	D.	b.	PCo	7 June 1882	3	5	
McGovern	D.	b.	PWA	15 Sept. 1883	3	6	
McGovern	D.	b.	SD	22 Sept. 1883	2	4	
McGovern	Daniel	m.	DR	15 Aug. 1881	3	2	
McGovern	Daniel	m.	PCo	20 July 1881	3	5	
McGovern	Daniel	m.	SD	6 Aug. 1881	3	8	
McGrath	John	b.	PCo	2 Nov. 1881	3	5	
McGregor	Frank	b.	CR	28 May 1881	5	5	
McGregor	Frank	b.	DR	24 May 1881	2	2	
McGregor	Frank	b.	SD	28 May 1881	3	8	
McGregor	Freddie	d.	SD	11 June 1881	3	8	
McGrew	J.	b.	CR	16 Apr. 1881	5	2	
McGrew	J.	b.	CR	16 Apr. 1881	5	3	
McGrew	James	b.	PCo	13 Apr. 1881	3	6	
McGrew	James	b.	SD	16 Apr. 1881	3	8	
McGrew	James	b.	SD	23 Apr. 1881	3	8	
McGrew	William	b.	DR	8 Dec. 1884	3	2	
McGrew	William	m.	PCo	14 June 1882	3	5	
McGrew	William	b.	PCo	3 Dec. 1884	3	5	
McGrew	William	m.	SD	17 June 1882	2	4	
McGrew	William	b.	SD	13 Dec. 1884	2	5	
McGuire	James	d.	SD	9 Apr. 1881	3	8	
McGuire	Lucius	d.	PCo	27 Aug. 1884	2	3	Cypress Hill Cem.
McGuire	Thomas	b.	PC	9 May 1883	3	5	
McGuire	Thomas	b.	PWA	5 May 1883	3	8	
McHatten	Robert	b.	PCo	16 July 1884	3	6	
McHatton	Rev.	m.	SD	8 Sept. 1883	3	4	
McHatton	Robert	b.	DR	5 July 1884	3	4	under heading "died"
McIlmoil	Miss	m.	CR	15 Jan. 1881	5	5	
McIlmoil	Nellie	m.	DR	12 Jan. 1881	3	2	

(1) Surname	(2) Given Name	(3)	(4)	(5) Date	(6) Pg	(7) Col	(8) Comments
McIlmoil	Nellie	m.	SD	15 Jun. 1881	3	8	
McIntosh	John	b.	PCo	1 Apr. 1885	3	6	
McIntosh	John	b.	PWA	4 Apr. 1885	3	6	
McKay	Andrew	m.	DD	4 Aug. 1883	3	2	
McKeadney	H., Mrs.	d.	HE	12 Jan. 1882	2	3	
McKeadney	H., Mrs.	d.	HE	19 Jan. 1882	3	4	
McKeadney	H., Mrs.	d.	PCo	18 Jan. 1882	3	5	
McKeadney	H., Mrs.	d.	RRF	12 Jan. 1882	2	2	
McKeadney	H., Mrs.	d.	SD	21 Jan. 1882	3	6	
McKeadney	Hugh	b.	DD	8 Dec. 1883	3	3	
McKeadney	Hugh	m.	PCo	14 Feb. 1883	3	6	
McKeadney	Hugh	b.	RRF	6 Dec. 1883	2	3	
McKeadney	Hugh	m.	RRF	8 Feb. 1883	2	4	
McKeadney	Hugh	m.	SD	10 Feb. 1883	2	7	
McKeague	A. J.	b.	SD	24 Oct. 1885	5	4	
McKeague	P. J.	b.	SIT	17 Oct. 1885	2	3	
McKee	Hattie	m.	DR	18 July 1882	3	2	
McKee	Hattie	m.	SD	22 July 1882	3	5	
McKenna	James	m.	DR	1 Feb. 1882	2	3	
McKenna	James	m.	SD	4 Feb. 1882	3	6	
McKenna	John	d.	SD	16 June 1883	2	6	
McKenney	E. C.	d.	PCo	9 Jan. 1884	3	6	
McKenney	E. C.	d.	PWA	12 Jan. 1884	3	7	
McKenney	E. C.	d.	SD	19 Jan. 1884	3	6	
McKenney	Susan	m.	DR	10 July 1884	3	3	
McKenny	Susan	m.	SD	5 July 1884	2	3	
McKeown	Margaret	m.	PCo	17 Jan. 1883	3	5	
McKeown	Margaret	m.	RRF	11 Jan. 1883	2	2	
McKericher	Duncan	b.	SD	19 Feb. 1881	3	8	
McKinght	John	m.	PCo	23 Nov. 1881	3	5	
McKinlay	Duncan E.	m.	PCo	23 Dec. 1885	3	3&4	
McKinley	Duncan E.	m.	DR	16 Dec. 1885	3	4	
McKinley	Duncan E.	m.	SD	19 Dec. 1885	3	1&4	
McKinna	Peter	b.	CR	29 Oct. 1881	5	3	
McKinna	Peter	b.	PCo	2 Nov. 1881	3	5	
McKinna	Peter	b.	SD	5 Nov. 1881	3	6	
McKinnon	Archie	b.	PCo	28 Jan. 1885	3	6	
McKinnon	Darden A.	m.	PCo	13 Aug. 1884	3	4	
McKinnon	Darden A.	m.	PWA	9 Aug. 1884	2	4	
McKnight	John	m.	DR	16 Nov. 1881	2	3	
McKnight	John	m.	PCo	30 Nov. 1881	3	5	
McKnight	John	b.	SD	26 Aug. 1882	3	5	

(1) Surname	(2) Given Name	(3)	(4)	(5) Date	(6) Pg	(7) Col	(8) Comments
McLaine	M. A.	b.	SIT	26 Sept. 1885	2	2	
McLane	George M.	m.	DR	21 July 1882	3	2	
McLean	Hector	m.	DR	21 Nov. 1884	3	2	
McLean	Hector	m.	PCo	19 Nov. 1884	3	5	
McLean	Hector	m.	PWA	22 Nov. 1884	3	4	
McLellan	David T.	m.	DR	3 Sept. 1885	3	4	
McLellan	David T.	m.	PCo	16 Sept. 1885	3	6	
McLellan	David T.	m.	SD	5 Sept. 1885	2	4	
McLellan	David T.	m.	SD	12 Sept. 1885	1	5	also p. 2 col. 4
Mclise	James	m.	DR	10 Nov. 1884	2	2	
McManies	John C.	d.	DD	.2 Nov. 1883	3	2	
McMannus	Eunice	m.	SD	6 June 1885	2	4	
McManus	John G.	d.	CR	3 Nov. 1883	3	1	
McManus	John G.	d.	DD	30 Oct. 1883	3	2	
McManus	John G.	d.	RRF	1 Nov. 1883	2	2	also p. 2 col. 3
McManus	John G.	d.	SD	3 Nov. 1883	3	3	
McManus	John G.	d.	SD	3 Nov. 1883	1	4	Healdsburg
McManus	John G.	d.	SD	10 Nov. 1883	3	5	
McManus	William	d.	RRF	14 Apr. 1881	2	3	
McMeans	A. C.	m.	DR	11 July 1885	3	4	
McMeans	A. C.	m.	SD	18 July 1885	5	5	also p. 5 col. 5
McMeans	C.	m.	PCo	15 July 1885	3	6	
McMeans	J. C., Mrs.	d.	SD	4 Nov. 1882	3	1	Rural Cemetery
McMichael	Mr. & Mrs.	b.	DR	2 Nov. 1885	3	4	
McMillen	Mary E.	m.	SD	3 Jan. 1885	2	7	
McMinn	Joseph A.	m.	SD	21 Mar. 1885	2	4&5	
McMinn	Joseph, Sr.	d.	DR	13 Dec. 1884	1	4	
McMinn	Mary	m.	PCo	11 Oct. 1882	3	6	
McMinn	Mary	m.	SD	7 Oct. 1882	1	3	also p. 3 col. 6
McMorey	Mary E.	m.	SD	25 July 1885	3	5	
McMorrey	Mary E.	m.	DR	17 July 1885	3	4	
McMorrey	Mary E.	m.	PCo	22 July 1885	3	6	
McMullin	John	d.	PCo	22 Feb. 1882	3	5	
McNab	Janet	m.	PCo	21 Mar. 1883	3	5	
McNab	Janet	m.	RRF	29 Mar. 1883	2	4	
McNabb	Janet	m.	SD	24 Mar. 1883	2	5	also p. 3 col. 2
McNally	J. W.	b.	PCo	19 July 1882	3	6	
McNally	J. W.	b.	SD	22 July 1882	3	5	
McNally	Mary	p.	DD	11 July 1883	3	2	
McNally	Mary	m.	PCo	28 Feb. 1883	3	5	
McNally	Mary	d.	PWA	3 Mar. 1883	3	6	
McNally	Mary	d.	SD	3 Mar. 1883	2	6	

(1) Surname	(2) Given Name	(3)	(4)	(5) Date	(6) Pg	(7) Col	(8) Comments
McNally	Matt	m.	PCo	10 Sept. 1884	3	6	
McNally	Matt	m.	PWA	13 Sept. 1884	3	6	
McNally	Matt	m.	SD	20 Sept. 1884	2	5	
McNamara	Lydia	m.	PCo	11 Mar. 1885	3	6	
McNamara	Lydia	m.	PWA	14 Mar. 1885	3	5	
McNamara	Maggie	m.	SD	23 Sept. 1882	3	6	
McNamara	Mary	m.	PCo	15 Oct. 1884	3	6	
McNamara	Mary	m.	PWA	18 Oct. 1884	3	4	
McNear	George P., Mrs.	d.	PWA	26 May 1883	3	1	
McNear	George P.	b.	DR	31 May 1881	2	2	
McNear	George P.	b.	PCo	1 June 1881	3	4	
McNear	George P.	b.	SD	4 June 1881	3	8	
McNear	Jennie	p.	DR	29 Nov. 1884	3	2	
McNear	Jennie	d.	PWA	2 June 1883	3	8	
McNear	Jennie Otis	d.	SD	2 June 1883	1	5	
McNear	Mae A.	m.	SD	8 Dec. 1883	3	1	
McNear	Mae	m.	PWA	24 Nov. 1883	3	2	
McNee	Alexander	m.	PCo	27 Dec. 1882	3	6	
McNee	Alexander	m.	SD	23 Dec. 1882	2	5	
McNeel	Ida May	d.	SD	1 June 1881	3	7	
McNeel	William	b.	SD	1 June 1881	3	7	
McNeil	Homer	m.	DR	27 Nov. 1885	3	4	
McNeil	Maggie M.	m.	PCo	21 June 1882	3	5	
McNeil	Maggie M.	m.	SD	17 June 1882	2	4	
McNeill	William H.	d.	DR	10 Dec. 1881	2	3	
McNew	Belle	m.	CR	26 Feb. 1881	5	3	
McNew	Belle	m.	CR	26 Feb. 1884	5	2	
McNew	Belle	m.	DR	1 Mar. 1881	3	2	
McNew	Belle	m.	SD	5 Mar. 1881	3	8	
McNight	John	m.	SD	3 Dec. 1881	3	8	
McPeake	Philip	d.	SD	23 Aug. 1884	2	4	
McPeake	Philip Warren	d.	PCo	3 Sept. 1884	2	5	
McPeake	Philip Warren	d.	SD	6 Sept. 1884	2	5	
McPhee	George S.	m.	DD	24 Dec. 1883	3	2	
McPhee	Mary	d.	DR	25 Jan. 1882	2	3	
McPhee	Mary	d.	SD	4 Feb. 1882	2	4	
McPherson	(male)	b.	DR	17 May 1884	3	2	
McPherson	John M.	b.	DR	21 Aug. 1882	3	2	
McPherson	Kirk	b.	RRF	15 May 1884	5	6	
McPherson	Kirk	b.	SD	24 May 1884	2	3	
McPherson	Lycurgus	b.	PCo	16 Aug. 1882	3	6	
McPherson	Lycurgus	b.	RRF	10 Aug. 1882	2	4	

(1) Surname	(2) Given Name	(3)	(4)	(5) Date	(6) Pg	(7) Col	(8) Comments
McPherson	Lycurgus	b.	SD	12 Aug. 1882	3	5	
McPherson	Richard	d.	RRF	20 Oct. 1881	2	3	
McPhillips	Frank	b.	SD	28 Jan. 1882	3	6	
McQuone	Andrew	d.	DR	29 July 1885	3	4	
McReynolds	(male)	b.	DR	20 Mar. 1884	3	3	
McReynolds	Clayborn Clay	d.	SD	7 May 1881	3	8	
McReynolds	Clayborn	d.	DR	5 May 1881	3	1	
McReynolds	David M.	d.	PCo	5 Jan. 1881	3	4	
McReynolds	David M.	d.	SD	8 Jan. 1881	3	8	
McReynolds	Jim	m.	SD	24 Jan. 1885	5	5	
McReynolds	L. M.	b.	PWA	8 Sept. 1883	3	8	
McReynolds	Louis	b.	PCo	12 Apr. 1882	3	5	
McReynolds	Louis	b.	SD	15 Apr. 1882	3	6	
McRunniels	David	d.	CR	15 Jan. 1881	5	5	
McRunniels	David M.	d.	DR	11 Jan. 1881	3	2	
McTaggart	M. F.	b.	PWA	28 July 1883	3	7	
McTaggart	M. F.	b.	SWI	21 July 1883	3	4	
McTaggart	M. F.	b.	SWI	23 July 1883	3	4	
McWhinney	Samuel	d.	DD	21 Aug. 1883	3	3	
McWhinney	Samuel	d.	SD	25 Aug. 1883	2	5	
McWhinnie	Helen A.	d.	DR	10 July 1885	3	4	
McWilliams	B. B.	b.	SD	20 Oct. 1883	3	4	
McWilliams	E. B.	b.	DD	12 Oct. 1883	3	3	in with deaths
McWilliams	E. B.	b.	HE	11 Oct. 1883	2	2	
McWilliams	E. B.	b.	RRF	11 Oct. 1883	2	5	
Meacham	W. H.	b.	DR	7 June 1881	2	2	
Meacham	W. H.	b.	SD	5 Aug. 1882	3	5	
Meacham	W.	b.	CR	11 June 1881	5	5	
Mead	Alice C.	m.	RRF	8 Nov. 1883	2	3	
Mead	Charles Albert	d.	SD	12 Mar. 1881	3	8	
Mead	Frank D.	d.	RRF	2 Nov. 1882	2	4	
Mead	Harry	d.	SD	2 May 1885	2	5	
Mead	Mr. & Mrs. (child of)	d.	SD	5 Mar. 1881	3	8	
Mead	S. P.	d.	PCo	22 Apr. 1885	3	6	
Mead	Susie E.	m.	RRF	10 Jan. 1884	2	4	
Mead	Susie E.	m.	SD	19 Jan. 1884	3	6	
Meade	Susie E.	m.	PCo	16 Jan. 1884	3	6	
Meador	Edward	b.	DD	27 Dec. 1883	3	3	
Meany	Mary	d.	SD	15 Oct. 1881	3	8	
Mears	John London	m.	DR	12 Oct. 1885	3	4	
Medini	I.	b.	PCo	8 Mar. 1882	3	5	
Meeker	A. P.	b.	DD	23 Aug. 1883	3	2	

(1) Surname	(2) Given Name	(3)	(4)	(5) Date	(6) Pg	(7) Col	(8) Comments
Meeker	A. P.	b.	PC	22 Aug. 1883	3	5	
Meeker	A. P.	b.	SD	25 Aug. 1883	2	5	
Meeker	Emeline	d.	PWA	18 Aug. 1883	3	7	
Meeker	J. O.	b.	PCo	3 Sept. 1884	2	5	
Meeker	J. O.	b.	PWA	6 Sept. 1884	3	4	
Meeker	J. O.	b.	SD	11 June 1881	3	8	
Meeker	Louisa Jane	d.	CR	26 Feb. 1881	5	3	
Meeker	Louisa Jane	d.	CR	26 Feb. 1884	5	2	
Meeker	Louisa Jane	d.	DR	19 Feb. 1881	3	2	
Meeker	Louvisa	o.	SD	12 Mar. 1881	3	1	
Meeker	Louvisa	d.	SD	19 Feb. 1881	3	8	
Meeker	S. A.	b.	DR	10 Nov. 1885	2	2	
Meeker	W. N.	d.	SD	25 Oct. 1884	2	5	also p. 3. col 1; Sebastopol
Meeker	William A.	d.	PCo	22 Oct. 1884	3	6	
Meeker	William A.	d.	PWA	25 Oct. 1884	3	4	
Meerser	J. O.	b.	DR	23 Aug. 1884	3	4	wt. 10 lbs.
Meldrum	George W.	d.	DR	1 Aug. 1881	3	2	
Melehan	Patrick	b.	PCo	3 Jan. 1883	3	4	
Melehan	Patrick	b.	PCo	6 Aug. 1884	2	4	
Melehan	Patrick	b.	PWA	5 Jan. 1883	2	5	
Melehan	Patrick	b.	SD	6 Jan. 1883	2	5	
Melehan	Patrick	b.	SD	9 Aug. 1884	3	4	
Meloche	Ida May	d.	DD	12 Oct. 1883	3	3	
Melson	J. R.	m.	DR	15 Oct. 1885	3	4	
Melson	J. R.	m.	SD	17 Oct. 1885	2	7	also p. 4 col. 5
Melville	Dora	m.	CR	27 Dec. 1884	3	2	
Mendel	John (son of)	d.	DD	8 Sept. 1883	3	3	
Mendenhall	A.	m.	SD	1 Oct. 1881	3	8	
Mendenhall	Henry	b.	PCo	9 Jan. 1884	3	6	
Mendenhall	Henry	b.	SD	19 Jan. 1884	3	6	
Mendenhall	Henry (son of)	d.	PCo	9 Jan. 1884	3	6	
Mendenhall	Henry (son of)	d.	PWA	12 Jan. 1884	3	7	
Mendenhall	Henry (son of)	d.	SD	19 Jan. 1884	3	6	
Mendenhall	Mr. & Mrs.	b.	PWA	5 Jan. 1884	3	7	
Menefee	Belle	m.	SD	23 June 1883	1	5	also p. 3 col. 5
Menefee	John W.	b.	DD	13 Nov. 1883	3	3	
Menefee	John W.	m.	DR	21 Dec. 1882	2	2	
Menefee	John W.	m.	PCo	27 Dec. 1882	3	6	
Menefee	John W.	b.	SD	17 Nov. 1883	3	5	
Menefee	Sarah Bell	m.	PC	20 June 1883	3	6	
Menihan	M.	b.	CR	22 July 1882	5	3	

(1) Surname	(2) Given Name	(3)	(4)	(5) Date	(6) Pg	(7) Col	(8) Comments
Menihan	M.	b.	DR	25 July 1882	2	3	
Menihan	M.	b.	PCo	2 Aug. 1882	3	6	
Menihan	M.	b.	RRF	27 July 1882	2	4	
Menihan	M.	b.	SD	5 Aug. 1882	3	5	
Menkel	Amelia L.	m.	RRF	12 Oct. 1882	2	3	
Menoz	Pedro	d.	SD	15 Oct. 1881	3	8	
Merchant	T. S.	m.	RRF	31 Aug. 1882	2	4	
Merchant	T. S.	m.	SD	2 Sept. 1882	3	6	
Meredith	Cyrus	b.	PC	25 Apr. 1883	3	5	
Meredith	Cyrus	b.	RRF	19 Apr. 1883	2	3	
Meredith	Cyrus	b.	SD	28 Apr. 1883	3	6	
Merrell	E. Clifford	d.	SD	29 Dec. 1883	3	6	
Merrell	F. Clifford	d.	DD	27 Dec. 1883	3	1	
Merrett	Minnie E.	m.	PCo	24 June 1885	3	6	
Merriam	George H.	d.	DR	2 Oct. 1885	3	4	
Merriam	George H.	d.	PCo	7 Oct. 1885	3	6	
Merriam	H. A.	b.	SD	19 Mar. 1881	3	8	
Merrick	M. D.	d.	RRF	2 Mar. 1882	3	4	
Merritt	Edwin B.	m.	PCo	27 Dec. 1882	3	6	
Merritt	Edwin B.	m.	SD	30 Dec. 1882	3	6	
Merritt	F. K.	m.	PWA	7 Apr. 1883	2	3	
Merritt	Frank K.	b.	PCo	16 Jan. 1884	3	6	
Merritt	Frank K.	b.	PWA	19 Jan. 1884	3	7	
Merritt	Frank K.	b.	SD	19 Jan. 1884	3	6	
Merritt	Frank K.	m.	SWI	7 Apr. 1883	3	5	
Merritt	Frank K. (son of)	d.	PCo	16 Jan. 1884	3	6	
Merritt	Frank K. (son of)	d.	PWA	19 Jan. 1884	3	7	
Merritt	Frank K. (son of)	d.	SD	19 Jan. 1884	3	6	
Merritt	John F.	b.	PCo	28 May 1884	2	4	
Merritt	John F.	b.	SD	31` May 1884	2	3	
Merritt	John T.	b.	PCo	11 May 1881	3	5	
Merritt	John T.	b.	SD	21 May 1881	3	8	
Merritt	Minnie E.	m.	CR	13 June 1885	3	2	
Merritt	Minnie E.	m.	SD	27 June 1885	5	4	
Merritt	R. D.	o.	DR	26 Oct. 1882	2	1	
Merryfield	A. A.	m.	PWA	31 Mar. 1883	2	4	
Mervill	E., Miss	m.	SD	13 Dec. 1884	2	5	
Mesa	Ramon	d.	PCo	23 Dec. 1885	2	5	also p. 3 col. 4
Messerlea	John	d.	SD	3 Nov. 1883	1	4	
Metcalf	Mary	m.	SD	21 Apr. 1883	2	6	
Metcalf	Mrs.	m.	CR	14 Apr. 1883	3	1&2	
Metz	Rosa	m.	DD	4 Dec. 1883	3	3	

(1) Surname	(2) Given Name	(3)	(4)	(5) Date	(6) Pg	(7) Col	(8) Comments
Metzgar	Joseph E.	o.	DR	11 Oct. 1882	3	1	
Metzgar	Joseph E.	o.	DR	26 Oct. 1882	2	2	
Metzger	(male)	b.	DR	27 June 1884	3	3	
Metzger	Catherina Elmer	d.	PCo	28 June 1882	3	5	
Metzger	Cathrina	d.	SD	8 July 1882	2	5	
Metzger	G.	b.	SD	5 July 1884	2	3	
Metzger	J. E.	b.	DR	3 Oct. 1881	2	3	
Metzger	J. E.	b.	PCo	24 Jan. 1883	3	5	
Metzger	J. E.	b.	RRF	29 Sept. 1881	2	6	
Metzger	J. E.	b.	RRF	18 Jan. 1883	2	3	
Metzger	J. E.	b.	SD	1 Oct. 1881	3	8	
Metzger	J. E.	b.	SD	27 Jan. 1883	3	6	
Metzser	William	d.	SD	1 July 1882	2	3	
Meyer	Annie G.	d.	DR	24 Mar. 1884	3	3	
Meyer	Fred	b.	PCo	3 May 1882	3	5	
Meyer	Fred	b.	SD	6 May 1882	3	6	
Meyer	George	d.	PCo	27 Feb. 1884	3	6	
Meyer	George	d.	PWA	1 Mar. 1884	3	6	
Meyer	George Homer	b.	DR	23 Aug. 1884	3	4	
Meyer	George Homer	m.	PC	20 June 1883	3	6	
Meyer	George Homer	b.	PCo	3 Sept. 1884	2	5	
Meyer	George Homer	m.	SD	23 June 1883	1	5	also p. 3 col. 5
Meyer	George Homer	b.	SD	6 Sept. 1884	2	5	
Meyer	Louis	b.	PCo	3 May 1882	3	5	
Meyer	Louis	b.	SD	6 May 1882	3	6	
Meyer	Marks	b.	DD	18 Aug. 1883	3	3	
Meyer	Marks	b.	PC	22 Aug. 1883	3	5	
Meyer	Marks	b.	SD	25 Aug. 1883	2	5	
Meyerholtz	Henry	b.	PCo	29 June 1881	3	5	
Meyers	Antonette	m.	PCo	30 Apr. 1884	2	6	
Meyers	Antonette	m.	PWA	3 May 1884	3	6	
Meyers	Antonette	m.	SD	10 May 1884	2	4	
Meyers	David	b.	PCo	4 Oct. 1882	3	6	
Meyers	J. A.	b.	SD	16 Apr. 1881	3	8	
Meyers	Lillie C.	m.	PCo	26 Mar. 1884	3	6	
Meyers	Lillie C.	m.	SD	29 Mar. 1884	2	5	
Meyers	Marcus	b.	DD	21 Aug. 1883	3	3	
Meyers	Marcus	b.	RRF	16 Aug. 1883	2	4	
Meyers	Marcus	b.	SD	25 Aug. 1883	2	5	
Michael	Emma	m.	HE	23 Feb. 1882	2	4	
Michael	Emma	m.	SD	25 Feb. 1882	3	6	
Michael	Emma J.	m.	DR	24 Feb. 1882	2	3	

(1) Surname	(2) Given Name	(3)	(4)	(5) Date	(6) Pg	(7) Col	(8) Comments
Michael	Emma J.	m.	PCo	1 Mar. 1882	2	4	
Michaels	George	b.	RRF	20 Apr. 1882	2	3	
Michaels	George W.	b.	DR	20 May 1882	3	2	
Michaels	George W.	b.	HE	18 May 1882	2	3	
Michaels	George W.	b.	PCo	24 May 1882	3	5	
Michaels	George W.	b.	SD	20 May 1882	2	4	
Michaels	Mrs.	m.	CR	18 Feb. 1882	5	2	
Michaels	Mrs.	m.	RRF	16 Feb. 1882	3	6	
Michelsen	Captain	d.	DR	9 Nov. 1882	3	2	
Michelsen	Captain	d.	RRF	2 Nov. 1882	2	4	
Michelson	Alice	m.	SD	14 June 1884	2	4	
Mickelson	Captain	d.	PCo	8 Nov. 1882	3	6	
Middaugh	W. A.	m.	SD	10 Jan. 1885	2	6	
Middlemas	James	b.	PCo	26 Jan. 1881	3	4	
Middlemas	James	b.	SD	5 Feb. 1881	3	8	
Middleton	Bertha	d.	SD	13 Sept. 1884	3	4	
Middleton	Lillie	m.	DR	9 Feb. 1882	2	3	
Middleton	Lillie	m.	PCo	22 Feb. 1882	3	5	
Middleton	Lillie	m.	SD	11 Feb. 1882	3	6	
Middleton	Walter (child of)	d.	PCo	10 Sept. 1884	3	6	
Milan	Joe	d.	CR	5 Mar. 1881	5	5	
Miles	D., Mrs.	d.	DR	25 July 1881	2	3	
Miles	D., Mrs.	d.	RRF	21 July 1881	2	4	
Miles	D., Mrs.	d.	SD	6 Aug. 1881	3	8	
Miles	Paul	o.	SD	4 July 1885	5	2	
Miles	Paul	d.	SD	25 July 1885	1	3	
Millan	Joseph	d.	RRF	17 Feb. 1881	3	4	
Millar	William S.	d.	RRF	28 Feb. 1884	2	3	Oak Mound Cemetery
Miller	Alonzo	m.	PCo	8 July 1885	3	6	
Miller	Annie	m.	DR	21 Nov. 1884	3	2	
Miller	Annie	m.	PCo	19 Nov. 1884	3	5	
Miller	Annie	m.	PWA	22 Nov. 1884	3	4	
Miller	Caspar	m.	DR	13 June 1884	3	3	
Miller	Casper	m.	PCo	11 June 1884	3	5	
Miller	Casper	m.	PWA	14 June 1884	3	6	
Miller	Casper	m.	SD	28 June 1884	3	4	
Miller	Charles L.	m.	DD	10 Nov. 1883	3	3	
Miller	D. S.	m.	SD	20 May 1882	2	4	
Miller	Frederick	m.	SD	25 Mar. 1882	3	6	
Miller	George E.	d.	PCo	20 May 1885	3	6	
Miller	George E.	d.	SD	6 June 1885	2	4	
Miller	George	b.	CR	28 May 1881	5	5	

(1) Surname	(2) Given Name	(3)	(4)	(5) Date	(6) Pg	(7) Col	(8) Comments
Miller	George	o.	DR	10 July 1882	3	1	
Miller	George	b.	PCo	13 Sept. 1882	3	7	
Miller	George	b.	RRF	26 May 1881	2	5	
Miller	George	b.	SD	4 June 1881	3	8	
Miller	George	d.	SD	28 Jan. 1882	3	3	
Miller	George T.	b.	DR	26 Jan. 1882	2	3	
Miller	George T.	b.	HE	26 Jan. 1882	2	3	
Miller	George T.	b.	RRF	26 Jan. 1882	2	2	
Miller	George T.	b.	SD	4 Feb. 1882	3	6	
Miller	George W.	b.	PC	23 May 1883	3	5	
Miller	George W.	b.	RRF	17 May 1883	2	3	
Miller	J. F.	b.	DR	30 Sept. 1881	2	3	
Miller	J. F.	b.	SD	22 Oct. 1881	3	6	
Miller	J.	b.	CR	19 Feb. 1881	4	2	
Miller	J. R.	m.	CR	27 Oct. 1883	3	1	
Miller	James	b.	SD	20 Sept. 1884	2	5	
Miller	James P.	m.	DR	30 Oct. 1882	3	1	
Miller	James P.	m.	PCo	1 Nov. 1882	3	5	
Miller	James P.	m.	SD	28 Oct. 1882	3	5	
Miller	James R.	m.	RRF	25 Oct. 1883	2	4	
Miller	Johanna	m.	CR	15 Jan. 1881	5	5	
Miller	Johanna	m.	DR	11 Jan. 1881	3	2	
Miller	Johanna	m.	SD	15 Jan. 1881	3	8	
Miller	John	m.	CR	7 May 1881	5	5	
Miller	John	b.	DR	12 Feb. 1881	3	2	
Miller	John	m.	DR	30 Apr. 1881	2	3	
Miller	John	b.	PCo	3 Sept. 1884	2	5	
Miller	John	b.	PCo	14 Oct. 1885	3	6	
Miller	John	b.	PWA	6 Sept. 1884	3	4	
Miller	John	m.	SD	14 May 1881	3	8	
Miller	John	b.	SD	19 Feb. 1881	3	8	
Miller	John	b.	SD	10 Feb. 1883	2	7	
Miller	John	b.	SD	6 Sept. 1884	2	5	
Miller	John	b.	SD	10 Oct. 1885	5	5	
Miller	John	b.	SD	13 June 1885	3	5	
Miller	John	b.	SD	24 Oct. 1885	5	4	
Miller	John	b.	SIT	3 Oct. 1885	2	3	
Miller	Joseph	b,	DR	22 July 1884	3	3	
Miller	Louisa	m.	PCo	7 Jan. 1885	3	6	
Miller	Louisa	m.	PWA	10 Jan. 1885	3	2&4	
Miller	Louisa	m.	SD	10 Jan. 1885	2	6	
Miller	Mary A.	m.	PCo	17 Jan. 1883	3	5	

(1) Surname	(2) Given Name	(3)	(4)	(5) Date	(6) Pg	(7) Col	(8) Comments
Miller	Mary A.	m.	SD	13 Jan. 1883	3	1	
Miller	Mary	m.	SD	12 July 1884	6	8	
Miller	Mary P.	d.	DR	1 May 1882	3	2	
Miller	Mary P.	d.	PCo	10 May 1882	3	5	
Miller	Maude	m.	SD	25 Oct. 1884	2	5	
Miller	Nannie E.	m.	DR	29 July 1884	3	3	
Miller	Nannie E.	m.	SD	9 Aug. 1884	3	4	
Miller	Rosa A.	m.	DR	16 Oct. 1885	3	4	
Miller	Rosa A.	m.	PCo	28 Oct. 1885	3	4	
Miller	Rosa A.	m.	SD	24 Oct. 1885	5	4	
Millerick	Michael	b.	PCo	20 Dec. 1882	3	5	
Millet	William H.	m.	SD	12 Mar. 1881	3	8	
Millett	G. E.	b.	PCo	21 Mar. 1883	3	5	
Millett	G. E.	b.	PWA	24 Mar. 1883	3	7	
Millett	G. E. (son of)	d.	PC	28 Mar. 1883	3	5	
Millett	G. E. (son of)	d.	PWA	24 Mar. 1883	3	7	
Millihan	P.	b.	DR	1 Aug. 1884	3	3	
Millington	J. B.	m.	DD	8 Sept. 1883	3	3	
Millington	J. B.	m.	SD	15 Sept. 1883	2	4	
Millington	Nancy	m.	DR	29 Dec. 1881	2	3	
Millington	Nancy	m.	PCo	11 Jan. 1882	3	6	
Millington	Nancy	m.	SD	7 Jan. 1882	3	8	
Mills	E. T.	o.	DR	25 Oct. 1882	3	2	
Mills	Ed	d.	CR	4 Oct. 1884	3	1	
Mills	Eliza	m.	SD	25 Oct. 1884	2	5	
Mills	James A.	m.	RRF	15 Sept. 1881	2	5	
Mills	Martha M.	d.	DR	2 Apr. 1884	3	3	
Mills	Martha M.	d.	PCo	9 Apr. 1884	3	6	
Mills	Myria Ellenor	d.	SD	18 Apr. 1885	2	5	
Mills	Myrie Ellenor	d.	PCo	22 Apr. 1885	3	6	
Mills	Robert	m.	DR	30 Jan. 1882	2	3	
Mills	Robert	m.	PCo	25 Jan. 1882	3	6	
Mills	Sadie	m.	PCo	27 May 1885	3	6	
Mills	Sadie	m.	SD	6 June 1885	2	4	
Mills	W. A.	b.	PCo	19 Oct. 1881	3	5	
Mills	W. A.	b.	PCo	4 Nov. 1885	2	5	
Mills	W. A.	b.	SD	29 Oct. 1881	3	6	
Mills	W. J., Mrs.	d.	PCo	24 Jan. 1883	3	5	
Mills	W. J., Mrs.	d.	SD	27 Jan. 1883	3	6	
Mills	William A.	b.	DR	2 Nov. 1885	3	4	
Mills	William	b.	DR	29 Sept. 1885	3	4	
Mills	William	m.	SD	22 Aug. 1885	6	2	

(1) Surname	(2) Given Name	(3)	(4)	(5) Date	(6) Pg	(7) Col	(8) Comments
Mills	William	b.	SRR	1 Oct. 1885	3	3	
Milton	Ruth L.	d.	CR	28 Feb. 1885	3	3	
Milton	Ruth L.	d.	PCo	4 Mar. 1885	3	6	
Milton	Ruth L.	d.	SD	14 Mar. 1885	5	5	
Milton	Ruth	d.	CR	25 Apr. 1885	5	2	Michigan
Minehan	M.	b.	SD	29 Aug. 1885	2	4	
Miner	E. E.	m.	PCo	7 Dec. 1881	3	5	
Miner	E. E.	m.	SD	17 Dec. 1881	3	7	
Miner	Edgar E.	m.	DR	3 Dec. 1881	2	3	
Minkel	Amelia L.	m.	PCo	18 Oct. 1882	3	6	
Minkel	Aurelia L.	m.	SD	14 Oct. 1882	3	6	
Minkel	Martha	m.	DD	10 Nov. 1883	3	3	
Minkel	Martha	m.	RRF	8 Nov. 1883	2	3	
Minkel	Martha	m.	SD	17 Nov. 1883	3	5	
Minor	M. P.	d.	SD	2 Apr. 1881	3	8	
Minor	M. P.	d.	SD	26 Mar. 1881	3	8	
Miranda	Isabella	d.	PCo	21 Mar. 1883	3	5	
Mise	F. D.	b.	DR	20 Mar. 1882	2	3	
Mise	F. D.	b.	PCo	29 Mar. 1882	3	5	
Mise	F. D.	b.	SD	25 Mar. 1882	3	6	
Miser	Henry S.	d.	PCo	27 May 1885	3	6	
Miser	Henry S.	d.	SD	30 May 1885	1	6	
Misner	D. R.	b.	PCo	16 Apr. 1884	3	5	
Misner	D. R.	b.	PWA	12 Apr. 1884	3	6	
Mitchell	George	b.	DR	17 Sept. 1885	3	4	
Mitchell	H. H.	b.	PC	18 Apr. 1883	3	5	
Mitchell	J. H.	m.	DR	27 Dec. 1881	2	2	
Mitchell	J. H.	m.	PCo	4 Jan. 1882	3	7	
Mitchell	J. H.	m.	SD	31 Dec. 1881	3	6	
Mitchell	J. H.	b.	SD	21 Apr. 1883	2	6	
Mitchell	Jennie	m.	RRF	20 Jan. 1881	2	5	
Mitchell	Jennie	m.	SD	29 Jan. 1881	3	8	
Mitchell	O. K.	b.	PCo	19 Apr. 1882	3	5	
Mitchell	O. K.	b.	SD	29 Apr. 1882	3	6	
Mitchell	William E.	b.	SD	8 Jan. 1881	3	8	
Mitchell	William	m.	SD	28 Nov. 1885	3	5	
Mize	Amelia	d.	PCo	18 Jan. 1882	3	5	dau. of Thompson
Mize	Aurelia	d.	SD	7 Jan. 1882	3	8	
Mize	John	b.	PCo	1 Nov. 1882	3	5	
Mize	John	b.	RRF	26 Oct. 1882	2	3	
Mize	Thompson (son of)	d.	PCo	18 Jan. 1882	3	5	
Mize	Thompson (son of)	d.	SD	7 Jan. 1882	3	8	

(1) Surname	(2) Given Name	(3)	(4)	(5) Date	(6) Pg	(7) Col	(8) Comments
Mizer	Henry	b.	PCo	6 Aug. 1884	2	4	
Mizer	Henry	b.	SD	9 Aug. 1884	3	4	
Moarbach	Nicholas	d.	RRF	22 June 1882	3	1	
Mock	Elizabeth	d.	PWA	21 Apr. 1883	3	8	
Mock	Elizabeth J.	d.	PC	18 Apr. 1883	3	5	
Mock	Theodore, Mrs.	d.	PWA	3 Mar. 1883	3	6	
Mock	Willie	m.	DR	19 Aug. 1881	2	2	
Mock	Willie	m.	SD	27 Aug. 1881	3	8	
Modini	L.	b.	PWA	8 Sept. 1883	3	8	
Modini	L.	b.	SD	4 Mar. 1882	3	6	
Modini	L.	b.	SWI	1 Sept. 1883	3	4	
Moffet	Charles	m.	SD	22 Jan. 1881	3	8	
Moffet	Charles I.	d.	CR	15 Jan. 1881	5	5	
Moffet	Charlie L.	d.	RRF	13 Jan. 1881	2	5	
Moffet	Charlie L.	d.	RRF	13 Jan. 1881	3	1	
Moffet	Dacia	m.	PCo	4 Mar. 1885	3	6	
Moffet	Dacia	d.	RRF	13 Jan. 1881	2	5	
Moffet	Dacia	m.	SD	14 Mar. 1885	5	5	
Moffet	John	d.	DR	3 Jan. 1884	3	2	
Moffet	John	d.	RRF	13 Jan. 1881	2	5	
Moffet	John	d.	RRF	3 Jan. 1884	2	1	
Moffet	Ramo L.	d.	CR	26 Mar. 1881	5	5	
Moffet	Ramo L.	d.	RRF	24 Mar. 1881	2	4	Oak Mound Cem.
Moffett	Dacia	m.	PWA	28 Feb. 1885	3	5	
Moffett	John	d.	PCo	2 Jan. 1884	3	4	
Moffett	John	d.	PCo	9 Jan. 1884	3	6	
Moffett	John	d.	PCo	13 Feb. 1884	3	4	
Moffett	John	d.	PWA	5 Jan. 1884	3	2&7	
Moffett	John	p.	RRF	28 Feb. 1884	2	2	text of will
Moffett	John	d.	SD	5 Jan. 1884	1	3&4	
Moffett	Ramo L.	d.	DR	26 Mar. 1881	3	2	
Moller	Henry, Jr.	m.	PCo	27 May 1885	3	6	
Moller	Henry, Jr.	m.	SD	6 June 1885	2	4	
Moller	Richard	b.	PCo	7 Feb. 1883	3	6	
Moller	Richard	b.	PCo	19 Aug. 1885	3	6	
Moller	Richard	b.	PWA	10 Feb. 1883	3	7	
Moller	Richard	b.	SD	10 Feb. 1883	2	7	
Molloch	J. B.	b.	DR	30 Jan. 1882	2	3	
Molloch	J. B.	b.	PCo	25 Jan. 1882	3	6	
Molseed	Jennie	m.	PCo	3 May 1882	3	5	
Molseed	Robert, Jr.	d.	DR	8 Dec. 1884	3	2	
Molseed	Robert, Jr.	d.	PCo	3 Dec. 1884	3	5	

(1) Surname	(2) Given Name	(3)	(4)	(5) Date	(6) Pg	(7) Col	(8) Comments
Molseed	Robert, Jr.	d.	PWA	6 Dec. 1884	3	4	
Molseed	Robert, Jr.	d.	SD	13 Dec. 1884	2	5	
Molseed	Sarah	m.	DR	26 Aug. 1885	3	4	
Molseed	Sarah	m.	PCo	19 Aug. 1885	3	6	
Moltzen	Margretta Elizabeth	d.	DR	8 Mar. 1882	2	3	
Moltzen	Margretta	d.	DR	4 Mar. 1882	2	3	
Monahan	Barney	d.	PCo	27 July 1881	3	5	
Monahan	Barney	d.	SD	6 Aug. 1881	3	8	
Mondragon	Ellen	d.	SD	14 May 1881	3	8	
Monmonier	Jennie M.	m.	DR	1 Apr. 1881	2	3	
Monmonier	Jennie M.	m.	RRF	31 Mar. 1881	2	3	
Monroe	D.	b.	SD	12 Mar. 1881	3	8	
Monroe	J. T.	d.	PCo	17 Jan. 1883	3	5	
Monroe	John	b.	DD	24 Dec. 1883	3	2	
Monroe	Peter	m.	SD	25 Apr. 1885	2	5	
Montgomery	Josephine	m.	PCo	19 July 1882	3	6	
Montgomery	William	b.	DD	24 Oct. 1883	3	3	
Moody	Daniel	d.	DD	13 Aug. 1883	3	3	
Moody	Hannah	d.	PCo	18 Oct. 1882	3	6	
Moody	Hannah	d.	RRF	12 Oct. 1882	2	3	
Moore	Alice V.	d.	PCo	7 Dec. 1881	3	5	
Moore	Allen	d.	SD	6 Dec. 1884	3	3	
Moore	Annie K.	d.	SD	9 Apr. 1881	3	8	
Moore	C. P.	d.	RRF	2 June 1881	2	3	
Moore	Electa	d.	PCo	14 Feb. 1883	3	6	
Moore	Electa	d.	RRF	8 Feb. 1883	2	4	
Moore	Electa	d.	SD	10 Feb. 1883	2	7	
Moore	Electra	b.	CR	10 Feb. 1883	3	1	
Moore	Ella	m.	PCo	26 Dec. 1883	3	5	
Moore	G. W.	d.	PCo	24 May 1882	3	5	
Moore	G. W.	d.	SD	20 May 1882	2	4	
Moore	George	m.	SD	12 Jan. 1884	3	6	
Moore	George W.	d.	DR	16 May 1882	3	2	
Moore	Gideon J.	m.	DR	3 Dec. 1881	2	3	
Moore	Henrietta	m.	DR	28 Sept. 1881	3	2	
Moore	Henrietta	m.	RRF	22 Sept. 1881	2	5	
Moore	Henrietta	m.	SD	8 Oct. 1881	3	8	
Moore	J.	m.	PCo	7 Dec. 1881	3	5	
Moore	J.	m.	SD	17 Dec. 1881	3	7	
Moore	James	d.	SD	8 Aug. 1885	2	4	
Moore	John P.	d.	DR	27 July 1881	3	2	
Moore	John P.	d.	PCo	27 July 1881	3	5	

(1) Surname	(2) Given Name	(3)	(4)	(5) Date	(6) Pg	(7) Col	(8) Comments
Moore	John P.	d.	SD	6 Aug. 1881	3	8	
Moore	Maud	m.	PCo	19 July 1882	3	6	
Moore	Maud	m.	SD	22 July 1882	3	5	
Moore	Maude	m.	RRF	13 July 1882	2	3	
Moore	T. B.	b.	DR	24 Nov. 1885	3	4	
Moore	T. B.	b.	PCo	2 Aug. 1882	3	6	
Moore	T. B.	b.	PCo	26 Mar. 1884	3	6	
Moore	T. B.	b.	PWA	22 Mar. 1884	3	6	
Moore	T. B.	b.	SD	12 Feb. 1881	3	8	
Moore	T. B.	b.	SD	5 Aug. 1882	3	5	
Moore	T. B.	b.	SD	29 July 1882	3	7	
Moore	T. B.	b.	SD	22 Mar. 1884	2	4	
Moore	T. B.	b.	SD	29 Mar. 1884	2	5	
Moore	T. B.	b.	SD	21 Nov. 1885	3	5	
Moore	Thomas M.	d.	PCo	3 Aug. 1881	3	5	
Moore	Thomas M.	d.	SD	13 Aug. 1881	3	8	
Moore	W. Jewett	m.	DD	23 Nov. 1883	3	2	
Moore	W. Jewett	m.	RRF	22 Nov. 1883	2	3	
Moore	W. Jewett	m.	SD	1 Dec. 1883	3	4	
Moore	W. Jewett	b.	SD	6 Sept. 1884	2	5	
Moore	William	m.	PCo	9 Mar. 1881	3	4	
Moore	William	m.	SD	5 Mar. 1881	3	8	
Moore	William	b.	SD	30 July 1881	3	8	
Moral	(female)	b.	DR	9 June 1884	3	3	
Moral	Louis	d.	PCo	25 Feb. 1885	3	6	
Moral	Louis	d.	SD	28 Feb. 1885	5	6	
Moral	S.	b.	PCo	22 Nov. 1882	3	5	
Moral	S.	b.	PCo	18 June 1884	3	4	
Moral	S.	b.	SD	6 Aug. 1881	3	8	
Moral	S.	b.	SD	11 Nov. 1882	3	7	
Moral	S.	b.	SD	14 June 1884	2	4	
Mordecai	Thomas	m.	DR	22 Dec. 1881	2	2	
Mordecai	Thomas	b.	DR	29 July 1885	3	4	
Mordecai	Thomas	b.	PCo	22 July 1885	3	6	
Mordecai	Thomas	m.	SD	24 Dec. 1881	2	3	
Morell	Hugh	m.	SD	4 Feb. 1882	3	6	
Morey	Joseph W.	d.	PCo	4 Feb. 1885	3	6	
Morey	Joseph W.	d.	PWA	7 Feb. 1885	3	3&5	
Morgan	Maggie	d.	DR	21 June 1884	3	3	
Morgan	R. H.	b.	SD	5 Mar. 1881	3	8	
Morin	Josiah	d.	DR	26 Oct. 1885	3	4	
Morin	Josiah	d.	PCo	28 Oct. 1885	2	2	

(1) Surname	(2) Given Name	(3)	(4)	(5) Date	(6) Pg	(7) Col	(8) Comments
Morin	Josiah	o.	SD	15 Nov. 1884	3	1	
Morin	Josiah	d.	SD	31 Oct. 1885	3	1&2	Pleasant Hill Cem.
Morin	Josiah	d.	SIT	31 Oc t. 1885	3	3	
Morril	James	b.	PCo	1 Oct. 1884	3	5	
Morris	Carrie	m.	DR	27 Nov. 1885	3	4	
Morris	Emma Alice	m.	DR	30 Dec. 1882	2	1	
Morris	Emma Alice	m.	RRF	28 Dec. 1882	2	2	
Morris	Emma Alice	m.	SD	30 Dec. 1882	3	6	
Morris	Flora K.	d.	PCo	27 Dec. 1882	3	6	
Morris	Flora K.	d.	SD	30 Dec. 1882	3	6	
Morrison	Alice	m.	DR	6 May 1882	2	3	
Morrison	Alice	m.	DR	20 Oct. 1885	3	4	
Morrison	Alice	m.	PCo	28 Oct. 1885	3	4	
Morrison	Alice	m.	SD	24 Oct. 1885	5	4	
Morrison	Laura	m.	CR	10 Feb. 1883	3	1	
Morrison	Laura	m.	SD	24 Jan. 1885	5	5	
Morrison	Mary E.	d.	DR	13 Sept. 1881	2	3	
Morrison	Mary E.	d.	DR	15 Jan. 1884	3	3	
Morrison	Mary E.	d.	DR	15 Jan. 1884	2	1	
Morrison	Mary	d.	PCo	23 Jan. 1884	3	5	
Morrison	Mary	d.	SD	19 Jan. 1884	3	6	
Morrison	Simon	d.	PWA	26 May 1883	3	7	
Morrison	Simon T.	d.	PC	23 May 1883	3	1&5	Cypress Hill Cem.
Morrison	Zeno	m.	DD	29 Dec. 1883	3	3	
Morrow	Ella F.	d.	PCo	22 Nov. 1882	3	5	
Morrow	George	m.	CR	30 Apr. 1881	5	5	
Morrow	George P.	b.	DD	23 Aug. 1883	3	2	
Morrow	George P.	m.	DR	29 Apr. 1881	3	2	
Morrow	George P.	b.	PC	22 Aug. 1883	3	5	
Morrow	George P.	m.	PCo	27 Apr. 1881	3	5	
Morrow	George P.	m.	RRF	5 May 1881	2	4	
Morrow	George P.	m.	SD	30 Apr. 1881	3	8	
Morrow	J. A.	m.	SD	22 July 1882	3	5	
Morrow	J.	d.	DR	29 Nov. 1882	3	2	
Morrow	J. (dau. of)	d.	PCo	28 May 1884	2	4	
Morrow	James	d.	CR	12 Aug. 1882	5	1	
Morrow	James	m.	PCo	25 Oct. 1882	3	5	
Morrow	James	d.	RRF	17 Aug. 1882	3	3	
Morrow	James	d.	SD	21 Nov. 1885	3	4&5	
Morrow	John	m.	DR	18 July 1882	3	2	
Morrow	John	m.	PCo	2 Mar. 1881	4	4	
Morrow	John	b.	PCo	28 May 1884	2	4	

(1) Surname	(2) Given Name	(3)	(4)	(5) Date	(6) Pg	(7) Col	(8) Comments
Morrow	John	m.	SD	5 Mar. 1881	3	8	
Morrow	Joseph A.	m.	DD	23 Nov. 1883	3	2	
Morrow	Joseph A.	m.	RRF	22 Nov. 1883	2	3	
Morrow	Joseph A.	m.	SD	1 Dec. 1883	3	4	
Morrow	William	b.	PWA	6 Dec. 1884	3	4	
Morse	E. E.	d.	DR	30 Aug. 1884	3	1	
Morse	E. E.	d.	PCo	3 Sept. 1884	2	5	
Morse	E. E.	d.	PWA	6 Sept. 1884	3	4	
Morse	E. E.	d.	SD	6 Sept. 1884	1	7	
Morse	E. E.	d.	SD	6 Sept. 1884	2	5	
Morse	George W.	b.	PCo	5 Aug. 1885	3	6	
Morse	George W.	m.	PWA	4 Apr. 1885	3	6	
Morse	J. B.	b.	DR	29 Aug. 1885	3	4	
Morshead	George	b.	PCo	9 Jan. 1884	3	6	
Morshead	George	b.	SD	5 Jan. 1884	1	4	
Mortier	Harvey	d.	CR	22 Oct. 1881	4	1	
Mortier	Harvey	d.	RRF	20 Oct. 1881	2	3	
Mortier	Harvey	d.	SD	22 Oct. 1881	3	3	
Morton		d.	PCo	16 Dec. 1885	3	6	
Morton	Bertha R.	d.	DR	5 Feb. 1884	3	3	
Morton	Bertha R.	d.	PCo	6 Feb. 1884	3	6	
Morton	Bertha R.	d.	PWA	9 Feb. 1884	3	6	
Morton	Bertha R.	d.	SD	16 Feb. 1884	2	5	
Morton	C. C.	o.	SIT	22 Aug. 1885	2	2	
Morton	E. H.	o.	SIT	22 Aug. 1885	2	2	
Morton	John	d.	DR	8 May 1884	3	2	
Morton	William	b.	RRF	5 Oct. 1882	3	2	
Mosher	Dr.	b.	SD	23 Apr. 1881	3	8	
Mosman	Jessie	m.	DR	10 June 1884	3	3	
Moss	Joseph	b.	PC	20 June 1883	3	6	
Moss	Joseph (son of)	d.	PC	20 June 1883	3	6	
Moss	Joseph (son of)	d.	RRF	14 June 1883	2	3	
Moss	Joseph (son of)	b.	RRF	14 June 1883	2	3	
Moss	Joseph (son of)	b.&d.	SD	23 June 1883	3	5	
Moss	Julia M.	d.	PC	25 July 1883	3	6	
Moss	Julia M.	d.	RRF	19 July 1883	2	4	Oak Mound Cemetery
Mothorn	C.	b.	DR	20 Oct. 1885	3	4	
Moulton	Louella	d.	SD	4 Mar. 1882	3	6	
Moulton	Luella	d.	CR	25 Feb. 1882	5	1&2	Cloverdale Cemetery
Moulton	Luella	d.	DR	27 Feb. 1882	2	3	
Moulton	Luella	d.	RRF	2 Mar. 1882	2	4	
Mountjoy	Lulu	m.	DR	1 Nov. 1881	2	3	filed after Nov. 29

(1) Surname	(2) Given Name	(3)	(4)	(5) Date	(6) Pg	(7) Col	(8) Comments
Mountjoy	Lulu	m.	PCo	26 Oct. 1881	3	4	
Mowbray	J. R.	p.	CR	1 Oct. 1881	5	4	
Mowbray	James	d.	DR	1 June 1881	2	3	
Mowbray	James R.	d.	CR	4 June 1881	5	5	
Mowbray	James R.	d.	RRF	9 June 1881	2	4	
Mowbray	James Ross	m.	SD	4 June 1881	3	8	
Muegge	Theos.	m.	SD	12 Mar. 1881	3	8	
Mueller	J. J.	b.	DR	23 June 1882	3	2	
Mueller	J. J.	b.	SD	24 June 1882	3	5	
Muldry	Martin	m.	DR	29 Aug. 1882	3	2	
Muldry	Martin	b.	PCo	5 Mar. 1884	3	6	
Muldry	Martin	b.	PWA	8 Mar. 1884	3	6	
Muldry	Martin	m.	SD	2 Sept. 1882	3	6	
Mulgrew	(male)	b.	DR	11 Mar. 1884	3	2	
Mulgrew	(male)	b.	DR	26 Mar. 1884	3	3	
Mulgrew	F. B.	b.	PCo	19 Mar. 1884	3	6	
Mulgrew	F. B.	b.	RRF	27 Mar. 1884	2	3	
Mulgrew	J. F.	b.	PCo	2 Apr. 1884	3	6	
Mulgrew	J. W.	b.	SD	29 Mar. 1884	2	5	
Mulgrew	John F.	b.	RRF	27 Mar. 1884	2	3	
Mulhaupt	F. S.	m.	SD	3 June 1882	2	4	
Mulhaupt	F. S.	b.	SD	24 Oct. 1885	5	4	
Mulhaupt	F. S.	b.	SIT	17 Oct. 1885	2	3	
Mullalley	Margaret	d.	DR	1 Aug. 1885	3	4	
Mullally	Bridget	d.	DD	14 Aug. 1883	3	2	
Mullally	Bridget	d.	PWA	18 Aug. 1883	3	7	
Mullally	Bridget	d.	SD	18 Aug. 1883	2	6	
Mullally	Maggie	d.	DR	26 Aug. 1885	3	4	
Mullally	Maggie	d.	PCo	19 Aug. 1885	3	6	
Mullen	Emma	m.	SD	12 Jan. 1884	3	6	
Mullen	William	d.	SD	2 Apr. 1881	3	4	
Muller	Frank M.	m.	SD	6 June 1885	2	4	
Muller	John	m.	DR	8 Aug. 1882	3	2	
Muller	John	m.	SD	12 Aug. 1882	3	5	
Muller	John, Jr.	m.	PCo	9 Aug. 1882	3	6	
Muller	Joseph	b.	DR	28 Jan. 1882	2	3	
Muller	Joseph	b.	PCo	23 July 1884	3	6	
Muller	Leo W.	d.	SD	19 July 1884	2	5	
Muller	Leonard William	d.	DR	12 July 1884	3	3	
Muller	Margrantha	d.	PCo	18 Jan. 1882	3	5	
Muller	Margratha	d.	DR	30 Dec. 1881	2	3	
Muller	Margratha	d.	SD	7 Jan. 1882	3	8	

(1) Surname	(2) Given Name	(3)	(4)	(5) Date	(6) Pg	(7) Col	(8) Comments
Muller	R.	b.	DR	26 Aug. 1885	3	4	
Mulligan	George V.	m.	SD	11 Oct. 1884	2	5	
Mulligan	William	b.	RRF	28 Dec. 1882	2	2	
Mulvaney	Mary E.	d.	PWA	1 Mar. 1884	3	6	
Mulvaney	Mary F.	d.	PCo	27 Feb. 1884	3	6	
Munday	Thomas B.	b.	DR	5 July 1884	3	4	under heading "died"
Munday	Thomas	b.	PCo	11 Jan. 1882	3	6	
Munday	Thomas	b.	PCo	2 July 1884	3	4	
Munday	Thomas	b.	PWA	5 July 1884	3	6	
Munday	Thomas	b.	SD	21 Jan. 1882	3	6	
Munday	Thomas	b.	SD	12 July 1884	6	8	
Mungor	Calvin A.	m.	SD	21 Jan. 1882	3	6	
Munroe	Peter	m.	CR	25 Apr. 1885	5	2	
Munsen	Peter	d.	DR	18 Apr. 1881	3	1	
Munson	Peter	d.	CR	23 Apr. 1881	1	3	
Munson	Peter	d.	RRF	14 Apr. 1881	3	6	
Murbur	Clara	m.	SD	3 Oct. 1885	5	4	also 10 Oct., p. 1 col. 3
Murdock	James W.	m.	PCo	28 Jan. 1885	3	6	
Murphy	A. J.	b.	DR	26 Sept. 1885	3	4	
Murphy	A. J.	b.	PCo	9 Jan. 1884	3	6	
Murphy	A. J.	b.	PCo	23 Sept. 1885	3	6	
Murphy	A. J.	b.	PWA	5 Jan. 1884	3	7	
Murphy	A. J.	b.	SD	19 Jan. 1884	3	6	
Murphy	A. J.	b.	SRR	1 Oct. 1885	3	3	
Murphy	Aggie	m.	DR	30 Sept. 1885	3	4	
Murphy	Aggie	m.	SRR	1 Oct. 1885	3	3	
Murphy	Alice	m.	DR	28 Sept. 1885	3	4	
Murphy	Alice	m.	PCo	30 Sept. 1885	3	6	
Murphy	Alice	m.	SD	3 Oct. 1885	5	4	
Murphy	Alice	m.	SRR	1 Oct. 1885	3	3	
Murphy	Bridget	d.	PCo	27 Apr. 1881	3	5	
Murphy	Ella	m.	DR	13 Feb. 1882	2	3	
Murphy	Ella	m.	SD	11 Feb. 1882	3	6	
Murphy	Ellen	d.	DR	17 Sept. 1885	3	4	
Murphy	Ellen	d.	PCo	16 Sept. 1885	3	6	
Murphy	James	d.	DR	17 Dec. 1881	2	2	
Murphy	James	d.	DR	29 Apr. 1881	3	2	
Murphy	James	d.	RRF	15 Dec. 1881	2	4	
Murphy	James	d.	SD	24 Dec. 1881	2	3	
Murphy	Katie	m.	DR	15 Aug. 1881	3	2	
Murphy	Katie	m.	PCo	20 July 1881	3	5	

(1) Surname	(2) Given Name	(3)	(4)	(5) Date	(6) Pg	(7) Col	(8) Comments
Murphy	Katie	m.	SD	6 Aug. 1881	3	8	
Murphy	Margaret	m.	PCo	28 June 1882	3	5	
Murphy	Margaret	m.	SD	1 July 1882	2	3	
Murphy	William	d.	RRF	15 Dec. 1881	2	4	
Murray	A. B., Mrs.	d.	CR	8 Oct. 1881	5	1	Cloverdale Cemetery
Murray	B. A., Mrs.	d.	DR	17 Oct. 1881	2	3	
Murray	B. A., Mrs.	d.	SD	29 Oct. 1881	3	6	
Murray	J.	b.	DR	20 Oct. 1885	3	4	
Murray	J.	b.	PCo	28 Oct. 1885	3	4	
Murray	M.	d.	DD	12 Nov. 1883	3	3	
Murray	M.	b.	PCo	14 Dec. 1881	3	4	
Murray	M.	b.	PWA	10 Nov. 1883	3	8	
Murray	M.	d.	SD	17 Nov. 1883	3	5	
Murray	Mary	d.	PCo	29 Oct. 1884	3	5	
Murray	Mary	d.	PWA	1 Nov. 1884	3	4	
Murray	Thomas	d.	DR	9 June 1884	3	3	
Murray	Thomas	d.	PCo	11 June 1884	3	5	
Murray	Thomas	d.	PWA	14 June 1884	3	6	
Murray	Thomas	d.	SD	14 June 1884	2	4	also p. 3 col. 1; Oddfellows Cem.
Murry		d.	PCo	5 Oct. 1881	3	5	
Muscio	David (dau. of)	d.	DR	18 July 1882	3	1	
Muse	G .W.	m.	DR	6 Dec. 1884	3	2	
Muse	G. W.	m.	PCo	10 Dec. 1884	3	5	
Muse	George W.	m.	SD	13 Dec. 1884	2	5	
Musgrave	James C.	d.	DR	8 Apr. 1881	2	3	
Musgrave	James C.	d.	SD	16 Apr. 1881	3	8	
Musselman	A., Mrs.	d.	SD	23 Nov. 1882	3	2	Sebastopol Cemetery
Musselman	Mrs.	d.	DR	18 Nov. 1882	3	1	Sebastopol Cemetery
Myers	Abraham H.	m.	SD	12 Mar. 1881	3	8	
Myers	Edwin P.	b.	DD	13 Oct. 1883	3	3	
Myers	Emily	m.	DR	4 Mar. 1882	2	3	
Myers	Emily	m.	PCo	8 Mar. 1882	3	5	
Myers	Emily	m.	RRF	2 Mar. 1882	2	4	
Myers	Emily	m.	SD	25 Feb. 1882	3	6	
Myers	Lillie C.	m.	PWA	29 Mar. 1884	3	6	
Myrick	D. B.	d.	RRF	3 Aug. 1882	2	4	
Myrick	Eliza	m.	RRF	15 Nov. 1883	2	3	

N & O

(1) Surname	(2) Given Name	(3)	(4)	(5) Date	(6) Pg	(7) Col	(8) Comments
Nahmans	Nicholas	d.	PCo	2 Mar. 1881	4	4	
Nahmans	Nicholas	d.	SD	5 Mar. 1881	3	8	
Nally	George A.	m.	DR	6 Nov. 1884	2	2	
Nally	George A.	m.	PCo	12 Nov. 1884	3	5	
Nally	George A.	m.	SD	8 Nov. 1884	2	5	
Nash	Alta B.	m.	CR	22 Oct. 1881	5	3	
Nash	Alta B.	m.	DR	25 Oct. 1881	3	2	
Nash	Alta B.	m.	PCo	2 Nov. 1881	3	5	
Nash	Alta B.	m.	SD	29 Oct. 1881	3	6	
Nash	Charles	m.	DR	19 Dec. 1881	2	2	
Nash	Charles	m.	PCo	28 Dec. 1881	3	6	
Nash	Charles	m.	SD	24 Dec. 1881	2	3	
Nash	Emma	m.	DR	18 Dec. 1882	2	1	
Nash	Emma	m.	PCo	27 Dec. 1882	3	6	
Nash	Emma	m.	SD	23 Dec. 1882	2	5	
Nash	James	m.	PCo	28 Jan. 1885	3	6	
Nau	Thomas	d.	PCo	3 June 1885	3	6	
Nauert	H. F.	b.	DD	12 Oct. 1883	3	3	
Nauert	H. F.	b.	PWA	14 Mar. 1885	3	5	
Nauert	H. F.	b.	SD	20 Oct. 1883	3	4	
Nauert	H. F.	b.	SD	21 Mar. 1885	2	5	
Nauert	Herman F.	m.	CR	1 Jan. 1881	5	5	
Nauert	Herman F.	b.	PCo	31 May 1882	3	5	
Nauert	Herman F.	b.	SD	10 June 1882	2	3	
Naughton	Hubert J.	d.	PWA	16 Feb. 1884	3	6	
Naughton	Hubert James	d.	PCo	6 Feb. 1884	3	6	
Naughton	Hubert James	d.	PCo	13 Feb. 1884	3	4	
Naughton	Hubert James	d.	SD	16 Feb. 1884	2	5	
Naughton	James	d.	PWA	9 Feb. 1884	3	6	
Naughton	John F.	m.	SD	25 Apr. 1885	2	5	
Nay	Heber	m.	PCo	11 June 1884	3	5	
Nay	Heber L.	m.	DR	5 June 1884	3	3	
Nay	L. G.	m.	DD	11 Oct. 1883	3	3	
Nay	L. G.	m.	SD	13 Oct. 1883	3	4	
Nay	M. A.	d.	PCo	11 May 1881	3	5	
Nay	M. A., Mrs.	d.	DR	14 May 1881	2	3	
Nay	M. A., Mrs.	d.	SD	21 May 1881	3	8	
Neal	W. W.	b.	CR	15 Jan. 1881	5	5	

(1) Surname	(2) Given Name	(3)	(4)	(5) Date	(6) Pg	(7) Col	(8) Comments
Neal	W. W.	b.	SD	5 Feb. 1881	3	8	
Neal	W. W.	b.	SD	22 Jan. 1881	3	8	
Near	John	b.	SD	14 Oct. 1882	3	6	
Neece	George, Sr.	d.	CR	1 Oct. 1881	1	3	
Needham	John C.	m.	PCo	18 Jan. 1882	3	5	
Needham	Mary A.	m.	DR	21 Jan. 1882	3	2	
Neeley	W. H.	b.	RRF	5 Apr. 1883	2	3	
Neer	Edith Ophelia	d.	PCo	14 June 1882	3	5	
Neer	Edith Ophelia	d.	SD	10 June 1882	2	3	
Neil	Alfred	d.	DR	2 July 1881	2	3	
Neil	Alfred	d.	PCo	29 June 1881	3	5	
Neil	Washington (son of)	d.	SD	9 July 1881	3	8	
Neilson	Nels	m.	CR	18 Aug. 1883	3	2	also 25 Aug., p. 3 col. 3
Neles	Owen	d.	PWA	22 Mar. 1884	3	2	
Nellis	Henry	d.	DR	23 Mar. 1884	3	3	
Nellis	Henry	d.	PCo	26 Mar. 1884	3	6	
Nellis	Henry	d.	PWA	29 Mar. 1884	3	6	
Nelson	Henry	m.	SD	4 Feb. 1882	3	6	
Nelson	John	d.	DR	28 Nov. 1882	3	2	
Nelson	John	d.	SD	2 Dec. 1882	3	2	
Nelson	Leonard	m.	SD	2 May 1885	2	5	
Nesbitt	Joseph	m.	DD	18 Oct. 1883	3	3	
Nesbitt	Joseph	m.	PWA	13 Oct. 1883	3	8	
Nesbitt	Joseph	m.	SD	20 Oct. 1883	3	4	
Neuman	William	d.	SD	9 May 1885	2	5	
Newcomb	Alice Mary	d.	SD	28 May 1881	3	8	
Newcum	John Wesley	d.	DD	4 Aug. 1883	3	2	
Newell	Anna L.	m.	PCo	7 Dec. 1881	3	5	
Newell	Anna L.	m.	SD	17 Dec. 1881	3	7	
Newell	Annie L. L.	m.	DR	14 Dec. 1881	2	2	
Newhall	H. M.	d.	RRF	23 Mar. 1882	2	2	
Newland	Frank D.	b.	PCo	7 Jan. 1885	3	6	
Newland	Frank D.	b.	PCo	14 Jan. 1885	3	6	
Newman	O. M.	b.	DR	14 Oct. 1885	3	4	
Newman	Oliver	m.	PCo	7 Jan. 1885	3	6	
Newman	Oliver	m.	SD	10 Jan. 1885	2	6	
Nichols	Elizabeth	m.	PCo	31 Aug. 1881	3	5	
Nichols	Elizabeth	m.	SD	10 Sept. 1881	3	8	
Nichols	Lizzie E.	m.	DR	21 May 1884	3	2	
Nichols	Lizzie	m.	DR	30 Aug. 1881	3	2	
Nichols	Lizzie	m.	PWA	24 May 1884	3	5	
Nichols	Lizzie	m.	SD	3 Sept. 1881	3	8	

(1) Surname	(2) Given Name	(3)	(4)	(5) Date	(6) Pg	(7) Col	(8) Comments
Nichols	Lizzie	m.	SD	24 May 1884	1	6	also p. 2 col. 3
Nichols	W. A.	m.	SD	25 Oct. 1884	2	5	
Nickerson	Addie L.	m.	PCo	11 Mar. 1885	3	6	
Nickerson	Addie L.	m.	PWA	14 Mar. 1885	3	5	
Nickerson	W. J.	b.	SD	30 July 1881	3	8	
Niles	Milton	b.	DR	21 July 1885	3	4	
Niles	Milton	b.	PCo	15 July 1885	3	6	
Niles	R.	b.	SD	24 Sept. 1881	3	8	
Nilson	Marita	m.	RRF	8 May 1884	5	6	
Nissen	Jurgen U.	d.	DR	11 Sept. 1885	3	4	
Nissen	Jurgen U.	d.	PCo	9 Sept. 1885	3	6	
Nissom	George	d.	CR	5 Sept. 1885	3	1	
Nobbs	David M.	m.	PCo	9 Nov. 1881	3	5	
Noble	Cynthia B.	m.	SD	15 Jun. 1881	3	8	
Noble	Cynthia	m.	CR	15 Jan. 1881	5	5	
Noble	Emma	m.	SD	19 Feb. 1881	3	8	
Noble	S. B.	d.	DR	27 Nov. 1882	3	1	
Noble	S. S.	d.	DR	23 Oct. 1885	3	4	
Noble	S. S.	d.	PCo	21 Oct. 1885	3	4	
Nobles	Christiana	d.	PCo	24 Sept. 1884	3	5	
Nobles	Christina	d.	SD	27 Sept. 1884	2	5	also p. 3 col. 2; Cloverdale
Nobles	Y.	d.	CR	20 Sept. 1884	3	1	
Noffsinger	M., Miss	m.	SD	3 May 1884	3	3	
Noffsinger	Melvina	m.	DR	30 Apr. 1884	3	2	
Noffsinger	S.	m.	RRF	8 May 1884	5	6	
Noffsinger	Wilbur	m.	SD	24 Feb. 1883	3	1	
Nolan	Sylvester D.	m.	PCo	21 June 1882	3	5	
Nolan	Sylvester D.	m.	SD	17 June 1882	2	4	
Nonelle	Philomena	m.	PCo	17 June 1885	3	6	
Nonelle	Philomena	m.	SD	13 June 1885	3	5	
Noonan	Charles J.	d.	PCo	10 June 1885	3	6	
Noonan	Charles J.	d.	SD	13 June 1885	3	5	
Noonan	G. F.	b.	DR	24 June 1881	2	3	
Noonan	G. P.	b.	CR	2 July 1881	5	5	
Noonan	George P.	b.	DD	25 Aug. 1883	3	3	
Noonan	George P.	b.	SD	25 June 1881	3	8	
Noonan	George P.	b.	SD	1 Sept. 1883	2	7	
Noonan	George P.	b.	SD	19 Sept. 1885	2	4	
Noonan	George T.	b.	PCo	16 Sept. 1885	3	6	
Noonan	Lila Alberta	d.	DR	6 June 1882	3	2	
Noonan	Lila Alberta	d.	PCo	14 June 1882	3	5	
Noonan	Lila Alberta	d.	SD	10 June 1882	2	3	also p. 3 col. 1

(1) Surname	(2) Given Name	(3)	(4)	(5) Date	(6) Pg	(7) Col	(8) Comments
Noonan	P. H.	b.	DR	8 May 1882	2	3	
Noonan	P. H.	b.	DR	5 Sept. 1885	3	4	
Noonan	P. H.	b.	SD	6 May 1882	3	6	
Norbom	Peter	b.	PCo	21 Mar. 1883	3	5	
Norbom	Peter	b.	PWA	24 Mar. 1883	3	7	
Norborm	P. G.	b.	PCo	17 June 1885	3	6	
Norborm	P. G.	b.	SD	27 June 1885	5	4	
Norris	Charles	d.	DR	19 Jan. 1884	3	3	
Norris	Charles	p.	DR	26 Dec. 1884	2	2	
Norris	Charles	d.	PCo	23 Jan. 1884	3	5	
Norton	F. C.	m.	PCo	12 July 1882	3	5	
Norton	F. C.	m.	SD	15 July 1882	2	4	
Norton	Lewis Cleveland	b.	SD	21 Feb. 1885	2	5	
Norton	Nellie	m.	SD	25 Apr. 1885	2	5	
Nosler	H. E.	b.	DR	29 July 1885	3	4	
Nosler	H. E.	b.	PCo	29 July 1885	3	4	
Nosler	H. E.	b.	RRF	8 May 1884	5	6	
Nosler	H. E.	b.	SD	17 May 1884	3	5	
Nosler	Katie Myrtle	d.	DD	12 Oct. 1883	3	3	
Nosler	Katie Myrtle	d.	HE	11 Oct. 1883	2	2	
Nosler	Katie Myrtle	d.	RRF	11 Oct. 1883	2	5	Oak Mound Cemetery
Nosler	Katie Myrtle	d.	SD	20 Oct. 1883	3	4	
Nosler	W. H.	b.	PCo	17 Jan. 1883	3	5	
Nosler	W. H.	b.	RRF	11 Jan. 1883	2	2	
Nowell	Hattie A.	m.	PCo	22 Apr. 1885	3	6	
Nowell	Hattie A.	m.	SD	25 Apr. 1885	2	5	
Nowlin	J. E.	b.	PWA	6 Dec. 1884	3	4	
Nowlin	J. F.	b.	PCo	10 Dec. 1884	3	5	
Nowlin	Josephine Irene	d.	DR	31 Aug. 1882	3	2	
Nunn	Albert	b.	PCo	24 June 1885	3	6	
Nunn	Albert	b.	SD	27 June 1885	5	4	
Nutting	Frank A.	d.	DR	23 May 1882	2	3	Colorado
Nutting	Frank A.	d.	PCo	17 May 1882	3	5	
Nutting	Frank A.	d.	SD	20 May 1882	2	4	
Ny	Jacob	m.	SD	26 Dec. 1885	3	4	
Nye	David	d.	PCo	7 Jan. 1885	3	6	
Oates	J. Wyatt	m.	SD	13 Aug. 1881	3	3	
Ocke	Mr. & Mrs.	b.	PCo	13 May 1885	3	6	
Odell	Josephine S.	m.	PCo	15 Mar. 1882	3	4	
Odell	L. G.	b.	PCo	8 July 1885	3	6	
Odell	L. G.	b.	SD	27 June 1885	5	4	
Odell	Lincoln G.	d.	SD	12 Sept. 1885	1	6	

(1) Surname	(2) Given Name	(3)	(4)	(5) Date	(6) Pg	(7) Col	(8) Comments
Odell	Lincon	m.	PCo	1 Oct. 1884	3	5	
Odell	Link	d.	PCo	9 Sept. 1885	2	4	
Odell	S. I.	m.	DR	29 Nov. 1884	3	2	
Odell	Sephrona J.	m.	PCo	3 Dec. 1884	3	5	
Odell	Squire	d.	RRF	7 Dec. 1882	2	4	
Odlum	George W.	m.	RRF	21 Sept. 1882	2	4	
Odlum	George W.	m.	SD	30 Sept. 1882	3	6	
Odlum	Gussie	m.	SD	14 May 1881	3	8	
Oettl	Frank	d.	PWA	14 Apr. 1883	3	7	
Oettl	Frank	d.	SWI	7 Apr. 1883	3	5	
Oettl	Mrs.	d.	SWI	1 Sept. 1883	3	4	Sonoma Cemetery
Oettle	Frank	d.	SWI	7 Apr. 1883	3	5	
Oettle	Mrs.	d.	PWA	25 Aug. 1883	3	1	
Offutt	John W.	m.	PCo	11 Mar. 1885	3	6	
Offutt	John W.	m.	PWA	14 Mar. 1885	3	5	
Ogden	Eliel	m.	DR	29 July 1884	3	3	
Ogden	Mary L.	d.	PCo	3 May 1882	3	5	
Ogden	Mary	d.	DR	1 May 1882	3	2	
Ogle	Edwin	m.	DR	29 July 1884	3	3	
Ogle	Edwin	m.	SD	9 Aug. 1884	3	4	
Oilar	J.	d.	SD	12 Mar. 1881	3	8	
Olbirch	Lou F.	m.	PCo	24 June 1885	3	6	
Olbrich	Lou F.	m.	SD	27 June 1885	5	4	
Olive	Albert	b.	PCo	26 Nov. 1884	3	5	
Olive	Albert	b.	PWA	29 Nov. 1884	3	4	
Olmstead	Edward	m.	PCo	26 Mar. 1884	3	6	
Olmstead	William E.	m.	CR	22 Mar. 1884	3	1	
Olmstead	William E.	m.	RRF	27 Mar. 1884	2	3	
Orender	William	b.	SD	16 June 1883	2	6	
Ornbaum	Will F.	o.	CR	18 Nov. 1882	3	3	
Orr	Richard D.	m.	PWA	2 Feb. 1884	3	2	
Ort	Clara	m.	DD	4 Oct. 1883	3	2	
Ort	Clara	m.	SD	6 Oct. 1883	2	6	
Orvold	J. J.	m.	CR	28 May 1881	5	5	
Orvold	James J.	m.	PCo	18 May 1881	3	5	
Orvold	James J.	m.	SD	28 May 1881	3	8	
Orvold	James	m.	DR	20 May 1881	2	3	
Orzi	Louisa	m.	SWI	7 June 1884	3	4	
Osborne	Herbert	d.	PCo	16 Nov. 1881	2	5	murder-suicide
Osborne	L.	b.	RRF	14 Feb. 1884	2	4	
Osborne	S. L.	b.	PCo	20 Feb. 1884	3	6	
Osborne	S. L.	b.	SD	1 Mar. 1884	6	6	

(1) Surname	(2) Given Name	(3)	(4)	(5) Date	(6) Pg	(7) Col	(8) Comments
Oster	Henry	m.	PCo	16 Dec. 1885	3	6	
Ottman	Alice V.	m.	CR	1 Jan. 1881	5	5	
Ottmer	Ida	m.	PCo	21 Mar. 1883	3	5	
Ottmer	Leora	m.	PCo	21 Mar. 1883	3	5	
Otto	Isabella	d.	DR	22 Aug. 1881	2	3	
Ottolini	Ciciglia	m.	PCo	18 Oct. 1882	3	6	
Ovendale	Harry	d.	PWA	22 Mar. 1884	3	6	
Ovendale	Henry	d.	PCo	26 Mar. 1884	3	6	
Overholser	Abraham	d.	DR	7 July 1884	3	3	
Overholser	Abraham W.	d.	PCo	2 July 1884	3	4	Cypress Hill Cem.
Overholser	Abraham W.	d.	PWA	5 July 1884	3	6	
Overholser	Abraham W.	d.	SD	12 July 1884	6	8	
Overholser	Abraham Whitmore	d.	PWA	28 June 1884	3	3	
Overholser	William R.	b.	PCo	15 Mar. 1882	3	4	
Overholser	William R.	b.	SD	25 Mar. 1882	3	6	
Overton	J. H.	b.	DD	18 Oct. 1883	3	3	
Overton	J. H.	b.	PCo	26 Apr. 1882	3	4	
Overton	J. H.	b.	PWA	20 Oct. 1883	3	8	
Overton	J. H.	b.	SD	29 Apr. 1882	3	6	
Overton	J. H.	b.	SD	20 Oct. 1883	3	4	
Overton	John P.	b.	DD	10 Dec. 1883	2	2	
Overton	John P.	m.	DR	18 May 1882	2	2	also p. 3 col. 1
Overton	John P.	m.	PCo	31 May 1882	3	5	
Overton	John P.	m.	SD	10 June 1882	2	3	
Overton	Nicholas R.	d.	PCo	7 Jan. 1885	3	6	
Overton	Nicholas Ragan	d.	SD	10 Jan. 1885	1	6	Rural Cemetery; also p. 2 col. 6; also p. 5 col. 5
Owen	Mary	m.	RRF	30 Nov. 1882	2	3	
Owendale	Harry	d.	SD	22 Mar. 1884	2	4	
Owens	Charles	d.	PCo	22 Apr. 1885	3	6	
Owens	Charles	m.	PCo	25 Feb. 1885	3	6	
O'Brien	George	b.	SD	6 Aug. 1881	3	8	
O'Brien	George (dau. of)	d.	SD	3 Sept. 1881	3	8	
O'Brien	Michael	b.	SD	12 Mar. 1881	3	8	
O'Casey	Edward	m.	CR	22 Oct. 1881	5	3	
O'Connell	W. J.	b.	PC	25 Apr. 1883	3	5	
O'Connell	W. J.	b.	PWA	28 Apr. 1883	3	8	
O'Conner	Thomas	b.	PCo	2 Dec. 1885	3	4	
O'Connor	J. B.	m.	SD	30 Apr. 1881	3	8	
O'Connor	J. B.	b.	SD	22 Aug. 1885	6	2	
O'Connor	Lucy A.	m.	SD	11 Aug. 1883	2	7	
O'Connor	Thomas	b.	PC	8 Aug. 1883	3	6	

(1) Surname	(2) Given Name	(3)	(4)	(5) Date	(6) Pg	(7) Col	(8) Comments
O'Connor	Thomas	b.	PWA	11 Aug. 1883	3	8	
O'Connor	Thomas	b.	SIT	28 Nov. 1885	2	3	
O'Dell	Link	d.	CR	29 Aug. 1885	3	5	
O'Donell	Jennie	m.	SD	12 Mar. 1881	3	8	
O'Farrell	Charles Francis	d.	SD	27 May 1882	3	5	
O'Ferrall	John M. C.	m.	SD	5 Mar. 1881	3	8	
O'Hara	B. E.	m.	DR	26 Sept. 1885	3	4	
O'Hara	B. E.	m.	PCo	23 Sept. 1885	3	6	
O'Hara	B. E.	m.	SRR	1 Oct. 1885	3	3	
O'Hara	Johana	d.	PCo	17 Sept. 1884	3	6	
O'Hara	Johana	d.	PWA	20 Sept. 1884	3	4	
O'Hara	John	b.	SD	16 Apr. 1881	3	8	
O'Hara	Mary	d.	SD	26 Feb. 1881	3	8	
O'Malley	Kate	m.	RRF	8 Feb. 1883	2	4	
O'Malley	Katie	m.	SD	10 Feb. 1883	2	7	
O'Mally	Kate	m.	PCo	14 Feb. 1883	3	6	
O'Melia	Bridget	d.	PCo	8 July 1885	3	6	
O'Neal	Parker	m.	DR	13 Feb. 1882	2	3	
O'Rear	A.B.	d.	SD	9 May 1885	2	5	also 16 May, p. 5 col. 4
O'Rear	Anjanette	d.	SD	6 June 1885	5	4	
O'Rear	W.E.	o.	DR	20 July 1882	3	1	
O'Rear	W.E.	o.	SD	22 July 1882	3	1	
O'Roarke	Jeremiah	d.	PCo	29 Mar. 1882	3	5	
O'Rourke	Jeremiah	d.	SD	1 Apr. 1882	3	6	

P & Q

(1) Surname	(2) Given Name	(3)	(4)	(5) Date	(6) Pg	(7) Col	(8) Comments
Pacheco	Elma Sarah	d.	PCo	9 Apr. 1884	3	6	
Packard	C. O.	b.	DD	23 July 1883	3	2	
Packard	Howard F.	m.	PCo	6 Dec. 1882	3	6	
Packard	J. E.	b.	DD	4 Dec. 1883	3	3	
Packard	Olive S.	m.	SD	25 Apr. 1885	2	5	
Paddock	Rebecca	d.	DR	10 Jun. 1881	2	2	
Paddock	Rebecca	d.	DR	15 June 1881	2	3	
Paddock	Rebecca	d.	SD	18 June 1881	3	8	
Page	C. A.	b.	SD	2 May 1885	2	5	
Page	R. H.	b.	SD	22 Jan. 1881	3	8	
Page	Wilfred	b.	DR	23 Oct. 1885	3	4	
Page	Wilfred	b.	PCo	21 Oct. 1885	3	4	
Page	Wilfred	b.	SD	7 Nov. 1885	3	4	
Paget	Lulu G.	m.	CR	27 Aug. 1881	5	4	
Paget	Lulu G.	m.	SD	3 Sept. 1881	3	8	
Paget	Lulu Genella	m.	DR	27 Aug. 1881	2	3	
Paget	Lulu Genella	m.	RRF	25 Aug. 1881	2	4	
Paget	Susie H.	m.	CR	27 Aug. 1881	5	4	
Paget	Susie Herron	m.	DR	27 Aug. 1881	2	3	
Paget	Susie Herron	m.	RRF	25 Aug. 1881	2	4	
Paine	Waldo John	d.	PCo	7 Jan. 1885	3	6	
Painter	J. M.	b.	PCo	5 Mar. 1884	3	6	
Painter	J. M.	b.	SD	1 Mar. 1884	6	6	
Palli	Fred	b.	PCo	13 Aug. 1884	3	4	
Palmer	A. B.	b.	CR	12 Mar. 1881	5	5	
Palmer	A. B.	b.	DR	5 Mar. 1881	3	2	
Palmer	A. B.	b.	SD	5 Mar. 1881	3	8	
Palmer	A. B.	b.	SD	19 Mar. 1881	3	8	
Palmer	Charles	d.	PC	30 May 1883	3	2	
Palmer	Charles	b.	SD	1 June 1881	3	7	
Palmer	J. A.	b.	PCo	2 Jan. 1884	3	6	
Palmer	J. A.	b.	PWA	5 Jan. 1884	3	7	
Palmer	J. A.	b.	SD	5 Jan. 1884	1	4	
Palmer	John A.	b.	PCo	5 Jan. 1881	3	4	
Palmer	John A.	b.	PCo	30 Dec. 1885	3	4	
Palmer	Percie	m.	DR	16 July 1881	2	2	
Palmer	Pierce, Miss	m.	PCo	20 July 1881	3	5	

(1) Surname	(2) Given Name	(3)	(4)	(5) Date	(6) Pg	(7) Col	(8) Comments
Palmer	Pierce	m.	SD	23 July 1881	3	8	
Palmer	S. G.	b.	DR	10 Oct. 1881	2	3	
Palmer	S. G.	b.	SD	8 Oct. 1881	3	8	
Palmer	Sarah L.	d.	DR	4 Nov. 1884	3	2	
Palmer	Sarah L.	d.	PCo	12 Nov. 1884	3	5	
Palmer	Sarah L.	d.	SD	8 Nov. 1884	2	5	
Palmer	Sarah P.	d.	SD	13 Dec. 1884	1	5	
Palmer	W. J.	m.	PWA	18 Oct. 1884	3	4	
Palmer	William J.	m.	PCo	15 Oct. 1884	3	6	
Palmer	William	d.	DR	20 Aug. 1881	2	3	
Palmer	William	d.	PCo	17 Aug. 1881	3	5	
Palmer	William	d.	SD	27 Aug. 1881	3	8	
Palocchi	Charles	m.	DR	1 Aug. 1884	3	3	
Palocchi	Charles	m.	PCo	6 Aug. 1884	2	4	
Palocchi	Charles	m.	SD	9 Aug. 1884	3	4	
Papera	Joseph	m.	SD	25 Apr. 1885	2	5	
Parker	C. L., Miss	m.	SD	26 Mar. 1881	3	8	
Parker	E. D.	b.	PCo	5 Aug. 1885	3	6	
Parker	E. S.	b.	DR	1 Aug. 1885	3	4	
Parker	Ella	m.	PCo	9 Mar. 1881	3	4	
Parker	Ella	m.	SD	5 Mar. 1881	3	8	
Parker	G. W.	b.	DR	29 Aug. 1885	3	4	
Parker	L.	b.	SD	21 May 1881	3	8	
Parkerson	(male)	b.	DR	10 May 1884	3	2	
Parkerson	Annabella	m.	PCo	28 June 1882	3	5	
Parkerson	Annabella	m.	SD	8 July 1882	2	5	
Parkerson	H.	b.	PCo	7 May 1884	3	5	
Parkerson	H.	b.	PCo	14 May 1884	3	4	
Parkerson	H.	b.	PWA	10 May 1884	3	5	
Parkerson	H.	b.	SD	17 May 1884	3	5	
Parkerson	Henry	m.	PCo	28 Feb. 1883	3	5	
Parkerson	Henry	m.	PWA	3 Mar. 1883	3	6	
Parkerson	Henry	m.	SD	3 Mar. 1883	2	6	
Parks	Alva W.	d.	DR	1 Apr. 1884	1	5	
Parks	Alvah M.	d.	PCo	9 Apr. 1884	3	6	
Parks	Alvah M.	d.	SD	5 Apr. 1884	2	5	Rural Cem.; also p. 3 col. 4
Parks	Kittie	m.	PCo	10 Jan. 1883	3	6	
Parks	Kittie	m.	PWA	12 Jan. 1883	3	6	
Parmeter	Bessie	m.	PWA	29 Dec. 1883	3	6	
Parmeter	Hattie	m.	DD	24 Dec. 1883	3	2	
Parmeter	Hattie	m.	PCo	26 Dec. 1883	3	5	

(1) Surname	(2) Given Name	(3)	(4)	(5) Date	(6) Pg	(7) Col	(8) Comments
Parmeter	Hattie	m.	SD	29 Dec. 1883	3	6	
Parrish	David	b.	DR	4 Sept. 1885	3	4	
Parrish	David F.	b.	PCo	2 Sept. 1885	3	6	
Parrish	Nancy A.	d.	SD	19 May 1883	3	5	
Parsons	Alfred H.	m.	DR	11 Feb. 1882	2	3	
Parsons	Alfred H.	m.	SD	18 Feb. 1882	3	6	
Parsons	Charles S.	d.	PCo	1 Nov. 1882	3	5	
Parsons	Charles S.	d.	PWA	15 Sept. 1883	3	6	
Parsons	Effie	m.	PCo	9 Jan. 1884	3	6	
Parsons	Effie	m.	PWA	12 Jan. 1884	3	7	
Parsons	Effie	m.	SD	19 Jan. 1884	3	6	
Parsons	Mary	d.	PCo	16 Feb. 1881	3	4	
Parsons	Mary	d.	SD	5 Mar. 1881	3	8	
Parsons	Mary	d.	SD	19 Feb. 1881	3	8	
Parsons	Olive May Brians	m.	DR	25 July 1884	3	3	
Parton	Mary	d.	DR	29 Aug. 1885	3	4	
Parton	Mary	d.	PCo	2 Sept. 1885	3	6	
Pasell	A. F.	p.	DR	16 July 1884	3	2	
Pasmore	family	o.	CR	27 Oct. 1883	3	3	
Passalacqua	Frank	b.	CR	12 Nov. 1881	5	3	
Passalacqua	Frank	b.	SD	19 Nov. 1881	4	8	
Passalaqua	Frank	b.	DR	14 Nov. 1881	2	3	
Passalaqua	Frank	b.	PCo	16 Nov. 1881	3	5	
Passalaqua	Frank	b.	RRF	17 Nov. 1881	2	3	
Patocchi	Charles	m.	PWA	9 Aug. 1884	2	4	
Patrick	Ada	m.	RRF	3 Feb. 1881	3	4	
Patrick	Henry	m.	SD	14 June 1884	2	4	
Patrick	James	b.	DR	16 Dec. 1881	2	2	
Patrick	James	b.	HE	15 Dec. 1881	2	4	
Patrick	James	b.	PCo	21 Dec. 1881	3	5	
Patrick	James	b.	RRF	15 Dec. 1881	2	4	
Patrick	James	b.	RRF	6 Sept. 1883	2	4	
Patrick	James	b.	SD	24 Dec. 1881	2	3	
Patrick	James	b.	SD	15 Sept. 1883	2	4	
Patrick	Joseph	b.	DD	8 Sept. 1883	3	3	
Patten	William S.	m.	DR	13 July 1885	3	4	
Patterson	C. L.	m.	CR	11 June 1881	5	5	
Patterson	C. L.	m.	DR	4 June 1881	2	2	
Patterson	C. L.	m.	RRF	2 June 1881	2	3	
Patterson	C. L.	m.	SD	11 June 1881	3	8	
Patterson	Edward	b.	DR	17 June 1882	3	2	

(1) Surname	(2) Given Name	(3)	(4)	(5) Date	(6) Pg	(7) Col	(8) Comments
Patterson	Edward	b.	PCo	21 June 1882	3	5	
Patterson	Edward	b.	RRF	15 June 1882	2	4	
Patterson	Edward	b.	SD	17 June 1882	2	4	
Patterson	G. H.	m.	SD	23 Dec. 1882	2	5	
Patterson	J. H.	b.	SD	5 May 1883	2	6	
Patterson	Joshua	m.	DR	26 Sept. 1881	3	2	
Patterson	Joshua	m.	RRF	22 Sept. 1881	2	5	
Patterson	Joshua	m.	SD	8 Oct. 1881	3	8	
Patterson	Mollie	m.	DR	5 Aug. 1881	2	2	
Patterson	Mollie	m.	SD	6 Aug. 1881	3	8	
Patterson	Mollie	m.	SD	20 Aug. 1881	3	8	
Patterson	Robert	m.	RRF	2 June 1881	3	2	
Patterson	Sol. (Solomon?)	b.	PCo	16 Aug. 1882	3	6	
Patterson	Walter F.	d.	SD	5 Mar. 1881	3	8	
Patteson	C. L.	b.	DD	.2 Nov. 1883	3	2	
Patteson	C. L.	b.	RRF	1 Nov. 1883	2	2	
Patteson	C. L.	b.	SD	10 Nov. 1883	3	5	
Patteson	Mollie	m.	RRF	11 Aug. 1881	2	5	
Patteson	Sol	b.	DR	12 Aug. 1882	3	2	
Patteson	Sol	b.	RRF	10 Aug. 1882	2	4	
Patteson	Sol	b.	SD	12 Aug. 1882	3	5	
Patton	A. R.	d.	CR	30 Apr. 1881	4	3	
Patton	Mary	o.	SIT	5 Sept. 1885	2	3	
Patton	Mary S.	d.	DR	15 June 1881	2	3	
Patton	Mary S.	p.	DR	6 Dec. 1884	2	1	
Patton	Mary S.	d.	SD	25 June 1881	3	8	
Patton	R. R.	o.	SIT	5 Sept. 1885	2	3	
Patton	Robert A.	d.	DR	29 Apr. 1881	3	2	
Patton	Robert A.	d.	PCo	27 Apr. 1881	3	5	
Patton	Robert A.	d.	RRF	5 May 1881	2	4	
Patton	Robert A.	d.	SD	7 May 1881	3	8	
Patton	William S.	m.	SD	18 July 1885	5	5	
Patty	D. L.	b.	PCo	16 Feb. 1881	3	4	
Patty	L. H.	b.	SD	19 Feb. 1881	3	8	
Paul	Lee	d.	DR	17 Dec. 1885	3	4	
Paul	Leo	d.	PCo	23 Dec. 1885	3	2&4	Cypress Hill
Paul	Louise K.	m.	CR	1 Jan. 1881	5	5	
Paulacei	A.	m.	PCo	1 Apr. 1885	3	6	
Paulacei	A.	m.	PWA	4 Apr. 1885	3	6	
Paulacei	A.	m.	SD	4 Apr. 1885	2	5	
Pauli	A. F.	m.	DR	16 Nov. 1885	3	4	

(1) Surname	(2) Given Name	(3)	(4)	(5) Date	(6) Pg	(7) Col	(8) Comments
Pauli	A. F.	m.	SIT	14 Nov. 1885	2	3	
Pauli	F. A.	b.	PCo	21 Mar. 1883	3	5	
Pauli	F. A.	b.	PWA	24 Mar. 1883	3	7	
Pauli	R. J.	b.	PCo	14 Feb. 1883	3	6	
Pauli	R. J.	b.	PWA	17 Feb. 1883	3	7	
Pauli	R. J.	m.	SD	15 Oct. 1881	3	1&8	
Pauli	R. J.	b.	SWI	10 Feb. 1883	2	3	
Pauli	Robert J.	m.	DR	12 Oct. 1881	2	3	
Pauli	Robert J.	m.	PCo	12 Oct. 1881	3	5	
Paxton	B. W.	m.	PCo	2 Aug. 1882	3	6	
Paxton	B. W.	m.	SD	5 Aug. 1882	3	5	
Paxton	Blitz	m.	RRF	15 June 1882	3	4	
Paxton	Blitz W.	m.	RRF	27 July 1882	2	4	
Paxton	D. E.	m.	SD	21 Apr. 1883	2	6	
Paxton	Maggie	d.	SD	18 Feb. 1882	3	6	
Pearce	George	b.	PCo	20 Sept. 1882	3	6	
Pearce	George	b.	SD	23 Sept. 1882	3	6	
Pearce	John	b.	PC	9 May 1883	3	5	
Pearce	John	b.	PWA	12 May 1883	3	8	
Pearce	John	b.	SD	19 May 1883	3	5	
Pearson	Walter	m.	SD	16 June 1883	2	6	
Peatross	John H.	m.	DR	1 Feb. 1884	3	3	
Peatross	John H.	m.	PCo	6 Feb. 1884	3	6	
Peatross	John H.	m.	PWA	9 Feb. 1884	3	6	
Peatross	John H.	m.	SD	9 Feb. 1884	1	3	
Peavey	Charles C.	d.	DR	19 Oct. 1885	3	4	
Peavey	Charles C.	d.	PCo	21 Oct. 1885	3	4	
Peck	H. W.	b.	DR	26 Aug. 1885	3	4	
Peck	H. W.	b.	PCo	28 Feb. 1883	3	5	
Peck	H. W.	b.	RRF	1 Mar. 1883	2	4	
Peck	H. W.	m.	SD	22 July 1882	3	5	
Peck	Harvey W.	m.	PCo	19 July 1882	3	6	
Peck	Harvey W.	m.	RRF	13 July 1882	2	3	
Peck	John, Jr.	b.	PCo	7 Oct. 1885	3	6	
Peck	John, Jr.	b.	SD	10 Oct. 1885	5	5	
Peck	John R.	m.	PCo	15 Oct. 1884	3	6	
Peck	Loring	b.	SD	19 Dec. 1885	3	4	
Peck	Morris	b.	DD	20 Oct. 1883	3	3	
Peck	P. S.	d.	RRF	9 Feb. 1882	3	1	Oak Mound, Healdsburg
Peck	Philip S.	d.	RRF	9 Feb. 1882	2	3	
Peck	Sarah A.	d.	DR	9 Feb. 1882	2	3	

(1) Surname	(2) Given Name	(3)	(4)	(5) Date	(6) Pg	(7) Col	(8) Comments
Peck	Sarah A.	d.	HE	9 Feb. 1882	3	2	also p. 2 col. 3
Peck	Sarah A.	d.	RRF	9 Feb. 1882	2	3	
Peck	Sarah A.	d.	SD	11 Feb. 1882	3	6	
Peck	Sarah A.	d.	SD	18 Feb. 1882	3	6	
Peck	Sarah	d.	PCo	15 Feb. 1882	3	4	
Peckenpah	Henry H.	d.	RRF	8 Dec. 1881	2	4	Pleasant Hill, Sebastopol
Peckenpah	Henry Harrison	d.	DR	5 Dec. 1881	2	3	
Peckenpah	Henry Harrison	d.	SD	10 Dec. 1881	3	7	
Peckinpah	H. H.	d.	CR	10 Dec. 1881	1	2	Pleasant Hill, Sebastopol
Peckinpah	H. H.	d.	CR	17 Dec. 1881	1	2	
Peckinpah	Henry H.	d.	PCo	14 Dec. 1881	3	4	
Pedrot	Louis	b.	PCo	4 Feb. 1885	3	6	
Pedrozini	Louis	b.	PCo	13 May 1885	3	6	
Peetrotti	Lewis	m.	SD	8 July 1882	2	5	
Peetrotti	Louis	m.	PCo	28 June 1882	3	5	
Pennington	William H.	m.	DD	10 Nov. 1883	3	3	
Peoples	Andrew	b.	PCo	21 Feb. 1883	3	5	
Peoples	Andrew	b.	PWA	17 Feb. 1883	3	7	
Peoples	Andrew	b.	SD	17 Feb. 1883	2	7	
Peoples	Nathan	d.	CR	4 Feb. 1882	1	3	
Peoples	Nathan	d.	SD	28 Jan. 1882	3	2&6	
Percival	E. C.	b.	PCo	4 Mar. 1885	3	6	
Percival	E. C.	b.	PWA	7 Mar. 1885	3	5	
Percival	E. C.	b.	SD	14 Mar. 1885	5	5	
Percival	Herbert	d.	DD	24 Sept. 1883	3	2	
Percival	Herbert	d.	PWA	22 Sept. 1883	3	6	
Percival	Margaret	d.	PCo	31 Jan. 1883	3	5	also col. 1
Percival	Margaret	d.	PWA	3 Feb. 1883	3	7	
Percival	Mrs.	d.	SD	3 Feb. 1883	3	3	
Percival	W. O.	d.	SD	29 Sept. 1883	2	6	
Percival	Walter C.	m.	PCo	2 Nov. 1881	3	5	
Percival	Walter C.	m.	SD	12 Nov. 1881	3	7	
Percival	Walter	m.	DR	7 Nov. 1881	2	3	
Perillat	Alexis	m.	SD	10 Feb. 1883	2	7	
Perin	Puabo	d.	CR	29 Jan. 1881	4	2	
Perinoni	Flippo	m.	DR	17 Aug. 1882	3	2	
Perkeson	William	d.	PC	18 Apr. 1883	3	5	
Perkins	Hazel	d.	DR	23 Dec. 1882	3	3	
Perkins	Hazel	d.	PCo	20 Dec. 1882	3	5	
Perkins	William L.	d.	DR	2 Oct. 1885	3	4	
Perreaud	Catherine	d.	PCo	7 Dec. 1881	3	5	

(1) Surname	(2) Given Name	(3)	(4)	(5) Date	(6) Pg	(7) Col	(8) Comments
Perry	A. C.	b.	SD	21 Apr. 1883	2	6	
Perry	Al	b.	PCo	11 Oct. 1882	3	6	
Perry	Al	b.	PCo	26 Dec. 1883	3	5	
Perry	Al	b.	PWA	29 Dec. 1883	3	6	
Perry	Al	b.	SD	29 Dec. 1883	3	6	
Perry	B.	m.	SD	16 June 1883	2	6	
Perry	Charles A.	m.	DR	14 Oct. 1885	3	4	
Perry	Elbridge G.	m.	DR	26 Jan. 1882	2	3	
Perry	Elbridge G.	m.	HE	26 Jan. 1882	2	3	
Perry	Ernest D.	b.	PCo	28 Oct. 1885	3	4	
Perry	Ernest W.	m.	PCo	31 Dec. 1884	3	4	
Perry	Ernest W.	m.	PWA	27 Dec. 1884	2	5	
Perry	Frank	m.	SD	12 Jan. 1884	3	6	
Perry	Frank O.	m.	DR	26 Aug. 1885	3	4	
Perry	Frank O.	m.	PCo	19 Aug. 1885	3	6	
Perry	George	m.	SD	17 Oct. 1885	2	7	also p. 4 col. 5
Perry	Grattan	m.	PCo	6 Dec. 1882	3	6	
Perry	H. R.	b.	PCo	3 Jan. 1883	3	4	
Perry	H. R.	b.	PWA	5 Jan. 1883	2	5	
Perry	H. R.	b.	SD	30 Dec. 1882	3	6	
Perry	H. R.	b.	SD	6 Jan. 1883	2	5	
Perry	Hattie M.	m.	DR	27 June 1882	2	3	
Perry	Lilian	m.	PCo	20 July 1881	3	5	
Perry	Lillian M.	m.	SD	23 July 1881	3	8	
Perry	Maggie	m.	SD	10 Jan. 1885	2	6	
Perry	Mira P. M.	m.	DR	11 Dec. 1884	3	2	
Perry	Mira P. M.	m.	PCo	17 Dec. 1884	2	4	
Perry	Mira P. M.	m.	SD	13 Dec. 1884	2	5	
Peter	Lillie B.	m.	RRF	8 Dec. 1881	2	4	
Peter	Lillie	m.	DR	9 Dec. 1881	2	3	
Peter	Lillie	m.	HE	8 Dec. 1881	2	3	
Peterey	J. B. A.	d.	SD	9 Sept. 1882	3	2	
Peterman	Christian	m.	SD	10 June 1882	2	3	
Peters	David	d.	PWA	2 Aug. 1884	3	4	
Peters	Freido	d.	DD	23 Aug. 1883	3	2	
Peters	Freido	d.	PC	22 Aug. 1883	3	5	
Peters	Freido	d.	PWA	25 Aug. 1883	3	8	
Peters	Freido	d.	SD	25 Aug. 1883	2	5	
Peters	Godfrey	b.	DD	20 July 1883	3	2	
Peters	Godfrey	b.	PC	18 July 1883	3	5	
Peters	Godfrey	b.	PWA	14 July 1883	3	6	

(1) Surname	(2) Given Name	(3)	(4)	(5) Date	(6) Pg	(7) Col	(8) Comments
Peters	Godfrey	b.	SD	28 July 1883	2	5	
Peters	Julius	b.	SD	19 Nov. 1881	4	8	
Peters	M.	b.	SD	28 June 1884	3	4	
Peters	Manuel	b.	PCo	11 June 1884	3	5	
Peters	Manuel	b.	PWA	7 June 1884	3	6	
Petersen	Julius	b.	PCo	9 Nov. 1881	3	5	
Petersen	Mr. & Mrs.	b.	PCo	2 Aug. 1882	3	6	
Petersen	Mr. & Mrs.	b.	SD	5 Aug. 1882	3	5	
Peterson	A.	b.	CR	19 Mar. 1881	4	3	
Peterson	A.	b.	DR	21 Nov. 1881	2	3	
Peterson	A.	b.	PCo	16 Mar. 1881	3	4	
Peterson	A.	b.	PCo	15 Mar. 1882	3	4	
Peterson	A.	b.	SD	19 Mar. 1881	3	8	
Peterson	A.	b.	SD	18 Mar. 1882	3	5	
Peterson	Albertine	m.	SD	13 June 1885	3	5	
Peterson	Allen J.	m.	PC	2 May 1883	3	5	
Peterson	C. D.	b.	PCo	12 Mar. 1884	3	6	
Peterson	Carl	b.	PCo	3 Sept. 1884	2	5	
Peterson	Carl	b.	SD	6 Sept. 1884	2	5	
Peterson	E.	b.	DR	23 June 1882	3	2	
Peterson	Frank	o.	SD	18 Nov. 1882	3	3	
Peterson	Frank	d.	SD	23 Nov. 1882	3	2	San Diego
Peterson	infant son	d.	SD	19 Aug. 1882	3	5	
Peterson	Joseph	b.	PCo	3 Sept. 1884	2	5	
Peterson	Joseph	b.	PWA	6 Sept. 1884	3	4	
Peterson	Joseph	b.	SD	13 Sept. 1884	3	4	
Peterson	Julius A.	b.	DD	26 July 1883	3	2	
Peterson	Julius A.	b.	PWA	28 July 1883	3	7	
Peterson	Julius A.	b.	SD	28 July 1883	2	5	
Peterson	Julius	b.	PCo	6 May 1885	3	6	
Peterson	Juluis A.	b.	PC	25 July 1883	3	6	
Peterson	Minnie H.	m.	DD	24 Sept. 1883	3	2	
Peterson	Minnie H.	m.	PWA	22 Sept. 1883	3	6	
Peterson	Minnie H.	m.	SD	29 Sept. 1883	2	6	
Peterson	Mr.	b.	CR	22 July 1882	5	3	
Peterson	Mr.	m.	RRF	1 June 1882	1	6	
Peterson	Mr.	b.	RRF	27 July 1882	2	4	
Peterson	Mr. & Mrs.	b.	DR	25 July 1882	2	3	
Peterson	Mr. & Mrs. (son of)	d.	PCo	16 Aug. 1882	3	6	
Peterson	P. G.	m.	DD	4 Dec. 1883	3	3	
Petery	J. B. A.	d.	SD	2 Sept. 1882	3	1	

(1) Surname	(2) Given Name	(3)	(4)	(5) Date	(6) Pg	(7) Col	(8) Comments
Petsersen	(female)	b.	DR	10 Mar. 1884	3	2	
Pettis	C. E.	b.	DD	24 Dec. 1883	3	2	
Pettis	Lillie May	d.	DR	28 Oct. 1884	2	3	
Pettis	Lillie May	d.	PCo	29 Oct. 1884	3	5	
Pettis	Lillie May	d.	SD	8 Nov. 1884	2	5	
Pettis	William	d.	PCo	24 Sept. 1884	3	5	
Pettit	A.	b.	PCo	14 Dec. 1881	3	4	
Pettit	A.	b.	SD	10 Dec. 1881	3	7	
Peugh	T. M.	d.	RRF	11 May 1882	3	2	
Peugh	T. M.	d.	SD	6 May 1882	3	2	
Peugh	Thomas M.	d.	DR	1 May 1882	3	1&2	
Peugh	Thomas	d.	HE	11 May 1882	3	3	
Pfefferley	L.	b.	PWA	28 Apr. 1883	3	8	
Pfefferley	L.	b.	SD	12 May 1883	2	6	
Pfeister	Julia	m.	DR	20 Aug. 1885	3	4	
Pfeister	Julia	m.	SD	29 Aug. 1885	2	4	
Pfifer	Minnie	m.	PCo	4 Feb. 1885	3	6	
Pflying	George	b.	DR	16 Aug. 1881	2	3	
Pflying	George	b.	SD	20 Aug. 1881	3	8	
Pflying	George (child of)	d.	DR	11 Oct. 1881	3	2	
Pflying	George (son of)	d.	SD	15 Oct. 1881	3	8	
Pfortner	Charles F.	m.	DD	21 Aug. 1883	3	3	
Pfortner	Charles F.	m.	SD	25 Aug. 1883	2	5	
Pharres	John, Mrs.	d.	PC	16 May 1883	3	5	
Pharris	Julia E.	d.	SD	19 May 1883	3	5	
Pharriss	John	d.	PWA	19 May 1883	3	8	
Phelps	Luthera	m.	RRF	19 July 1883	2	4	
Philbee	James	p.	DD	19 July 1883	3	2	
Philbee	James	d.	SD	21 June 1883	3	3	
Philbee	Mary E.	m.	DD	10 Oct. 1883	3	3	
Philbee	Mary E.	m.	SD	13 Oct. 1883	3	4	
Philbrick	D. O.	m.	DD	21 Aug. 1883	3	3	
Philbrook	D. C.	m.	DR	5 Oct. 1881	2	3	
Philbrook	D. C.	m.	SD	8 Oct. 1881	3	8	
Philbrook	Ernest E.	o.	SD	25 July 1885	1	3	
Philbrook	Herbert L.	d.	PCo	8 July 1885	3	6	
Philbrook	Herbert L.	d.	SD	4 July 1885	5	2	
Philbuck	D. O.	m.	SD	25 Aug. 1883	2	5	
Philip	John W.	m.	PCo	26 Oct. 1881	3	4	
Philip	John W.	m.	SD	22 Oct. 1881	3	6	
Philips	Edward	b.	RRF	26 Oct. 1882	2	3	

(1) Surname	(2) Given Name	(3)	(4)	(5) Date	(6) Pg	(7) Col	(8) Comments
Phillip	John W.	m.	DR	18 Oct. 1881	3	1	
Phillippini	Angelica	m.	PCo	26 Oct. 1881	3	4	
Phillippini	P.	m.	PCo	26 Oct. 1881	3	4	
Phillips	Clarence	m.	DR	20 Oct. 1885	3	4	
Phillips	E.	b.	PCo	14 Oct. 1885	3	6	
Phillips	E.	b.	SD	10 Oct. 1885	5	5	
Phillips	Ed	m.	CR	15 Jan. 1881	5	5	
Phillips	Ed	m.	RRF	6 Jan. 1881	2	5	
Phillips	Edward	m.	SD	8 Jan. 1881	3	8	
Phillips	Fred	b.	PCo	23 Jan. 1884	3	5	
Phillips	Fred	b.	RRF	17 Jan. 1884	2	4	
Phillips	George K.	m.	PCo	2 Aug. 1882	3	6	
Phillips	H. E.	b.	DR	8 Mar. 1882	2	3	
Phillips	H. E.	b.	PCo	15 Mar. 1882	3	4	
Phillips	H. E.	b.	SD	18 Mar. 1882	3	5	
Phillips	H. E. (son of)	d.	PCo	14 June 1882	3	5	
Phillips	H. E. (son of)	d.	SD	10 June 1882	2	3	
Phillips	Hattie W.	m.	PCo	2 Aug. 1882	3	6	
Phillips	Margaret	p.	DD	11 July 1883	3	2	
Phillips	Margaret	d.	DR	9 Nov. 1882	3	2	
Phillips	Margaret	d.	PCo	8 Nov. 1882	3	6	
Phillips	Susan E.	d.	DR	7 June 1882	3	2	
Phillips	Susan E.	d.	SD	10 June 1882	2	3	
Phillips	Theodore Frederick	m.	SD	3 Sept. 1881	3	8	
Phillips	V. W.	d.	DR	22 Mar. 1882	2	3	
Phillips	V. W.	d.	PCo	29 Mar. 1882	3	5	
Phillips	V. W.	d.	SD	25 Mar. 1882	3	6	
Phillips	Walter	b.	DR	22 Aug. 1882	3	2	
Phillips	Walter	b.	SD	2 Sept. 1882	3	6	
Phinney	Ann	m.	CR	17 Feb. 1883	3	1	
Phlips	Ed. (Edward?)	b.	PCo	1 Nov. 1882	3	5	
Pholey	F.	b.	PCo	6 Aug. 1884	2	4	
Pholey	F.	b.	SD	9 Aug. 1884	3	4	
Pickerell	Joseph W.	m.	DD	17 Oct. 1883	3	3	
Pickerell	W.	m.	SD	20 Oct. 1883	3	4	
Pickett	Betsy H.	d.	PCo	4 Feb. 1885	3	6	
Pickett	Betsy H.	d.	PWA	7 Feb. 1885	3	5	
Pickett	Remington F.	d.	PCo	10 Dec. 1884	3	5	
Pickett	Remington F.	d.	PWA	13 Dec. 1884	3	4	
Pickett	Remington Frazier	d.	SD	13 Dec. 1884	2	5	
Pickett	Remington	d.	DR	6 Dec. 1884	3	2	

(1) Surname	(2) Given Name	(3)	(4)	(5) Date	(6) Pg	(7) Col	(8) Comments
Pickle	Frances Isabel	d.	SD	18 Apr. 1885	2	5	
Pickle	J. F.	b.	RRF	28 Apr. 1881	2	3	
Picknell	C. M.	m.	SD	18 Apr. 1885	2	4	
Pidancet	Adrien	m.	SD	12 Mar. 1881	3	8	
Pieratt	A. L.	b.	SD	22 Jan. 1881	3	8	
Pieratt	John	o.	SD	4 Feb. 1882	2	4	
Pieratt	Mary Elizabeth	d.	DR	23 Apr. 1884	3	2	
Pieratt	Mary Elizabeth	d.	PWA	26 Apr. 1884	3	6	
Pierce	Abraham J.	d.	PC	2 May 1883	3	2	also May 9 p. 3 col. 4 & 5
Pierce	Abraham Jewell	d.	PWA	5 May 1883	3	2&8	Cypress Hill Cem.
Pierce	Abraham Jewell	d.	PWA	19 May 1883	3	2	
Pierce	Arthur L.	d.	CR	11 Feb. 1882	1	3	
Pierce	Arthur L.	d.	SD	4 Feb. 1882	3	2	
Pierce	John C.	m.	DR	21 Jan. 1882	3	2	
Pierce	Mary A.	m.	PCo	18 Jan. 1882	3	5	
Piercey	Samuel	o.	CR	23 Apr. 1881	1	3	
Pierson	Lillie	m.	RRF	11 Jan. 1883	2	2	
Piezzi	S.	b.	DR	6 July 1882	3	2	
Piezzi	S.	b.	PCo	12 July 1882	3	5	
Piezzi	V.	b.	DR	7 Apr. 1881	2	3	
Piezzi	V.	b.	SD	16 Apr. 1881	3	8	
Piggott	James K.	m.	DR	27 Nov. 1885	3	4	
Piggott	James K.	m.	SD	5 Dec. 1885	1	7	
Pimm	H.	o.	PWA	9 Feb. 1884	3	3	
Piner	Rosa	d.	SD	21 Apr. 1883	2	6	
Piper	Maria	d.	SD	12 Mar. 1881	3	8	
Pizze	J.	b.	SD	24 June 1882	3	5	
Plag	F.	b.	RRF	2 Feb. 1882	3	7	
Plag	F.	b.	SD	4 Feb. 1882	3	6	
Plagge	George W.	d.	CR	28 July 1883	3	1	
Platt	Annie	m.	PWA	28 Apr. 1883	3	2	
Plow	Georgina Sophie	m.	PCo	12 Oct. 1881	3	5	
Plow	Georgina Sophy	m.	DR	14 Oct. 1881	2	3	
Plow	Georgina Sophy	m.	SD	22 Oct. 1881	3	6	
Plumb	Clara Starr	m.	DR	16 Nov. 1882	2	3	
Plumb	Clara Starr	m.	RRF	16 Nov. 1882	2	4	
Poe	Mattie	d.	SD	28 Jan. 1882	3	6	
Poehlman	Henry	b.	PCo	21 Jan. 1885	2	5	
Poehlman	Henry	b.	PWA	17 Jan. 1885	2	4	
Poehlman	Henry J.	m.	PCo	26 Mar. 1884	3	6	
Poehlman	Henry J.	m.	PWA	29 Mar. 1884	3	6	

(1) Surname	(2) Given Name	(3)	(4)	(5) Date	(6) Pg	(7) Col	(8) Comments
Poehlman	Henry J.	m.	SD	29 Mar. 1884	2	5	
Poggie	Frank	b.	RRF	16 Nov. 1882	2	4	
Pola	Mary	d.	DR	9 Nov. 1882	3	2	
Pola	Mary	d.	PCo	8 Nov. 1882	3	6	
Polack	Mary	o.	CR	21 Nov. 1885	1	4	
Polk	C. E.	b.	DR	1 Aug. 1885	3	4	
Polk	J. J.	d.	PCo	1 June 1881	3	4	
Poncet	J.	b.	SD	11 Mar. 1882	3	6	
Ponset	J.	b.	PCo	15 Mar. 1882	3	4	
Pontius	R. W.	m.	SD	13 Dec. 1884	2	5	
Pool	Abbey	m.	RRF	22 Dec. 1881	2	3	
Pool	Abbie	m.	SD	24 Dec. 1881	2	3	
Pool	Abby	m.	DR	17 Dec. 1881	2	2	
Pool	Abby	m.	HE	15 Dec. 1881	2	4	
Pool	Abby	m.	PCo	21 Dec. 1881	3	5	
Pool	Noah	d.	DR	17 Aug. 1882	3	2	
Pool	Noah	d.	RRF	31 Aug. 1882	2	4	
Pool	Noah	d.	SD	2 Sept. 1882	3	6	
Pool	Robert	b.	DD	4 Dec. 1883	3	3	
Pool	Robert	b.	RRF	29 Nov. 1883	2	3	
Pool	Robert	b.	SD	8 Dec. 1883	3	1	
Pope	Charles J.	b.	PWA	8 Mar. 1884	3	6	
Poppe	Charles J.	m.	PC	4 Apr. 1883	3	5	
Poppe	Charles J.	b.	PCo	5 Mar. 1884	3	6	
Poppe	Charles J.	m.	PWA	7 Apr. 1883	2	3	
Poppe	E. A.	o.	DR	26 Oct. 1882	2	1	
Poppe	Emma	m.	SWI	25 Aug. 1883	3	2	
Poppe	Katherine	m.	DR	17 Dec. 1881	2	2	
Poppe	Katherine	m.	PCo	28 Dec. 1881	3	6	
Poppe	Katherine	m.	SD	24 Dec. 1881	2	3	
Porch	H.	b.	DR	4 Nov. 1881	2	3	
Porter	A. A.	b.	DD	1 Sept. 1883	3	2	
Porter	A.	b.	SD	19 Mar. 1881	3	8	
Porter	James L.	d.	HE	19 Jan. 1882	3	4&2	Oak Mound Cemetery
Porter	James L.	d.	RRF	19 Jan. 1882	3	2	Oak Mound Cemetery
Porter	Sarah	m.	DD	15 Dec. 1883	3	1	
Porter	Sarah	m.	PCo	19 Dec. 1883	3	4	
Porter	Sarah	m.	SD	22 Dec. 1883	3	5	
Porterfield	J. W.	o.	CR	28 May 1881	5	4	
Porterfield	William H.	b.	PCo	1 July 1885	3	6	
Porterfield	William	m.	PCo	4 June 1884	3	5	

(1) Surname	(2) Given Name	(3)	(4)	(5) Date	(6) Pg	(7) Col	(8) Comments
Porterfield	William	m.	DR	30 May 1884	3	2	
Poso	(Indian)	d.	PCo	28 Feb. 1883	3	3	
Post	Rachael	d.	SD	16 July 1881	3	8	
Post	Rachel	d.	PCo	6 July 1881	3	5	
Potter	Maggie	m.	DD	18 Oct. 1883	3	3	
Potter	Maggie	m.	SD	20 Oct. 1883	3	4	
Potter	Margaret	m.	PWA	13 Oct. 1883	3	8	
Potter	Samuel	d.	CR	3 Nov. 1883	3	1	
Potter	Samuel	d.	DD	25 Oct. 1883	3	2	
Potter	Samuel	d.	PWA	27 Oct. 1883	3	1	
Potter	Samuel	d.	SD	27 Oct. 1883	3	3&4	
Powell	Moses	b.	SD	23 July 1881	3	8	
Powell	Robert	d	SD	5 Dec. 1885	1	6	
Powers	David P.	m.	DR	12 Mar. 1884	3	2	
Powers	David P.	m.	PCo	19 Mar. 1884	3	6	
Powers	David P.	m.	SD	22 Mar. 1884	2	4	
Pozzi	Mary C.	d.	PCo	7 June 1882	3	5	
Pozzi	Morris C.	d.	SD	3 June 1882	2	4	
Pozzi	Morris C., Mrs.	d.	DR	7 June 1882	3	2	
Prather	W. J.	m.	DD	29 Dec. 1883	3	3	
Prescott	Asa	d.	PCo	2 Dec. 1885	3	2&4	
Prescott	Asa	d.	SD	12 Dec. 1885	4	1	
Prescott	Sophia	d.	PC	23 May 1883	3	5	
Prescott	Sophia	d.	PWA	26 May 1883	3	7	
Pressey	Daniel	d.	SD	11 Mar. 1882	3	4	
Pressey	R. W.	d.	DR	4 Nov. 1881	2	3	
Pressy	D.	d.	RRF	16 Mar. 1882	2	3	
Preston	J. M.	b.	PCo	1 June 1881	3	4	
Preston	J. M.	b.	PCo	6 Feb. 1884	3	6	
Preston	J. M.	b.	PWA	9 Feb. 1884	3	6	
Preston	J. M.	b.	SD	4 June 1881	3	8	
Preston	J. M.	b.	SD	16 Feb. 1884	2	5	
Preston	R. M.	d.	DR	23 Mar. 1882	2	3	
Preston	R. M.	d.	PCo	29 Mar. 1882	3	5	
Preston	R. M.	d.	PCo	29 Mar. 1882	3	2	
Preston	R. M.	d.	SD	1 Apr. 1882	3	6	
Preston	R. M.	d.	SD	25 Mar. 1882	3	2	
Prewett	James, Sr.	d.	CR	15 Apr. 1882	1	2	
Price	A.	b.	PCo	7 Jan. 1885	3	6	
Price	A.	b.	PCo	14 Jan. 1885	3	6	
Price	Andrew	b.	RRF	15 Nov. 1883	2	3	

(1) Surname	(2) Given Name	(3)	(4)	(5) Date	(6) Pg	(7) Col	(8) Comments
Price	E.	b.	CR	22 Jan. 1881	5	5	
Price	E.	b.	DR	24 Jan. 1881	3	2	
Price	E.	b.	RRF	20 Jan. 1881	2	5	
Price	E.	b.	SD	29 Jan. 1881	3	8	
Price	Lucetta	d.	DR	24 Nov. 1885	3	4	
Price	W. F.	m.	PWA	14 June 1884	3	6	
Price	W. G.	m.	DR	7 June 1884	3	3	
Prick	Herbert Austin	d.	DR	9 Nov. 1885	2	2	
Prince	Beatrice	d.	DD	16 Jan. 1884	3	3	
Prince	Mrs.	d.	PCo	16 Nov. 1881	2	5	murder-suicide
Prince	Peter	b.	DR	6 July 1881	2	5	
Prince	Peter	b.	SD	16 July 1881	3	8	
Prince	Peter	b.	SD	7 Oct. 1882	3	6	
Prindle	Henry (son of)	d.	PCo	22 Apr. 1885	3	6	
Pritchett	Eleanor E.	m.	HE	29 Nov. 1883	3	3	also p. 2 col. 4
Pritchett	Eleanor	m.	CR	1 Dec. 1883	3	1	
Pritchett	Eleanor	m.	DD	4 Dec. 1883	3	3	
Pritchett	Eleanor	m.	RRF	29 Nov. 1883	2	3	
Pritchett	Eleanor	m.	SD	8 Dec. 1883	3	1	
Pritz	William	d.	CR	4 Mar. 1882	1	3	
Pritz	William	d.	HE	23 Feb. 1882	3	4	
Proctor	Effie L.	m.	PCo	18 Feb. 1885	3	6	
Proctor	Effie L.	m.	PWA	21 Feb. 1885	3	5	
Proctor	Effie L.	m.	SD	21 Feb. 1885	2	5	
Proctor	Ira	b.	RRF	5 Apr. 1883	2	3	
Proctor	Lou Emma	m.	SD	3 Sept. 1881	3	8	
Proctor	Thomas A.	m.	DR	15 May 1884	3	2	
Proctor	Thomas A.	m.	SD	24 May 1884	1	6	
Proctor	William M.	d.	SD	19 July 1884	1	8	Rural Cemetery
Prouse	Sylvester	m.	RRF	18 Jan. 1883	2	3	
Prouse	Sylvester W.	m.	PCo	24 Jan. 1883	3	5	
Prows	(male)	b.	DR	17 May 1884	3	2	
Prows	A.	m.	PCo	17 Jan. 1883	3	5	
Prows	S. W.	b.	RRF	15 May 1884	5	6	
Prows	S. W.	b.	SD	24 May 1884	2	3	
Prows	Sylvester W.	m.	SD	13 Jan. 1883	3	5	
Pullen	Annie R.	m.	SD	10 Jan. 1885	2	6	
Purine	William	b.	SD	13 Dec. 1884	2	5	
Purkerson	Emma Rose	m.	SD	21 Jan. 1882	3	6	
Purkinson	Emma R.	m.	HE	26 Jan. 1882	3	3	
Purrington	Samuel	m.	PCo	7 Jan. 1885	3	6	

(1) Surname	(2) Given Name	(3)	(4)	(5) Date	(6) Pg	(7) Col	(8) Comments
Purrington	Samuel	m.	SD	10 Jan. 1885	2	6	
Purrington	Samuel W.	m.	PWA	10 Jan. 1885	3	2&4	
Purvine	T. B.	m.	PCo	27 Sept. 1882	3	6	
Purvine	T. B.	b.	PWA	10 Nov. 1883	3	8	
Purvine	T. E.	m.	DR	2 Oct. 1882	2	3	
Purvine	W. B.	m.	CR	19 Mar. 1881	4	3	
Purvine	W. B.	m.	DR	21 Nov. 1881	2	3	
Purvine	W. B.	m.	PCo	16 Mar. 1881	3	4	
Purvine	W. B.	m.	SD	19 Mar. 1881	3	8	
Purvine	William	b.	DR	21 Dec. 1882	2	2	
Purvine	William	b.	DR	8 Dec. 1884	3	2	
Purvine	William	b.	PCo	21 Dec. 1881	3	5	
Purvine	William	b.	PCo	20 Dec. 1882	3	5	
Purvine	William	b.	PCo	3 Dec. 1884	3	5	
Purvine	William	b.	PWA	6 Dec. 1884	3	4	
Purvine	William	b.	SD	31 Dec. 1881	3	6	
Putnam	Charles B.	m.	DD	4 Oct. 1883	3	2	
Putnam	Charles S.	m.	PWA	6 Oct. 1883	3	8	
Putnam	Hattie	m.	PCo	1 Oct. 1884	3	5	
Putnam	Hattie	m.	SD	4 Oct. 1884	3	5	
Putnam	Lillian I.	m.	DR	24 June 1884	3	3	
Putnam	Lillian I.	m.	PWA	21 June 1884	3	5	
Putnam	Marcus M.	d.	PC	4 July 1883	3	5	
Putnam	Marcus M.	d.	PWA	7 July 1883	3	6	
Pyatt	John	b.	SD	1 Apr. 1882	3	6	
Pyne	H. H.	b.	PC	13 June 1883	3	6	
Pyne	H. H.	b.	RRF	7 June 1883	2	3	
Pyne	H. H.	b.	SD	16 June 1883	2	6	
Pyne	Henry H.	m.	PCo	14 Dec. 1881	3	4	
Pyne	Henry H.	m.	RRF	1 Dec. 1881	2	3	
Pyne	Henry H.	m.	SD	10 Dec. 1881	3	7	
Quackenbush	Alfred	o.	SD	2 Apr. 1881	3	4	murder trial
Quackenbush	R. M.	m.	DR	25 July 1885	3	3	
Queen	C.	m.	SD	2 June 1883	2	7	
Queen	C.	b.	SD	19 July 1884	2	5	
Quick	William	d.	SD	2 Apr. 1881	3	8	
Quick	William	d.	SD	26 Mar. 1881	3	8	
Quill	John	d.	DR	18 Dec. 1882	2	3	
Quinlan	M.	b.	PCo	21 Mar. 1883	3	5	
Quinlan	Martin	b.	PCo	28 Dec. 1881	3	6	
Quinlan	Martin	m.	SD	19 Mar. 1881	3	8	

(1) Surname	(2) Given Name	(3)	(4)	(5) Date	(6) Pg	(7) Col	(8) Comments
Quinlan	Martin	b.	SD	24 Dec. 1881	2	3	
Quinlin	Martin	d.	DR	17 Dec. 1881	2	2	
Quinliven	D.	b.	SD	19 Feb. 1881	3	8	
Quinn	P. H.	b.	PCo	2 Aug. 1882	3	6	
Quinn	P. H.	b.	RRF	27 July 1882	2	4	
Quinn	P. H.	b.	SD	5 Aug. 1882	3	5	
Quitzow	Carolina	d.	DD	.2 Nov. 1883	3	2	
Quitzow	Carolina	d.	SD	10 Nov. 1883	3	5	

R

(1) Surname	(2) Given Name	(3)	(4)	(5) Date	(6) Pg	(7) Col	(8) Comments
Raabe	Detlef	b.	SD	12 Mar. 1881	3	8	
Rabstock	John	d.	DR	20 Aug. 1885	3	4	
Rackliff	Eugene	m.	RRF	6 Jan. 1881	2	5	
Rackliff	Eugene	m.	SD	8 Jan. 1881	3	8	
Rackliffe	Eugene	m.	CR	1 Jan. 1881	5	5	
Rackliffe	Eugene	m.	DR	11 Jan. 1881	3	2	
Radcliffe	Viola	m.	DR	23 Feb. 1882	2	3	
Rader	John	m.	SD	2 Apr. 1881	3	8	
Rafter	James	d.	CR	19 Feb. 1881	1	4	
Rafter	Jerome	b.	SD	13 Aug. 1881	3	8	
Ragle	Alexander	m.	PCo	17 Jan. 1883	3	5	
Ragle	Alexander	m.	SD	13 Jan. 1883	3	1	
Ragsdale	J. W. (son of)	d.	CR	18 Mar. 1882	5	1	
Ragsdale	J. W. (son of)	d.	DR	20 Mar. 1882	2	3	
Ragsdale	J. W. (son of)	d.	PCo	22 Mar. 1882	3	5	
Ragsdale	J. W. (son of)	d.	SD	18 Mar. 1882	3	5	
Ragsdale	J. W.	b.	PCo	22 Mar. 1882	3	5	
Ragsdale	J. W.	b.	PCo	25 Feb. 1885	3	6	
Ragsdale	J. W.	d.	RRF	16 Mar. 1882	2	4	
Ragsdale	J. W.	b.	RRF	16 Mar. 1882	2	4	
Ragsdale	J. W.	b.	SD	18 Mar. 1882	3	5	
Ragsdale	J. W.	b.	SD	21 Feb. 1885	2	5	
Rahlves	A.	b.	DD	23 July 1883	3	2	
Railsback	F. A.	m.	SD	13 June 1885	3	5	
Railsback	Frank A.	m.	PCo	10 June 1885	3	6	
Rains	Gallant	d.	CR	24 Nov. 1883	3	1	
Rains	Gallant	b.	PCo	27 July 1881	3	5	
Rains	Gallant	b.	SD	6 Aug. 1881	3	8	
Rains	Margaret Morton	d.	PCo	10 Jan. 1883	3	6	
Rains	Margaret Morton	d.	PWA	12 Jan. 1883	3	6	
Rains	Margaret Morton	d.	SD	13 Jan. 1883	3	5	
Ramey	Lizzie B.	m.	DD	20 Oct. 1883	3	3	
Ramos	J. F.	m.	PCo	1 Apr. 1885	3	6	
Ramos	J. F.	m.	PWA	4 Apr. 1885	3	6	
Ramos	J. F.	m.	SD	4 Apr. 1885	2	5	
Ramos	Jose Francis	d.	DR	16 Sept. 1882	3	4	
Ramsey	Robert Lee	d.	SD	30 Apr. 1881	3	8	
Ranard	Anderson	d.	CR	8 Oct. 1881	1	2	

(1) Surname	(2) Given Name	(3)	(4)	(5) Date	(6) Pg	(7) Col	(8) Comments
Ranard	Anderson	d.	DR	3 Oct. 1881	2	3	
Ranard	Belle	m.	PCo	15 Oct. 1884	3	6	
Ranard	Isabella	m.	PWA	11 Oct. 1884	3	4	
Ranard	James Anderson	d.	PCo	28 Sept. 1881	3	5	
Ranard	James Anderson	d.	SD	8 Oct. 1881	3	8	
Rand	W. J.	d.	DR	25 Nov. 1882	3	1	
Rand	W. J.	d.	SD	2 Dec. 1882	3	5	
Randal	James S.	b.	CR	1 Jan. 1881	5	5	
Randall	Mary	m.	DR	1 Dec. 1885	3	4	
Rankin	Blanche	m.	SWI	22 Sept. 1883	2	3	
Rankin	Blanche	m.	SWI	22 Sept. 1883	3	3	
Ransom	George C.	b.	PWA	19 May 1883	3	8	
Ranson	George C.	b.	PC	16 May 1883	3	5	
Rasmussen	Mary	m.	PCo	1 Oct. 1884	3	5	
Rasmussen	Mary	m.	PWA	27 Sept. 1884	2	4	
Rasmussen	Mary	m.	SD	4 Oct. 1884	3	5	
Rawles	A. N.	b.	DD	18 Aug. 1883	3	3	
Rawles	A. N.	b.	DD	28 Aug. 1883	3	3	
Rawles	A. N.	m.	DR	19 Aug. 1881	2	2	
Rawles	A. N.	b.	PC	22 Aug. 1883	3	5	
Rawles	A. N.	b.	SD	1 Sept. 1883	2	7	
Rawles	A. N.	b.	SD	25 Aug. 1883	2	5	
Rawls	Joseph	d.	RRF	28 Apr. 1881	2	4	
Ray	George	b.	SD	24 Sept. 1881	3	8	
Ray	Lily	d.	SD	19 July 1884	2	5	
Ray	R. Belle	m.	PCo	4 Mar. 1885	3	6	
Ray	R. Belle	m.	PWA	28 Feb. 1885	3	5	
Ray	R. M.	b.	SD	13 Dec. 1884	2	5	
Ray	Robert	m.	CR	17 Mar. 1883	3		
Ray	Robert	m.	PCo	21 Mar. 1883	3	5	
Ray	Robert	m.	RRF	15 Mar. 1883	3	4	
Ray	Robert	m.	SD	17 Mar. 1883	3	5	
Raymond	C. F.	b.	SD	24 Jan. 1885	5	5	
Raymond	G.	b.	SD	12 Mar. 1881	3	8	
Raymond	M. A., Miss	m.	DR	5 Nov. 1885	3	4	
Raymond	M. A., Miss	m.	SD	7 Nov. 1885	2	2	also p. 3 col. 4
Raynard	P. B.	b.	DR	22 Feb. 1882	2	3	
Raynard	P. B.	b.	PCo	1 Mar. 1882	2	4	
Raynard	P. B.	b.	SD	25 Feb. 1882	3	6	
Rea	T. E.	b.	DR	29 Aug. 1882	3	2	
Rea	T. L.	b.	SD	19 Aug. 1882	3	5	
Read	May F.	d.	DR	28 Jan. 1884	3	3	

(1) Surname	(2) Given Name	(3)	(4)	(5) Date	(6) Pg	(7) Col	(8) Comments
Read	May F.	d.	PCo	30 Jan. 1884	3	6	
Read	Walter Howard	d.	DD	16 July 1883	3	2	
Reading	Lizzie	m.	DR	3 Sept. 1885	3	4	
Reading	Lizzie	m.	PCo	16 Sept. 1885	3	6	
Reading	Lizzie	m.	SD	5 Sept. 1885	2	4	
Reading	Lizzie	m.	SD	12 Sept. 1885	1	5	also p. 2 col. 4
Reardon	David	b.	DR	12 Aug. 1882	3	2	
Reardon	David	b.	PCo	16 Aug. 1882	3	6	
Reardon	David	b.	RRF	10 Aug. 1882	2	4	
Reardon	David	b.	SD	12 Aug. 1882	3	5	
Redmond	Martin D.	d.	CR	7 Nov. 1885	3	2	
Redmond	Martin D.	m.	DR	22 June 1882	3	1	
Redmond	Martin D.	m.	SD	24 June 1882	3	3&5	
Redmond	Martin David	d.	SD	7 Nov. 1885	2	2	also p. 3 col. 4
Redwine	Sam	b.	SD	21 Apr. 1883	2	6	
Reed	A. K.	b.	SD	19 Mar. 1881	3	8	
Reed	John (son of)	d.	DR	18 Sept. 1882	3	1	
Reed	Pliny W.	m.	DR	2 Nov. 1881	2	3	
Reed	Pliny W.	m.	PCo	9 Nov. 1881	3	5	
Reed	Pliny W.	m.	SD	12 Nov. 1881	3	7	
Reeves	Edward L.	m.	DD	15 Dec. 1883	3	1	
Regan	Daniel	d.	PCo	28 Feb. 1883	3	5	
Reid	Joseph B.	d.	SD	25 Aug. 1883	2	5	
Reiger	V.	b.	PCo	30 Jan. 1884	3	6	
Reilly	Mary A.	m.	SD	27 Oct. 1883	1	6	
Reinking	John W.	m.	DR	6 Sept. 1881			
Remmel	William A.	d.	PCo	6 Aug. 1884	2	4	
Remmel	William A.	d.	PCo	13 Aug. 1884	3	4	
Remmel	William A.	d.	SD	9 Aug. 1884	3	4	
Renault	Josephine	m.	PCo	1 Apr. 1885	3	6	
Renault	Josephine	m.	PWA	4 Apr. 1885	3	6	
Renault	Josephine	m.	SD	4 Apr. 1885	2	5	
Rendall	Nellie	d.	CR	30 Apr. 1881	5	5	
Rendall	Nellie	d.	DR	25 Apr. 1881	3	2	
Rendall	Nellie	d.	SD	30 Apr. 1881	3	8	
Rendall	S. A.	d.	CR	30 Apr. 1881	5	5	
Rendall	S. A.	b.	DR	7 June 1882	3	2	
Rendall	S. A.	b.	PCo	21 June 1882	3	5	
Rendall	S. A.	b.	SD	24 June 1882	3	5	
Renfrew	Annie	m.	PCo	10 Jan. 1883	3	6	
Renfrew	Annie	m.	RRF	4 Jan. 1883	2	2	
Rex	William	b.	DD	17 Oct. 1883	3	3	

(1) Surname	(2) Given Name	(3)	(4)	(5) Date	(6) Pg	(7) Col	(8) Comments
Rex	William	b.	SD	20 Oct. 1883	3	4	
Reynolds	C. F.	m.	RRF	4 Oct. 1883	2	3	
Reynolds	C. W.	m.	HE	11 Oct. 1883	2	2	
Reynolds	Eliza	d.	RRF	23 Mar. 1882	2	5	
Reynolds	Ezekial	m.	RRF	6 Jan. 1881	2	5	
Reynolds	Fannie B.	m.	PCo	22 June 1881	3	5	
Reynolds	Fannie M.	m.	DR	15 June 1881	2	3	
Reynolds	Fannie N.	m.	SD	18 June 1881	3	8	
Reynolds	H. J., Mrs.	m.	RRF	15 Nov. 1883	2	3	
Reynolds	Hannah	m.	CR	15 Jan. 1881	5	5	
Reynolds	Hannah	m.	RRF	6 Jan. 1881	2	5	
Reynolds	Hannah	m.	SD	8 Jan. 1881	3	8	
Reynolds	Minnie M.	m.	SD	24 Oct. 1885	1	4	
Reynolds	Sarah Jane	m.	DR	25 July 1885	3	3	
Reynolds	W. B., Mrs.	d.	PCo	4 Feb. 1885	3	6	
Reynolds	William B.	m.	PCo	9 Nov. 1881	3	5	
Reynolds	William B.	m.	SD	12 Nov. 1881	3	7	
Reynolds	William H.	m.	DR	5 Nov. 1881	2	3	
Rhoades	Alfred Alphonso	m.	CR	11 Oct. 1884	3	3	
Rhoades	Alzina	m.	PCo	14 Feb. 1883	3	6	
Rhoades	Alzina	m.	PWA	10 Feb. 1883	3	7	
Rhoades	Alzina	m.	SD	10 Feb. 1883	2	7	
Rhoades	Mary	m.	CR	1 July 1885	3	2	
Rhodes	Caroline	m.	CR	18 Nov. 1882	3	3	
Rhodes	Caroline	m.	PCo	29 Nov. 1882	3	6	
Rhodes	James	d.	DR	25 July 1884	3	3	
Rhodes	James	d.	PCo	30 July 1884	3	6	
Rhodes	James	d.	PWA	2 Aug. 1884	3	4	
Rhodes	Mary	m.	DR	13 July 1885	3	4	
Rhodes	Mr.	b.	CR	28 May 1881	5	1	
Rhodes	Mr. & Mrs.	b.	DR	16 May 1882	3	2	
Rhodes	Mr. & Mrs.	b.	PCo	17 May 1882	3	5	
Rhodes	Mr. & Mrs.	b.	SD	20 May 1882	2	4	
Rhodes	Nancy	m.	PCo	31 May 1882	3	5	
Rhodes	Nancy	m.	RRF	25 May 1882	2	3	
Rhodes	Nancy	m.	SD	3 June 1882	2	4	
Rhorer	Nellie	m.	SD	12 May 1883	2	6	
Ribli	(dau.)	d.	PCo	3 June 1885	3	6	
Ricabaugh	Seth	b.	SD	4 Mar. 1882	3	6	
Rice	James I.	d.	PCo	1 Oct. 1884	3	5	
Rice	James L.	d.	SD	4 Oct. 1884	3	5	

(1) Surname	(2) Given Name	(3)	(4)	(5) Date	(6) Pg	(7) Col	(8) Comments
Rice	John W.	d.	RRF	14 June 1883	2	3	Oak Mound Cemetery
Rich	H. J.	b.	DD	8 Sept. 1883	3	3	
Rich	H. J.	b.	RRF	6 Sept. 1883	2	4	
Rich	H. J.	b.	SD	15 Sept. 1883	2	4	
Rich	William B.	m.	DD	27 Aug. 1883	3	3	
Rich	William B.	m.	SD	1 Sept. 1883	2	7	
Richard	Josie	m.	SD	28 May 1881	3	8	
Richards	Helen	m.	PCo	10 Sept. 1884	3	6	
Richards	Helen	m.	SD	13 Sept. 1884	3	1	
Richards	Joseph	d.	DR	6 June 1882	3	2	
Richards	Josephine	m.	CR	28 May 1881	5	5	
Richards	Josephine	m.	DR	21 May 1881	2	3	
Richards	Josephine	m.	RRF	19 May 1881	2	4	
Richards	Josephine	m.	SD	4 June 1881	3	8	
Richardson	Alice E.	m.	SD	25 Mar. 1882	3	6	
Richardson	Belle E.	m.	SD	12 Mar. 1881	3	8	
Richardson	J. H.	d.	SD	13 Jan. 1883	3	5	
Richardson	Margaret	d.	DR	25 Nov. 1881	2	3	
Richardson	Margaret	d.	PCo	23 Nov. 1881	3	5	
Richardson	Margaret	d.	SD	3 Dec. 1881	3	8	
Richey	Ella E.	m.	DR	3 Nov. 1885	3	4	
Richie	John	d.	DR	17 Sept. 1885	3	4	
Richman	George W.	d.	RRF	21 July 1881	2	4	Oak Mound, Healdsburg
Richmond	G. W.	d.	DR	25 July 1881	2	3	
Rickett	Clara	m.	PCo	28 Jan. 1885	3	6	
Rickman	James	m.	PWA	6 Dec. 1884	3	4	
Rickman	James T.	m.	DR	6 Dec. 1884	3	2	
Rickman	James T.	m.	PCo	3 Dec. 1884	3	5	
Rickman	Lewis	b.	DR	24 Nov. 1885	3	4	
Rickman	Lewis	b.	PCo	18 Nov. 1885	3	4	
Rickman	Mr. & Mrs.	b.	DR	9 Nov. 1885	2	2	
Rickman	Thomas H.	d.	DR	9 Nov. 1885	2	2	
Rickman	Thomas H.	d.	SD	21 Nov. 1885	1	7	
Ricksecker	Mary A.	m.	PCo	7 Jan. 1885	3	6	
Ricksecker	Mary A.	m.	SD	3 Jan. 1885	2	7	
Ridenhauer	Ella	m.	PCo	22 Nov. 1882	3	5	
Ridenhour	Ella	m.	DR	17 Nov. 1882	2	3	
Ridgway	Jeremiah	d.	SD	18 Apr. 1885	1	6	
Ridgway	Jeremiah	d.	SD	21 Feb. 1885	2	5	also p. 5 col. 5
Ridgway	Jeremiah	p.	SD	25 Apr. 1885	5	2	text of will
Ridley	James F.	m.	PCo	30 Sept. 1885	3	6	
Ridley	James F.	m.	SD	3 Oct. 1885	5	4	

(1) Surname	(2) Given Name	(3)	(4)	(5) Date	(6) Pg	(7) Col	(8) Comments
Ridley	James	m.	DR	28 Sept. 1885	3	4	
Ridley	James	m.	SRR	1 Oct. 1885	3	3	
Ried	Joseph B.	d.	DD	20 Aug. 1883	3	3	
Riegels	Mary E.	d.	SD	10 Oct. 1885	1	4	
Riegles	Mary E.	d.	DR	3 Oct. 1885	3	4	
Riggs	Mattie	m.	SD	8 Oct. 1881	3	8	
Righetti	Isolina	m.	DR	17 Aug. 1882	3	2	
Riley	E. F.	b.	SD	14 Jan. 1882	3	8	
Riley	Lucy	m.	DD	23 July 1883	3	2	
Riley	Lucy	m.	SD	28 July 1883	2	5	
Risega	Franci	d.	PCo	26 Oct. 1881	3	4	
Rising	H.	b.	SD	30 Apr. 1881	3	8	
Risley	Eva Francis	m.	SD	19 Mar. 1881	3	8	
Ritchie	Maggie J.	m.	SD	3 Jan. 1885	2	7	
Roach	Jennie E.	m.	PCo	11 Jan. 1882	3	6	
Roach	Jennie E.	m.	SD	21 Jan. 1882	3	6	
Roach	Robert	m.	SD	12 July 1884	6	8	
Robbins	Ira A.	m.	DR	17 Nov. 1881	2	3	
Robbins	Ira A.	m.	PCo	23 Nov. 1881	3	5	
Robbins	Ira A.	m.	RRF	17 Nov. 1881	2	3	
Robbins	Ira A.	m.	SD	26 Nov. 1881	3	8	
Robbins	Nettie	d.	SD	10 Jan. 1885	2	6	
Roberson	J. P.	m.	PWA	23 June 1883	3	7	
Roberto	Samuel	b.	SD	25 Mar. 1882	3	6	
Roberts	Charles	b.	PCo	1 Oct. 1884	3	5	
Roberts	D., Miss	m.	DR	30 Jan. 1882	2	3	
Roberts	D., Mrs.	m.	PCo	25 Jan. 1882	3	6	
Roberts	E. N.	m.	DR	9 Nov. 1885	2	2	
Roberts	Emma	m.	DD	20 Oct. 1883	3	3	
Roberts	Emma	m.	DR	22 Dec. 1884	2	2	
Roberts	Emma	m.	PCo	24 Dec. 1884	3	4	
Roberts	Emma	m.	PWA	20 Dec. 1884	3	4	
Roberts	Frank	b.	DR	22 Aug. 1882	3	2	
Roberts	Frank	b.	SD	2 Sept, 1882	3	6	
Roberts	Hattie	m.	DR	21 Jan. 1884	3	2	
Roberts	Hattie	m.	PCo	23 Jan. 1884	3	5	
Roberts	Hattie	m.	PWA	19 Jan. 1884	3	7	
Roberts	Hattie	m.	SD	26 Jan. 1884	3	5	
Roberts	Herbert	d.	DD	10 Sept. 1883	3	3	
Roberts	Herbert	d.	PWA	8 Sept. 1883	3	8	
Roberts	Herbert	d.	SD	15 Sept. 1883	2	4	
Roberts	Mary	d.	CR	6 Oct. 1883	3	1	

(1) Surname	(2) Given Name	(3)	(4)	(5) Date	(6) Pg	(7) Col	(8) Comments
Roberts	Mary	d.	DD	6 Oct. 1883	3	3	
Roberts	Mary	d.	DD	29 Sept. 1883	3	2	
Roberts	O. J.	b.	PCo	23 Dec. 1885	3	4	
Roberts	Oliver	b.	PCo	28 June 1882	3	5	
Roberts	Oliver	b.	SD	1 July 1882	2	3	
Roberts	Oliver P.	m.	DR	13 Sept. 1881	2	3	
Roberts	Oliver P.	m.	PCo	7 Sept. 1881	2	4	
Roberts	Oliver P.	m.	SD	17 Sept. 1881	3	8	
Roberts	Samuel	b.	PCo	15 Mar. 1882	3	4	
Roberts	Samuel	b.	PCo	6 Feb. 1884	3	6	
Roberts	Samuel	b.	PWA	9 Feb. 1884	3	6	
Roberts	Samuel	b.	SD	16 Feb. 1884	2	5	
Roberts	William R.	d.	DR	3 May 1881	2	2	also p. 3 col. 1
Roberts	William R.	d.	PCo	4 May 1881	3	4	
Roberts	William R.	d.	SD	14 May 1881	3	8	
Roberts	William	d.	DR	6 May 1881	3	2	Petaluma
Robertson	A. B.	b.	PCo	5 July 1882	3	5	
Robertson	Dr.	d.	DR	25 Feb. 1882	3	2	
Robertson	Henry A.	m.	CR	18 Nov. 1882	3	1	
Robertson	Henry A.	d.	PCo	15 Nov. 1882	3	5	
Robertson	J. P.	m.	PC	27 June 1883	3	6	
Robertson	J. P.	m.	SD	30 June 1883	3	5	
Robertson	Lillie E.	d.	PCo	17 June 1885	3	6	
Robertson	Lucy E.	d.	DD	23 July 1883	3	2	
Robertson	Lucy E.	d.	SD	28 July 1883	2	5	
Robertson	Olive	m.	CR	11 June 1881	5	5	
Robertson	Olive	m.	DR	3 June 1881	2	3	
Robertson	Olive	m.	RRF	16 June 1881	2	5	
Robertson	Olive	m.	SD	4 June 1881	3	8	
Robin	Amelia H.	d.	DR	5 Feb. 1884	3	3	
Robin	Amelia Honorado	d.	PCo	6 Feb. 1884	3	6	
Robin	Amelie Honnorado	d.	SD	16 Feb. 1884	2	5	
Robin	Honorado	d.	PWA	9 Feb. 1884	3	6	
Robinson	Agnes	m.	PCo	3 Sept. 1884	2	5	
Robinson	Agnes	m.	PWA	30 Aug. 1884	3	5	
Robinson	Agnes	m.	SD	6 Sept. 1884	2	5	
Robinson	Alice Annie	m.	PCo	18 Oct. 1882	3	6	
Robinson	Benjamin	m.	PCo	3 Jan. 1883	3	4	
Robinson	Benjamin	m.	SD	6 Jan. 1883	2	5	
Robinson	Benjamin F.	m.	DD	10 Nov. 1883	3	3	
Robinson	Benjamin F.	m.	SD	17 Nov. 1883	3	5	
Robinson	Bnjamin	m.	PWA	5 Jan. 1883	2	5	

(1) Surname	(2) Given Name	(3)	(4)	(5) Date	(6) Pg	(7) Col	(8) Comments
Robinson	Carrie B.	d.	SD	1 Oct. 1881	3	8	
Robinson	Carrie	d.	DR	23 Sept. 1881	2	3	
Robinson	Carrie	d.	PCo	21 Sept. 1881	3	5	
Robinson	Charles	d.	PCo	2 Apr. 1884	3	6	
Robinson	Charley	d.	PWA	5 Apr. 1884	3	2&6	
Robinson	D	b.	PC	4 Apr. 1883	3	5	
Robinson	D.	m.	DR	27 June 1882	2	3	
Robinson	D.	b.	PWA	7 Apr. 1883	2	3	
Robinson	D. L.	m.	PCo	6 Feb. 1884	3	6	
Robinson	D. L., Miss	m.	PCo	30 Jan. 1884	3	6	
Robinson	David	d.	PCo	12 Dec. 1883	2	4	
Robinson	Eliza	m.	PCo	20 July 1881	3	5	
Robinson	Eliza H.	m.	SD	6 Aug. 1881	3	8	
Robinson	Eliza H.	m.	SD	23 July 1881	3	8	
Robinson	Frank	m.	PC	6 June 1883	3	4	
Robinson	Frank	b.	PCo	2 Apr. 1884	3	6	
Robinson	Frank	m.	PWA	9 June 1883	3	7	
Robinson	Frank	b.	SD	29 Mar. 1884	2	5	
Robinson	Henry A.	d.	DR	15 Nov. 1882	2	3	
Robinson	Henry	d.	DR	14 Nov. 1882	3	1	Santa Rosa Cem.
Robinson	J. R., Mrs.	m.	DR	24 Oct. 1882	3	2	
Robinson	Laura F.	m.	SD	21 Apr. 1883	2	6	
Robinson	Laura	m.	RRF	26 Apr. 1883	2	3	
Robinson	Lillie Emeline	d.	SD	13 June 1885	3	5	
Robinson	Mary M	d.	DR	27 Nov. 1885	3	4	
Robinson	Mattie	m.	DR	2 Oct. 1882	2	3	
Robinson	Minnie J.	m.	PC	27 June 1883	3	6	
Robinson	Minnie J.	m.	PWA	23 June 1883	3	7	
Robinson	Minnie J.	m.	SD	30 June 1883	3	5	
Robinson	Sallie	m.	PCo	27 Sept. 1882	3	6	
Robinson	T. A.	m.	DR	20 Aug. 1885	3	4	
Robinson	T. A.	m.	SD	29 Aug. 1885	2	4	
Robinson	Ulysses F.	d.	PCo	24 Jan. 1883	3	5	
Robinson	Ulysses F.	d.	SD	27 Jan. 1883	3	6	
Robinson	W. I.	b.	DR	2 Nov. 1885	3	4	
Robinson	W. L.	o.	DR	26 Oct. 1882	2	2	
Robinson	Willie E.	d.	DR	12 Aug. 1882	3	2	
Robinson	Willie E.	d.	PCo	9 Aug. 1882	3	6	
Robinson	Willie E.	d.	SD	12 Aug. 1882	3	5	
Robson	Jeannette	m.	PWA	1 Nov. 1884	3	4	
Robuson	George	d.	DD	18 Oct. 1883	3	3	
Robuson	George	d.	PWA	20 Oct. 1883	3	8	

(1) Surname	(2) Given Name	(3)	(4)	(5) Date	(6) Pg	(7) Col	(8) Comments
Robuson	George	d.	SD	20 Oct. 1883	3	4	
Robuson	George	d.	SWI	27 Oct. 1883	3	3	Cypress Hill Cem.
Rochford	Jennie	m.	SD	5 Mar. 1881	3	8	
Rockford	Jennie	m.	PCo	2 Mar. 1881	4	4	
Rodd	Samuel	m.	PWA	19 May 1883	3	8	
Rodehaver	Lulu	m.	PCo	4 Oct. 1882	3	6	
Rodgers	Alice	d.	PCo	27 May 1885	3	6	
Rodgers	Alice R.	d.	SD	6 June 1885	2	4	
Rodgers	Alice R.	d.	SD	30 May 1885	5	4	
Rodgers	E.	b.	DR	23 Sept. 1881	2	3	
Rodgers	E.	b.	PCo	21 Sept. 1881	3	5	
Rodgers	E.	b.	SD	1 Oct. 1881	3	8	
Rodgers	John P.	b.	PWA	1 Dec. 1883	3	6	
Rodgers	Mary A.	d.	DR	3 Nov. 1885	3	4	
Rodgers	Mary A.	d.	SD	7 Nov. 1885	3	1&4	Petaluma
Rodgers	Warren	m.	PCo	31 May 1882	3	5	
Rodgers	Warren	m.	RRF	25 May 1882	2	3	
Rodgers	Warren	m.	SD	3 June 1882	2	4	
Roger	J. P. (mother of)	d.	CR	7 Nov. 1885	3	2	
Rogers	Albert Emmet	d.	DR	21 July 1885	3	4	
Rogers	Bessie	m.	PC	4 Apr. 1883	3	5	
Rogers	Bessie	m.	RRF	29 Mar. 1883	2	4	
Rogers	E. H., Mrs.	d.	DR	12 Aug. 1882	3	2	
Rogers	E. H., Mrs.	d.	PCo	9 Aug. 1882	3	6	
Rogers	E. H., Mrs.	d.	SD	12 Aug. 1882	3	5	
Rogers	Edward	b.	PC	11 July 1883	3	5	
Rogers	Edward	b.	PCo	15 Apr. 1885	3	6	
Rogers	Edward	b.	PWA	14 July 1883	3	6	
Rogers	Edward	b.	PWA	18 Apr. 1885	3	6	
Roher	Susan	d.	PCo	23 Sept. 1885	3	6	
Rohl	Oscar	b.	SD	13 Sept. 1884	3	4	
Rohrer	Benard A.	d.	DR	30 Nov. 1885	3	4	
Rohrer	Bernard A.	d.	SD	5 Dec. 1885	1	7	also p. 3 col. 1 & 2
Rohrer	Frederick	o.	SD	21 Nov. 1885	1	7	
Rohrer	Nellie	m.	PC	9 May 1883	3	5	
Rohrer	Nellie	m.	PWA	12 May 1883	3	8	
Rohrer	Susan	d.	DR	17 Sept. 1885	3	4	
Roix	J. A.	m.	PCo	20 Aug. 1884	3	4	
Roix	L.	m.	PWA	23 Aug. 1884	3	4	
Romine	Thomas	m.	PCo	12 Mar. 1884	3	6	
Romine	Thomas	m.	RRF	6 Mar. 1884	2	3	
Roney	A. S.	d.	SD	1 Dec. 1883	1	3	

(1) Surname	(2) Given Name	(3)	(4)	(5) Date	(6) Pg	(7) Col	(8) Comments
Roney	George W.	d.	CR	2 Apr. 1881	4	1	
Roney	George W.	d.	CR	2 Apr. 1881	4	1	
Roney	Henrietta F. L.	d.	DR	7 June 1882	3	2	
Roney	Henrietta F. L.	d.	PCo	7 June 1882	3	5	
Ronsheimer	John	b.	PCo	13 Sept. 1882	3	7	
Ronsheimer	John	b.	SD	9 Sept. 1882	3	6	
Rosasco	John	b.	PC	4 Apr. 1883	3	5	
Rosasco	John	b.	PCo	26 Oct. 1881	3	4	
Rosasco	John	b.	PCo	29 July 1885	3	4	
Rosasco	John	b.	RRF	20 Oct. 1881	2	4	
Rosasco	John	b.	RRF	29 Mar. 1883	2	4	
Rosasco	John	b.	SD	29 Oct. 1881	3	6	
Rosasco	John (dau. of)	d.	RRF	7 June 1883	2	3	14 June, p 2. col. 3 says wrongly reported
Rosasco	John (child of)	d.	SD	16 June 1883	2	6	
Rose	A., Mrs.	d.	DR	2 Nov. 1884	2	2	
Rose	A., Mrs.	d.	PCo	5 Nov. 1884	3	5	
Rose	Anne Kenworthy	d.	PWA	5 Jan. 1883	2	5	
Rose	Benjamin F.	d.	CR	17 Dec. 1881	1	3	
Rose	Emma	m.	DR	1 May 1882	3	2	
Rose	J. W.	b.	DR	2 Oct. 1882	2	3	
Rose	J. W.	b.	PCo	26 Mar. 1884	3	6	
Rose	J. W.	b.	RRF	28 Sept. 1882	2	3	
Rose	J. W.	b.	RRF	20 Mar. 1884	2	4	
Rose	J. W.	b.	SD	29 Mar. 1884	2	5	
Rose	J. W.	b.	SWI	29 Mar. 1884	3	5	
Rose	Martha A.	d.	PCo	12 Nov. 1884	3	5	
Rose	Martha A.	d.	SD	8 Nov. 1884	2	5	
Rose	Randolph D.	d.	PC	30 May 1883	3	4	
Rose	Randolph D.	d.	PWA	26 May 1883	3	7	
Rose	Randolph D.	d.	RRF	17 May 1883	2	3	also 24 May, p. 2 col. 4
Rosebraugh	Charles	b.	CR	22 Dec. 1883	3	1	
Rosenberg	W.	b.	DD	.2 Nov. 1883	3	2	
Rosenberg	W.	b.	PCo	28 Oct. 1885	3	4	
Rosenberg	W.	b.	RRF	1 Nov. 1883	2	2	
Rosenberg	W.	b.	SD	10 Nov. 1883	3	5	
Rosenthal	Joseph	b.	RRF	22 Sept. 1881	2	6	
Rosenthal	Julius	b.	PCo	6 Aug. 1884	2	4	
Rosenthal	Julius	b.	SD	9 Aug. 1884	3	4	
Rosett	A. F.	m.	RRF	16 June 1881	2	5	
Rosett	Ada F.	m.	SD	18 June 1881	3	8	
Rosette	A. F., Miss	m.	CR	25 June 1881	4	3	

(1) Surname	(2) Given Name	(3)	(4)	(5) Date	(6) Pg	(7) Col	(8) Comments
Rosette	A. F., Miss	m.	DR	18 June 1881	2	3	
Ross	A. O.	b.	SD	22 Jan. 1881	3	8	
Ross	C. A.	b.	SD	19 Feb. 1881	3	8	
Ross	D.	b.	DD	12 Nov. 1883	3	3	
Ross	D.	b.	PWA	10 Nov. 1883	3	8	
Ross	D.	b.	SD	17 Nov. 1883	3	5	
Ross	David	m.	DR	18 Nov. 1882	3	2	
Ross	David	m.	PCo	22 Nov. 1882	3	5	
Ross	Frank	m.	PCo	10 Dec. 1884	3	5	
Ross	Frank	m.	PWA	6 Dec. 1884	3	4	
Ross	George W.	m.	PCo	3 Dec. 1884	3	5	
Ross	Gillie	d.	PCo	30 Dec. 1885	3	4	
Ross	I. D.	b.	DR	10 Nov. 1885	2	2	
Ross	J. D.	m.	SD	25 Oct. 1884	2	5	
Ross	M.	b.	SD	28 May 1881	3	8	
Ross	Robert	b.	DR	12 Aug. 1884	3	3	
Ross	Robert	b.	PCo	12 Apr. 1882	3	5	
Ross	Robert	b.	SD	8 Apr. 1882	3	6	
Ross	Robert	b.	SD	13 Aug. 1884	2	4	
Ross	Thomas	d.	PC	30 May 1883	3	4	
Ross	Thomas	d.	SD	26 May 1883	2	7	
Rossan	Fred	d.	RRF	12 Jan. 1882	2	4	
Rossan	Fred	d.	SD	7 Jan. 1882	3	4	
Rossan	Fred	d.	SD	28 Jan. 1882	3	2	
Rosse	Rafael	m.	PCo	13 May 1885	3	6	
Rosse	Rafael	m.	SD	23 May 1885	2	5	
Roth	M.	b.	PCo	17 May 1882	3	5	
Roth	M.	b.	SD	20 May 1882	2	4	
Roth	Maximillian	m.	PCo	6 July 1881	3	5	
Roth	Maximillian	m.	SD	16 July 1881	3	8	
Rothermel	I. Y.	d.	PWA	3 Mar. 1883	3	6	
Rothermel	V.	d.	PCo	7 Mar. 1883	3	5	
Rothschild	Charles	m.	DD	29 Sept. 1883	3	2	
Rothschild	Charles	m.	SD	6 Oct. 1883	2	6	also p. 3 col. 1
Roussan	Fred	d.	CR	7 Jan. 1882	1	3	
Roux	A. F.	m.	DR	5 Dec. 1882	3	2	
Roux	A. F.	m.	PCo	6 Dec. 1882	3	6	
Roux	A. F.	m.	SD	9 Dec. 1882	2	5	
Rovia	Frank	b.	SIT	19 Dec. 1885	2	3	
Rovia	Pedro	m.	SWI	7 June 1884	3	4	
Rowe	N.	b.	DR	8 Aug. 1882	3	1&2	
Rowe	N.	b.	PCo	16 Aug. 1882	3	6	twins

(1) Surname	(2) Given Name	(3)	(4)	(5) Date	(6) Pg	(7) Col	(8) Comments
Rowe	N.	b.	RRF	10 Aug. 1882	2	4	
Rowe	N.	b.	SD	12 Aug. 1882	3	5	
Rowland	Ida C.	d.	DD	4 Aug. 1883	3	2	
Rowland	Ida C.	d.	PC	8 Aug. 1883	3	6	
Rowland	Ida C.	d.	RRF	2 Aug. 1883	2	4	Oak Mound Cemetery
Rowland	Ida C.	d.	SD	11 Aug. 1883	2	7	
Rowland	T. B.	b.	DR	29 Nov. 1882	3	2	
Rowland	Thomas B.	b.	SD	2 Dec. 1882	3	5	
Rowlinson	Virginia L.	m.	PCo	19 Nov. 1884	3	5	
Rubke	Henry	b.	DR	13 Dec. 1882	2	3	
Rubke	Henry	b.	DR	21 Dec. 1882	2	2	
Rubke	Henry	b.	PCo	20 Dec. 1882	3	5	
Ruch	Michael	d.	DR	13 Sept. 1882	3	1	
Rudd	Samuel	m.	PC	16 May 1883	3	5	
Ruddock	J. C.	b.	SD	2 Apr. 1881	3	8	
Ruddock	James Carroll	d.	DD	11 Oct. 1883	3	3	
Ruddock	Kate Siddons	d.	DR	28 July 1884	3	3	
Ruddock	Kate Siddons	d.	PCo	6 Aug. 1884	2	4	
Rude	T. E.	d.	DR	4 Feb. 1882	2	3	
Rude	T. G.	d.	SD	4 Feb. 1882	3	2&6	
Rue	(male)	b.	DR	25 Jan. 1884	3	3	
Rue	James O.	m.	CR	10 Feb. 1883	3	1	
Rue	James O.	b.	DR	28 Nov. 1885	3	4	
Rue	James O.	b.	PCo	6 Feb. 1884	3	6	
Ruffner	Annie	m.	DR	25 Apr. 1884	3	2	
Ruffner	Annie	m.	PCo	23 Apr. 1884	2	6	
Ruffner	Annie	m.	RRF	24 Apr. 1884	1	4	
Ruffner	Annie	m.	SD	26 Apr. 1883	3	5	
Ruffner	James, Mrs.	d.	DR	16 Nov. 1885	3	4	
Ruffner	Jennie	m.	CR	10 Feb. 1883	3	1	
Ruffner	Jessie	m.	RRF	8 Feb. 1883	2	4	also p. 3 col. 3
Ruffner	Jessie	m.	SD	10 Feb. 1883	2	7	
Ruffner	N. M., Mrs.	d.	SIT	14 Nov. 1885	2	3	
Rufner	Jessie	m.	PCo	14 Feb. 1883	3	6	
Rufus	Bertha A.	m.	SWI	7 June 1884	3	4	
Rufus	Bertie A.	m.	DR	7 June 1884	3	3	
Rufus	Bertie A.	m.	PCo	11 June 1884	3	5	
Rufus	Bertie A.	m.	PWA	14 June 1884	3	6	
Rufus	Bertie A.	m.	SD	14 June 1884	1	6	also p. 2 col. 4
Rufus	E.	o.	SIT	22 Aug. 1885	2	2	
Rugg	W. H.	d.	CR	7 Jan. 1882	1	3	14 Jan. p. col. 1 says he did not drown

(1) Surname	(2) Given Name	(3)	(4)	(5) Date	(6) Pg	(7) Col	(8) Comments
Rule	E. J.	b.	SD	19 July 1884	2	5	
Rulle	William	m.	SD	10 June 1882	2	3	
Rummel	Frederick E.	d.	DR	31 Aug. 1881	2	3	
Rummelsbereg	Aleck	b.	SD	12 Feb. 1881	3	8	
Runyan	Mary J.	m.	DR	20 June 1884	3	3	
Runyan	R. B.	d.	DR	6 Nov. 1882	3	2	
Runyon	Amelia	m.	PCo	20 Feb. 1884	3	6	
Runyon	Emelia	m.	PWA	23 Feb. 1884	3	2&6	
Runyon	Emelie	m.	SD	16 Feb. 1884	2	5	also p. 3 col. 4, 5, 6
Runyon	Mary J.	m.	SD	5 July 1884	2	3	
Runyon	Mellie J.	m.	SD	4 Mar. 1882	3	6	
Runyon	Miss	m.	DR	14 Feb. 1884	3	2	
Runyon	Mollie J.	m.	PCo	8 Mar. 1882	3	5	
Runyon	Mollie	m.	DR	3 Mar. 1882	2	3	
Runyon	Mollie	m.	DR	8 Mar. 1882	2	3	
Rupe	Dr.	d.	CR	29 Jan. 1881	4	2	
Rupe	Judith	m.	DR	7 Feb. 1882	2	3	
Rupe	Judith	m.	PCo	15 Feb. 1882	3	4	
Rupe	Judith	m.	SD	11 Feb. 1882	3	6	
Rupe	S. H.	d.	RRF	27 Jan. 1881	3	4	
Russ	Mary E.	m.	DR	8 Dec. 1882	3	2	
Russ	Mary E.	m.	PCo	13 Dec. 1882	3	4	
Russel	Minnie A.	d.	SD	5 Nov. 1881	3	6	
Russel	Nettie	m.	DR	18 Dec. 1884	2	2	
Russell	A.	b.	DR	17 Aug. 1881	2	3	
Russell	L. M.	d.	PCo	10 Jan. 1883	3	6	
Russell	L. M.	d.	SD	13 Jan. 1883	3	5	
Russell	M.	d.	PWA	12 Jan. 1883	3	6	
Russell	Marion	m.	SD	24 Sept. 1881	3	8	
Russell	Minnie M.	d.	DR	31 Oct. 1881	2	3	
Russell	Minnie M.	d.	PCo	9 Nov. 1881	3	5	
Rutherford	Sadie	m.	DR	28 Jan. 1882	2	3	
Rutherford	Sadie	m.	PCo	25 Jan. 1882	3	6	
Rutherford	Silva C.	m.	PCo	30 Apr. 1884	2	6	
Rutherford	Thomas	d.	PCo	23 Dec. 1885	3	4	
Rutherford	Thomas	d.	SD	26 Dec. 1885	3	2	
Rutherford	W. S.	m.	SD	29 Dec. 1883	3	6	
Rutledge	Clara	m.	DR	1 May 1884	3	2	
Rutledge	Clara	m.	PCo	7 May 1884	3	5	
Rutledge	Clara	m.	PWA	10 May 1884	3	2&5	
Rutledge	Clara	m.	RRF	8 May 1884	5	6	
Rutledge	Clara	m.	SD	3 May 1884	3	1	

(1) Surname	(2) Given Name	(3)	(4)	(5) Date	(6) Pg	(7) Col	(8) Comments
Ryan	James W.	m.	PWA	15 Dec. 1883	3	6	
Ryan	M. J.	b.	CR	15 Apr. 1882	5	1	also death of son
Ryan	Mary	d.	DR	26 Sept. 1885	3	4	
Ryan	Mary	m.	PCo	17 Jan. 1883	3	5	
Ryan	Mary	d.	PCo	23 Sept. 1885	3	6	
Ryan	Mary	m.	PWA	12 Jan. 1883	3	2&6	
Ryan	Mary	d.	SRR	1 Oct. 1885	3	3	
Ryan	Michael S.	m.	SD	8 Oct. 1881	3	8	
Ryan	Roger	b.	PCo	7 Feb. 1883	3	6	
Ryan	Roger	b.	PWA	10 Feb. 1883	3	7	
Ryan	Roger	b.	SD	10 Feb. 1883	2	7	
Ryan	T.	b	SD	7 Nov. 1885	3	4	
Ryan	T.	b.	SIT	31 Oct. 1885	2	3	
Ryder	Charles H.	m.	PWA	27 Oct. 1883	3	8	

S

(1) Surname	(2) Given Name	(3)	(4)	(5) Date	(6) Pg	(7) Col	(8) Comments
Sachs	Samuel L.	o.	DR	12 Sept. 1882	2	1	
Sackett	Daisy Alberta	d.	PCo	21 Sept. 1881	3	5	
Sacray	William	b.	PCo	7 June 1882	3	5	
Sacray	William	b.	SD	10 June 1882	2	3	
Sacru	Mrs.	d.	RRF	1 Dec. 1881	3	5	Oak Mound Cem.
Sacry	Susan M.	d.	PCo	7 Dec. 1881	3	5	
Sacry	Susan M.	d.	SD	3 Dec. 1881	3	8	
Sacry	Susan	d.	DR	28 Nov. 1881	2	3	also p. 3 col. 1
Safley	James	b.	SD	16 July 1881	3	8	
Sales	Henry	d.	PCo	24 Sept. 1884	3	5	
Sales	Henry	d.	PWA	20 Sept. 1884	3	4	
Sales	Henry	d.	SD	4 Oct. 1884	3	5	
Salliner	Gertley	m.	DD	29 Dec. 1883	3	3	
Salvo	M. A., Mrs.	d.	SD	30 Apr. 1881	3	8	
Samuels	Elizabeth	m.	SD	13 Aug. 1881	3	8	
Samuels	James M.	b.	DR	10 May 1881	2	2	
Samuels	James M.	b.	SD	14 May 1881	3	8	
Sanborn	Fannie	m.	CR	28 May 1881	5	5	
Sanborn	Fannie	m.	RRF	19 May 1881	2	4	
Sanborn	Fannie	m.	SD	4 June 1881	3	8	
Sanborn	Fannie	m.	SD	28 May 1881	3	8	
Sanborn	W. B.	b.	RRF	5 Apr. 1883	2	3	
Sanborn	W. B.	m.	SD	21 Jan. 1882	3	6	
Sanborn	William	m.	HE	26 Jan. 1882	3	3	
Sanders	Joseph	b.	DR	9 Apr. 1882	3	2	
Sanders	Joseph	b.	RRF	6 Apr. 1882	2	4	
Sandford	H. T.	b.	RRF	27 Mar. 1884	2	3	
Sanford	(male)	b.	DR	28 Mar. 1884	3	3	
Sanford	H. T.	b.	PCo	2 Apr. 1884	3	6	
Sanford	H. T.	b.	SD	5 Apr. 1884	3	4	
Sansbury	Mrs.	d.	CR	22 Dec. 1883	3	3	
Sansbury	Mrs.	d.	DD	27 Dec. 1883	3	3	
Sansbury	Mrs.	d.	PCo	2 Jan. 1884	3	6	
Sansbury	Mrs.	d.	RRF	27 Dec. 1883	2	2	Oak Mound Cemetery
Sanson	William	m.	CR	1 Jan. 1881	5	5	
Sanson	William	m.	SD	1 June 1881	3	7	
Santee	L.	m.	PCo	30 Nov. 1881	3	5	

(1) Surname	(2) Given Name	(3)	(4)	(5) Date	(6) Pg	(7) Col	(8) Comments
Santee	Levi	m.	SD	26 Nov. 1881	3	8	
Sargeant	Mattie L.	d.	PCo	24 May 1882	3	5	
Sargent	Charlotte A.	d.	PC	18 Apr. 1883	3	5	
Sargent	Charlotte A.	d.	SD	14 Apr. 1883	2	5	
Sargent	J. C.	d.	DR	7 Dec. 1885	3	4	
Sargent	J. C.	d.	SD	19 Dec. 1885	4	1	
Sargent	Mattie L.	d.	DR	16 May 1882	3	2	
Sargent	Minnie L.	d.	SD	20 May 1882	2	4	
Sartori	Lavina	d.	DR	10 Jun. 1881	2	2	
Sartori	P.	b.	DR	24 Nov. 1885	3	4	
Sartori	P.	b.	PCo	23 Nov. 1885	3	4	
Sass	C. D. F.	b.	SD	16 Apr. 1881	3	8	
Satori	Savina	d.	SD	11 June 1881	3	8	
Saul	Rod M.	m.	PCo	26 Dec. 1883	3	5	
Saul	Rod M.	m.	PWA	22 Dec. 1883	3	6	
Saunders	W. S.	m.	DD	15 Dec. 1883	3	1	
Savage	C. W.	b.	DR	6 July 1885	3	3	
Savage	C. W.	b.	SD	11 July 1885	5	6	
Savage	Florence Willie	d.	SD	21 Mar. 1885	2	5	
Savage	J.	b.	PCo	31 Dec. 1884	3	4	
Savage	J.	b.	PWA	3 Jan. 1885	3	4	
Savage	J.	b.	SD	10 Jan. 1885	2	6	
Savage	John	b.	PCo	23 Nov. 1881	3	5	
Savage	John	b.	PWA	5 May 1883	3	8	
Savage	John	b.	SD	3 Dec. 1881	3	8	
Savage	John	b.	SD	5 May 1883	2	6	
Savage	Mr. & Mrs.	b.	PC	2 May 1883	3	5	
Savage	Nelson E.	m.	SD	14 Mar. 1885	5	5	
Savage	Nelson F.	m.	PCo	11 Mar. 1885	3	6	
Scanlan	Margaret	d.	DR	17 Sept. 1885	3	4	
Scanlan	Margaret	d.	PCo	16 Sept. 1885	3	6	
Schaaf	H.	d.	DR	1 May 1882	3	2	
Schaff	Andrew	d.	PCo	3 May 1882	3	5	
Schallenberger	Vesta	m.	SD	19 Jan. 1884	3	6	
Schaumloeffel	Lizzie	m.	SD	12 Mar. 1881	3	8	
Scheidecker	Carolina	m.	SD	27 June 1885	5	4	
Schetter	O.	b.	PCo	5 Mar. 1884	3	6	
Schetter	O.	b.	PWA	8 Mar. 1884	3	6	
Schetter	Otto	b.	DR	25 Oct. 1881	3	2	
Schetter	Otto	b.	SD	29 Oct. 1881	3	6	
Schiedecker	Carolina	m.	PCo	24 June 1885	3	6	
Schiller	Albert W.	m.	SD	25 Mar. 1882	3	6	

(1) Surname	(2) Given Name	(3)	(4)	(5) Date	(6) Pg	(7) Col	(8) Comments
Schlopke	H.	b.	PCo	11 May 1881	3	5	
Schlopke	H.	b.	SD	21 May 1881	3	8	
Schloss	Amelia	m.	DR	16 May 1882	3	1	
Schloss	Amelia	m.	PCo	31 May 1882	3	5	
Schloss	Amelia	m.	RRF	25 May 1882	2	3	
Schloss	Amelia	m.	SD	3 June 1882	2	4	
Schloss	Minnie	m.	DD	29 Sept. 1883	3	2	
Schloss	Minnie	m.	SD	6 Oct. 1883	2	6	also p. 3 col. 1
Schloss	Miss	m.	RRF	1 June 1882	1	6	
Schloss	S.	o.	SD	11 July 1885	5	5	
Schlosser	W. P.	d.	CR	2 Apr. 1881	5	3	
Schlosser	Willie	d.	CR	2 Apr. 1881	5	3	
Schlosser	Willie	d.	PCo	30 Mar. 1881	3	4	son of Frank
Schlosser	Willie	d.	SD	9 Apr. 1881	3	8	
Schluckebier	H.	b.	PCo	16 Dec. 1885	3	6	
Schluckebier	Henry	m.	DR	25 Apr. 1884	3	2	
Schluckebier	Henry	m.	PCo	23 Apr. 1884	2	6	
Schluckebier	Henry	m.	PWA	26 Apr. 1884	3	6	
Schluckebier	Henry	m.	RRF	1 May 1884	5	6	
Schluckebier	Henry	m.	SD	26 Apr. 1883	3	5	
Schmidli	Joseph	m.	DR	18 Dec. 1882	2	1	
Schmidli	Joseph	m.	PCo	27 Dec. 1882	3	6	
Schmidli	Joseph	m.	SD	23 Dec. 1882	2	5	
Schmidt	Arthur F.	d.	PWA	21 Feb. 1885	3	5	
Schmidt	Arthur F.	d.	SD	28 Feb. 1885	5	6	
Schmidt	Arthur Theodore	d.	PCo	25 Feb. 1885	3	6	
Schmidt	Auguste	m.	PCo	5 July 1882	3	5	
Schneider	Elizabeth	m.	SD	14 Apr. 1883	2	6	
Schoenagel	Jacob	m.	DR	27 May 1882	2	3	
Schoenagel	Mr. & Mrs.	b.	SD	24 Mar. 1883	2	5	
Schoenaglel	Jacob	m.	PCo	31 May 1882	3	5	
Schoenaglel	Jacob	m.	SD	27 May 1882	3	5	
Schofield	Mrs.	d.	PCo	12 Jan. 1881	2	2	
Schriver	J.	b.	PCo	15 Mar. 1882	3	4	
Schriver	J.	b.	SD	25 Mar. 1882	3	6	
Schroyer	Benjamin	d.	DR	22 May 1884	3	2	
Schroyer	Benjamin	d.	PCo	21 May 1884	3	4	
Schroyer	Benjamin	d.	SD	24 May 1884	2	3	
Schuerer	Henry	b.	SD	25 June 1881	3	8	
Schuhman	Anton	m.	RRF	25 May 1882	2	3	
Schuhman	Mr.	m.	RRF	1 June 1882	1	6	
Schuler	C. O.	b.	PCo	13 May 1885	3	6	

(1) Surname	(2) Given Name	(3)	(4)	(5) Date	(6) Pg	(7) Col	(8) Comments
Schulte	W. H.	m.	CR	5 Mar. 1881	4	2	
Schulte	W. H.	m.	DR	25 Feb. 1881	3	2	
Schultz	E.	b.	PCo	7 Mar. 1883	3	5	
Schultz	Mr.	o.	CR	3 Mar. 1883	3	1	
Schultz	Mr. & Mrs.	b.	CR	24 Feb. 1883	3	1	
Schumaker	Joseph	b.	SD	8 Oct. 1881	3	8	
Schuman	Annie E.	d.	SD	24 June 1882	3	5	
Schuman	Anton	m.	PCo	31 May 1882	3	5	
Schuman	Anton	m.	SD	3 June 1882	2	4	
Schumann	Antone	m.	DR	16 May 1882	3	1	
Schupe	Antone	o.	CR	19 Feb. 1881	1	2	
Schwab	F. J.	b.	PC	23 May 1883	3	5	
Schwab	F. J.	b.	RRF	22 Sept. 1881	2	6	
Schwab	F. J.	b.	SD	1 Oct. 1881	3	8	
Schwab	F. J.	b.	SD	18 Apr. 1885	2	4	
Schwarz	Henry	d.	RRF	6 Oct. 1881	2	3	
Schwarz	Hubert John Francis	d.	RRF	6 Oct. 1881	2	3	
Schwobeda	John B	d.	SD	11 Oct. 1884	2	5	
Schwobeda	John B.	d.	PCo	8 Oct. 1884	3	6	
Schwobeda	John B.	d.	PWA	11 Oct. 1884	3	1	Two Rock Cemetery
Scofield	Mrs.	d.	RRF	20 Jan. 1881	3	2	
Scott	Albert	m.	PC	18 Apr. 1883	3	5	
Scott	Albert	m.	RRF	12 Apr. 1883	2	5	
Scott	Dellah	m.	PCo	16 July 1884	3	6	
Scott	Elizabeth	m.	CR	11 Aug. 1883	3	1	
Scott	Elizabeth	m.	PC	8 Aug. 1883	3	6	
Scott	Elizabeth M.	m.	DD	11 Aug. 1883	3	1	
Scott	Elizabeth M.	m.	SD	18 Aug. 1883	2	6	
Scott	Ella	d.	DR	12 July 1881	3	2	
Scott	Ella	d.	SD	23 July 1881	3	8	
Scott	Elsie May	d.	DR	1 May 1882	3	2	
Scott	Elsie May	d.	PCo	26 Apr. 1882	3	4	
Scott	Elsie May	d.	SD	29 Apr. 1882	3	6	
Scott	Fannie	d.	PWA	29 Mar. 1884	3	6	
Scott	Fannie	d.	SD	29 Mar. 1884	2	5	
Scott	Fanny	d.	PCo	26 Mar. 1884	3	6	
Scott	Florence E.	m.	RRF	26 May 1881	2	5	
Scott	Florence E.	m.	SD	21 May 1881	3	8	
Scott	Florence	m.	SD	2 Apr. 1881	3	8	
Scott	Frances E.	d.	PCo	12 Mar. 1884	3	6	
Scott	Frances E.	d.	SD	8 Mar. 1884	6	5	

(1) Surname	(2) Given Name	(3)	(4)	(5) Date	(6) Pg	(7) Col	(8) Comments
Scott	J. F.	d.	DR	18 July 1884	3	3	
Scott	J. F.	d.	PCo	30 July 1884	3	6	
Scott	J. F.	d.	PWA	27 July 1884	2	3	
Scott	Rosetta	d.	PCo	2 Aug. 1882	3	6	
Scott	Rosetta	d.	SD	22 July 1882	3	5	
Scovill	Kate	m.	DR	24 Oct. 1884	3	3	
Scoville	Katie	m.	PCo	22 Oct. 1884	3	6	
Scoville	Katie	m.	PWA	25 Oct. 1884	3	4	
Scoville	Katie	m.	SD	8 Nov. 1884	2	5	
Scribner	T. S.	b.	SD	12 Mar. 1881	3	8	
Scriver	J.	b.	CR	11 Mar. 1882	5	1	
Scriver	J.	b.	RRF	16 Mar. 1882	2	4	
Scudder	Nancy B.	d.	DR	15 Oct. 1885	3	4	
Seafer	George (son of)	d.	SD	7 May 1881	3	8	
Seafer	Lavinia	m.	SD	26 Mar. 1881	3	8	
Seamen	Edgar	m.	SD	26 Mar. 1881	3	8	
Sears	M. B.	m.	PCo	8 Oct. 1884	3	6	
Sears	M. B.	m.	SD	11 Oct. 1884	2	5	
Seavey	Robert	b.	PCo	11 Jan. 1882	3	6	
Seavey	Robert	b.	SD	21 Jan. 1882	3	6	
Seawell	George	b.	DR	16 Dec. 1882	2	3	
Seawell	George	b.	PCo	20 Dec. 1882	3	5	
Seawell	George	b.	RRF	14 Dec. 1882	2	3	
Seawell	George	b.	SD	16 Dec. 1882	3	6	
Seawell	James	o.	RRF	17 Jan. 1884	33	4	
Seawell	Nettie V.	m.	DR	26 Dec. 1884	2	2	
Seawell	Nettie V.	m.	PCo	7 Jan. 1885	3	6	
Seawell	Nettie V.	m.	SD	3 Jan. 1885	2	4	also p. 2 col. 7
Sebring	Alfred H.	d.	SWI	29 Mar. 1884	3	5	
Sebring	Alfred Thomas	d.	DR	14 Mar. 1884	3	2	
Sebring	Alfred Thomas	d.	PCo	19 Mar. 1884	3	6	
Sebring	Alfred Thomas	d.	PWA	22 Mar. 1884	3	6	
Sebring	Alfred Thomas	d.	SD	22 May 1884	2	4	
Sedgeley	Joseph	b.	CR	24 Feb. 1883	3	1	
Sedgeley	Joseph	b.	PCo	28 Feb. 1883	3	5	
Sedgley	Joseph	b.	SD	22 Aug. 1885	6	2	
Seegelkem	A. D.	o.	SD	17 Dec. 1881	3	3	
Seffins	George	d.	RRF	17 Feb. 1881	2	4	
Seffins	Mary	d.	RRF	17 Feb. 1881	2	4	
Sefton	A. W.	d.	RRF	20 Jan. 1881	3	5	
Selimer	Annie	m.	PWA	29 Sept. 1883	3	8	
Sellars	Annie	m.	SD	13 June 1885	3	5	

(1) Surname	(2) Given Name	(3)	(4)	(5) Date	(6) Pg	(7) Col	(8) Comments
Sellmer	Annie	m.	DD	15 Sept. 1883	3	3	
Sellmer	Annie	m.	DD	27 Sept. 1883	3	3	
Sellmer	Annie	m.	SD	29 Sept. 1883	2	6	
Semple	William	d.	DR	25 Apr. 1884	3	2	
Semple	William	d.	PCo	7 May 1884	3	5	
Semple	William	d.	RRF	1 May 1884	5	6	
Semple	William	d.	SD	3 May 1884	3	3	
Severance	Margaret	m.	PCo	26 Oct. 1881	3	4	
Seward	M. V.	m.	DR	16 Nov. 1882	2	3	
Seward	M. V.	m.	PCo	22 Nov. 1882	3	5	
Seward	M. V.	m.	RRF	16 Nov. 1882	2	4	
Seward	W. V.	b.	PCo	5 Mar. 1884	3	6	
Seward	W. V.	b.	RRF	28 Feb. 1884	2	3	
Seward	W. V.	b.	SD	8 Mar. 1884	6	5	
Sewell	James Long	d.	SD	27 Oct. 1883	1	7	
Sewell	John Long	d.	CR	27 Oct. 1883	3	1	
Sewell	John Long	d.	RRF	25 Oct. 1883	3	4	
Seymore	Fred	b.	SD	23 Apr. 1881	3	8	
Seymore	George	d.	PCo	26 Nov. 1884	3	5	
Seymour	George	d.	DR	15 Nov. 1884	3	2	
Seymour	George	d.	PCo	19 Nov. 1884	3	5	
Seymour	George	d.	SD	23 Nov. 1884	2	6	
Shadle	Henry	m.	DD	7 Dec. 1883	3	2	
Shaeffer	Ignatz	m.	CR	13 May 1882	5	2	
Shaffer	James	d.	CR	26 Dec. 1885	3	2	
Shaffer	James	d.	SD	26 Dec. 1885	1	7	
Shane	Adam	o.	DR	17 Jan. 1881	3	1	
Shane	Rebecca	d.	CR	30 Apr. 1881	5	5	
Shane	Rebecca	d.	CR	30 Apr. 1881	5	5	
Shane	Rebecca	d.	DR	27 Apr. 1881	2	3	
Shane	Rebecca	d.	SD	30 Apr. 1881	3	8	
Shannon	A. G.	b.	DR	8 May 1882	2	3	
Shannon	A. G.	b.	SD	6 May 1882	3	6	
Sharon	Sarah Althea	o.	SD	10 Jan. 1885	2	1	
Sharon	William	o.	SD	10 Jan. 1885	2	1	
Sharp	Joseph	b.	DR	25 Nov. 1881	2	3	
Sharp	Joseph	b.	PCo	7 Dec. 1881	3	5	
Sharpe	C.	b.	CR	16 Apr. 1881	5	2	
Sharpe	C.	b.	CR	16 Apr. 1881	5	3	
Sharpe	Charles	b.	CR	30 Apr. 1881	5	5	
Sharpe	Charles	b.	DR	11 Apr. 1881	2	3	
Sharpe	Charles	b.	DR	25 Apr. 1881	3	2	

(1) Surname	(2) Given Name	(3)	(4)	(5) Date	(6) Pg	(7) Col	(8) Comments
Sharpe	Charles	b.	SD	16 Apr. 1881	3	8	
Sharpe	Charles	b.	SD	23 Apr. 1881	3	8	
Shattuck	D. O.	o.	SIT	22 Aug. 1885	2	2	
Shattuck	Lizzie	m.	CR	17 Mar. 1883	3		
Shattuck	Lizzie	m.	PCo	21 Mar. 1883	3	5	
Shattuck	Nellie	m.	DR	8 Dec. 1884	3	2	
Shattuck	Olivia E.	d.	DR	30 Aug. 1882	3	1	
Shattuck	Olivia E.	d.	PCo	30 Aug. 1882	3	7	
Shattuck	Olivia E.	d.	SD	2 Sept. 1882	3	1	
Shattuck	W. F.	b.	PCo	14 Mar. 1883	3	5	
Shattuck	W. F.	b.	PWA	17 Mar. 1883	3	7	
Shattuck	W. F.	b.	SD	17 Mar. 1883	3	3	
Shaver	Eli	b.	PCo	28 June 1882	3	5	
Shaver	Eli	b.	PWA	28 Mar. 1885	3	5	
Shaver	Eli	b.	SD	1 July 1882	2	3	
Shaver	George	m.	PCo	4 Feb. 1885	3	6	
Shaw	F. D.	o.	RRF	3 Jan. 1884	3	3	
Shaw	Julia M.	m.	CR	1 Jan. 1881	5	5	
Shaw	Julia M.	m.	DR	11 Jan. 1881	3	2	
Shaw	Julia M.	m.	RRF	6 Jan. 1881	2	5	
Shaw	Julia M.	m.	SD	8 Jan. 1881	3	8	
Shaw	M., Miss	m.	PCo	21 Mar. 1883	3	5	
Shaw	Mollie	m.	DD	4 Dec. 1883	3	3	
Shaw	Mollie	m.	SD	8 Dec. 1883	3	1	
Shay	B. J.	d.	SD	19 Dec. 1885	3	1 & 3	
Shay	Frank	d.	PCo	10 Sept. 1884	3	2	
Shay	Patrick	d.	PCo	10 Sept. 1884	3	2	
Shay	Willie	d.	PCo	10 Sept. 1884	3	2	
Shea	family	o.	PWA	4 Oct. 1884	3	3	
Shea	Frank	d.	SD	13 Sept. 1884	3	3	
Shea	Patrick	d.	SD	13 Sept. 1884	3	3	
Shea	William	d.	SD	13 Sept. 1884	3	3	
Shear	Hattie Bell	d.	DR	31 Oct. 1881	2	3	
Shear	Hattie Bell	d.	RRF	27 Oct. 1881	2	5	
Shear	Hattie Bell	d.	SD	12 Nov. 1881	3	7	
Shear	Mattie Bell	d.	PCo	2 Nov. 1881	3	5	
Shear	Orrin (dau. of)	d.	CR	28 May 1881	4	1	Mark West Cemetery
Shear	Orrin	d.	RRF	27 Oct. 1881	2	5	
Shearer	Cynthia A.	d.	RRF	2 June 1881	2	3	Mark West Cem.
Shearer	Cynthia L.	d.	DR	30 May 1881	2	3	
Shearer	Cynthia L.	m.	SD	4 June 1881	3	8	

(1) Surname	(2) Given Name	(3)	(4)	(5) Date	(6) Pg	(7) Col	(8) Comments
Shearer	D. M.	b.	SD	16 Sept. 1822	3	7	
Shearer	M. M.	b.	PCo	20 Sept. 1882	3	6	
Shearer	Orren	d.	RRF	2 June 1881	2	3	
Shedd	E. D.	d.	PCo	27 May 1885	3	6	
Shedd	Edward D.	m.	DR	11 Dec. 1884	3	2	
Shedd	Edward D.	m.	PCo	17 Dec. 1884	2	4	
Shedden	John	d.	PWA	2 June 1883	3	8	
Sheddon	John	d.	PC	30 May 1883	3	2	
Sheddon	John	d.	PWA	26 May 1883	3	1	
Shedon	John	d.	SD	2 June 1883	1	5	
Sheidckee	Caroline	m.	DR	1 Aug. 1885	3	4	
Sheldon	Dexter B.	m.	PCo	7 Jan. 1885	3	6	
Sheldon	Dexter B.	m.	SD	3 Jan. 1885	2	7	
Shelford	(infant daughter)	d.	SD	10 June 1882	2	3	
Shelford	E. M.	b.	DD	16 July 1883	3	2	
Shelford	E. M.	b.	PC	18 July 1883	3	5	
Shelford	E. M.	b.	RRF	12 July 1883	2	4	
Shelford	E. M.	b.	SD	21 June 1883	2	4	
Shelford	Erastus	m.	CR	28 May 1881	5	5	
Shelford	Erastus M.	m.	DR	30 May 1881	2	3	
Shelford	Erastus M.	m.	RRF	26 May 1881	2	5	
Shelford	Erastus M.	m.	SD	4 June 1881	3	8	
Shelford	L., Miss	m.	PCo	1 July 1885	3	6	
Shelford	Letitia	m.	CR	27 June 1885	3	2	
Shelford	Levi	b.	CR	12 Nov. 1881	5	3	
Shelford	Levi	b.	CR	22 Dec. 1883	3	1	
Shelford	Levi	b.	DR	14 Nov. 1881	2	3	
Shelford	Levi	b.	PCo	16 Nov. 1881	3	5	
Shelford	Levi	b.	RRF	17 Nov. 1881	2	3	
Shelford	Levi	b.	SD	19 Nov. 1881	4	8	
Shelford	Mr. & Mrs.	b.	PCo	7 June 1882	3	5	
Shelford	Mr. & Mrs.	b.	SD	10 June 1882	2	3	
Shelford	Mr. & Mrs. (dau. of)	d.	PCo	7 June 1882	3	5	
Shelford	P.	b.	DR	31 Jan. 1882	2	3	
Shelford	P.	b.	RRF	2 Feb. 1882	3	7	
Shelford	P.	b.	SD	4 Feb. 1882	3	6	
Shelford	Peter	b.	PCo	3 Sept. 1884	2	5	
Shelford	Peter	b.	SD	6 Sept. 1884	2	5	
Shelton	A. C.	b.	DR	8 Mar. 1882	2	3	
Shelton	A. C.	b.	PCo	1 Mar. 1882	2	4	
Shelton	A. C.	b.	SD	11 Mar. 1882	3	6	
Shelton	Elizabeth	d.	DR	1 May 1882	3	2	

(1) Surname	(2) Given Name	(3)	(4)	(5) Date	(6) Pg	(7) Col	(8) Comments
Shelton	Elizabeth	d.	PCo	3 May 1882	3	5	
Shelton	Elizabeth	d.	PCo	10 May 1882	3	5	
Shelton	Elizabeth	d.	RRF	11 May 1882	2	3	
Shelton	Elizabeth	d.	SD	29 Apr. 1882	3	6	
Shelton	Fred	m.	PWA	4 Oct. 1884	3	4	
Shelton	Fred	m.	SD	11 Oct. 1884	2	5	
Shepherd	M. F.	b.	DR	26 July 1881	2	2	
Shepherd	M. F.	b.	SD	30 July 1881	3	8	
Shepherd	Melville	d.	DR	1 May 1882	3	2	
Shepherd	William	b.	PCo	1 Nov. 1882	3	5	
Shepherd	William	b.	RRF	26 Oct. 1882	2	3	
Sheppard	Hattie E.	m.	DR	23 Jan. 1882	2	3	
Sheppard	Hattie E.	m.	SD	28 Jan. 1882	3	6	
Sheriff	Annie	d.	SD	12 Mar. 1881	3	8	
Sherman	Ida J.	m.	PCo	3 May 1882	3	5	
Sherman	Mamie	m.	SD	12 Mar. 1881	3	8	
Sherow	Eva	m.	PCo	2 Aug. 1882	3	6	
Sherow	Eva	m.	PCo	16 Aug. 1882	3	6	
Sherow	Eva	m.	RRF	27 July 1882	2	4	
Sherow	Eva	m.	SD	5 Aug. 1882	3	5	
Sherwood	Ethan A.	m.	SD	24 Oct. 1885	1	4	
Sheurer	Felicia	d.	PCo	2 Aug. 1882	3	6	
Shield	Edward D.	m.	SD	13 Dec. 1884	2	5	
Shiell	Agnes	m.	SD	12 May 1883	2	6	
Shiell	Agnes J. W.	m.	PC	16 May 1883	3	5	
Shiell	Agnes J. W.	m.	PWA	19 May 1883	3	8	
Shiell	Frank R.	m.	PCo	21 Mar. 1883	3	5	
Shier	Jake	m.	SD	28 May 1881	3	8	
Shinn	John	d.	CR	19 Dec. 1885	3	3&4	Big Springs Cem.
Shinn	John	o.	PCo	16 Dec. 1885	3	2	
Shinn	John	d.	SD	19 Dec. 1885	3	1	
Shinn	Mary	d.	DR	6 Aug. 1884	3	2	
Shipley	M. A., Mrs.	d.	RRF	17 Feb. 1881	2	5	
Shipley	Mary A.	d.	CR	12 Mar. 1881	5	4&5	
Shipley	Mary A.	m.	DR	14 Mar. 1881	2	3	
Shipley	Mrs.	d.	RRF	17 Feb. 1881	3	5	Cloverdale
Shipley	R. J.	m.	CR	4 Mar. 1882	5	1&2	
Shipley	R. J.	m.	DR	28 Feb. 1882	2	3	
Shipley	R. J.	m.	PCo	8 Mar. 1882	3	5	
Shipley	R. J.	d.	RRF	17 Feb. 1881	2	5	
Shipley	R. J.	m.	SD	4 Mar. 1882	3	6	
Shipley	R. J., Mrs.	d.	CR	12 Mar. 1881	5	4&5	

(1) Surname	(2) Given Name	(3)	(4)	(5) Date	(6) Pg	(7) Col	(8) Comments
Shippy	B. J.	b.	SD	13 Aug. 1881	3	8	
Shippy	Burton	b.	PCo	6 Dec. 1882	3	6	
Shire	Jacob	m.	CR	28 May 1881	5	5	
Shire	Jacob	m.	RRF	19 May 1881	2	4	
Shire	Jacob	m.	SD	4 June 1881	3	8	
Shirley	Almira	d.	DR	1 Dec. 1885	3	4	
Shirley	Almira	d.	PCo	23 Nov. 1885	3	4	
Shiveley	Jennie May	o.	DR	26 Feb. 1881	3	2	
Shiveley	William B.	o.	DR	26 Feb. 1881	3	2	
Shively	J. H.	m.	RRF	26 Apr. 1883	2	3	
Shively	J. H.	m.	SD	21 Apr. 1883	2	6	
Shoat	L.	b.	SD	26 Mar. 1881	3	8	
Shobridge	Eugene	d.	SD	27 Sept. 1884	3	2	
Shoemake	Omar	b.	SD	1 June 1881	3	7	
Sholes	Eva A.	m.	DR	2 June 1884	3	2	
Sholes	Eva A.	m.	PCo	4 June 1884	3	5	
Sholes	Pearl J.	m.	DR	26 Jan. 1882	2	3	
Sholes	Pearl J.	m.	HE	26 Jan. 1882	2	3	
Sholes	Pearl J.	m.	RRF	26 Jan. 1882	2	2	
Sholes	Pearl J.	m.	SD	4 Feb. 1882	3	6	
Shone	Edwin	b.	CR	29 Jan. 1881	5	5	
Shone	Edwin	b.	DR	26 Jan. 1881	3	2	
Shone	Edwin	b.	SD	29 Jan. 1881	3	8	
Short	Caroline	m.	SD	5 Mar. 1881	3	8	
Shortridge	(female)	b.	DR	21 Apr. 1884	3	2	
Shortridge	E.	b.	PCo	16 Apr. 1884	3	5	
Shortridge	E.	b.	SD	12 Apr. 1884	2	5	
Shortridge	E. S.	b.	SD	3 May 1884	3	3	
Shortridge	Elisha S.	m.	PC	13 June 1883	3	6	
Shottie	J. R.	b.	DR	9 Oct. 1885	3	4	
Shottie	J. R.	b.	PCo	7 Oct. 1885	3	6	
Showalter	Victoria	m.	DR	1 Aug. 1882	3	2	
Showalter	Victoria	m.	PCo	2 Aug. 1882	3	6	
Showalter	Victoria	m.	SD	29 July 1882	3	7	
Shriver	Lorena	m.	PCo	21 Mar. 1883	3	5	
Shuler	Ella	m.	DR	11 July 1881	2	3	
Shuler	Ella	m.	RRF	7 July 1881	2	4	
Shuler	Florence M.	m.	DR	17 Nov. 1881	2	3	
Shuler	Florence M.	m.	PCo	23 Nov. 1881	3	5	
Shuler	Florence M.	m.	RRF	17 Nov. 1881	2	3	
Shuler	Florence M.	m.	SD	26 Nov. 1881	3	8	
Shulte	W. H.	b.	SD	2 Sept. 1882	3	6	

(1) Surname	(2) Given Name	(3)	(4)	(5) Date	(6) Pg	(7) Col	(8) Comments
Shulte	William	m.	SD	26 Feb. 1881	3	8	
Shuster	John	d.	PC	1 Aug. 1883	3	6	
Shuster	John	d.	PWA	28 July 1883	3	7	
Sibbald	John	b.	PCo	20 Aug. 1884	3	4	
Sibbald	John	b.	PWA	23 Aug. 1884	3	4	
Sibbald	John	b.	SD	6 Sept. 1884	2	5	
Sides	Catherine	m.	SD	10 May 1884	2	4	
Sieman	Emil	m.	DD	4 Dec. 1883	3	3	
Silberhorn	Addie	m.	DD	29 Dec. 1883	3	3	
Silva	F. A.	b.	PCo	4 Mar. 1885	3	6	
Silva	F. A.	b.	PWA	7 Mar. 1885	3	5	
Silva	Frank A.	d.	PCo	16 Dec. 1885	3	6	
Silva	John A.	b.	DD	29 Sept. 1883	3	2	
Silvers	Lizzie	m.	SD	3 Dec. 1881	3	8	
Simmons	A. R.	b.	DR	26 Sept. 1881	3	2	
Simmons	A. R.	b.	SD	1 Oct. 1881	3	8	
Simmons	B. O.	b.	SD	6 Aug. 1881	3	8	
Simmons	Ben	b.	PCo	23 Jan. 1884	3	5	
Simmons	Ben	b.	RRF	17 Jan. 1884	2	4	
Simmons	Charles Emerson	m.	SD	19 Jan. 1884	3	6	
Simmons	Horace F.	m.	DR	26 Aug. 1885	3	4	
Simonds	Mr. & Mrs.	b.	DD	4 Dec. 1883	3	3	
Simonson	Ole (dau. of)	d.	DD	27 Oct. 1883	3	3	
Simpson	A. W.	b.	PCo	17 Jan. 1883	3	5	
Simpson	A. W.	b.	SD	13 Jan. 1883	3	5	
Simpson	Everett	d.	DD	13 Aug. 1883	3	3	
Simpson	Everett S.	d.	SD	18 Aug. 1883	2	6	
Simpson	G. B.	b.	PCo	6 Dec. 1882	3	6	
Simpson	G. R.	b.	DR	13 Dec. 1882	2	3	
Simpson	G. R.	b.	SD	16 Dec. 1882	3	6	
Simpson	Hattie A.	m.	PWA	9 Feb. 1884	3	6	
Simpson	Hattie A.	m.	SD	16 Feb. 1884	2	5	
Simpson	J.	b.	SD	28 Jan. 1882	3	6	
Simpson	James (infant dau.)	d.	SD	29 Jan. 1881	3	8	
Simpson	James	b.	CR	15 Jan. 1881	5	5	
Simpson	James	b.	DR	12 Aug. 1882	3	2	
Simpson	James	b.	RRF	13 Jan. 1881	2	5	
Simpson	James	b.	RRF	10 Aug. 1882	2	4	
Simpson	James	b.	SD	12 Aug. 1882	3	5	
Simpson	James, Mrs.	d.	RRF	28 Sept. 1882	3	6	
Simpson	James (dau. of)	d.	CR	22 Jan. 1881	5	5	
Simpson	Janus	b.	SD	22 Jan. 1881	3	8	

(1) Surname	(2) Given Name	(3)	(4)	(5) Date	(6) Pg	(7) Col	(8) Comments
Simpson	Mary J.	d.	RRF	5 Oct. 1882	2	3	Healdsburg
Simpson	Mattie A.	m.	PCo	6 Feb. 1884	3	6	
Simpson	W. B.	b.	PCo	8 Oct. 1884	3	6	
Simpson	W. B.	b.	SD	11 Oct. 1884	2	5	
Sinclair	Annie F.	m.	SD	11 Aug. 1883	2	7	
Sinclair	Lena	m.	DR	5 Aug. 1884	3	4	
Sinclair	Lena	m.	SD	9 Aug. 1884	3	4	
Sing	Ah	d.	CR	1 July 1885	3	1	
Sink	William	b.	DR	27 Jan. 1882	2	3	
Sink	William	b.	SD	28 Jan. 1882	3	6	
Sitton	Grant B.	d.	PCo	4 Mar. 1885	3	6	
Sitton	Grant B.	d.	PWA	7 Mar. 1885	3	5	
Sitton	Grant B.	d.	PWA	14 Mar. 1885	3	1	
Siveed	Philip	b.	PWA	6 Oct. 1883	3	8	
Skaggs family		o.	SD	9 Aug. 1884	3	4	
Skaggs	Charles Walter	d.	PC	30 May 1883	3	4	
Skaggs	Charles Walter	d.	RRF	24 May 1883	2	4	Skaggs Springs
Skaggs	E.	m.	DR	28 Sept. 1885	3	4	
Skaggs	E.	m.	PCo	7 Oct. 1885	3	6	
Skaggs	E.	m.	SRR	1 Oct. 1885	3	3	
Skaggs	Eben	m.	SD	3 Oct. 1885	5	4	
Skaggs	Nancy	d.	CR	8 Sept. 1883	3	1	
Skaggs	Nancy	d.	DD	8 Sept. 1883	3	3	
Skaggs	Nancy	d.	RRF	6 Sept. 1883	2	4	Oak Mound Cemetery
Skaggs	Walter	b.	PCo	18 Oct. 1882	3	6	
Skaggs	Walter	b.	RRF	12 Oct. 1882	2	3	
Skaggs	William W.	o.	SD	21 Feb. 1885	1	4	
Skaggs	Wilson W.	m.	RRF	4 Oct. 1883	2	3	
Skaggs	Wilson	m.	HE	4 Oct. 1883	2	3	
Skillman	Eva	m.	CR	5 Mar. 1881	4	2	
Skillman	Eva	m.	DR	1 Mar. 1881	3	2	
Skillman	Eva	m.	PCo	9 Mar. 1881	3	4	
Skillman	Eva	m.	SD	5 Mar. 1881	3	8	
Skillman	Mary C.	d.	DR	12 May 1884	3	2	
Skillman	Mary C.	d.	PCo	7 May 1884	3	5	
Skillman	Mary C.	d.	SD	17 May 1884	3	5	
Skillman	Mary Catherine	d.	PWA	10 May 1884	3	2&5	Cypress Hill Cem.
Skillman	Mary Catherine	d.	RRF	15 May 1884	5	6	
Skinner	Annie	d.	SD	9 Aug. 1884	3	4	
Skinner	Annie F.	d.	PCo	6 Aug. 1884	2	4	
Skinner	Annie Peoples	m.	DR	5 Aug. 1884	3	4	

(1) Surname	(2) Given Name	(3)	(4)	(5) Date	(6) Pg	(7) Col	(8) Comments
Skinner	Annie Peoples	d.	PWA	9 Aug. 1884	2	4	
Skinner	Hugh R.	m.	DR	17 Aug. 1882	3	2	
Skinner	Hugh R.	m.	SD	2 Sept. 1882	3	6	
Skinner	W. G.	m.	CR	28 May 1881	5	5	
Skinner	W. G.	m.	DR	24 May 1881	2	2	
Skinner	W. G.	m.	SD	28 May 1881	3	8	
Skinner	William G.	m.	PCo	25 May 1881	3	5	
Sl\pencer	Nannie	m.	SD	9 Aug. 1884	3	4	
Slater	Rhoda	d.	SD	25 Oct. 1884	2	5	
Slattery	Wilham J.	d.	DR	24 Feb. 1882	2	3	
Slattery	William J.	d.	HE	23 Feb. 1882	3	1	
Slattery	William J.	d.	PCo	22 Feb. 1882	3	5	
Slattery	William	d.	CR	4 Mar. 1882	1	4	
Slattery	William	d.	SD	25 Feb. 1882	3	3&6	
Slayton	C. W.	o.	SIT	5 Sept. 1995	2	3	
Slayton	Margaret	o.	SIT	5 Sept. 1995	2	3	
Slepka	Henry	b.	DD	26 Oct. 1883	3	3	
Slepka	Henry	b.	PWA	27 Oct. 1883	3	8	
Sloane	M. S., Miss	m.	SD	22 July 1882	3	5	
Sloane	M. S.	m.	PCo	19 July 1882	3	6	
Slocum	George	b.	DR	9 Nov. 1882	3	2	
Slocum	George	b.	PCo	8 Nov. 1882	3	6	
Slocum	George	b.	PCo	25 Feb. 1885	3	6	
Slocum	George	b.	RRF	2 Nov. 1882	2	4	
Slocum	George	b.	SD	21 Feb. 1885	2	5	
Slocum	Maud	d.	DR	30 Dec. 1881	2	3	
Slocum	Maud	d.	HE	29 Dec. 1881	2	3	
Slocum	Maud	d.	SD	31 Dec. 1881	3	6	
Slocum	Roy	d.	PCo	8 July 1885	3	6	
Slocum	Roy	d.	SD	27 June 1885	5	4	
Sloper	David	b.	PCo	20 Sept. 1882	3	6	
Sloper	David	b.	SD	23 Sept. 1882	3	6	
Slopka	Henry	b.	SD	3 Nov. 1883	3	3	
Slusser	Bayard B.	d.	SD	11 Oct. 1884	2	5	also p. 3 col. 4
Slusser	Baynard B.	d.	PCo	15 Oct. 1884	3	6	
Slusser	L. B.	o.	SD	19 May 1883	3	2	
Slusser	L. B., Mrs.	d.	CR	19 May 1883	3	2	
Slusser	M. E.	b.	DR	5 May 1882	2	2	
Slusser	M. E.	b.	SD	6 May 1882	3	6	
Slusser	Martin	b.	DD	27 Oct. 1883	3	3	
Slusser	Martin	b.	SD	3 Nov. 1883	3	3	
Slusser	Sarah	d.	PWA	19 May 1883	3	2&8	Healdsburg

(1) Surname	(2) Given Name	(3)	(4)	(5) Date	(6) Pg	(7) Col	(8) Comments
Slusser	Sarah	d.	RRF	17 May 1883	2	3	Oak Mound Cemetery
Slusser	W. P.	b.	PCo	18 Feb. 1885	3	6	
Slusser	William P.	m.	PCo	13 Dec. 1882	3	4	
Slusser	William P.	m.	RRF	7 Dec. 1882	2	3	
Slusser	William	m.	DR	7 Dec. 1882	2	3	
Slusser	William	m.	SD	16 Dec. 1882	3	6	
Small	E. P.	m.	DR	4 Dec. 1881	2	3	
Small	E. P.	m.	PCo	30 Nov. 1881	3	5	
Small	E. P.	m.	SD	3 Dec. 1881	3	4&8	
Small	J. B.	b.	DR	29 July 1884	3	3	
Small	J. B.	b.	PCo	30 July 1884	3	6	
Small	J. B.	b.	PWA	2 Aug. 1884	3	4	
Small	Joseph B.	m.	SWI	25 Aug. 1883	3	2	
Smallwood	L. W., Mrs.	d.	SD	31 Mar. 1883	3	2	
Smissaert	Jacob H.	m.	SD	2 Apr. 1881	3	8	
Smissert	Baron Jacob H.	m.	CR	2 Apr. 1881	5	3	
Smissert	Jacob H.	m.	CR	2 Apr. 1881	5	3	
Smissert	Jacob H.	m.	DR	30 Mar. 1881	3	2	
Smith	(female)	b.	DR	28 June 1884	3	2	
Smith	A. A.	b.	PCo	10 Dec. 1884	3	5	
Smith	A. A.	b.	PWA	13 Dec. 1884	3	4	
Smith	A. A.	b.	SD	27 Dec. 1884	2	4	
Smith	Ada	d.	DD	12 Oct. 1883	3	3	
Smith	Ada	d.	PWA	6 Oct. 1883	3	8	
Smith	Ada	d.	SD	20 Oct. 1883	3	4	
Smith	Al	b.	PCo	31 May 1882	3	5	
Smith	Al	b.	SD	10 June 1882	2	3	
Smith	Annie	m.	DR	4 Mar. 1882	2	3	
Smith	Annie	m.	DR	8 Mar. 1882	2	3	
Smith	Annie	m.	PCo	15 Mar. 1882	3	4	
Smith	Annie	m.	RRF	9 Mar. 1882	2	4	
Smith	Annie	m.	SD	11 Mar. 1882	3	6	
Smith	Asa	m.	SD	16 June 1883	2	6	
Smith	Bud	b.	RRF	15 Nov. 1883	2	3	
Smith	C. W. (dau. of)	d.	CR	1 Nov. 1884	3	1	
Smith	Carrie E.	m.	SD	1 June 1881	3	7	
Smith	Carrie M.	m.	CR	1 Jan. 1881	5	5	
Smith	Charles C.	d.	CR	10 June 1882	5	2	
Smith	Charles C.	d.	RRF	15 June 1882	3	5	
Smith	Delos	b.	DD	26 Oct. 1883	3	3	
Smith	Delos	b.	PWA	27 Oct. 1883	3	8	

(1) Surname	(2) Given Name	(3)	(4)	(5) Date	(6) Pg	(7) Col	(8) Comments
Smith	Dollie A.	m.	PC	30 May 1883	3	4	
Smith	Dollie A.	m.	SD	26 May 1883	2	7	
Smith	Elizabeth	d.	RRF	10 Feb. 1881	3	6	
Smith	Elizabeth	d.	SD	19 Feb. 1881	3	8	
Smith	Ella	m.	CR	12 July 1884	3	1	
Smith	Ella	m.	DR	17 July 1884	3	3	
Smith	Ella	m.	PCo	23 July 1884	3	6	
Smith	Elward	d.	SD	1 June 1881	3	7	
Smith	Emma E.	m.	CR	29 Jan. 1881	5	5	
Smith	Emma E.	m.	RRF	27 Jan. 1881	2	4	
Smith	Emma E.	m.	SD	5 Feb. 1881	3	8	
Smith	Fanny	m.	CR	22 Mar. 1884	3	1	
Smith	Fanny	m.	SD	29 Mar. 1884	2	5	
Smith	Fillmore	m.	RRF	20 Jan. 1881	2	5	
Smith	G. W.	b.	PCo	23 Jan. 1884	3	5	
Smith	G. W.	b.	RRF	17 Jan. 1884	2	4	
Smith	George	b.	PCo	29 Oct. 1884	3	5	
Smith	George M.	b.	PWA	1 Nov. 1884	3	4	
Smith	George N.	m.	DR	1 May 1882	3	2	
Smith	George N.	m.	PCo	26 Apr. 1882	3	4	
Smith	George N.	m.	SD	29 Apr. 1882	3	6	
Smith	George T.	p.	DD	24 July 1883	3	2	
Smith	George T.	p.	DR	6 Dec. 1884	2	1	
Smith	H.	b.	CR	25 June 1881	4	3	
Smith	H.	b.	SD	2 July 1881	3	8	
Smith	H. J.	b.	DD	17 Nov. 1883	3	2	
Smith	H. J.	b.	SD	24 Nov. 1883	3	4	
Smith	Harriet C.	d.	DR	23 Oct. 1885	3	4	
Smith	Howard Eugene	d.	SD	5 Aug. 1882	3	5	
Smith	Inez B.	m.	SD	1 July 1882	2	3	
Smith	Inez C.	m.	PCo	28 June 1882	3	5	
Smith	J. F.	b.	CR	28 May 1881	5	5	
Smith	J. F.	b.	PC	16 May 1883	3	5	
Smith	J. F.	b.	RRF	26 May 1881	2	5	
Smith	J. F.	b.	SD	4 June 1881	3	8	
Smith	J. F.	b.	SD	5 May 1883	2	6	
Smith	J. Fillmore	m.	PCo	19 Jan. 1881	3	4	
Smith	J. Fillmore	m.	SD	29 Jan. 1881	3	8	
Smith	J. L.	m.	DD	23 Nov. 1883	3	2	
Smith	J. L.	m.	PWA	24 Nov. 1883	3	6	
Smith	J. L.	m.	SD	1 Dec. 1883	3	4	
Smith	J. V.	d.	DR	2 Aug. 1881	2	2	

(1) Surname	(2) Given Name	(3)	(4)	(5) Date	(6) Pg	(7) Col	(8) Comments
Smith	J. Y.	d.	PCo	3 Aug. 1881	3	5	
Smith	J. Y.	d.	SD	13 Aug. 1881	3	8	
Smith	James	b.	SD	4 June 1881	3	8	
Smith	Jennie	m.	PCo	12 July 1882	3	5	
Smith	Jennie	m.	SD	15 July 1882	2	4	
Smith	John	d.	CR	2 July 1881	5	5	
Smith	John	d.	DR	28 June 1881	2	2	
Smith	John	d.	SD	9 July 1881	3	8	
Smith	Julia	d.	PCo	28 June 1882	3	5	
Smith	L.	d.	SD	22 Sept. 1883	3	1	
Smith	Lawrence	d.	HE	4 Oct. 1883	3	3	
Smith	Legrande	m.	CR	24 Sept. 1881	1	3	
Smith	Lillian C.	m.	PCo	14 Oct. 1885	3	6	
Smith	Lizzie A.	d.	DR	2 Nov. 1885	3	4	
Smith	Lizzie A.	d.	PCo	28 Oct. 1885	3	3&4	Cypress Hill Cem.
Smith	M. J.	b.	SD	2 Apr. 1881	3	8	
Smith	Manuela T.	b.&m.	SD	19 Mar. 1881	3	1	
Smith	Maria H.	m.	DD	15 Dec. 1883	3	1	
Smith	Mertie	m.	PCo	18 Mar. 1885	3	2	
Smith	Mertle H.	m.	PWA	28 Mar. 1885	3	5	
Smith	Mr.	m.	RRF	3 Feb. 1881	3	4	
Smith	N. O.	b.	CR	23 Apr. 1881	5	3	
Smith	N. O.	b.	DR	25 Apr. 1881	3	2	
Smith	N. O.	b.	DR	22 Apr. 1882	3	2	
Smith	N. O.	b.	HE	20 Apr. 1882	2	2	
Smith	N. O.	b.	PCo	26 Apr. 1882	3	4	
Smith	N. O.	b.	RRF	20 Apr. 1882	2	3	
Smith	N. O.	b.	SD	29 Apr. 1882	3	6	
Smith	N. (dau. of)	d.	SD	25 June 1881	3	8	
Smith	Norman	b.	RRF	14 Apr. 1881	2	4	
Smith	Norman	d.	RRF	16 June 1881	2	5	
Smith	Norman	b.	SD	30 Apr. 1881	3	8	
Smith	Norman	b.	SD	18 Apr. 1885	2	4	
Smith	O. C.	b.	DR	4 Nov. 1884	3	2	
Smith	O. C.	b.	PCo	12 Nov. 1884	3	5	
Smith	Olive	m.	SD	5 Mar. 1881	3	8	
Smith	Perry C.	m.	PCo	14 Mar. 1883	3	5	
Smith	Perry C.	b.	PCo	3 June 1885	3	6	
Smith	Perry C.	m.	PWA	17 Mar. 1883	3	7	
Smith	Perry C.	m.	SD	17 Mar. 1883	3	5	
Smith	Perry C.	b.	SD	6 June 1885	2	4	
Smith	Press	b.	PCo	20 Aug. 1884	3	4	

(1) Surname	(2) Given Name	(3)	(4)	(5) Date	(6) Pg	(7) Col	(8) Comments
Smith	R. Press	b.	DR	18 Aug. 1884	3	3	
Smith	R. W.	b.	PCo	24 May 1882	3	5	
Smith	Richard	d.	PCo	30 Apr. 1884	2	6	
Smith	Richard	d.	PWA	3 May 1884	3	6	
Smith	Richard	d.	SD	10 May 1884	2	4	
Smith	Rufus	b.	PCo	28 June 1882	3	5	
Smith	Rufus	b.	SD	1 July 1882	2	3	
Smith	S. V.	b.	DR	2 Oct. 1885	3	4	
Smith	Samuel	d.	CR	28 May 1881	4	1	Oak Mound Cemetery
Smith	Samuel	d.	DR	30 May 1881	2	3	
Smith	Samuel	d.	RRF	2 June 1881	2	3	
Smith	Samuel	m.	SD	4 June 1881	3	8	
Smith	Sarah E.	m.	DR	21 Dec. 1882	2	2	
Smith	Sarah F.	m.	PCo	27 Dec. 1882	3	6	
Smith	Sarah	m.	SD	19 Mar. 1881	3	8	
Smith	Susan	d.	PCo	7 June 1882	3	5	
Smith	Susan	d.	SD	10 June 1882	2	3	
Smith	T. F.	m.	CR	22 Jan. 1881	5	5	
Smith	T. F.	b.	DR	20 Jan. 1882	3	2	
Smith	T. F.	b.	HE	19 Jan. 1882	2	3	
Smith	T. F.	b.	RRF	19 Jan. 1882	2	3	
Smith	T. F.	b.	SD	28 Jan. 1882	3	6	
Smith	W. C.	d.	SD	13 June 1885	3	5	
Smith	W. F.	d.	PCo	12 Apr. 1882	3	5	
Smith	W. F.	d.	SD	15 Apr. 1882	3	6	
Smith	William C.	d.	SD	20 June 1885	5	4	
Snedaker	E.	m.	PCo	28 May 1884	2	4	
Sneed	R.	o.	SIT	22 Aug. 1885	2	2	
Snider	Annie	m.	PC	6 June 1883	3	4	
Snider	Lillie	d.	PCo	31 Jan. 1883	3	5	
Snider	Naomi	m.	CR	26 Mar. 1881	5	5	
Snider	Naomi	m.	CR	26 Mar. 1881	5	5	
Snider	Naomi	m.	SD	2 Apr. 1881	3	8	
Snider	Naomi	m.	SD	26 Mar. 1881	3	8	
Snow	Joshua	d.	DR	18 Mar. 1884	3	3	
Snow	Joshua	d.	PCo	19 Mar. 1884	3	2&6	
Snow	Joshua	d.	PWA	15 Mar. 1884	3	6	
Snyder	John	m.	CR	7 Nov. 1885	3	5	
Snyder	John	m.	DR	9 Nov. 1885	2	2	
Snyder	Maomi	m.	DR	26 Mar. 1881	3	2	
Snyder	Maomi	m.	RRF	24 Mar. 1881	2	4	

(1) Surname	(2) Given Name	(3)	(4)	(5) Date	(6) Pg	(7) Col	(8) Comments
Sock	(Indian)	d.	CR	23 July 1881	4	1	
Sock	George	o.	CR	23 Apr. 1881	1	3	
Soldate	John	b.	PCo	6 Sept. 1882	3	7	
Soldate	John	b.	PWA	4 Apr. 1885	3	6	
Soldate	John	b.	SD	18 Apr. 1885	2	4	
Soldati	A.	m.	DR	21 July 1885	3	4	
Soldati	A.	m.	PCo	15 July 1885	3	6	
Solley	S. J.	b.	PCo	25 Oct. 1882	3	5	
Solly	S. J.	b.	DR	18 July 1884	3	3	
Solly	S. J.	b.	PCo	16 July 1884	3	6	
Solly	S. J.	b.	PWA	19 July 1884	3	4	
Soloman	Mattie A.	m.	SD	13 Aug. 1881	3	3	
Solomon	C.	b.	DR	13 Dec. 1884	1	4	
Solomon	Emma J.	m.	SD	9 Apr. 1881	3	8	
Som	Ah	o.	DR	13 Nov. 1882	3	1	
Somes	Alpheus	m.	PCo	28 Jan. 1885	3	6	
Sommer	Annie	d.	SD	14 Mar. 1885	5	5	
Sorenson	Hans	d.	PCo	3 Aug. 1881	3	5	
Sorenson	Hans	d.	SD	13 Aug. 1881	3	8	
Sorenson	S.	b.	SD	15 Jan. 1881	3	8	
Sorrenson	Stephen	d.	PC	1 Aug. 1883	3	6	
Soule	Frank	d.	RRF	13 July 1882	1	6	
Soules	Jessie	m.	PCo	19 Mar. 1884	3	6	
Soules	Jessie	m.	PWA	22 Mar. 1884	3	6	
Soules	Jessie	m.	SD	22 Mar. 1884	2	4	
Soules	L. O.	d.	RRF	11 May 1882	2	3	
Soules	L. O.	m.	RRF	13 Mar. 1884	2	2	
Soules	Marian	d.	DR	13 May 1882	2	3	
Soules	Marian	d.	HE	11 May 1882	2	3	
Soules	Marian	d.	PCo	17 May 1882	3	5	
Soules	Marian	d.	SD	20 May 1882	2	4	
Soules	Stephen	d.	DR	13 May 1882	2	3	
Soules	Stephen	d.	HE	18 May 1882	2	3	
Soules	Stephen	d.	PCo	24 May 1882	3	5	
Soules	Stephen	d.	RRF	11 May 1882	2	3	
Soules	Stephen	d.	RRF	18 May 1882	2	3	
Sowerly	E. M.	m.	PCo	15 Feb. 1882	3	4	
Sowerly	E. P.	m.	DR	7 Feb. 1882	2	3	
Sowerly	E. P.	m.	SD	11 Feb. 1882	3	6	
Sowers	W. R.	b.	PCo	24 Sept. 1884	3	5	
Sowers	William R.	m.	PC	27 June 1883	3	6	
Sowers	William R.	m.	SD	23 June 1883	3	5	

(1) Surname	(2) Given Name	(3)	(4)	(5) Date	(6) Pg	(7) Col	(8) Comments
Sparrow	E. D.	b.	PCo	30 Jan. 1884	3	6	
Spaulding	L. F.	d.	PWA	15 Sept. 1883	3	2	
Spaulding	Maud E.	m.	DR	3 Dec. 1881	2	3	
Spaulding	Maud E.	m.	PCo	7 Dec. 1881	3	5	
Spaulding	Maud E.	m.	SD	3 Dec. 1881	3	8	
Spear	S. (son of)	d.	PCo	1 Oct. 1884	3	5	
Spears	C.	b.	PCo	27 Sept. 1882	3	6	
Spears	Cy	b.	RRF	28 Sept. 1882	2	3	
Spears	Cy	b.	SD	30 Sept. 1882	3	6	
Spence	W. O., Miss	m.	SD	7 Nov. 1885	3	1	
Spence	W. Olive	m.	DR	4 Nov. 1885	3	4	
Spencer	Homer T.	d.	CR	5 July 1884	3	1	
Spencer	Homer T.	b.	DD	8 Oct. 1883	3	2	
Spencer	Homer T.	d.	DR	1 July 1884	3	3	
Spencer	Homer T.	m.	SD	11 Feb. 1882	3	6	
Spencer	Homer Thomas	d.	SD	5 July 1884	2	3	
Spencer	Nannie	m.	DR	29 July 1884	3	3	
Spencer	Nannie	m.	PCo	30 July 1884	3	6	
Spencer	Nannie	m.	PWA	2 Aug. 1884	3	4	
Spencer	Nonie	m.	PCo	7 Oct. 1885	3	6	
Spencer	Nonie	m.	SD	10 Oct. 1885	5	5	
Spencer	Nonie	m.	SIT	3 Oct. 1885	2	3	
Spencer	T.	m.	DR	13 Feb. 1882	2	3	
Spielman	L. W.	b.	SD	12 Mar. 1881	3	8	
Spillone	John	b.	DR	27 Jan. 1882	2	3	
Spillone	John	b.	SD	28 Jan. 1882	3	6	
Spivy	Mrs.	d.	SD	16 Apr. 1881	3	8	
Splaunn	John	b.	DD	16 July 1883	3	2	
Splaunn	John	b.	PC	18 July 1883	3	5	
Sponogle	Olive J.	d.	RRF	19 July 1883	2	4	
Sponogle	Olive	d.	RRF	5 July 1883	2	4	Ohio
Sponogle	Ollie J.	d.	PC	11 July 1883	3	5	
Spotswood	Ernest	d.	PCo	17 Sept. 1884	3	6	
Spotswood	Ernest	d.	PWA	20 Sept. 1884	3	4	
Spotswood	George	b.	PCo	16 Nov. 1881	3	5	
Spotswood	George	b.	PCo	28 Feb. 1883	3	5	
Spotswood	George	b.	SD	26 Nov. 1881	3	8	
Spotswood	George	b.	SD	3 Mar. 1883	2	6	
Spotswood	James M.	d.	PCo	12 Apr. 1882	3	5	
Spotswood	James M.	d.	SD	15 Apr. 1882	3	6	
Spottswood	Ernest	d.	SD	27 Sept. 1884	2	5	
Spottswood	George	d.	PWA	3 Mar. 1883	3	6	

(1) Surname	(2) Given Name	(3)	(4)	(5) Date	(6) Pg	(7) Col	(8) Comments
Sprague	Edward E.	m.	PCo	31 Jan. 1883	3	5	
Sprague	Edward E.	m.	RRF	25 Jan. 1883	2	4	
Sprague	Edwin E.	m.	SD	27 Jan. 1883	3	6	
Sprague	Kate Chase	o.	DR	29 May 1882	3	1	
Sprague	William A.	m.	SD	23 May 1885	2	5	
Springer	Mary E.	d.	PWA	1 Nov. 1884	3	4	
Springer	Tim	m.	DR	8 Mar. 1882	2	3	
Springer	Timothy	m.	PCo	1 Mar. 1882	2	4	
Springer	Timothy	m.	SD	11 Mar. 1882	3	6	
Springsteen	Emma	m.	DR	5 Oct. 1881	2	3	
Springsteen	Emma	m.	SD	8 Oct. 1881	3	8	
Sproehnle	Frank	d.	DR	30 Aug. 1882	3	2	Chicago, IL
Sproenhle	Frank	d.	DR	14 Sept. 1882	3	1	Chicago, IL
Sproule	Frank	b.	SD	3 Sept. 1881	3	8	
Spurr	Allen H.	m.	CR	27 Dec. 1884	3	1	
Spurr	Rose R.	m.	PCo	1 Oct. 1884	3	5	
Squires	M. E., Mrs.	m.	RRF	2 Mar. 1882	3	6	
Squires	Mary E.	m.	SD	4 Mar. 1882	3	6	
St. Clair	F. C.	b.	DR	9 Feb. 1882	2	3	
St. Clair	F. C.	b.	HE	9 Feb. 1882	2	3	
St. Clair	F. C.	b.	PCo	15 Feb. 1882	3	4	
St. Clair	F. C.	b.	RRF	16 Feb. 1882	2	4	
St. Clair	F. C.	b.	SD	11 Feb. 1882	3	6	
St. Clair	Frank C.	d.	RRF	3 Jan. 1884	1	6	
St. Clair	Frank Chapel	d.	RRF	13 Dec. 1883	3	3	Oak Mound Cemetery
St. Clair	Frank	d.	PCo	19 Dec. 1883	3	4	
St. Clair	John F.	b.	PCo	1 Oct. 1884	3	5	
St. Clair	John F.	b.	PWA	27 Sept. 1884	2	4	
St. Clair	John F.	b.	SD	4 Oct. 1884	3	5	
St. Clair	Nancy	b.	PCo	14 May 1884	3	4	
St. Clair	Nancy	b.	RRF	8 May 1884	5	6	
St. Clair	Nancy	b.	SD	17 May 1884	3	5	
St. John	Adia C.	b.	PWA	1 Nov. 1884	3	4	
St. John	Adin C.	m.	PCo	20 Sept. 1882	3	6	
St. John	Adin C.	b.	PCo	29 Oct. 1884	3	5	
St. John	Adin C.	m.	SD	23 Sept. 1882	3	6	
St. John	Anna	m.	PCo	29 Nov. 1882	3	6	
St. John	S. C.	b.	PCo	22 Oct. 1884	3	6	
St. John	S. C.	b.	PWA	25 Oct. 1884	3	4	
St. John	S. C.	b.	SD	8 Nov. 1884	2	5	
St. Ores	Libbie	m.	SD	25 July 1885	3	5	

(1) Surname	(2) Given Name	(3)	(4)	(5) Date	(6) Pg	(7) Col	(8) Comments
Stakemire	G.	b.	SD	9 July 1881	3	8	
Staley	Charles	m.	SD	24 Jan. 1885	5	5	
Staley	Jennie	m.	PC	13 June 1883	3	6	
Stanley	Ina May	m.	PCo	30 Nov. 1881	3	5	
Stanley	Ina May	m.	SD	26 Nov. 1881	3	8	
Stanley	J. D.	m.	PC	11 July 1883	3	5	
Stanley	J. D.	m.	PWA	14 July 1883	3	6	
Stanley	Jefferson D.	m.	SD	7 July 1883	2	5	
Stanley	L. R.	b.	SD	18 Feb. 1882	3	6	
Staples	John	b.	DD	15 Sept. 1883	3	3	
Stapp	I. N.	m.	RRF	2 Mar. 1882	3	6	
Stapp	I. N.	m.	SD	4 Mar. 1882	3	6	
Stapp	Nettie	d.	HE	12 Apr. 1883	2	4	
Stapp	Nettie	d.	PC	18 Apr. 1883	3	5	
Stapp	Nettie	d.	RRF	12 Apr. 1883	2	5	Oak Mound Cemetery
Stapp	Nettie	d.	SD	28 Apr. 1883	3	6	
Starett	Robert	m.	DR	23 Mar. 1882	2	3	
Stark	Thomas	b.	CR	23 Apr. 1881	5	3	
Stark	Thomas	b.	DR	25 Apr. 1881	3	2	
Stark	Thomas	b.	RRF	28 Apr. 1881	2	3	
Stark	Thomas	b.	SD	14 May 1881	3	8	
Stark	Thomas	b.	SD	30 Apr. 1881	3	8	
Starke	F. J.	b.	PCo	10 Jan. 1883	3	6	
Starke	F. J.	b.	PWA	12 Jan. 1883	3	6	
Starke	F. J.	b.	SD	13 Jan. 1883	3	5	
Starke	Fred	p.	DR	26 Dec. 1884	2	2	
Starke	Frederick	d.	DR	21 Nov. 1884	3	2	
Starke	Frederick	d.	PCo	19 Nov. 1884	3	5	
Starke	Frederick	d.	PWA	22 Nov. 1884	3	4	
Starke	Wilhelmina Friedreke	d.	PCo	31 Aug. 1881	3	5	
Starke	Wilhelmini Fredreke	d.	SD	10 Sept. 1881	3	8	
Starkey	Elizabeth K.	m.	SD	8 Jan. 1881	3	8	
Starr	E. G.	d.	DR	3 Dec. 1881	2	3	
Starr	E. G.	d.	PCo	30 Nov. 1881	3	5	
Starr	Elmon G.	d.	SD	10 Dec. 1881	3	3 & 7	
Starrett	Robert (son of)	d.	DR	19 Dec. 1882	3	2	
Starrett	Robert (son of)	d.	PCo	27 Dec. 1882	3	6	
Starrett	Robert	b.	DR	19 Dec. 1882	3	2	
Starrett	Robert	b.	PCo	27 Dec. 1882	3	6	
Starrett	Robert	m.	PCo	29 Mar. 1882	3	5	
Starrett	Robert	m.	SD	25 Mar. 1882	3	6	

(1) Surname	(2) Given Name	(3)	(4)	(5) Date	(6) Pg	(7) Col	(8) Comments
Steadman	Clara	d.	PCo	25 Oct. 1882	3	5	
Steamer	Charles	m.	DR	16 Sept. 1882	3	4	
Stearns	Charles	m.	SRR	1 Oct. 1885	3	3	
Stearns	Charles D.	m.	DR	28 Sept. 1885	3	4	
Stearns	Charles D.	m.	SD	19 Sept. 1885	2	4	
Stedman	Clara	d.	DR	24 Oct. 1882	3	2	
Stedman	Clara	d.	RRF	19 Oct. 1882	2	3	
Steel	M. A.	m.	SD	17 Oct. 1885	2	7	also p. 4 col. 5
Steel	M. A., Miss	m.	DR	14 Oct. 1885	3	4	
Steele	J. A.	b.	SD	19 July 1884	2	5	
Steele	J. H.	m.	RRF	20 Oct. 1881	2	4	
Steele	J.	m.	PCo	12 Oct. 1881	3	5	
Steele	Julius A.	m.	DR	7 Oct. 1881	2	3	
Steele	Julius A.	m.	SD	15 Oct. 1881	3	8	
Steiger	Ed	b.	SD	23 July 1881	3	8	
Stein	A. H.	d.	DR	9 Apr. 1882	3	2	
Steinbach	Fred	m.	DR	17 Feb. 1882	2	3	
Steinbach	Fred	m.	PCo	22 Feb. 1882	3	5	
Steinbach	Fred	m.	RRF	16 Feb. 1882	2	4	
Steinbach	Fred	m.	SD	18 Feb. 1882	3	6	
Steinbach	Marguerita	d.	DR	9 Nov. 1885	2	2	
Steinberger	Charles M.	m.	SD	31 Dec. 1881	3	6	
Steitz	Henry	o.	DR	2 Nov. 1882	2	2	
Steitz	Henry	o.	DR	26 Oct. 1882	2	2	
Stelend	Peter	m.	PCo	22 July 1885	3	6	
Stelend	Peter	m.	SD	18 July 1885	5	5	
Stemmons	A., Mrs.	d.	SD	24 Jan. 1885	5	5	
Stemple	A. P.	m.	DR	9 Nov. 1882	3	2	
Stemple	A. P.	m.	PCo	8 Nov. 1882	3	6	
Stemple	Charles	d.	DR	3 July 1884	2	2	
Stemple	Henrietta E.	m.	DR	12 Jan. 1882	3	2	
Stemple	Henrietta G.	m.	PCo	18 Jan. 1882	3	5	
Stemple	Henriette G.	m.	SD	14 Jan. 1882	3	8	
Stephenson	John	d.	DR	28 Aug. 1882	3	2	
Stephenson	John	d.	RRF	24 Aug. 1882	2	3	
Stephenson	John	d.	SD	2 Sept. 1882	3	6	
Sterling	L. W.	b.	PC	18 Apr. 1883	3	5	
Sterling	P. W.	b.	CR	23 Apr. 1881	5	3	
Sterling	P. W.	b.	DR	25 Apr. 1881	3	2	
Sterling	P. W.	b.	HE	12 Apr. 1883	2	4	
Sterling	P. W.	b.	RRF	14 Apr. 1881	2	4	
Sterling	P. W.	b.	RRF	5 Apr. 1883	2	3	

(1) Surname	(2) Given Name	(3)	(4)	(5) Date	(6) Pg	(7) Col	(8) Comments
Sterling	P. W.	b.	SD	30 Apr. 1881	3	8	
Sterling	William H.	b.	SD	3 Feb. 1883	3	3	
Sternberg	Rebecca	m.	SD	28 Mar. 1885	5	6	
Stettee	Livia	m.	SD	6 Aug. 1881	3	8	
Steudeman	John J.	b.	SD	12 Mar. 1881	3	8	
Stevens	Lucy	m.	DR	4 Jan. 1884	3	3	
Stevens	Lucy	m.	PCo	23 Jan. 1884	3	5	
Stevenson	John E.	d.	DR	3 Oct. 1881	2	3	
Stevenson	John E.	d.	PCo	28 Sept. 1881	3	5	
Stevenson	John E.	d.	SD	8 Oct. 1881	3	8	
Steward	Marion	d.	SD	10 Feb. 1883	2	7	
Steward	Morton	d.	PCo	14 Feb. 1883	3	6	
Stewart	Charles	b.	PCo	7 June 1882	3	5	
Stewart	Charles	b.	SD	17 June 1882	2	4	
Stewart	Jehu	d.	PCo	13 Dec. 1882	3	1&4	
Stewart	Julia	m.	DR	25 Apr. 1884	3	2	
Stewart	Julia	p.	DR	29 Nov. 1884	3	2	
Stewart	Julia	m.	PCo	7 May 1884	3	5	
Stewart	Julia	m.	RRF	1 May 1884	5	6	
Stewart	M., Mrs.	d.	RRF	8 Feb. 1883	2	4	Oak Mound Cemetery
Stewart	William	d.	SD	10 Dec. 1881	3	2	
Stiers	Warren G.	d.	DD	18 Dec. 1883	3	1	accident at Gualala
Stiles	R. T.	b.	PC	23 May 1883	3	5	
Stiles	R. T.	b.	PWA	26 May 1883	3	7	
Stiles	R. T.	b.	SD	2 Apr. 1881	3	8	
Stiles	R. T.	b.	SD	26 Mar. 1881	3	8	
Stillwagon	Fannie	m.	SD	10 Sept. 1881	3	8	
Stine	Abram	d.	PCo	12 Apr. 1882	3	5	
Stine	Abram	d.	SD	15 Apr. 1882	3	6	
Stine	Charles	b.	PCo	9 Nov. 1881	3	5	
Stine	Charles	b.	SD	19 Nov. 1881	4	8	
Stine	Etta	m.	DR	18 Apr. 1884	3	2	
Stine	Etta	m.	PWA	26 Apr. 1884	3	6	
Stine	Etta	m.	SD	19 Apr. 1884	3	4	
Stocking	Dexter	d.	PCo	4 Mar. 1885	3	6	
Stocking	Dexter	d.	SD	7 Mar. 1885	1	6	also p. 5 col. 5
Stockstill	Eugene	d.	RRF	25 Aug. 1881	2	4	
Stockstill	Eugene	b.	RRF	25 Aug. 1881	2	4	
Stockstill	Eugene	b.	SD	3 Sept. 1881	3	8	
Stockstill	Eugene (dau. of)	d.	SD	3 Sept. 1881	3	8	
Stockton	I. N.	m.	SD	21 May 1881	3	8	

(1) Surname	(2) Given Name	(3)	(4)	(5) Date	(6) Pg	(7) Col	(8) Comments
Stockwell	Willard	m.	CR	3 Sept. 1881	5	2	
Stockwell	Willard	b.	CR	1 Dec. 1883	3	1	
Stockwell	Willard	d.	CR	24 Nov. 1883	3	1 & 2	
Stockwell	Willard	d.	DD	4 Dec. 1883	3	3	
Stockwell	Willard	d.	HE	29 Nov. 1883	3	4	
Stoddard	Harlow	d.	SD	18 Feb. 1882	3	3	
Stoddard	J.	d.	DR	18 Feb. 1882	2	3	
Stoddard	J.	d.	PCo	15 Feb. 1882	3	4	
Stoddard	William	b.	DR	18 May 1881	2	3	
Stofen	Dora Alice Engeberg	d.	SD	14 Mar. 1885	5	5	
Stofen	P. N.	b.	PWA	3 Nov. 1883	3	8	
Stofen	P. N.	b.	SWI	27 Oct. 1883	3	5	
Stone	Flora Belle	d.	CR	26 Mar. 1881	5	5	
Stone	Flora Belle	d.	DR	21 Nov. 1881	2	3	
Stone	Flora Belle	d.	RRF	17 Feb. 1881	2	5	
Stone	Flora Belle	d.	SD	2 Apr. 1881	3	8	
Stone	Flora Belle	d.	SD	19 Mar. 1881	3	8	
Stone	Hallie L.	m.	RRF	29 June 1882	2	5	
Stone	Harry	d.	RRF	17 Feb. 1881	2	5	
Stone	Hattie L.	m.	SD	24 June 1882	3	5	
Stone	J. W.	b.	PCo	9 Apr. 1884	3	6	
Stone	J. W.	b.	PWA	12 Apr. 1884	3	6	
Stone	John	m.	DD	14 Sept. 1883	3	2	
Stone	John	b.	PCo	30 July 1884	3	6	
Stone	John	b.	PWA	2 Aug. 1884	3	4	
Stone	John	m.	RRF	13 Sept. 1883	2	4	
Stone	John	m.	SD	22 Sept. 1883	2	4	
Stone	John	b.	SD	9 Aug. 1884	3	4	
Stone	N. J.	b.	CR	19 Feb. 1881	4	2	
Stone	N. J.	b.	DR	16 Feb. 1881	3	2	
Stone	N. J.	b.	DR	22 Feb. 1882	2	3	
Stone	N. J.	b.	PCo	1 Mar. 1882	2	4	
Stone	N. J.	b.	SD	19 Feb. 1881	3	8	
Stone	N. J.	b.	SD	25 Feb. 1882	3	6	
Stone	O. M. (dau. of)	d.	PC	4 July 1883	3	5	
Stone	O. M. (dau. of)	d.	SD	30 June 1883	3	5	
Stone	Oscar	d.	PCo	19 Dec. 1883	3	4	
Stone	R. A., Mrs.	m.	SD	21 May 1881	3	8	
Stone	T. B.	b.	PCo	19 Mar. 1884	3	6	
Stone	T. B.	b.	RRF	13 Mar. 1884	2	2	
Stone	T. P.	m.	PCo	21 Mar. 1883	3	5	
Stone	Thomas	b.	PCo	22 Apr. 1885	3	6	

(1) Surname	(2) Given Name	(3)	(4)	(5) Date	(6) Pg	(7) Col	(8) Comments
Stone	Thomas	d.	SD	9 May 1885	2	5	
Stone	W.	b.	PCo	14 Dec. 1881	3	4	
Stone	W.	b.	SD	17 Dec. 1881	3	7	
Stone	William	b.	DR	22 Dec. 1884	2	2	
Stone	William	b.	PC	1 Aug. 1883	3	6	
Stone	William	b.	PWA	28 July 1883	3	7	
Stone	William	b.	SD	4 Aug. 1883	2	5	
Stone	William	b.	SWI	21 July 1883	3	4	
Stone	William	b.	SWI	23 July 1883	3	4	
Stoner	Sarah E.	m.	DR	29 July 1884	3	3	
Stout	H. L.	m.	DR	11 Jan. 1881	3	2	
Stout	H. L.	m.	SD	15 Jan. 1881	3	8	
Stout	Mary E.	m.	DR	6 Aug. 1881	2	3	
Stout	Mary E.	m.	SD	20 Aug. 1881	3	8	
Stout	S. T.	m.	SD	22 Jan. 1881	3	8	
Strom	William	d.	SD	21 Feb. 1885	1	4	Weiser City, ID
Strong	Lulu A.	d.	SD	16 Apr. 1881	3	8	
Strong	Lulu	d.	CR	16 Apr. 1881	5	3	
Strong	Lulu	d.	CR	16 Apr. 1881	5	2	
Strong	Lulu	d.	DR	18 Apr. 1881	3	2	
Strong	Mary E.	d.	DR	1 Dec. 1884	3	2	under "born" heading
Strong	Mary E.	d.	PCo	3 Dec. 1884	3	5	
Struckman	Caroline	d.	DR	26 Sept. 1881	3	2	
Stuart	Mary	d.	DD	23 Aug. 1883	3	2	
Stuart	Mary	d.	SD	1 Sept. 1883	1	6	Rural Cemetery
Stuart	Mary	d.	SD	25 Aug. 1883	2	5	
Stuart	Mary	d.	SD	19 Jan. 1884	2	5	
Stuart	Nettie	m.	DR	29 Jan. 1884	3	3	
Stuart	Nettie	m.	PCo	6 Feb. 1884	3	6	
Stuart	Nettie	m.	PWA	2 Feb. 1884	3	6	
Studdert	Burton	b.	PCo	26 Jan. 1881	3	4	
Studdert	Burton	b.	SD	5 Feb. 1881	3	8	
Stump	Alameda E.	m.	CR	12 Mar. 1881	5	5	
Stump	Alameda E.	m.	DR	9 Mar. 1881	3	2	
Stump	Alameda E.	m.	SD	19 Mar. 1881	3	8	
Stump	Arnold B.	m.	DR	17 Apr. 1884	3	2	
Stump	Arnold B.	m.	SD	19 Apr. 1884	3	4	
Stump	Ella	m.	CR	12 Feb. 1881	5	5	
Stump	Ella	m.	DR	7 Feb. 1881	3	2	
Stump	Ella	m.	PCo	16 Feb. 1881	3	4	
Stump	Ella	m.	SD	12 Feb. 1881	3	8	

(1) Surname	(2) Given Name	(3)	(4)	(5) Date	(6) Pg	(7) Col	(8) Comments
Stump	Fannie A.	m.	DR	9 Nov. 1882	3	2	
Stump	Fannie A.	m.	PCo	8 Nov. 1882	3	6	
Stump	James	d.	DR	27 May 1884	3	2	
Stump	James	d.	SD	31` May 1884	2	3	
Stump	Katie	m.	DR	6 Dec. 1884	3	2	
Stump	Katie	m.	PCo	10 Dec. 1884	3	5	
Stump	Katie	m.	SD	13 Dec. 1884	2	5	
Stump	Leonard T. (son of)	d.	SD	13 Dec. 1884	2	5	
Stump	Lester B.	d.	DR	9 Dec. 1884	3	2	
Stump	Truman W.	m.	SD	2 July 1881	3	8	
Sturgeon	George L.	d.	DR	1 Feb. 1882	2	3	
Sturgeon	George L.	d.	SD	4 Feb. 1882	3	6	
Sturges	Eliza D.	d.	DR	1 July 1884	3	3	
Stussey	David	d.	CR	30 Apr. 1881	4	1	
Stussy	David	d.	DR	30 Apr. 1881	3	2	
Stussy	David	d.	RRF	14 July 1881	3	1	
Stussy	David	d.	RRF	28 Apr. 1881	3	1	
Stussy	David	d.	SD	30 Apr. 1881	3	4	
Stussy	Margaret	m.	DR	17 Feb. 1882	2	3	
Stussy	Margaret	m.	PCo	22 Feb. 1882	3	5	
Stussy	Margaret	m.	RRF	16 Feb. 1882	2	4	
Stussy	Margaretta	m.	SD	18 Feb. 1882	3	6	
Suers	Manuel	d.	DR	1 Dec. 1885	3	4	
Sulivan	Annie F.	m.	CR	10 June 1882	5	2	
Sullivan	(male)	b.	DR	15 May 1884	3	2	
Sullivan	Anna F.	m.	DR	9 June 1882	2	2	
Sullivan	Anna F.	m.	PCo	21 June 1882	3	5	
Sullivan	Anna F.	m.	SD	24 June 1882	3	5	
Sullivan	Annie	o.	CR	2 Apr. 1881	4	1	
Sullivan	C. G.	b.	PCo	21 May 1884	3	4	
Sullivan	C. G.	b.	SD	17 May 1884	3	5	
Sullivan	Denis J.	d.	PC	25 Apr. 1883	3	5	
Sullivan	Mary	m.	DD	4 Dec. 1883	3	3	
Sullivan	Mary	d.	DR	16 Nov. 1885	3	4	
Sullivan	Priscilla M.	m.	DR	21 July 1884	2	2	
Sullivan	Priscilla M.	m.	PCo	23 July 1884	3	6	
Sullivan	William	o.	DR	1 Dec. 1882	3	1	
Surer	Manuel	d.	PCo	23 Nov. 1885	3	4	
Surmifrank	Levi	m.	PCo	30 Apr. 1884	2	6	
Surryhne	Edward	b.	DR	21 Feb. 1882	3	2	
Surryhne	Emily J.	m.	DR	7 June 1884	3	3	
Surryhne	Emily J.	m.	PWA	14 June 1884	3	6	

(1) Surname	(2) Given Name	(3)	(4)	(5) Date	(6) Pg	(7) Col	(8) Comments
Sutherland	H., Mrs.	d.	SIT	21 Jan. 1888	3	2	
Sutherland	Jay	d.	DR	16 Nov. 1885	3	4	
Sutherland	Jay	d.	PCo	11 Nov. 1885	3	4	
Sutherland	Sarah M.	m.	SD	1 Sept. 1883	2	7	
Sutherland	W. H.	d.	PWA	7 Mar. 1885	3	5	
Sutherland	William H.	d.	PCo	4 Mar. 1885	3	6	
Sutherland	William H.	d.	SD	28 Feb. 1885	5	6	
Sutluffe	Harriet	m.	SD	24 Jan. 1885	5	5	
Sutton	Mary A.	m.	SD	19 Sept. 1885	2	4	
Sutton	Mary F.	m.	DR	28 Sept. 1885	3	4	
Sutton	Mary F.	m.	SRR	1 Oct. 1885	3	3	
Sutton	Mary	m.	DR	16 Sept. 1882	3	4	
Sutton	Nancy M.	m.	DR	15 Aug. 1881	3	2	
Sutton	Nancy M.	m.	SD	6 Aug. 1881	3	8	
Swain	James	d.	DR	10 Feb. 1882	2	3	
Swain	James	d.	PCo	22 Feb. 1882	3	5	
Swain	James	d.	SD	25 Feb. 1882	3	6	
Swan	Dora	m.	CR	7 May 1881	5	5	
Swan	Dora	m.	DR	30 Apr. 1881	2	3	
Swan	Dora	m.	SD	14 May 1881	3	8	
Swartz	Isadore	m.	RRF	21 Dec. 1882	3	4	
Swayze	Winfield	m.	DR	20 Oct. 1885	3	4	
Swayze	Winfield	m.	PCo	28 Oct. 1885	3	4	
Swayze	Winfield	m.	SD	24 Oct. 1885	5	4	
Sweed	Philip	b.	SD	17 Dec. 1881	3	7	
Sweed	Phillip	b.	PCo	7 Dec. 1881	3	5	
Sweeney	Charles H.	d.	PCo	16 Aug. 1882	3	6	
Sweeney	Charles H.	d.	SD	19 Aug. 1882	3	5	
Swetland	Nancy	d.	DR	25 Nov. 1881	2	3	
Swetland	Nancy	d.	PCo	23 Nov. 1881	3	5	
Swetland	Nancy	d.	SD	3 Dec. 1881	3	8	
Swinson	Gyda	m.	DR	15 Oct. 1885	3	4	
Swinson	Gyda	m.	SD	17 Oct. 1885	2	7	also p. 4 col. 5
Swisher	J. R.	b.	DR	15 Nov. 1881	2	3	
Swisher	J. R.	b.	PCo	16 Nov. 1881	3	5	
Swisher	J. R.	b.	RRF	10 Nov. 1881	2	4	
Swisher	J. R.	b.	SD	19 Nov. 1881	4	8	
Swisher	Sarah May	d.	DR	5 Jan. 1884	3	3	
Sydnor	Clara	m.	DR	7 June 1881	2	2	
Sydnor	Clara	m.	SD	11 June 1881	3	8	
Sydnor	Sabrina C.	m.	PCo	15 June 1881	3	5	
Sylva	Frank A.	b.	PCo	31 Jan. 1883	3	5	

(1) Surname	(2) Given Name	(3)	(4)	(5) Date	(6) Pg	(7) Col	(8) Comments
Sylva	Frank	b.	PWA	3 Feb. 1883	3	7	
Sylvester	J. W. (dau. of)	d.	DR	25 Nov. 1881	2	3	
Sylvester	J. W. (dau. of)	d.	PCo	23 Nov. 1881	3	5	
Sylvester	J. W.	b.	PCo	23 Nov. 1881	3	5	
Sylvester	J. W.	b.	RRF	24 Nov. 1881	2	4	
Sylvester	J. W.	d.	RRF	24 Nov. 1881	2	4	
Sylvester	J. W.	b.	SD	26 Nov. 1881	3	8	
Symonds	C. W.	d.	CR	2 July 1881	5	5	
Symonds	C. W.	m.	PCo	19 July 1882	3	6	
Symonds	C. W.	m.	SD	22 July 1882	3	5	
Symonds	Elizabeth	d.	CR	2 July 1881	5	5	
Symonds	Elizabeth	d.	DR	27 June 1881	2	2	
Symonds	Elizabeth	d.	PCo	15 June 1881	3	5	
Symonds	Elizabeth	d.	SD	9 July 1881	3	8	
Symonds	Elizabeth	d.	SD	18 June 1881	3	8	
Symth	Pashie	m.	PWA	4 Apr. 1885	3	6	

T

(1) Surname	(2) Given Name	(3)	(4)	(5) Date	(6) Pg	(7) Col	(8) Comments
Tabbett	F. B.	b.	CR	5 Feb. 1881	5	5	
Taber	Wing H.	d.	PCo	12 Aug. 1885	3	2&6	
Taft	H. F.	b.	PCo	13 Sept. 1882	3	7	
Taft	Herbert Allen	d.	PCo	28 June 1882	3	5	
Taft	Herbert Allen	d.	SD	1 July 1882	2	3	
Taggard	Frederick A.	m.	DR	18 Aug. 1885	3	4	
Taggard	Frederick	m.	SD	22 Aug. 1885	5	5	
Taggart	W. F.	m.	DR	15 Aug. 1881	3	2	
Taggart	William F.	m.	SD	6 Aug. 1881	3	8	
Talbot	Coleman	d.	DR	18 June 1881	2	3	
Talbot	Holman	b.	SD	21 Mar. 1885	2	5	
Talbot	J.	b.	CR	25 June 1881	4	3	
Talbot	Lou	d.	SD	5 May 1883	3	2	
Talbott	J. M.	b.	DR	16 May 1882	3	2	
Tallner	Henry	o.	DR	31 Aug. 1881	2	3	
Talmadge	Florence C.	d.	DR	28 July 1884	3	3	
Talmadge	Florence C.	d.	PCo	30 July 1884	3	6	
Talmadge	Florence C.	d.	PWA	2 Aug. 1884	3	4	
Tanner	James C.	m.	DR	8 Dec. 1884	3	2	
Tanner	James C.	m.	PCo	3 Dec. 1884	3	5	
Tanner	James C.	m.	PWA	29 Nov. 1884	3	4	
Tanner	James C.	m.	SD	13 Dec. 1884	2	5	
Tanner	James	d.	DR	25 Jan. 1884	2	1	
Tarbet	F. B.	b.	PCo	16 Feb. 1881	3	4	
Tarbett	F. B.	b.	CR	12 Feb. 1881	5	5	
Tarbett	F. B.	b.	DR	10 Feb. 1881	3	2	
Tarbett	F. B.	b.	RRF	10 Feb. 1881	2	5	
Tarbett	F. H.	b.	SD	19 Feb. 1881	3	8	
Tarwater	M. W.	b.	DR	9 Nov. 1882	3	2	
Tate	A. E.	b.	DD	18 Sept. 1883	3	2	
Tate	A. E.	b.	SD	22 Sept. 1883	2	4	
Tate	Augustus	b.	DR	16 Aug. 1881	2	3	
Tate	G.	b.	CR	19 Mar. 1881	5	5	
Tate	Gus	b.	SD	20 Aug. 1881	3	8	
Tate	J.	b.	CR	19 Mar. 1881	4	3	also p. 5 col. 5
Tate	J.	b.	PCo	3 Jan. 1883	3	4	
Tate	J.	b.	RRF	24 Mar. 1881	2	4	
Tate	J.	b.	RRF	4 Jan. 1883	2	2	

(1) Surname	(2) Given Name	(3)	(4)	(5) Date	(6) Pg	(7) Col	(8) Comments
Tate	J.	b.	SD	26 Mar. 1881	3	8	
Tate	J. T.	b.	CR	8 Nov. 1884	3	1	
Tate	T. J.	b.	PCo	26 Nov. 1884	3	5	
Tauzer	Albert	m.	RRF	13 Jan. 1881	2	5	
Taylor	Ada	m.	DR	5 Nov. 1884	2	2	
Taylor	Ada	m.	PCo	12 Nov. 1884	3	5	
Taylor	Ada	m.	SD	8 Nov. 1884	2	5	
Taylor	Annie	m.	SD	25 Apr. 1885	2	5	
Taylor	Charles D.	o.	DR	5 Feb. 1881	3	1	
Taylor	Cordelia W.	d.	DR	18 Mar. 1882	2	3	
Taylor	Cordelia W.	d.	SD	1 Apr. 1882	3	6	
Taylor	Elizabeth	d.	SD	26 Jan. 1884	3	5	
Taylor	George S.	d.	PCo	16 Jan. 1884	3	6	
Taylor	George S.	d.	PWA	19 Jan. 1884	3	7	
Taylor	George S.	d.	SD	19 Jan. 1884	3	6	
Taylor	Gus	b.	CR	21 Feb. 1885	3	1	
Taylor	Gus	b.	PCo	25 Feb. 1885	3	6	
Taylor	Gus	b.	SD	28 Feb. 1885	5	6	
Taylor	James A.	m.	DR	2 June 1884	3	2	
Taylor	James A.	m.	PCo	4 June 1884	3	5	
Taylor	James	m.	SD	22 Jan. 1881	3	8	
Taylor	John S.	b.	DR	2 Feb. 1882	2	3	
Taylor	John S.	b.	PCo	15 Feb. 1882	3	4	
Taylor	John S.	b.	SD	4 Feb. 1882	3	6	
Taylor	Lizzie	m.	SD	9 July 1881	3	8	
Taylor	Marian Ruth	d.	PWA	26 Jan. 1884	3	2&6	
Taylor	Mary	d.	DR	22 Jan. 1884	3	2	
Taylor	Mary	d.	PCo	30 Jan. 1884	3	6	
Taylor	Mary	d.	SD	12 July 1884	6	8	
Taylor	Mr.	d.	DR	14 Jan. 1884	3	3	
Taylor	Mrs.	m.	CR	25 Apr. 1885	5	2	
Taylor	Nellie L.	d.	PCo	3 Jan. 1883	3	4	
Taylor	Nellie L.	d.	SD	30 Dec. 1882	3	6	
Taylor	Orson A., Mrs.	d.	PCo	29 Mar. 1882	3	5	
Taylor	P. D.	d.	DR	1 Dec. 1885	3	4	
Taylor	P. D.	d.	PCo	23 Nov. 1885	3	4	
Taylor	Townsend E.	d.	PCo	7 Mar. 1883	3	5	
Taylor	W. E.	o.	SD	12 Mar. 1881	3	1	
Taylor	Wesley S.	b.	DD	14 Aug. 1883	3	2	
Taylor	Wesley S.	b.	PC	22 Aug. 1883	3	5	
Taylor	Wesley S.	b.	SD	18 Aug. 1883	2	5	
Teague	C. P., Mrs.	d.	DR	11 Oct. 1881	3	2	

(1) Surname	(2) Given Name	(3)	(4)	(5) Date	(6) Pg	(7) Col	(8) Comments
Teague	C. P., Mrs.	d.	SD	15 Oct. 1881	3	8	
Teague	Olive O.	m.	DR	28 Dec. 1881	2	2	
Teague	Olive O.	m.	PCo	4 Jan. 1882	3	7	
Teague	Olive O.	m.	SD	31 Dec. 1881	3	6	
Teale	Charles L.	b.	SD	16 July 1881	3	8	
Teale	George	b.	SD	25 Feb. 1882	3	6	
Tempel	C.	b.	PCo	26 Jan. 1881	3	4	
Temple	C.	b.	SD	5 Feb. 1881	3	8	
Temple	Edith Hood	d.	DR	1 Feb. 1882	2	3	
Temple	Edith Hood	d.	PCo	15 Feb. 1882	3	4	
Temple	Edith Hood	d.	RRF	9 Feb. 1882	2	3	
Temple	Edith Hood	d.	SD	4 Feb. 1882	3	6	
Temple	J. W.	d.	SD	29 Aug. 1885	5	3	
Temple	Jackson	o.	DR	22 Sept. 1882	2	1	
Temple	Jackson	d.	RRF	9 Feb. 1882	2	3	
Temple	Rufus A.	m.	DD	4 Oct. 1883	3	2	
Temple	Rufus A.	b.	DR	11Dec. 1884	3	2	
Temple	Rufus A.	b.	PCo	17 Dec. 1884	2	4	
Temple	Rufus A.	m.	SD	6 Oct. 1883	2	6	
Templeman	John	b.	PC	9 May 1883	3	5	
Templeman	John	b.	RRF	10 May 1883	2	3	
Templeton	John	b.	SD	12 May 1883	2	6	
Tente	William	d.	SWI	25 Aug. 1883	3	2	
Tente	William	b.	SWI	25 Aug. 1883	3	2	
Terry	America M.	d.	DD	4 Aug. 1883	3	2	
Terry	America M.	d.	PC	8 Aug. 1883	3	6	
Terry	America M.	d.	RRF	2 Aug. 1883	2	4	
Terry	America M.	d.	SD	11 Aug. 1883	2	7	
Terry	Michael	p.	DD	24 July 1883	3	2	
Terry	William, Mrs.	d.	SWI	27 Oct. 1883	3	5	
Terry	William	b.	DR	26 Sept. 1881	3	2	
Terry	William	d.	PWA	3 Nov. 1883	3	8	
Terry	William	b.	SD	1 Oct. 1881	3	8	
Tescher	Elizabeth	m.	DD	10 Nov. 1883	3	3	
Tescher	Elizabeth	m.	SD	17 Nov. 1883	3	5	
Teute	William	p.	DR	29 Nov. 1884	3	2	
Tharp	J. W.	b.	PWA	21 Apr. 1883	3	8	
Theill	Frank R.	m.	PWA	24 Mar. 1883	3	7	
Theilman	Mamie	m.	DR	4 Dec. 1881	2	3	
Thelan	J. J.	b.	SIT	28 Nov. 1885	2	3	
Thelen	J. J.	b.	PCo	2 Dec. 1885	3	4	
Theobald	William W.	b.	PCo	7 Dec. 1881	3	5	

(1) Surname	(2) Given Name	(3)	(4)	(5) Date	(6) Pg	(7) Col	(8) Comments
Therp	James	m.	CR	19 Jan. 1884	3	2	
Thevenet	Marie	d.	SD	6 Sept. 1884	2	5	
Thielman	Mamie	m.	PCo	30 Nov. 1881	3	5	
Thielman	Mamie	m.	SD	3 Dec. 1881	3	8	
Thing	Arthur	d.	PCo	11 Oct. 1882	3	6	
Thing	Arthur	d.	RRF	5 Oct. 1882	2	3	Healdsburg
Thing	Arthur	d.	SD	7 Oct. 1882	1	4	Healdsburg
Thistle	Lizzie	m.	SD	6 June 1885	2	4	
Thomas	Abigail	d.	CR	23 Apr. 1881	5	3	
Thomas	Ben	p.	DD	25 July 1883	3	2	
Thomas	Ben	m.	DR	9 Nov. 1882	3	2	
Thomas	Ben	b.	PC	1 Aug. 1883	3	6	
Thomas	Ben	m.	SD	28 Oct. 1882	3	5	
Thomas	Ben	b.	SD	28 July 1883	2	5	
Thomas	Benjamin	d.	CR	30 June 1883	3	2	
Thomas	Benjamin	d.	PC	4 July 1883	3	5	
Thomas	Benjamin	m.	PCo	8 Nov. 1882	3	6	
Thomas	Benjamin	d.	SD	7 July 1883	2	5	
Thomas	Charles	b.	DD	13 Oct. 1883	3	3	
Thomas	Isaac	m.	CR	17 Feb. 1883	3	1	
Thomas	Joseph	d.	PC	23 May 1883	3	5	
Thomas	Joseph	d.	PWA	26 May 1883	3	7	
Thomas	L. D., Mrs.	d.	PCo	29 Nov. 1882	3	6	
Thomas	Mary	d.	CR	25 Nov. 1882	3	1	Roseville, CA
Thomas	R. B.	b.	SIT	19 Dec. 1885	2	3	
Thomas	Thomas	d.	SD	15 Oct. 1881	3	1	Lower Lake
Thomas	W. S., Mrs.	d.	SIT	19 Dec. 1885	3	1	
Thomas	W.	o.	SIT	22 Aug. 1885	2	2	
Thompson	A. B.	o.	SD	11 Apr. 1885	1	3	
Thompson	A. W.	b.	SD	21 Apr. 1883	2	6	
Thompson	Annie M.	m.	DD	21 Aug. 1883	3	3	
Thompson	Annie M.	m.	SD	25 Aug. 1883	2	5	
Thompson	Eliza A.	d.	CR	21 Apr. 1883	3	1	
Thompson	Eliza A.	d.	PC	2 May 1883	3	5	
Thompson	Eliza A.	d.	RRF	19 Apr. 1883	2	3	
Thompson	Eliza A.	d.	SD	28 Apr. 1883	3	6	
Thompson	Henry	d.	CR	22 Dec. 1883	3	3	
Thompson	J. G.	b.	DR	17 June 1882	3	2	
Thompson	J. G.	b.	HE	8 June 1882	2	3	
Thompson	J. G.	b.	RRF	15 June 1882	2	4	
Thompson	J. G.	d.	RRF	31 Aug. 1882	2	4	
Thompson	J. G.	b.	SD	17 June 1882	2	4	

(1) Surname	(2) Given Name	(3)	(4)	(5) Date	(6) Pg	(7) Col	(8) Comments
Thompson	J. M.	b.	DR	24 Oct. 1882	3	2	
Thompson	J. M.	b.	PCo	25 Oct. 1882	3	5	
Thompson	J. M.	b.	RRF	19 Oct. 1882	2	3	
Thompson	John	m.	DR	2 Oct. 1885	3	4	
Thompson	John	m.	PCo	30 Sept. 1885	3	6	
Thompson	Mary C.	m.	CR	25 June 1881	4	3	
Thompson	Mary Mercer	m.	DR	12 Oct. 1885	3	4	
Thompson	Mary O.	m.	CR	25 June 1881	4	3	
Thompson	Mattie B.	m.	PCo	16 Jan. 1884	3	6	also 23 Jan., p. 3 col. 3
Thompson	Mattie B.	m.	PWA	19 Jan. 1884	3	7	
Thompson	Mattie B.	m.	SD	19 Jan. 1884	3	6	
Thompson	May C.	m.	DR	17 June 1881	2	2	
Thompson	May C.	m.	DR	21 June 1881	2	2	
Thompson	May C.	m.	SD	18 June 1881	3	4&8	
Thompson	May	m.	PCo	22 June 1881	3	5	
Thompson	May	m	RRF	23 June 1881	3	3	
Thompson	Meda	d.	DR	2 July 1881	2	3	
Thompson	Page E.	m.	DD	10 Oct. 1883	3	3	
Thompson	Page E.	m.	SD	13 Oct. 1883	3	4	
Thompson	Ralph P.	d.	SD	13 Aug. 1881	3	8	
Thompson	Retta	d.	RRF	21 Sept. 1882	3	2	
Thomson	Abigail	d.	CR	23 Apr. 1881	5	3	
Thomson	Abigail	d.	DR	26 Apr. 1881	2	2	
Thomson	Abigail	d.	RRF	28 Apr. 1881	2	3	
Thomson	Abigail	d.	SD	30 Apr. 1881	3	8	
Thomson	Alma	d.	RRF	21 June 1883	2	3	Oak Mound Cemetery
Thomson	John	m.	DR	26 Sept. 1885	3	4	
Thomson	John	m.	SRR	1 Oct. 1885	3	3	
Thomson	Meda	d.	RRF	30 June 1881	3	6	Oak Mound, Healdsburg
Thomson	R. Herber	m.	RRF	13 Sept. 1883	2	4	
Thomson	Retta	m.	RRF	9 Feb. 1882	3	4	
Thomson	S. H.	d.	DR	14 Sept. 1882	3	2	
Thomson	S. H.	m.	RRF	30 June 1881	3	6	
Thomson	S. H.	d.	RRF	7 Sept. 1882	2	4	
Thon	Charles	d.	PCo	3 Sept. 1884	2	5	
Thon	Charles	d.	PWA	6 Sept. 1884	3	4	
Thon	Charles	d.	SD	13 Sept. 1884	3	4	
Thorne	Charley	o.	DR	13 Feb. 1882	3	2	
Thornton	Ellen	d.	DR	30 Dec. 1882	2	1	
Thornton	Ellen	d.	PCo	3 Jan. 1883	3	4	
Thornton	Ellen	d.	SD	6 Jan. 1883	2	5	also p. 3 col. 2
Thornton	Ellie Roberts	d.	SD	20 Jan. 1883	3	2	

(1) Surname	(2) Given Name	(3)	(4)	(5) Date	(6) Pg	(7) Col	(8) Comments
Thornton	G. A.	b.	PCo	18 Jan. 1882	3	5	
Thornton	G. A.	b.	SD	14 Jan. 1882	3	8	
Thornton	Laura A.	m.	DD	4 Sept. 1883	2	2	
Thornton	Laura A.	m.	SD	8 Sept. 1883	2	7	
Thornton	Theresa	m.	DR	15 Aug. 1885	3	4	
Thornton	Thusa	m.	SD	22 Aug. 1885	6	2	
Thorpe	Louisa E.	m.	PCo	14 Mar. 1883	3	5	
Thorpe	Louisa E.	m.	SD	10 Mar. 1883	2	6	
Thrasher	Annie	m.	PCo	29 Mar. 1882	3	5	
Thrasher	Annie	m.	SD	25 Mar. 1882	3	6	
Thrasher	N. J.	m.	DR	23 Mar. 1882	2	3	
Thrift	Mollie	d.	DR	23 May 1881	2	2	
Thrift	Mollie	d.	SD	28 May 1881	3	8	
Throop	Althea	d.	DR	8 Mar. 1882	2	3	
Throop	Althea	d.	PCo	1 Mar. 1882	2	4	
Throop	Althea	d.	SD	25 Feb. 1882	3	6	
Throop	Emily M.	m.	PC	16 May 1883	3	5	
Thrum	James	b.	DD	23 July 1883	3	2	
Thrum	James	b.	DD	28 July 1883	3	2	
Tibbey	Anna	m.	SD	26 Mar. 1881	3	8	
Tierney	Mary	m.	PCo	25 Oct. 1882	3	5	
Tilden	Lulu	m.	DR	26 Sept. 1885	3	4	
Tilden	Lulu	m.	PCo	23 Sept. 1885	3	6	
Tilden	Lulu	m.	SRR	1 Oct. 1885	3	3	
Tillipin	James	d.	CR	2 Dec. 1882	3	3	
Timms	A.	d.	PC	25 Apr. 1883	3	2	
Tindall	C. W.	b.	SD	13 Aug. 1884	2	4	
Tipple	Joseph	d.	DD	1 Sept. 1883	3	2	
Tipple	Joseph	d.	SD	8 Sept. 1883	2	7	
Tiven	Sobrida Clara	d.	SD	15 Apr. 1882	3	6	
Tivnan	John	m.	PCo	15 June 1881	3	5	
Tivnen	Clara	d.	PCo	12 Apr. 1882	3	5	
Tivnen	J.	b.	DR	5 Apr. 1882	3	2	
Tivnen	J.	b.	PCo	12 Apr. 1882	3	5	
Tivnen	J.	b.	SD	15 Apr. 1882	3	6	
Tivnen	John	m.	DR	7 June 1881	2	2	
Tivnen	John	m.	SD	11 June 1881	3	8	
Tivnen	Sebrina Clara	d.	DR	10 Apr. 1882	2	2	
Tobin	Edward	b.	PC	1 Aug. 1883	3	6	
Tobin	Edward	b.	PWA	4 Aug. 1883	3	7	
Tobin	Edward	b.	SD	4 Aug. 1883	2	5	
Tobin	Mark	d.	SWI	26 May 1883	3	4	also 23 June, p. 3 col. 4

(1) Surname	(2) Given Name	(3)	(4)	(5) Date	(6) Pg	(7) Col	(8) Comments
Tobin	Mr. & Mrs.	b.	DR	26 Aug. 1885	3	4	
Todd	Allen J. M.	m.	SD	8 Nov. 1884	2	5	
Todd	Hugh	d.	CR	12 Feb. 1881	5	5	
Todd	Hugh	d.	DR	7 Feb. 1881	3	2	
Todd	Hugh	d.	PCo	2 Feb. 1881	3	4	
Todd	Hugh	d.	SD	12 Feb. 1881	3	8	
Todd	J. M.	m.	DR	24 Oct. 1884	3	3	
Todd	J. M.	m.	PCo	22 Oct. 1884	3	6	
Todd	J. M.	m.	PWA	25 Oct. 1884	3	4	
Todd	J. W.	d.	PCo	2 Dec. 1885	3	1	
Todd	James W.	d.	PCo	23 Dec. 1885	3	2	Florence Camp, ID
Toley	Milton A.	m.	DR	17 Nov. 1881	2	3	
Toley	Milton A.	m.	RRF	17 Nov. 1881	2	3	
Tomane	Maggie	d.	SD	9 Apr. 1881	3	8	
Tomasini	Louis	b.	PC	27 June 1883	3	6	
Tomasini	Louis	b.	SD	30 June 1883	3	5	
Tombes	Minnie	m.	HE	11 Oct. 1883	2	2	
Tomblinson	John	m.	PCo	2 Sept. 1885	3	6	
Tomblison	John	m.	DR	4 Sept. 1885	3	4	
Tombs	Frank, Mrs.	d.	SD	17 Nov. 1883	1	7	
Tombs	J. F.	m.	PCo	22 Nov. 1882	3	5	
Tombs	J. Frank	m.	RRF	30 Nov. 1882	3	4	
Tombs	John F.	m.	RRF	23 Nov. 1882	2	4	
Tombs	Mary Hendricks	d.	RRF	15 Nov. 1883	2	3	Oak Mound Cemetery
Tombs	Minnie	m.	RRF	11 Oct. 1883	2	5	
Tombs	Minnie	m.	RRF	25 Oct. 1883	2	4	
Tomer	Maggie	d.	SD	26 Mar. 1881	3	8	
Tomlinson	John T.	o.	DR	30 Oct. 1882	3	1	also 1 Nov., p. 2 col. 2
Toms	Samuel	b.	DR	23 Oct. 1885	3	4	
Toms	Samuel	b.	PCo	2 Nov. 1881	3	5	
Toms	Samuel	b.	PCo	21 Oct. 1885	3	4	
Toner	Emma	m.	RRF	15 Sept. 1881	2	5	
Toney	Calvin C.	m.	SD	10 Jan. 1885	2	6	
Toney	Elias B.	d.	DD	31 Oct. 1883	3	3	
Toney	Elias B.	d.	SD	3 Nov. 1883	3	3	
Tonini	R. (son of)	d.	PCo	1 Mar. 1882	2	4	
Tontam	William	d.	SD	15 Oct. 1881	3	1	Lower Lake
Toombs	J. E.	m.	DR	16 Nov. 1882	2	3	
Toomey	T.	b.	RRF	27 Oct. 1881	2	5	
Toomey	T.	b.	SD	27 June 1885	5	4	
Toomey	Thomas (child of)	d.	PCo	7 Oct. 1885	3	6	
Tooms	J. P.	m.	CR	18 Nov. 1882	3	3	

(1) Surname	(2) Given Name	(3)	(4)	(5) Date	(6) Pg	(7) Col	(8) Comments
Toomy	Maggie	d.	PCo	16 Apr. 1884	3	5	
Toomy	T.	b.	PCo	27 Feb. 1884	3	6	
Toomy	Thomas	b.	RRF	21 Feb. 1884	2	4	
Toomy	Thomas	b.	SD	1 Mar. 1884	6	6	
Toppilla	Brita	m.	SD	19 Mar. 1881	3	8	
Toppilla	Josephine	m.	DD	11 Aug. 1883	3	1	
Torr	L. D.	m.	PCo	20 May 1885	3	6	
Torrance	Maggie	m.	PC	6 June 1883	3	4	
Torrance	Maggie	m.	PWA	9 June 1883	3	7	
Torrence	William H.	b.	CR	1 Jan. 1881	5	5	
Toulouse	H. P.	m.	PCo	16 July 1884	3	6	
Toumey	Augusta	d.	CR	29 Jan. 1881	5	5	
Toumey	Augusta	d.	DR	26 Jan. 1881	3	2	
Toumy	Thomas	b.	DR	31 Oct. 1881	2	3	
Toumy	Thomas	b.	PCo	2 Nov. 1881	3	5	
Toumy	Thomas	b.	SD	5 Nov. 1881	3	6	
Tout	Joseph	d.	PCo	26 Oct. 1881	3	4	
Towel	Ada	m.	PCo	26 Nov. 1884	3	5	
Towey	Mr. & Mrs.	b.	DR	7 Sept. 1882	3	4	
Towey	Mr. & Mrs.	b.	PCo	16 Sept. 1885	3	6	
Towey	Peter	b.	DR	22 Apr. 1882	3	2	
Towey	Peter	b.	PCo	19 Apr. 1882	3	5	
Towey	Peter	b.	SD	15 Apr. 1882	3	6	
Towle	Emma	m.	CR	19 Mar. 1881	4	3	
Towle	Emma	m.	DR	14 Mar. 1881	2	3	
Towle	Emma	m.	RRF	17 Feb. 1881	2	5	
Towle	Ida	m.	DR	29 Nov. 1884	3	2	
Towne	Amanda H.	d.	DD	19 Nov. 1883	3	3	
Towne	Amanda H.	d.	PWA	24 Nov. 1883	3	3&6	
Towne	Amanda H.	d.	SD	24 Nov. 1883	1	5	also p. 3 col. 4
Trefren	Frank A.	b.	RRF	22 June 1882	2	3	
Trefren	Frank A.	b.	SD	24 June 1882	3	5	
Tregido	Alfonso A.	m.	SD	24 Sept. 1881	3	8	
Triplett	Henry	b.	DD	1 Sept. 1883	3	2	
Tripp	H. L.	m.	SD	27 Sept. 1884	2	5	
Trott	Joseph	m.	SD	14 Apr. 1883	2	5	
Trowbridge	Eliza H.	d.	DR	8 Nov. 1884	2	2	
Trowbridge	Eliza H.	d.	SD	8 Nov. 1884	2	5	
Trudgen	William	b.	PWA	18 Apr. 1885	3	6	
Truett	Harry	d.	PCo	4 Mar. 1885	3	6	
Truett	Harry, Mrs.	d.	CR	28 Feb. 1885	3	1	
Truitt	(female)	b.	DR	18 Mar. 1884	3	3	

(1) Surname	(2) Given Name	(3)	(4)	(5) Date	(6) Pg	(7) Col	(8) Comments
Truitt	Harry, Mrs.	d.	SD	14 Mar. 1885	5	5	
Truitt	Harvey	b.	RRF	19 Apr. 1883	2	3	
Truitt	Harvey	b.	SD	28 Apr. 1883	3	6	
Truitt	Hattie I.	m.	SD	5 Jan. 1884	1	8	
Truitt	Hattie L.	m.	DD	29 Dec. 1883	3	3	
Truitt	Hattie L.	m.	PCo	2 Jan. 1884	3	6	
Truitt	Hattie L.	m.	RRF	27 Dec. 1883	2	2	
Truitt	Henry	b.	PC	25 Apr. 1883	3	5	
Truitt	J. H.	b.	RRF	13 Jan. 1881	2	5	
Truitt	J. H.	b.	SD	8 Jan. 1881	3	8	
Truitt	M. K.	b.	CR	15 Mar. 1884	3	1	
Truitt	M. K.	b.	PCo	19 Mar. 1884	3	6	
Truitt	M. K.	b.	SD	22 Mar. 1884	2	4	
Truitt	William R.	d.	PCo	26 Oct. 1881	3	4	
Truitt	William R.	b.	RRF	13 Oct. 1881	2	4	
Truitt	William R.	d.	SD	22 Oct. 1881	3	6	
Truitt	William	d.	DR	11 Oct. 1881	3	2	
Truitt	William	d.	SD	15 Oct. 1881	3	8	
Tucker	Cornelia	d.	SD	17 Feb. 1883	2	7	
Tucker	J. E.	b.	SD	26 Mar. 1881	3	8	
Tucker	Joshua D.	m.	SD	11 Aug. 1883	2	7	
Tullis	E.	m.	DD	27 Oct. 1883	3	3	
Tully	Agnes	d.	DR	28 Nov. 1881	2	3	
Tully	Agnes	d.	PCo	7 Dec. 1881	3	5	
Tully	C. H.	b.	SD	10 Feb. 1883	2	7	
Tully	Frank	d.	SD	3 Dec. 1881	3	8	
Tully	James	m.	SD	26 Mar. 1881	3	8	
Tuomey	Augusta A.	d.	SD	29 Jan. 1881	3	8	
Tuomey	Catherine A.	d.	SD	5 Feb. 1881	3	8	
Tupper	Ellen	m.	DD	13 July 1883	3	3	
Tupper	Ellen	m.	PC	18 July 1883	3	5	
Tupper	Ellen	m.	PWA	14 July 1883	3	6	
Tupper	Etta	m.	PCo	13 Aug. 1884	3	4	
Tupper	Etta	m.	PWA	9 Aug. 1884	2	4	
Tupper	John B.	m.	PCo	20 July 1881	3	5	
Tupper	John B.	m.	SD	23 July 1881	3	8	
Tupper	John B.	b.	SD	1 July 1882	2	3	
Tupper	John B., Jr.	b.	PCo	28 June 1882	3	5	
Tupper	John B., Jr.	b.	PCo	20 Feb. 1884	3	6	
Tupper	John B., Jr.	b.	PWA	23 Feb. 1884	3	6	
Tupper	John B., Jr.	b.	SD	1 Mar. 1884	6	6	
Turkeson	J. W.	d.	PC	25 Apr. 1883	3	5	

(1) Surname	(2) Given Name	(3)	(4)	(5) Date	(6) Pg	(7) Col	(8) Comments
Turkeson	J. W.	d.	SD	28 Apr. 1883	3	6	
Turner	Alfred	m.	DR	29 Nov. 1884	3	2	
Turner	Alfred	m.	PCo	26 Nov. 1884	3	5	
Turner	Alfred	b.	PCo	16 Sept. 1885	3	6	
Turner	Charles	d.	DR	9 Nov. 1885	2	2	
Turner	P.	m.	SD	9 Apr. 1881	3	8	
Turner	Thomas	b.	SD	16 July 1881	3	8	
Tustin	Wayne	m.	DD	15 Dec. 1883	3	1	
Tustin	Wayne	m.	PCo	19 Dec. 1883	3	4	
Tustin	Wayne	m.	SD	22 Dec. 1883	3	5	
Tuttle	Alice	m.	SD	17 Nov. 1883	3	5	
Tuttle	Alice M.	m.	PWA	17 Nov. 1883	3	2&8	
Tuttle	Benjamin	d.	DR	14 Nov. 1882	3	1	
Tuttle	Benjamin	d.	SD	18 Nov. 1882	3	1	
Tuttle	Cyrus	m.	DD	4 Dec. 1883	3	3	
Tuttle	Cyrus	b.	PCo	10 Sept. 1884	3	6	
Tuttle	Cyrus	b.	PWA	13 Sept. 1884	3	6	
Tuttle	Cyrus	b.	SD	20 Sept. 1884	2	5	
Tuttle	Daisy	m.	PWA	8 Sept. 1883	3	8	
Tuttle	Ella	m.	PCo	10 Jan. 1883	3	6	
Tuttle	Ella	m.	PWA	12 Jan. 1883	3	6	
Tuttle	Ella	m.	SD	13 Jan. 1883	3	5	
Tuttle	J. T.	b.	SD	19 Feb. 1881	3	8	
Tuttle	Sarah E.	d.	DR	3 Dec. 1881	2	3	
Tuttle	Sarah E.	d.	PCo	30 Nov. 1881	3	5	
Tuttle	Sarah E.	d.	SD	10 Dec. 1881	3	7	
Twist	A. G.	m.	DD	28 July 1883	2	2	
Twist	J. P.	b.	DR	17 Sept. 1881	2	3	
Twist	J. P.	b.	PCo	14 Sept. 1881	2	4	
Twist	J. P.	b.	SD	24 Sept. 1881	3	8	
Twist	John	b.	DD	12 Oct. 1883	3	3	
Twist	John	b.	PWA	13 Oct. 1883	3	8	
Twist	John	b.	SD	20 Oct. 1883	3	4	
Tyler	George	m.	SD	18 Apr. 1885	2	5	
Tyler	J. N.	m.	PCo	20 July 1881	3	5	
Tyler	J. N.	m.	SD	6 Aug. 1881	3	8	
Tyler	J. N.	m.	SD	23 July 1881	3	8	
Tyler	John N.	b.	DD	10 Sept. 1883	3	3	
Tyler	John N.	b.	PWA	15 Sept. 1883	3	6	
Tyler	John N.	b.	SD	15 Sept. 1883	2	4	
Tyther	Honore	d.	DR	27 Oct. 1885	3	4	
Tyther	Mrs.	d.	SD	31 Oct. 1885	3	2&3	

U & V

(1) Surname	(2) Given Name	(3)	(4)	(5) Date	(6) Pg	(7) Col	(8) Comments
Udell	Henry, Mrs.	d.	PCo	31 Jan. 1883	3	5	
Udell	Henry, Mrs.	d.	RRF	25 Jan. 1883	2	4	
Ulrich	Charles	m.	DD	31 Aug. 1883	3	3	
Ulrich	Charles	m.	RRF	30 Aug. 1883	2	4	
Unckless	C. F.	d.	PCo	9 July 1884	3	5	
Unckless	C. F.	d.	PWA	12 July 1884	3	6	
Underhill	John G.	d.	DR	16 Aug. 1882	2	2	
Underhill	John G.	d.	PCo	16 Aug. 1882	3	6	
Underhill	John G.	d.	RRF	17 Aug. 1882	3	5	
Underhill	John Green	d.	SD	12 Aug. 1882	3	2&5	Rural Cemetery
Underhill	John	d.	DR	9 Aug. 1882	3	2	
Ungerwitter	Henry W.	m.	SD	17 Mar. 1883	3	5	
Ungewitter	Henry W.	m.	PCo	14 Mar. 1883	3	5	
Upson	W. F.	b.	PCo	24 June 1885	3	6	
Upson	W. F.	b.	SD	27 June 1885	5	4	
Urton	(female)	b.	DR	10 Jan. 1884	3	3	
Urton	C. M., Miss	m.	PCo	8 Oct. 1884	3	6	
Urton	C. M., Miss	m.	PWA	11 Oct. 1884	3	4	
Urton	C. M., Miss	m.	SD	4 Oct. 1884	3	5	
Urton	J. H.	m.	PCo	13 Sept. 1882	3	7	
Urton	J. H.	b.	PCo	16 Jan. 1884	3	6	
Urton	J. H.	m.	SD	9 Sept. 1882	3	6	
Urton	J. H.	b.	SD	19 Jan. 1884	3	6	
Utt	Mary E.	m.	SD	23 Nov. 1884	2	6	
Utt	Mary	m.	DR	17 Nov. 1884	3	2	
Utt	Mary	m.	PCo	26 Nov. 1884	3	5	
Vail	F. J.	b.	CR	15 Jan. 1881	5	5	
Vail	F. K.	b.	CR	15 Jan. 1881	5	5	
Vail	F. K.	b.	SD	22 Jan. 1881	3	8	
Vail	Fred K.	b.	RRF	6 Jan. 1881	2	5	
Vail	Fred K.	b.	SD	1 June 1881	3	7	
Vail	S. R.	p.	DD	24 July 1883	3	2	
Vale	Joseph	m.	SD	27 Sept. 1884	2	5	
Valensuela	Mary	m.	PWA	23 Aug. 1884	3	4	
Valentine	Mary G.	d.	DD	8 Sept. 1883	3	3	
Valentine	Mary	d.	SD	15 Sept. 1883	1	5	Rural Cem., also p. 2 col. 4
Valenzuela	Mary	m.	DR	18 Aug. 1884	3	3	
Valenzuela	Mary	m.	SD	23 Aug. 1884	2	4	

(1) Surname	(2) Given Name	(3)	(4)	(5) Date	(6) Pg	(7) Col	(8) Comments
Vallejo	M. G.	o.	SIT	22 Aug. 1885	2	2	
Vallejo	Mariano G.	o.	SD	18 Mar. 1882	3	1	golden wedding celebration
Van Alen	Henry	m.	SD	13 Sept. 1884	3	1	
Van Allen	Harry	m.	PCo	10 Sept. 1884	3	6	
Van Allen	Mary	d.	RRF	31 Jan. 1884	2	3	
Van Alstine	Maria	d.	HE	19 Feb. 1880	2	4	
Van De Bogart	A. A. Mrs.	d.	PCo	16 Jan. 1884	3	6	
Van De Bogart	A. A., Mrs.	d.	SD	19 Jan. 1884	3	6	
Van De Bogart	Annie A.	d.	PWA	19 Jan. 1884	3	7	
Van Geldern	Charles	d.	SD	2 July 1881	3	8	
Van Geldern	Otto	b.	SIT	26 Sept. 1885	2	2	
Van Graffen	Louise	m.	PC	2 May 1883	3	5	
Van Horn	Sarah B.	d.	SD	18 Apr. 1885	2	5	
Van Marter	William H.	m.	PCo	2 Jan. 1884	3	6	
Van Marter	William H.	m.	PWA	5 Jan. 1884	3	7	
Van Marter	William H.	m.	SD	5 Jan. 1884	1	4	
Van Mehr	Alfred de R.	m.	PWA	2 Feb. 1884	3	6	
Van Owen	M.	d.	SD	2 Apr. 1881	3	3	
Van Schaick	Beulah	m.	SD	16 June 1883	2	6	
Van Slyke	D. S.	b.	DR	4 Apr. 1881	2	3	
Van Slyke	Lavina	m.	DD	23 Aug. 1883	3	2	
Van Slyke	Lavina	m.	PC	22 Aug. 1883	3	5	
Van Slyke	Lavina	m.	PWA	25 Aug. 1883	3	8	
Van Slyke	Lavina	m.	SD	25 Aug. 1883	2	5	
Van	E. S.	m.	RRF	20 Oct. 1881	2	4	
Van Vost	William	m.	RRF	4 Aug. 1881	2	5	
Van Winkle	Ida	m.	DR	20 Nov. 1884	3	2	
Van York	Mr.	m.	CR	27 Dec. 1884	3	2	
Vance	A. W.	b.	PC	4 July 1883	3	5	
Vance	Elizabeth	m.	PCo	26 Oct. 1881	3	4	
Vance	Elizabeth	m.	RRF	20 Oct. 1881	2	4	
Vance	Elizabeth F.	m.	DR	20 Oct. 1881	2	2	
Vance	John B.	m.	PCo	26 Oct. 1881	3	4	
Vance	John	m.	DR	1 Nov. 1881	2	3	filed after Nov. 29
Vance	John	b.	PCo	1 Nov. 1882	3	5	
Vancil	(infant son)	b.	DR	4 Mar. 1884	3	3	
Vancil	(infant son)	d.	DR	4 Mar. 1884	3	3	
Vancil	C. N.	b.	PCo	12 Mar. 1884	3	6	
Vancil	C. N. (son of)	d.	PCo	12 Mar. 1884	3	6	
Vancil	G. W.	m.	SD	14 Apr. 1883	2	5	
Vanderhoff	M. V.	b.	SD	14 Jan. 1882	3	8	
Vanderhoof	M. V.	b.	PCo	18 Jan. 1882	3	5	

(1) Surname	(2) Given Name	(3)	(4)	(5) Date	(6) Pg	(7) Col	(8) Comments
Vann	E. S.	m.	PCo	26 Oct. 1881	3	4	
Vann	Edward S.	m.	DR	20 Oct. 1881	2	2	also p. 3 col. 1
Varner	(female)	b.	DR	12 Apr. 1884	3	2	
Varner	S.	b.	PCo	16 Apr. 1884	3	5	
Vassar	Benjamin	b.	CR	6 Dec. 1884	3	1	
Vassar	Benjamin	b.	PCo	10 Dec. 1884	3	5	
Vassar	J. P.	d.	CR	19 Sept. 1885	3	3	
Vassar	J. P.	d.	DR	21 Sept. 1885	3	4	
Ver Mehr	Alfred de R.	m.	DR	29 Jan. 1884	3	3	
Ver Mehr	Alfred de R.	m.	PCo	6 Feb. 1884	3	6	
Veria	Joseph F.	d.	PCo	1 Apr. 1885	3	6	
Veria	Joseph F.	d.	PWA	4 Apr. 1885	3	6	
Vestal	Alice	m.	SD	29 Jan. 1881	3	8	
Vestal	Lem	b.	DD	20 Dec. 1883	2	2	
Vestal	Lem	b.	PCo	19 Dec. 1883	3	4	
Vestal	Lem	b.	PWA	22 Dec. 1883	3	6	
Vestal	Lem	b.	SD	22 Dec. 1883	3	5	
Vicari	Augustine	d.	DR	21 Oct. 1885	3	3	
Vicari	Augustine	d.	SIT	31 Oct. 1885	3	2	
Volkerts	E. A.	b.	PCo	16 Sept. 1885	3	6	
Volkirts	E. A.	b.	PCo	21 Feb. 1883	3	5	
Volkirts	F. A.	b.	PWA	24 Feb. 1883	3	7	
Von Compvanee	Mr.	d.	DR	30 July 1884	3	3	
Von Graffen	Louisa	m.	SD	5 May 1883	3	1	
Von Tagen	Annie J.	d.	DR	21 July 1885	3	4	
Von Tagen	Arthur	d.	DR	21 July 1885	3	4	
Von Vost	William	m.	DR	8 Aug. 1881	3	2	
Vonsen	Caludane	d.	PCo	16 Aug. 1882	3	6	
Vonsen	Clandane	d.	SD	19 Aug. 1882	3	5	
Vonson	Emil	d.	PCo	13 Sept. 1882	3	7	
Voss	C.	b.	DR	2 Nov. 1885	3	4	twins
Vragnisan	A.	b.	CR	25 Oct. 1883	3	1	
Vragnisan	A.	b.	DR	28 Oct. 1884	2	3	

W

(1) Surname	(2) Given Name	(3)	(4)	(5) Date	(6) Pg	(7) Col	(8) Comments
Waddell	Alex J.	b.	DR	7 June 1882	3	2	
Waddell	Alex J.	b.	PCo	7 June 1882	3	5	
Waddell	Alex J.	b.	RRF	8 June 1882	2	3	
Waddell	Alex J.	b.	SD	3 June 1882	2	4	
Waddell	Joseph	m.	SD	12 Mar. 1881	3	8	
Wade	Henry	b.	DD	28 Aug. 1883	3	3	
Wages	A.	b.	SD	24 Jan. 1885	5	5	
Wagner	Ophelia	m.	SD	19 Apr. 1884	3	4	
Waite	Parthenia	m.	CR	31 Oct. 1885	3	4	
Waite	Parthenia	m.	DR	29 Oct. 1885	3	4	
Waite	Thomas	b.	RRF	20 Jan. 1881	2	5	
Waldron	Kate	m.	DR	23 Mar. 1882	2	3	
Waldron	Kate	m.	SD	8 Apr. 1882	3	6	
Waldron	Katie	m.	PCo	5 Apr. 1882	3	5	
Waldvogel	Alfred	d.	DR	19 Jan. 1884	3	3	
Waldvogel	Alfred	d.	PCo	23 Jan. 1884	3	5	
Waldvogel	Alfred	d.	SD	26 Jan. 1884	3	5	
Walgamot	E. J. T.	b.	DR	14 July 1885	3	4	
Walgamot	E. J. T.	b.	PCo	22 July 1885	3	6	
Walgamot	E. J. T.	m.	SD	25 Oct. 1884	2	5	
Walgamot	E. J. T.	b.	SD	18 July 1885	5	5	
Walker	A.	b.	CR	28 May 1881	5	5	
Walker	A.	b.	DR	23 May 1881	2	2	
Walker	A.	b.	SD	28 May 1881	3	8	
Walker	Almira	o.	SD	25 Aug. 1883	1	4	
Walker	Dovey	m.	DR	23 Mar. 1884	3	3	
Walker	Dovey	m.	PCo	26 Mar. 1884	3	6	
Walker	E. S.	b.	DR	16 Dec. 1882	2	3	
Walker	E. S.	b.	PCo	20 Dec. 1882	3	5	
Walker	E. S.	b.	RRF	14 Dec. 1882	2	3	
Walker	E. S.	b.	SD	16 Dec. 1882	3	6	
Walker	Fred	m.	DR	27 June 1884	3	3	
Walker	Fred	m.	PCo	15 June 1884	3	4	
Walker	Fred	m.	PWA	28 June 1884	3	5	
Walker	George	d.	PCo	7 Jan. 1885	3	6	
Walker	George	d.	PWA	10 Jan. 1885	3	4	
Walker	George	d.	SD	10 Jan. 1885	2	6	
Walker	Isabel H.	m.	SD	17 Nov. 1883	3	5	

(1) Surname	(2) Given Name	(3)	(4)	(5) Date	(6) Pg	(7) Col	(8) Comments
Walker	J. L. (infant)	d.	DR	30 Dec. 1884	2	2	
Walker	J. L.	m.	DR	12 May 1882	3	2	
Walker	J. L.	m.	HE	11 May 1882	2	3	
Walker	J. L.	m.	PCo	17 May 1882	3	5	
Walker	J. L.	m.	SD	20 May 1882	2	4	
Walker	J. L.	b.	SD	12 May 1883	2	6	
Walker	J. L.	b.	SD	18 Apr. 1885	2	4	
Walker	J. L. (son of)	d.	SD	3 Jan. 1885	2	7	
Walker	Joel M.	m.	SD	27 Dec. 1884	2	4	
Walker	John	b.	RRF	3 May 1883	2	3	
Walker	John K.	d.	PWA	17 Jan. 1885	2	4	also p. 3 col. 2
Walker	John L.	m.	CR	13 May 1882	5	1	
Walker	John L.	b.	PC	9 May 1883	3	5	
Walker	John L.	m.	RRF	11 May 1882	3	4	
Walker	John L.	b.	SD	19 May 1883	3	5	
Walker	John L.	d.	SD	17 Jan. 1885	5	4	Guerneville
Walker	John King, Mrs.	d.	CR	25 Apr. 1885	3	1	
Walker	John, Mrs.	d.	PCo	22 Apr. 1885	3	6	
Walker	Joseph	b.	CR	1 Jan. 1881	5	5	
Walker	Joseph	b.	DR	12 June 1881	2	2	
Walker	Joseph	b.	SD	2 July 1881	3	8	
Walker	Joseph	b.	SD	18 June 1881	3	8	
Walker	Joseph M.	m.	DR	23 Dec. 1884	3	2	
Walker	Lou	m.	SD	29 Dec. 1883	3	6	
Walker	Louie B.	m.	SD	27 Dec. 1884	2	4	
Walker	Louisa	m.	DR	23 Dec. 1884	3	2	
Walker	Morin H.	d.	PCo	7 Jan. 1885	3	6	
Walker	Mr. & Mrs.	o.	DR	19 Dec. 1882	3	1	60th anniversary
Walker	Mrs.	d.	SD	25 Apr. 1885	1	4	Guerneville
Walker	Polina	d.	PCo	15 Apr. 1885	3	6	
Walker	S. P.	m.	DD	4 Sept. 1883	2	2	
Walker	S. P.	m.	SD	8 Sept. 1883	2	7	
Walker	Samuel B.	o.	SD	25 Aug. 1883	1	4	
Walker	W.	b.	PC	2 May 1883	3	5	
Walker	W.	b.	SD	5 May 1883	3	6	
Walkup	Emily	d.	DR	26 Apr. 1881	2	2	
Walkup	Emily	d.	SD	23 Apr. 1881	3	8	
Wall	Ella	m.	DR	28 Mar. 1884	3	3	
Wall	Ella	m.	PCo	2 Apr. 1884	3	6	
Wall	Ella	m.	SD	5 Apr. 1884	3	4	
Wall	John	m.	CR	24 Oct. 1885	3	3	
Wallace	Glen A.	m.	PWA	22 Mar. 1884	3	6	

(1) Surname	(2) Given Name	(3)	(4)	(5) Date	(6) Pg	(7) Col	(8) Comments
Wallace	Glen A.	m.	RRF	13 Mar. 1884	2	2	
Wallace	Glenn A.	m.	PCo	19 Mar. 1884	3	6	
Wallace	Glenn A.	m.	SD	22 Mar. 1884	2	4	
Wallace	James	b.	DR	6 July 1882	3	2	
Wallace	James	b.	PCo	12 July 1882	3	5	
Wallace	James	b.	SD	24 June 1882	3	5	
Wallace	Margaret	m.	SD	1 Oct. 1881	3	8	
Wallace	Willia A.	b.	DR	16 Nov. 1885	3	4	
Walldorf	Philip	b.	PCo	16 Nov. 1881	3	5	
Walls	Grace	d.	PCo	4 May 1881	3	4	
Walls	Thomas	d.	RRF	11 Aug. 1881	2	5	
Walsh	Fannie A.	m.	SD	11 Oct. 1884	2	5	
Walsh	M.	b.	CR	2 Apr. 1881	5	3	
Walsh	M.	b.	PCo	30 Mar. 1881	3	4	
Walsh	M.	d.	PCo	30 Apr. 1884	2	6	
Walsh	M.	b.	PCo	30 Apr. 1884	2	6	
Walsh	M.	b.	PWA	26 Apr. 1884	3	6	
Walsh	M.	b.	SD	9 Apr. 1881	3	8	
Walsh	M.	b.	SD	10 May 1884	2	4	
Walsh	M. (son of)	d.	PWA	26 Apr. 1884	3	6	
Walsh	M. (son of)	d.	SD	10 May 1884	2	4	
Walsh	Theresa C.	d.	PCo	14 Dec. 1881	3	4	
Walter	F. M.	m.	PCo	20 Aug. 1884	3	4	
Walter	F. M.	m.	PWA	23 Aug. 1884	3	4	
Walter	F. M.	m.	SD	6 Sep. 1884	2	5	
Walter	Hannah	m.	PCo	7 Jan. 1885	3	6	
Walter	Hannah	m.	SD	10 Jan. 1885	2	6	
Walters	Frank	b.	SD	12 Mar. 1881	3	8	
Walters	S.	b.	PCo	7 Jan. 1885	3	6	
Warboys	(female)	b.	DR	5 May 1884	3	2	
Warboys	J. W.	m.	DR	4 Dec. 1882	3	2	
Warboys	J. W.	m.	PCo	6 Dec. 1882	3	6	
Warboys	J. W.	b.	PCo	7 May 1884	3	5	
Warboys	J. W.	b.	RRF	8 May 1884	5	6	
Warboys	J. W.	m.	SD	9 Dec. 1882	2	5	also p. 3 col. 6
Ward	A. E.	b.	SD	18 Apr. 1885	2	4	
Ward	Benjamin F.	d.	PCo	14 Jan. 1885	3	6	
Ward	Benjamin F.	d.	PWA	17 Jan. 1885	2	4	
Ward	Frank	b.	PCo	14 Mar. 1883	3	5	
Ward	Frank	d.	PCo	28 Jan. 1885	3	2	
Ward	Frank	b.	SD	17 Mar. 1883	3	3	
Ward	Hannah	d.	DR	25 Apr. 1884	3	2	

(1) Surname	(2) Given Name	(3)	(4)	(5) Date	(6) Pg	(7) Col	(8) Comments
Ward	Hannah	d.	PCo	23 Apr. 1884	2	6	
Ward	Hannah	d.	RRF	1 May 1884	5	6	
Ward	Hannah	d.	SD	26 Apr. 1884	3	5	
Ward	John H.	b.	CR	1 Jan. 1881	5	5	
Ward	John H.	m.	PCo	9 Dec. 1885	3	6	
Ward	John H.	b.	SD	15 Jan. 1881	3	8	
Ward	John W.	o.	DR	26 Oct. 1882	2	2	
Ward	Matilda	d.	SD	3 Mar. 1883	2	6	
Ward	Mina	m.	PCo	30 Dec. 1885	3	4	
Ward	N.	b.	PCo	8 Mar. 1882	3	5	
Ward	N.	b.	RRF	2 Mar. 1882	2	4	
Ward	Naomi	d.	DD	18 Oct. 1883	3	3	
Ward	Naomi	d.	PWA	20 Oct. 1883	3	8	
Ward	Naomi	d.	SD	20 Oct. 1883	3	4	
Ward	Porter	m.	PCo	1 July 1885	3	6	
Ward	Thomas	m.	PCo	2 Nov. 1881	3	5	
Ward	William H.	b.	SD	17 Sept. 1881	3	8	
Warders	Minnie B.	m.	PCo	15 Mar. 1882	3	4	
Warders	Minnie	m.	DR	20 Mar. 1882	2	3	
Warders	Minnie	m.	SD	25 Mar. 1882	3	6	
Ware	(male)	b.	DR	9 Apr. 1884	3	3	
Ware	A. B.	b.	PCo	16 Apr. 1884	3	5	
Ware	Emma	d.	PCo	27 Dec. 1882	3	6	
Ware	Emma	m.	SD	23 Dec. 1882	2	5	
Ware	Preserved	d.	DR	19 Sept. 1885	3	4	
Ware	Preserved	d.	PCo	23 Sept. 1885	3	6	
Warfield	R. H.	b.	RRF	27 Jan. 1881	2	4	
Warfield	R. H.	b.	SD	5 Feb. 1881	3	8	
Warfield	R.	b.	CR	29 Jan. 1881	5	5	
Warner	Cora E.	m.	DR	9 Apr. 1882	3	2	
Warner	Cora E.	m.	PCo	12 Apr. 1882	3	5	
Warner	Cora E.	m.	RRF	6 Apr. 1882	2	4	
Warner	Cora E.	m.	SD	15 Apr. 1882	3	6	
Warner	Elam	m.	RRF	11 Jan. 1883	2	2	
Warner	Gustavus	o.	PCo	31 Dec. 1884	3	1	
Warner	Gustavus	d.	PCo	14 Jan. 1885	3	6	
Warner	Gustavus	d.	PWA	17 Jan. 1885	2	4	
Warner	Gustavus	d.	SD	17 Jan. 1885	5	5	
Warner	John	b.	RRF	10 Feb. 1881	2	5	
Warner	John	b.	SD	19 Feb. 1881	3	8	
Warner	Olive	d.	PCo	14 Oct. 1885	3	6	
Warner	Olive	d.	SD	10 Oct. 1885	5	5	

(1) Surname	(2) Given Name	(3)	(4)	(5) Date	(6) Pg	(7) Col	(8) Comments
Warner	Rebecka	m.	PCo	4 Feb. 1885	3	6	
Warren	E. H.	m.	SD	7 Jan. 1882	3	8	
Warwick	Mr. & Mrs.	b.	CR	22 Jan. 1881	5	5	
Warwick	Thomas	b.	DR	17 Jan. 1881	3	2	
Warwick	Thomas	b.	PCo	12 Jan. 1881	3	2	
Warwick	Thomas	b.	SD	22 Jan. 1881	3	8	
Waters		d.	PCo	5 Oct. 1881	3	5	
Waters	J. U.	d.	SIT	19 Dec. 1885	3	3	
Waters	Jacob	d.	PCo	21 Dec. 1881	3	5	
Waters	Jacob	d.	SD	31 Dec. 1881	3	6	
Waters	John T.	d.	SD	15 Oct. 1881	3	8	
Waters	S. J.	m.	DD	11 Oct. 1883	3	3	
Waters	S. J., Mrs.	m.	SD	13 Oct. 1883	3	4	
Watkins	Henry	b.	DD	15 Dec. 1883	3	1	
Watora	J. U.	d.	SIT	21 Jan. 1888	3	2	
Watriss	George E.	d.	PC	1 Aug. 1883	3	6	
Watriss	George E.	d.	PWA	28 July 1883	3	7	
Watriss	George E.	d.	SWI	21 July 1883	3	4	
Watriss	George E.	d.	SWI	23 July 1883	3	4	
Watson	Albert	m.	DD	29 Dec. 1883	3	3	
Watson	Alex	b.	PC	30 May 1883	3	4	
Watson	Alex	b.	SD	2 June 1883	2	7	
Watson	Alexander (son of)	d.	SD	12 Sept. 1885	1	5	
Watson	Cynthia	d.	DR	18 Nov. 1885	3	4	
Watson	H. H.	m.	DR	29 May 1884	3	2	
Watson	Henry H.	m.	PCo	11 June 1884	3	5	
Watson	Henry H.	m.	SD	31` May 1884	2	3	
Watson	Henry	d.	DR	5 Sept. 1885	3	4	
Watson	J. H.	m.	PCo	1 Nov. 1882	3	5	
Watson	J.	d.	PCo	31 Jan. 1883	3	5	
Watson	J.	d.	SD	27 Jan. 1883	3	6	
Watson	James	b.	PCo	7 Dec. 1881	3	5	
Watson	John H.	m.	SD	28 Oct. 1882	3	5	
Watson	Josie	m.	PCo	16 Jan. 1884	3	6	
Watson	Josie	m.	RRF	27 Dec. 1883	2	2	
Watson	Josie	m.	SD	19 Jan. 1884	3	6	
Watson	Minnie A.	m.	SD	6 Sept. 1884	2	5	
Watson	Silas	d.	SD	19 Feb. 1881	3	8	
Watson	Valentine	m.	DR	27 Oct. 1884	3	3	
Watson	Valentine	m.	PCo	29 Oct. 1884	3	5	
Watson	Valentine	m.	SD	8 Nov. 1884	2	5	
Watt	Richard I.	d.	SIT	11 Jan. 1888	2	5	also p. 3 col. 3

(1) Surname	(2) Given Name	(3)	(4)	(5) Date	(6) Pg	(7) Col	(8) Comments
Watts	Claydie A.	m.	SD	12 Feb. 1881	3	8	
Watts	Claydie	m.	DR	21 Feb. 1881	3	1	
Wearmouth	Mr. & Mrs.	b.	PCo	15 June 1884	3	4	
Wearworth	(female)	b.	DR	24 June 1884	3	3	
Weatherington	William	b.	PCo	17 Jan. 1883	3	5	
Weatherington	William	b.	SD	20 Jan. 1883	2	5	
Weaver	Albert W.	m.	SD	1 Sept. 1883	2	7	
Webb	Ira	b.	PC	13 June 1883	3	6	
Webb	Ira	b.	RRF	7 June 1883	2	3	
Webb	Ira	b.	SD	16 June 1883	2	6	
Webb	W. R.	b.	DR	10 Apr. 1882	2	2	
Webb	W. R.	b.	PCo	12 Apr. 1882	3	5	
Webb	W. R.	b.	SD	15 Apr. 1882	3	6	
Webber	Henry	b.	PC	18 Apr. 1883	3	5	
Webber	Henry	b.	PWA	21 Apr. 1883	3	8	
Weber	Catherine	m.	SD	3 June 1882	2	4	
Webster	C. B.	m.	DR	20 Nov. 1885	3	4	
Webster	Calvin B.	m.	PCo	23 Nov. 1885	3	4	
Webster	H. F.	b.	PC	9 May 1883	3	5	
Webster	W. W. L.	m.	SD	1 July 1882	2	3	
Webster	William	d.	DR	18 Jan. 1884	3	1	
Webster	William	d.	DR	21 Jan. 1884	3	2	
Webster	William	d.	PCo	23 Jan. 1884	3	5	
Webster	William	d.	PWA	26 Jan. 1884	3	6	
Webster	William	d.	SD	26 Jan. 1884	3	3	inquest report
Weeks	Effie	m.	DD	31 Oct. 1883	3	3	
Weeks	Effie	m.	SD	3 Nov. 1883	3	3	
Weeks	Frank P.	m.	SD	25 Oct. 1884	2	5	
Weeks	George B. McClellan	d.	DR	27 July 1881	3	2	
Weeks	George B. McClellan	d.	PCo	27 July 1881	3	5	
Weeks	George B. McClellan	d.	SD	6 Aug. 1881	3	8	
Weeks	James	d.	SD	15 Oct. 1881	3	1	Lower Lake
Weeks	S. S.	m.	CR	15 Jan. 1881	5	5	
Weeks	Solomon S.	m.	SD	15 Jan. 1881	3	8	
Wege	Joseph	b.	PCo	28 Jan. 1885	3	6	
Wehrspon	August	b.	SD	24 May 1884	2	3	
Weiberts	H. M., Mrs.	d.	RRF	6 Apr. 1882	2	4	
Weigand	Charles	b.	DR	10 Apr. 1882	2	2	
Weigand	Charles	b.	PCo	5 Apr. 1882	3	5	
Weigand	Frank	m.	PCo	22 Oct. 1884	3	6	
Weigand	Frank	b.	PCo	29 July 1885	3	4	
Weigand	Frank	m.	PWA	25 Oct. 1884	3	4	

(1) Surname	(2) Given Name	(3)	(4)	(5) Date	(6) Pg	(7) Col	(8) Comments
Weigand	Frank	m.	SD	8 Nov. 1884	2	5	
Weil	Eva	m.	SD	29 Jan. 1881	3	8	
Weir	J. G.	m.	SD	24 Jan. 1885	5	5	
Weise	Eliza J.	d.	PCo	22 Mar. 1882	3	5	
Wells	Edith	m.	RRF	10 Nov. 1881	3	4	
Wells	Edith May	m.	DR	8 Nov. 1881	2	3	
Wells	Edith May	m.	PCo	16 Nov. 1881	3	5	
Wells	Edith May	m.	RRF	10 Nov. 1881	2	4	
Wells	George	b.	SD	19 Sept. 1885	2	4	
Wells	George W.	b.	DR	15 Sept. 1882	3	4	
Wells	O. T.	m.	DD	23 July 1883	3	2	
Wells	Philip	b.	PCo	15 Mar. 1882	3	4	
Wells	Philip	b.	RRF	9 Mar. 1882	2	4	
Wells	Philip	b.	SD	11 Mar. 1882	3	6	
Wells	R. R.	d.	RRF	26 Oct. 1882	2	3	Oak Mound Cem.
Wells	S.	b.	DR	13 June 1882	3	2	
Wells	S.	b.	PCo	21 June 1882	3	5	
Wells	S.	b.	SD	24 June 1882	3	5	
Wells	Winnie	m.	SD	24 Jan. 1885	5	5	
Welsh	Anna	m.	PCo	14 June 1882	3	5	
Welsh	Anna	m.	SD	17 June 1882	2	4	
Welty	Z.	m.	SD	8 Oct. 1881	3	8	
Wenquist	Emma C.	m.	SD	14 Apr. 1883	2	5	
Wentworth	Ida H.	m.	SD	14 Mar. 1885	5	5	
Wentworth	Lillie	m.	DD	24 Sept. 1883	3	2	
Wentworth	Lillie	m.	PWA	22 Sept. 1883	3	6	
Wentworth	Lillie	m.	SD	29 Sept. 1883	2	6	
Wertz	G. W.	d.	CR	11 Feb. 1882	1	2	
Wertz	G. W.	d.	HE	2 Feb. 1882	3	1	
Wertz	G. W.	d.	RRF	2 Feb. 1882	3	7	
Wertz	G. W.	d.	SD	4 Feb. 1882	3	4&6	
Wescoatt	O. K.	b.	SD	3 Jan. 1885	2	7	
Wescott	Freddie	d.	DR	13 Dec. 1882	2	3	
Wescott	Freddie	d.	PCo	20 Dec. 1882	3	5	
Wescott	Oscar	m.	PCo	9 Jan. 1884	3	6	
Wescott	Oscar	m.	SD	19 Jan. 1884	3	6	
West	Charles	d.	PCo	27 May 1885	3	6	
West	Edward	d.	PCo	25 Feb. 1885	3	6	
West	Edward	m.	PWA	28 Feb. 1885	3	5	
West	Rachel H.	d.	PC	27 June 1883	3	6	
West	Rachel H.	d.	SD	23 June 1883	3	5	
West	William Mark	o.	SD	11 Apr. 1885	1	3	

(1) Surname	(2) Given Name	(3)	(4)	(5) Date	(6) Pg	(7) Col	(8) Comments
West	William	d.	DR	28 Nov. 1881	2	3	
West	William	d.	PCo	7 Dec. 1881	3	5	
West	William	d.	SD	3 Dec. 1881	3	8	
Westcoatt	O. K.	b.	PCo	7 Jan. 1885	3	6	
Westcott	Oscar	m.	PWA	12 Jan. 1885	3	7	
Weston	R. K.	b.	SD	29 Jan. 1881	3	8	
Wetmore	F. R.	b.	PCo	22 Apr. 1885	3	6	
Weyhe	P.	b.	PCo	19 July 1882	3	6	
Weyhe	P.	b.	SD	22 July 1882	3	5	
Weyhe	Paul	b.	PC	20 June 1883	3	6	
Weyhe	Paul	b.	PWA	23 June 1883	3	7	
Weyhe	Pauline	d.	PC	23 May 1883	3	5	
Weyhe	Pauline	d.	PWA	26 May 1883	3	7	
Weyl	Henry	b.	DR	23 Jan. 1882	2	3	
Weyl	Henry	b.	SD	28 Jan. 1882	3	6	
Weymouth	W. C., Mrs.	m.	SD	27 Sept. 1884	2	5	
Whaley	(male twins)	b.	DR	31 Mar. 1884	3	3	
Whaley	Margaret E.	d.	PCo	19 Mar. 1884	3	6	
Whaley	Margaret E.	d.	PWA	15 Mar. 1884	3	6	
Whaley	Margaret E.	d.	SWI	29 Mar. 1884	3	5	
Whaley	Samuel	b.	PCo	9 Apr. 1884	3	6	
Whaley	Samuel	b.	PWA	5 Apr. 1884	3	6	
Whallon	Harry	d.	SD	30 Apr. 1881	3	8	
Whallon	Harry S.	d.	CR	30 Apr. 1881	5	5	
Whallon	Harry S.	d.	DR	26 Apr. 1881	2	2	
Whallon	James B.	d.	DR	18 July 1884	3	3	
Whallon	James B.	d.	PCo	23 July 1884	3	6	
Wharff	P. B.	m.	PWA	23 Aug. 1884	3	4	
Wheeler	D. R.	b.	SD	9 May 1885	2	5	
Wheeler	David	m.	SD	5 July 1884	2	3	
Wheeler	David R.	m.	DR	3 July 1884	2	2	
Wheeler	David R.	m.	PCo	16 July 1884	3	6	
Wheeler	G. W.	b.	DR	2 Dec. 1882	3	2	
Wheeler	G. W.	m.	DR	27 July 1882	2	3	
Wheeler	John S.	m.	DD	8 Dec. 1883	3	3	
Wheeler	Sam (dau. of)	d.	CR	3 Sept. 1881	5	1	
Whipple	E. L.	m.	DR	17 June 1881	2	2	
Whipple	E. L.	m.	DR	21 June 1881	2	2	
Whipple	E. L.	d.	DR	8 Dec. 1882	3	2	
Whipple	E. L.	m.	PCo	22 June 1881	3	5	
Whipple	E. L.	m.	RRF	23 June 1881	3	3	
Whipple	E. L.	d.	RRF	14 Dec. 1882	3	3	Santa Rosa

(1) Surname	(2) Given Name	(3)	(4)	(5) Date	(6) Pg	(7) Col	(8) Comments
Whipple	E. L.	m.	SD	18 June 1881	3	4 & 8	
Whipple	E. L.	d.	SD	9 Dec. 1882	3	3	
Whipple	Edwin L.	m.	CR	25 June 1881	4	3	
Whipple	Edwin Laurens	d.	PCo	13 Dec. 1882	3	4	
Whipple	Edwin Laurens	d.	SD	16 Dec. 1882	3	1,4,6	also p. 4 col. 2
Whisman	M. H., Mrs.	o.	CR	6 Aug. 1881	5	2	
Whitaker	John B.	m.	PCo	19 Apr. 1882	3	5	
Whitaker	John B.	m.	SD	15 Apr. 1882	3	6	
Whitcomb	Ethelbert	m.	SD	8 Jan. 1881	3	8	
White	C. H.	b.	DR	19 Dec. 1882	3	2	
White	C. H.	b.	PCo	27 Dec. 1882	3	6	
White	C. H.	b.	SD	23 Dec. 1882	2	5	
White	Delos	b.	SD	3 Nov. 1883	3	3	
White	E. J.	b.	PCo	7 June 1882	3	5	
White	E. J.	b.	SD	10 June 1882	2	3	
White	E. J. (dau. of)	d.	PCo	7 June 1882	3	5	
White	E. J. (dau. of)	d.	SD	10 June 1882	2	3	
White	E. W.	b.	SD	12 Mar. 1881	3	8	
White	Francis D.	d.	DR	1 Dec. 1884	3	2	
White	Francis D.	d.	PCo	3 Dec. 1884	3	5	
White	Francis D.	d.	SD	6 Dec. 1884	3	5	
White	Frankie	m.	CR	6 Aug. 1881	1	2	
White	George	m.	CR	6 Aug. 1881	1	2	
White	George	d.	PCo	15 Feb. 1882	3	4	
White	George W.	d.	DR	8 Feb. 1882	2	3	
White	J. S.	m.	PCo	5 Aug. 1885	3	6	
White	J. S.	m.	SD	22 Aug. 1885	6	2	
White	James	d.	RRF	8 Sept. 1881	3	3	
White	John	b.	PCo	3 June 1885	3	6	
White	John	b.	SD	6 June 1885	2	4	
White	L. P.	b.	DR	26 Jan. 1882	2	3	
White	L. P.	b.	HE	26 Jan. 1882	2	3	
White	Maria	m.	PWA	24 Feb. 1883	3	7	
White	Nancy C.	d.	SD	31 Oct. 1885	4	1	
White	Nancy	d.	DR	2 Oct. 1885	3	4	
White	Nancy	d.	PCo	7 Oct. 1885	3	6	
White	Nancy	d.	SD	10 Oct. 1885	5	5	
White	Nellie	d.	PC	30 May 1883	3	4	
White	Nellie	d.	SD	26 May 1883	2	7	also p. 3 col. 2
White	Olive Edith	m.	DR	9 Nov. 1882	3	2	
White	Olive Edith	m.	PCo	8 Nov. 1882	3	6	
White	Olive Edith	m.	SD	28 Oct. 1882	3	5	

(1) Surname	(2) Given Name	(3)	(4)	(5) Date	(6) Pg	(7) Col	(8) Comments
White	W. H.	b.	SD	8 Jan. 1881	3	8	
White	W. P.	m.	CR	22 Jan. 1881	5	5	
White	W. P.	m.	DR	25 Jan. 1881	3	2	
White	W. P.	b.	HE	5 Jan. 1882	2	3	
White	W. P.	b.	PCo	11 Jan. 1882	3	6	
White	W. P.	m.	RRF	13 Jan. 1881	3	5	
White	W. P.	m.	RRF	20 Jan. 1881	2	5	
White	W. P.	b.	RRF	5 Jan. 1882	2	3	
White	W. P.	m.	SD	29 Jan. 1881	3	8	
White	W. P.	b.	SD	7 Jan. 1882	3	8	
White	W. P.	b.	SD	21 Jan. 1882	3	6	
Whiteman	Elizabeth J.	m.	PCo	12 Nov. 1884	3	5	
Whiting	Walter C.	d.	DR	21 Sept. 1885	3	4	
Whitman	H. H.	b.	SD	11 June 1881	3	8	
Whitmore	H.	d.	CR	13 July 1882	1	2	
Whitmore	J. H.	m.	PCo	10 Dec. 1884	3	5	
Whitmore	J. H.	b.	PCo	28 Oct. 1885	3	4	
Whitmore	J. H.	m.	PWA	13 Dec. 1884	3	4	
Whitmore	J. H.	m.	SD	13 Dec. 1884	2	5	
Whitney	(male)	b.	DR	9 June 1884	3	3	
Whitney	A. L.	b.	PCo	11 June 1884	3	5	
Whitney	A. L.	b.	PWA	7 June 1884	3	6	
Whitney	A. L.	b.	SD	28 June 1884	3	4	
Whitney	A. P.	d.	CR	16 Feb. 1884	3	2	
Whitney	A. P.	d.	DR	11 Feb. 1884	3	3	
Whitney	A. P.	d.	PWA	16 Feb. 1884	3	6	
Whitney	A. P.	p.	SD	8 Mar. 1884	3	2	text of will
Whitney	A. P.	d.	SD	16 Feb. 1884	2	5	Cypress Hill; also p. 3 col. 3
Whitney	Albion Paris	d.	PWA	1 Mar. 1884	3	4	
Whitney	Albion Paris	d.	PWA	8 Mar. 1884	3	4	
Whitney	Albion Paris	d.	PWA	29 Mar. 1884	3	4	
Whitney	Arthur L.	m.	PCo	29 Nov. 1882	3	6	
Whitney	Calvin E.	m.	PWA	20 Oct. 1883	3	2	
Whitney	Charles W.	d.	PCo	23 Sept. 1885	3	6	
Whitney	Edgar	b.	DR	23 June 1882	3	2	
Whitney	Edgar	b.	PCo	21 June 1882	3	5	
Whitney	F.	m.	PC	22 Aug. 1883	3	5	
Whitney	Inez Louella	m.	PCo	14 Dec. 1881	3	4	
Whitney	Inez Luella	m.	RRF	1 Dec. 1881	2	3	
Whitney	Inez Luella	m.	SD	10 Dec. 1881	3	7	
Whitney	Jennie	m.	CR	30 Apr. 1881	5	5	

(1) Surname	(2) Given Name	(3)	(4)	(5) Date	(6) Pg	(7) Col	(8) Comments
Whitney	Jennie	m.	DR	29 Apr. 1881	3	2	
Whitney	Jennie	m.	PCo	27 Apr. 1881	3	5	
Whitney	Jennie	m.	SD	30 Apr. 1881	3	8	
Whitney	Jenny	m.	RRF	5 May 1881	2	4	
Whitney	Justinia	m.	DR	11 Feb. 1884	3	3	
Whitsitt	Charles	d.	SD	10 Jan. 1885	1	3	
Whitson	Eddie	d.	PCo	15 Nov. 1882	3	5	
Whitson	Frank	b.	DD	18 Oct. 1883	3	3	
Whitson	Frank	b.	DR	28 Jan. 1882	2	3	
Whitson	Frank	b.	DR	26 Aug. 1885	3	4	
Whitson	Frank	b.	PCo	25 Jan. 1882	3	6	
Whitson	Frank	b.	PCo	19 Aug. 1885	3	6	
Whitson	Frank	b.	PWA	13 Oct. 1883	3	8	
Whitson	Frank	b.	SD	20 Oct. 1883	3	4	
Whitson	Frank (son of)	d.	DR	16 Nov. 1882	2	3	
Whittaker	T. B.	m.	DR	14 Apr. 1882	3	2	
Whitton	James L.	m.	DD	8 Sept. 1883	3	3	
Whorspon	August	b.	PCo	28 May 1884	2	4	
Whysman	Mariah	d.	PCo	26 Oct. 1881	3	4	
Whysman	Mariah	d.	SD	22 Oct. 1881	3	6	
Wiars	Lewis	m.	CR	10 June 1882	5	2	
Wiars	Lewis	m.	DR	9 June 1882	2	2	
Wiars	Lewis	m.	PCo	21 June 1882	3	5	
Wiars	Lewis	m.	SD	24 June 1882	3	5	
Wicker	H. J.	m.	SD	14 June 1884	1	6	also p. 2 col. 4
Wicker	Henry J.	m.	DR	7 June 1884	3	3	
Wicker	Henry J.	m.	PCo	11 June 1884	3	5	
Wicker	Henry J.	m.	PWA	14 June 1884	3	6	
Wicker	Henry J.	m.	SWI	7 June 1884	3	4	
Wieberts	H. M., Mrs.	d.	HE	13 Apr. 1882	2	3	
Wieland	Bertha	d.	PCo	7 Jan. 1885	2	3	
Wieland	John	d.	PCo	7 Jan. 1885	2	3	
Wigand	Frank	b.	DR	1 Aug. 1885	3	4	
Wilber	Alonzo	m.	PCo	15 July 1885	3	6	
Wilber	R. A., Mrs.	d.	DR	6 Feb. 1882	2	3	
Wilber	R. A., Mrs.	d.	PCo	15 Feb. 1882	3	4	
Wilber	R. A., Mrs.	d.	RRF	9 Feb. 1882	2	3	
Wilbur	R. A., Mrs.	d.	SD	11 Feb. 1882	3	6	
Wilcox	Dr. & Mrs.	b.	PCo	15 Oct. 1884	3	6	
Wilcox	Dr. & Mrs.	b.	SD	25 Oct. 1884	2	5	
Wilde	Frederica	d.	SD	1 June 1881	3	7	
Wilder	William	m.	PCo	3 May 1882	3	5	

(1) Surname	(2) Given Name	(3)	(4)	(5) Date	(6) Pg	(7) Col	(8) Comments
Wiley	J. M.	m.	DD	24 Dec. 1883	3	2	
Wiley	J. M.	m.	PCo	26 Dec. 1883	3	5	
Wiley	J. M.	b.	PCo	4 Feb. 1885	3	6	
Wiley	J. M.	m.	PWA	29 Dec. 1883	3	6	
Wiley	J. M.	m.	SD	29 Dec. 1883	3	6	
Wiley	J. N.	b.	CR	26 Feb. 1881	5	3	
Wiley	J. N.	b.	CR	26 Feb. 1884	5	2	
Wiley	J. N.	b.	DR	22 Feb. 1881	3	2	
Wiley	J. N.	b.	SD	26 Feb. 1881	3	8	
Wilkerson	Lewis	d.	DR	9 Aug. 1881	2	3	
Wilkes	Minnie G.	m.	PCo	3 Jan. 1883	3	4	
Wilkes	Minnie G.	m.	SD	30 Dec. 1882	3	6	
Wilkes	Mollie E.	m.	DR	26 Dec. 1882	3	1	
Wilkes	William	d.	PWA	17 Feb. 1883	3	1	
Wilkes	William	d.	SD	24 Feb. 1883	3	1	
Wilkins	W. W.	b.	PCo	13 Sept. 1882	3	7	
Wilkinson	T. D.	m.	PCo	23 Nov. 1885	3	4	
Wilkinson	Thomas	m.	DR	19 Nov. 1885	3	4	
Wilkinson	Thomas	m.	SD	21 Nov. 1885	3	5	
Wilkinson	William	b.	DR	21 Jan. 1882	3	2	
Wilkinson	William	b.	PCo	18 Jan. 1882	3	5	
Wilkinson	William	b.	SD	28 Jan. 1882	3	6	
Willapoli	John	d.	DD	6 Oct. 1883	3	3	
Willard	George I.	d.	PCo	19 Dec. 1883	3	4	
Willard	George L.	d.	DD	20 Dec. 1883	2	2	
Willard	George L.	d.	PWA	22 Dec. 1883	3	6	
Willard	John	d.	SD	22 Dec. 1883	3	5	
Willard	John W.	b.	PCo	6 Dec. 1882	3	6	
Willard	John W.	b.	SD	16 Dec. 1882	3	6	
Willard	Olive Josephine	d.	PCo	28 June 1882	3	5	
Willets	Mary Ballard (Dolly)	d.	PCo	10 Jan. 1883	3	6	
Willey	Leonora E.	m.	CR	22 Mar. 1884	3	1	
Willey	Leonora E.	m.	RRF	27 Mar. 1884	2	3	
Willey	M. B., Miss	d.	PCo	7 June 1882	3	5	
Willey	M. B., Miss	d.	SD	10 June 1882	2	3	
Willey	Mary Bates	d.	DR	7 June 1882	3	2	
Willey	Norah	m.	PCo	26 Mar. 1884	3	6	
Williams	(male)	b.	DR	30 May 1884	3	2	
Williams	A. D.	b.	PC	27 June 1883	3	6	
Williams	A. D.	b.	RRF	21 June 1883	2	3	
Williams	A. F.	d.	DR	22 May 1884	3	2	
Williams	Allen	b.	PCo	4 June 1884	3	5	

(1) Surname	(2) Given Name	(3)	(4)	(5) Date	(6) Pg	(7) Col	(8) Comments
Williams	Betsey	d.	SD	25 Feb. 1882	3	2&6	
Williams	Betsy	d.	DR	24 Feb. 1882	2	3	
Williams	Betsy	d.	PCo	22 Feb. 1882	3	5	
Williams	Charles H.	m.	DR	27 Oct. 1882	3	1	
Williams	Isabelle	m.	SD	16 Apr. 1881	3	8	
Williams	J. M., Jr.	m.	DR	9 Nov. 1882	3	1&2	
Williams	James M.	m.	PCo	15 Nov. 1882	3	5	
Williams	James M.	m.	SD	11 Nov. 1882	3	7	
Williams	Joe	o.	SD	31 Dec. 1881	3	2	
Williams	John D.	m.	CR	12 Mar. 1881	5	5	
Williams	John D.	m.	DR	9 Mar. 1881	3	2	
Williams	John D.	m.	SD	19 Mar. 1881	3	8	
Williams	John	m.	SD	17 June 1882	3	1	
Williams	John L.	d.	DR	10 Aug. 1882	3	1	
Williams	Joseph A.	d.	DR	2 Nov. 1884	2	2	
Williams	Joseph A.	d.	PCo	5 Nov. 1884	3	5	
Williams	Joseph A.	d.	PWA	8 Nov. 1884	3	4	
Williams	L. L.	m.	DR	17 Sept. 1885	3	4	
Williams	Maria	m.	DR	31 Dec. 1881	2	3	
Williams	Maria	m.	PCo	4 Jan. 1882	3	7	
Williams	Maria	m.	SD	7 Jan. 1882	3	8	
Williams	Mary	m.	DR	6 Aug. 1881	2	3	
Williams	Mary	m.	SD	20 Aug. 1881	3	8	
Williams	Peter	d.	RRF	15 Sept. 1881	2	5	Healdsburg
Williams	Peter	m.	SD	24 Sept. 1881	3	8	
Williams	Peter W.	d.	DR	15 Sept. 1881	2	3	
Williams	Sarah J.	m.	DD	10 Oct. 1883	3	3	
Williams	Sarah J.	m.	SD	13 Oct. 1883	3	4	
Williams	Susie	m.	SD	12 Jan. 1884	3	6	
Williams	T. T.	m.	PCo	11 Mar. 1885	3	6	
Williams	T. T.	m.	PWA	7 Mar. 1880	3	5	
Williams	Thomas T.	m.	SD	14 Mar. 1885	5	5	
Williams	William	d.	CR	9 July 1881	5	4	Cloverdale Cemetery
Williamson	Emma	m.	PC	4 July 1883	3	5	
Williamson	Emna	m.	SD	30 June 1883	3	5	
Williamson	Kate	m.	DR	8 May 1884	3	2	
Williamson	Kate	m.	SD	10 May 1884	2	4	
Williamson	Thomas D.	d.	DR	28 Apr. 1881	2	2	
Williamson	Thomas D.	d.	DR	29 Apr. 1881	3	1	
Williamson	Thomas D.	d.	SD	30 Apr. 1881	3	8	
Williamson	W. M.	d.	SD	8 Apr. 1882	3	3	
Williard	Charles A.	m.	PWA	14 Mar. 1885	3	5	

(1) Surname	(2) Given Name	(3)	(4)	(5) Date	(6) Pg	(7) Col	(8) Comments
Williard	Charles	m.	PCo	11 Mar. 1885	3	6	
Williard	John W.	b.	DR	13 Dec. 1882	2	3	
Williard	Olive Josephine	d.	SD	1 July 1882	2	3	
Williford	Henry	b.	SD	29 Aug. 1885	2	4	
Williford	Mary E.	m.	PCo	21 June 1882	3	5	
Williford	Mary E.	m.	SD	17 June 1882	2	4	
Williford	Mary E.	m.	SD	24 June 1882	3	5	
Williges	Ehler	d.	PC	18 Apr. 1883	3	5	
Williges	Ehler	d.	PWA	21 Apr. 1883	3	8	
Willis	E. H.	m.	PWA	19 July 1884	3	4	
Willis	E. R.	m.	DR	18 July 1884	3	3	
Willis	E. R.	m.	PCo	16 July 1884	3	6	
Willitts	Annie	m.	DD	22 Oct. 1883	3	3	
Willitts	Annie	m.	SD	27 Oct. 1883	3	4	
Willitts	Dolly	d.	DR	29 Dec. 1882	3	1	
Wills	George W.	m.	DR	20 Nov. 1884	3	2	
Wills	Mary E.	d.	DR	4 Nov. 1881	2	3	
Wilmot	Mrs.	d.	DR	23 Aug. 1884	3	4	
Wilmot	Mrs.	d.	PCo	3 Sept. 1884	2	5	
Wilsey	Ella J.	m.	PCo	21 June 1882	3	5	
Wilsey	Ella J.	m.	SD	24 June 1882	3	5	
Wilsey	Francis	d.	DR	23 Dec. 1882	3	3	
Wilsey	Francis	d.	PCo	27 Dec. 1882	3	6	
Wilsey	Francis	d.	SD	30 Dec. 1882	3	6	
Wilson	Aleck	o.	SD	21 Mar. 1885	1	7	
Wilson	Alex	b.	DR	12 Aug. 1882	3	2	
Wilson	Alexander	b.	RRF	10 Aug. 1882	2	4	
Wilson	Alice May	m.	SD	23 May 1885	2	5	
Wilson	Ann Jane	d.	DD	25 Sept. 1883	3	3	
Wilson	Ann Jane	d.	SD	29 Sept. 1883	2	6	
Wilson	Anna	m.	DR	13 Nov. 1885	3	2	article on marriage
Wilson	Anna	m.	DR	16 Nov. 1885	3	4	article on marriage
Wilson	Annie E.	m.	DR	7 Nov. 1881	2	3	
Wilson	Charles	d.	DR	19 June 1882	3	1	
Wilson	Emma	d.	CR	21 July 1883	3	3	
Wilson	Emma	d.	DD	23 July 1883	3	2	
Wilson	Emma	d.	PC	25 July 1883	3	6	
Wilson	Emma	d.	SD	28 July 1883	2	5	
Wilson	Fowler E.	d.	DR	16 Dec. 1882	3	1	
Wilson	Fowler E.	d.	SD	23 Dec. 1882	3	3	
Wilson	Frances Lenora	d.	RRF	15 Mar. 1883	2	4	
Wilson	George W.	b.	PCo	4 June 1884	3	5	

(1) Surname	(2) Given Name	(3)	(4)	(5) Date	(6) Pg	(7) Col	(8) Comments
Wilson	Henry Felix	d.	RRF	15 Mar. 1883	2	4	
Wilson	John	b.	PCo	9 Jan. 1884	3	6	
Wilson	John	b.	PWA	5 Jan. 1884	3	7	
Wilson	John	b.	SD	19 Jan. 1884	3	6	
Wilson	Johnson	d.	SD	12 Apr. 1884	1	4	
Wilson	Julia	d.	PC	18 Apr. 1883	3	5	
Wilson	Julia	d.	SD	14 Apr. 1883	2	5	
Wilson	Logan M.	d.	PCo	22 Oct. 1884	3	6	
Wilson	Logan M.	d.	PWA	25 Oct. 1884	3	4	
Wilson	Logan M.	d.	SD	25 Oct. 1884	2	5	
Wilson	Margaret A.	d.	PCo	21 May 1884	3	4	
Wilson	Marguerite A.	d.	PCo	14 Dec. 1881	3	4	
Wilson	Marguerite Aileen	d.	DR	6 Dec. 1881	2	3	
Wilson	Marguerite Aileen	d.	SD	10 Dec. 1881	3	7	
Wilson	Mary C.	m.	DR	19 June 1884	3	3	
Wilson	Mary C.	m.	PCo	18 June 1884	3	4	
Wilson	Mary C.	m.	PWA	14 June 1884	3	6	
Wilson	Mary C.	m.	SD	28 June 1884	3	4	
Wilson	Mattie E.	m.	PCo	7 Mar. 1883	3	5	
Wilson	Mattie E.	m.	SD	10 Mar. 1883	3	1	
Wilson	Mr.	m.	DR	5 Apr. 1882	3	2	
Wilson	Mr.	m.	PCo	29 Mar. 1882	3	5	
Wilson	Mr.	m.	SD	25 Mar. 1882	3	6	
Wilson	Mr. & Mrs.	b.	DD	6 Oct. 1883	3	3	
Wilson	Ralph B.	d.	DR	30 Nov. 1885	3	4	
Wilson	Samuel	d.	PC	4 July 1883	3	5	
Wilson	Samuel	d.	SD	30 June 1883	3	5	
Wilson	Santa	m.	SD	12 Jan. 1884	3	6	
Wilson	Serena A.	m.	PCo	8 Oct. 1884	3	6	
Wilson	Serena A.	m.	PWA	11 Oct. 1884	3	4	
Wilson	Serena A.	m.	SD	4 Oct. 1884	3	5	
Wilson	Susan E.	m.	DR	17 Nov. 1884	3	2	
Wilson	W. C.	m.	DD	24 Dec. 1883	3	2	
Wilson	W. C.	m.	PCo	26 Dec. 1883	3	5	
Wilson	W. C.	m.	SD	29 Dec. 1883	3	6	
Wilson	W. H.	b.	DR	8 July 1882	3	2	
Wilson	W. H.	b.	PCo	12 July 1882	3	5	
Wilson	W. P., Mrs.	d.	CR	27 Aug. 1881	1	4	
Wilson	Will	o.	SD	6 Sept. 1884	5	1	
Wilson	William H.	b.	SD	8 July 1882	2	5	
Wilson	William J.	d.	CR	2 Apr. 1881	5	3	
Wilson	William J.	d.	DR	1 Apr. 1881	2	3	

(1) Surname	(2) Given Name	(3)	(4)	(5) Date	(6) Pg	(7) Col	(8) Comments
Wilson	William J.	d.	PCo	30 Mar. 1881	3	4	
Wilson	William J.	d.	SD	9 Apr. 1881	3	8	
Wilson	William	b.	DR	23 Aug. 1881	3	2	
Wilson	William	b.	SD	27 Aug. 1881	3	8	
Winans	J. E.	b.	PCo	7 Feb. 1883	3	6	
Winans	J. E.	b.	PWA	10 Feb. 1883	3	7	
Winans	J. E.	b.	SD	10 Feb. 1883	2	7	
Winchell	Charles	m.	SD	16 Apr. 1881	3	8	
Winder	Eva	m.	SD	28 Oct. 1882	3	5	
Windor	Eva	m.	PCo	1 Nov. 1882	3	5	
Windsor	Maggie M.	m.	SD	19 Feb. 1881	3	8	
Winslow	A. J.	d.	CR	28 May 1881	5	5	
Winslow	A. J.	d.	DR	23 May 1881	2	2	
Winslow	A. J.	p.	DR	29 Nov. 1884	3	2	
Winslow	A. J.	d.	PCo	1 June 1881	3	4	
Winslow	A. J.	m.	SD	4 June 1881	3	8	
Winslow	A. J.	d.	SD	11 June 1881	3	8	
Winslow	A. J.	d.	SD	28 May 1881	3	8	
Winter	Alice	m.	CR	24 Oct. 1885	3	3	
Winter	Max	o.	DR	15 July 1881	2	2	
Wise	Henry	o.	SD	24 Dec. 1881	3	3	
Wise	Meyer	d.	DD	23 July 1883	3	2	
Wise	Meyer	d.	SD	28 July 1883	2	5	
Wisecarver	James	b.	RRF	26 Jan. 1882	2	2	
Wisecarver	Joseph	m.	PCo	31 May 1882	3	5	
Wisecarver	Joseph	m.	RRF	25 May 1882	2	3	
Wisecarver	Joseph	m.	SD	3 June 1882	2	4	
Wisener	George C.	d.	DR	22 Mar. 1882	2	3	
Wisener	George C.	d.	PCo	29 Mar. 1882	3	5	
Wisener	George C.	d.	SD	25 Mar. 1882	3	6	
Wiser	Henry	d.	DR	7 July 1884	3	3	
Wiser	Henry	d.	PCo	2 July 1884	3	4	
Wiser	Henry	d.	SD	12 July 1884	6	8	
Witham	George F.	b.	DR	28 Mar. 1882	2	3	
Witham	George	b.	PCo	5 Apr. 1882	3	5	
Withers	Robert	d.	DR	24 Feb. 1882	2	3	
Withers	Robert	d.	PCo	22 Feb. 1882	3	5	
Wittenstein	F. C.	m.	SD	25 Oct. 1884	2	5	
Wittenstein	Fred C.	b.	DR	3 Aug. 1885	3	4	
Wittenstein	Fred C.	b.	PCo	5 Aug. 1885	3	6	
Wittenstein	Fred C.	b.	SD	22 Aug. 1885	6	2	
Wittenstein	Mary E.	d.	DR	17 Sept. 1885	3	4	

(1) Surname	(2) Given Name	(3)	(4)	(5) Date	(6) Pg	(7) Col	(8) Comments
Wittenstein	Mary E.	d.	PCo	23 Sept. 1885	3	6	
Wolcott	Alice	d.	PC	9 May 1883	3	5	
Wolcott	Alice	d.	RRF	3 May 1883	2	3	
Wolcott	Alice	d.	SD	12 May 1883	2	6	
Wolf	John	b.	PC	1 Aug. 1883	3	6	
Wolf	John	b.	RRF	26 July 1883	2	4	
Wolfe	Ben	d.	RRF	15 Dec. 1881	2	4	
Wolfe	Ben (child of)	d.	DR	16 Dec. 1881	2	2	
Wolfe	Ben (infant of)	d.	PCo	28 Dec. 1881	3	6	
Wolfe	Ben (child of)	d.	SD	24 Dec. 1881	2	3	
Wolfe	Buck	b.	PCo	22 Apr. 1885	3	6	
Wolfe	Ida Murtle	d.	RRF	1 May 1884	5	6	
Wolfe	Ida Murtle	d.	SD	3 May 1884	3	3	
Wood	B. S.	o.	DR	26 Aug. 1882	3	1	
Wood	Ben S.	o.	RRF	31 Aug. 1882	3	6	
Wood	Ben S.	o.	SD	2 Sept. 1882	3	2	
Wood	C. H.	d.	DR	1 Dec. 1884	3	2	under "born" heading
Wood	C. H.	d.	PCo	3 Dec. 1884	3	5	
Wood	Colonel	m.	CR	2 Dec. 1882	3	2	
Wood	Henry	d.	SD	12 Mar. 1881	3	8	
Wood	John	b.	DR	26 Aug. 1885	3	4	
Wood	John	b.	PCo	19 Aug. 1885	3	6	
Wood	M. D.	m.	PCo	10 Jan. 1883	3	6	
Wood	M. D.	m.	SD	6 Jan. 1883	2	5	
Wood	Martha E.	d.	SD	11 Oct. 1884	1	4	Shiloh Church
Wood	Martha	d.	SD	4 Oct. 1884	3	5	
Wood	Seneca B.	m.	DR	16 Nov. 1882	2	3	
Wood	Seneca B.	m.	RRF	16 Nov. 1882	2	4	
Wood	Thomas	m.	DR	7 Nov. 1881	2	3	
Wood	Thomas	m.	SD	12 Nov. 1881	3	7	
Wood	Wesley	b.	DR	2 June 1882	3	2	
Wood	Wesley	b.	PCo	14 June 1882	3	5	
Wood	Wesley	b.	SD	10 June 1882	2	3	
Wood	William H.	b.	PWA	17 Feb. 1883	3	7	
Wood	William	d.	DD	8 Oct. 1883	3	2	
Wood	William	d.	SD	13 Oct. 1883	3	4	
Woodman	Everett I.	b.	DR	8 Dec. 1884	3	2	
Woodman	Everett I.	b.	SD	6 Dec. 1884	3	5	
Woodman	Everett J.	b.	PCo	3 Dec. 1884	3	5	
Woods	Clara W.	d.	DR	24 Oct. 1882	3	2	
Woods	Clara W.	d.	PCo	25 Oct. 1882	3	5	
Woods	Clara W.	d.	RRF	19 Oct. 1882	2	3	

(1) Surname	(2) Given Name	(3)	(4)	(5) Date	(6) Pg	(7) Col	(8) Comments
Woods	K.	b.	CR	1 Jan. 1881	5	5	
Woods	K.	b.	SD	1 June 1881	3	7	
Woods	William	m.	PCo	15 Mar. 1882	3	4	
Woodson	Belle	m.	DR	10 Apr. 1882	2	2	
Woodson	Belle	m.	PCo	5 Apr. 1882	3	5	
Woodson	Frank	b.	PC	4 July 1883	3	5	
Woodson	Frank	b.	PWA	7 July 1883	3	6	
Woodson	Mary F.	m.	PCo	30 Nov. 1881	3	5	
Woodson	Mary F.	m.	SD	31 Dec. 1881	3	6	
Woodward	E. F.	b.	DR	21 Dec. 1885	3	4	
Woodward	E. F.	b.	PCo	10 Sept. 1884	3	6	
Woodward	E. F.	b.	SD	26 Dec. 1885	3	4	
Woodward	J. M.	d.	PCo	14 Jan. 1885	3	6	
Woodward	James	m.	DR	4 Mar. 1882	2	3	
Woodward	James	m.	DR	8 Mar. 1882	2	3	
Woodward	James	m.	PCo	15 Mar. 1882	3	4	
Woodward	James	m.	RRF	9 Mar. 1882	2	4	
Woodward	James	m.	SD	11 Mar. 1882	3	6	
Woodward	L. B.	p.	DD	11 July 1883	3	2	
Woodward	L. B., Mrs.	d.	PCo	16 Aug. 1882	3	6	
Woodward	L. B., Mrs.	d.	SD	5 Aug. 1882	3	5	
Woodward	Lucina	d.	DR	4 Aug. 1882	3	1	
Woodward	Mattie M.	m.	PC	4 Apr. 1883	3	5	
Woodward	Orrin T.	m.	DR	26 Aug. 1884	3	4	
Woodward	Orrin T.	m.	PCo	3 Sept. 1884	2	5	
Woodward	T. H.	b.	PCo	2 Jan. 1884	3	6	
Woodward	T.	m.	DR	8 Mar. 1882	2	3	
Woodward	Thomas	d.	SD	18 Apr. 1885	5	2	
Woodward	Walter Frear	d.	PC	8 Aug. 1883	3	6	
Woodward	William A.	d.	PWA	18 Apr. 1885	3	6	
Woodworth	Clara	m.	PWA	4 Apr. 1885	3	6	
Woodworth	James	m.	DR	17 Sept. 1885	3	4	
Woodworth	Marilla	d.	PCo	21 Mar. 1883	3	5	Cypress Hill Cem.
Woodworth	Marilla	d.	PWA	24 Mar. 1883	3	1&7	Cypress Hill Cem.
Woodworth	Marilla	d.	SD	24 Mar. 1883	2	5	
Woodworth	Mary	m.	DR	17 Sept. 1885	3	4	
Woodworth	S. P.	m.	PCo	15 July 1885	3	6	
Woodworth	Samuel P.	m.	DR	14 July 1885	3	4	
Woodworth	Samuel	m.	SD	18 July 1885	5	5	
Wooley	J. A.	d.	DR	15 Nov. 1884	3	2	
Wooley	J. A.	d.	PCo	19 Nov. 1884	3	5	
Wooley	J. A.	d.	PWA	22 Nov. 1884	3	4	

(1) Surname	(2) Given Name	(3)	(4)	(5) Date	(6) Pg	(7) Col	(8) Comments
Wooley	J. A.	d.	SD	23 Nov. 1884	2	6	
Wooley	William C.	m.	DD	11 Dec. 1883	2	2	
Wooley	William	b.	DR	13 Dec. 1884	1	4	
Wooley	William	m.	PCo	19 Dec. 1883	3	4	
Woolly		d.	HE	4 Oct. 1883	3	3	
Woolsey	Marie Louise	m.	SD	13 June 1885	3	5	
Wooster	M.	o.	SIT	22 Aug. 1885	2	2	
Wooster	Mark	d.	SIT	7 Jan. 1888	2	5	also p. 3 col. 2
Worthington	W. A.	b.	CR	1 Jan. 1881	5	5	
Worthington	W. A.	b.	SD	1 June 1881	3	7	
Wren	E., Miss	m.	RRF	27 Mar. 1884	2	3	
Wren	E. A., Miss	m.	SD	5 Apr. 1884	3	4	
Wright	(female)	b.	DR	26 Apr. 1884	3	2	
Wright	C. A.	b.	DR	10 June 1882	3	2	
Wright	C. A.	b.	DR	16 Sept. 1882	3	4	
Wright	C. A.	b.	PCo	21 June 1882	3	5	
Wright	C. A.	b.	PCo	7 May 1884	3	5	
Wright	C. A.	b.	RRF	1 May 1884	5	6	
Wright	C. A.	b.	SD	24 June 1882	3	5	
Wright	C. A. (son of)	d.	SD	24 June 1882	3	5	
Wright	Celia	m.	PCo	11 Mar. 1885	3	6	
Wright	Celia	m.	SD	14 Mar. 1885	5	5	
Wright	Charles A.	b.	SD	3 May 1884	3	3	
Wright	Charles	b.	SD	19 Sept. 1885	2	4	
Wright	Elsie	d.	DR	2 Feb. 1884	3	3	
Wright	Elsie	d.	PCo	6 Feb. 1884	3	6	
Wright	Elsie	d.	SD	16 Feb. 1884	2	5	
Wright	Fanny P.	d.	SD	19 Feb. 1881	3	2&8	
Wright	Isaac	m.	DD	18 Aug. 1883	3	3	
Wright	Isaac	m.	PC	15 Aug. 1883	3	6	
Wright	Isaac	m.	SD	25 Aug. 1883	2	5	
Wright	Jesse	m.	PWA	11 Aug. 1883	3	8	
Wright	Jones	m.	SD	24 Dec. 1881	2	3	
Wright	Joseph	o.	DR	13 May 1882	3	2	
Wright	Lydia	d.	PC	9 May 1883	3	5	
Wright	Lydia	d.	PWA	5 May 1883	3	8	
Wright	Miss	m.	RRF	16 Feb. 1882	3	5	
Wright	Mr. & Mrs.	b.	DD	15 Dec. 1883	3	1	
Wright	Mr. & Mrs.	b.	RRF	17 Apr. 1884	2	4	
Wright	Mr. & Mrs.	b.	SD	26 Apr. 1883	3	5	
Wright	S. B.	m.	DR	9 May 1881	2	2	
Wright	S. B.	b.	DR	20 Jan. 1882	3	2	

(1) Surname	(2) Given Name	(3)	(4)	(5) Date	(6) Pg	(7) Col	(8) Comments
Wright	S. B.	m.	RRF	12 May 1881	2	4	
Wright	S. B.	b.	RRF	26 Jan. 1882	2	2	
Wright	S. B.	d.	RRF	26 Jan. 1882	2	2	
Wright	S. B.	b.	RRF	4 Jan. 1883	2	2	
Wright	S. B.	b.	SD	21 Jan. 1882	3	6	
Wright	S. B. (son of)	d.	DR	20 Jan. 1882	3	2	
Wright	S. B. (son of)	d.	SD	21 Jan. 1882	3	6	
Wright	Sadie E	m.	SD	11 Oct. 1884	2	5	
Wright	Sadie E.	m.	PWA	4 Oct. 1884	3	4	
Wright	Sampson B.	m.	RRF	16 Feb. 1882	3	5	
Wright	Sylvanus	d.	DD	24 Oct. 1883	3	3	
Wright	Sylvanus	d.	SD	27 Oct. 1883	3	1&4	
Wristen	Annie	m.	SD	18 Apr. 1885	2	5	
Wunderlich	H. F.	m.	SD	19 Feb. 1881	3	8	
Wunderlich	Henry F.	d.	SD	21 Feb. 1885	2	5	
Wunderlich	Henry	m.	DR	15 Feb. 1881	3	1	
Wunderlich	Henry	b.	PC	9 May 1883	3	5	
Wunderlich	Henry	b.	PWA	12 May 1883	3	8	
Wyatt	Frank	b.	DD	4 Dec. 1883	3	3	
Wyatt	Frank	b.	RRF	29 Nov. 1883	2	3	
Wyatt	Frank	b.	SD	8 Dec. 1883	3	1	
Wyatt	Frank W.	m.	PC	4 Apr. 1883	3	5	
Wyatt	Frank W.	m.	RRF	29 Mar. 1883	2	4	
Wyatt	M. O.	m.	CR	27 June 1885	3	2	
Wyatt	M. O.	m.	PCo	1 July 1885	3	6	
Wyche	Kathleen	m.	DD	20 July 1883	3	2	
Wyche	Kathleen	m.	PC	18 July 1883	3	5	
Wyche	Kathleen	m.	PWA	21 July 1883	3	7	
Wyche	Kathleen	m.	SD	28 July 1883	2	5	
Wyckoff	G.	b.	SD	23 July 1881	3	8	
Wykoff	H. H.	b.	SD	19 Mar. 1881	3	8	
Wyman	B.	m.	DR	22 Aug. 1881	2	3	
Wyman	B.	m.	SD	13 Aug. 1881	3	8	
Wynne	Owen G.	d.	SWI	22 Sept. 1883	3	2	
Wynne	Owen G.	d.	SWI	22 Sept. 1883	3	4	
Wyrich	Luella	m.	PWA	14 July 1883	3	6	
Wyrick	Ella	m.	PC	11 July 1883	3	5	
Wyrick	Lewelen M.	m.	SD	7 July 1883	2	5	

Y & Z

(1) Surname	(2) Given Name	(3)	(4)	(5) Date	(6) Pg	(7) Col	(8) Comments
Yancy	Emma B.	m.	DD	23 Nov. 1883	3	2	
Yancy	Emma B.	m.	RRF	22 Nov. 1883	2	3	
Yancy	Emma B.	m.	SD	1 Dec. 1883	3	4	
Yates	Alice	m.	DR	26 Sept. 1881	3	2	
Yates	Alice	m.	DR	28 Sept. 1881	3	2	
Yates	Alice	m.	RRF	22 Sept. 1881	2	5	
Yates	Charles	b.	SD	4 Feb. 1882	3	6	
Yell	Archibald	m.	DR	28 Nov. 1881	2	3	
Yengling	Arthur	d.	PC	6 June 1883	3	4	
Yengling	Jason	b.	PWA	14 Apr. 1883	3	7	
Yengling	Jason	d.	SD	16 June 1883	2	6	
Yerger	(inf. son)	d.	DR	30 May 1884	3	2	
Yerger	Theodore (son of)	d.	PCo	28 May 1884	2	4	
Yerger	Theodore	m.	HE	4 Oct. 1883	2	3	
Yerger	Theodore	b.	PCo	28 May 1884	2	4	
Yonker	G. G.	m.	DD	27 July 1883	3	2	
Yordi	Fred	b.	CR	22 Dec. 1883	3	1	
York	A. A.	b.	PCo	31 Jan. 1883	3	5	
York	A. A.	b.	RRF	25 Jan. 1883	2	4	
York	A. A.	b.	SD	27 Jan. 1883	3	6	
York	Augustus A.	m.	CR	22 Jan. 1881	5	5	
York	Augustus A.	m.	DR	25 Jan. 1881	3	2	
York	Augustus A.	m.	RRF	20 Jan. 1881	2	5	
York	Augustus A.	m.	SD	29 Jan. 1881	3	8	
York	Dick, Jr.	b.	CR	24 Jan. 1885	3	1	
York	Leona	m.	SD	17 Oct. 1885	4	5	
Youker	G. G.	m.	PC	1 Aug. 1883	3	6	
Youker	G. G.	m.	SD	4 Aug. 1883	2	5	
Young	C. M.	b.	PCo	1 Nov. 1882	3	5	
Young	Carrie	m.	CR	19 Mar. 1881	5	4	
Young	D. C.	d.	PC	8 Aug. 1883	3	4&6	
Young	D. C.	d.	PWA	11 Aug. 1883	3	8	
Young	D. C.	d.	SD	11 Aug. 1883	2	7	
Young	D. C.	d.	SWI	11 Aug. 1883	3	3	
Young	George C.	m.	DR	10 July 1885	3	4	
Young	J. B.	m.	PCo	7 Jan. 1885	3	6	
Young	J. H.	m.	SD	3 Jan. 1885	2	7	
Young	J. S.	m.	DR	3 Jan. 1884	3	2	

(1) Surname	(2) Given Name	(3)	(4)	(5) Date	(6) Pg	(7) Col	(8) Comments
Young	J. S.	m.	PCo	9 Jan. 1884	3	6	
Young	J. S.	b.	PCo	15 Oct. 1884	3	6	
Young	J. S.	m.	RRF	3 Jan. 1884	2	4	
Young	J. S.	m.	SD	5 Jan. 1884	1	1	
Young	John	d.	RRF	10 Feb. 1881	3	6	
Young	Josephine	m.	DR	13 Feb. 1882	2	3	
Young	L. A.	b.	SD	16 July 1881	3	8	
Young	Michael	d.	SD	13 Sept. 1884	3	4	
Young	Minnie E.	m.	SD	25 Apr. 1885	2	5	
Young	Minnie	m.	PCo	22 Apr. 1885	3	6	
Young	N. A.	b.	RRF	14 Sept. 1882	2	4	
Young	Olivia	d.	DR	17 May 1881	2	2	
Young	Olivia	d.	SD	21 May 1881	3	8	
Young	T. L.	b.	SD	15 Jun. 1881	3	8	
Young	W. H.	b.	DD	15 Dec. 1883	3	1	
Young	Willie Frederick	d.	RRF	10 Feb. 1881	3	6	
Youngs	Naomi E.	m.	PCo	9 Dec. 1885	3	6	
Zartman	G. W.	b.	PCo	13 May 1885	3	6	
Zartman	George W.	b.	DR	9 Nov. 1882	3	2	
Zartman	George W.	b.	PCo	8 Nov. 1882	3	6	
Zartman	George W.	m.	SD	1 June 1881	3	7	
Zelhart	J., Miss	m.	SD	6 Sept. 1884	2	5	
Zelheart	Mattie J.	m.	PWA	6 Sept. 1884	3	4	
Zellheart	Mattie J.	m.	PCo	3 Sept. 1884	2	5	
Zellner	Prof. & Mrs.	b.	PCo	22 Nov. 1882	3	5	
Zellner	Professor	b.	DR	14 Nov. 1882	2	3	
Zellner	Professor	b.	RRF	16 Nov. 1882	2	4	
Zillheart	Mattie J.	m.	DR	23 Aug. 1884	3	4	
Zimmerman	J. M.	b.	PCo	8 Oct. 1884	3	6	
Zook	F. K.	b.	PCo	13 Dec. 1882	3	4	
Zuck	Cassie I.	d.	PWA	29 Nov. 1884	3	4	
Zurmiller	Elizabeth	d.	SD	14 Mar. 1885	5	5	
Zurnes	Job	d.	PWA	14 July 1883	3	6	
Zurnes	John	d.	PC	18 July 1883	3	5	
Zuver	John	d.	PC	27 June 1883	3	6	
Zweifel	Walter	m.	PCo	24 June 1885	3	6	
Zweifel	Walter	m.	SD	27 June 1885	5	4	
Zweifle	Walter	m.	DR	1 Aug. 1885	3	4	

Heritage Books by the Sonoma County Genealogical Society, Inc.:

CD: *Sonoma County [California] Records, Volume 1*

Early School Attendance Records of Sonoma County, California, Beginning 1858

Early School Attendance Records of Sonoma County, California, Volume II: 1874–1932

Homestead Declarations: Amended Index, Sonoma County, California, Second Edition

Index and Abstracts of Wills, Sonoma County, California: 1850–1900

Index to Naturalization Records in Sonoma County, California, Volume 1: 1841–1906

Naturalization Records in Sonoma County, California, Volume II: 1906–1930

Index to The Sonoma Searcher: *Volume 16, No. 1 to Volume 28, No. 3*
(Including Index to The Sonoma Searcher: *Volume 1, No. 1 to Volume 15, No. 4, SCGS, August 1993)*

Index to Vital Data in Local Newspapers of Sonoma County, California, Volume 1: 1855–1875

Index to Vital Data in Local Newspapers of Sonoma County, California, Volume 2: 1876–1880

Index to Vital Data in Local Newspapers of Sonoma County, California, Volume 3: 1881–1885

Index to Vital Data in Local Newspapers of Sonoma County, California, Volume 4: 1886–1890

Index to Vital Data in Local Newspapers of Sonoma County, California, Volume 5: 1891–1899

Index to Vital Data in Local Newspapers of Sonoma County, California, Volume 6: 1900–1903

Index to Vital Data in Local Newspapers of Sonoma County, California, Volume 7: 1904–1906

Index to Vital Data in Local Newspapers of Sonoma County, California, Volume 8: 1907–1909

Index to Vital Data in Local Newspapers of Sonoma County, California, Volume 9: 1910–1912

Index to Vital Data in Local Newspapers of Sonoma County, California, Volume 10: 1913–1915

Index to Vital Data in Local Newspapers of Sonoma County, California, Volume 11: 1916–1918

Indigent Records in Sonoma County, California 1878 to 1926, Volume 1: The Indigents

Indigent Records in Sonoma County, California 1878 to 1926, Volume 2: Taxpayers Who Certified Indigent Need

Militia Lists of Sonoma County, California, 1846 to 1900

Probate Records, Sonoma County, California Index for 1847 to 1959

Santa Rosa Rural Cemetery, 1853–1997

Sonoma County, California Cemetery Records, 1846–1921, Third Edition

Sonoma County, California Death Records, 1873–1905, Second Edition

Sonoma County California Reconstructed 1890 Census

The 1930 School Census of Sonoma County, California

www.ingramcontent.com/pod-product-compliance
Lightning Source LLC
Chambersburg PA
CBHW080413270326
41929CB00018B/3011